A Dictionary of Stylistics

Second edition

Studies in language and linguistics

General editors: GEOFFREY LEECH, *Lancaster University*
and
JENNY THOMAS, *University of Wales, Bangor*

Already published:

A Dictionary of Stylistics

Second edition

KATIE WALES

Longman

An imprint of **Pearson Education**

Harlow, England · London · New York · Reading, Massachusetts · San Francisco
Toronto · Don Mills, Ontario · Sydney · Tokyo · Singapore · Hong Kong · Seoul
Taipei · Cape Town · Madrid · Mexico City · Amsterdam · Munich · Paris · Milan

Pearson Education Limited
Edinburgh Gate
Harlow
Essex CM20 2JE
England

and Associated Companies throughout the world

Visit us on the World Wide Web at:
www.pearsoned.co.uk

First published by Longman Group Limited 1990
Second edition published by Pearson Education Limited 2001

© Pearson Education Limited 1990, 2001

ISBN 978-0-582-31737-6

British Library Cataloguing-in-Publication Data

A catalogue record for this book is available from the British Library

Library of Congress Cataloging-in-Publication Data

A catalog record for this book is available from the Library of Congress

11 10 9 8
10 09

Set in Palatino 9.5 / 12pt by 35
Printed in Malaysia, GPS

Introduction to Second Edition

At the beginning of a new century and a new millennium it is exhilarating to look back as well as forwards. No discipline stands still, and the 10 years or so since the first edition of this *Dictionary* appeared have witnessed the rise of many new perspectives and schools of thought with particular impact on stylistic studies and methodologies (e.g. COGNITIVE LINGUISTICS; SCHEMA THEORY; CRITICAL DISCOURSE ANALYSIS), each concerned with language in relation to broader issues, e.g. of reality, cognition, power and ideology. The last 10 years have also consolidated approaches, essentially contextual also, that were just beginning to emerge as the *Dictionary* was being written (e.g. RELEVANCE THEORY; POLITENESS THEORY). Looking back to the 1980s nonetheless, there is no doubting the long-lasting significance still of reader response/reception theory with the idea of the reader actively negotiating meaning, text-creating; and the resonance still also of a Bakhtinian approach to language which sees it as socially stratified and polyphonic. One significant consequence of this is that the Formalist and Structuralist theories of such importance to stylistics at its first flourishing in the 1960s now seem a long way away in time, although questions of 'literariness' are still much debated, and the formal linguistic analysis of particular texts or kinds of discourse as a means towards a fuller appreciation and interpretation still lies at the heart of stylistic study. Increasingly, however, as befitting the present postmodern *Zeitgeist* some of the many structuralist oppositions that have marked language and literary studies of many different persuasions are now collapsing or blurring: e.g. *langue* v. *parole; text* v. *context; form* v. *content; literary* v. *nonliterary; reality* v. *fantasy; mimesis* v. *diegesis; standard* v. *non-standard.* In general, looking back over 40 years of stylistics, I realized that stylistic perspectives are continually being refined, reshaped, re-assessed, re-oriented, but at the same time had to acknowledge once again the abiding influence on the foundations of the subject of 2000 years of literary criticism and rhetorical theory.

Stylistics is frequently described metaphorically as a kind of 'tool-kit', and this new second edition, like the first, certainly has unashamedly practical aims: to elucidate relevant but often difficult, ambiguous or conflicting terms; and to demonstrate by exemplification potentially valuable ways into the techniques of diverse kinds of texts, spoken, written or media, literary and non-literary. Its aim is to show the value of stylistics for sharpening analytical skills and for encouraging sensitive and pleasurable responses to what is read or listened to. So this new edition is designed to be of use not only to students and teachers in higher education of what is specifically called stylistics, but also to those engaged in related or overlapping courses, for example in basic literary theory, practical criticism, the history of literary language, rhetoric of composition, rhetoric and politics, textlinguistics, cultural and media studies, critical linguistics and discourse analysis. There are, as in the first edition, many basic terms of linguistic analysis described (lexical and phonological as well as grammatical) specifically in order to help the many secondary-level students in the UK and undergraduates in their studies of English language, present-day and historical; and to help foreign students and teachers of English language and literature.

For reasons of space many terms from the first edition have had to be omitted, but I have tried to restrict the omissions to those terms no longer much used or more at home in a dictionary of literary terms. Still, don't throw away your first edition! Most of the remaining entries have been revised, some quite significantly (e.g. ANAPHORA; FACE; FICTIONALITY; LITERAL; REGISTER; STYLISTICS, of course); many terms have new senses added (e.g. AFFECT; BLENDING; DISCOURSE STYLISTICS; GENRE ANALYSIS; NARRATIVITY); and there are many new entries (e.g. ACCOMMODATION; CARNIVAL; INTEGRATIONAL LINGUISTICS; LIMINALITY; STANCE; TEXTUAL INTERVENTION). I have tried to make the second edition clearer than the first edition in the lay-out of many of the entries; and in the interests of clarity also I have removed the italic small capitals convention in reference to other subject areas that are not separately defined. Otherwise, the conventions remain as before: terms defined within an entry and their related forms are printed in **bold-face**; SMALL CAPITALS indicate a word is defined elsewhere in the Dictionary. This cross-referencing is inevitable for a subject like stylistics, at the interface of linguistic, literary and other approaches; but inevitable too at a time when inter-disciplinarity and inter-textuality are so prominent.

I have benefited greatly from encouraging and constructive comments on the first edition by reviewers and colleagues (e.g. Frances Austen, Michael Barry, Elizabeth Black, Klaus Hansen, Tom McArthur, John McRae, the late Paul Salmon, Michael Vinogradis, Tuija Virtanen, Susan Wright, Bo Yonglin); and from helpful comments in the preparation of the revisions for this new edition. In particular I would note Sylvia Adamson, David Bovey, Cathy Emmott, Anthea Fraser Gupta, Andrew Gibson, Geoffrey Leech, John Mcleod and Catriona McPherson. This new edition is dedicated to all my friends and colleagues in the Poetics and Linguistics Association (PALA), in Britain and overseas, who will enthusiastically ensure that stylistics continues to flourish in this new millennium.

January 2001

List of Abbreviations and Symbols

adj.	adjective
cf.	compare
ch.	chapter
d.	died
et al.	and others
f.	following; onwards
Fr.	French
Ger.	German
Gk	Greek
It.	Italian
Lat.	Latin
ME	Middle English
NE	Modern (New) English
OE	Old English
OED	*The Oxford English Dictionary*
op. cit.	in the work already quoted
OF	Old French
ON	Old Norse
pub.	published
q.v.	which see
sg.	singular
TLS	*Times Literary Supplement*
*	ungrammatical or unacceptable form
[ ]	enclose semantic components (e.g. [– (human)])
< >	enclose graphic symbols (letters of the alphabet)
/ /	enclose phonemic symbols

List of Phonemic Symbols

/ɪ/ as in h<u>i</u>t (Received Pronunciation, RP)
/iː/ as in h<u>ea</u>t
/e/ as in h<u>e</u>n
/ə/ as in v<u>a</u>nill<u>a</u>
/ɜː/ as in b<u>ir</u>d
/æ/ as in c<u>a</u>t
/ɑː/ as in c<u>ar</u>d
/ɒː/ as in d<u>o</u>g
/ɔː/ as in p<u>aw</u>
/uː/ as in f<u>oo</u>d
/ʊ/ as in s<u>u</u>gar
/ʌ/ as in b<u>u</u>d
/aɪ/ as in n<u>igh</u>t
/eɪ/ as in d<u>ay</u>
/ɒɪ/ as in b<u>oy</u>
/ɒʊ/ as in h<u>ou</u>se
/əʊ/ as in r<u>oa</u>d
/ɪə/ as in <u>ear</u>
/ɛə/ as in c<u>are</u>
/ʊə/ as in t<u>our</u>
/p/ as in <u>p</u>in
/b/ as in <u>b</u>in
/t/ as in <u>t</u>in
/d/ as in <u>d</u>in
/k/ as in <u>k</u>in

/g/ as in <u>g</u>un
/s/ as in <u>s</u>in
/z/ as in <u>z</u>oo
/θ/ as in <u>th</u>in
/ð/ as in <u>th</u>is
/f/ as in <u>f</u>in
/v/ as in <u>v</u>ine
/ʃ/ as in <u>sh</u>in
/ʒ/ as in <u>g</u>enre
/tʃ/ as in <u>ch</u>in
/dʒ/ as in ju<u>dg</u>e
/h/ as in <u>h</u>ouse
/m/ as in <u>m</u>ouse
/n/ as in <u>n</u>ice
/ŋ/ as in si<u>ng</u>ing
/l/ as in <u>l</u>u<u>ll</u>
/r/ as in <u>r</u>oll
/j/ as in <u>y</u>awn
/w/ as in <u>w</u>in

OLD ENGLISH GRAPHIC
SYMBOLS USED

<Ð>/<ð> as in <u>th</u>is
<Þ>/<þ> as in <u>th</u>orn
<Æ>/<æ> as in c<u>a</u>t

A

---

a-verse

The first **half-line** or **hemistich** of a line of Old English verse (see also B-VERSE: the second half-line). The half-lines are separated by a CAESURA or pause, and typically contain two strong STRESSES each. But the rhythmic balance is offset by the linear pattern of ALLITERATION, which in OE poetry is FORMAL rather than STYLISTIC. In the **a-verse** both stressed words are normally alliterative; in the b-verse only the first, e.g.:

```
      /        /  /      /
Þær wæs gidd ond gleo. Gomela Scilding,
 /  /      /      /
felaþricgende, feorran rehte (Beowulf)
```
('There was song and mirth. The old Dane, much-knowing, told of far times')

(See also ALLITERATIVE VERSE.)

absence

In the work of Macherey (1966) and in DECONSTRUCTION THEORY, as well as novel theory, the concept that what is meaningful is as much what is not said as what is physically present (see also DIFFÉRANCE).

Our expectations of what is 'usual' in novel techniques may lead us to note, for example, the **absence** of expressive speech markers in Woolf's *The Waves* (only *said* is used); and of speech phrases of any kind in Joyce's *Ulysses* (see also FREE DIRECT STYLE). Both novels are also marked by the significant absence of a narratorial voice for much of the text. Significant absence of a character's voice is illustrated in Faulkner's *The Sound and The Fury*: Caddy is presented totally from the viewpoint of her brothers.

Absence can be seen to highlight the process of ideological CHOICE that is involved in the creation of a fictional world however seemingly 'complete' or 'natural'. It should be considered, therefore, with the related (textual and interpretative) concepts of GAP and INDETERMINACY, and the notion of INFERENCE.

1

abstract nouns

Abstract nouns are a subclass of NOUNS which refer to qualities or states, i.e. they have non-material REFERENCE, unlike **concrete nouns**.

Characteristically, they lack the number and ARTICLE contrast of concrete nouns (*eagernesses; *a bravery) but some can be 'individualized' (*difficulty/-ies; experience(s); a temptation*, etc.). Many are derived from ADJECTIVES, VERBS and other nouns by the addition of specific SUFFIXES of Germanic and Latin origin: e.g. *child-hood; scholarship; free-dom; dull-ness; classic-ism; pedestrian-ization*, etc.

Abstract DICTION is characteristic of many FORMAL types of (written) language technical or intellectual in nature (see also NOMINALIZATION; JARGON).

In LITERATURE, especially poetry and ALLEGORY, abstract nouns are highlighted in the RHETORICAL FIGURE of PERSONIFICATION (q.v.), where the semantic COMPONENTS of 'ANIMATE' and 'human' become contextually associated with them: as in Gray's

> Disdainful Anger, pallid Fear,
> And Shame that sculks behind

> (*Ode on a Distant Prospect of Eton College*)

accent; accentuation

Accent is widely used in various branches of linguistics, LITERARY CRITICISM and ordinary speech, in different senses; but broadly referring to aspects of 'pronunciation', or 'prominence', or both.

(1) Most commonly, those features of pronunciation (e.g. choice of vowel, INTONATION) which identify a speaker's place of origin regionally (as in 'She has a Birmingham/Norfolk accent'). Accents can also be national ('American'), and social ('She has a BBC accent').

The term is popularly confused with DIALECT, but linguists stress that accent is but one aspect of dialect, the PHONETIC or PHONOLOGICAL, as above. In present-day spoken English it is an important aspect, for many regional speakers otherwise use STANDARD syntax and vocabulary. **Accent-switching**, like **dialect-switching**, can be exploited for humorous purposes: i.e. the shift of one mode of pronunciation to another. But it also occurs quite naturally in certain social SITUATIONS where **degrees of** FORMALITY vary (e.g. switching between standard and regional forms).

(2) In PHONETICS, **accent** (singular) is usually applied to syllables or words which are prominent, whether by loudness and intensity (STRESS); pitch change (INTONATION); length; or all such factors (e.g. the first syllable of *prominent*; the third syllable of *intonation*). Hence:

(3) The term is used for the GRAPHEMIC or written symbol or diacritic above letters in certain languages (e.g. French, Greek to indicate quality of vowel sound, pitch, or length, etc. (e.g. *écriture*).

(4) What makes the RHYTHM of English speech is the pattern of **accented** and **unaccented** syllables in polysyllabic words; and of accented and unaccented words in SENTENCES (usually LEXICAL ITEMS v. FUNCTION WORDS).

The rhythm of English poetry is characteristically based on natural speech rhythms. The mainstream of English verse from the OE period is **accentual**, more properly **accentual syllabic**: highly regular in the number of accents per line (reasonable so in the number of syllables), e.g.:

```
×  /  ×  /  ×  / × /
A slumber did my spirit seal
```

(Wordsworth: *Lucy Poems*)

```
/ ×  ×  / × / × × / ×
Little Miss Muffet sat on a tuffet
```

(5) **Accent** and its related forms, **accented** and **accentuation**, are used figuratively in literary criticism to mean 'intensity', 'emphasis' or 'highlighting'. So fog is accented in the opening of Dickens's *Bleak House*, where it is repeated 13 times in the second paragraph. (See also FOREGROUNDING.)

acceptability

(1) In its narrowest sense, the term refers to the extent to which a native speaker would regard an UTTERANCE as conforming to the rules of the language: hence GRAMMATICAL.

(2) However, **acceptability** is not to be identified too closely with GRAMMATICALITY (q.v.). A well-formed utterance may be 'unacceptable' CONTEXTUALLY or SITUATIONALLY: e.g. if it is too formal, or too technical, or spoken in a STANDARD ACCENT. (See also APPROPRIATENESS.) Conversely, an ungrammatical utterance may be acceptable if, for example, the speaker or writer is a foreigner, a toddler, highly excited, or inebriated.

And generally, there is a high tolerance of DEVIANT or unusual forms and meanings in LITERARY, especially POETIC, LANGUAGE.

(3) In TEXT LINGUISTICS the term refers to the judgment of a TEXT in respect of COHERENCE and functional relevance. De Beaugrande & Dressler (1981) make it one of their (stringent) standards of TEXTUALITY (q.v.). Thus, presumably, an instruction leaflet for DIY double-glazing 'fails' as a text if the reader cannot make enough sense of it to fulfil the task.

(See also CORRECTNESS.)

accommodation

(1) In sociolinguistics a useful term to describe the very common phenomenon in social encounters, and often unconscious, where people alter their STYLE of speech or ACCENT to make it similar to that of their interlocutor, perhaps as a sign of identification. So the British Prime Minister Tony Blair was noted as using 'Cockney' glottalization, unusual for him normally, in a TV chat-show

interview with the comedian Des O'Connor. The context, and the speech-act frame of anecdote, probably also influenced this 'street-wise' informality.

(2) For the linguistic philosopher David Lewis (1979), the 'rules' of conversation are more **accommodating** than those of sport. According to context, the scope and salience of reference can shift, for example; and what is accurate enough on one occasion may not be on another. This idea of accommodation has recently been taken up in TEXTWORLD THEORY and DISCOURSE processing. (See further Werth 1999, ch. 5.)

acronym

From Gk 'beginning-name'; **acronyms** are a very popular twentieth-century method of word formation, by which words and especially names are formed from the initial letters of a group of words. A less common term is **protogram** (= 'first-letter').

Acronyms are commonly used to label scientific inventions (*laser* = 'Light Amplification by Stimulated Emission of Radiation'; *BASIC* = 'Beginners All-purpose Symbolic Instruction Code'). They also identify succinctly the names of organizations, etc. (*WASP* = 'White Anglo-Saxon Protestant'). It is fashionable to suggest a word already in the language, and one which is humorous or punningly appropriate (e.g. *CISSY*: 'Campaign to Impede Sexual Stereotyping in the Young').

They are sometimes confused with simple abbreviations or alphabetisms, which maintain the sequence of initials as letters, e.g. *MIT* (/em aɪtiː/) (Massachussetts Institute of Technology), *BSE* (bovine spongiform encephalopathy).

act

(1) Most often **act** refers to the major division of a play or opera. Traditionally tragedies have had five acts, following classical precedence, which generally reflect a pattern of action rising to a climax and ending with a catastrophe and final resolution (see also DÉNOUEMENT).

(2) In DISCOURSE ANALYSIS, **act** as developed by Sinclair & Coulthard (1975) refers to the smallest identifiable unit of conversational behaviour, as distinct from move, the smallest by which discourse is developed. Emphasis is placed on the FUNCTION of acts in the structure of discourse, on the way they take up what has gone before or solicit further activity: so TAG QUESTIONS like *don't you?*, *isn't it?* operate as 'appeals' for TURN-TAKING. Hence an alternative name is **interactional act**. But as labels like 'elicitation', 'directive', 'accept', etc., suggest for different types of act, interest is also taken in their PRAGMATIC function or communicative intent, arising out of the study of exchanges in classroom, surgery, dramatic text, etc., e.g. (spoken by a doctor): *Let's have a look at you. What seems to be the trouble?* ('starter' + 'elicitation').

They are therefore similar to ILLOCUTIONARY ACTS (q.v.); and both have been seen as subtypes of COMMUNICATIVE **acts**.

(3) The term **act** is also found in NARRATOLOGY in the analysis of CHARACTER. 'Acts of commission' refer to deeds done; 'of omission' to deeds not done; 'contemplated acts' to mere plans or intentions. (See Rimmon-Kenan 1983.)

(4) The DISCOURSE(E) phrases 'act of telling', 'act of writing', 'act of narration', refer to the actual activity of producing utterances (or ÉNONCIATION) within the whole context of teller, tale and reader.

(See also NARRATION.)

actant

Actant was introduced by the French linguist Tesnière (1959), but is particularly associated in NARRATOLOGY with the work of Greimas (1966f). As in the writings of the **Russian** FORMALISTS, Greimas views characters FUNCTIONALLY as actants or participants in a series of ACTIONS. The theory has also been applied to dramatic texts, and has its origins, in fact, in Aristotle's analysis of dramatic action in his *Poetics* (see also DRAMATIS PERSONA).

Actantial theory uses a framework or model analogous to a functional GRAMMAR of the SENTENCE: so the actant 'Sender' would correspond to grammatical SUBJECT; 'Receiver' to OBJECT, etc., and the PLOT itself would correspond to the standard sentence. Indeed, terms like 'actor', 'action' and 'goal' have been traditionally used by grammarians (not without criticism) to refer to subject, VERB, object, respectively.

The theory is designed to have universal significance, implying that different STORIES have the same DEEP or 'underlying' structural configurations. (See Propp's work, 1928, on the MORPHOLOGY of folk-tales, and the ROLES of 'hero', 'dispatcher', 'helper', 'villain', etc.) Yet the study has also been criticized for its schematization and reductiveness, its failure to account for other aspects of CHARACTER and its underestimation of the possible manipulation of roles and functions. Still, even if, for example, Magwitch, in Dickens's *Great Expectations* is both 'villain', 'donor' and 'helper', it is precisely our awareness of conventional and basic NARRATIVE structures which enables us to appreciate the variation.

The term *acteur* (from Greimas *op. cit.*) can be used for a character in any individual work with more than one role: an aspect of the SURFACE STRUCTURE. (See further Fowler 1977.)

action; actional code

(1) **Action** (singular) is traditionally used as a synonym for PLOT to describe the series of significant events in a play, film, novel, etc. (See also SJUŽET).

(2) In Barthes (1970) the **actional** (*actantiel*) CODE or **level** of a story refers to the successive stages of the action, and also the **actions** (plural) of the characters. This is also termed the **proairetic code**. Using this code we can also take account of type, manner, purpose and setting of actions; of sequences (connected actions); and series (unconnected actions).

(3) **Actions** in this sense can refer to physical acts or activities, speeches and thoughts. Dramatic 'action' therefore does not necessarily imply dynamic movement. SPEECH ACTS in DIALOGUE serve economically to verbalize actions (e.g. love-making, quarrelling, etc.); and actions important in the plot may be indirectly reported in description or discourse (e.g. the reconciliation of Leontes and Perdita in Shakespeare's *The Winter's Tale*).

active

Widely used in the GRAMMARS of many languages to describe a category concerned with the relations of SUBJECT and OBJECT, and the 'action' expressed by the VERB, i.e. VOICE (q.v.). An **active** CLAUSE or SENTENCE typically has a grammatical subject in the ROLE of AGENT of the action, which is expressed by a TRANSITIVE VERB; and an object in the role of 'affected' participant, e.g. *The Prime Minister claims a Brussels victory*.

Since agentive and affected roles are most characteristic of subjects and objects, it is natural for the active to be regarded as the **un**MARKED or neutral voice, as opposed to the PASSIVE (q.v.).

actualization

(1) **Actualization** or **realization** is used by linguists to refer to the physical manifestation of any underlying or ABSTRACT form. So, for example, the 'plural' MORPHEME <s> may be actualized by /s/ (*cat-s*), /z/ (*dog-s*), /ɪz/ (*horse-s*), etc. And a TEXT is an actualization of the potential CHOICES from the linguistic system.

(2) By analogy, the term came to be used in the work of Riffaterre (1978) as part of his TRANSFORMATIONAL theory of poetic composition, reinforced by its more dynamic connotations of action or process. In a poem the underlying THEME or idea is **actualized** in a complex text by the LEXICAL forms and references. Many of Shakespeare's sonnets present actualizations of the same ideas: e.g. the mutability of beauty; the inexorability of time.

(3) The sense of giving 'physical substance' or 'reality' is underlined by the use of **actualization** in READER-RESPONSE CRITICISM, where it is argued that works of art only exist as such, are only actualized, in the process of reading. In dramatic criticism, a performance of a play is an actualization of the reading of the text.

(4) More specifically, **actualization** appears in the NARRATIVE theory of Brémond (e.g. 1973). Here he describes the three logical stages in a sequence of actions: the aim or objective (first stage); putting the objective into action (second stage); success or failure (third stage). So Hamlet's delay in the actualization of revenge provides the central tension of the play.

(5) **Actualization** also came to be used by some translator-critics as the direct equivalent of the PRAGUE SCHOOL term *aktualisace*, traditionally and more popularly known as FOREGROUNDING (q.v.). The characteristic function of POETIC LANGUAGE is seen to be the 'throwing into relief' of the linguistic SIGN or UTTERANCE, which ordinarily is prone to AUTOMATIZATION (q.v.), or unconscious familiarity.

address, terms of

Forms used to refer to, or to name a person directly in speech or writing (see also VOCATIVE). They include titles (*your Ladyship*), kinship terms (*mother, mum*), endearments and insults (*darling, bitch*), as well as first name (*Cherie*), surname (*Blair*), and title and last name (*Mrs Blair*).

CHOICE of forms, which clearly vary in **degree of** FORMALITY, is dependent upon the speaker's relationship with, and attitude towards, the ADDRESSEE, and the kind of SITUATION in which the interchange takes place (e.g. private v. public; formal v. intimate). In sociolinguistics it is argued that two main relations governing choice are **power** or status (cf. office worker addressing boss); and **solidarity** or social intimacy (cf. terms used between school-friends; football players, etc.).

addressee; addresser

Terms referring to the two distinctive participants in any verbal ACT of COMMUNICATION or SPEECH EVENT (q.v.). Other equivalent terms (borrowed from French) are **locutor (addresser)** and **allocutor (addressee)**.

The addresser is normally the speaker/writer and sender of the MESSAGE (cf. **first** PERSON PRONOUN, *I, We*); the addressee, the person spoken/written to and receiver of the message (cf. **second** person *you*). (See also AUDIENCE.)

However, these ROLES of speaker/sender; hearer/receiver are not entirely interchangeable: for example, an official letter may be sent by a special messenger, and be intercepted by a secret agent or delivered to the wrong address. Moreover, a speaker may not always have the direct authority to speak: he or she may simply be a spokesperson (e.g. for the Ministry of the Environment), and the power be in the figure of an **addressor** (*sic*) (the Minister). In SOLILOQUY addresser and addressee are actually the same person.

In LITERARY DISCOURSE, especially poetry, these participants need not be human: rivers, birds and crosses, etc., speak (see PERSONIFICATION), or are addressed in invocation and APOSTROPHE: *No, Time, thou shalt not boast that I do change* (Shakespeare: Sonnet 123).

Literary discourse itself may be seen to be a complex act of communication involving more than one addresser and addressee. For example, the novelist as IMPLIED AUTHOR may address himself or herself to READERS (e.g. Fielding or George Eliot). In novels with an *I*-figure as NARRATOR the CHARACTERS are addressed, and a 'reader' may be (e.g. in Sterne's *Tristram Shandy*). In both third person and first person novels it could be argued that even without direct address to a reader, an image of a reader is still created, which is reflected in the TONE of the discourse (see also VOICE; MODALITY).

(For addressee-oriented criticism, see AFFECTIVE STYLISTICS; see also AVERAGE READER; IDEAL READER.)

adjacency pair

Adjacency pair was coined in sociolinguistics by Sacks *et al.* in the 1970s to refer to conversational sequences in which an UTTERANCE by one speaker depends upon an utterance made by another (i.e. a kind of TURN-TAKING). It is also known as a **tied pair** and in SPEECH ACT THEORY an ILLOCUTIONARY **sequel**, in DISCOURSE ANALYSIS an **exchange**.

In their simplest form adjacency pairs characterize such rituals as greetings (e.g. *How are you? – 'Fine, thank you'*); invitations (e.g. *'Can you come to dinner?' – 'Yes, I'd love to'*); and questions and answers generally. Cross-examinations, catechisms, quiz-games and joke-books present extensive examples of the latter, and also illustrate **chaining**, i.e. the linking of more than one pair in a sequence (cf. 'Knock-knock' jokes).

adjective

Adjective is a word class or part of speech which characteristically PREMODIFIES a NOUN in the so-called **attributive** position following the ARTICLE (e.g. *The White Peacock*); or which occurs in the so-called **predicative** position, following the VERB as a COMPLEMENT (e.g. *Roses are red, violets are blue, sugar is sweet, and so are you*). Unlike French, for example, adjectives in English do not characteristically occur in **postposition**, i.e. after the noun, but one can note their occurrence here in phrases borrowed from French (like *heir apparent*); and in **adjective phrases** (e.g. *a child easy to please*). In FORMAL, especially LITERARY LANGUAGE, a succession of adjectives may follow the noun in a CO-ORDINATED phrase: *The water, cold and grey . . .* (cf. *the cold grey water*). And in poetry, postposition of adjectives is quite common:

> She found me roots of relish sweet
> And honey wild . . .
>
> (Keats: *La Belle Dame Sans Merci*)

As *the cold grey water* illustrates, more than one adjective can premodify a noun, yet in ordinary usage multiple premodification is relatively rare. It is, however, characteristic of descriptive prose, eye-catching advertisements, auction catalogues, fashion journalism, etc. Adjectives in sequence generally conform to patterns of ordering, rather than random choice: based on semantic factors such as 'size', 'colour', 'age', etc. *A little brown jug*, or *a little red hen* (size + colour) seems more natural or **un**MARKED compared with *a brown little jug*, etc. Generally, evaluative or subjective adjectives like *charming, splendid*, come first in a string, e.g. *For sale: a very attractive large old Tudor brick farmhouse*.

(See also **poetic** EPITHET.)

adjunct

(1) Usually **adjunct** designates an element in the structure of a SEN which refers to a circumstance (e.g. reason, place, manner, etc.) rather t[ ] direct participant, e.g. *Farmers dig in* (*for battle*).

(2) By extension, it is sometimes used (especially in SYSTEMIC GRAMMAR) [ ] any structure loosely appended to a CLAUSE or sentence, e.g. connectors an[ ] MODIFIERS (e.g. *however, actually,* etc.); and even interpolations (e.g. *She has big* *– and I mean big – feet*). (See Winter 1982 on **ad hoc adjuncts**.)

(3) Since certain word classes such as ADVERBS and PREPOSITIONAL PHRASES are characteristically associated with circumstantial functions, it is often used synonymously with ADVERBIAL (q.v.).

(4) Confusingly, however, some grammarians (e.g. Quirk *et al.* 1985) use **adjunct** to refer to a subclass of the larger group adverbial (e.g. *slowly, greedily*), which is more integrated into the clause structure than either **disjunct** (e.g. words like *actually*) and CONJUNCT (connectives like *however*).

adnominatio

See POLYPTOTON.

adverb; adverbial

(1) **Adverb** is a word-class which is commonly marked by the SUFFIX *-ly* (for ADJECTIVE derivatives) and which refers to circumstances such as 'how' or 'why' or 'when', etc., an action is done. It characteristically occurs as an ADJUNCT in the CLAUSE structure, e.g. *quickly; now*.

(2) **Adverbial** is frequently used to embrace a larger group of constructions such as PREPOSITIONAL PHRASES, FINITE and NON-FINITE CLAUSES, which function in the same way as adverbs.

(3) Some grammarians also use the term as an equivalent to adjunct, i.e. for an element of SENTENCE structure.

Adverb(ials) as adjuncts generally have greater freedom of position in the clause than other elements. Choice of WORD ORDER for adverbs of 'manner', for instance, may be a matter of FOCUS or EMPHASIS:

<u>Suddenly</u> the door opened.
The door <u>suddenly</u> opened.
The door opened <u>suddenly</u>.

With adverbs of direction and place, INVERSION of SUBJECT and VERB can accompany the adverb in initial position, in literary and/or dramatic narrative (e.g. <u>Down came the rain</u>; <u>Here lies Farmer Brown</u>). Initial position is often used in sentences for sequences of adverbials, to avoid 'jamming' at the end, e.g. <u>Every year without fail</u> she comes here to Austria for winter skiing.

ADVERBIAL

TENCE
han a

or

~ value; ~ function; ~ code, etc.;

word meaning 'perceptive' **aesthetic** describes the
of what is 'beautiful', and is most used in the
Aesthetics is a branch of philosophy concerned with
.y.

what is 'beautiful' is a problem; and whether beauty is intrinsic,
of the beholder, or both. FORM especially is considered to be of
aesthetic value, and poetry, with its formal complexity and unity, is
ently described with reference to the aesthetic. The **Russian** FORMALISTS,
nd Roman Jakobson in particular, see poetry as language in its **aesthetic** FUNC-
TION: i.e. language used autonomously for the sake of the work of art itself, with
textual and thematic reference, rather than for an extra-textual communicative
or informational purpose. (On the autonomy of literary works, see also NEW
CRITICISM.) Yet allowance must be made for kinds of poems (e.g. love poems;
verse epistles; epigrams, etc.) which have a practical function. Conversely, an
aesthetic effect may be associated with 'functional' advertisements, with their
word-play, structural unity and fictional WORLDS.

(2) **Aesthetic** CODE therefore is a term used in SEMIOTICS to refer to any kind
of language in any situation which is self-conscious, or innovative. The aesthetic
is also a matter of response as well as what is intrinsic. Tastes in 'beauty' vary
from culture to culture, period to period. For some critics therefore, an aesthetic
object is not the same as an artefact, a physical object: it is rather our interpretation of it.

(3) **Aesthetic distance** has sometimes been used in LITERARY CRITICISM
to refer to the objectivity demanded by writer and reader with reference to
the literary work, lest art be confused with reality. Hence the attitudes of the
NARRATOR Stephen Dedalus need not be taken as Joyce's in *Portrait of the Artist
as a Young Man.*

(4) **Aestheticism** refers to a literary and artistic movement of the late nineteenth century introduced from France by Walter Pater, and influential on the
work of writers such as Swinburne, Arthur Symons, Oscar Wilde and Yeats. 'Art
for art's sake' was the catchword for a hedonistic philosophy alienated from
traditional religion and from commercialized society.

(See further Eagleton 1990.)

affect; affective: ~ criticism; ~ fallacy; ~ stylistics; ~ meaning, etc.

Basically **affective** refers to feelings, hence it means 'emotional'. In its COLLOCA-
TIONS as listed for this entry, however, it can apply (rather confusingly) either to
the emotions of the speaker/writer; or to the responses of the listener/reader
(**affected**).

(1) Traditionally **affective criticism** describes a kind of criticism which evaluates or explains literary texts in terms of their degree of success in producing appropriate emotional, even physical, responses in the reader (e.g. inducing tears, goose-pimples, etc.). Aristotle's theory of **catharsis**, or the purging of emotions, is an ancient and celebrated example. NEW CRITICS like Wimsatt & Beardsley (see Wimsatt 1954) who dislike this kind of judgment because it is too subjective, refer to it as the **affective fallacy**.

(2) However, the term **affective criticism** or **affective** STYLISTICS has been revived in America and France as part of a broader KINETIC approach to READER RESPONSE CRITICISM, itself a reaction to the 'narrow' text-orientated criticism advocated by such critics as Wimsatt & Beardsley. So Stanley Fish (e.g. 1970) is interested not only in emotional responses, but more particularly in the mental operations involved in the process of reading. Such an approach can also be criticized for its 'subjectivity', for it is difficult to verify.

(3) By some linguists the term **affective meaning** refers to the emotional associations or effects of words evoked in the reader/listener: e.g. *home; mother; solidarity* (see also EMOTIVE MEANING).

(4) By others, e.g. Leech (1974), **affective meaning** refers also to the emotional associations that words may have for the speaker/writer, and specifically what they (and clauses and phrases) may express of personal feelings and attitudes, etc. (e.g. *Speaking personally; I hate you; You idiot*). ATTITUDINAL MEANING is a possible alternative here; but it clearly also overlaps with EXPRESSIVE MEANING (q.v.). (See also CONNOTATION.)

(5) Related to this sense of affective is the use of the noun **affect** by some linguists to refer to the emotive aspect of SUBJECTIVITY, or what Halliday (1978) calls 'the degree of emotive charge' between interlocutors or participants. This can also include feelings, moods, dispositions and attitudes. Studies of affect are interested in lexical and grammatical **affect markers** or **keys**, and differences between GENRES (e.g. Biber & Finegan 1989); or diachronically changes in affect across periods, e.g. in scientific writing. (See also STANCE.)

(6) **Affective rhythm** and **affective function of rhythm** are terms used in the criticism of verse to refer to RHYTHMS which express or suggest moods or emotional states (see, e.g., Attridge 1982). Thus there appears even in ordinary speech a kind of ICONIC relationship between rapid rhythms and excitement; slow rhythms and seriousness or misery. In Herbert's

I struck the board, and cry'd, No more.
I will abroad.
What? Shall I ever sigh and pine?

(*The Collar*)

the jerky rhythm suggests the emphasis of heated feelings.

However, it must be stressed that the same rhythmic pattern can express different effects; and that affective functions must be judged in conjunction with the meaning suggested by other linguistic features in the poem.

affix; affixation

Affix is used in LEXICOLOGY for a MORPHEME or form which can be added to the base or root of a word, usually at the beginning (i.e. PREFIX) or end (i.e. SUFFIX), to make new words: e.g. *pre-war; kindness*.

Affixation or DERIVATION is a valuable and productive means of word formation in English, for deriving words from other parts of speech. It is commonly found in technical and official REGISTERS (cf. *pedestrian-iz-ation; de-oxyribonucle-ic*). In the POETIC DICTION of earlier periods from Spenser to the nineteenth century are found affixes such as *en-* and *be-* to form verbs (e.g. *en-slumber; be-dew*) and *-y* and *-ed* to form adjectives (e.g. *fleec-y; honey-ed*).

affricate

In PHONETICS this term describes a consonant articulated with initial complete stoppage of air followed by its gradual release to produce a kind of friction.

In English **affricates** are typical **palato-alveolar**, i.e. the blade of the tongue is in contact with the teeth (ALVEOLAR) ridge, and the front of the tongue is raised towards the hard palate: hence /tʃ/ usually written *ch* (VOICELESS) as in *Choose Cheese*; and /dʒ/ usually *dge* or *j* (VOICED) as in *jingle-jangle*.

agent; agentive

(1) In LEXICOLOGY an **agent** NOUN denotes the 'doer' of an action: e.g. *driver; publisher; cleaner; She's a heavy smoker/drinker*, etc. Typically such nouns are marked by an agentive SUFFIX, such as *-er*, but they need not be: e.g. *coach; referee*.

(2) In GRAMMAR **agent** refers to one of the semantic ROLES of nouns and PRONOUNS in relation to the PREDICATE. The (ANIMATE) instigator or doer of an action would thus be contrasted with, for example, the 'instrument', i.e. the means (INANIMATE) by which an action is done: e.g. *The princess opened the chest* v. *The key opened the chest* (cf. *The princess opened the chest with the key*).

Such concepts are independent of syntactic structure, yet clearly the grammatical SUBJECT is frequently an agentive (e.g. *She took a train to London*). In PASSIVE sentences the agentive phrase can be deleted, e.g. *The chest was opened (by the princess)*.

(3) In CASE GRAMMAR (q.v.), developed by Fillmore (1968), **agentive** is one of his basic categories (also **locative; instrumental**, etc.) to account for supposedly universal semantic, rather than MORPHOLOGICAL, relationships between sentence elements.

The concept of semantic roles is of interest and value in the STYLISTIC analysis of NARRATIVES (see, e.g., Fowler 1977). NARRATORS and CHARACTERS can be seen to be active instigators, or passive experiencers, according to whether they are 'agents' or 'patients'. And villains are often obvious agents; but characters may well have more than one role. (See also ACTANT.)

alexandrine

A six-BEAT line or **hexameter** introduced into English poetry in the sixteenth century after French models, but never accepted as a regular structural form like the four-beat line (**tetrameter**) or five-beat line (**pentameter**), probably because of its unusual length. It commonly occurs in isolation as part of a stanzaic METRICAL pattern, e.g. the last line of the stanzas in Byron's *Childe Harold's Pilgrimage*, or Spenser's *The Faerie Queene*:

> Full fast she flies, and farre afore him goes,
> /   /   /   /   /   /
> Ne feeles the thorns and thickets pricke her tender toes
>
>   (Book IV, canto vii)

Its MARKEDNESS is simultaneously commented upon and illustrated in Pope's *Essay on Criticism*:

> A needless Alexandrine ends the song
> That like a wounded snake, drags its slow length along.

alienation: ~ devices; alien

Alienation broadly refers to the 'act of ESTRANGING' or the 'state of ESTRANGEMENT'. From what, or whom, one can be estranged (self; God; society etc.) varies according to discipline: psychology, theology, MARXIST CRITICISM, etc.

(1) In LITERARY CRITICISM **alienation** refers to the 'gap' felt between the reader and a character as a result of an external PERSPECTIVE reinforced by words suggestive of ESTRANGEMENT (q.v.). So it is difficult for a reader to 'identify' with Gradgrind in the first chapter of Dickens's *Hard Times*, since his name is not given, and he is only and consistently referred to impersonally as 'the speaker'.

(2) **Alienation** or **alienation effect** is also used in dramatic theory to translate the concept of Ger. *Verfremdung* as defined and developed by Bertolt Brecht in the 1930s. Here theatrical devices are designed to distance the audience from the action so that the 'familiar should become strange'; so that they look afresh at the society they have become accustomed to. Estranging may therefore involve lighting effects, freezing of action, nonsensical dialogue, etc.

The alienation effect is based on the **Russian** FORMALIST principle of poetic art, that its FUNCTION is to 'make strange' the object described, to DEFAMILIARIZE (q.v.). (See also AUTOMATIZATION; FOREGROUNDING.)

(3) **Alienation devices** have been exploited in other disciplines for the same purpose, e.g. DISCOURSE ANALYSIS. The transcription of ordinary conversation into written form, for example, can show by this 'reification' aspects of its structure which might normally not be noticed. (See further Burton 1980.)

(4) The adjective **alien**, as translated from the Russian *cuzoj*, is used idiosyncratically in the work of the linguist-philosopher Mikhail Bakhtin in the 1930s to mean 'other', 'someone else's'. It does not necessarily imply 'estranged'. He suggests that generally the words we use are half someone else's; and that the

transmission and assessment of the alien word is one of the fundamental topics of speech. The mixture of 'own-ness' and 'other', what Bakhtin sees as a kind of DIALOGUE, is very characteristic of the DISCOURSE of the novel. For him the prose-writer welcomes the alien tones and CONNOTATIONS embedded in the words appropriated.

allegory

A NARRATIVE which is not simply a narrative; it is a TEXT which has a level of meaning other than the superficial one, whether political, historical, ethical, religious, etc., as in Spenser's *The Faerie Queene*. It can be seen to be a kind of extended METAPHOR (FIGURATIVE V. LITERAL MEANING); or AMBIGUITY (double/multiple meaning). While it might be argued that all literature is ethical, and that it demands a kind of allegorical process of INTERPRETATION, **allegory** proper is anti-MIMETICAL. The narrative level is not as significant as the **analogical** level or meaning. Related literary forms are beast-fables and parables, and 'examples' (*exempla*) in sermons.

In some works can be found explicit devices such as PERSONIFICATIONS and ABSTRACT places and settings: Giant Despair and the Slough of Despond in Bunyan's *Pilgrim's Progress*; the Seven Deadly Sins in *Piers Plowman* and *The Faerie Queene*. Often, however, the surface text provides no such obvious clues to other interpretations: e.g. Dryden's poem *Absalom and Achitophel*, which is an allegory satirical of the political situation of the day.

Allegory in the nineteenth century was frequently contrasted with SYMBOLISM (q.v.), and unfavourably, on the grounds that the allegorical SIGN is tied to one specific meaning, whereas a SYMBOL is more suggestive. But allegory can itself be seen as a systematic, structural kind of symbolism.

alliteration; alliterative verse

(1) Sometimes rather loosely paraphrased as 'initial RHYME', **alliteration** is the REPETITION of the initial consonant in two or more words.

As a deliberate PHONOLOGICAL device, it is associated mostly with LITERARY, especially POETIC, LANGUAGE; but it is also found in popular idioms (e.g. *rack and ruin; as dead as a doornail*), tongue twisters (*Peter Piper picked a peck of pickled pepper,* etc.) and advertising language (*Guinness is good for you*). The FOREGROUNDING of the sounds can be used for EMPHASIS, and to aid memorability. In poetry alliteration is characteristically used also for ONOMATOPOEIC effects, to suggest by the association of sounds what is being described, e.g.:

> While melting music steals upon the sky,
> And soften'd sounds along the waters die
>
> (Pope: *The Rape of the Lock*)

(2) Occurrences of more than two alliterated words seem MARKED to the modern reader, even over-emphatic. Yet extensive alliteration was regularly used as

a means of COHESION in so-called **alliterative verse**, which flourished in England before the Norman Conquest; and again in the north and west of the country in the fourteenth century (e.g. *Piers Plowman, Sir Gawain and the Green Knight*). The alliterated syllables are also the strongly ACCENTED or STRESSED syllables, and so are related to the RHYTHMIC pattern. As well as what can be seen as **continuous alliteration** (x x x x) there are patterns of **transverse alliteration** (x y x y), etc.

The extent to which alliteration in such poetry can also be EXPRESSIVE is a matter of dispute. It seems hard to deny associations in such lines as:

The snaw snitered ful snart, that snayped the wilde
                                        (*Sir Gawain and the Green Knight*)
(i.e. 'The snow came shivering down very bitterly, so that it nipped the wild animals').

Alliteration as a device of FORM has occasionally been exploited in later literature by poets such as Hopkins and Auden. For Hopkins in particular it takes its significance from its co-occurrence with other phonological patterns such as ASSONANCE, e.g.:

I caught this morning morning's minion, kingdom of daylight's dauphin, dapple-dawn-drawn Falcon, in his riding . . .

                                                        (*The Windhover*)

alveolar

In PHONETICS, a consonant articulated when the tip and blade of the tongue touch the ridge (*alveolum*) behind the upper teeth; which is one of the significant parts of the mouth for English consonants. Hence the PLOSIVES /t/ and /d/ are **alveolar**; also the FRICATIVES /s/ and /z/, and the nasal /n/ (pronounced with the nose passage open).

ambiguity; ambivalence

Ambiguity is double (or multiple) meaning: an ambiguous expression has more than one interpretation. The concept has, however, special implications in different disciplines.

(1) Linguists would see **ambiguity** as a linguistic universal, common to all languages, one of the inevitable consequences of the arbitrariness of language, i.e. the lack of one-to-one correspondence between SIGNS and meanings.

They often distinguish between the GRAMMATICAL ambiguity of phrases or SENTENCES, and the LEXICAL ambiguity of words. Grammatically ambiguous units admit the possibility of more than one structural interpretation: e.g. *Free women* as an IMPERATIVE in a slogan can be seen also as an ADJECTIVE plus NOUN (hence the graffitist's comment: *Where?*). In RHETORIC this would have been termed **amphibologia**. Lexical ambiguity arises because of POLYSEMY (words having more than one meaning) or HOMONYMY (words having the same form, but different origins). *I need new glasses* might mean something different to a short-sighted reader and a publican.

Ambiguity is more often potential than real: normally in speech and writing natural communicative REDUNDANCY, and the SITUATIONAL or TEXTUAL CONTEXT, will lead to the required interpretation of a MESSAGE. It is only forced on our attention when such clues are absent; and even then disambiguation may quickly occur by reassessment (e.g. *Piano sold to lady with carved legs; Dogs must be carried on escalators*).

(2) But when ambiguity does occur in discourse, it may not be tolerated if it hinders interpretation seriously. One of the 'rules' arising from the general CO-OPERATIVE PRINCIPLE of conversation (and indeed of writing), is that of clarity of meaning (see **maxim of** MANNER). Newspaper headlines are sometimes ambiguous in this derogatory sense (e.g. *British teachers amongst poorest in Europe*). **Ambiguity** in this sense is regarded as a 'fault' of STYLE, akin to vagueness and obscurity.

In certain REGISTERS, however, ambiguity may be exploited for humorous effect, especially in PUNS, e.g. in jokes, riddles and advertisements, e.g. *Buy a House with a Mouse* (Estate agent website); *Rest assured* (advertisement for beds); *How do you get down from elephants? You don't, you get it from ducks.*

(3) **Ambiguity** is also exploited in LITERARY, especially POETIC, LANGUAGE, and has been seen as one of the special or defining features of the latter. But here the reader is expected neither to be deceived or misled, or amused or irritated, but to hold the different interpretations in mind, and to give them equal serious meaningful value. The poetic context, in fact, does not always eliminate ambiguity, but can heighten it. Poetic ambiguity includes not only puns and double SYNTAX, but any expression which allows for alternative reactions or associations. In this sense it means multiplicity of meaning, and was popularized in LITERARY CRITICISM chiefly as a result of the work of Empson (1930).

(4) Ambiguity in this last sense is sometimes replaced by **ambivalence**, as suggesting the property of having more than one meaning of equal value. Some literary critics, however, would restrict it more narrowly to two meanings (cf. Lat. *ambo* 'both'), and so lose the Empsonian open-endedness.

(5) In ordinary use **ambivalence** is usually applied to (often contradictory) feelings or attitudes, and can imply uncertainty, or equivocation. But like *equivocation* also it can suggest deliberate ambiguity, e.g. to conceal the truth.

(6) In PRAGMATICS **ambivalence** has therefore come to be usefully employed for FUNCTIONAL ambiguity: an utterance may have more than one ILLOCUTIONARY FORCE. So in Shakespeare's *Richard II* Exton interpret's Bolingbroke's *Have I no friend will rid me of this living fear?* (V.iv) as a command to kill Richard; Bolingbroke, however, is able publicly to claim it as merely a wish (at V.vi).

amplificatio, also amplification

Amplificatio in RHETORIC refers to the use of devices and FIGURES OF SPEECH such as PERIPHRASIS, APOSTROPHE, HYPERBOLE, etc., to extend or expand an argument or narrative or to intensify its emotional impact.

It was much favoured by English prose writers and poets from the Middle Ages to the eighteenth century (e.g. Chaucer; John Lyly), and was not merely designed to be ornamental but also to heighten, and to 'win favour or move affections' (Thomas Wilson 1553).

(See also GRAND STYLE.)

anachronism; anachrony

(1) In literary and film studies **anachronism** is usually used critically to refer to any event or object which shows some discrepancy in temporal placing with respect to the period described. It is not a term, however, which can be usefully applied to medieval literature, since it reflects a concern for chronology and perspective that developed much later. Hence the characters in the Old English poem *Beowulf*, ostensibly set in the non-Christian Scandinavia of the sixth century, speak easily of the Christian God.

(2) **Linguistic anachronism** has sometimes been used, following Leech (1969), to refer to a kind of ARCHAISM (q.v.) whereby older forms of the language are deliberately revived or imitated, e.g. *eftsoons* ('soon afterwards'), *wist* ('know'), etc., in Coleridge's *The Rime of the Ancient Mariner*.

(3) In the study of NARRATIVE following Genette (1972) the special coinage **anachrony** is a general term to cover types of discrepancy between the (logical) STORY (HISTOIRE) order and the actual order of events in the DISCOURS(E). The two main kinds are ANALEPSIS and PROLEPSIS, i.e. 'flashback' and 'anticipation'. In this sense *Beowulf* is certainly full of **anachronies**. What may be of relevance is the distance of time forwards or backwards from the point reached in the narrative at any given moment; or the duration of the anachrony. More significant, perhaps, will be its function: to fill in information, to create a special kind of suspense (Beowulf will be killed by the dragon undoubtedly; but when, where and how?). Anachronies serve usefully in STREAM OF CONSCIOUSNESS writing, for example, to suggest the disordered play of recollections.

anacoluthon

From Gk 'inconsistent', **anacoluthon** is used in RHETORIC and modern GRAMMAR to refer to a grammatical sequence which begins in one way, and finishes in another, e.g.: *She was responsible for – had to interview me.*

It is often marked as above by a pause (or dash in writing), but changes in structure are not always immediately obvious. They are part of the habitual non-fluency of casual speech, arising from unclear formulation, heightened emotion, etc.; or, in longer and more complex sentences, from a failure perhaps to keep the whole construction intended in mind. In the dialogue of novels and plays **anacolutha** (plural) rarely appear unless to suggest some 'MARKED' feeling.

(See also APOSIOPESIS; BLENDING.)

anacrusis

In METRICAL studies **anacrusis** describes an unSTRESSED syllable at the beginning of a verse, which serves as a kind of metrical introduction, e.g. *O* | *come, all ye faithful.*
    An alternative term is **upbeat** (see Attridge 1982).

anadiplosis

In RHETORIC (from Gk 'to double back'), the REPETITION of the last part of one verse line or sentence at the beginning of the next. **Anadiplosis** was a device much favoured in Elizabethan poetry to link lines, and to reinforce the progression of ideas:

> My words I know do well set forth <u>my mind</u>;
> <u>My mind</u> bemoans his sense of inward <u>smart</u>;
> Such <u>smart</u> may pity claim of any <u>heart</u>;
> Her <u>heart</u>, sweet heart, is of no tiger's kind.

(Sidney: Astrophel and Stella)

It was also used as a device to link stanzas. The Middle English ALLITERATIVE poem *Pearl* presents an extensive illustration: its one hundred and one stanzas are arranged in 20 groups of five (one has six), each group clearly marked by anadiplosis of a 'key' word linking last and first lines in successive stanzas.

analepsis

One of a pair of terms coined by Genette (1972) to refer to the break in the telling of a story for a 'flashback' or retrospective NARRATION (v. ANTICIPATION of future events, i.e. PROLEPSIS). Such disruptions of normal (chronological) ordering he calls generally ANACHRONIES (q.v.). **Analepses** serve characteristically to fill in what now appear to be 'gaps', to provide necessary information about a character or event, etc., and are often framed realistically in the recollections of characters or narrators (e.g. Woolf's *Mrs Dalloway*). Analepsis is often a consequential feature of beginning a story IN MEDIAS RES, i.e. in the apparent 'middle' of a story.
    An alternative name from traditional rhetoric would appear to be **anamnesis** (Gk 'remind'). Dramatists have found it a useful, if sometimes 'stagey', device to present necessary information, especially at the beginning of a play (e.g. Prospero's conversation with Miranda in Shakespeare's *The Tempest*, I.ii).

anapaest

In the metrical study of verse, **anapaest** is the classical term for a FOOT or MEASURE which consists of three syllables, the first two unSTRESSED, the last stressed ($\times \times /$). The anapaestic foot can be distinguished from the DACTYL ($/ \times \times$). For example:

```
xx / x x   /    x x / x   x /
```
The Assyrian came down like the wolf on the fold,

```
x   x / x  x  / x x / xx  /
```
And his cohorts were gleaming in purple and gold.

(Byron: *The Destruction of Sennacherib*)

anaphora; anaphoric reference

(1) In RHETORIC **anaphora** (Gk 'carrying back') is a popular FIGURE OF SPEECH involving REPETITION of the same word at the beginning of successive clauses, sentences or verses (also known as **epanaphora**). It is found in verse and prose of all periods, and can be effectively deployed to underline descriptive and emotional effects, e.g.:

> The rain fell heavily on the roof, and pattered on the ground . . . The rain fell, heavily,
> drearily. It was a night of tears.

(Dickens: *Little Dorrit*, ch. 17)

It is common in public oratory to give structure to an argument, and to 'hammer home' a point, e.g.:

> We said we would get more money into schools . . .we have, . . . We said we'd sign
> the Social Chapter; we did . . . etc.

(Tony Blair, Labour Party Conference, 1 October 1997)

(2) In GRAMMAR and TEXT studies, anaphora (adj. **anaphoric**) popularly denotes a kind of REFERENCE which is 'backward-looking' (as distinct from CATAPHORIC (q.v.) 'forward-looking'), both important aspects of the COHESION or connectedness of DISCOURSE (Halliday & Hasan 1976). So the **third** PERSON PRONOUNS (*she, he, it, they*) function typically with **anaphoric reference**, for NOMINALS as **antecedents** in the CO-TEXT:

> Little Bo-Peep has lost her sheep,
> And doesn't know where to find them

The DEFINITE ARTICLE (*the*) and DEMONSTRATIVES like *that* can also be anaphoric; as also in FORMAL or legal English, are explicit phrases like *the aforesaid, the former*, etc. SUBSTITUTE forms like *do* and *one* usefully avoid repetition, e.g. *I thought you were changing your car. No, my flat-mate did. She found a new one, actually.*

ELLIPSIS can also be seen as a kind of anaphora in contexts where the 'complete' structure precedes it:

> The world's too little for thy tent,
> A grave [is] too big for me

(Herbert: *The Temper*)

With the development of DISCOURSE ANALYSIS, COGNITIVE LINGUISTICS and PRAGMATICS, formal approaches to anaphora have been reassessed, with emphasis given to discourse processing. So building on the work of Brown & Yule (1983), linguists like Wales (1996, ch. 3) and Emmott (1997) argue that third person pronouns in particular refer not to an 'antecedent' but to a mental representation of an entity. Both full nominals and pronouns are therefore 'pro-referents'.

What at first sight appears to be anaphoric reference sometimes occurs at the beginning of stories, poems or plays, and yet technically there are no 'antecedents'. Since it implies previous mention, and therefore existence, it helps to create the illusion of a WORLD into which the reader is dramatically thrust, IN MEDIAS RES (q.v.), e.g.: _He was struggling in every direction, he was the centre of the writhing and kicking knot of his own body_ . . . (the opening of Golding's _Pincher Martin_).

With the possible 'anticipation' of fuller information, the pronoun may be described as having CATAPHORIC REFERENCE, but see that entry for problems.

(3) Some uses of the term **anaphora** (**-ic**) are confusing, and are best avoided, since these senses are usefully named by other terms. It is sometimes used (e.g. Lyons 1977) to include both anaphoric and cataphoric reference, for which the general term ENDOPHORIC (q.v.) is otherwise favoured: reference within the text or discourse. Elam's (1980) notion of anaphora includes EXOPHORIC REFERENCE (q.v.), i.e. reference outside the text, in the CONTEXT OF SITUATION.

animate; animateness hierarchy

(1) A basic semantic distinction is that between human beings and animals which possess life or **animacy**, and objects which are INANIMATE (q.v.). (The distinction is not, however, clear-cut: e.g. plants, thunder, etc.) We thus expect the selection, for example, of an **animate** SUBJECT with the verb _smile_ (e.g. _Why is no-one smiling?_), but an inanimate subject with _sizzle_ (e.g. _The sausages were sizzling nicely in the pan_); and we also expect appropriate COLLOCATES for the adjectives _stale_ (e.g. _bread; air_) versus _mischievous_ (_child; imp_, etc.).

Violation of these norms or SELECTIONAL RULES, however, occurs frequently in FIGURATIVE LANGUAGE, both LITERARY and popular. In PERSONIFICATION inanimate objects are made animate (and also human), and can be seen as a kind of METAPHOR (cf. _the eye of needle; the hand of a clock; inflation threatens the economy; the pound suffers_, etc.). Less common perhaps, and more dramatic, is **de-animation**, which impersonalizes, 'deadens': troops referred to as the _remnant_ of a battle, for example.

(2) The concept of an **animateness hierarchy** has become popular through the work of COGNITIVE LINGUISTS like Lakoff & Turner (1989), to describe the tendency towards culturally determined anthropocentrism and personification. So NOUNS in English can be ranked conceptually on a scale of animateness, where human beings usually precede animals, animals precede plants, and plants precede objects, etc. This Lakoff and Turner term the Great Chain of Being, so invoking the medieval and Elizabethan world order with God and angels at the apex. Some common metaphors reflect this conceptual hierarchy. Human beings can be 'down-graded' by being equated with animals ('She's a pig'), or even objects ('He's got a heart of _stone_').

In English this hierarchy strongly influences the selection of **third** PERSON PRONOUNS: so, for example, culturally determined 'higher' animals like cats, dogs and horses will normally be referred to by *he/she*; but ants and worms by *it* (unless personification is involved). (See further Wales 1996, ch. 6.)

(See also COMPONENTIAL ANALYSIS.)

anomaly

(1) A term which covers all kinds of semantic incompatibility or contradiction. It depends by contrast on the principle of the normal conceptual classification of the features of the world around us.

However, **anomaly** is tolerated, even approved, in many situations, and it is often difficult to distinguish it from certain FIGURES OF SPEECH, such as METAPHOR, or IDIOMS. *She has green ears*, for instance, might make better sense on Mars; whereas *She has green fingers* is perfectly acceptable in a garden.

(2) Todorov (1967), in fact, has taken the term as a count noun (i.e. **anomalies**) to refer to what are traditionally known as TROPES (e.g. metaphor), i.e. 'rule-violating' devices

Anomaly is exploited for its attention-arresting possibilities in the naming practices of pop music bands, e.g. *Prefab Sprout*; *Aztec Camera*; and it is a regular feature of children's nonsense verse and zany riddles:

Q: What is grey and lights up?
A: An electric elephant.

antanaclasis

See PUN.

anticipation; anticipatory: ~ structure, etc.

(1) **Anticipation** is often used with various nuances in the analysis of NARRATIVES. For example, it is a gloss for Genette's (1972) term PROLEPSIS, the NARRATION of an event at a point earlier than its strict chronological place (as distinct from ANALEPSIS, the narration of an event at a later point). (See also ANACHRONY.) So in *Berlin Alexanderplatz* Döblin writes:

. . . The boy, Max Rüst, will later on become a tin-smith, father of seven more Rüsts, he will go to work for the firm Hallis & Co., Plumbing and Roofing, in Grünau . . .

Such a device, with the use of the 'prophetic' *will*, is unusual in the European novel tradition; readers would seem to prefer the element of suspense.

However, anticipation of a less strict kind than Genette's prolepsis certainly occurs: what can be seen as 'foreshadowing', often with the special dramatic

21

connotation of 'foreboding'. Later events are subtly hinted at, or prepared for by clues the reader re-evaluates later. The use of explicit prophecy is one obvious device (e.g. that of the witches in *Macbeth*).

Chatman (1978) uses the term **anticipatory satellite** for 'units' of a narrative which anticipate later outcomes.

(2) Anticipation is also built into non-literary discourse. ADDRESSERS are continually and continuously aware of the potential responses of their inter-locutors, who in turn like to predict the rest of the utterance. We anticipate explanations, refusals, objections, etc., and often make our fears explicit by special **anticipatory strategies** (e.g. *Before you object; I'm sorry to be a nuisance, but . . .*). Conversely, much overlapping and interruption occurs in conversation because the hearer has worked out what will follow (see Edmondson 1981).

Anticipation is basic to the Russian linguist-philosopher Bakhtin's notion of DIALOGISM (q.v.). Any utterance anticipates or provokes an answer, whether in speech or writing. For the social theorist Bourdieu such an anticipation of recep-tion can provoke a kind of self-censorship or EUPHEMISM: we may 'tone down' what we say. Politeness markers are another manifestation: what we might say could be potentially FACE-threatening. (See Bourdieu 1991.)

(3) Leech & Short (1981) use **anticipatory structure/constituent** in the special-ized sense of a SUBORDINATE or dependent CLAUSE which is non-final in a sen-tence, especially a COMPLEX or PERIODIC SENTENCE. Final constituents they term **trailing**. Sentences with more than one anticipatory constituent are generally characteristic of a FORMAL, written style, since the main clause and PROPOSITION are delayed. The syntactic pattern can underline a movement of suspense and resolution: cf. the very first sentence of Dickens's *David Copperfield*:

> Whether I shall turn out to be the hero of my own life, / or whether that station will be held by anybody else, / these pages must show.

anti-climax

See BATHOS.

anti-intentionalist approach

Underlying most modern LITERARY CRITICISM is the supposition that the 'mean-ing' of a work is primarily to be derived from the text itself (internal evidence), and not the INTENTIONS of its AUTHOR (external evidence). A writer may, of course, proclaim his intentions or design (as in Wordsworth's Prefaces to the *Lyrical Ballads*); but precept, it is argued, must ultimately be matched against practice.

(See also INTENTIONAL FALLACY. See further Wimsatt 1954.)

anti-language

(1) Coined by Halliday (1978) to refer to all those VARIETIES of language such as thieves' ARGOT or CANT, public-school SLANG, 'private' language of love-letters, etc., which are known only to exclusive initiates. They create an 'alternative' world, a counter-culture, whether as a badge of social resistance, or for secrecy, or both. Their distinction is often mainly LEXICAL: their users typically coin new equivalents for 'standard' terms, or for concepts of prime importance (e.g. *police* (*fuzz*); *booty* (*ice*); *informer* (*grass*); (**re-lexicalization**)). Lively examples of the **anti-language** of Elizabethan vagabonds and cut-purses are found in the pamphlets of the period by writers such as Dekker and Greene: e.g. *crashing-cheats* ('teeth'); *smelling-cheats* ('nose'); *queer-ken* ('prison'), etc. (See also Fowler 1979.)

(2) By extension the term could be applied to the radical linguistic DEVIATION and NEOLOGISM which characterize many modern so-called **anti-novels** like Joyce's *Finnegans Wake*, for whom reader 'initiates' are few.

(3) However, by a kind of metaphoric extension, it is possible, as Halliday *op. cit.* himself argues, to apply the term to the language of all novels, and of all literature. As readers we enter a unique WORLD of the writer's creation, verbalized in a unique way: 'Literature is both language and anti-language at the same time.' (See also MIND STYLE.)

antimetabole

See CHIASMUS.

antistrophe

(1) In Greek drama **antistrophe** (Gk 'turning about') seems originally to have referred to the returning movement of the Chorus, and then extended to the verses sung simultaneously. The first movement was the **strophe**, and a final movement (the Chorus standing still), was the **epode**.

(2) These terms were also applied to the structure of the poetic genre of ode: the **antistrophe** was the second strophe or **stanza**, in the same METRE as the first.

(3) **Antistrophe** was also used more generally in RHETORIC for inverse relations or parallels, the REPETITION of words in reverse order, e.g. *You must say what you mean and mean what you say*. (See Leech 1969.) Related terms are **antimetabole**, CHIASMUS and EPANODOS.

(4) Confusingly, **antistrophe** was also used in rhetoric for the repetition of a word at the end of successive clauses or lines (also known as **epiphora** or EPISTROPHE): e.g. the catalogue of Richard's deeds in Shakespeare's *Richard III* (IV.iv), where the repetition underscores the violence of the War of the Roses:

> *Queen Margaret*: I had an Edward, till a Richard killed him;
> I had a Harry, till a Richard killed him:

Thou hadst an Edward, till a Richard killed him;
Thou hadst a Richard, till a Richard killed him . . .

This also illustrates SYMPLOCE, initial and final repetition.

antithesis

Antithesis effectively contrasts ideas by contrasting LEXICAL ITEMS in a formal structure of PARALLELISM.

An extended example involving explicit ANTONYMY occurs at the opening of Dickens's *A Tale of Two Cities: It was the best of times, it was the worst of times, it was the age of wisdom, it was the age of foolishness* . . .

Many famous quotations are often based on witty or satirical antitheses; e.g. *Marriage has many pains, but celibacy has no pleasures* (Johnson: *Rasselas*).

The CONJUNCTION *but* is here used as an **antithetical conjunct**; other explicit markers in ordinary discourse include *on the contrary; by comparison; on the other hand*, etc.

(See also OXYMORON; PARADOX.)

antonomasia

From Gk 'name instead', **antonomasia** was used as a term in RHETORIC for usages which are still common today:

(1) Substitution of an ADJECTIVE phrase or NOUN PHRASE for a (well-known) proper name: e.g. *The Iron Duke* (The Duke of Wellington); *The Iron Chancellor* (Gordon Brown).

It is frequent in POETIC DICTION: cf. Gray's *Hymn to Adversity*:

Daughter of Jove, relentless Power,
Thou Tamer of the human breast . . .

and in religious language: e.g. *The Almighty* (God); *The Prince of Darkness* (Satan).

It can also be seen to operate in verbal TABOO, where a descriptive phrase or EUPHEMISM is substituted for the name of revered or feared objects, spirits, etc., e.g. the *Eumenides* (= 'gracious ones') for the Greek Furies, avenging spirits.

(2) The use of a proper name GENERICALLY as a common noun, to refer to a class or type: e.g. *He's a Casanova*. Many brand names have been popularly 'de-properized' in this way in ordinary speech: e.g. *biro; hoover*.

antonymy

Antonymy is well established in SEMANTICS to refer to contrasts of word meaning, chiefly in ADJECTIVES, but also NOUNS, and occasionally VERBS.

There are different kinds of antonymy, the most common involving opposites which are **gradable**, e.g. (*very*) *hot/cold*. Conjoined **antonyms** of this kind are characteristic of popular verse as expressions to suggest inclusiveness, or 'everyone': e.g. *young and old; high and low; streets wide and narrow.*

Other antonyms can be **ungraded** (also known as **complementaries** or **complementarity**). Here the contrast must be 'either/or', e.g. *alive/dead; female/male,* etc. To be dead is not to be alive (ungradable); whereas not to be hot (gradable) can be as much warm as cold.

Another kind of antonymy is found in so-called **converse pairs/converseness** or **relational opposites**. To *buy*, for example, asserts the converse *sell*; to be a *parent* is also to have a *child*.

It is possible for many words to be used as opposites in what can be seen as **contextual antonymy**: e.g. *look* and *act* in the ANTITHETICAL *She looks like an angel, but acts like a little devil.*

(See also OXYMORON. See further Cruse 1986; Lyons 1977; Rusiecki 1985.)

aphesis

In RHETORIC a kind of ELISION or CLIPPING process, in which the initial syllable of a word is omitted. Less common is the term **aphaeresis**, which the *OED* at least reserves for special (NONCE) loss, rather than gradual loss (**aphesis**).

For METRICAL needs it is often found in POETIC LANGUAGE (e.g. (*be*)'*twixt;* (*a*)'*gainst*); but it is also common in informal speech, for economy of effort (e.g. (*tele*)'*phone*; (*aero*)'*plane*). For some words (e.g. *bus*), the fuller form (*omnibus*) is no longer used as the FORMAL alternative.

(See also APOCOPE; SYNCOPE.)

aphorism

(1) An **aphorism** is a pithy statement or maxim expressing some general or gnomic truth about (human) nature. It is usually marked by the PRESENT TENSE, as in Pope's

A little learning is a dangerous thing;
Drink deep, or taste not the Pierian spring

(*An Essay on Criticism*)

Impersonal and authoritative, it is characteristic of many ancient literatures and appears frequently in seventeenth and eighteenth-century prose essays. Yet as Fowler (1977) notes, in the novel it is a sign of the intrusive or assertive author–narrator (e.g. in the works of Fielding and George Eliot).

(2) **Aphoristic sentence** in GRAMMAR refers to a minor SENTENCE type (i.e. without a FINITE VERB) where there are two equivalent or parallel constructions: as in the proverbial *Easy come, easy go; First come, first served.*

Sometimes regarded as an unproductive sentence type, it is, however, quite common in ordinary speech and REGISTERS such as advertising (e.g. *Fill trolley, save lolly; No homework, no pocket money*).

apocope

In RHETORIC **apocope** refers to the omission or ELISION of the last syllable(s) of a word, as in POETIC DICTION, e.g. *oft(en)*. It can usefully be applied to the CLIPPING in informal speech in words like *ad(vert)(isement)*; *photo(graph)*.

(See also APHESIS; SYNCOPE.)

apophony

Also known as **vowel gradation** or **antiphony, apophony** refers to variation in vowels where the consonants of the word or syllable remain constant:

(1) in words relating to roughly the same semantic FIELD (e.g. *tip, top; slit, slot*).

(2) in COMPOUNDS like *flip-flop; tick-tock; pitter-patter*, where the alternation of vowel symbolizes alternation of movement or sound (also known as **ablaut-combinations** in Strang 1970; and classed generally as **reduplicatives** by Quirk *et al.* 1985).

(3) between words in verse for EXPRESSIVE effects: what Hopkins calls **vowelling off**, and a device much exploited in his poetry, along with related devices of ALLITERATION and ASSONANCE, e.g.

> . . . throned behind
> Death with a sovereignty that <u>heeds</u> but <u>hides</u>, <u>bodes</u> but <u>abides</u> . . .
> > (*The Wreck of the Deutschland*)

(See also PARARHYME.)

Antiphony as a LEXICAL feature seems to be related to what linguists term **ablaut**, the ancient Indo-European grammatical phenomenon surviving in Germanic languages generally of vowel alternation to indicate the different categories of irregular VERBS: e.g. NE *ring, rang, rung*.

aporia

(1) From Gk 'impassable path', a term in RHETORIC to describe a moment of deliberation or hesitation on the part of a speaker, particularly when confronted by an apparently insolvable problem or conundrum. Hamlet's famous 'To be or not to be' soliloquy in III.i provides a striking extended example.

(2) This soliloquy also illustrates, in the movement of Hamlet's logical reasoning, the revival of the term in DECONSTRUCTION THEORY, in the sense of a textual impasse, a moment when the logic is unravelled. It can also refer to a

clash or a GAP between the LITERAL and FIGURATIVE senses of an utterance or sentence, when the meaning of a text is really undecidable, and potentially richly AMBIVALENT. So in this way the last sentence of Larkin's *The Whitsun Weddings* with the image of the arrow-shower actually resists the poem's CLOSURE:

> We slowed again,
> And as the tightened brakes took hold, there swelled
> A sense of falling, like an arrow-shower
> Sent out of sight, somewhere becoming rain.

aposiopesis

A RHETORICAL term for the sudden breaking off of an utterance before it is completed, usually in moments of emotion (e.g. *What the* . . .).

In the normal flow of LITERARY DISCOURSE **aposiopesis** is rare, but MARKED when it appears. A striking example helps form the climax of Fitzgerald's *The Great Gatsby*, as the narrator Nick Carraway sums up Gatsby's aspirations. It is as if the unfinished sentence ENACTS the hope, and also the vanity, of Gatsby's dreams:

> Gatsby believed in the green light, the orgastic future that year by year recedes before us. It eluded us then, but that's no matter – tomorrow we will run faster, stretch out our arms further . . . And one fine morning –
> So we beat on, boats against the current, borne back ceaselessly into the past.

(See also ANACOLUTHON.)

apostrophe

A RHETORICAL FIGURE in traditional poetic and dramatic language. From Gk meaning 'turning away', **apostrophe** originated in the orator's turning aside from his immediate audience to address some other person, whether physically present or not. It then came to signify a VOCATIVE address to an absent, or dead person, or to an INANIMATE object or quality as if PERSONIFIED. No longer fashionable in oratory or poetry, apostrophe is typically exclamatory and emotive, and is particularly striking in SOLILOQUY, or at the opening of poems, e.g.

> Busie old foole, unruly Sunne,
> Why dost thou thus,
> Through windowes, and through curtaines call on us?
>
> (Donne: *The Sun Rising*)

apposition

Apposition is commonly used in GRAMMAR to refer to a sequence of units (usually NOUN PHRASES) with identical REFERENCE and grammatical FUNCTION, e.g. *Tom, the piper's son, stole a pig.*

The **appositional phrase** is commonly marked off by commas in writing, or a separate TONE UNIT in speech. It has many functions: to provide, in a kind of POSTMODIFICATION, additional information or description by way of identification (*The author, Katie Wales*); designation (*Katie Wales, the author*); explanation; reformulation, etc. Appositional phrases consisting of title and proper name are extremely common in journalism, e.g. *The local National Lottery winner, Vera Bloggs, 44 year-old mother of two* . . .

Apposition is often explicitly marked by **apposition markers** or CONNECTIVES such as *namely; that is; i.e.; that is to say; or rather*, etc., especially in REGISTERS where explicitness and clarity are important (e.g. scientific articles; official reports).

appropriateness: ~ conditions

Generally meaning 'suitability', **appropriateness** has been a pervasive concept in STYLISTIC theory since classical times, and has been extended into sociolinguistics, and FUNCTIONAL approaches to the study of language.

(1) The **appropriateness** or propriety of FORM and STYLE to subject matter was regarded as a virtue in RHETORIC from Aristotle onwards. Its most important realization is in the concept of DECORUM (q.v.), a doctrine of propriety in style, form, theme, characterization, audience, etc.

(2) **Appropriateness** is also an important aspect of non-literary language, and the term REGISTER (q.v.) has been used in senses very similar to (literary) decorum. It is part of their COMMUNICATIVE COMPETENCE that native speakers are aware that certain kinds of language or expressions are more suitable or efficient in some situations or for some functions than others (e.g. SLANG in informal speech, rather than in a legal document). (See also ACCEPTABILITY.) Inappropriate language may seem to be inept, even offensive (e.g. lecturing to students as if they were in a nursery school), but can be exploited for striking effect in **register-borrowing**. Features of language deemed appropriate can often become conventionalized in certain situations over a period of time (e.g. FORMULAS in condolences, business letters, invitations, etc.).

Appropriateness as a working concept in linguistics has replaced the older concept of CORRECTNESS (q.v.).

(3) In SPEECH ACT THEORY, appropriateness and competence come together under the term **appropriateness conditions**. These are the different kinds of PRAGMATIC constraints that must be fulfilled in order for an UTTERANCE or speech act to achieve its communicative purpose. (See also FELICITY CONDITIONS.) So in giving a command, or making a request, the speaker must have the appropriate status or authority to do so, and in the appropriate CONTEXT.

In a novel or a play, such appropriateness conditions must normally be recreated by the author in the construction of DIALOGUE, itself subjected to the reader's judgment of literary appropriateness and thematic relevance (see (1) above).

archaism

(1) **Archaism** and its derivative adjective **archaic** reflect an awareness of language change, and belong to a set of terms which range from 'obsolescence'/ 'obsolete' to 'innovation/innovatory'.

Archaism is the retention or survival of linguistic features no longer generally current, usually in VARIETIES that are themselves 'unusual' in some way. So archaisms and archaic grammatical features are commonly found in regional DIALECTS. They are found also in the language of the liturgy (*forthwith; ye; thou; takest*, etc.), although they have now been expunged (controversially) from revised versions of the Bible and Prayer Book. They occur also in legal language still (e.g. *witnesseth; aforesaid; hereunder*), and in linguistic situations that are characteristically conservative or ceremonial. It is thus very difficult to dissociate archaisms from words which are simply rare or formal (e.g. *cavalcade* in a report on a royal wedding). This is particularly true in POETIC LANGUAGE, where at least until the early twentieth century archaism was an accepted part of standard poetic usage, along with APOSTROPHE, PERSONIFICATION and POETIC DICTION: e.g.

Thou still unravished bride of quietness,
Thou foster-child of Silence and slow Time,
Sylvan historian, who canst thus express
A flowery tale more sweetly than our rhyme

(Keats: *Ode on a Grecian Urn*)

(2) Archaism in poetry is complicated by an additional factor that reflects a subtle distinction in the sense of the term itself. For it can mean not only the retention of what is old, but its imitation: not survival, but revival, for which the appropriate adjective is **archaistic** (cf. also to **archaize**). This is also known as **linguistic** ANACHRONISM. Many poets from Spenser onwards (and possibly as far back as Laʒamon in the twelfth century), have deliberately revived words such as *eld* ('age') and *quoth* ('said') in their recreations of a bygone age (e.g. *The Faerie Queene*); or of an ancient genre such as pastoral (with its additional rural associations). Another motive was the imitation of the language of past poets: Spenser of Chaucer, Milton of Spenser.

archetype

From Gk meaning 'original pattern', and so close in meaning to **prototype**, this word is often colloquially used to refer to something 'typical', or the perfect example. However, in LITERARY CRITICISM it is particularly associated with the work of Northrop Frye (1957), who identified recurrent units, quasi-mythical images, symbols or themes in literature, of universal significance, integrating one text with another, and with which readers subconsciously identify: e.g. the cycle of the seasons, and old age.

Archetypal criticism of this kind is indebted to the work of the anthropologist Sir James Fraser at the turn of the twentieth century, and of the psychiatrist Carl

Gustav Jung, particularly his theory of the 'collective unconscious'. For Jung dreams, as well as literature, universally make use of primordial archetypes: mountain peaks, towers, river valleys; a theory much exploited by James Joyce in his last work, the 'dream-vision' *Finnegans Wake*.

argot

Borrowed from French (but of unknown origin) **argot** refers to the special linguistic usages of certain (usually anti-social) groups of people, such as thieves. Words such as *porridge* and *stir* for prison (sentence) have become widely known.

JARGON and SLANG are sometimes used synonymously with this term, but slang is more usefully applied to the colloquial usages of all native speakers; and jargon is better applied to the technical vocabulary of occupations and disciplines (e.g. STYLISTICS). Admittedly it is not always easy to make distinctions. Does the terminology of that 'élite' group of 'hackers' who break into other people's computer systems constitute jargon or an argot? (For example, the grades of hackers have been termed *novice, student, tourist, crasher* and *thief*.)

ANTI-LANGUAGE (q.v.) as a technical term itself has tended to replace **argot** in present-day language study, just as **argot** has tended to replace the earlier term CANT (q.v.).

(See also RE-LEXICALIZATION.)

article

Article (Lat. *articulus* 'joint') refers to a small class of grammatical items which function solely as MODIFIERS of the NOUN and which simply, if significantly, indicate the DEFINITENESS or INDEFINITENESS of the noun. The two most important articles are the DEFINITE (*the*) and INDEFINITE (*a*), whose main TEXTUAL functions are to signal either that the noun is 'known' already (definite), or that it is being introduced for the first time (indefinite). (See also GIVEN V. NEW.) For example: *A documentary on London's police was released today. The film will be shown in local youth-clubs.*

However, since articles have little lexical meaning, in certain contexts they can easily be omitted to save space or time, e.g. newspaper headlines, small ads, note-taking, etc.

Articles are sometimes called DETERMINERS (q.v.), although the term is also used generically to refer to a larger class of items which 'determine' noun status in similar ways (e.g. *this; that*), but which can be used more flexibly (e.g. as PRONOUNS) than the articles proper.

(See also GENERIC REFERENCE; ZERO ARTICLE.)

aside

(1) A dramatic and theatrical convention in which an actor turns to address the audience directly.

Asides are often emotional or sarcastic, functioning as comments on the action, or providing explicit motivations. Although it might be argued that they 'break FRAME', destroy the illusion of MIMESIS, it is also true that the audience become involved in the play, and are not mere passive spectators. However, it is a licence not much used in modern, naturalistic drama.

(2) **Aside** is also found in DISCOURSE ANALYSIS. Like the dramatic aside, a **conversational aside** does not belong to the interchange proper, and there is usually a distinct change in tone or voice quality; but analysts seem to see it as a kind of self-address by a speaker, with very little purpose except as a PHATIC signal, a gap-filler (e.g. *Let's see what we've got; Oh come on, why not?*). Commentative asides by listeners similar to those in drama can occur in conversation, but may often appear sarcastic (e.g. *Oh no, not that joke again*).

aspect

(1) A grammatical category applied to VERBS, referring to particular ways of viewing the temporal constraints of an activity or event. In English the two kinds of **aspect** which are marked formally in the verb phrase are:

(a) the PROGRESSIVE (q.v.), which indicates whether an action is in progress (*be + ing: She is changing the gear-box*);

(b) the PERFECT or PERFECTIVE (q.v.), which indicates whether an action is completed (*have + ed/en: She has changed the gear-box*).

It is difficult to dissociate aspect from TENSE, the verbal category that denotes temporal distinctions. It is not only that aspect combines with tense to give the present progressive (e.g. *She is changing the gear-box*) or the past progressive (e.g. *She was changing the gear-box*), but also that in present-day English the progressive is more usual (**un**MARKED) to describe a single action done at the present time, than the simple PRESENT TENSE itself (cf. *the kettle's boiling* v. *the kettle boils*).

Although the relationship between perfect and simple past tense is complex (see PERFECT), in NARRATIVES where the past tense is the 'norm', the significance of the (past) perfect (or **pluperfect**) for aspect is apparent. It is not so much a sense of completion that emerges, but of setting or ORIENTATION v. story-line, e.g.:

> The trusser and his family proceeded on their way, and soon entered the Fair-field, which showed standing-places and pens where many hundreds of horses and sheep had been exhibited . . . At present, as their informant had observed, but little real business remained on hand . . .
>
> (Hardy: *The Mayor of Casterbridge*, ch. 1)

A shift from tense to aspectual distinctions can also mark a shift from narrative to FREE INDIRECT STYLE, to indicate a character's thoughts, e.g.: *I pressed the door gently. It had always been left open at night in the old days.* (Murdoch: *The Italian Girl*, opening sentences.)

(2) The term **aspect** was borrowed by Todorov (1966) and applied to the study of NARRATIVE: the PERSPECTIVE from which a story is viewed by the NARRATOR. A much more widely used term is POINT OF VIEW (q.v.).

assimilation

A term in PHONETICS to refer to the change of one sound into another at word boundaries in connected speech, under the influence of an adjacent sound.

For example, final ALVEOLAR consonants (e.g. /t d n/) readily change their place of articulation in this way: as in *good* (/b/) *morning*, where the (BILABIAL) /m/ bilabializes the preceding PLOSIVE /d/ by anticipation. (See further Gimson 1989.)

Such variant pronunciations as *breb 'm butter* and *reg* (/g/) *currants* occur extremely frequently in informal speech, but are hardly ever recorded in writing. However, some novelists may record them for comic or colloquial effect: so Kingsley Amis in *Girl 20* has an aging composer speaking of *corm beef* and *tim peaches*.

Assimilations are perhaps less noticeable in speech than ELISIONS or losses of sounds, which are also a feature of normal colloquial speech, but which are represented in informal spellings such as *I'm; she's; can't*, etc.

(See also COALESCENCE.)

associative: ~ meaning; ~ engineering, etc.

(1) **Associative meaning** for Leech (1981) is an inclusive term for kinds of AFFECTIVE or EMOTIVE MEANINGS or CONNOTATIONS which words commonly attract other than their CONCEPTUAL MEANINGS.

In politics, for example, many words acquire partisan **associations**, and can be exploited for propaganda purposes (e.g. *Vietnam; imperialism*). In advertising and sales promotions, brand names are frequently coined which evoke associations of luxury (Lux soap), macho-man (Brut aftershave) or wealth (All Gold chocolates): what Leech calls **associative engineering**. (See also EUPHEMISM.)

(2) In his analysis of the FUNCTIONS of RHYTHM in poetry, Attridge (1982) points out how different rhythms come to acquire particular associations, which are conventionalized. So it is difficult for us not to associate the rhythm and FORM of a limerick with humour and exaggeration. IAMBIC PENTAMETER, by contrast, has associations with the serious mainstream verse inherited from Shakespeare.

assonance

(1) A partial or HALF-RHYME much used in POETIC LANGUAGE as an aspect of sound patterning and COHESION. The same (STRESSED) vowel is repeated in words, but with a different final consonant (e.g. *cough drop; fish 'n' chips*).

Assonance is used for a variety of EXPRESSIVE effects. In the poem by Tennyson beginning

Break, break, break,
On thy cold grey stones, O Sea!

the double assonance of the diphthongs /eɪ/ and /əʊ/ enforces the LEXICAL links of *break* and *grey*, *cold* and *stone*; and also suggests (by the vowel length) the steady, inexorable movement of the sea, as well as the narrator's anguish.

(2) **Assonance** is sometimes more loosely used to refer to all kinds of PHONO-LOGICAL recurrence or juxtaposition, e.g. ALLITERATION and RHYME.

asyndeton; asyndetic co-ordination

Asyndeton in traditional GRAMMARS and RHETORIC refers to CO-ORDINATED CLAUSES or phrases without explicit CONJUNCTIONS or CONNECTIVES (Gk 'uncon-nected'). In Quirk *et al.* (1985, 13.1) it is termed **asyndetic co-ordination**. For example:

At Mr. Wackford Squeers's Academy, Dotheboys Hall . . . Youth are boarded, clothed, booked, furnished with pocket-money, provided with all necessaries, instructed in all languages living and dead.

(Dickens: *Nicholas Nickeby*, ch. 3)

Asyndeton is common as a rhetorical device of listing in Renaissance poetry; so in Donne's *Holy Sonnet* 7 the poet urges souls to arise from death:

All whom warre, dearth, age, agues, tyrannies,
Despaire, law, chance, hath slaine . . .

also known as **brachylogia**.

attitude; attitudinal meaning

(1) **Attitudinal meaning** as used in semantics and PHONETICS reflects the fact that we use language not only to communicate factual information, but also feelings and **attitudes**.

PROSODIC and PARALINGUISTIC FEATURES of speech are important indicators of attitudes: loudness, voice quality, and INTONATION can show boredom, excite-ment, anger or sarcasm. High pitch levels and dramatic 'rise' or 'fall' contours of TONE are more readily associated with passionate feelings than low pitch levels, which suggest reserve, detachment, or simply neutrality.

Attitudes in face-to-face interactions can also be conveyed by body language: facial expressions of disgust, pleasure, etc.; hand gestures of triumph ('thumbs up') or ill luck ('thumbs down').

Some attitudinal meanings are difficult to convey in writing: exclamation marks, capital letters and more explicit choices of LEXIS and SYNTAX supplant prosodic devices (e.g. *Thanks ever so much for the lovely present!*). At the same time, however, the attitudes of one's ADDRESSEE(s) cannot be perceived, which would be part of the natural FEEDBACK in DISCOURSE.

(2) In NARRATIVE theory the study of the NARRATOR's **attitude** to the story being told to the IMPLIED READER can be seen as an important aspect of the study of POINT OF VIEW. The narrator of Sterne's *Tristram Shandy*, for instance, is self-conscious about his ability to tell his own life story; and is variously deferent to, intimate with and teasing of his 'reader(s)'.

audience

(1) In its basic collective sense of an 'assembly of listeners', we think of a lecture **audience**, or a theatre audience, or the MASS audiences of radio and TV networks and commercial advertising.

Speakers will adjust their language to suit the size and/or social ROLE of their audiences. Scientists can assume their audience, whatever the size, will share a similar background of knowledge and PRESUPPOSITIONS, and will neither seek to ingratiate themselves, nor provide unnecessary explanations. DJs, however, address their unknown audience of millions in a friendly, even intimate manner, to transcend potential IMPERSONALITY. But the very heterogeneity of a broadcast audience in respect of sex, age, race, creed, etc. means that CHOICE of subject matter and language is limited (see Goffman 1981).

The members of theatre audiences are, in one sense, merely bystanders and overhearers to the ACTION; yet in another sense their presence (as patrons) is vital to the performance. Plays are cancelled and considered failures if no-one goes to see them; and the audience's applause at the conclusion is a kind of 'blessing'. Moreover, in some plays the audience becomes part of the action (as in *Noises Off* by Michael Frayn), or is addressed in ASIDES.

(2) With the spread of literacy over the centuries, **audience** has also come to be used to refer to an assembly of READERS. **Readership** and **reading public** are alternatives, but sound too abstract and impersonal.

Authors have no control over their readership or audience, although they may well write with an IDEAL READER or audience in mind (e.g. Eliot for *The Wasteland*); they may also have their NARRATORS address a fictional IMPLIED READER or audience, as in the opening to Dickens's *Martin Chuzzlewit*:

As no lady or gentleman, with any claims to polite breeding, can possibly sympathise with the Chuzzlewit family without being first assured of the extreme antiquity of the race . . .

(See also ADDRESSEE; NARRATEE.)

aureate: ~ diction; ~ style

Aureate diction is a poetic vocabulary much favoured by fifteenth-century poets and followers of Chaucer. The adjective **aureate**, i.e. 'golden', seems first to have been used by Lydgate, and describes a decorative **style** characterized by polysyllabic Latinate words and coinages such as *celicall* ('heavenly'), *nebule* ('cloudy'). Through aureate diction the so-called Scottish Chaucerian poets like Dunbar, Henryson and James I wished to 'enrich' and elevate the VERNACULAR language as a medium for poetry.

(See also INKHORN TERM.)

author; authority

For the production of LITERATURE there must be an **author**, a TEXT and a READER. Theoretical and critical approaches have been variously centred upon each of these three 'nodes' (see, e.g., Eagleton 1983). Traditional LITERARY CRITICISM, inherited from the nineteenth century, has been preoccupied with the author; and more recently AFFECTIVE STYLISTICS and RECEPTION THEORY have been preoccupied with the responses and responsibilities of the reader. In between, the analysis of texts as texts has been popular in twentieth-century criticism in NEW CRITICISM, **Russian** FORMALISM and STYLISTICS. As a result the role and significance of the author have been much discussed.

(1) It is a commonplace now to distinguish the real author from the IMPLIED AUTHOR (q.v.): the 'Fielding' or 'Sterne' who may (or may not) intrusively address the 'reader', and whose opinions and POINT OF VIEW as NARRATOR may not coincide with those of the historical author Henry Fielding or Laurence Sterne. The **authorial** VOICE is thus a textual construct.

It is also a commonplace to adopt an ANTI-INTENTIONALIST approach to the study of the meaning of the text: to argue that the real author's INTENTIONS are largely impossible to ascertain, and are critically irrelevant.

(2) Combined with views popular in French STRUCTURALISM and beyond (see, e.g., Barthes 1970, 1977), that the text is in any case created not by an author but by the reader, it is not surprising that the 'death of the author' should have been announced, and be the slogan in vogue since the late 1970s. Literally, of course, authors die, but their works survive; and there are literary texts which we read, but whose authors are unknown (e.g. the fourteenth-century ALLITER-ATIVE poem *Sir Gawain and the Green Knight*).

(3) Nonetheless, the (real) authorial presence cannot utterly be banished. Literary texts are not produced in a social vacuum, nor written by robots. Since medieval times we expect literature to be 'signed', and we respect the authors' rights to the financial fruits of their labours. We also tend to respect their **author-ity** as reliable critics of society and human nature although FEMINIST CRITICS seek to deconstruct any patriarchal connotations of such **authoritative discourse**.

r, if the implied author is a fiction, it is also partly constructed from
ie reader knows about the real author: the IDEOLOGICAL 'authority' of
ased on the author-figure or PERSONA and something behind that:
or posited real author, or EXTRAFICTIONAL VOICE (q.v.) in Lanser's
;. In her view, the notion of author, far from disappearing, actually
expands.

(4) In non-literary VARIETIES of language the role and significance of the
author is less important. Indeed, it might be argued that the more important
the notion of authorship, the more 'literary' the text (e.g. travel books and bio-
graphies, reviewed in the *Times Literary Supplement*). But notions of authority are
also important, for texts such as learned articles, scientific theories or theological
interpretation, etc. In public notices and advertisements, on the other hand, no
authorship is claimed or demanded; in radio and TV announcing, the ADDRESSER
is not necessarily the author of the words spoken.

Film studies raise the issue of multiple authorship: e.g. of director as well
as screen-writer as the source of creativity and authority: in so-called 'auteur-
theory' (Sarris 1968), adopting French film theory of the 1950s. (For other views
see Caughie 1981.)

automatization

As used by the **Russian** FORMALISTS and PRAGUE SCHOOL in opposition to
FOREGROUNDING (q.v.), **automatization** refers to the process of over-familiarity
to which linguistic SIGNS are prone in everyday communication, so that users
of a language are no longer aware of their AESTHETIC possibilities. Poetry, by
contrast, DE-AUTOMATIZES, it ACTUALIZES or foregrounds the linguistic utterance
consciously and dynamically.

But even within the field of poetic language a tension arises between forces of
innovation and conventionalization: poetic phrases can become stock CLICHÉS,
part of a POETIC DICTION (e.g. *purling brooks; fleecy care*), which new generations
of poets react against.

(See also BACKGROUNDING.)

auxiliary verb

(1) **Auxiliaries** are a CLOSED subclass of VERBS which help to make distinctions
of ASPECT, VOICE, etc. in the VERB PHRASE and which normally cannot occur
independently of other (**main** or **lexical**) **verbs**.

One of the most important is *do*, which is used in Modern Standard English
with lexical verbs simply as an **operator**, to form INTERROGATIVES or questions
(e.g. *Do you take sugar?*); and negative statements (*I don't like milk*). The other
primary auxiliaries are *be* and *have* (*I am shivering; I have stopped now*); and the
group of so-called MODAL (q.v.) **auxiliaries**, such as *can, could, will, would*, which

have some lexical meaning, and which are generally used to qualify PROPOSI-TIONS to express possibility, obligation, ability, etc. *Will* and *shall* are also two important indicators of future time in Modern English, which lacks a future TENSE.

(2) In some versions of TRANSFORMATIONAL GRAMMAR (TG), auxiliary, abbreviated to AUX, has included not only the verbs but also markers of tense, etc. (e.g. *-s; -ed*).

average reader

Coined by Riffaterre (1959) to refer to a composite READER-figure, and what he later (1966) termed a **super-reader** or *archi-lecteur*: based on the sum of reactions by informants to linguistic features of texts in terms of their STYLISTIC (or non-stylistic) value.

More generally, Riffaterre's work on the images of texts in readers' minds was a counter-movement to the text-orientated analyses of the kind favoured by Jakobson (e.g. Jakobson & Lévi-Strauss 1962), and was paralleled in the AFFECTIVE STYLISTICS of, amongst others, Stanley Fish (1970), with his own concept of the **informed** or IDEAL READER (q.v.).

(For a critique, see further Posner 1983, ch. 6; Taylor 1981.)

B

---

b-verse

The second **half-line** or **hemistich** of a line of Old English verse (see also A-VERSE: the first half-line).

The half-lines are separated by a CAESURA or pause, and typically contain two strong STRESSES each. In the a-verse both stressed words are normally ALLITERATIVE; in the **b-verse** only the first. This is sometimes termed the **head-stave** (Ger. *Hauptstabe*), since this word provides the KEY alliteration to the line. It is also common for many sentences to begin with the b-verse and so give rise to ENJAMBMENT. The following a-verse often contains 'filler' material, of a descriptive or amplificatory nature: e.g.

> . . . ðær fyrgenstream
> [under næssa genipu] niðer gewiteð,
> [flod under foldan] . . .
>
> *(Beowulf)*
>
> ('there where the mountain-stream [under the mists of the nesses] downwards falls,
> [the flood under the earth] . . .')

back-formation

In LEXICOLOGY the creation of new words or LEXEMES by deletion of the SUFFIXES or endings of longer words: e.g. *rotovate* (from *rotovator*); *paramedic* from *paramedical*. Well-established words are *edit* (from *editor*), and *televise* (from *television*). Back-formation is a very popular source of COMPOUND verbs from nouns: e.g. *dry-clean; soft-land; brain-wash*.

backgrounding

Backgrounding came into English in opposition to FORE-GROUNDING (q.v.), a much-used STYLISTIC term from the **Russian** FORMALISTS and PRAGUE SCHOOL of linguists.

(1) Commonly, foregrounding applies to the dynamic ACTUALIZATION or DE-AUTOMATIZATION of ordinary language in POETIC LANGUAGE; hence ('normal')

non-aesthetic language is the **background**. The natural RHYTHMS of speech, for example, provide the background to the foregrounding in poetry of a selection and regularization of them as the patterns of METRE.

(2) But within the poetic or literary text features of literary language can themselves be foregrounded, or made prominent, for specific effects, by a variety of means, e.g. by DEVIATION, by REPETITION, etc. These are thus set against the (subordinated) **background** of the rest of the text. So, in this first stanza of Herbert's poem *Vertue*, the adjective phrases of the first line are foregrounded by syntactic repetition:

Sweet day, so cold, so calm, so bright,
The bridall of the earth and skie:
The dew shall weep thy fall to night;
For thou must die.

(3) Foregrounding is essentially a dynamic process, and one which aims for DE-FAMILIARIZING, for 'making strange'. Over-familiarity, AUTOMATIZATION, affects even poetic language, so that poetic innovation attracts imitation, as in POETIC DICTION. Many poets (e.g. Wordsworth, T. S. Eliot) therefore set their work against the **background** of the poetic tradition.

In general, however, the background of literary tradition is an important influence on any writer's work, for good as well as ill.

(See also INTERTEXTUALITY.)

ballad metre; ballad stanza

Ballad metre is so called because of its great frequency of use in popular and literary ballads, i.e. folk-songs or narrative poems which are dramatic and formulaic in nature. It is also known as **common metre**. The **ballad stanza** consists of four lines, with alternations of four and three BEATS or STRESSES in each line, rhyming abab, or abcb, e.g. in Coleridge's *The Ancient Mariner*:

```
  ×  /  ×    /    / ×  ×  /
The Wedding-Guest sat on a stone:
  ×  /  ×     /  ×    /
He cannot chuse but hear;
×      ×   /  /   × /  ×      /
And thus spake on that ancient man,
  ×  /     /    / × ×
The bright-eyed Mariner.
```

bathos, also anti-climax

This FIGURE OF SPEECH depends on a sudden lowering or deflation from a heightened TONE for IRONIC effect. It has thus been much exploited in literature for humour and satire.

39

From the Gk meaning 'depth', the movement of the **bathetic** sentence is paralleled in the popular phrase 'from the sublime to the ridiculous'. It was Pope in the eighteenth century who introduced the word, and in his own poem *The Dunciad*, for example, **bathos** is a key device as part of the poem's mock-epic structure in 'celebration' of bad writing:

> Poetic justice, with her lifted scale,
> Where, in nice balance, truth with gold she weighs,
> And solid pudding against empty praise (Book 1)

Bathos may also lie in the eye (and ear) of the reader, in the sense of a sudden deflating discrepancy between subject matter and EXPRESSION: e.g. this couplet from Keats's *Isabella*:

> For they resolved in some forest dim
> To kill Lorenzo, and there bury him.

beat

(1) Commonly used in METRICS to refer to the basic strongly ACCENTED or STRESSED syllable which helps to determine the RHYTHM of the verse line. Rather confusingly, however, it is used in the National Literacy Strategy (1998) to refer to any syllable.

Popular kinds of verse (e.g. nursery rhymes, ballads) favour **four-beat** lines (*Mary, Mary, quite contrary*); the BLANK VERSE tradition favours **five-beats** (also known as IAMBIC PENTAMETER. The unstressed syllables are correspondingly called **off-beats**. (See also FOOT; MEASURE. See further Attridge 1982, 1995.)

(2) In theatrical terminology **beat** has been used by the disciples of the director Konstantin Stanislavsky to refer to a segment or unit of action, for instance with a single subject and dominant emotion. So the famous 'pilgrim'-sonnet dialogue sequence in *Romeo and Juliet* (I.v) could be regarded as a beat.

bilabial consonant

A consonant articulated with both lips: in English the PLOSIVES /p/ and /b/ and the nasal /m/, as in *bumble bee*.

bilingualism; bidialectalism

(1) **Bilingualism** refers to the ability to speak two languages, but a bilingual speaker is normally regarded as someone who speaks two languages fluently and regularly as a native speaker.

What is of particular interest, however, is which language is used in which situations: i.e. where so-called CODE-SWITCHING occurs, and why. For example, an immigrant in Britain may use Urdu at home and English at school; a Welsh child may use Welsh at school, but English at home. A whole community, not just an individual, may be bilingual, with one language associated with official REGISTERS and education, the other with informal or private discourse (e.g. English v. Ibo in West Africa). Sociolinguists speak here of 'high' v. 'low' variation, and term the phenomenon DIGLOSSIA (q.v.).

(2) Diglossic situations also apply to co-existing DIALECTS of the same language. In the West Indies, for instance, there are different VARIETIES of CREOLE which speakers regularly shift between. Sociolinguists like Trudgill (1995) would see the opposition between regional dialect and STANDARD ENGLISH as one of **bidialectalism**, for those speakers who speak their dialect at home, and who switch to the standard in public.

binarism; binary opposition, etc.

(1) **Binarism** or **binarity** as a structural principle of language, a CHOICE or dichotomy between two mutually exclusive contrasting constituents or COMPONENTS, was first developed by Roman Jakobson and the PRAGUE SCHOOL, with particular reference to PHONOLOGY. For example, many consonants in English are in opposition to each other through the contrasting features of VOICE (voice present) and voicelessness (voice absent): i.e. whether the vocal chords vibrate or not (e.g. /b/ v. /p/; /d/ v. /t/, etc.).

(2) **Binarism** has been extended to the analysis of all levels of language. As the cross-referencing in this Dictionary reveals, binary choices can be found in grammatical theory (ACTIVE V. PASSIVE; SUBJECT V. PREDICATE; COMPETENCE V. PERFORMANCE, etc.) and in semantic theory. ANTONYMY is an obvious example of the apparently universal tendency to dichotomize: *rich* and *poor*; *big* and *little*, etc. So-called COMPONENTIAL ANALYSIS of meaning treats semantic features or components of LEXICAL ITEMS typically in terms of **binary oppositions** such as 'animate' v. 'inanimate', 'male' v. 'female', etc. (See also SEME.)

(3) STRUCTURALISTS, including Jakobson himself, interested in the analysis of kinds of cultural activity other than language, have used the principle of **binarism** in their studies of myth and literature. (See Culler 1975.) It may well be that binary contrasts are fundamental to human thought and categorization of experience: one has only to think of the basic opposition between 'good' and 'evil' which dominates religious philosophies and moral codes throughout the world, and which has been a pervasive theme in literature in various SYMBOLIC transformations (hero v. villain; cowboy v. Indian; monarch v. usurper; rose v. worm, etc.).

However, as critics such as Riffaterre (1966) have argued about Jakobson's own analyses of poetry (e.g. Jakobson & Lévi-Strauss 1962), it is possible to reduce almost everything to sets of pairs. (See also Werth 1976.) And as FEMINIST CRITICS and POST-COLONIAL THEORISTS have argued, binarism is a provocative concept for other reasons also. The two terms in an opposition may not simply be neutral: one may have a positive, the other a negative value (e.g. *good* v. *evil*; *West* v. *East*; *male* v. *female*).

It has also been argued that even if binarism is a fundamental principle of the human mind, it is not the only one; nor is it the only structural principle in language. Very often it appears too simplistic. Multiple taxonomies are a more satisfactory way to categorize species of plants, animals, etc.; and there are many objects which present problems for binary analysis, whether at physical or cultural levels (If mercury is liquid, how can it be a metal? Do we eat Heinz Big soups, or drink them? Why are frogs edible to the French, but inedible to the English?) So pervasive is binarism, however, in our IDEOLOGY that INDETER-MINACIES or ambiguities of this kind can become socially disturbing: e.g. homosexuals, single-parent families, non-trade union members ('whose side are you on?').

binomial

In LEXICOLOGY **binomial** describes a particular kind of IDIOMATIC phrase con-sisting of two LEXEMES normally linked by the CONJUNCTION *and*. The two items so associated or in COLLOCATION may rarely occur out of this context (e.g. *spick and span; kith and kin*) and are often irreversible (**ruin and rack*).

As these examples reveal, binomials are often marked by ALLITERATION or by RHYME (*toil and moil, wheeling and dealing*); and are often near-SYNONYMS, although the meaning of individual lexemes may have become obscured through time.

A special category of binomials is found in legal language: *law and order, goods and chattels, rape and pillage,* etc. These groups can perhaps be distinguished from those linked collocates, however habitual, which simply mark the common situational association of two entities (*fish and chips, bangers and mash*).

Conjoined phrases have also been a feature of prose styles in different periods: what are traditionally termed **doublets**. Pairs of synonyms were used for copiousness and emphasis in medieval homiletic prose or sermon, and they recur as a stylistic marker of Johnson's reflective essays, e.g.: *An even and unvaried tenour of life always hides from our apprehension the approach of its end* (*The Idler*, no. 103).

blank verse

Verse that does not rhyme; and particularly, verse with five-BEAT or -STRESS lines, rather than four beats. (See also IAMBIC PENTAMETER.)

Blank verse was introduced into the English poetic tradition by the Earl of Surrey in his translation of parts of the *Aeneid* in the mid-sixteenth century. The combination of five beats and non-rhyme gives it a flexibility and a suggestive-ness of 'ordinary' speech which dramatists in particular have exploited, notably Shakespeare and his contemporaries.

blending

(1) In LEXICOLOGY a **blend** is a word formed from the parts of two others. An alternative popular name is **portmanteau-word**, after Humpty Dumpty's definition in Lewis Carroll's *Through the Looking-Glass*: 'two meanings packed up into one word'.

Blends coined for striking effect are found in advertising language (*swimsation* and IT (e.g. *emoticon*). Yet many blends coined in journalism, science, etc., have passed into ordinary speech (*smog = smoke + fog; motel = motor + hotel*). Many older, expressive words in the language may owe their origin to blending: e.g. *splotch* (*spot + blotch*).

(2) By extension, the term is sometimes applied to other linguistic structures where a fusion of elements occurs. **Syntactic blends** present a combination of two possible clauses, and are not uncommon in colloquial, unpremeditated speech: *The child seems sleeping* (. . . *seems to be asleep + is sleeping*). (See also ANACOLUTHON.)

(3) In DISCOURSE ANALYSIS **blending** denotes the phenomenon whereby a MOVE by one speaker (i.e. an utterance significant for the development of the conversation) is taken over and completed by another, e.g.:

> A: I don't think we're getting anywhere in this discussion, we've gone over the same arguments all morning. I think the best thing probably is that we should all –
> B: Yes, all have a break for lunch.

(4) More recently, in MENTAL SPACE THEORY (q.v.) developed in COGNITIVE LINGUISTICS **blending** is seen as a basic cognitive operation for creating new meanings: a kind of conceptual integration. It can be most obviously seen in COMPOUNDING, where meanings and assumptions from different fields merge together (e.g. *working mother; computer virus*); in cultural icons (*Father Christmas*, for example, blending European and American beliefs); and METAPHOR. In *She looked daggers at him*, for example, the ideas of perceiving and throwing objects are fused together, the 'target' (TENOR) and 'source' (VEHICLE).

block language

A useful term to cover kinds of restricted structures (usually NOMINAL or ADJECTIVE PHRASES) in the written medium which yet have specific pragmatic functions. An alternative term is **little texts** (Halliday 1985: Appendix 2). Examples include labels (*fragile; dry-cleanable*); notices (*No dogs allowed; exit*); and advertising slogans (*The car in front is a Toyota*), etc. Restrictions of space are obviously the main constraint on length and structuring.

Block language is also used to describe newspaper headlines. While space is also at a premium here, and nominal groups are common (*Mortgage blow; Low-key protest*), nonetheless complete clauses or sentences are found (*Talks fail to resolve Geneva deadlock*). What tend to be ELIDED, however, are grammatical items easily redundant in their contexts, e.g. ARTICLES.

border crossing

A term introduced by Fairclough (1996) in the field of CRITICAL DISCOURSE ANALYSIS to describe forms of language associated with one situation or REGISTER 'crossing the border' into new ones. The increasing INFORMALITY of much public discourse is a very obvious and general example; the spread of the language of sales and marketing is a more specific case. Railway passengers are now 'customers'; British universities have logos and slogans comparable to those on the sides of lorries, e.g. Open University: *Altogether a better place to work*; South Bank University London: *Central to your success*.

bound clause

Used by some grammarians (e.g. Sinclair 1972) to refer to what is more commonly termed a SUBORDINATE or **dependent** CLAUSE. It cannot be a MAIN CLAUSE, and is often marked by a CONJUNCTIVE element or **binder** (e.g. *when*; *until*; *which*; *that*) as in:

When my love swears/ *that* she is made of truth/,
I do believe her, / *though* I know she lies . . .

(Shakespeare: Sonnet 138)

The term **bound** is probably used by analogy with **bound** MORPHEME, a grammatical form which is not 'free', i.e. which occurs only in conjunction with another (base) form, e.g. SUFFIXES.

branching

(1) A metaphorical term introduced into early TRANSFORMATIONAL GRAMMAR (TG) to refer to the hierarchy of elements in a SENTENCE that can be represented as a 'tree'; e.g.:

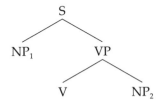

where NP_1 refers to a NOUN PHRASE (as SUBJECT), VP to a PREDICATE or VERB PHRASE, V to a verb and NP_2 to a noun phrase as OBJECT. **Trees** are a representation, therefore, of what are termed **Phrase Structure** (PS) **Rules**.

(2) In particular, **branching** refers to the implicit or underlying complexity of dependency or EMBEDDING of some constructions. **Left-branching** structures show complexity to the 'left', e.g. of a **head** or main word in a phrase, or heavy PREMODIFICATION: possessive-genitive phrases like *My flat-mate's mother's motor-bike*; or

Our heart's charity's hearth's fire,
Our thought's chivalry's throng's Lord

(Hopkins: *Wreck of the Deutschland*)

Strings of ADJECTIVES are also left-branching (*a charming old Jacobean thatched cottage*); and the noun MODIFIERS in the BLOCK LANGUAGE of newspaper headlines (*Clinton arms talk call*) and placards (*Railway station murder inquiry verdict challenge*).

Supposedly easier for our minds to process are **right-branching** structures. 'The House that Jack Built' is well-known for its repeated or RECURSIVE RELATIVE CLAUSES (*This is the dog that ate the cat that ate the rat that . . .*); and heavy POST-MODIFICATION of the noun occurs in the song *The flea on the hair of the tail of the dog of the nurse of the child . . . (etc.) has just come to town.*

(3) **Branching** is often used to refer to complexity in clause and sentence structure, and the placing of SUBORDINATE or BOUND CLAUSES in relation to the MAIN CLAUSE. Left-branching structures, which delay the main clause, are traditionally termed PERIODIC (q.v.); in contrast, right-branching structures, which begin with the main clause, are traditionally termed LOOSE (q.v.).

bricolage

(1) A French word meaning 'patchwork', popularized in the 1960s by the structural anthropologist Lévi-Strauss to refer metaphorically to the thought patterns of so-called, 'primitive', non-literate man. These are based on concrete yet rather *ad hoc* responses to the natural world. (For a critique, see Derrida 1967a, 1978b.)

(2) **Bricolage** has also been applied to the composition of non-literate, i.e. oral, poetry (see Ong 1982), to refer to the corrections made in performance by rephrasing and additions, etc.

(3) It has also aptly been applied to the TEXTURE of MODERNIST and POST-MODERNIST writing, e.g. the experimental, surrealistic prose of novels like Joyce's *Finnegans Wake*, with its distorted interweavings of words and phrases borrowed from various languages, registers, and genres:

. . . Pro clam a shun! Pip! Peep! Pipitch! Ubipop jay piped, ibipep goes the whistle. Here Tyeburn throttled, massed murmars march: where the bus stops there shop I: here which ye see, yea reste. On me, your sleeping giant. Estoesto! Estote sunto! . . .

C

cadence

As a term common in LITERARY CRITICISM from the sixteenth to the nineteenth century, **cadence** has now largely dropped out of use. Since it runs the risk of vagueness, it is really best avoided.

(1) In RHETORIC it described the falling patterns of TONE and RHYTHM at the ends of sentences (cf. Lat. *cadere* 'to fall'; It. *cadenza*, the conclusion of a musical movement or phrase).

(2) In older works on PHONETICS **cadence** is sometimes used to describe what is more usually known as the NUCLEUS, i.e. the final most prominent syllable of an utterance, and the one associated with its most significant tone changes (falling, rising, etc.).

(3) Generally, it has been used to mean '(prose) rhythm' (as in Chaucer); or the so-called 'flow' or modulation of sentences or verses, especially referring to marked sequences of STRESSED and unstressed syllables.

caesura

A classical term introduced into traditional English PROSODY to refer to a pause in the middle of a line of verse.

In English verse such pauses are determined by SYNTAX, sense or punctuation rather than METRICAL form, and so there are no 'rules' determining their occurrence. However, in Old and Middle English ALLITERATIVE VERSE a regular pause or **caesura** divides the line into two half-lines.

canon; canonical; canonization

(1) In LITERARY CRITICISM and TEXT STUDIES, **canon** is a term commonly used to refer to the collection of works which are generally regarded as being the genuine work of a particular author: hence the adjective **canonical**, meaning 'accepted, authoritative, standard'.

(2) The **Russian** FORMALISTS and PRAGUE SCHOOL LINGUISTS use **canon** in a wider sense to refer to those works which are generally accepted as upholding the (main) literary or poetic tradition. Innovation comes from a reaction to this canon, which has a tendency to 'harden', to be AUTOMATIZED. Many innovations are linguistic (e.g. reactions against POETIC DICTION), and also generic: in the novel, for instance, 'low' or popular sub-genres (e.g. epistle, travelogue, horror story) may become incorporated. Such innovations and others are said to be **canonized**, elevated to the (new) literary NORM (Shklovsky 1925).

But, ironically, the very process of **canonization** involves a 'hardening' of forms. A contemporary of the Formalists, Mikhail Bakhtin (1981), speaks of what he calls the **centripetal** (v. the **centrifugal**) forces in culture: the homogenizing v. the dispersive influences of subversive literary forms. For him the novel as a genre is not quite as subject to the pressures of canonization as poetry. By its very nature it is more alert to 'alternative' art forms.

(3) **Canonization** may be seen as the characteristic feature of a STANDARD language or dialect. Any dialect which is accepted as the authoritative speech of the nation is elevated, as it were, above other dialects; and accepted as the 'norm' for USAGE. So much so, that many speakers will resist, or resent changes.

(4) For some radical critics, **canon** and **canonization** carry distinct political and IDEOLOGICAL implications in studies of (English) literature. So Eagleton (1983) sees the study of English in higher education as mainly based on the authority of a literary canon of texts, itself based on a mixed set of assumptions (cultural, social, moral, as well as formal) of a kind much influenced by Leavis (1948).

Under the influence of cultural studies, FEMINIST CRITICISM and POST-COLONIAL THEORY, the idea of the canon has been 'exploded', and a wider range of texts are now taught in British schools and universities. Questions of **de-canonization** and **canon formation** have inevitably reinvigorated issues of LITERARINESS and the nature of LITERATURE.

(5) **Canonical** is used in linguistics as a synonym for 'standard' or 'non-deviant' or 'ideal'. So words are given in their **canonical forms** in dictionaries, irrespective of how they may actually be pronounced in speech. The **canonical** SITUATION **of utterance** is a spoken encounter between two people; a non-canonical situation would be written communication, and where the participants are far away from each other, etc. In SEMIOTICS **canonical orientation** is spoken about: phrases like *back to front* and *upside down* reflect our intuitions about what are our (ab)normal perspectives on certain objects (see further Lyons 1977).

cant

(1) In ordinary usage today this word is most likely to be derogatory, referring to insincerity or hypocrisy in language and thought.

(2) *OED* suggests that the word is probably ultimately derived from Lat. *cantus* 'song, chant'. In the seventeenth century, when it first appears, it was frequently applied pejoratively to the whining speech of beggars; and it has since then most

usually been applied to the special languages or vocabularies used by the misfits or outcasts of society, such as thieves (see also ANTI-LANGUAGE; ARGOT); but also by religious sects like the Quakers, and by certain professions (e.g. lawyers).

(See also JARGON; SLANG.)

captatio benevolentiae

See EXORDIUM.

carnival(esque)

A term in LITERARY CRITICISM popularized through the writing of the Russian theorist Mikhail Bakhtin (1968) on Rabelais, to signal any demotic HETERO-GLOSSIC or 'multi-voiced' counter-culture in comic or exuberant opposition to a hegemonic official culture: a kind of subversive anti-culture, often with its own ANTI-LANGUAGE.

case: ~ grammar

(1) **Case** is used in the description of inflected languages like Latin or Modern German to describe the different forms assumed by NOUNS and other members of the NOUN PHRASE (PRONOUNS; ADJECTIVES, etc.) according to their different syntactic FUNCTIONS in the sentence. Hence the **nominative case** is used for nouns as grammatical SUBJECTS; **accusative** for DIRECT OBJECTS, etc.

In Modern English, unlike Old English, such case forms are rare, and terms like **nominative, accusative** and **dative case** are discouraged by grammarians. Only the **genitive** (denoting possession) is left to mark (ANIMATE) nouns: *girl's* is thus opposed to the unmarked form *girl*, which is sometimes referred to as the **common case**.

In the pronouns the old accusative survives also (now known as the OBJECTIVE **case**): e.g. *them, her, me, him,* which can thus be distinguished from the genitive case (*theirs, hers,* etc.), and the so-called SUBJECTIVE **case** (*they, she,* etc.).

The grammatical functions denoted by former case forms have generally come to be indicated by other means, e.g. WORD ORDER (subjects precede VERBS, which precede objects); and PREPOSITIONS (e.g. *of* (possession); *to/for* (INDIRECT OBJECT: formerly in the dative case)).

(2) From the late 1960s onwards, following Fillmore (1968), the term **case** acquired a new extended meaning in a grammatical theory called **case grammar**. It is used in what can be seen as a DEEP rather than SURFACE sense, to refer to semantic relationships or ROLES which may or may not be realized by the surface MORPHEMES of the traditional cases. The particular significance of case grammar lies in the fact that apparently unrelated sentences can be regarded as sharing

the same configuration of 'deep' cases or arguments (what Lyons (1977), calls **valency roles**). So *Ethel hit the alien on the head with a rolling-pin* (ACTIVE) is related to *The alien was hit on the head (by Ethel) with a rolling-pin* (PASSIVE); and *A rolling-pin hit the alien on the head* since in each example the 'participants' in the action are the same: AGENTIVE (*Ethel*), 'Patient' and 'Possessor' (*alien*), 'Locative' or 'Goal' (*head*), and 'Instrument' (*rolling-pin*).

The concept of semantic roles in case grammar resembles other theories, notably Halliday's system of TRANSITIVITY in his SYSTEMIC-FUNCTIONAL GRAMMAR (e.g. 1985). It has proved of value in STYLISTICS, epecially for those studying NARRATIVE (see Fowler 1977). Many STRUCTURALIST approaches to CHARACTER and PLOT have adopted independently semantic and functional frameworks very similar to case grammar (e.g. ACTANTIAL **theory**).

catachresis

(1) From Gk meaning 'misuse' or 'abuse', **catachresis** was used in RHETORIC by Puttenham (1589) and others, as a kind of TROPE which involved unusual or far-fetched METAPHORS. So, part of the dynamism of Shakespeare's language comes from (NONCE) applications of words outside their normal contexts to metaphorical, often compressed, uses:

> . . . for supple knees
> *Feed* arrogance
>
> *(Troilus and Cressida*, III.iii)

> . . . my face I'll grime with filth,
> . . . *elf* all my hairs in knots
>
> *(King Lear*, II.iii)

(2) As the French philosopher Foucault (1966) has argued, **catachresis** is basic to the FIGURES of rhetoric, since so many of them depend on DEVIATIONS from 'normal' (non-poetic) usage, or on the play of LITERAL v. FIGURATIVE sense. Indeed, he would go so far as to maintain that all language is **catachretic**: literal meanings are not inherent in the SIGNIFIER–SIGNIFIED relationship, but have simply come to be conventionalized by society. Moreover, paraphrased as 'error', catachresis symbolizes the origin of language: the naming of the multiplicities of experience and environment under broader, single SIGNS.

(3) As definitions like 'error' and 'abuse' suggest, **catachresis** is also an evaluative term, part of the prescriptive linguistic tradition concerned with notions of CORRECTNESS (q.v.), with 'right' and 'wrong', 'proper' and 'improper' usages.

(4) However, **catachresis/catachretic** meaning 'error', 'erroneous' are terms still used in lexicography or dictionary making as part of the usage labelling system for lexical entries (symbolized by a paragraph mark in the *OED*, for example).

It is certainly true that many linguistic changes and innovations are due to error and ignorance (e.g. of ETYMOLOGIES); but, once accepted by a majority of educated people, they become sanctioned by custom, and their origins eventually obscured (e.g. *primrose* from Fr. *primerole; crayfish* from *crevisse*).

(See also MALAPROPISM.)

catalyst, also catalyser

Catalyst is one of a pair of terms popularized in NARRATOLOGY by Barthes (1966), influenced by the work of the **Russian** FORMALISTS. A *catalyse* (in French) is the kind of event or description which amplifies, upholds, or even delays the main thread of an ACTION; as distinct from the *noyau* or KERNEL (q.v.) which advances the action in some way.

In his own work on narrative influenced by Barthes, Chatman (e.g. 1978) preferred the term **satellite** on the justifiable grounds that **catalyst**, because of its more usual meaning of 'aiding' a change or effect, implies a degree of functional importance it does not actually possess: such a narrative element can easily be deleted.

Catalysts are thus typically minor details of behaviour; although whole episodes might be seen as (relatively) insignificant in terms of any advance in PLOT (e.g. the scenes of magic tricks between Faustus and his servants in Marlowe's play). Significantly perhaps, Barthes himself did not persist in using the term, although other critics have done so.

As Culler (1975) maintains, one problem posed by the distinction between kernel and catalyst is the difficulty in many cases of establishing their relative significance for the plot except in retrospective reading. In any case, one would like also to admit the possibility of an element having the two functions.

(See also FUNCTION; INDEX.)

cataphora; cataphoric reference

In GRAMMAR and TEXT studies, CATAPHORA as introduced by Bühler (1934) denotes a kind of linguistic REFERENCE which is 'forward-looking' rather than 'backward-looking' (ANAPHORA, q.v.).

(1) In particular, it is used for PERSONAL PRONOUNS and other **proforms** which 'anticipate' the NOUN PHRASES with which they co-occur, e.g.: *If she's thinking of applying for that job, Kate had better apply quickly.* Specific **cataphoric reference** like this is more common between clauses than between sentences (unlike **anaphoric reference**); and is, in any case, replaceable by anaphoric reference itself: cf. *If Kate's thinking of applying for the job, she had better apply quickly.*

With its delay of more precise information, cataphora lends itself to STYLISTIC exploitation in the interests of suspense; or with the pattern of (light) pronoun followed by (heavier) noun phrase, it can provide a useful FOCUSSING device. Both effects can be seen in utterances favoured in journalism and broadcasting:

And slowly down the steps in <u>her</u> primrose-coloured outfit comes <u>the great lady</u> of the moment we have all been waiting for, the Queen Mother herself.

In literature, the device of delayed NPs and the use of 3rd person pronouns and other items of definite or familiar reference is frequently exploited at the beginning of texts in the technique known as IN MEDIAS RES (q.v.). What is interesting about the opening of Golding's *Pincher Martin*, cited in the entry for ANAPHORIC reference, is that a definite NP (*the man*) is not found until the beginning of the third paragraph on the second page. This suggests that, from a discourse processing point of view, we are actually looking for more information about the *he* in the universe of discourse, not waiting for a 'master' or 'co-referential' NP to appear. So, as with anaphora, Wales (1996, ch. 2) would argue that in many such examples reference is text-'inward-looking' rather than 'forward-looking' for cataphora (or 'backward-looking' for anaphora).

(2) Cataphora is used commonly for reference to aspects of the discourse itself, rather than specific objects or people. The pronoun *it* characteristically anticipates following clauses or sentences, as in: *It's a pity [that she can't come with us]*; or *I don't like it. [The cat's gone missing for the third day running.]*

(3) Superficially cataphoric reference can be found in certain 'self-repair' utterances in conversation, when speakers correct themselves fearing potential ambiguity, rather like an afterthought. Sometimes such 'afterthoughts' are for EMPHASIS or FOCUS: what Quirk *et al.* (1985) term **postponed identification** and **amplificatory tags**, and what Halliday & Hasan (1976) call **substitute themes**. These are common in dialectal speech: e.g. *She's brilliant, <u>that girl</u>.*

channel

While linguists as scrupulous as Lyons (1977) have argued that **channel** should be distinguished from MEDIUM (q.v.), it is frequently not: the terms are often used synonymously.

(1) **Channel** is used in descriptions of COMMUNICATION systems to refer to the route along which a SIGNAL or MESSAGE or CODE is transmitted from sender to receiver: e.g. telephone cables and radio waves.

(2) Engineering terminology has been borrowed by linguists to describe human communication, so that language is primarily transmitted via the medium or physical means of speech along the **channel** of sound waves in the air. Literate societies make significant use of writing as a medium of transmission, whose channel is the visual mode of the written or printed page.

Technology has opened up new media for language (telephone, radio, television, e-mail, etc.) and new channels, visual and aural; although the theatre since ancient times has exploited voice and body, as well as music and scenery, in its expression of meanings. Ordinary spoken language itself does not depend entirely on the 'vocal–auditory' channel alone: in the context of face-to-face discourse we assimilate reinforcing messages which are visual (e.g. facial expressions), even tactile (body contact or touch). This **multiple channel** effect, to borrow the Goffman (1974) phrase, is lost in the transmission of speech by telephone, for example.

(3) In sociology the term is used as in the phrase **channel(s) of communication**, to refer to the various means (e.g. newspaper, bulletin, White Paper) by which information passes from one group of people to another, particularly amongst those in authority (e.g. the Government, a board of directors, a local council, etc.).

character; characterization

Character defined simply as the fictional representation of a person belies a multiplicity and complexity of methods of **characterization**. Yet it suggests two key issues: the degree of MIMESIS or IMITATION involved in the 'representation'; and the verbal mechanics, the 'fictions', upon which characters depend for their existence.

(1) A popular traditional distinction inherited from E. M. Forster (1927) is between **flat** and **round characters**. While there are problems with these metaphorical terms, the distinction does accord with readers' intuitions that there are different kinds of characterization, even within one text.

Flat characters are based on a single quality, and tend to remain static, undeveloped throughout a work. They correspond in the novel to the dramatic 'humour' characters popularized by play-wrights like Jonson, whose very proper names (Downright, John Littlewit) symbolize their predominant trait, which is realized in their speech and actions. Functionally, they usually have minor ROLES in the action of a novel. However, as many of the characters in Dickens's novels reveal (Mrs Micawber, Silas Wegg, Vincent Crummles) these characters are often vividly and dramatically portrayed, so that their very dynamism and idiosyncracy create an illusion of lifelike individuality. At the other extreme are characters who are simply 'speaking names'; what have been called **characteronyms** (e.g. the many lovers and husbands in Defoe's *Moll Flanders*).

Round characters are said to be more complex, presenting several traits or SEMES (q.v.) and often undergoing some sort of development or change as the plot progresses (e.g. Hardy's Mayor of Casterbridge or George Eliot's Dorothea in *Middlemarch*). In TEXTWORLD THEORY these would be **enactors** rather than **bystanders** ('flat'). In the twentieth-century novel in particular the reader is given access to the inner thoughts of such characters (see also FREE DIRECT THOUGHT; INTERIOR MONOLOGUE); but even in novels of earlier periods the 'inner life', if only indirectly reported by the narrator, was an important means of verisimilitude (e.g. Fanny Price in Jane Austen's *Mansfield Park*; or Jude in Hardy's *Jude the Obscure*).

For such characters (usually major) we are less ready to accept stereotyping in action or speech, etc., but more willing to flesh them out by analogy with real people and the social and political or moral conventions of their apparent milieu, and of the period. In a sense, then, characterization is achieved, an illusion of reality created, by what is ABSENT in the text, by what we will supply or supplement for ourselves. (See also GAP; INDETERMINACY.)

(2) Some, notably STRUCTURALIST, approaches to character incline more to analysis in terms of the structure of the text itself, rather than relations with the world outside it. A simple illustration would be the contrast of characters for the highlighting of opposing traits (e.g. Henchard and Farfrae in Hardy's *The Mayor of Casterbridge*).

(3) An extreme approach is to see characterization subordinated to plot structure, a set of functional roles or ACTANTS (q.v.). Much of the work on NARRATIVE by the **Russian** FORMALISTS (see, e.g., Propp 1928) is along these lines, itself a strong influence on later theorists (especially French), e.g. Barthes, Brémond, Greimas and Todorov in the 1960s. Folk-tales and fairy-tales certainly lend themselves to analysis of character in terms of such roles as 'hero', 'villain', 'helper', etc.; and indeed, present obvious kinds of 'flat' characters.

Many MODERNIST novels reveal a minimum of characterization from the realist perspective of individuality and apparent 'depth' (e.g. Joyce's *Finnegans Wake*; or the novels of Robbe-Grillet or Borges). Any valuable theory of character must be able to account for the conventions accrued in the established tradition, against which these essentially reactionary modes are FOREGROUNDED.

(See also DRAMATIS PERSONA; POINT OF VIEW.)

character zone

Coined by Mikhail Bakhtin in the 1930s to refer to the distinctive NARRATIVE style which can surround the DIRECT SPEECH of a character, and which suggests his or her voice or consciousness. Thus the **zone** of a character's influence need not simply cover what is quoted, but a broader area of the text. Jane Austen, for instance, characteristically intersperses direct DIALOGUE between characters with INDIRECT SPEECH and NARRATIVE REPORT, so that we remain aware of the characters' continual involvement with each other. In *Emma*, for example, in the scene where Knightley plucks up courage to propose to Emma, Emma's reactions to his words are expressed both in speech, and (more significantly) in (FREE) INDIRECT STYLE:

> Emma could not bear to give him pain. He was wishing to confide in her – perhaps to consult her; – cost her what it would, she would listen. She might assist his resolution, or reconcile him to it . . .

(See also COLOURED NARRATIVE; POINT OF VIEW.)

chiasmus

From Gk meaning 'cross-wide', **chiasmus** is a RHETORICAL term to describe a construction involving the REPETITION of words or elements in reverse order (ab:ba); also known as **antimetabole**. It is often used for witty or APHORISTIC effect: '*Before New Labour, politicians fought elections in order to govern. This administration governs in order to fight elections*' (Conservative leader William Hague, November 1998).

Syntactic INVERSION is common in the couplets of eighteenth-century poetry: e.g. *Renown'd / for conquest, and in council / skilled* (Addison: *The Campaign*).

Possibly under the influence of NEW HISTORICISM's catchphrase 'the history of texts and the textuality of history', chiasmus has become a popular figure in academic book-titles: see, e.g., Fludernik (1993) and Bex (1996).

(See also ANTISTROPHE; EPANODOS.)

choice

A very popular view of STYLE (q.v.) is to see it involving **choice**. An author is seen to select features from the whole resources of the language at his or her disposal; a choice also partly governed presumably by the demands of GENRE; FORM; THEME; etc. (See also DOMAIN.)

In this wide sense, however, writers are no different from all language users: it is part of our COMPETENCE as native speakers that we select for our utterances the relevant PHONEMES, SYNTAX, LEXICAL ITEMS, etc., appropriate for what we mean to say, and appropriate for the CONTEXT in which it will be uttered.

Not all selections, however, would necessarily be called stylistic, by those who use the concept of choice. To select, for example, a negative rather than the positive construction in identical contexts affects meaning radically, cf.:

Waiter, please bring me the sweet trolley.
Waiter, please don't bring me the sweet trolley.

Conversely, the English speaker's choice of *anyone* rather than *anybody* or the spelling *grey* rather than *gray*, makes no difference in meaning whatsoever, and is simply a matter of whim or personal idiosyncracy. Stylistic choice, therefore, is generally concerned with expressions that have more or less the same meaning, but which may be subtly distinguished in semantic nuance or CONNOTATION, or **degree of** FORMALITY, etc., cf.:

Smokers are kindly requested to sit in the rear.
We ask smokers to sit at the back.

As the entries for CONTENT; FORM; PARAPHRASE also reveal, linguists and stylisticians have differed over the extent to which 'the same meaning' can be expressed in different words. (See also DUALISM; MONISM.) Certainly it is possible to argue, as Fowler *et al.* (1979) and Fairclough (1989f) have done, that in some contexts (e.g. newspaper headlines) choice of expression reflects a particular 'bias' or view of reality which raises questions of IDEOLOGY rather than simple connotation, cf.:

Vice-Chancellor's plans for merger rejected.
Dons defy College closure threat.

In literary texts the choice of features overall determines the particular WORLD-VIEW communicated by the narrator.

(For choice as a linguistic principle, see also SYSTEMIC GRAMMAR.)

chronotope

In the Russian theorist Mikhail Bakhtin's work on the novel (1981), **chronotope**, lit. 'time-space', refers to the potentially complex nature of, and relationship between the represented dimensions of time and space. Different novels and genres create different world pictures according to different chronotopes: the epic versus the novel, for example. Spenser's epic *The Faerie Queene* conveys a vivid sense of space, but little sense of time (as with dream-visions.) The recent critical concept of LIMINALITY can be seen to have a temporal, as well as spatial, significance.

circumlocution

See PERIPHRASIS.

clause

Traditional and modern GRAMMARS alike recognize the **clause** as an important grammatical unit, but find it difficult in some respects to distinguish from the SENTENCE. Indeed, the two terms are often used interchangeably, in phrases like **clause/sentence structure**; or IMPERATIVE **sentence/clause**.

The clause is sometimes defined in terms of size, as being smaller than the sentence, but larger than the **phrase** (itself larger than the other units or RANKS of **word** and MORPHEME). However, it is more satisfactory to define it in terms of its structural features, namely that it normally consists of a SUBJECT and PREDICATE (which phrases lack). A sentence also contains a subject and predicate normally; but its distinguishing characteristic is that it can consist of more than one clause. The clause, therefore, is only a sentence-like structure; it functions as part of a sentence. Superficially, structures like

I have seen roses damask'd, red and white

and

I have seen roses damask'd, red and white,
[But no such roses see I in her cheeks]

are identical, but a clause on its own is properly a SIMPLE SENTENCE; in the second example it functions as a MAIN CLAUSE followed by a CO-ORDINATE CLAUSE (introduced by the CONJUNCTION *but*) in what is called a COMPOUND SENTENCE (q.v.).

As this example shows, many clauses are introduced by a CONNECTIVE element. The other major type of non-main clause is the SUBORDINATE or **dependent** or BOUND CLAUSE, which with the main clause forms a COMPLEX SENTENCE. Major types of subordinate clauses are functionally NOMINAL (introduced by the conjunction *that*, for example); ADVERBIAL (introduced by *when, if,* etc.); and ADJECTIVAL or RELATIVE (introduced by *who, which, that,* etc.). Much formal writing is characterized by strings of subordinate clauses, occurring before and after the main clause. (See also PERIOD(IC); BRANCHING.)

Dependent clauses can also be classified as FINITE (q.v.) or NON-FINITE (q.v.), i.e. whether the verb is marked for TENSE and MOOD or not. INFINITIVES and PARTICIPLES (*-ing* and *-ed* forms) occur in non-finite clauses, which do not necessarily have subjects like finite clauses:

> Spend'st thou thy fury on some worthless song,
> Darkening thy power/to lend base subjects light?
>
> (Shakespeare: Sonnet 99)

clause relations

Developed by Winter in the 1970s in his work on aspects of TEXT analysis or CONTEXTUAL GRAMMAR (q.v.) and taken up by his colleagues (e.g. Hoey 1983). **Clause relations** refer to how we understand sequences of CLAUSES and SENTENCES in the context of the grammatical features and meaning of adjoining clauses and sentences. Alternative names are **interclausal relations**, or **propositional relations**.

Simple examples would be 'cause' and 'effect', 'condition' and 'consequence', which are specifically marked within sentences by SUBORDINATORS and ADVERBIALS such as *because* and *therefore, if* and *then,* etc. Between sentences, however, a wider and subtler range of relational signals may be used; and even simple juxtaposition of sentences may be enough to set up a pattern of expectation and fulfilment; e.g.:

> The tenor and soprano had totally contrasting approaches to their roles. Cianella produced some amazing heroic high notes. If his Arrigo was forceful, Olivia Stapp's Elena was restrained and ladylike.
>
> (from a *Times* review)

Clause relations, therefore, are an important aspect of textual COHERENCE (q.v.).

(See also INFORMATION PROCESSING.)

clefting; cleft sentence

A term originating from Jespersen (1949), **clefting** is used in GRAMMAR to describe a process whereby for EMPHASIS or FOCUS a simple SENTENCE appears to have been 'cleft' or divided into two CLAUSES. One contains CATAPHORIC *it* + AUXILIARY VERB *be*, the other a RELATIVE CLAUSE. So *The sparrow killed Cock Robin* can yield:

It was the sparrow/who killed Cock Robin (focus on logical SUBJECT).
It was Cock Robin/(whom) the sparrow killed (focus on OBJECT).

Alternative names are **predicated** THEME or **theme predication** (Halliday 1985); *it*-**theme** (Young 1980) and *it*-**cleft** (Biber *et al.* 1999). These terms indicate that it is 'natural' to highlight items in the PREDICATE, i.e. after a verb (*was*); and that the pronoun *it* is the **dummy** subject, as it were, an **empty theme** or point of initiation.

In speech, extra prominence on certain elements can be made simply by STRESS and TONE of voice, possibilities denied in writing. But clefting is found in speech as well as writing: it provides, as it were, an extra degree of emphasis, and so is popularly exploited in the rhetorical or impassioned discourses of public oratory: *It was the last Government who were responsible for our present rate of unemployment.* In newscasting and narratives ADVERBIALS of time are commonly focussed in this way, to present what Quirk *et al.* (1985) see as a kind of 'scene-setting': *It was early this morning that the hostages were released.*

There are other motivations for clefting. For example, it seems to occur very naturally in contexts where one speaker wishes to contradict another, e.g.:

A: I hear Jenny Wren killed Cock Robin.
B: (No), it was the sparrow (who killed Cock Robin).

In other words, the item of focus presents NEW INFORMATION against the residue which is GIVEN, or PRESUPPOSED. Note also question–answer sequences of the type:

A: Who killed Cock Robin?
B: It was the sparrow (who killed Cock Robin).

In each case the given information can be easily omitted.

(See also PSEUDO-CLEFT.)

cliché

From the Fr. verb meaning 'stereotyped', this well-known term is used pejoratively to refer to COLLOCATIONS or IDIOMS which have been used so often that they have lost their precision or force.

Readers of and listeners to FORMAL or serious discourse (politics; journalism) are particularly irritated by **clichés**, because their apparent triteness or REDUNDANCY suggests lack of originality, slackness of thought, etc. (*at this moment in time; at the end of the day*). Similarly, we expect originality of thought and expression in POETIC LANGUAGE, and the term POETIC DICTION is also sometimes used pejoratively to refer to the well-used collocations of poetic tradition such as *purling brooks* and *feathered songsters*.

Yet in ordinary colloquial and familiar speech clichés frequently pass unnoticed, and it is difficult to see how we can do without them, any more than the thousands of habitual collocations (*deep feeling; slim chance*), SIMILES (*as dead as a doornail*) and FORMULAS (*many happy returns*) where PRAGMATIC motivation (consolation, politeness, etc.) is paramount.

(See also PHATIC COMMUNION.)

climax

(1) **Climax** is widely used to refer to the point of greatest importance and intensity in a story, play, film, etc.

(2) From Gk 'ladder', **climax** in RHETORIC as a FIGURE OF SPEECH is a dramatic means of persuasion. Also known as **gradatio**, it presents arguments in an ascending order of importance, reserving the best point till last. (ANTI-CLIMAX, as its name suggests, puts the best point first.) For example: *What light is to the eyes, what air is to the lungs, what love is to the heart, liberty is to the soul of man* (R. G. Ingersoll).

(3) A specific kind of rhetorical gradation involves the linking of words between CLAUSES, the last LEXICAL ITEM of one clause beginning the next. It thus resembles ANADIPLOSIS, but the climactic buildup of the argument is important. So Thomas Wilson (1553) gives the following illustration:

> Of sloth cometh pleasure, of pleasure cometh spending, of spending cometh whoring, of whoring cometh lack, of lack cometh theft, of theft cometh hanging, and here an end for this world.

(4) Leech & Short (1981) refer to a PHONOLOGICAL **principle of climax** in discourse, whereby in a sequence of TONE UNITS, the final position will be the major FOCUS of information. In effect, this seems to be an extension of the notion of END-FOCUS (q.v.), and is also manifested in SYNTAX as well as phonology. PERIODIC SENTENCES frequently present a climax with the delay of the main clause; and they are most prominent in writing rather than speech.

clipping

(1) In LEXICOLOGY, the process of shortening lexical items. It usually occurs mostly in colloquial speech, so that **clippings** present informal stylistic variants of fuller forms. Occasionally these become the established forms, ousting the longer (e.g. *bus* from *omnibus*). Either the first syllable(s) or the last is ELIDED, as in *bus* and *perm(anent wave)*. COMPOUNDS can also be shortened: e.g. *sci(ence)-fi(ction)* (now the abbreviation *sf.*) and *sit(uation)-com(edy)*.

Economy of effort in speaking and of space in writing, is obviously a strong motivation for shortening, as it is for ACRONYMS; but memorability, and EUPHONY, etc., are also involved. Orwell, noting the 'telescoping' of words and phrases in political language, satirizes the practice in his B vocabulary of NEWSPEAK in *1984*. Hence the Fiction Department is *Ficdep*, the Records Department *Recdep*, etc. (See also APHESIS; APOCOPE.)

(2) In PHONETICS **clipping** describes a kind of pronunciation in which syllables are spoken very quickly and/or abruptly without slurring, to produce a staccato rhythm (e.g. the speech of the Daleks in the British TV series *Doctor Who*).

Although this tends to be thought of as an individual or IDIOLECTAL feature, to American ears, for example, British English speech (especially the STANDARD ACCENT) sounds clipped, as the occasional imitations of British English in American films suggest.

closed: ~ class; ~ system, etc.

(1) Phrases used in the description of the LEXIS or vocabulary of a language of those parts of speech whose membership is **closed** or 'finite', in that new words (by borrowing, coinage, etc.) are not readily created. OPEN CLASSES, by contrast, do admit innovation or renewal. **Closed classes** contain the main FUNCTION WORDS: PRONOUNS, ARTICLES, PREPOSITIONS, CONJUNCTIONS, part of the ancient and persistent word stock of English, and important in the skeletal, syntactic structure of sentences.

(2) In the work of Smith (1968) on poetic CLOSURE (q.v.) the phrase **closed system** refers to a poetic STYLE which becomes too familiar or predictable, and has nothing new to say (e.g. eighteenth-century POETIC DICTION). This seems to correspond to PRAGUE SCHOOL notions of AUTOMATIZATION (q.v.).

closed text

One of a pair of terms (see also OPEN TEXT) popularized by Eco (e.g. 1979) to refer to kinds of readers and interpretations. A **closed text** is aimed at a specific reader in a specific social context; unlike an open text. Popular fiction (romance; thrillers) would fall into the category of a closed text: characters and relationships are identified explicitly and directly, and there is no great complexity of theme or structure.

Rather confusingly, however, Eco sees such texts as being potentially 'open' to every possible kind of misreading (what he calls 'aberrant DECODING'), whereas open texts define their own readers (and are thus 'closed'), and cannot afford just any sort of interpretation. (Look at OPEN TEXT, if it helps!)

(See also READERLY; WRITERLY.)

closing

Closings or **closing routines** as a feature of DISCOURSE (types) have been the subject of much ETHNOMETHODOLOGICAL research by Sacks *et al.* (e.g. 1974): for instance, how we take leave in telephone conversations, and (less obviously) conclude our face-to-face interchanges. No-one, out of politeness, really likes to bring talk to an end, so various strategies are employed, characteristically prefaced by a FRAMING signal such as *Well*, or *OK* (*It's been really nice bumping into you; I better go, because I've a bus to catch*, etc.). (See also Traugott & Pratt 1980.)

Closings are easier to achieve in the impersonal MEDIUM of writing, and obvious FORMULAIC routines, or what Kermode (1978) describes as CLOSURE **tagmemes** have been evolved for letters (*yours faithfully*, etc.), stories (. . . *and they all lived happily ever after*), prayers (*Amen*), etc. The EPILOGUE is a formal closing structure for many plays.

(See also CODA.)

closure

Closure has been popular in LITERARY CRITICISM and LITERARY THEORY, but with varying connotations.

(1) Defined as 'sense of completion', it provides opportunities in poetry and narrative for the study of their realizations of FORM, i.e. the different strategies of achieving 'completion' (see, e.g., Smith 1968; Torgovnick 1981).

Couplets and end-stopped lines are common METRICAL devices, as is the return to an initial RHYTHMICAL and RHYME pattern (e.g. the last line of a limerick). One simple form in narratives is based on ANTITHESIS: the poor become rich; the ugly are made beautiful; the wicked made good. In novels, as distinct from fairy-tales, **closure** comes from the 'tying up' of all the strands of the PLOT, the resolution of all the ENIGMAS, or apparent contradictions. (See also DÉNOUEMENT.)

(2) It might be argued that there are degrees of **closure** or **finalization** (Rimmon-Kenan 1983); and more significantly, that some narratives work against closure in favour of **anti-closure** or OPENNESS, especially in the modern period. Closure for some novelists (and also critics), because of its associations with the nineteenth-century 'realist' or classical novel, has become identified generally with plots or themes of political conservatism, and lack of formal or linguistic experimenting.

At an extreme, Derrida has argued that all LITERARY LANGUAGE lacks closure, that the concept is IDEOLOGICAL.

(3) The term is sometimes applied to non-literary texts (e.g. newspaper reports, television programmes) to refer to the fact that stories of all kinds are constructed according to particular ideologies, other possible interpretations being 'closed'.

(See also GESTALT.)

coalescence

Used in PHONETICS to refer to the coming together of two PHONEMES to form a single, different phoneme. In English this has mainly affected the ALVEOLAR consonants: the PLOSIVES /t/, /d/, and the FRICATIVES /s/, /z/, all when adjacent to the semi-vowel /j/. There are two kinds of coalescence:

(1) Historically, and medially in a word, /t/ and /d/ + /j/ became the AFFRICATES /tʃ/ and /dʒ/ by the eighteenth century in words like *virtue* and *grandeur*. In very slow or careful speech, or in some IDIOLECTS, certain of these words can now be heard **de-coalesced**. Coalescence also affects medial /s/ and /z/ + /j/, which in words like *special* and *occasion*, came to be pronounced as /ʃ/ and /ʒ/ from the seventeenth century onwards. Today there are variant pronunciations of *issue, casual*, etc.

(2) In contemporary colloquial speech **coalescence** occurs at word boundaries, so that, for instance, *would you . . .* or *what do you . . .*, etc., are heard as /wudʒu/ and /wotʃu/.

Coalescence is rarely recorded in writing, unlike ELISION (forms like *I'll, she's*, etc.), except perhaps in attempts to suggest **non**-STANDARD or DIALECT speech (*betcha; wotcha got*).

coda

Taken from music theory and used in NARRATOLOGY to refer to the final structural or thematic unit of a NARRATIVE, following the resolution of the ACTION. In a novel, for example, the **coda** typically moves away from the close perspective of the action to resolve all the loose ends of the PLOT, or summarize the later events in the hero(ine)'s life (e.g. the FORMULAIC *They all lived happily ever after*).

(See also CLOSURE; EPILOGUE.)

code

Commonly used in SEMIOTICS and COMMUNICATION THEORY, **code** has become popular in other fields, including STRUCTURALISM, sociolinguistics and LITERARY THEORY. Its extensive COLLOCATIONAL range (**aesthetic code; cultural code; linguistic code; pictorial code; theatrical code**, etc.) testifies to its value, but also it must be said, a certain vagueness, even pretentiousness. It is sometimes used as a synonym for language, VARIETY, or DIALECT (see CODE-SWITCHING); but with the emphasis on 'system', which is one of the fundamental elements of its meaning.

(1) In semiotics a **code** is a systematic set of rules which assigns meanings to SIGNS: e.g. we can speak of **Morse code** or a **secret code**. Because all aspects of human behaviour function as signs, there are codes of all kinds in society, with

differing degrees of complexity of structure and information: e.g. the BINARY code of computers (1/0), traffic lights, dress, gesture, algebra. Not all are inventions, but all are cultural constructs.

(2) Human language presents a highly sophisticated **code**, or rather, a set of codes or **subcodes**: as well as the PHONOLOGICAL, SYNTACTICAL and LEXICAL rules, there are PROSODIC and PARALINGUISTIC rules, etc., each of which help to assign meaning to utterances, but some of which also can function as meaning-systems in their own right (e.g. the paralanguage of snorts, giggles, *tut-tuts*, etc.). Watching television or attending a play, we engage in processing a variety of **representational codes**: visual (lighting, costume, image), aural (music, sound effects), as well as linguistic (and AESTHETIC CODES).

(3) In Jakobson's (1960) notion of the SPEECH EVENT **code** is one of the basic aspects of human COMMUNICATION. The MESSAGE that is sent between ADDRESSER and ADDRESSEE requires a CONTEXT and a code: the system of meaning which structures it. For Jakobson the main FUNCTIONS of speech are orientated towards the different components of the speech event. So a code-orientated utterance has a METALINGUISTIC function (e.g. talking about someone's accent; defining a word, etc.).

In recent years the code model or metaphor of human language has been questioned, both in RELEVANCE THEORY (Sperber & Wilson 1995 [1986]), and INTEGRATIONAL LINGUISTICS (see Harris 1997, Toolan 1996). The former theory argues, for example, that the codedness of language needs to be supplemented by a level of inferencing, in order to account for full communication of meaning. The latter rejects 'code-mindedness' completely.

(4) A combination of semiotic and communicative approaches informs the sociolinguistic theory of **codes** as espoused by Halliday (1978), much influenced by Bernstein (1971f). Codes are seen as types of meaning or cultural values generated by the social system, ACTUALIZED or realized in language VARIETIES, and transmitted by different social groups (e.g. family, school, golf club). Extreme examples would be the ANTI-LANGUAGES of underworld or tight-knit organizations.

Much of Bernstein's own work has centred on his now notorious concept of ELABORATED CODE (q.v.) and RESTRICTED CODE (q.v.). These terms have been rather misleadingly used and applied, even by Bernstein himself, and code taken in the sense simply of a '(social) variety' or 'dialect' rather than a **semiotic style** (Halliday's paraphrase).

(5) A characteristic feature of codes is that one sign system (**primary code**) can be used to convert messages into another (**secondary code**): e.g. Morse code based on verbal language. In this sense a code is a SYMBOLIC system, as phrases like *heraldic code* also imply. In literature, especially poetry, systems of symbols are a pervasive and unifying feature, so that, following Riffaterre (1978), we could see a geographical code, for example, informing the IMAGERY and word-play of Donne's elegies:

> The brow becalms us when 'tis smooth and plain,
> And when 'tis wrinkled, shipwracks us again . . .

('Love's Progress')

O my America! my new-found-land,
My kingdome safeliest when with one man man'd . . .

('Going to Bed')

In a general sense, however, it might be argued, as Leech & Short (1981) argue, that all literature is a code: the message of a text a 'second order' symbolization, since we expect it to mean something beyond itself, something of universal significance.

(6) **Code** in literary theory is probably best known from the early work of Barthes (1970), on how we make sense of a text, particularly the novel. It is part of our COMPETENCE as readers to draw for our understanding, consciously or not, on certain literary and cultural FRAMES OF REFERENCE, models or codes. Barthes distinguishes five: the ACTIONAL or **proairetic** CODE concerned with sequencing of actions; the HERMENEUTIC with narrative ENIGMAS and solutions; the SEMIC with the meanings of CHARACTERS; the SYMBOLIC with thematic oppositions; and the REFERENTIAL or cultural with the body of general knowledge outside the text. Culler (1975, 1983) thinks further codes are necessary: e.g. a code of NARRATION: the construing of the text as a particular discourse between NARRATOR and NARRATEE.

(See also DECODING; ENCODING.)

code-switching; ~ -crossing

(1) **Code-switching** is used in sociolinguistics to refer to the shifting adopted by speakers between one VARIETY or DIALECT or LANGUAGE and another. (See also CODE.)

BILINGUAL speakers regularly switch languages systematically and APPROPRIATELY: according to the person addressed (e.g. father v. mother), or the SITUATION (e.g. home v. office), or even the topic (pleasure v. business). This latter variation is sometimes termed **metaphorical code-switching**. In informal conversations some bilingual speakers will shift from language to language many times, even within sentences, for emphasis and feeling (called **conversational code-switching**). But even monolingual speakers can code-switch: usually according to situation and/or **degree of** FORMALITY: e.g. shifting from regional speech within the family circle to the STANDARD form outside it.

In DIGLOSSIC communities, where there is an 'official' variety (e.g. High German) and the VERNACULAR (e.g. Swiss German) code-switching occurs for similar functional and stylistic reasons. This has been termed **high** and **low** variation (following Ferguson 1959): shifts occurring between languages in REGISTERS or DOMAINS of public and formal discourse (government, education, journalism) and informal discourse (family, humour, popular songs, etc.).

Code-switching in literary texts provides an interesting field for analysis, both in terms of its possible reflection of social reality, and its manipulation as a literary device. There is a strong correlation, for example, between the voice of the NARRATOR and the standard dialect or 'official' language (code of the norm?

of authority?), and between the voice of the characters in direct speech and regional dialect (the code of the DEVIANT? of subversion?).

(2) In the SEMIOTICS of the theatre, **code-switching** or **transcodification** refers to the replacement of one code by another, e.g. pictorial scenery replacing scenic indication by gesture or verbal language (as in the Restoration theatre); or vice versa (as in mime). (See further Elam 1980.)

(3) **code-crossing** is Rampton's term (1995) based on a study of South Asians in an East Midland town for a kind of code-switching across cultures or ethnic groups. So a speaker will use a language variety of a group he or she does not normally 'belong' to. Code-crossing is particularly associated with LIMINAL periods: for example, by adolescents wanting either to resist or affirm certain ritual activities, or to challenge authority. The 1999 cult TV comic Ali G can be seen to be a parodic version of white or Asian adolescents trying to get in to black street culture, with his stereotypical vocabulary, syntax and accent of a gangster rapper: 'These unemployed – they just chillin', innit man?'

cognitive: linguistics; ~ poetics; ~ stylistics; ~ discourse analysis

(1) **Cognitive linguistics** has proved to be one of the most stimulating new disciplines to have emerged in the 1990s, of potential value for DISCOURSE studies and STYLISTICS, and confirming general interest in this decade in the idea of reading as a creative negotiation between writer, text, reader and context to construct a TEXT WORLD. As well as cognitive science itself, its origins lie variously in anthropology, psychology, SEMANTICS, PRAGMATICS and artificial intelligence (AI), for example, and there is no one line of approach. However, it can broadly be said to be associated with Langacker (1987) and the writings of Lakoff, Turner and Johnson since the 1980s, particularly their work on COGNITIVE METAPHOR THEORY (q.v.). Very broadly also cognitive linguistics aims in a theoretical way to account for principles of language behaviour and interpretation from the perspective of general principles of cognition, with particular regard to perception and categorization, and based on what is known about how the mind works. Traditional 'oppositions' are neutralized: e.g. GRAMMAR V. LEXICON; syntax v. meaning; semantic v. pragmatic meaning; LITERAL V. FIGURATIVE.

(2) It is in this latter domain of discussion that a **cognitive poetics** or **stylistics** or **rhetoric** can be said to have recently emerged in the 1990s, generally concerned with the cognitive effects of style, but particularly concerned with METAPHOR: see the entry for cognitive metaphor theory below. Cognitive linguistics and poetics are much concerned with the role of 'conventional' metaphors in cognition and language, and with FIGURATION generally in thought and speech as well as literature.

(3) Another branch of cognitive poetics, building on cognitive research into discourse comprehension (e.g. Chafe 1973f), is essentially a **cognitive discourse analysis** or **grammar**. Particularly influential is work on FRAMES and SCHEMAS (q.v.), which has been applied to readers' comprehension and interpretation of

literary and non-literary texts by Cook (1994); of poetry by Semino (1997); and of NARRATIVES by Emmott (1997) and Werth (1999).

(See also MENTAL SPACE THEORY.)

cognitive meaning

See CONCEPTUAL MEANING.

cognitive metaphor theory

As their title suggests (*Metaphors we live by*, 1980), Lakoff and Johnson (and later Turner) argue that the metaphoric impulse is basic to human thought processes, stimulating the formation of ideas and actually fundamental to many concepts. A **cognitive metaphor theory** they have developed, which attempts to group so-called 'conventional' metaphors together on the basis of a set of fundamental and schematized real or vicarious bodily experiences, which are yet culturally conditioned. For example, in English what is 'good' is commonly portrayed in terms of 'up' (*She's in high spirits/ on cloud nine/ on a high*); and what is 'bad' as 'down' (*She's down in the dumps/ under the weather/ in low spirits/ has an inferiority complex*). Very common metaphors, in both conversation and literature, show LIFE is a JOURNEY; LOVE is a DISEASE, etc. In a **cognitive stylistic** approach (q.v.) it is possible to show how such **root analogies** (Goatly 1997) are basic to the designs of imagery in literary texts, however elaborated and creative their realization; and also therefore to suggest that such patterns can help in the underlining of significant themes. (See further Freeman 1993 on *King Lear*; for a critique see Downes 1993. See also SCHEMA.)

coherence; cohesion

Coherence and **cohesion** have been two very prominent terms in DISCOURSE ANALYSIS and TEXT LINGUISTICS, but they are difficult to distinguish. They are related etymologically, and share the same verb (**cohere**). That there are grounds for a useful distinction, however, is indicated by the derived adjectives **coherent** and **cohesive**, which, even in common usage, have different meanings.

(1) Popularized by Halliday & Hasan (1976), **cohesion** refers to the means (PHONOLOGICAL, GRAMMATICAL, LEXICAL, SEMANTIC) of linking SENTENCES into larger units (paragraphs, chapters, etc.), i.e. of making them 'stick together'. Other equivalent terms popular at one time or another have been **inter-sentence linkage/concord; supra-sentential relations**; and CONNECTIVITY.

Cohesive ties can be overt or explicit; or covert or implicit; and there are several patterns or processes: (i) explicit lexical REPETITION as in: *Fog everywhere. Fog up the river, where it flows among green aits and meadows; fog down the river, where it rolls defiled* . . . (Dickens: *Bleak House*).

(ii) CO-REFERENCE (q.v.):

'Always the same. Have the little bitches into your bed. Lose all sense of proportion.'
'They're students?'
'The Mouse. God knows what the other thinks she is.'
But Breasley clearly did not want to talk about them . . .

(Fowles: *The Ebony Tower*)

(iii) ELLIPSIS as an implicit device:

'Are you a cricketer?' inquired Mr Wardle of the marksman.
. . . Mr Winkle . . . modestly replied, 'No' [I am not a cricketer].
'Are you [a cricketer], sir?' inquired Mr Snodgrass.
'I was [a cricketer] once upon a time', replied the host; 'but I have given it up now.
I subscribe to the club here, but I don't play [cricket].'

(Dickens: *Pickwick Papers*)

(For a detailed discussion of cohesive strategies, see Halliday & Hasan *op. cit.* and Quirk *et al.* 1985, ch. 19.)

The examples above illustrate one of the main PRAGMATIC functions of cohesion, which is to avoid exact repetition in the interests of ease and economy of communication, unless it is rhetorically necessary, and therefore MARKED (e.g. the quotation above from *Bleak House*). Other functions include the furthering of an argument by progression, contrast or by explanation; and CONJUNCTS are useful linking devices here, especially in complex or technical texts (*however; in addition; so,* etc.). Certain REGISTERS are characterized by particular kinds of cohesive ties: SUBSTITUTION in colloquial speech; RHYME, stanza schemes, ALLITERATION, etc., as phonological patterns of cohesion in poetry.

(2) **Coherence** has sometimes been seen, after Widdowson (1979), as referring to the underlying development of propositions in terms of SPEECH ACTS, in contrast to cohesion, concerned with SURFACE features of connectivity.

But his further distinction, namely that cohesion has to do with TEXT (q.v.) and coherence with DISCOURSE (q.v.) is unsatisfactory. Text, no less than discourse, is 'coherent' if it makes sense, has a unity, and is therefore well-formed. Indeed, a text without coherence is hardly a 'text' at all; and we certainly expect even conversation to be coherent in the sense of being relevant and clear. (See also CO-OPERATIVE PRINCIPLE.) In the following example, there are no obvious cohesive ties, yet the text is coherent as text: *Beckham's high pass was headed to the right. The forward shot at once, and scored a goal. The referee declared the kick offside.* It has been argued that a kind of 'semantic cohesion', or 'connectivity of content' is involved here, and hence the confusion between the two concepts. Coherence without cohesion depends considerably on INFERENCE (q.v.).

Coherence has obvious significance for literary forms. Aside from DECONSTRUCTION THEORISTS, most readers expect logical consistency and clarity in the working out of PLOT, for instance (NARRATIVE coherence), as we expect clear and plausible NARRATION (discourse coherence). Novels like Joyce's *Finnegans Wake*, therefore, which appear to lack coherence, are particularly frustrating, and come close to 'incoherence' in the sense of 'unintelligibility'. Discourse coherence is a marked feature of dramatic DIALOGUE, which tends to lack the non-sequiturs, the digressions and REDUNDANCIES which can occur in ordinary conversation.

Culler (1975) uses the term **models of coherence** to refer to the various ways in which readers make sense of texts and naturalize them, by drawing on their familiarity with other texts, their cultural knowledge, etc. (See also FRAME.)

collective discourse

(1) Lambert (1975) uses the phrase to refer to the practice by medieval writers of ascribing speech to two or more characters in unison (as in Malory's *Morte d'Arthur*). Functioning not unlike the chorus of classical drama (although usually participating in the action, rather than merely observing it), this collective voice dramatically emphasizes unanimity of opinion: e.g. of the 163 knights in the last Tale.

(2) **Collective discourse** might appear incompatible with 'realistic' narrative, yet related forms are certainly characteristic of the novel tradition. These provide interesting examples of COLOURED NARRATIVE (q.v.), and FREE INDIRECT SPEECH, as the work of Mikhail Bakhtin (1981) reveals on the STYLES of the novel. So what is taken as the common view of a social group, public opinion reflecting certain social values, can be exploited for (IRONIC) effect in the presentation or exposure of character or theme. Dickens's portrayal of the hypocritical Pecksniffs in *Martin Chuzzlewit*, for example, leans heavily on passages such as the following:

> Mr. Pecksniff was observed too; closely. When he talked to the Mayor, they said, Oh really, what a courtly man he was! When he laid his hand upon the mason's shoulder, giving him directions, how pleasant his demeanour to the working classes: just the sort of man who made their toil a pleasure to them, poor dear souls! (ch. 35)

collocation; collocative meaning

(1) **Collocation** is a frequently used term in LEXICOLOGY, derived from the work of Firth (1957) and developed especially by Halliday from the 1960s onwards. It refers to the habitual or expected co-occurrence of words, a characteristic feature of LEXICAL behaviour in language, testifying to its predictability as well as its IDIOMATICITY. Associations are most commonly made contiguously (e.g. ADJECTIVE + NOUN: *old man; saucy postcard*); or proximately in phrases (*herd of cows; as cool as a cucumber*), but they also occur over a larger span, such as CLAUSE and SENTENCE, and even beyond.

Statistically, given a big enough corpus of material, it might be possible to estimate the **collocational range** or **cluster** of an item, i.e. its **collocates** ranked in order of probability of occurrence (e.g. *elephant: grey, white, pink, green*). Those words which show similar ranges are said to belong to the same LEXICAL SET (q.v.).

Habitual collocations are a recognizable feature of different REGISTERS (*warm front; soaring prices; beat the eggs*), and in LITERARY LANGUAGE form the basis of the POETIC DICTION of many periods (OE *atol yðagewealc* 'dark wave-surge'; eighteenth-century *finny tribe* 'fish', etc.).

But poetic effect often depends more on the exploitation of the non-habitual, the unusual, as in Eliot's:

I am aware of the <u>damp souls</u> of housemaids
<u>Sprouting despondently</u> at area gates

('*Morning at the Window*')

And note the memorability of pop group names like *Aztec Camera* and *Prefab Sprout*. (See also ANOMALY.)

(2) In this connection, the RHETORICAL term **collocatio** refers to a special kind of lexical incongruity which juxtaposes different levels of TONE or STYLE. Shakespeare's plays have many examples, notoriously Macbeth's:

No, this my hand will rather
The <u>multitudinous seas incarnadine</u>,
Making the <u>green one red</u> (II.ii)

(3) It might be argued that lexical (in)congruity is dependent on semantic (in)compatibility: the meaning of *soul*, for example, normally excludes ideas of 'dampness' and 'sprouting'. The degree of dependence of collocations upon the senses of the lexical items themselves is much debated, and the extent to which we can talk, as Leech (1981) does, of **collocation meaning** as a distinct from CONCEPTUAL MEANING. (Why, for example, do we say *big business*, but not *large* or *great*?)

But an investigation of clustering can be of use in lexicography or dictionary-making for the refinement of dictionary definitions, of particular benefit for foreign learners of English (what kinds of words do the verbs *evade, scold* and *erase* take as OBJECTS? What *boggles* apart from the *mind*? Does Laurel and Hardy's *lonesome pine* exist?).

(See also CLICHÉ; IDIOM; SELECTION RESTRICTIONS; SYNONYMY.)

coloured narrative

A term introduced by Hough (1970) to refer to a kind of NARRATIVE discourse in the novel which suggests the speech of characters, without the framework of DIRECT or INDIRECT SPEECH. It is close to FREE INDIRECT SPEECH (q.v.), but in the latter it is the speech which is 'coloured' by the narrative VOICE, not vice versa. So, in this sentence from Dickens's *Dombey and Son*:

The Chicken himself attributed this punishment to his having had the misfortune to get into Chancery early in the proceedings, when he was severely <u>fibbed by the Larkey one</u>, and heavily <u>grassed</u> . . . (ch. 44)

the words underlined function as **pseudo-quotations** (Pascal 1977), echoing what we assume to be Chicken's actual phraseology. In contrast, a COLLECTIVE voice may be assumed to colour the opening of *A Tale of Two Cities*, that of the current general or journalistic opinion: *It was the best of times, it was the worst of times, it was the age of wisdom, it was the age of foolishness* . . . (etc.).

Coloured narrative, with its highlighting of speech, is often exploited for IRONY; although it is not always easy to distinguish between the voices of character and narrator if their IDIOLECTS are similar: e.g. in Jane Austen's novels.

(See also CHARACTER ZONE; DUAL VOICE; HYBRIDIZATION.)

common core

(1) Traditionally used in LEXICOLOGY to refer to the basic and characteristically stable stock of LEXICAL ITEMS in any language. Thus the **common core vocabulary** of English comprises mostly words of Old English origin (as distinct from French and Latin), which reflect the concerns of everyday life. Items less central are more likely to be stylistically MARKED: e.g. words of Latin or Greek origin or derivation (e.g. *hubris*; *depolymerize*), found in FORMAL or technical REGISTERS.

So-called **core vocabularies** (of about 1000 words) have often been used in language teaching, on the principle that the frequency of core words aids comprehension of texts. C. K. Ogden's 'Basic English', a LINGUA FRANCA well known for a time in the thirties, also depends on the idea of a lexical core (see also Orwell's NEWSPEAK).

(2) **Common core** has increasingly come to be used in studies of VARIETIES of English to refer to any linguistic features (not only vocabulary) which are 'neutral', or which are 'common' to all varieties, or used by the majority of speakers. Forms like *whosoever, zymurgy, maiden over*, etc., would fall outside the core.

(3) In Quirk *et al.* (1985) **common core** is used specifically with reference to grammatical features of STANDARD ENGLISH, as a metaphor for an unmarked nucleus of forms which are also attitudinally neither formal nor informal (ch. 1, *passim*).

(4) The same term, however, is also used by Quirk *et al.* to describe the common characteristics of British and American English. This usage is perhaps derived from Hockett's (1958) use of the term to refer to linguistic features shared by two or more DIALECTS.

communication: ~ theory

(1) **Communication** is broadly the process of exchanging INFORMATION or MESSAGES, and human language, in speech and writing, is the most significant and most complex communication system.

(2) Yet, in some basic respects this system is comparable, if controversially, to technical systems as described in the influential **communication theory** of Shannon & Weaver (1949): messages are transmitted as SIGNALS from transmittor or sender to receiver via the MEDIUM of speech, for example, along the CHANNEL of sound-waves. The human 'transmittor', however, is (normally) also the creator of the message; and what may be 'communicated' may not only be factual, or even verbal, but also ATTITUDINAL, social, or cultural information. Indeed, it is very difficult for people not to communicate anything to each other, even when they are silent.

(3) A more influential model for the analysis of DISCOURSE has been Jakobson's (1960), which outlines the key constituents of **communication**, and also their related FUNCTIONS. The SPEECH EVENT requires an ADDRESSER and ADDRESSEE (q.v.) and the message sent between them a CONTEXT and a CODE (the system of meaning).

In conversation, addresser and addressee are usually the speaker and hearer; but as the entries for these terms reveal, in literature the situation is more complex. LITERARY DISCOURSE itself is a double, even multiple speech event, requiring more than one addresser (AUTHOR to READER; NARRATOR to NARRATEE or IMPLIED READER, etc.); just as dramatic discourse enacts speech events between (performers as) fictional participants in the larger speech event between dramatist and AUDIENCE. One important difference, however, between literary communication and everyday communication is that the roles of addresser/addressee cannot be reversed.

(See also NON-VERBAL COMMUNICATION.)

communicative competence

See COMPETENCE.

communicative dynamism (CD)

A TEXTUAL principle developed particularly in the post-war PRAGUE SCHOOL by Firbas, to describe the extent to which elements of a sentence contribute to the dynamic 'development' of the communication.

This involves, for example, the CONTEXTUAL interplay of GIVEN and NEW INFORMATION, the semantic value or weight of the elements, and WORD ORDER. THEMES (q.v.) usually bear the lowest degree of CD, RHEMES the highest. **Transitional elements** linking theme and rheme are frequently VERBS. The overall pattern of dynamism is called the FUNCTIONAL SENTENCE PERSPECTIVE (FSP) (q.v.). The commonest perspective is to move from 'low' to 'high' in a sentence, as in the following examples:

> Once upon a time there (all **thematic**) lived (**transition**) a beautiful princess (**rhematic**). She (**theme**) had (**transition**) many suitors from far countries (**rhematic**).

Alternative orderings seem odd or MARKED here:

> A beautiful princess lived once upon a time. Many suitors from far countries she had.

(See also END-FOCUS. See further Firbas 1992.)

competence: linguistic ~; communicative ~; literary ~, etc.

(1) **Competence** was made famous by the theory of GENERATIVE GRAMMAR by Chomsky (1965), along with its opposition PERFORMANCE (q.v.). These are often

compared with Saussure's terms LANGUE (q.v.) and PAROLE (q.v.), but they taken their particular significances from quite different frameworks.

Linguistic competence is the internalized knowledge users of a language supposedly have about its system, which enables them to construct and interpret an infinite number of grammatically CORRECT (*sic*) and meaningful sentences (see also IDEAL SPEAKER). This implicit knowledge is to be distinguished from what we do when we actually speak, i.e. performance: the process of speaking and writing. Performance is seen as secondary to competence, because it depends on it. By this dichotomy, STYLE is a matter of performance, whereas what possibilities of stylistic CHOICE exist are a matter of competence.

(2) However, since the 1960s many linguists have found the distinction unsatisfactory as attention has come more and more to be focussed on aspects of linguistic behaviour and 'rules' largely ignored by Chomsky and his followers. One result has been to extend the notion of competence to a general **communicative competence**, which recognizes our ability to construct and interpret APPROPRIATE utterances in particular linguistic and social CONTEXTS, with specific goals or purposes (see Hymes 1971). Our awareness of what we normally take for granted is made explicit in learning a foreign language (e.g. making a polite request or a telephone call), or in reading a text or watching a play which violates normal communicative rules (e.g. an ABSURDIST drama).

In this sense, 'competence' comes close to its common meaning of 'skill': communicative competence depends on social and cultural interaction, on relations of power, and must be acquired. It is easier to think of 'incompetent' communicators (unable to make small talk, rude to superiors, etc.) than Chomskyan incognizants.

(3) Even the ability to tell stories is a skill, an aspect of what might be termed **narrative competence**. Various kinds of (sub-) competence terms now proliferate by analogy, and the concept became popular in LITERARY CRITICISM. As early as 1966 Halle & Keyser in their GENERATIVE METRICS presented the reader's ability to judge the metrical ACCEPTABILITY of lines of verse as analogous to linguistic competence.

Literary competence was popularized by Culler (1975) in his model of a LITERARY THEORY or POETICS which would make explicit the (IDEAL) READER's knowledge of the set of conventions needed for the INTERPRETATION of literary texts. These are in part linguistic (e.g. use of METAPHOR, DEVIANT structure, etc.), in part extra-textual: derived from the cultural situation, or other texts within the same GENRE, etc. (see also INTERTEXTUALITY). However, the whole process of reading and comprehension is far from being understood, let alone described.

complement; complementation

(1) In some GRAMMARS, especially SYSTEMIC, **complement** (C) designates a NOMINAL GROUP functioning as an element in the PREDICATE structure of CLAUSES which essentially completes the construction. In some grammars it includes DIRECT OBJECTS (DO) and INDIRECT OBJECTS (IO), as in *The agent quickly passed James Bond* (IO) *the microfilm* (DO).

(2) Traditionally, however, and in some late twentieth-century grammars (e.g. Quirk *et al.* 1985) **complement** is restricted to nominals or ADJECTIVES which are linked specifically to the SUBJECT or OBJECT of the clause (**ascriptive** or **attributive complements**). **Subject complements** follow so-called COPULAR or equative VERBS like *be, become, seem*: *A thing of beauty is a joy forever*; and **object complements** refer to the object in structures like *They declared her* (DO) chairman (C) *unanimously*.

Clearly, there is the possibility of confusion. (And see also (4) below.) An object complement may mean 'object (as) complement' in some descriptions. Crystal & Davy (1969), who use complement in the generic sense of (1) call structures involving DO and C **intensive**; whereas structures with IO and DO are called **extensive**:

> She called her mother (DO) an idiot (C) (= intensive)
> She called her mother (IO) a taxi (DO) (= extensive)

Other problems arise with the distinction between complements and ADJUNCTS. Quirk *et al.* (*op. cit.*), for example, classify PREPOSITIONAL PHRASES normally as adjuncts; but, as they admit, in certain structures following copular and other verbs they are obligatory rather than optional, as they complete the sense: *She says she's in love, The Church lies in a valley*. In this last example, however, where position is specified, Quirk *et al.* prefer to see the phrase as a subject-related ADVERBIAL. Other grammarians have called it a **prepositional complement** (e.g. Young 1980). Unfortunately, there can be confusion even here: Quirk *et al.* use **prepositional complement** to refer simply to the nominal phrase which follows a preposition.

(3) In GENERATIVE GRAMMAR particularly, and American grammars generally, **complement** and **complementation** refer to nominal SUBORDINATE CLAUSES, both FINITE and NON-FINITE functioning as (object) nominal groups, e.g.: *I hear* [*that petrol prices are going up*]. *I don't know* [*what I'll do*]. *We've decided* [*to sell the car*]. A form like *that* which introduces the complement is called a **complementizer**. Such clauses are frequently found in INDIRECT DISCOURSE after verbs like *affirm, announce, explain, declare, state, conjecture, wish*, etc.

(4) For Quirk *et al.*, however, **complementation** is used in a general sense to refer to various kinds of syntactic and semantic completion. Thus certain adjectives require phrasal or clausal completion (*The pan's easy to clean*). Rather confusingly (see (2) above) **complementation** is used particularly with reference to verbs: e.g. TRANSITIVE VERBS (*hate, hit*) require obligatory complementation by direct objects; whereas INTRANSITIVE VERBS (*come, go*, etc.) lack it completely.

complex sentence; compound sentence

Term reflecting a common classification of SENTENCE types according to kinds of CLAUSES. They are opposed to the **simple sentence**, which consists of one clause only. Quirk *et al.* (1985) call them both **multiple sentences**; Halliday (1978) **clause**

complexes. Young (1984) uses the term **complex sentence** to cover both types, but this is misleading.

(1) A **complex sentence** has at least two clauses: a MAIN CLAUSE and one (or more BOUND/SUBORDINATE CLAUSE(s). It is not necessarily 'complex' in the familiar sense, as many everyday sentences testify: [*If you go out for the day*] *please feed the cat*. However, so-called PERIODIC SENTENCES found in FORMAL or LITERARY prose are characterized by several bound clauses, often EMBEDDED one within another.

(2) A **compound sentence** consists of two or more conjoined or CO-ORDINATED main clauses. *And, or* and *but* are the commonest CONJUNCTIONS. Because of their fairly simple logic (mainly expressing 'addition' or 'contrast'), such sentences occur frequently in everyday usage; but excessive use of co-ordination is regarded as unsophisticated in formal writing. Compound sentences occur commonly in (oral) narratives and chronicles, e.g. Malory's *Morte d'Arthur*.

(3) Sentences containing both subordination and co-ordination of clauses are sometimes called **mixed sentences**.

(See also HYPOTAXIS; PARATAXIS.)

componential analysis; component

Componential analysis is an approach to meaning once favoured by some semanticists (e.g. Nida 1975) whereby LEXICAL ITEMS are distinguished and defined by sets of inherent **distinctive features** or **components** or SEMES possibly common to all languages (universal). It is less commonly known as **lexical decomposition**. It was first developed in anthropology in the 1950s for the study of kinship systems, although an interest in components, especially in PHONOLOGY, was developed in Europe by the PRAGUE SCHOOL.

The features are usually analysed in terms of BINARY (q.v.) contrasts e.g. [+/- (concrete)]; [+/- (animate)]; [+/- (human)], etc. Textbooks tend to give fairly simple examples: so *boy* can be decomposed into the bundle of features [+ (human)], [- (adult)], [+ (male)]. It is not always easy to define lexical items in this way, for there seems no limit to the number of oppositions one might establish, granted that they can be posited at all. The **semantic** FIELD of 'chair-ness' lends itself to some useful distinctive lexical items in English (*chair* [+ (back)], [+/- (arms)] v. *stool* [- (back)], [- (arms)]); but how to distinguish *armchair* from *sofa* in terms of components?

Nonetheless, semantic features might usefully explain our intuitions about compatibility and incompatibility which lie, for example, behind METAPHOR and PERSONIFICATION. SELECTION RESTRICTIONS will normally permit nouns marked by [+ (concrete)] or [+ (animate)] to be SUBJECTS with certain relevant VERBS (e.g. *eat, walk*); hence in *Portrait of a Lady* Eliot's *My self-possession gutters*, with its [+ (ABSTRACT)] subject and verb of movement normally associated with melting candles, has to be interpreted metaphorically.

73

compound: ~ing; ~ epithet

(1) By **compounding** (or **composition**), a productive means of word-formation in English, two LEXICAL ITEMS are combined to make a new one, which is regarded as a single fixed unit, often with a meaning different from its (separate) 'parts': e.g. *greenhouse* v. *green house*. This unity is an important feature: along with it usually goes the single main STRESS pattern of simple words, as in the example above (with corresponding FOCUS on the first element). Confusingly (especially to foreign learners of English), **compounds** may be written either 'solidly' as a single word (*greenfly*); hyphenated (*green-fee*); or even 'openly' as a phrase (*green belt*).

The various grammatical word classes freely combine together: e.g. NOUN + noun (*apple-tree*); ADJECTIVE + noun (*red-brick*); adjective + adjective (*ready-made*); noun + VERB (*brick-laying*); and compounds are commonly analysed and classified according to the underlying CLAUSE structures such combinations reflect (e.g. *brick-laying* = object + verb: 'X lays bricks'). Compounds can also be more simply classified according to their grammatical FUNCTION, mainly as nouns (*greenhouse, green belt*), adjectives (*man-made, waterproof*) and verbs (*brain-wash, push-start*).

Although many compounds are well-established in the language, some are largely restricted to certain REGISTERS. So-called **neoclassical compounds**, made up of Latin or Greek roots, originate often in technical discourse (*astronaut; telephone*). Descriptive compound adjectives are favoured in advertising (*jungle-fresh; sun-kissed*).

(2) Descriptive compounding is usually associated with LITERARY LANGUAGE, especially poetry. Old English poetry is characterized by metaphoric, though FORMULAIC, compounds called KENNINGS (e.g. 'swan-path' = 'sea'; 'battle-adder' = 'sword'). So-called **compound epithets** (see also EPITHET) are a pervasive feature of POETIC DICTION from the Renaissance: compound adjectives such as *cloud-capped, pity-pleading* (Shakespeare); *ivy-mantled* (Gray); *flake-laden* (Hardy). Hopkins draws inspiration from the Old English and later poetic tradition for his own dense coinages: e.g. *fire-folk* and *circle-citadels* (in 'The Starlight Night'); *dapple-dawn-drawn Falcon* (in 'The Windhover').

compound sentence

See COMPLEX SENTENCE.

computational: ~ linguistics; ~ stylistics

Computational stylistics, as particularly developed since the late 1960s, uses statistical and computer-aided methods and analyses in the study of different problems of STYLE, a subdiscipline of **computational linguistics**. Computers have proved invaluable in dictionary-making or lexicography and GRAMMAR in the analysis of large samples of data; and INFORMATION technology is widely applied in such areas as automatic speech synthesis and machine translation.

One popular study in computational stylistics has been that known as STY-LOMETRY (q.v.), the investigation of features such as COLLOCATIONS, word length and sentence length in different texts to determine authorship. The discipline as a whole is traditionally very much concerned with style as IDIOLECT: so a work like Milic's (1967) is concerned to establish the distinctive features of Swift's prose style by an 'objective' analysis of selected grammatical categories.

Many stylistic studies generally count word frequencies, for example, in order to establish DEVIATIONS from the NORM, or to verify intuitions about FOREGROUNDING. In studies of GENRE, statistical variation of key features is noted across speech and writing.

(See also CORPUS LINGUISTICS. See further Aitken *et al.* 1973; Biker & Finegan 1989; Williams 1970. For a critique of Milic's approach, see Fish 1973.)

conative function

Introduced by Jakobson (1960) as one of his key FUNCTIONS of COMMUNICATION in the SPEECH EVENT.

An utterance with **conative function** is orientated towards the ADDRESSEE. Commands, VOCATIVES and questions typically have a conative function, as do any utterance generally which aim to have a specific effect or influence on the addressee (e.g. propaganda discourse).

Similar distinctions have been made by other linguists interested in the functions of language (q.v.), chiefly Bühler 1934, whose *appel* or 'appeal' corresponds to the conative function.

However, granted that most **communicative** ACTS involve both ADDRESSER and addressee, it is not always easy to distinguish functions clearly; and any utterance may have more than one orientation. In a certain context *I feel very cold* may ostensibly have an EXPRESSIVE FUNCTION and speaker-orientation, but also have the ILLOCUTIONARY FORCE of a request for the window to be shut. A love poem may well express the speaker's feelings; at the same time it may be a warning (e.g. the CONCEIT that beauty fades); or complaint (about indifference); or an exhortation (to sexual compliance); or a mixture of all three. Consider, for example, many of Shakespeare's sonnets, or the poems of Donne, Herrick and Marvell.

conceit

Originally meaning 'thought' (cf. *conceive*), **conceit** came to be used in the later sixteenth century for a popular FIGURE OF SPEECH in Elizabethan and Metaphysical (love) poetry as well as in French and Italian poetry which depended on wit or ingenuity of idea for its effect.

SIMILE, METAPHOR, HYPERBOLE, OXYMORON are some of the forms of a conceit, which may even extend over a whole poem (e.g. Donne's 'The Flea'). In the vogue for sonnet-writing, conceits tended to become conventionalized: e.g. the **catalogue** or **blazon** of the mistress's qualities; the passing of time and youth. The most striking conceits are the oft-quoted recondite or far-fetched IMAGES of poets like Donne and Herbert (souls as compasses, tears as globes), which return in the intellectual poetic tradition of the twentieth century, in a poet like Eliot:

> April is the cruellest month, breeding
> Lilacs out of the dead land
>
> *(The Waste Land)*

> When the evening is spread out against the sky
> Like a patient etherised upon a table
>
> *(Love Song of J. Alfred Prufrock)*

conceptual meaning, also cognitive meaning; conceptualization

(1) In SEMANTICS the terms **conceptual** or **cognitive meaning** are widely used (see, for example, COMPONENTIAL ANALYSIS and SYNONYMY). Conceptual meaning is the basic PROPOSITIONAL or REFERENTIAL MEANING of words, the DENOTATIONAL MEANING, that which corresponds to the primary dictionary definition.

It is also argued that such meaning is stylistically neutral, objective; opposed to other kinds or ASSOCIATIVE MEANINGS (e.g. AFFECTIVE, CONNOTATIONAL, EMOTIVE) which are more peripheral, more subjective, and stylistically MARKED. So the sentence *The bitch won't eat her food* has two quite distinct meanings and overtones according to whether the conceptual meaning of *bitch* is prominent ('female dog'), or an emotive one ('woman (derogatory)').

However, it is not always easy to maintain a distinction on these grounds: for the words *lad* and *lass*, for example, the connotations of familiarity seem hard to dissociate from the basic meaning. In EUPHEMISM the very associations to be avoided frequently become attached to the conceptual meaning (*undertaker* = 'one who manages funerals'). The question also arises whether stylistic 'neutrality' actually exists. Even informational language can become a 'loaded weapon' (Bolinger 1980) in the discourse of propaganda, as Leech (1981) acknowledges in his discussion of what he terms **conceptual engineering**.

(2) The manipulation of language, consciously and unconsciously, is an important factor in the consideration generally of **conceptualization**, i.e. the way language is used in the classification and interpretation of the world around us. The extent to which different societies conceptualize experience in the same way is a much discussed point; as is the extent to which language restrains as well as helps the representation of reality (see also DETERMINISM). Linguistic innovation in poetry often correlates with novelty of conceptualization. It can be argued that all texts, however, create a particular conceptual WORLD-VIEW, whether this is the daily life in Mansfield Park, or the Russian battlefield, or the hallucinatory scenes of an opium-eater. (See also MIND-STYLE.)

conjunction; conjunct

(1) **Conjunction** is well-established in GRAMMAR to refer to a part of speech or word-class consisting of a CLOSED set of items which link CLAUSES and phrases. They are commonly grouped into **co-ordinating** (e.g. *and, or, but*) and **subordinating** (e.g. *that, when, since*, etc.), since they introduce CO-ORDINATE and SUBORDINATE CLAUSES, and express relations of addition, contrast, time, place, result, etc.

Traditionally it has often been stated that SENTENCES cannot begin with a co-ordinating conjunction; but in advertising copy and popular FICTION, for example, rhetorical linkage of sentences is often made in this way for a dramatic effect: *Many years passed as they went their separate ways. But he never forgot that day in Brighton.*

Sentence linkage by conjunction is also found in NARRATIVES, e.g.: *So they came to a lake that was a fair water and broad. And in the midst Arthur was ware of an arm clothed in white samite . . .* (Malory: *Morte d'Arthur*).

(2) Conjunctions themselves can be seen as part of a general abstract category of **conjunction**, or of a class of **(con)junctives** which function as CONNECTIVES (q.v.) in discourse.

Certain ADVERBIAL elements, sometimes called **sentence adverbials**, or **conjuncts** (Quirk *et al.* 1985), are used in this way. Their usual function is to link sentences as well as clauses, and so they are an important means of COHESION, used for listing (*first, lastly*), reasoning (*therefore*) and contrast (*rather*), etc. Like conjunctions proper they are often found initially in the clause or sentence (e.g. *so, yet, then*); but most of them can occur medially and finally as well, often separated by a comma in writing or by an INTONATION boundary in speech, as in: *I'd like you to come tomorrow. There's just one problem, however/though.*

Conjuncts and conjunctions can co-occur (*and so, but yet*), and are sometimes used (especially in FORMAL or LITERARY DISCOURSE) in **correlation**: a conjunction in one clause is followed by a linked conjunct in the next, which makes the relations between the clauses quite explicit (e.g. *because . . . therefore; when . . . then; and just as . . . so* of EPIC SIMILE).

(3) In the work on TEXT LINGUISTICS of de Beaugrande & Dressler (1981) the term **conjunction** is close to its sense in logic. It refers to links between units with the same status, i.e. which are 'both true' in the textual world, and contrasts with **disjunction** (= 'or'). Conjunction in this co-ordinate sense is most commonly signified by *and*; as well as (conjuncts like) *moreover, also, besides*.

connectivity; connected speech

(1) **Connectivity** is commonly used in the analysis of DISCOURSE and TEXT as an aspect of COHESION, the linkage of UTTERANCES or SENTENCES. Other terms are **connection, connectedness** and **connexity**.

Connectivity may be both implicit and explicit. The simple juxtaposition of sentences is enough to imply some sort of semantic connection: we expect it in a text or speech. Implicit connectivity works best for sequences of events:

The rain set early in to-night,
The sullen wind was soon awake . . .

(Browning: *Porphyria's Love*)

and also reason:

Little boy blue,
Come blow up your horn,
The sheep's in the meadow,
The cow's in the corn.

However, explicit connectivity aids clarity and underlines the structure of an argument, so that it is common in all discourse types for dealing with relations other than the simply sequential. In INTERIOR MONOLOGUE the absence of connectivity is sometimes exploited to suggest the fragmentation or disjointedness of thought processes.

(2) **Connectives** are explicit means of linkage: e.g. lexical REPETITION, pronominal CO-REFERENCE and CONJUNCTIVES (q.v.). In LITERARY LANGUAGE syntactic PARALLELISM, RHYME and RHYTHM are obvious means of connectivity.

(3) The phrase **connected speech** is used in PHONETICS to refer to speech analysable as a continuous sequence, not as a succession of individual discrete items. ASSIMILATION and ELISION are two processes, for example, which affect pronunciation in connected speech so that word boundaries are obscured: *I've gotta get sm brebm butter* ('I have got to get some bread and butter').

connotation; connotative meaning

(1) In SEMANTICS and LITERARY CRITICISM **connotation** and **connotative meaning** are commonly used to refer to all kinds of ASSOCIATIONS words may evoke: emotional, situational, etc., particularly in certain CONTEXTS, over and above the basic DENOTATIONAL or CONCEPTUAL MEANING. Thus *home* defined as 'dwelling-place' has to many people connotations also of 'domesticity' and 'warmth'. In literature, such 'second order' meanings are particularly exploited: in horror comics night and thunder connote evil or mystery; in poetry dew-drops connote fragility, stars steadfastness, and other meanings prompted by the context.

The extent to which connotations can be distinguished from the 'basic' meaning is controversial. In words like *woe, betwixt, billow*, a poetic quality seems part of the basic meaning. Many words seem to have either a favourable meaning (*He expired*); or a derogatory meaning (*He snuffed it*). Certainly connotations are often said to distinguish apparent SYNONYMS. Thus *house* is also a 'dwelling-place', but does not have the same connotations as *home* (Builders, in fact, no longer build houses, but homes . . .). Still, there is an element of subjectivity involved: some words may evoke different connotations to different people.

(2) In SEMIOTICS reference is made to **connotations** or 'additional' meanings not only in language, but in other SIGN systems, visual and aural, such as art, dress and music (see Barthes 1967b). Advertising depends for its success on 'promise': shampoos, soaps and hair-sprays are promoted by images connoting

glamour, romance or adventure, which may well become part of the denotation of the brand name.

consonance

(1) From Lat. 'to harmonize', **consonance** in LITERARY CRITICISM refers to a kind of HALF-RHYME or end-ALLITERATION or consonantal ASSONANCE whereby final consonants are repeated, but with different preceding vowels, e.g. *sing, rang; sin, run; 'Beanz meanz Heinz'*.

(2) Confusingly, Turner (1973) and Cuddon (1998) use the term for what others call APOPHONY and Leech (1969) calls PARARHYME: where both initial as well as final consonants remain constant, with variation in the medial vowels, e.g. *sing, sang; sin, sun*. Cummings & Simmons (1983) cover both (1) and (2) under this term.

constative utterance

The term **constative utterance**, as introduced by the philosopher J. L. Austin (1961), is essentially a statement which describes a state of affairs and which is 'true' or 'false' (e.g. the kind of sentence reproduced in textbooks; or an utterance like *The kettle's boiling* in ordinary speech). Statements which 'say' something were to be distinguished from MARKED utterances which 'do' something verbally, i.e. PERFORMATIVES (q.v.): *promise, threaten, command*, etc.

Austin eventually came to the conclusion that constatives themselves 'do' something: not *I promise/threaten you that . . .*, but *(I tell you that) the kettle's boiling*. They were now re- or down-graded to a class of performatives; and the whole basis of his theorizing thus shifted from the truth concerns of philosophy to the notion of SPEECH ACTS, with a now three-fold distinction between LOCU-TIONARY ACT ('act of saying'), ILLOCUTIONARY ACT ('act performed in saying something') and also PERLOCUTIONARY ACT ('act performed as a result of saying something').

contact

(1) In Jakobson's (1960) model of COMMUNICATION or the SPEECH EVENT **contact** refers to the relations between ADDRESSER and ADDRESSEE, not only the physical connections by CHANNEL (e.g. voice and body), but also the psychological and situational connections.

It is a useful term, but one which strangely has not been taken up by linguists, unlike the other terms in his model. (But see Lanser 1981 on the novel.) The study of DISCOURSE certainly involves the consideration of the relations between speaker and hearer, or narrator and reader, and the influence on the **degree of FORMALITY** of utterances for instance: what is also called TENOR.

Language orientated towards contact is said to have a PHATIC FUNCTION, i.e. it serves solely and socially to keep 'contact' between the participants, to keep the 'channels of communication' open (e.g. discussing health or the weather).

(2) **Contact** is also used in sociolinguistics in phrases like **language(s) in contact** and **contact language(s)**, to refer to the influence of one language upon another due to geographical or social closeness. So, as a result of the contact between English and French after the Norman Conquest, BILINGUALISM was common amongst certain social groups for a time, and many words were borrowed from French. Special contact languages, such as PIDGINS, arise from limited contacts such as trading, where bilingual speakers are few or non-existent.

content

A widely used term in LITERARY CRITICISM, but one much debated in linguistics and STYLISTICS. It is normally opposed, by collocation or implication, to terms such as FORM (q.v.) or EXPRESSION (q.v.): what the classical rhetoricians termed *res* as distinct from *verba*.

(1) Following Saussure's work on the SIGN, the levels of language can be seen as consisting of a **content** or 'meaning' plane, the traditional concern of SEMANTICS; and an expression plane (SYNTAX and PHONOLOGY), which 'expresses' content through the mediation of form: the sound patterns and grammatical patterns. It is not easy to keep the levels apart: much work in grammatical and semantic theory, for example, has shown the extent to which content can be formalized and form semanticized.

(2) Nonetheless, meaning has been studied independently of expression, and in literary criticism the **content** discussed of literary works. One of the aims of stylistics has been to analyse how elements of content (PLOT, CHARACTER, THEME, etc.) are ACTUALIZED in linguistic forms. (See also FABULA V. SJUŽET.)

(3) The extent to which STYLE itself can be defined in terms of CHOICES of form ('manner') rather than **content** ('matter') has been much discussed, in art as well as in literature. The DUALIST (q.v.) approach, based on a dichotomy between form and content, assumes that the 'same content' can be expressed in different forms. This assumption also lurks behind the notion of PARAPHRASE (and SYNONYMY) and translation. So a sentence like:

> There was an altercation between him and the manager, as a consequence of which he was dismissed from his post.

means the same as

> He had a row with the manager, so he got the sack.

The MONIST (q.v.) view, popular in stylistics following STRUCTURALIST influence, argues for the ultimate inseparability of form and content, and the very instability of content itself. Language is said not only to communicate meaning, but also to create it. Certainly translations of poetic texts are always difficult (but seemingly not impossible), precisely because alternative formalizations tend to become alternative CONCEPTUALIZATIONS; whether of the 'same' event is a matter of dispute.

The two views are not entirely incompatible, and compromises are often reached. Content itself is in any case loosely used, with different degrees of 'depth': from PROPOSITIONAL MEANING to subject matter. The study of style need not only be concerned with possible variations in the SURFACE STRUCTURES of syntax and CONNOTATION, but also with the realization of DEEP STRUCTURE elements of story and IDEOLOGY (see further Leech & Short 1981).

content word

A LEXICAL ITEM which has lexical meaning: typically a NOUN, ADJECTIVE or VERB (but not AUXILIARY). It is opposed to a form or FUNCTION WORD (e.g. ARTICLE; CONJUNCTION), which has grammatical meaning, contributing to the structure of the sentence or phrase. Alternative terms are **full** or **lexical words** or **pleremes** v. **empty** or **grammatical words** or **kenemes**. **Content words** belong to the OPEN CLASSES of words in a language: they admit innovation by borrowing or coinage, for example.

Content words are normally ACCENTED or STRESSED, function words unaccented or unstressed in speech. English poetic RHYTHM is based on the natural accentual patterns of these words. In addition, in ALLITERATIVE VERSE, alliteration falls on the content words rather than the function words.

context; contextualization; contextual grammar; context-of-situation, etc.

Context with its numerous variants or modifiers is one of the most widely used terms both in linguistics and in LITERARY CRITICISM, and one of the most comprehensive in its range of meanings.

(1) Most narrowly (but vaguely) defined, it refers to 'something which precedes or follows something'. In an UTTERANCE or a SENTENCE this could be the sounds, words, phrases or clauses surrounding another sound, word, phrase or clause; in a TEXT (non-literary or literary), the words, sentences or utterances, paragraphs or chapters, etc. This is also known as the **verbal context**, or (usefully) the CO-TEXT (q.v.). The so-called **third** PERSON PRONOUNS (*she, he, they, it*) are typically used with co-textual reference, backward (ANAPHORIC) and forward (CATAPHORIC).

Context in this sense is an important factor in the processing of INFORMATIONAL value or weight. The terms GIVEN and NEW, for instance, refer respectively to items or ideas which have already been mentioned in previous sentences, and which are newly introduced (see also COMMUNICATIVE DYNAMISM; FUNCTIONAL SENTENCE PERSPECTIVE). The **contextual grammar** developed by Winter in the 1970s is concerned with how we understand sequences of clauses or sentences in terms of relevant grammatical features and meaning (see Winter 1982; Hoey 1983). Emmott (1997) is concerned with how we monitor co(n)textual information in NARRATIVES in order to keep track of continuity and change in the fictional world.

As it is argued in SEMANTICS, context also has an important function in determining the actual meaning of words. Definition by **contextualization** is well illustrated by the practice of quotations in large dictionaries. Contextualization helps in the resolution of AMBIGUITY arising from POLYSEMY and HOMONYMY, for example, for words like *light* and *flounder*. In PUNS and jokes two different contexts may come together:

Q: Why don't skeletons go to scary films?
A: They don't have the guts.

(2) Given an apparently meaningless utterance such as *The elephant is a funny bird* we will try and contextualize it, imagine a context in which it would have meaning; a kind of FRAMING ability is presupposed in the semantic ANOMALIES of fantasy literature and many poetic METAPHORS. Contextualization here, however, draws upon an extended notion of context beyond textual or ENDOPHORIC REFERENCE to SITUATIONAL or EXOPHORIC REFERENCE (q.v.).

Situational reference is very broad indeed, and linguists vary amongst themselves as to what they include under the heading 'context' here. It normally can include:

(a) the immediate DISCOURSE situation of 'here and now' in which a text or utterance is produced (e.g. casual conversation between friends; a quarrel between two neighbours). The so-called **first** and **second** person pronouns (*I*, *we* and *you*) typically function in this **context-of-utterance**, or **communicative context**.

(b) the immediate **situational context** in which the discourse occurs (e.g. at a dinner party or at a bus-stop).

(c) increasingly 'remote' environments beyond these, such as the geographical, social and cultural; also the cognitive context of background or shared knowledge and beliefs: the **macro-context**, then, of the world at large. In RELEVANCE THEORY the focus is on the cognitive aspects of context, how **contextual implications** are derived from the processing of existing information and assumptions.

All these meanings of context have been subsumed under the term **context-of-situation**, which was popularized from the 1930s to the 1950s in the work of Firth, who took it from the anthropologist Malinowski (1923). Firth stressed the importance of context for the very process of acquiring language. Also, utterances of the kind *What's that?* are entirely context-dependent; and social contexts are an important determinant of REGISTER and linguistic APPROPRIATENESS. Shared knowledge means certain kinds of information can be presupposed between interlocutors, which makes for linguistic economy. DETERMINERS such as *the, this* and *that* are significant DEICTIC markers or pointers to both textual and contextual reference.

(3) In LITERATURE there are two main kinds of situational **context**: the context WORLD created and INFERRED in the text, IDEOLOGICAL as well as concrete; and broad situational context of the non-fictional world, on the given knowledge which authors and readers inevitably draw (even in science fiction). (See also REFERENTIAL CODE.)

Our INTERPRETATION of the meaning and theme of a text depends on our judgment of readings appropriate in the co-text and the world of the text, mediated by our knowledge of reality, and of the relevant historical context for non-contemporary literature. The context of critical reception itself may also be significant. Clearly, as the DECONSTRUCTIONIST Derrida (1977a) has observed, this restricting contextual determination of meaning pulls against the almost infinite extendability of contexts themselves (see also Culler 1983).

For our appreciation of drama particularly, the more immediate contexts of situation and utterance involved in the theatrical performance are important. Dramatic devices such as the ASIDE and EPILOGUE explicitly relate the world of the play to the real world of the audience.

(See also PRAGMATICS.)

contrastive rhetoric

A relatively recent yet important subdiscipline of language teaching and textual studies, elaborated by Kaplan in the 1960s, for example, which is based on the belief that there are significant differences between languages in the ways in which texts and GENRES are constructed, originating in deeply-embedded cultural practices or ways of thinking. English academic articles, for example, in the identifying and development of a topic, follow a structural pattern, essentially 'linear' and non-digressive, that is inherited from the classical Greek rhetorical tradition and centuries of educational inculcation. Other languages (e.g. Arabic) see parallelism as an important feature; Romance language favour 'digression'.

(See further Connor & Kaplan (eds) 1987; Connor 1996.)

conversational: ~ maxims; ~ implicature; co-operative principle

Related terms introduced by the linguistic philosopher Grice (1975), which have proved extremely popular in conversational analysis and the study of dramatic DIALOGUE.

(1) The **co-operative principle** (CP) appears to be fundamental to normal COMMUNICATION, an aspect of our COMPETENCE, at least in western societies. It is a kind of tacit agreement to work together to achieve a COHERENT and effective exchange. Ideal, perhaps: informal conversation is often aimless and incoherent; but the fact that it is judged to be so suggests that the CP is a valid 'norm'.

The importance of the principle, to a greater or lesser degree, is reflected in the fact that total non-co-operation is rare, and regarded as 'anti-social' behaviour (or political or tactical evasion). The CP is certainly in evidence in situations of giving advice and information, etc., as it is in LITERARY DISCOURSE.

The reader expects consistency of representation, just as the writer assumes our 'willing suspension of disbelief', for example, or our willingness to tolerate linguistic DEVIATION.

(2) Within the terms of this global principle, communication is further governed by more particular principles or **maxims,** of which Grice distinguishes four:

(a) **The maxim of** QUANTITY (q.v.) concerns the degree of INFORMATION normally demanded. Participants should be as informative as required; but not more than is required.

(b) **The maxim of** QUALITY (q.v.) concerns truthfulness. We should not tell lies, for instance.

(c) **The maxim of** RELATION (q.v.) describes normal expectations of RELEVANCE.

(d) **The maxim of** MANNER (q.v.) concerns clarity. We should avoid obscurity, AMBIGUITY, prolixity, and be orderly.

These amount to a kind of 'sincerity principle': 'Say what you mean and mean what you say.' Grice does not list them in order of importance, although they are usually reproduced as above. In different situations different maxims may be crucial: we expect relevance in literature, for example, but not truth. And as Grice himself was quick to point out, these maxims don't always apply and are easily violated. Yet they do serve as an implicit model of ordinary communicative behaviour, at least in so far as the exchange of information is concerned, by which we assess the violations themselves. Common terms like TAUTOLOGY and 'contradiction' and 'ambiguity' testify to our awareness.

(3) Grice himself distinguishes between 'violating' a maxim (i.e. unconsciously or unavoidably, as in telling lies) and blatantly 'flouting' it or exploiting it; but the term 'violation' is commonly used by others in the latter sense. The important point is that it is on the basis of these implicit conversational rules we may exploit the maxims in certain contexts in order to mean more than we actually say: such 'extra meanings' Grice calls **conversational implicatures.** So if speaker A, for example, knows that B has read her letter to *The Times* and asks for an opinion of it, and B's response is *It was easy to spot, wasn't it,* A can legitimately assume that the maxim of quantity has been broken (lack of sufficient information). What is implied is B's unwillingness to express a critical opinion. (See also INFERENCE; RELEVANCE THEORY.)

Here, clearly, constraints of POLITENESS are also dominant, and their importance for conversational behaviour has led some linguists (e.g. Leech 1983) to suggest a **politeness principle.**

Some FIGURES OF SPEECH appear to flout maxims: IRONY the maxim of quality (*That's very nice of you, I must say*); HYPERBOLE the maxims of manner and quality (*He's as old as the hills*). (See also LITOTES; PERIPHRASIS.)

conversion

(1) Also known as **functional shift/change, transfer** and ZERO-AFFIXATION/ DERIVATION, **conversion** is a common productive lexical process in English

whereby one part of speech or word-class changes to another, with no change in its form. So frequently NOUNS become VERBS (*elbow, eye, finger*); also verbs become nouns (*spy, kill*); and ADJECTIVES become nouns (*better, dirty*).

Conversions, effective for economy and impact, occur frequently in advertising and the media. In American English conversions figured prominently in the political speeches of Alexander Haig in the 1970s: hence 'Haig-Speak' featuring words like *caveat* and *context* as verbs, and the question *Will you burden share*? As *The Guardian* later observed, he paradoxed his auditioners by abnormalling his responds.

In Elizabethan RHETORIC conversion was known as **anthimeria**. Shakespeare's conversions are most frequently noun to verb, reflecting a dynamic WORLD-VIEW (*window, climate, monster*). Many POETIC conversions remain NONCE WORDS (e.g. Hardy's *goddess* as a verb).

(2) In Riffaterre's (1978) theory of poetry, **conversion** is one of the rules that apply to the GENERATION of a text. Several SIGNS are TRANSFORMED into one overall collective sign; or the whole text is one sign. It thus lies behind poetic SYMBOLISM. So in Donne's *Hymn to God in My Sickness*, the theme of the narrator as God's Music is conveyed in words like *tune, instrument, choir*, etc.

co-operative principle

See CONVERSATIONAL MAXIMS.

co-ordinate clause; co-ordination

A **co-ordinate structure** is related to, but not SUBORDINATE to, or dependent on, another. Thus a COMPOUND SENTENCE consists of two or more conjoined or **co-ordinated** MAIN **clauses**. So-called **co-ordinating** CONJUNCTIONS link the clauses: chiefly *and, or* and *but*.

Co-ordination provides the simplest and most straightforward means of CONNECTIVITY, and semantically links ideas which are not complex and are sequentially or chronologically related. It is common, therefore, in NARRATIVES, conversational anecdotes and lists:

And the muttering grew to a grumbling;
And the grumbling grew to a mighty rumbling:
And out of the houses the rats came tumbling
(Browning: The Pied Piper of Hamelin)

In terms of INFORMATION PROCESSING, co-ordinated structures have equal weight, and the cumulative effect of excessive co-ordination is often monotonous. It is possible to rephrase certain kinds of co-ordination by subordinate clauses, e.g. of 'result': *Jack fell down and broke his crown* (. . . *so that he* . . .); or 'concession': *She was poor but she was honest* (*Although she was poor, she was honest*).

copula

A **copula** is a linking VERB such as *be, seem, become* which relates the grammatical SUBJECT of a CLAUSE **ascriptively** or **attributively** to the (subject) COMPLEMENT, as in *She is a professional pianist.*

Copulative verbs are not universal (cf. Russian, Hungarian). In African American VERNACULAR English, as in some CREOLE LANGUAGES, sentences like *She nice* without *is* are found in casual speech. In British English omission of the copula, as indeed of other FUNCTION WORDS, is found in newspaper headlines (*Jogging a hazard, warns health chief*).

co-reference, also cross-reference

(1) **Co-reference** is used in GRAMMAR to describe the relations between two NOUN PHRASES that have the same REFERENCE, i.e. identify the 'same thing'. So, e.g. APPOSITIONS (*Tom, Tom, the piper's son*) and reflexive PRONOUNS (*She washed herself*) typically contain **co-referential** structures.

(2) **Co-reference**, or **cross-reference**, can operate between sentences in a TEXT, to provide structural and semantic continuity. Hence it is often defined in terms of the means of referring to something elsewhere in the CO-TEXT: either already mentioned (ANAPHORA), or yet to come (CATAPHORA).

Backward-reference is far commoner than forward-reference and is signalled chiefly by the **third** PERSON pronouns, and by the DEFINITE ARTICLE, as in:

The Thane of Fife had a wife: where is <u>she</u> now?

> (Shakespeare: *Macbeth*, v.i)

And ice, mast-high, came floating by . . .
The <u>ice</u> was here, the <u>ice</u> was there,
The <u>ice</u> was all around . . .

> (Coleridge: *The Ancient Mariner*)

Pronominal co-reference illustrates a common progression of INFORMATION from most specific (the noun phrase) to least (the pronoun) for economy of reference without unnecessary REPETITION: the definite article illustrates another common pattern of NEW INFORMATION followed by GIVEN.

In some contexts it is not always easy to tell whether definite articles are co-referential, or situation-referring, or both. In Yeats's poems, for example, the noun phrases of his openings seem to specify objects in the WORLD described; but can be seen to link textually with the title (e.g. in *Leda and the Swan*).

(3) **Co-reference** is also an inclusive term for all those cohesive devices such as linkage, which permit 'already used' structures to be 're-used' or modified economically in a text (see, e.g., de Beaugrande & Dressler 1981). So ELLIPSIS (q.v.) and SUBSTITUTION (q.v.) by proforms (e.g. *so, do, one*) would be included here, and formal REPETITION (e.g. *ice* in the quotation above).

corpus linguistics

A relatively recent branch of COMPUTATIONAL LINGUISTICS which uses large-scale text corpora for a better empirical understanding of different aspects of language patterning and use. Pioneers in the field include Quirk *et al.* at University College London, who established the Survey of English Usage 40 years ago, as a basis for one of the first comprehensive corpora (London-Lund) of twentieth century spoken and written varieties, a stimulus to descriptions of British grammar (especially Quirk *et al.* 1972, 1985); followed in the 1990s by Greenbaum's project on an International Corpus of English (ICE). The investigation and codification of international varieties of English are productive areas for future corpora-based studies.

In the field of **corpus pedagogy**, in language learning and teaching, universities have regularly combined resources and expertise with publishers: the University of Birmingham with Collins to produce the COBUILD dictionary (1987); the University of Nottingham with Cambridge University Press in the late 1990s for the CANCODE spoken grammar project. With the technical help of Lancaster University, the British National Corpus (BNC) of the mid-1990s (10 million spoken words, 90 million written) was designed to help the EFL lexicographers of Longmans and Oxford University Press improve their definitions, and explanations of COLLOCATIONS and IDIOMS etc. In 1999 a part BNC-based grammar was published by Longman (Biber *et al.*).

In the area of historical linguistics, the Helsinki corpus of Early Modern English texts has stimulated research into socio-stylistic features of a variety of genres. In STYLISTICS, Short *et al.* at Lancaster University have recently established a corpus of fiction and journalism to investigate methods of the REPRESENTATION OF SPEECH/THOUGHT. Biber & Finegan (e.g. 1989) have drawn on the London-Lund corpus in their studies of the probability of occurrence of certain features for a typology of GENRES across speech and writing.

(See further Thomas & Short (eds) 1996.)

correctness

Although long cherished in GRAMMAR and RHETORIC from Quintilian (first century AD) to the early years of this century, **correctness** is not much favoured by linguists today because it is EVALUATIVE and absolute, presupposing that USAGES in grammar, pronunciation or meaning can be 'right' or 'wrong' according to some ideal standard. This is not to say that linguists are libertines: rules of GRAMMATICALITY, for example, are determined by observation of actual usages and patterns. Hence *elephants have big ears* is grammatical, but **elephants ears have big* is not. Chomsky has termed this as correctness, in fact, in his GENERATIVE GRAMMAR (q.v.).

Allowance has to be made, however, for DIALECTAL or STYLISTIC variation: *He's a quick sort of a bairn is that*, is grammatical in Tyne-side; *Irks care the crop-full bird*? in Browning's *Rabbi ben Ezra*. In such cases the notions of ACCEPTABILITY and APPROPRIATENESS are important: apparently ill-formed utterances may be tolerated in certain contexts, or considered APPROPRIATE to a SITUATION or FUNCTION.

For the ordinary language users, however, notions of 'correctness' based on the PRESCRIPTIVE grammatical tradition die hard, and are confirmed by the continuing popularity of handbooks such as Fowler (1998). In FORMAL writing particularly, certain usages which have been traditionally regarded as 'incorrect' are often avoided: e.g. using *who for whom*; or *than I* for *than me*.

(See also ETYMOLOGICAL FALLACY.)

co-text

Especially common in TEXT LINGUISTICS (see Petöfi 1975) **co-text** is a useful alternative to CONTEXT (q.v.). It describes the verbal or linguistic context as distinct from situational context.

The co-text of an item helps to determine its form and meaning. So-called **colligational ties** account for the grammatical restraints that fit, for example, appropriate VERB forms to SUBJECTS. COHESIVE devices such as CO-REFERENCE link one part of the text with another; ELLIPSIS depends on the co-text for its interpretation. The habitual co-textual occurrence of words accounts for COL-LOCATIVE MEANING (e.g. *desirable detached residence with attractive Cotswold stone elevations*).

counterfactive; counterfactual

(1) Terms used in GRAMMAR and SEMANTICS as part of the categorization of VERBS, PREDICATES and MOODS, etc., according to the truth-values with which they are associated.

So-called **factive verbs**, for example, presuppose 'facts' or truth (*know, agree*, etc., as in the Biblical *I know that my Redeemer liveth*); **non-factives** are non-committal as to the truth of the PROPOSITION (*think, suspect*, etc., as in Carroll's *He thought he saw a Banker's Clerk descending from the bus*); and **counter-** (or **contra-**) **factives** presuppose the falsity of the following proposition (*wish, pretend*, etc., as in Raleigh's *I wish I loved the Human Race* (. . . *but I don't* implied)).

(2) **Counterfactual** is especially applied to conditional clauses (commonly introduced by the SUBORDINATOR *if* and expressing contingency), or rather, the particular class of conditional clauses which denotes hypothetical and unfulfilled conditions; e.g.: *If you'd listened to me, then this wouldn't have happened* implies that the addressee has not listened to the speaker; and utterances of the kind *If I were a rich man* or *If I ruled the world* counter or oppose the unreal with the (negative) true state of affairs (*but I'm not; but I don't*).

(3) **Counterfactual** conditions can be seen to underlie many of the logical arguments of mathematics and philosophy, and provide the basis (*if only*) of fantasy, dream and vision, of *Alice in Wonderland* and *Kubla Khan*; and indeed, of the whole imaginative process of FICTION generally.

Readers readily and aesthetically accept the norms and truths of the counterfactual world, whatever the degree of 'realism', and as Coleridge says, 'willingly suspend their disbelief'. At an extreme, however, the counterfactual worlds of drama and the media with their realistic visual and kinetic ENACTMENT in the present, are not unknown to be taken for actuality: hence the subject of satire, for instance, in Beaumont & Fletcher's *The Knight of the Burning Pestle*; and the inspiration for Woody Allen's film *The Purple Rose of Cairo*.

(See also POSSIBLE WORLDS (THEORY) and further Lewis 1973.)

counterpointing

(1) Sometimes used in METRICS, the term **counterpoint** is borrowed from musical theory, where it refers to a melody added as a strict accompaniment to another, main melody, to produce POLYPHONIC effect.

In metrical theory, however, **counterpointing** is mostly used in the sense of 'tension', between a regular and a varied RHYTHMICAL pattern (see Attridge 1982); or, in earlier studies, a (simple) DEEP and a (complex) SURFACE pattern.

(2) By extension, it sometimes describes the juxtaposition or interweaving of STYLES, THEMES or VOICES in a novel, the playing off of one feature against another: e.g. the 'Sirens' episode in Joyce's *Ulysses*; or, structurally, the voices of the narrator and of Esther Summerson in Dickens's *Bleak House*.

cratylism

Particularly favoured by French critics such as Genette (1980), to describe what is also known as SOUND SYMBOLISM, namely the belief in the MOTIVATION of the SIGN or sound by its 'resemblance' to the object signified.

The term is derived from Plato's *Cratylus*, in which the whole subject of naming is discussed. Hermogenes holds the (long agreed) view that names are the result of convention; Cratylus suggests that there is a natural harmony between name (FORM) and referent (CONTENT).

Genette argues that poets in particular have been seduced by the 'myth' of a universal MIMESIS, seeking to remedy the 'defect' of ordinary language in the (non-conventional) language of poetry. See the work and ideas of the SYMBOLIST poets Mallarmé, Rimbaud and Valéry, for instance, where colours are among the associations evoked SYNAESTHETICALLY by different sounds: *A black, E white, I red, U green, O blue, vowels* (Rimbaud: *Voyelles*).

(See also ENACTMENT; ICONICITY; ONOMATOPOEIA; PHONAESTHESIA.)

creativity

(1) In linguistics and particularly Chomsky's TRANSFORMATIONAL GRAMMAR (TG), **creativity** refers to our open-ended ability to produce and understand (an infinite number of) sentences that have never been heard before from the finite set of linguistic resources. This ability seems to be confined to human language, not the COMMUNICATION systems of animals or machines.

In ordinary everyday interchanges this capacity or COMPETENCE is not usually much in evidence: our speech may be highly predictable, repetitive, FORMULAIC. It may also be, in Bakhtin's terms (1981) ALIEN, i.e. borrowed, half someone else's.

Linguistic creativity is most evident in words rather than sentences, in the innovations of meaning and of word creation in the LEXICON, to keep pace with new technological developments and social fashions. An alternative term is **productivity** (Lyons 1977). It is also a feature of wordplay (see PARONOMASIA; PUN).

(2) **Creativity** is also used for artistic originality of idea or inventiveness in form: it is connected with DEVIATION and FOREGROUNDING, the departure from what is expected in language. It is much associated with poetry and literary prose, and REGISTERS such as advertising.

creole (language); creolization

In sociolinguistics a distinction is made between a PIDGIN language and a **creole language**. Pidgins are HYBRID languages which arise naturally out of the needs for practical communication, e.g. in trading, between groups of people who do not know each others' languages, and which combine the features of one language (e.g. English) with another (e.g. African or Chinese VERNACULARS).

However, if a pidgin becomes the mother tongue of a speech community, as has happened in Jamaica and Haiti, then it is said to have become **creolized**. The word **creole** itself is also (traditionally) applied to the descendants of European or African settlers in the tropics.

Inevitably, with the extension of its functions beyond trading, a creole language is structurally and lexically more complex than a pidgin, although the number of grammatical inflections (e.g. word-endings) remains characteristically small.

However, in communities where the 'official' or STANDARD language may well be a world language, like English or French, creoles are often socially stigmatized, and VARIETIES of speech revealing degrees of standardization or **de-creolization** frequently arise. Bickerton in the 1970s popularized the notion of a **creole continuum** (Bickerton 1973), with the 'deepest' creole as the **basi**LECT, and the local standard as the **acrolect**. One theory about the disputed origins of **African-American** VERNACULAR English (AAVE) is that it has been de-creolized and that a creole was the native language of its earliest speakers.

critical: ~ linguistics; ~ discourse analysis

Critical linguistics and **critical discourse analysis (CDA)** have been profoundly influential on the teaching of STYLISTICS and media studies in many British universities. Similarly named, and with similar aims, it is not therefore surprising that they are often seen as synonymous. Indeed, *critical discourse analysis* is sometimes used as an 'umbrella' or generic term to cover both schools of thought. However, there are some differences of perspective and slant.

(1) **Critical linguistics** was proposed by Roger Fowler and his colleagues at the University of East Anglia (e.g. Fowler *et al.* 1979), arising out of their work on language and IDEOLOGY, the way social patterns of language can influence thought.

Drawing heavily on SYSTEMIC GRAMMAR for a 'tool-kit', it is precisely concerned to analyse critically the (inseparable) relationship between language and social meanings. Newspaper headlines and advertising are obvious examples of discourses where particular assumptions or ideologies are perhaps unconsciously embodied. (See further Fowler 1996, ch. 3.)

(2) **Critical discourse analysis** is particularly associated with the writings of Norman Fairclough at the University of Lancaster 10 years later (1989f). Also interested in the ways linguistic CHOICES are ideologically constructed, Fairclough is also deeply indebted to the work of Foucault on DISCOURSE, and the ways different discourses are constructed by social systems. And with an emphasis on discourse as an instrument of power and control, there are distinct evocations of MARXIST CRITICISM and also FEMINIST CRITICISM. Like critical linguistics, it presupposes that ideology is usually 'invisible' or 'neutralized', and is likewise a 'critical' movement in that it wishes to protest at bias, inequalities, obfuscation, etc., to raise 'critical language awareness', and to change discursive practices by intervention, e.g. in the media, and institutional or bureaucratic documents. (See further Fairclough 1992a, 1992b, 1995.)

Critical discourse analysis has most recently been subjected to critique, notably by Widdowson (1995, 1996) and Toolan (1997). It is argued, for example, that the kinds of texts chosen for analysis tend to be easy targets; that interpretations are negatively monovalent, biased by the political views of the analyst, and based on prior political readings; although the question of whether any interpretations in any discipline can actually be value-free, is a moot point. More problematic for CDA and critical linguistics also is the role of readers: as passive, compliant consumers of ideologically-biassed texts, or free agents capable of diverse interpretative positions, and of actually constructing their own representation.

(See also DETERMINISM; ETHICAL STYLISTICS; IDEOLOGY; RADICAL STYLISTICS.)

cross-reference

See CO-REFERENCE.

cultural materialism

Like NEW HISTORICISM, this relatively recent movement in LITERARY CRITICISM is deeply indebted to Continental theorists such as Foucault, Althusser, Derrida, Bakhtin and Benjamin, as well as the British MARXIST CRITIC Raymond Williams (1980), and likewise engaged in the process of 'de-mystifying' LITERATURE as a privileged discourse. As its name suggests, **cultural materialism** is interested in the material and technological conditions of the production and reception of literature and other cultural forms in their appropriate historical contexts. It has also engaged with theoretical issues of the relations between cultural CODES and political power: see, e.g., Dollimore and Sinfield (1985) on Elizabethan and Jacobean drama. Yet cultural materialism also stresses the significance of the historical or 'present' location of the critic and reader in textual interpretation: as the different readings of *Hamlet* though the centuries bear witness to. (See also HERMENEUTICS.)

(See further Hawthorn 1998; Ryan (ed.) 1996.)

curt style

Introduced into traditional LITERARY CRITICISM by Morris Croll (1929) to describe a kind of prose STYLE in the seventeenth century whose sentences are characteristically short or assymmetrical in length and structure. ASYNDETIC CO-ORDINATION of clauses is common, i.e. with no explicit CONJUNCTIVE ties. It is opposed to the LOOSE STYLE (q.v.), and is supposedly modelled on the classical prose style of Seneca.

However, it is not always easy to distinguish different kinds of prose style, especially on the basis of supposed classical models, and in any case there can be variations within any one work. Hence these terms should be used with care, if used at all.

D

---

dactyl

In terminology borrowed from classical PROSODY a **dactyl** is a type of FOOT or METRICAL unit which consists of a STRESSED syllable followed by two unstressed syllables (/ x x), as in the phrase

```
/  x x   /  x x
Ladies and gentlemen
```

to be distinguished from the ANAPAEST which is the reverse (x x /). It is a characteristic of the Homeric hexameter (with six feet), and distinguished in Greek, as in Latin, verse by length, not stress, i.e. a long syllable plus two short ones. It is rare for English poems to be composed consistently in **dactyllic metre**, perhaps because of its rhythmic jauntiness, though Tennyson's *Charge of the Light Brigade* is a celebrated example:

```
/  x  x /  x   x
Cannon to right of them,
/  x  x /  x   x
Cannon to left of them,
/  x x  /  x   x
Cannon in front of them
/ x   x   /   x
Volleyed and thundered . . .
```

de-automatization, also de-familiarization

Terms used by the RUSSIAN FORMALISTS and PRAGUE SCHOOL linguists in their discussions of LITERARY, especially POETIC, and non-literary language; and in particular, of the AUTOMATIZING tendencies of everyday communication and its consequent over-familiarity.

(1) Poetry by constrast **de-automatizes**, it ACTUALIZES or FOREGROUNDS (q.v.) utterances consciously and makes the reader aware of the linguistic medium, by what the Formalists called **devices**: e.g. METAPHOR, unusual patterns of SYNTAX, or REPETITION (see Havránek 1932; Mukařovský 1932).

(2) Literary language not only highlights or foregrounds, but also it ALIENATES or ESTRANGES (*ostranenie*). Readers must look afresh at what has become familiarized (see Shklovsky 1917). So Blake's *Tyger* in its IMAGERY and RHETORICAL QUESTIONS forces on the reader a radical and dynamic re-conceptualization of the animal. And Hopkins's poetry generally, in language and subject, makes us feel the essence of things (inscape): an apt illustration of Shklovky's own description of the function of literature, namely that it should reveal the 'stoniness' of a stone.

However, as these same critics acknowledge, what is novel or strange can itself become automatized, familiar. Literary language through the ages reveals successive reactions, revolutions, against equally successive tendencies to conventionalization.

(See further Cook 1994; Fowler 1996.)

declarative sentence; declaration

(1) **Declarative** is commonly used in GRAMMAR to distinguish one of the major SENTENCE-structure types, the others being IMPERATIVE (q.v.) and INTERROGATIVE (q.v.).

In many languages, as in English, these sentence types are characterized by differences of FORM. So declaratives in English have a WORD ORDER of SUBJECT–VERB–OBJECT normally, and a falling INTONATION pattern.

It is usual to distinguish sentence types in this way from their meanings, or FUNCTIONS in terms of SPEECH-ACTS. Although there is a strong correlation between declarative and its use to make a 'statement' or 'assertion', nonetheless the semantic functions possible far outnumber the three sentence types; and the sentence types themselves may have overlapping functions. So in different CONTEXTS the declarative *You're washing the dishes* may be a statement, question (with rising intonation) or directive.

Nonetheless, declarative sentences are by far the commonest category, and the staple of most REGISTERS, especially those where information is paramount (e.g. reports, journalism, textbooks, etc.). They are taken as CANONICAL, as the 'norm' for illustrations of grammatical points in grammar books. In some versions of TRANSFORMATIONAL GRAMMAR, the positive declarative has been taken as the basic sentence type from which the others are derived, including negatives, e.g. *You're not washing the dishes*. It is also implied that utterances such as

Peter will type the letter
Will Peter type the letter?
Type the letter, Peter

express the same PROPOSITION, or underlying meaning.

(2) In speech-act theory (see Searle 1979), a **declaration** is a special, rather conventional kind of ILLOCUTIONARY ACT which directly constitutes an action,

e.g. dismissing, sentencing, naming (e.g. a ship). It is often uttered within some particular social context by a person of authority (e.g. judge, member of the royal family, etc.): e.g. *I hereby sentence you to two years' imprisonment.*

decoding

(1) A term from COMMUNICATION THEORY especially used in SEMIOTICS to refer to the interpretation of MESSAGES (spoken, written, visual) by the receiver or ADDRESSEE which have been formed or ENCODED (q.v.) as TEXT by the transmitter or ADDRESSER according to a set of rules or CODE (e.g. language).

(2) **Code** and its derivatives became popular in STYLISTICS and LITERARY CRITICISM in the 1960s and 1970s, both concerned with the whole communication process of writer, text and reader. However, they are often no more than technical-sounding equivalents of commoner terms: **decodification** used to mean 'understanding' or INTERPRETATION, for instance.

The model of encodification and decodification has more recently been questioned, and the extent to which a 'message' exists independently of these processes. So the reader can be seen to create or 're-code' the very message of a text in the process of reading, each reader producing a different message.

deconstruction (theory)

A reactionary intellectual movement in philosophy and LITERARY THEORY which began in France in the 1960s amongst the writers of the journal *Tel Quel* (Kristeva, Barthes and Sollers), and chiefly associated with the philosophy of Jacques Derrida from 1967 onwards. It attracted considerable attention, not all of it favourable, and was mostly influential on the work of American critics rather than British: e.g. Paul de Man, and J. Hillis Miller amongst others, who developed their own kind of deconstructive criticism known as the **Yale School**.

Deconstruction is sometimes used synonymously with POST-STRUCTURALISM (q.v.), but in fact deconstruction is one (dominant) version of a larger movement, which sets out to challenge some of the long-held tenets of STRUCTURALISM. One of its main aims is to 'de-construct' a text, undermine its PRESUPPOSITIONS, de-stabilize it, de-centre it. INTERPRETATION of a text is not seen as recovering some deeper 'given' objective meaning which controls and unifies the text's structure, but as exposing what is usually suppressed, namely the infinite possibilities, the 'free play' of meanings (**ludism**). Each deconstruction opens itself to further deconstruction. Text itself gives way to INTERTEXTUALITY, the play of meanings are disseminated across the text's sources, and as a result the boundaries are dissolved between LITERARY and other kinds of DISCOURSE. Moreover, FIGURATIVE LANGUAGE is not seen as primarily literary: all language is figurative.

As might be expected, deconstruction has been seen as 'destruction': nihilistic, counter-intuitive, open to fanciful interpretative licences/licentiousness, what

Geoffrey Hartman wittily calls 'Derridadaism'. And as Peter Mullen expressed it in the *TLS* (1985):

> D'ya wanna know the creed'a
> Jacques Derrida?
> Dere ain't no reada
> Dere ain't no wrider
> Eider.

It is also truistic. If reality is an illusion, if texts, authors and readers can be deconstructed, then we are left with nothing; but, of course, if we believe they do exist, then we can discuss them as if they do. Water can be deconstructed by the scientists into hydrogen and oxygen, and an amazing number of particles; but it can be discussed as a liquid on a different level. Even a deconstructive essay cannot avoid the presuppositions and foundations which it seeks to undermine, however brilliant its own rhetorical displays, and however much Derrida would wish to keep the term 'deconstruction' itself and its associates (see, e.g., DIFFÉRANCE) from stabilizing their reference.

Nonetheless, for those who are prepared to grapple with the complexities and self-indulgences of Derridan style and thought, there is much that has rightly challenged critical orthodoxy and offered a fresh perspective on language as a system of SIGNS; on speech and writing; on notions of 'literary' language; and on the activity of interpretation itself. American deconstructionists in particular did much to re-instate RHETORIC as a subject worthy of serious critical attention.

(See also ABSENCE; APORIA; LOGOCENTRISM.)

decorum

An important RHETORICAL principle governing STYLE: the doctrine of fitness or APPROPRIATENESS of style matched to GENRE, subject matter, CHARACTERIZATION, or SITUATION, etc.

From Horace to the Renaissance and beyond the styles were usually formalized to three major types: GRAND, MIDDLE and PLAIN STYLE (q.v.). The grand style was, for example, considered suitable for epic, with its heroic deeds and grand passions. However, the use of the three styles together in one work was not uncommon (the variations between, and within, Chaucer's *Canterbury Tales*, for example); and the growth of 'mixed' genres such as tragi-comedy, melodrama and the novel meant inevitably that style-switching occurred.

Perhaps because of its connotations of CORRECTNESS and accepted conventions, the term **decorum** (first used in English by Ascham in the sixteenth century) is no longer much used, at least in its literary sense, although appropriateness (q.v.) itself is still a valid aspect of our communicative behaviour, in non-literary as well as literary REGISTERS. And Grice's CO-OPERATIVE PRINCIPLE (q.v.) can be seen as a kind of decorum of conversational interaction.

deep structure

(1) One of a pair of terms (see also SURFACE STRUCTURE) made famous by Chomsky's GENERATIVE or TRANSFORMATIONAL GRAMMAR from 1965.

For his so-called 'standard theory', SENTENCES were held to have a **deep** or **underlying** syntactic **structure**, the surface form generated from the deep by means of **transformational rules** of addition or deletion, etc. Arguments in favour of a deep structure were based on the native speaker's intuitions about SYNTAX itself: that, for example, grammatically AMBIGUOUS sentences, i.e. with the same surface forms, can be related to different (deep) structures, e.g.: *Moving chairs can be a nuisance* = 'Chairs that move can be a nuisance'; or 'The act of moving chairs can be a nuisance'; and also that sentences with different surface forms are felt to have the same deep structure, are PARAPHRASES of each other: notably ACTIVE and PASSIVE sentences, such as:

Local TV star awards first prize.
First prize awarded by local TV star.

Violations of deep grammatical structure would produce 'ungrammatical' sentences such as *She flung slowly* or *She astounded the pale blue*. Such DEVIANT structures, however, can be occasionally found in LITERARY, especially POETIC LANGUAGE (notably the works of modern poets such as e.e. cummings). (See also GRAMMATICAL.)

In Chomsky's standard theory the deep structure is the source of the **semantic interpretation** of a sentence (just as the surface structure is the source of its **phonetic interpretation**), yet it remains a syntactic or structural concept. For other linguists, however, even those working within the theory of generative grammar, the deep structure has often been regarded as semantic, more abstract, composed also of the PROPOSITIONAL elements of the sentence. Outside generative grammar it thus came loosely to be equated simply with the propositional 'meaning' or CONTENT.

Whatever the precise nature of deep structure, and however 'deep' it is, its important place in generative theory aligned Chomsky's views in the 1960s with the so-called DUALIST approach to STYLE, with the assumption that there are 'different ways' of saying the 'same thing'.

(2) The metaphors of **deep** and **surface** were extended to the structure of the novel as part of NARRATIVE GRAMMAR (see especially the work of Greimas 1966f). Stories can be seen to have underlying basic configurations of PLOT structures, and characters deep functional ROLES (see also ACTANT). However, the 'rules' connecting deep with surface structures are by no means clear.

de-familiarization

See DE-AUTOMATIZATION.

definite article; definiteness

(1) The **definite article** *the*, one of the most commonly used words in English, and grammatically classed as a DETERMINER (q.v.), functions as a modifier of a NOUN to indicate its **definiteness**, i.e. the fact that it is already known or identified, uniquely, from either the textual or situational CONTEXT or common knowledge.

The INDEFINITE ARTICLE (*a, an*), by contrast, is used when no such definite identification has been made, e.g. when the noun is being introduced for the first time. All nouns in English must be marked for **(in)definiteness**. (See also ZERO-ARTICLE.) Articles are therefore important indicators of GIVEN and NEW INFORMATION.

With CO-TEXTUAL reference, the definite article is chiefly used ANAPHORICALLY:

Three wise men of Gotham
Went to sea in a bowl;
And if the bowl had been stronger,
My song would have been longer.

CATAPHORIC (forward) REFERENCE is found with POST-MODIFYING phrases or RELATIVE CLAUSES: *Sweet are the uses of adversity*.

Situational identification may be specific and immediate (*Pass me the salt*), or vaguer, indicating something in the broader context of situation or culture, or of assumed general knowledge of speaker and hearer: *I've been to London to see the Queen; What did you do in the war, Daddy?* This assumption of familiarity of reference is common in notices (*Mind the step*), and in poetry, where the illusion may be created of a dramatic situation upon which the reader 'intrudes', or is assumed to be familiar with: or of an experience or values shared by narrator and reader alike. So, e.g.:

The river glideth at his own sweet will:
Dear God the very houses seem asleep . . .

(Wordsworth: *Upon Westminster Bridge*)

Similar uses of *the* found in the opening sentences of novels are an important indicator of the IN MEDIAS RES technique, by which the reader appears to be drawn into a 'world' already existing: the definite article assuming previous mention or assumed knowledge: *Dombey sat in the corner of the darkened room in the great armchair by the bedside* . . . (Dickens: *Dombey and Son*).

(2) **Definiteness** is not regarded by linguists as exclusive to the definite article. Lyons (1977), for instance, would add proper names and PERSONAL PRONOUNS as definite expressions of REFERENCE; and others would add DEICTIC words such as the DEMONSTRATIVES *this* and *that*, and the ADVERBS *here* and *there*, *now* and *then*. Then **past** TENSE is more definite than the PERFECT ASPECT: *I met a man with seven wives* refers to a specific occasion; *I have met a man with seven wives* has indefinite temporal reference in the past.

degrees of formality

See FORMALITY.

deixis; deictic

(1) From the Gk 'pointing' or 'showing', **deixis** in linguistics refers generally to all those features of language which orientate or 'anchor' our utterances in the context of proximity of space (*here* v. *there*; *this* v. *that*), and of time (*now* v. *then*), relative to the speaker's viewpoint.

DISCOURSE is therefore multi-dimensional, heavily dependent on the SITUATION or CONTEXT OF UTTERANCE: *Come here and look at this mess*, and *Go over there and look at that mess* point to two quite different scenarios, the choice of elements shifting accordingly.

In dramatic discourse such **deictic** elements help to create the WORLD of the play, re-contextualizing real speech behaviour. In poetry also a situation can be INFERRED which the reader watches, as it were, or is made to participate in, e.g.:

> Say what you will, there is not in the world
> A nobler sight than from this upper down.
> No rugged landscape here . . .

> (Wilfrid Blunt: *Chanclebury Ring*)

The indicative elements themselves are often called **deictics**, and include the **first** and **second** PERSON PRONOUNS *I*, *we* and *you*; the DEMONSTRATIVES *this* and *that*; ADVERBS of place and time; and TENSE (present v. past).

In the reporting of DIRECT SPEECH into INDIRECT SPEECH, any 'here' and 'now' elements can be transposed into 'there' and 'then', hence:

> The manager said: 'This car is on special offer today'.

becomes

> The manager said that that car was on special offer that day.

(2) Since TEXTS occupy time and space, it is also possible to have **textual** or **secondary deixis**: words like *this* and *that*, or *the former* and *the latter*, for example, locating items, or facts, or even linguistic structures themselves, in the CO-TEXT, ANAPHORICALLY or CATAPHORICALLY: *This is a true story. A certain king had a son and a daughter. The former was idle, the latter was hard-working . . .*

(3) Another kind of **secondary deixis** involves a metaphorical, expressive displacement in terms of emotional nearness and distance. So *that* is commonly used to indicate dislike, e.g.: *Get that dog out of here!* whereas *this* indicates, e.g. familiarity: *There was this tiny elephant . . .* (in joke-telling).

(4) Some grammarians (e.g. Halliday 1985; Sinclair 1972) have used the term **deictic(s)** to refer to a class of 'identifying' modifiers of the NOUN, which are more usually called DETERMINERS. In this sense, the ARTICLES *the* and *a*, as well as the possessives *his*, *her*, etc., would be deictics.

The DEFINITE ARTICLE was once deictic in the 'stronger' sense of (1): it developed out of the demonstrative in Early Middle English (post-AD 1000), if not earlier. In Modern English, however, it is unmarked semantically for a 'pointing' element, except in so far as it possibly invites us to find its referent in the context or co-text; or points to an aspect of shared knowledge.

demonstrative

(1) A tiny subgroup of grammatical items associated with the NOUN PHRASE and comprising *this* (plural *these*) and *that* (plural *those*). They have a DEICTIC (q.v.) meaning of 'nearness' v. 'distance', and can function both (a) as MODIFIERS or DETERMINERS of the noun and (b) independently, as PRONOUNS, as in:

(a) That affable familiar ghost (Shakespeare: Sonnet 86)
(b) Tired with all these, for restful death I cry (Shakespeare: Sonnet 66)

The term **demonstrative** (the Latin translation of Gk 'deictic') also reflects the function of pointing to something in the situation (EXOPHORIC REFERENCE), as in *I'll take this one, not that one*, often accompanied, indeed, by a physical pointing gesture. Demonstratives are also used to indicate something in the TEXT (ENDOPHORIC REFERENCE): usually preceding (ANAPHORIC), but also following (CATAPHORIC), at least for *this*, e.g.:

'Here's the rule for bargains: "Do other men, for they would do you." That's the true business precept.' (Dickens: *Martin Chuzzlewit*)
Just listen to this. They've found gold on the moon.

denotation; denotative meaning

Denotation is one of a pair of terms from philosophy (see also CONNOTATION) used in SEMANTICS and SEMIOTICS to distinguish what is seen as the basic or central CONCEPTUAL or REFERENTIAL MEANING of words or signs, without the associations (connotations) or METAPHORIC meanings which they can acquire in particular contexts. Dictionary definitions of LEXICAL ITEMS are based on **denotative** or **denotational meaning**. In popular parlance we speak of a word's LITERAL MEANING.

The term **denotatum** is sometimes used for REFERENT, i.e. the 'object', etc., in the external world referred to by a lexical item. (NB: this is a broad generalization: 'object' covers abstractions such as love and hate; and 'external world' includes the world of fiction and fantasy, where unicorns and Father Christmas exist.)

The semantic concepts of SYNONYMY and PARAPHRASE depend on the assumption that words may **denote** the same referent or proposition, but vary in their connotational meaning. However, it is often difficult to maintain a clear distinction between denotation and connotation. The dictionary definitions of *charger* and *steed* may well be 'horse', but their respective military and archaic/poetic associations seem basic to their interpretation and use.

In POETIC LANGUAGE generally such 'second order' meanings are exploited and expected. Mountains and cuckoos, rivers and nightingales exceed their scientific definitions. In contrast, in the REGISTER of science itself, and other technical or informative registers, associative meanings are suppressed in favour of denotations pertinent to the context and subject matter. Some linguists, therefore, speak of denotative meaning as being stylistically 'neutral', but all words can be seen to have differential values in their different contexts. And strict denotation is in any case probably confined to the logical CODES of mathematical SYMBOLS, or to utilitarian codes such as traffic lights.

dénouement

From the French 'unknotting', **dénouement** is a metaphorical term in LITERARY CRITICISM referring to the 'resolution' of the PLOT of a play or novel. It is derived from Aristotle's image in his *Poetics* describing the knotted and unknotted thread of the narrative line. For Aristotle, the *dénouement* followed the 'complication' of the ACTION and its CLIMAX, and brought the action to a conclusion. Here revenge could be finally achieved, or villains exposed, or marriages planned, etc.

The unravelling image evoked by the word aptly describes the (re)solution of detective fiction; but, in another sense, the *dénouement* is as much a 'tying up' of the action as an untying, providing a sense of CLOSURE: cf. the very image of the last chapter of Trollope's *The Warden*:

> Our tale is now done, and it only remains to us to collect the scattered threads of our little story, and to tie them in a seemly knot.

derivation

Popularly used in the study of word formation to describe the common and productive process of creating new LEXICAL ITEMS by adding meaningful AFFIXES or BOUND forms to pre-existing word bases or stems, at the beginning (PREFIX) or end (SUFFIX).

It is also known as AFFIXATION by Quirk *et al.* (1985), who would prefer to keep **derivation** as a very general term to embrace all methods of word creation.

French, Latin and Greek affixes have been freely used and adapted in English since the Middle Ages (*re-, in-, -ize, -ation*, etc.), as well as native (Germanic) affixes: *un-, -ness, -y*, etc.).

Some **derivations** involve a change of word class or part of speech, e.g. VERBS are derived from ADJECTIVES in *en-rich*. Such derivation types, and others, were a common feature of POETIC DICTION from the sixteenth to the late nineteenth century: *enghosted, abrim* from Hardy's poems, for example. But derivation is found in many registers: brand names (*Kleen-ex, Tipp-ex; Ox-o, Brill-o*, etc.); shop names (*cafeteria, washeteria*); journalism and the MEDIA (*Euro-jargon, Euro-crat; telethon, jog-athon; kissa-gram, santa-gram*, etc.); and science (*nitr-ate, carbo-hydr-ate,*

101

etc.). Indeed, it is hard to imagine any area of the LEXICON of English where derivatives are not found.

determiner

In many modern GRAMMARS the term **determiner** covers a CLOSED class of grammatical items in the NOMINAL GROUP or noun phrase, including ARTICLES (q.v.) and DEMONSTRATIVES (q.v.) (e.g. *the, a, this, that*), which 'determine' or specify the reference of the noun. MODIFIERS expressing quantity (*some, much, every*, etc.), and the possessives (*my, your, their*, etc.) are also classed as determiners.

If the nominal group also contains one or more ADJECTIVES, determiners precede them. Determiners themselves can be preceded by a small set of items known as **predeterminers** or **noun phrase initiators**: e.g. *all* and *half* as in *All the President's Men*; or *Half a Sixpence*. Some grammars or textbooks (e.g. Cummings & Simmons 1983) would class such predeterminers, and also numerals, as determiners, using the term therefore in a wider sense: e.g. *All my six children*.

Unlike adjectival modifiers, determiners in the narrower sense are mutually exclusive, i.e. they cannot co-occur with each other: **The my new car* is unacceptable in English.

determinism: linguistic

A recurring theory in linguistics that language 'determines' or constrains, even constitutes, thought and WORLD-VIEW (q.v.). It is also known as **linguistic relativity**, **Whorfianism**, or the **Sapir-Whorf hypothesis**, after the early twentieth-century American anthropologists and linguists Edward Sapir and Benjamin Lee Whorf, notable proponents of **determinism**. (For a reassessment of Whorf's position, however, see O'Halloran 1997.)

That differences in world-views between societies are to be attributed to differences in linguistic systems is difficult to prove or to disprove; but that language influences forms of thought in some way, or 'blinkers' our perception of the world, is certainly plausible, and various kinds or degrees of determinism have been continually advocated. Early work in FEMINIST CRITICISM (e.g. Spender 1980) was clearly based on a deterministic position.

Innovation in POETIC LANGUAGE has often come about because of the 'frustration' felt by poets with the existing norms or resources of expression. Poets like Mallarmé and Wallace Stevens see language as a potential 'barrier' to the real world. The image of the 'prison-house of language' is also propounded by those literary critics who see the world as TEXT(UALITY), nothing standing behind it.

The possibility also that reduction in linguistic choices could lead to impoverishment of thought is one of the premises lying behind Orwell's NEWSPEAK in *1984*, where the ultimate aim of the pruned vocabulary is to make 'Thoughtcrime' impossible. (Newspeak also depends on the notion that any thought is impossible without language.) And it is plausibly argued (e.g. by Lacan) that in the process of acquiring language, of 'languaging' experience, children are influenced in their concepts by this very same (pre-existing) linguistic system, just as they are by the system of social meanings around them.

Fowler *et al.* (1979), see determinism working within a language, within different VARIETIES. It is part of their CRITICAL LINGUISTICS to investigate the way social patterns of language, in politics and journalism, for example, can (unconsciously) influence thought and determine or reinforce particular, non-neutral, world-views.

(See further Cameron 1995; Lee 1992; Simpson 1993, ch. 6.)

deviation; deviance

Deviation has been very commonly used in early work in STYLISTICS, and has appeared in definitions of STYLE (q.v.) itself. It has also been used in GENERATIVE GRAMMAR to refer to any unit which is not GRAMMATICAL or is ill-formed, i.e. which does not conform to the 'rules' of the language.

Although some writers (e.g. Leech & Short 1981) have tried to make a distinction between **deviation** and **deviance**, preferring **deviance** in sense (1) below, for the most part the terms are used synonymously (at least in linguistics).

(1) Strictly, **deviation** refers to divergence in frequency from a NORM, or the statistical average. Such divergence may depend on: (a) the breaking of normal rules of linguistic structure (whether phonological, grammatical, lexical or semantic) and so be statistically unusual/infrequent; or (b) upon the over-use of normal rules of usage, and so be statistically unusual in the sense of over-frequent. So an ungrammatical sentence like *The clock elapsed fat* is **deviant** according to (a), and *The House that Jack Built*, with its recurrent RELATIVE CLAUSES (*This is the dog that worried the cat that ate the rat that ate the malt . . . etc.*) is deviant according to (b). Halliday (1971) calls this category **deflections**.

(2) Not surprisingly, statistical deviance easily becomes associated with what is unusual, unpredictable, unexpected, unconventional.

Deviation is particularly associated with POETIC LANGUAGE: our expectations and tolerance of the unusual, in structuring and CONCEPTUALIZATIONS, are high (see also POETIC LICENCE). But marked deviations are also found in advertising language, as in such eye- and attention-catching devices as: *Beanz meanz Heinz; Crack a can of Carnation.*

The idea that poetry characteristically violates the norms of everyday language was much propounded by the PRAGUE SCHOOL (see also FOREGROUNDING). As the entry for NORM reveals, it is important to know what kind of norm a deviation is taken to diverge from. Norm itself is very much a relative concept. A sentence like *I am here since five years* is grammatically deviant measured against the English language as a whole; whereas *I ain't done nothing* is ungrammatical only when DIALECTAL usage is measured against STANDARD ENGLISH. Similarly, a line like *Irks care the crop-full bird?* (Browning: *Rabbi ben Ezra*) is deviant against the 'norms' of prose.

(3) Thus the definition of style itself as a **deviation** from a norm (common in the 1960s) is rather unsatisfactory, since there are as many norms as there are varieties of language, non-literary, as well as literary. (It is, moreover, misleading to think of style as being essentially 'abnormal', or that 'normal' usage(s) lack 'style'.) Conversational, everyday language is often regarded as a norm; but it is perhaps better to think of a 'scale' or 'degrees' of deviance/normality, and of a 'set' of norms against which we judge, for example, the deviation(s) of poetic language.

(4) It is also possible to argue that all texts, whatever the degree of deviance, establish their own particular 'secondary' or 'second order' norms; and some early stylisticians, following Levin (1965), distinguish between **external** and **internal deviation**. External deviation measures the language of the text against the 'norms' outside it; internal deviation refers to the features within a text that differ from the expected, set up by the norm of the text itself: what is also known as **defeated expectancy** (Leech 1969f). In e.e. cummings's poems, it is thus quite normal for deviant language to be normal, and normal language to be deviant, as this example shows:

> light's lives lurch
> a once world quickly from rises
> army the gradual of unbeing fro
> on stiffening greenly air and to ghosts go
> drift slippery hands tease slim float twitter faces
> Only stand with me, love! against these its
> until you are, and until i am dreams . . .

Here the words underlined are foregrounded (linguistically and thematically) by their very 'normality'. It may not be so easy, however, especially on first reading, to establish the linguistic 'norms' of other texts except in a rough and ready way. Many texts, especially novels, depend on linguistic variety and also on COUNTERPOINTING, the localized playing-off of one feature against another.

(See further Leech 1985; Widdowson 1972.)

diachrony; diachronic linguistics, etc.

(1) **Diachrony** is a historical perspective for studying language, as it changes through time, in sounds, syntax, vocabulary, etc. We can trace the development of English from Old to Middle (eleventh century) to Early Modern (sixteenth century) to Modern English. Diachrony is opposed, following Saussure (1916), to SYNCHRONY: the study of language as it functions at a given period of time. Systematic synchronic linguistics owes its origins largely to Saussure (see also STRUCTURALISM); whereas the nineteenth century was the great period of **diachronic linguistics**, especially in PHONOLOGY.

But, as Roman Jakobson continually stressed, it is important to see the distinction as one of perspective, and not inherent in language itself. Language is never static: changes in pronunciation and vocabulary in particular take place from one generation to another. At any given moment there are obsolescent forms in circulation with innovatory ones, even though their FIELDS of use may vary.

An awareness of diachronic variation is important for any linguist working on aspects of earlier periods of English, and for any student of earlier literature. If Old English must be learned as a 'foreign language', even Shakespeare's language presents pitfalls to the unwary in syntax (*Stand not upon the order of your going*) and meaning (*coast* 'region'; *perfection* 'performance'), etc. And anyone studying earlier English must also be aware of the synchronic variations in any one period, in so far as evidence is available: variations arising from different REGISTERS, degree of FORMALITY, etc.

(2) A diachronic perspective is found in STYLISTICS and LITERARY CRITICISM as well as linguistics. It is certainly useful to know something about the values by which texts have been judged, and about the expectations of readers, to avoid misunderstandings and to heighten our appreciation of unfamiliar traditions or conventions (e.g. of medieval ALLEGORY; of Old English or eighteenth-century POETIC DICTION).

Some earlier critics have presented a study of the changes in a literary style or genre from one period to the next (e.g. Gordon 1966, on the development of prose; Miles 1967, on poetic language). Chambers (1932) traces the continuity of homilectic prose from the Old English period to the Renaissance; Groom (1955) the tradition of poetic diction from Chaucer to the early twentieth century. European writers like Bakhtin in the 1930s and Auerbach (1957) adopt a more theoretical approach to their work of typologizing literary styles in different epochs: a **diachronic** POETICS.

Inevitably, any studies of supposed literary and linguistic evolution must be simplified. Poets may represent distinct literary traditions, even if they belong to the same generation (e.g. poets of the first decades of this century); and trends may by no means be straightforward. One must be wary of relating stylistic trends too closely to the political and social movements of the period (see Spitzer 1948).

On the cycle of exuberance and innovation in poetic language followed by conservatism, see also AUTOMATIZATION and DE-AUTOMATIZATION.

dialect; dialectism; dialectology

(1) **Dialect** refers to a VARIETY of language associated with subsets of users: in a geographical area (**rural dialect**, e.g. Cornwall, Leicestershire; **urban dialect** if a town or city, e.g. Tyneside, Cockney); or with a social group (**class dialect** if associated with socio-economic status, e.g. working class; **occupational dialect** if associated with a profession or trade, e.g. train-drivers, coal-miners, etc.). (See also SOCIOLECT; VERNACULAR.)

While many rural dialects have virtually disappeared during the last century (and hundreds of local dialect words), urban varieties remain distinctive, if often difficult to describe. In some communities, for instance, many varieties (foreign as well as English) co-occur. Speech varies here between the people themselves, rather than between regions or villages. The study of urban dialects developed relatively late in twentieth-century sociolinguistics (e.g. the work of Labov and Trudgill), whereas regional **dialectology**, based largely on rural informants has been well-established for a century (e.g. the work at Leeds University associated with Orton *et al.* 1962–71).

With each dialect is associated a distinctive set of GRAMMATICAL and/or LEXICAL features, and also very commonly a distinctive ACCENT (q.v.) or pronunciation. Indeed, many regional speakers may keep only their accent, otherwise using the grammar and vocabulary of STANDARD ENGLISH (q.v.). (See also CODE-SWITCHING.)

The term 'dialect' as used by linguists carries no implications that one dialect is inferior to another, or that all are inferior to Standard English (or, in matters of pronunciation, to the RECEIVED PRONUNCIATION (q.v.)). Yet as **perceptual dialectology** reveals, many people rate dialects and accents in impressionistic or aesthetic terms; and in older literature and drama regional varieties in particular were often exploited in DIALOGUE for comic and social effect, especially when uttered by characters (bumpkins, labourers) low in social status. (See also (2) below.)

Halliday (1978) popularly distinguished dialect from REGISTER on the basis that the latter varies according to use, not user, and so there is the possibility of CHOICE of forms, not open to the dialect user. But there are interesting overlaps between the two. Common is the **code-** or **dialect-switching** that occurs from one situation to another (e.g. home v. place of work). Certain dialects or accents have come to be associated with particular registers: e.g. sports' commentaries (rugby – North of England; darts – Tyneside). For DJs a kind of 'mid-Atlantic' accent is common.

(2) The use of dialect in literature has sometimes been known, following Leech (1969), as **dialectism** or **dialectal** DEVIATION. In the novel and drama dialect is used in DIRECT SPEECH and dialogue as a MIMETIC device to indicate provenance, and as a means of CHARACTERIZATION. Most frequently, only a selection of features is used (often overused), features of SYNTAX and special terms, in the interests of readability. Deviations of spelling and punctuation may indicate accent, if only in a rather impressionistic sense. What may result, however, is a kind of stereotyping, or artificial form: 'stage dialect', for instance, as a crude 'south-west' hotch-potch. (See also EYE-DIALECT.) Another kind of distortion may result from 'dialect suppression' (Leech & Short 1981) in the interest, again, of readability: major characters will use the standard variety, even if their social or regional background might have warranted dialect (e.g. Oliver Twist, Adam Bede). So too the narrator, if (s)he is not to be treated in any MARKED way, e.g. as a humorous character or social misfit.

While novelists like Lawrence and Emily Bronte had first-hand knowledge of the dialects they represent (Nottinghamshire and the West Riding of Yorkshire respectively), as did poets such as William Barnes (Dorset) and Tennyson (Lincolnshire), other authors, like Dickens, have felt free to imitate the speech forms of a number of varieties, social as well as regional.

Dialectism, like ARCHAISM has sometimes been used in POETIC DICTION as a means of heightening poetic language: it is particularly associated with 'pastoral'. Despite a revival of interest in Scots recently, literature in the British Isles since the Renaissance has mostly been written in standard English; earlier, in the absence of a definite standard variety, writers wrote in the dialect of their own area, so dialectism as a literary device was but little exploited.

(3) The adjective derived from **dialect** is **dialectal**; not to be confused with DIALECTIC(S) (noun) and DIALECTICAL (adj.) below.

dialectic(al): ~ materialism

(1) **Dialectic**, from GK 'across' and Lat. 'reading', refers to the ancient philosophical method of logical disputation, as illustrated in Plato's *Dialogues* (see entry below). It is also used for the kind of logical argument with thesis, antithesis and synthesis, well illustrated in Donne's love poems.

(2) **Dialectical materialism** is a term coined at the end of the nineteenth century to describe Marxist philosophy. It suggests a dynamic model of beliefs, concerned as Marx was with the continual conflicts and transformations of social and political life. In particular, it is argued that what appears to be universal and immutable is challenged and changed through negation; and what is challenged and thus reified in this way will in turn be itself negated. As Pope (1995) concludes, at an extreme this leads to ceaseless scepticism or a belief in permanent revolution; but many theorists representing marginal groups have used this kind of dialectical method to deconstruct dominant social and political IDEOLOGIES.

(See further Hawthorn 1998.)

dialogue; dialogic(al)

(1) In ordinary usage we are likely to think of (a) **dialogue** as a kind of conversational interaction or DISCOURSE, earnest rather than chatty, involving an exchange of views. (So Foreign Ministers, for instance, are often said to be engaged in a 'dialogue' with each other.) We are also likely to think of there being just two participants; perhaps under the (mistaken) impression that the first syllable of the word derives from the Greek prefix meaning 'two'. But the word is actually derived from the Greek word 'to converse'. While two participants, ADDRESSER and ADDRESSEE, would seem to be the CANONICAL situation, any number of people can take part (e.g. at parties, board meetings, etc.). The term **duologue**, however, has sometimes been employed when only two participants are involved (e.g. Kennedy 1983). (See also EXCHANGE.)

A dialogue is to be distinguished from a MONOLOGUE (q.v.): UTTERANCES by a single speaker with no expectation of a response from another speaker.

Although dialogues are normally spoken, it is perhaps plausible to think of the exchange of letters, for instance, as being a kind of dialogue, or filling in official forms and questionnaires.

(2) In literature, **dialogue** describes the reproduction of apparently serious conversations, a genre that goes back to Plato's *Dialogues* (fourth century BC), with their questions and answers. Dryden's *Essay of Dramatic Poesy* is an English example.

(3) More commonly, **dialogue** describes all the speech found in NARRATIVES in the delineation of character; and the interchanges that dominate drama.

In the novel, representation of speech is frequently DIRECT (q.v.), MIMETIC of real dialogue; but other modes of representation are used, with differing degrees of directness. But even direct speech, given the nature of the MEDIUM, presents an 'edited' or stylized version of what actual dialogue in real life would be like; and, in any case, is subordinated, like dramatic dialogue, to the structure and theme of the work as a whole. Moreover, unlike real-life dialogue, it is designed to be 'overheard' by reader or audience.

Even the dialogue of drama, which is intended to be performed orally, has few of the hesitations and lapses of natural speech. In poetic drama indeed, e.g. of Shakespeare, the rhythms are of verse, not conversation. STICHOMYTHIA (q.v.) presents a markedly formal kind of dramatic dialogue.

It was Aristotle who first stressed the significance of dialogue in drama: verbal action as well as the action of the PLOT. Dialogue is virtually obligatory in drama, at least in the mainstream Western tradition; it is optional in fiction. (See further Herman 1995.)

(4) **Dialogue** and its formatives such as **dialogic, dialogization**, etc., are used in the widest possible sense by the Russian linguist and philosopher Mikhail Bakhtin and his circle (1920s onwards). What has come to be known as the **dialogical principle** informs much of Bakhtin's philosophy of language. Every utterance, every sentence (and hence even monologue) is orientated dynamically, towards an anticipated implied response, is in 'dialogue' with utterances that have already been made, and also in interaction with the social situation around it. In the novel, a special kind of dialogization is its main characteristic: the interrelation of social styles and voices (characters and narrator, for instance). (See also HETEROGLOSSIA; INTERTEXTUALITY; POLYPHONY.)

diction

A literary term referring to LEXIS or vocabulary, mainly used in discussions of STYLE, to mean:

(1) all the LEXICAL ITEMS in a text or as used by an author, e.g. the '**diction** of Shakespeare's sonnets'; 'Milton's diction', etc.

(2) more specifically, the characteristic or IDIOLECTAL patterns in the lexis of a text or oeuvre: so the **diction** of Shakespeare's sonnets may differ from the diction of his tragedies, etc.; or a text may reveal a predominance of ABSTRACT diction, etc.

(3) very commonly, in the phrase POETIC DICTION (q.v.), the (stock) vocabulary and phraseology of poetry.

diegesis; diegetic

Diegesis is a RHETORICAL term derived from Plato and Aristotle, which has been revived in novel theory under the influence of the work of Genette (e.g. 1972).

(1) Although the word means 'narrative' in Greek, Plato's interest in *The Republic* Bk. III, is in POETIC LANGUAGE, and in the mode of NARRATION: either by 'telling' (the poet as narrator), i.e. **diegesis**; or by 'showing' (in the persona of another character, by another's speech), i.e. MIMESIS (q.v.). Dramatic DIALOGUE is clearly mimetic in this sense; the epic is both diegetic and mimetic; the novel primarily diegetic.

In his *Poetics* Aristotle maintained a distinction between pure NARRATIVE or diegesis and 'direct' representation, but saw them both as kinds of mimesis. Modern critics of narrative would certainly argue that there are degrees of directness: that narrative modes run from the authority of a controlling narratorial report (**diegetic summary**), through 'indirect' modes (e.g. INDIRECT SPEECH) to the forms of DIRECT and FREE DIRECT SPEECH, etc. (see McHale 1978). It is possible to argue that mimesis is a kind of diegesis: that a narrator is 'implied', and also may explicitly provide the TAGGING ('he said', etc.).

(2) As Lanser (1981) says, the distinction relates to notions of POINT OF VIEW or PERSPECTIVE: **diegesis** leads to summary, and distance from an event. It is precisely this aspect which informs Genette's use of the concept: diegesis as a narrative method. Moreover, within any one work there may be a number of diegetic levels, corresponding to narratives within narratives.

In Genette's work **diegetic** spawned new terms, such as **heterodiegetic** for a narrative told in the **third** PERSON (*he, she*); and **autodiegetic** for a first PERSON (*I*) narrative. (See also EXTRADIEGETIC.)

différance; difference

Différance, a neologism coined by Derrida (1967a), reflects a central, if complex, aspect of his DECONSTRUCTION THEORY. The term is used with many nuances, but these largely relate to the word's blend of meanings. The spelling (with an *a* in the final syllable and not the expected *e* in French, as in English), is meant to evoke ambiguously both the normal senses of 'difference' or 'differentiation', and also 'deferral'.

For the sense 'difference', Derrida is indebted to the STRUCTURALIST principle associated with Saussure, that language is really an economical network of **differences**; that difference, not some object in the outside world, determines meaning. The difference in signification between the words *pig* and *fig*, for instance, that exercised Alice and the Cheshire Cat, depends at the linguistic level upon a simple difference of sound (PHONEME).

109

Derrida would emphasize that what appears here to be a BINARY OPPOSITION between what is present (say the /p/ in *pig*) and what is absent (i.e. what it is not) is not really so: it is not simply that /p/ can be replaced by a number of different phonemes in English (/d/, /b/, /w/, etc.), but that it carries 'traces' of what is not uttered: difference is neither present nor absent.

For Derrida, any kind of identity, any kind of signification, depends upon the play of differences, which not only differ but 'defer'. 'Deferral' or 'deferment' is the semantic instability that comes from meaning delayed, or postponed. The meaning of the word *pig*, for instance, depends not only upon phonemic contrasts, but upon a whole series of contrasts or CHOICES made (*pig* v. *hog, boar; pig* v. *dog, cat*; etc.) which are significant because they are systematically differentiated; but these contrasts themselves are SIGNS, linguistic SYMBOLS, not actual objects. Theoretically, the chain or process of SIGNIFICATION is therefore (potentially) endless.

In the IMAGERY and SYMBOLISM of literary, especially poetic, texts we may well sense something of an infinite possibility of signification; but in ordinary discourse, as Culler indicates (1983), the pragmatic function of the communication clearly overrides the play of differences.

diglossia

(1) A term coined by Ferguson (1959) to refer to a BIDIALECTAL or multi-dialectal situation in certain speech communities.

Typically certain distinct social functions are regarded as APPROPRIATE for different DIALECTS, and have become standardized, grouped largely under FORMAL or **high**, and informal or **low**. The high VARIETY is usually a STANDARD (written) dialect, used in education, government, religion, serious literature, etc.: e.g. in Egypt, classical Arabic and Egyptian colloquial Arabic; in Switzerland, High German and Swiss-German. CODE-SWITCHING by speakers will regularly take place between the different varieties.

(2) The term has been extended to cover comparable functional variation between languages in a community: e.g. English and Hawaiian Pidgin; Spanish and Guarani in Paraguay.

In medieval Europe what can be seen as **cultural diglossia** (Ong 1984) existed: Latin used for education, religion and serious literature; the VERNACULARS for oral and popular literature and everyday speech.

(3) Some sociologists (e.g. Sankoff 1972) use the term for similar situational code-switching of a less institutionalized kind, with changes of **degrees of FORMALITY** for different REGISTERS within one variety. Although this rather undermines the usefulness of the concept, clearly STYLE-switching in writing and speech, in serious and comic literature, etc., can be seen to be related to **diglossic** code-switching. Hudson (1996) would prefer to call this **social dialectia**.

However, the terms **high** and **low** have been criticized (see Fowler *et al.* 1979) on the grounds that they reinforce notions of superiority and inferiority. Even if the standard dialect has prestige value, the competing dialect is not usually a stigmatized dialect in its own sphere of usage.

direct object

Common in GRAMMAR to describe the NOUN PHRASE which normally follows the grammatical SUBJECT and VERB, and which refers to an entity normally directly 'affected' by the action denoted in the CLAUSE or SENTENCE.

If the noun phrase is a PERSONAL PRONOUN, it is marked by a special **objective** CASE, e.g.: *I like him; he likes me.*

The **direct object** (DO) is usually distinguished from the INDIRECT OBJECT (IO) (q.v.), a similar nominal element occurring in the PREDICATE, but which refers semantically to the 'recipient' or 'beneficiary' (ANIMATE) of the action, if required. In the examples above there are no indirect objects, but in *I gave him* (IO) *a Porsche* (DO) *for Christmas; he gave me* (IO) *a box of chocolates* (DO), the IO precedes the DO.

In some grammars, especially SYSTEMIC GRAMMAR, both kinds of OBJECT are included under COMPLEMENT (q.v.).

In PASSIVE sentences, the subject has been seen as the DEEP STRUCTURE object of an equivalent ACTIVE construction:

> The Tiddlywinks World Championship match was won by Cambridge University; Cambridge University won the Tiddlywinks World Championship match.

FOCUS on the DO can be achieved by variation in WORD ORDER, or by FRONTING, and is especially common in POETIC LANGUAGE, as well as emphatic or emotional:

> Strange fits of passion have I known (Wordsworth: *Lucy Poems*) (Do, V, S, V)
> That remark I refuse to consider (DO, S, VP)

Verbs which are followed by the DO are TRANSITIVE VERBS (q.v.).

direct speech

One of the commonest methods of the REPRESENTATION of SPEECH (q.v.) in writing, especially FICTION. We normally assume, especially for non-literary discourse, e.g. journalism and report-writing, that a writer is claiming to represent the actual words of a speaker within quotation marks, which are also explicitly marked as such by an accompanying reporting clause or TAG (q.v.). This commonly precedes the reported clause, and contains a reference to the speaker, and a SPEECH ACT verb, e.g. *say, state, reply, shout,* etc.: e.g. *She said, 'I have some surprising news for you'.* Graphemically it is conventional to separate the two clauses by a comma or colon, and mark the first 'quoted' word by a capital letter.

Since the tags especially in fictional writing, also frequently contain information about the manner in which an utterance is supposedly spoken (*She giggled/ whispered/said in an Irish accent,* etc.) they confirm the overall impression that direct speech, however 'direct', is merely an approximation of actual spoken language in the written MEDIUM.

Some writers, however, do attempt to mark DIALECTAL or IDIOLECTAL pronunciations using DEVIATIONS of punctuation and spelling: e.g. Dickens for Sam

Weller in *Pickwick Papers*: *Wery glad to see you, indeed, and hope our acquaintance may be a long 'un, as the gen'l'm'n said to the fi' pun' note* . . .

Direct speech is certainly more EXPRESSIVE than INDIRECT SPEECH (q.v.), since it admits exclamations, **terms of** ADDRESS, interjections, etc. which are normally omitted there:

> 'Oh Peter!' she exclaimed, 'What a lovely surprise!'
> *She exclaimed that oh Peter what a lovely surprise.

Direct speech not only FOREGROUNDS the nature of the utterance itself, but its truth value: whether in the journalistic reporting of parliamentary proceedings in the real world, or the fictional world of the novel. Hence by a kind of ICONIC resemblance, direct speech can appear 'direct' (i.e. honest, straightforward), indirect speech 'indirect' (evasive, dishonest), and the opposition exploited on the printed page in the representation of DIALOGUE. So Gregory (1965) notes how in Dickens's *A Tale of Two Cities*, Lucy and Dr Manette are 'allowed to speak for themselves'; whereas the witnesses Barsad and Cly, for example, are given indirect modes.

Interestingly, in the headlines of popular newspapers, where direct speech frequently occurs as an attention-catching device, the obligation to record the original words and content of the **anterior discourse** is sometimes violated (see Short 1988). Even Hansard, the official record of the British Parliament, is not actually verbatim. (Slembrouck 1992.)

(See also DIRECT THOUGHT; FREE DIRECT SPEECH; FREE DIRECT THOUGHT; FREE INDIRECT SPEECH; FREE INDIRECT THOUGHT. See further Steinberg (1982a) on the **direct discourse fallacy**.)

direct thought

By analogy with DIRECT SPEECH **direct thought** is a category proposed by Leech & Short (1981); although others subsume it under direct speech itself, or **direct** DISCOURSE/STYLE (e.g. McHale 1978).

In form direct speech and direct thought may be seen to be identical, except that the VERB in the reporting clause indicates mental activity, not spoken (*think, ponder, wonder*, etc.): e.g. *'Is there life on Mars?', she wondered.*

Indeed, direct speech itself represents thought, in so far as speech itself is assumed to be the result of mental activity. And there are times when we 'think aloud': conventionally exploited in SOLILOQUY (q.v.). Conversely, thought is often described as 'inner speech'.

Yet functionally a fundamental distinction can be made between what is uttered and what is thought. For the representation of thoughts is a literary device, characteristic of the novel, unlike other REGISTERS; the OMNISCIENT NARRATOR has 'privileged' and convenient access to the minds of the characters, implausible in real life. Moreover, what appears in quotation marks, cannot be an 'accurate' representation of actual thought processes, since there are different levels of conceptualization and rationalization, in which IMAGERY as well as language plays a part.

(See also FREE DIRECT THOUGHT; FREE INDIRECT THOUGHT; INDIRECT THOUGHT.)

discours

One of a pair of terms (see also HISTOIRE) introduced into French linguistics and LITERARY THEORY by Benveniste (1966) and frequently used untranslated in British and American theory. This is advisable, since translated literally as 'DISCOURSE' and 'STORY' they add to the semantic overload of these already multi-valent terms (especially DISCOURSE (q.v.)).

(1) Benveniste himself distinguished two modes of UTTERANCE: *histoire*, the 'objective' mode, concerned with the narration of events in the past; and **discours** the SUBJECTIVE mode, highlighting the present moment, indicating the act of ÉNONCIATION and the ADDRESSER (*I*) and ADDRESSEE (*you*) and their SITUATION: comparable in a way to the classical distinction between MIMESIS (q.v.) and DIEGESIS (q.v.), 'showing' and 'telling'.

The problem is that these two modes would hardly ever appear in their 'pure' state: a novel told in the third person may well appear to be in the neutral or anonymous mode of *histoire*, and conversation in the mode of *discours*; but many conversations recount happenings or stories, and many third PERSON novels (e.g. *Tom Jones*) have a characteristic *discours* framework involving IMPLIED AUTHOR and IMPLIED READER.

(2) Other critics, therefore (e.g. Todorov, Genette, Greimas), prefer to think of levels rather than modes or classes: so that the level of FORM crudely corresponds to *discours*, and CONTENT to *histoire* (see also SURFACE V. DEEP STRUCTURE). *Discours* would not only include NARRATIVE mode, but also TONE, POINT OF VIEW, ordering of events and the realization of the wider relations between implied author and reader. (See also FABULA V. SJUŽET; PLOT; RÉCIT.)

discourse: ~ analysis; ~ stylistics; ~ genre; ~ marker, etc.

Discourse is one of the most widely used and overworked terms in many branches of linguistics, STYLISTICS, cultural and critical theory. It generally seems to be used for all those senses of language which, in the words of Bakhtin, emphasize its 'concrete living totality' (1981); the term 'language' itself being orientated more towards a linguistic system. Discourse is also used in more (inter-) active senses.

(1) Its technical uses appear to have really little to do with the senses recorded in the *COD*, for instance: namely a formal written 'treatise' or 'dissertation'; or (archaically) 'talk' or 'conversation', except in so far as all of these could be included. In fact, the current emphasis is more on spoken than written language, reviving under a new guise the 'archaic' sense. And in so far as 'treatise' or

'conversation' implies more than one SENTENCE or UTTERANCE, this is also significant for the technical uses of **discourse**.

(2) One prominent and comprehensive sense, for which there is indeed no other direct equivalent, covers all those aspects of COMMUNICATION which involve not only a MESSAGE or TEXT but also the ADDRESSER and ADDRESSEE, and their immediate CONTEXT OF SITUATION. Leech & Short (1981), emphasize its INTERPERSONAL or transactional nature, and also its social purpose. **Discourse** would therefore refer not only to ordinary conversation and its context, but also to written communications between writer and reader: hence terms like **literary** or **narrative discourse**, **discourse** WORLD, etc.

In this sense it is equivalent to the French term DISCOURS (see sense (2) especially), and is so used by Chatman (1978), for instance.

In the novel as discourse other discourses can be EMBEDDED: e.g. DIALOGUE. A novel, like a poem, can also engage in discourse, or be part of a larger discourse, involving other texts in the tradition (see INTERTEXTUALITY).

(3) Out of sense (2) in the 1980s came the term **discourse stylistics**, made popular in the 1990s through the sub-title of Carter & Simpson (1989), and marking a new direction in STYLISTICS (q.v.) away from formal analysis to contextualized, discourse-oriented approaches, including sociolinguistic, pragmatic and feminist.

(4) With the emphasis on communication in speech or writing it is often used simply as an alternative to VARIETY or REGISTER: LITERARY v. non-literary **discourse**, dramatic, philosophical, etc. And the terms **discourse genre/type** are now commonly used instead of register, for instance. (See also SPEECH EVENT.) Out of Swales's work on genre analysis (e.g. 1990) came the term **discourse community**, by analogy with the term 'speech community', to refer to socio-rhetorical networks of people all engaged in the same communicative pursuit, united by common public goals, discourse expertise, familiarity with relevant genres necessary for the pursuit of their goals, etc. It is arguable, however, whether a university, for example, can be seen as one such discourse community or several, comprising administrators, academics, librarians, students, etc.

(5) With the emphasis on communication, or on mode of communication, it is sometimes used in discussions of novel discourse to refer to the representation of speech and thought; hence terms like FREE DIRECT or INDIRECT **discourse**.

(6) **Discourse** is popularly used in linguistics and LITERARY THEORY in a more loaded sense after the work of Foucault. Discourse transmits social and institutionalized values or IDEOLOGIES, and also creates them. Thus we can speak of the discourse of New Labour, of the tabloids, of regulations, etc. (See further CRITICAL LINGUISTICS/CRITICAL DISCOURSE ANALYSIS.) Foucault (1972) also uses the term **discursive practices** as a general label for the larger discourse frameworks which reflect and inscribe sets of significant social, cultural and political beliefs at any one period: e.g. education, politics, information technology. Diachronically, we can see how one kind of discursive practice can come to eclipse another: e.g. currently 'New Age' philosophy over orthodox religion and medicine.

(7) In the broad sense of (2), **discourse** 'includes' TEXT (q.v.), but the two terms are not always easily distinguished, and are often used synonymously.

Some linguists would restrict discourse to spoken communication, and reserve text for written: the early discourse analysts, for instance (see (8) below; and Coulthard 1977). Others see discourse as 'process', and text as 'product'.

A well-established definition of discourse views it as a series of connected utterances, a unit of potential analysis larger than a sentence. Thus, if conversation is discourse in (2), here it can include discourse (see Crystal & Davy 1969), if it is seen as a continuous stretch of speech preceded and followed by silence or a change of speaker (see also UTTERANCE). However, most linguists who use the term with particular reference to speech, would include all turns, etc., and emphasize its transactional nature as in sense (2).

(8) This is particularly true in the discipline of **discourse analysis**, which has exposed the different kinds of structure, interactional as well as linguistic, in stretches of spoken interchange in particular. (See ACT; ADJACENCY PAIR; EXCHANGE, for example.) The analysis of written discourse is often subsumed under TEXT LINGUISTICS (q.v.).

The work of Harris, 1952, on linear 'strings' of utterances is widely held to be the precursor of discourse analysis, which in Britain has been prominently associated since the 1970s with the work at Birmingham University by Sinclair, Coulthard *et al.* on relatively formalized types of discourse such as classroom and doctor–patient interchanges. For an attempt to apply their discourse model to (non-natural) dramatic dialogue, see Burton (1980). The Birmingham emphasis is PRAGMATIC, concerned with the FUNCTION and COHERENCE of discourse units. (See also ETHNOGRAPHY.)

More recently, discourse analysis has taken a COGNITIVE perspective. Here interest is in the mental activity of the reader of a written text to actually 'construct' a far richer text than the literal words on the page, by various sorts of INFERENCE. (See further Emmott 1997.)

(9) Discourse analysis has highlighted elements of speech which are often disregarded in GRAMMARS, but which have important discourse functions. Usually CLOSED-CLASS items, but difficult to classify as traditional parts of speech, or (parenthetic) CLAUSES, for example, they are called **discourse markers** or **signals**: *well, I mean, you know, yes*, etc., following Schiffrin 1987.

While these may have little INFORMATION value, and are seldom reproduced in FORMAL writing, they are nevertheless part of the native speaker's communicative fluency. They can act as significant FRAMING and editing devices in face-to-face interaction, and serve usefully as 'floorholders', for example, or to monitor FEEDBACK (e.g. *OK?*). Sometimes they simply indicate hesitation or nervousness; or the desire to make contact (see also PHATIC COMMUNION). (See further Biber *et al.* 1999; Hughes 1996.)

dispositio

A classical term for the arrangement and structure of an argument, one of the major **divisions** of RHETORIC, and one of the necessary skills in oratory and written composition.

A common pattern was an introduction or EXORDIUM, a set of propositions, the 'proof' and a conclusion (**peroratio**). But other 'parts' were common depending on the nature of the work: e.g. a 'narration' or 'exposition' and a 'moral' (as in a fable); arguments and counter-arguments (as in a debate). Evidence of such ordering is clearly seen in the 'songs' of Donne, and the sonnets of Shakespeare, for example; and comparable structures form the basis of technical and critical articles in academic discourse today.

(See also ELOCUTIO.)

domain

Generally meaning 'scope' or 'field of influence':

(1) **domain** in sociolinguistics, following the work of Fishman (e.g. 1971), refers to general areas of language use which are socially and functionally significant, often institutionalized.

In DIGLOSSIC communities, for instance, domains of public and FORMAL discourse (government, education) frequently contrast with domains of informal or private (family, humour, popular literature), labelled **high** and **low** respectively, giving rise to CODE-SWITCHING (q.v.).

It is a term broader than REGISTER, and it overlaps with **semantic** FIELD (q.v.). For bilingual speakers, domains such as 'school', 'religion', or 'home', for example, can cause code-switching, even as conversational topics. For monolingual speakers domain can be seen as an important factor in APPROPRIATENESS of usage, determining, e.g. formal v. informal variants.

(2) In TEXT LINGUISTICS, the semantic slant of **domain** is also emphasized in its COLLOCATIONS, **shared domain** and **referential domain**. Here it means simply FRAME OF REFERENCE. Every discourse is firmly anchored in its own particular domain, with its own time–space orientation, PERSPECTIVE, topics and assumed knowledge, etc. So the domain of cricket commentary differs from that of boxing; and both differ from a lecture on small British mammals.

(3) In the sense of CONTEXT, the term is employed by Leech & Short (1981) in their discussion of STYLE, as a relational term. Judgments about the style of a poem or of a novel, for example, are often made in explicit or implicit comparison with CHOICES of features in other texts in the writer's oeuvre; or the GENRE; or the period, i.e. various stylistic **domains**.

(4) In GRAMMAR, **domain** is sometimes used to mean 'scope' or 'sphere of activity' within the narrower frames of TEXT or SENTENCE context: see, e.g., Taglicht (1985) on FOCUS devices. Thus words like *only* and *also* are notorious for their ambiguity of scope or domain, depending on construction or position:

> At the party, only Kate wore a bikini.
> At the party, Kate wore only a bikini.

These sentences have different domains for *only*, and different emphases and PRESUPPOSITIONS.

(5) In POSSIBLE WORLD THEORY the term **semantic domain** is used by Ryan (1991) to describe the sum of meanings evoked by any fictional text, to include all the varied INFERENCES, generalizations and symbolic interpretations, etc., as well as the actual 'reality' or WORLD of the text.

dominant

(1) Particularly associated with the LITERARY THEORY of the **Russian** FORMAL-ISTS and the PRAGUE SCHOOL, and defined by Jakobson (1935), for instance, as the 'focussing component' of a work of art, which 'rules, determines and transforms' the remaining components. The notion of the **dominant** is closely related to the notion of FOREGROUNDING (q.v.).

For poetry, the obvious example of the dominant which makes it what it is would be its verse structure. But clearly, this in itself is a complex of elements, and hence of potential dominant features, just as 'poetry' overall comprises a variety of subgenres. So a set of dominants can characterize or define a genre: the fourteen lines and limited RHYME patterns of the sonnet, for example. Moreover, what is the dominant in poetry of one period may not be so in the poetry of another: ALLITERATION in Old English poetry replaced by end-rhyme in Middle English.

The term 'dominance' implies a dynamic quality, a struggle or conflict even. One element is seen as prevailing over others in competition, providing unity and harmony.

The Formalist emphasis is very much on the dominant as a formal inherent property of the text. Yet it might be argued that it also involves what is perceived or felt to be dominant by the reader. Hence the appreciation and judgment of dominant (and subordinate) elements may vary from one period to another: e.g. Elizabethan CONCEITS or PUNS.

(See further Matejka & Titunik (eds) 1976.)

double voice(d)

See DUAL VOICE.

dramatic irony

See IRONY.

dramatic monologue

See MONOLOGUE.

117

dramatis persona

From Lat. 'mask of drama' **dramatis persona** in LITERARY CRITICISM refers to a dramatic CHARACTER (q.v.). It was also borrowed by Propp (1928), for FUNCTIONAL characterization in NARRATIVES.

The theory of dramatic character is as complex as that of the novel, compounded by the relationship of dramatic ROLE to the actor in performance, commonly regarded as an ICON of the character. Actually, a *dramatic persona* need not be present on stage (e.g. Godot in Beckett's *Waiting for Godot*); nor need it be acted by human beings (e.g. in puppet plays).

In the criticism of dramatic characterization the question of the degree of MIMESIS involved in the representation is as central an issue as in novel criticism. The playwright, however, has no narrative framework for 'filling out' the character, which must instead be realized in the DIALOGUE and the action, and in the actor's interpretation in performance.

Characters in early drama tended to be based on a dominant trait: the PERSONIFICATION of a quality in the ALLEGORICAL 'morality' plays of the late medieval period (e.g. *The Seven Deadly Sins*); or the humours and stock types of the Elizabethan and Jacobean playwrights (the braggart, cuckold, Justice Overdo, etc.). This is transformed into a 'ruling passion', and held up for awe and pity, not ridicule in the ambition, jealousy and pride of the tragic heroes.

Aristotelian theory viewed 'character' (*ethos*) as less significant than AGENCY in the action. Twentieth-century and FORMALIST and STRUCTURALIST criticism has also analysed dramatic (and narrative) texts in terms of structural configurations of functional or ACTANTIAL roles (e.g. of hero, villain, etc.). For a resumé of approaches, e.g. of Souriau and Greimas, see Elam (1980).

Other approaches to drama prefer to see characterization from a wider viewpoint, especially in plays which reveal a complexity of structure and THEME. Our appreciation of Shakespeare's *Richard III* involves not only a consideration of his dual role of 'hero' as well as 'villain', but also an assessment in terms of psychological realism, historical background, and Richard's INTERTEXTUAL relations with Shakespeare's 'History' kings.

dualism

Dualism has been a popular theory of meaning in LITERARY CRITICISM and STYLISTICS based on the premise that FORM (q.v.) and CONTENT (q.v.) can be distinguished in language, and that the same content or 'meaning' therefore can be expressed in various ways (see also notions of PARAPHRASE and SYNONYMY). A sentence like *Would you kindly extinguish your cigarettes* means the same as *Please put your cigarettes out* and the distinction is regarded as stylistic, in a common use of the term.

Native speakers may well feel that in certain situations they have a CHOICE of structures to express their meaning, yet at the SURFACE level of discourse, variations do suggest different CONNOTATIONS, which play a not insignificant role in our interpretation of utterances even in ordinary speech. These can, indeed, be politically and socially exploited (e.g. in journalism and advertising).

In POETIC LANGUAGE in particular, the extent to which expressions might be changed without a change in 'content' is more arguable, and is a matter much discussed in translation theory. Since the AESTHETIC focus of poetry is as much on the form as on the content, the notion of potential equivalence in DEEP STRUC- TURE, or in PROPOSITIONAL MEANING between 'versions' of a poem really means very little.

In contrast, MONISM (q.v.) argues for the inseparability of form and content, and has been advocated by the NEW CRITICS for instance, and by the proponents of RADICAL STYLISTICS. For monists and dualists alike, stylistic choices are clearly significant, but are 'meaningful' in different ways.

dual voice

(1) **Dual voice** is particularly associated with the work of Pascal 1977, on FREE INDIRECT STYLE (FIS) (q.v.). He argues that in the REPRESENTATION OF THE SPEECH OR THOUGHTS of characters through the mode of the NARRATIVE, the VOICE of the NARRATOR is an essential presence: hence the duality of PERSPECTIVE.

The very terms 'free' (i.e. without explicit TAGGING, so that the discourse and experiences of the characters are presented dramatically) and 'indirect' (i.e. in the words of the narrator, not the 'actual' words of the characters) imply critical recognition of the dual voice, but Pascal argues for a stronger, non-neutral narratorial voice, heard as a TONE of irony, or sympathy, etc., underlying the statements of the characters. Clearly, the reader's awareness of the voice and its tone is heavily dependent on CONTEXT, which could include the novel as a whole. So the representation of Maria and Julia Bertram's enthusiasm for producing a play in Jane Austen's *Mansfield Park* can be seen to have an ironic perspective in the light of subsequent events: *Their mother had no objection to the plan, and they were not in the least afraid of their father's disapprobation.*

While Banfield (1982) raised doubts about distinguishing the narratorial voice on a linguistic basis, Pascal's thesis does raise interesting questions about the functions of FIS generally, its relations with other modes of speech representa- tion, and its potential SYMBOLIC role as a means of subordination and indirect- ness in the presentation of viewpoints.

(2) The concept of **dual voice** also illustrates an important notion of Bakhtin (1973, 1981): namely that of the DIALOGICAL principle of discourse, with his own use of the terms **double-styled/-accented/-voiced**. For Bakhtin the discourse of the novel is characteristically heterogeneous, interactive, even conflictive: styles and voices are interwoven, of social groups, of characters and narrator. CHARACTER ZONE, COLOURED NARRATIVE, the 'concealed speech' of COLLECTIVE DISCOURSE, and FIS are all manifestations of this double voice. PARODY is also double-voiced, depending on the manipulation of the discourses or styles of texts or genres. (See also HYBRIDIZATION; POLYPHONY.)

E

elaborated code

One of a pair of controversial terms (see also RESTRICTED CODE) coined by the sociolinguist Basil Bernstein in the 1960s as part of a theory of educational development and social class (see especially 1971), and replacing his earlier terms **formal** and **public language**.

As the entry for CODE suggests, the two terms refer to types of meaning or cultural values generated by the social system and ACTUALIZED in VARIETIES of language; but the terms have been frequently used (even in Bernstein's own work) in the sense simply of variety or DIALECT (e.g. Labov 1970). The assumption then is that social class determines the 'variety' of English available to the child (see also Fowler 1981).

Elaborated code users, it was argued, are orientated towards universalistic or context-free meanings, restricted code users towards particularistic or context-tied meanings. Elaborated code is seen to be more complex and more abstract than restricted code, as well as being more impersonal, less REDUNDANT, concrete and personal.

On the face of it, the distinction seems to have uncontroversial sociostylistic implications: that elaborated code is a feature of the discourses of literature and technology, for example, and common in writing; that restricted code is a common aspect of ordinary PHATIC speech. CODE-SWITCHING could occur between one situation and another, depending on the degree of 'elaboration' or explicitness needed. This is, of course, to see it in purely linguistic terms. But Bernstein claimed that the education system as a whole was dominated by the elaborated code semiotic; and that certain children, predominantly from working-class backgrounds, were prevented from educational success by their lack of 'access' to this code or use of it.

It is this conclusion that aroused most controversy. In any case, the terms themselves seem to have implicit value judgments, 'elaborated' having more favourable connotations than 'restricted'.

elision

A term used in PHONETICS and METRICS (from Lat. 'striking out'); not to be confused with ELLIPSIS, although it commonly is, especially since its verb form **elide** is common to both.

(1) In verse, two syllables may be run together to regularize the metre, and so sounds may be elided or omitted: e.g. medial FRICATIVES as in the *o'er* and *ne'er* of POETIC DICTION; and commonly the (unstressed) word-final vowels preceding other vowels: e.g. Milton's *th' eclipse; t'augment.* (Also known as **synaloepha** in RHETORIC.)

Medial **elision** was technically termed SYNCOPE in rhetoric. APHESIS was the term for the elision of initial syllables: e.g. *(be)twixt;* APOCOPE for the omission of final syllables: e.g. *oft(en).* Elision is frequently marked by an apostrophe in writing.

(2) Other **elisions** in verse, however useful metrically, reflect the natural omissions of unstressed vowels in colloquial connected speech: Milton's *heav'n, fall'n, liv'st,* for example; or of consonants in unstressed words: Shakespeare's *heat o' the sun.*

In modern English, forms like *she's, I'll, fish 'n' chips,* so represented in informal writing, are elidable because they carry little INFORMATIONAL value, which can be derived from the CONTEXT. Elision of syllables for ease or economy of effort is common in polysyllabic words, if rarely recorded GRAPHEMICALLY: *a temporary secretary* may be pronounced /ə temprı sekrətrı/.

ellipsis; elliptical

(1) **Ellipsis** (Gk 'leaving out') can be seen as grammatical omission, rather than phonological ELISION: i.e. omission of part of an utterance or grammatical structure, which can be readily understood by the hearer or reader in the CO-TEXT or the CONTEXT, and which can be 'recovered' explicitly. In a wine-bar we can point to a bottle of wine and say *Two glasses [of wine] please.*

Answers to questions are commonly **elliptical**:

Q: Where is the tiger's head?
A: [The tiger's head is] five foot from his tail.

and ellipsis of SUBJECT is common in CO-ORDINATE CLAUSES:

Jack fell down,
And [ ] broke his crown . . .

Elided or **ellipted** elements constitute GIVEN INFORMATION, and ellipsis helps to focus on NEW INFORMATION, or more important information. It is common in registers where economy of expression is needed, e.g. note-taking, newspaper adverts (*Home wanted for German shepherd. House-trained. Good with children*). Such a 'telegraphic' style, with the omission of grammatical words (ARTICLES, AUXILIARIES, etc.), is common in the representation of INTERIOR MONOLOGUE in novels, suggesting the quick succession of thoughts or images. So in Joyce's *Ulysses,* Bloom raised his eyes and met the stare of a bilious clock. Two. Pub clock five minutes fast. Time going on. Hands moving. Two. Not yet.

Ellipsis in normal discourse is possible because of the latter's REDUNDANCY or surplus and predictability of meaning; and it is a common means of implicit COHESION between sentences or utterances, usefully avoiding unnecessary and possibly tedious REPETITION. It is thus typically ANAPHORIC, i.e. dependent on prior full reference. (See also ZERO ANAPHORA.)

Ellipsis is extremely common, especially in speech, to the extent that it could inspire a CONVERSATIONAL MAXIM 'reduce as much as possible'. But where economy could lead to AMBIGUITY, ellipsis is avoided: in legal contracts, for example. Also, dramatic DIALOGUE tends to be less elliptical than natural conversation, because it lacks the same context-dependence.

(2) In narratives or plays **ellipsis** or omission of events assumed to happen but not described or enacted is a means of speeding up the action or pace of the discourse. In Genette's (1972) terms it is a kind of ANACHRONY, i.e. a discontinuity or discrepancy between STORY and DISCOURS. Act, scene or chapter divisions may serve as ICONIC, if implicit, signs of omission or gaps of time (as in Shakespeare's *The Winter's Tale*); but explicit markers are also common (*Beowulf had ruled over the Geats for 50 years; two years later*, etc.).

elocution, also elocutio

(1) In ordinary usage **elocution** refers to a type of speech training which encourages people to speak clearly, especially on public occasions, or to speak with a prestigious ACCENT, such as RECEIVED PRONUNCIATION.

(2) It is, in fact, a rare survivor of the ancient RHETORICAL tradition, and not far removed from the sense in which Aristotle uses it in his *Rhetoric*, Book III, namely a manner of oral delivery which is clear and APPROPRIATE.

(3) **Elocutio** became one of the main **divisions** of rhetoric, and was increasingly identified, indeed, over the centuries with the subject itself. **Dispositio**, for example, was to do with the arrangement of ideas, *elocutio* provided the STYLE of their expression: the choice of appropriate rhythms, rhetorical FIGURES, etc.

embedding

(1) **Embedding**, taken from GENERATIVE GRAMMAR, refers to the process whereby one sentence is included in another; what other grammars term SUBORDINATION. One clause is regarded as dependent on, or a constituent of, another clause: e.g. *I regret [that I am unable to attend]*. (See also RANK-SHIFT.) RELATIVE CLAUSES can be seen to be **embedded** within the NOUN PHRASE in the MAIN CLAUSE:

Happy [the man [whose wish and care
A few paternal acres bound]]

(Pope: *On Solitude*)

(2) Halliday (1985) appears to restrict **embedding** to relative clauses, and other such structures where a clause or phrase functions within a group (e.g. POSTMODIFICATION); what Quirk *et al.* (1985) term **indirect embedding**.

(3) But Halliday's use perhaps reinforces the sense of 'medial inclusion', and **embedding** is sometimes used instead of subordination as a synonym for **nesting**, e.g. for dependent clauses which split main clauses rather than precede or follow them in BRANCHING structures. The frequent use of embedding is a particular feature of formal prose, and a marker of structural complexity. So the first sentence of James's *The Ambassadors* has two such embedded clauses:

> Strether's first question, [when he reached the hotel], was about his friend; yet on his learning [that Waymarsh was apparently not to arrive till evening] he was not wholly disconcerted.

(4) **Embedding** is used in the study of NARRATIVE to refer to the insertion of one STORY within another (see Todorov 1971). *The Arabian Nights* offers a good illustration of complex embedding: Scheherazade will tell a story about a character who will tell a story about a tailor who tells a story about a baker, etc. (See also EXTRADIEGETIC; FRAMING.)

As this very summary reveals, such embedding can be directly compared with grammatical structures. Indeed, the process of storytelling itself can be seen to be a complex SPEECH ACT of the structure X (the author) tells that Y (the narrator) tells that Z (the character) . . . etc.

emotive: ~ meaning; ~ function

Emotive is an adjective that is often vaguely used in traditional SEMANTICS and LITERARY CRITICISM to describe meaning or use of language, and is difficult to distinguish from AFFECTIVE (q.v.) and EXPRESSIVE (q.v.), even CONNOTATIVE.

(1) In semantics, basic CONCEPTUAL or REFERENTIAL MEANINGS of words are opposed to more peripheral or subjective kinds or ASSOCIATIONS. **Emotive meaning** refers to the effect that a word might have on the emotions of the reader or listener: e.g. the word *home* to a sailor or long-distance lorry-driver. If this seems too subjective, certain words do seem to have emotive CONNOTATIONS 'built into' them: EVALUATIVE words of approval (*darling; sweetheart*) and disapproval (*hooligan; vandal*). Over a period of time such associations may change: *enthusiast* is no longer a term of abuse, but *villain* now is. Obviously the use of **emotive language** may tell us something about the feelings and attitudes of the speaker or writer.

The PRAGUE SCHOOL linguists argue that emotive 'colouring' is also found with PHONEMES. /h/, which is only found in pre-vowel position in NE anyway, is dropped in many dialects, or wrongly inserted (e.g. *hour Enry* for *our Henry*), and has become a marker of social status. Grammatical forms too can be emotive: many people, especially women, dislike and avoid *he* with GENERIC reference, and the notion of CORRECTNESS in usage is an emotive issue.

(2) Clearly such **emotive meanings** or associations may be exploited in certain REGISTERS for particular reasons. The manipulation of emotions has been important in traditional RHETORIC, and continues to be so in advertising and political propaganda. I. A. Richards argued influentially in the 1920s and 1930s that emotive meaning distinguished LITERARY, especially POETIC, LANGUAGE from that of science (factual, referential): a broad distinction taken up by the NEW CRITICS.

The function of poetic language, it is argued, is to arouse feelings, by the IMAGERY, SYMBOLISM and CHOICE of words, by patterns of RHYTHM; whereas scientific discourse is primarily directed towards readers' beliefs. Even if the distinction can be largely accepted, there are many kinds of discourse where it can't, and where emotive and factual meaning work together (e.g. advertising). And at word-level, scientific terms which pass into common parlance may easily acquire subjective or emotive connotations (e.g. *nuclear deterrent; mastectomy; clone*).

(3) In Jakobson's (1960) model of the SPEECH EVENT (q.v.), the **emotive function** of language describes the set of language towards the ADDRESSER: namely, that it communicates his or her emotions, attitudes, status, etc.; what others call the EXPRESSIVE FUNCTION.

emphasis; emphatic stress

(1) In PHONETICS **emphasis** or **emphatic stress** is an extra intensity and prominence given to words or syllables for special significance, often involving extra loudness or a high falling (or rising) TONE. In writing and print this can be indicated by (small) capitals, italics, underlining and/or exclamation marks (e.g. *you* BLOODY GREAT IDIOT*!!!*). Emphasis is common in speech for denials and corrections, for indicating enthusiasm, or intensity of feeling.

In verse, emphasis is hard to recognize above the 'neutral' rhythmic stress patterns, themselves marked against the rhythms of ordinary speech, but the sense can help. So with Donne's punning address to God; *When thou hast done, thou has not done, (A Hymn to God the Father)* the sense demands emphatic stress on the (otherwise unstressed) negative.

(2) As a kind of FOCUS device, **emphasis** on certain significant parts of an utterance can be conveyed by syntactic means: e.g. AUXILIARY VERB *do* (*But she does like elephants*); INVERSION of SUBJECT and VERB; FRONTING of elements (*Down came the rain*); CLEFTING and PSEUDO-CLEFTING (*It was the butler who killed her; What we want is a cup of tea*); arrangement of clauses to provide a CLIMAX, etc.

(See also END-FOCUS; HYPERBOLE.)

empirical study of literature

A European-based subject in origins (see Schmidt 1981) and popular in the Netherlands particularly, which aims to develop theories and models of literary communication based on the responses of READERS in empirical testing. Of particular relevance to STYLISTICS are van Peer 1986 on FOREGROUNDING, and Steen (1994) on the understanding of literary METAPHOR.

enactment

(1) Uncontroversially, **enactment** in the sense of acting something out, turning it into action, can be seen to lie at the heart of drama, and can be equated with the Greek concept of MIMESIS (q.v.) or 'showing'. But the enactment of human experience, turning it into words, giving it verbal and structural form, applies to all kinds of literature.

LITERARY THEORY has tended to use the term, however, like mimesis itself, in more precise senses which involve these very linguistic forms:

(2) A common critical and stylistic assumption is that literary language will directly **enact** or mime the meaning it expresses: FORM mirrors CONTENT.

This is certainly possible if the experience is auditory or KINETIC: variations in PHONETIC, RHYTHMIC and CLAUSE structures, for example, can suggest quick movement, noise and confusion, as in this sentence from Dickens's *Oliver Twist*:

Away they ran, pell-mell, helter-skelter, slap-dash, tearing, yelling, screaming, knocking down the passengers as they turn corners, rousing up the dogs, and astonishing the fowls: and streets, squares and courts re-echo with the sound.

A simple **enactment** is a (temporal) progression of actions mirrored in a temporal (spoken) or linear (written) sequence of clauses: found not only in NARRATIVES (*Solomon Grundy, born on a Monday, christened on Tuesday,* . . . , etc.) but also in instruction manuals: *First, check that the gear lever is in neutral. Then insert the key in the lock, and turn till the engine fires,* . . . , etc.

The principle of enactment or ICONICITY (q.v.) is invoked most frequently with respect to sounds (see ONOMATOPOEIA; SOUND SYMBOLISM). While it might be argued that correspondences of PHONEME and real-world auditory phenomena are easily identified (buzzing bees, sizzling sausages), many sound correspondences (concerning objects, themes, etc.) that are made by critics are often highly subjective and impressionistic. Critics like Barry (1984) therefore, see the concept of enactment as a **fallacy**, yet frequent and commonly accepted instances of different kinds of enactment in literature seem hard to deny, as part of its EXPRESSIVITY, and as a kind of DECORUM.

(3) Viewed in this way, **enactment** can be seen to suggest a special involvement of writer and subject, which the reader also is drawn into as a 'mediary'. In the AFFECTIVE STYLISTICS and READER-RESPONSE CRITICISM of Stanley Fish, for instance, it is the reader who enacts or re-creates the experience described. It might be argued, for example, that the voyage or 'odyssey' in Joyce's *Ulysses* is as much the reader's as Leopold Bloom's, i.e. a voyage of discovery and education.

encoding

A term in SEMIOTICS from COMMUNICATION theory to refer to the process whereby an ADDRESSER or transmitter converts a MESSAGE into a TEXT by means of a set of rules or CODE, to be received or DECODED by an ADDRESSEE.

Each speech community can be viewed in general as registering and **encoding** the world and experience through its language system. And as Fiske (1982) argues, the perception of reality is itself an encoding process: making sense of it.

More specifically, speakers **encode** their ideas through spoken language, and writers through writing. Also encoded will be the sender's values, beliefs and assumptions, personal, social, cultural and moral.

Attention in LITERARY CRITICISM is now focussed on 'decoding' or INTERPRE- TATION of texts rather than encoding; and the extent to which the reader may be seen, in fact, as 'encoding' or **re-coding** (i.e. creating) the meaning in the process of reading, has also been much debated.

end-focus; end-weight

(1) The **principle** or **maxim of end-focus** illustrates the important interrela- tions between SYNTAX, INTONATION and TEXT structure. It is based on the general fact that different parts of utterances have different communicative values or degrees of COMMUNICATIVE DYNAMISM (q.v.), and that normally NEW or import- ant INFORMATION is reserved for the end, corresponding to the NUCLEUS in speech: e.g. *Good food costs less at Sainsbury's.*

End-focus can be seen to be an important factor in the choice of ACTIVE and PASSIVE sentences, for instance: in

9 out of 10 cats prefer Whiskas

the focus is on the cat-food; in

Whiskas is preferred by 9 out of 10 cats

the focus is on the (high) proportion of cats.

The principle of end-focus can also be applied to a succession of clauses: what Quirk *et al.* (1985) call **resolution**. So the final clause will have the maximum EMPHASIS: *If a wife dies, her husband has to cope with all those household chores, look after the children, and keep his own job going* (insurance advertisement). A careful 'grading' of importance in clauses is exploited in the RHETORICAL FIGURE of CLIMAX (q.v.).

(2) End position is also important for the **principle** or **maxim of end-weight**, which involves syntax. Here complex or 'heavy' sentence constituents will tend to follow simpler or lighter ones. Potential **left**-BRANCHING structures are often avoided in favour of **right**-BRANCHING as a result (what is sometimes called **extraposition**): so instead of:

That it was a good idea to propose her for President,/no-one doubted will be found

No-one doubted / that it was a good idea to propose her for President.

In the following example it is the SUBJECT which is moved from its normal initial or pre-verbal position to the end of the sentence: *Just introduced to the market from a Watford Company are/coated polycarbonate prescription safety lenses with a scratch-resistant coating.*

As this very example reveals, the principle of end-focus seems also to be at work, since the subject is undoubtedly the most important part of the information.

(See also EXISTENTIAL SENTENCE; FOCUS.)

endophoric reference

One of a pair of terms popularized by Halliday (e.g. Halliday & Hasan 1976) to refer to TEXTUAL reference, as distinct from EXOPHORIC (i.e. CONTEXTUAL, REFERENCE (q.v.)).

Items with **endophoric reference** are important means of COHESION, and are subdivided into ANAPHORIC (i.e. backward) and CATAPHORIC (forward) REFERENCE. The third PERSON PRONOUNS (*she, it, he, they*) are typically **endophoric**; whereas the **first** and **second** person pronouns (*I, we, you*) are typically exophoric. The ARTICLES can have either endophoric reference (*The girl came into the room*) or exophoric (*the sun; the moon*, etc.).

enigma

Sometimes used in NARRATOLOGY to describe one of the commonest PLOT lines: suspense followed by 'resolution' or 'deferred' significance (see Barthes 1970; see also HERMENEUTIC CODE).

Just how much information should be given to readers at any one stage must be the continual preoccupation of a story-teller, and it is particularly crucial in detective fiction, for instance: hence the label 'whodunnit'.

If the very beginning of a novel normally presents the ORIENTATION stage, i.e. the setting or background, and the introduction of the characters, the adoption of the IN MEDIAS RES technique thrusts **enigma** to the forefront of the novel. So the opening sentence of Murdoch's *The Italian Girl* invites questions about the person 'narrating', and where (s)he is: *I pressed the door gently.*

Novels which apparently have no enigma are unusual, but consider the opening of *A Judgment in Stone* by Ruth Rendell: *Eunice Parchman killed the Coverdale family because she could not read or write.* Here, however, there is still a sense of suspense: we seek to know not what happens, but how it happens.

enjamb(e)ment

Taken into METRICS and PROSODY from the French to refer to the 'striding over' (cf. *jambe* 'leg') of a sentence from one line of poetry to the next.

Originally, **enjambment** applied to the continuation of a sentence beyond the second line of a **couplet**, but it is now almost invariably used with the more general meaning. Alternative names are **run on** or **straddled lines** (the latter used by Keats). In Germanic and Old English verse it is sometimes referred to as *Hakenstil* or *Bogenstil* ('hook-' or 'bow-style').

Enjambed lines are opposed to **end-stopped lines**, or **line junctures**, where the last word coincides with a normal grammatical break, such as the end of a clause or sentence, marked GRAPHEMICALLY by <,>, or <.>. Line juncture is itself to be distinguished from a CAESURA, which is a pause created by the SYNTAX within a verse line.

With enjambment there is thus a COUNTERPOINT or tension between metrical and syntactical boundaries. Tension is more acute the more a grammatical pause would be abnormal: e.g. between parts of a word (not very common, but see Hopkins's poems); less extreme forms would be separate phrases, e.g. SUBJECT away from PREDICATE. Deliberate AMBIGUITY can be exploited in line 'breaks' as in Carlos Williams's:

> I saw a girl with one leg
> over the rail of a balcony

Frequent use of end-stopped lines is found in popular verse and ballads:

> Hickory, dickory dock
> The mouse ran up the clock, . . .

whereas frequent use of enjambment is found in the (five-BEAT) BLANK VERSE of Shakespeare and Milton. In dramatic verse it suggests the natural rhythms of speech, and a more flowing movement of thought than the 'staccato' effect of end-stopped lines: see Macbeth's soliloquy:

> If it were done when 'tis done, then 'twere well →
> It were done quickly; if the assassination →
> Could trammel up the consequence, and catch →
> With his surcease success; that but this blow →
> Might be the be-all and the end-all here, . . . (I.vii)

énonciation (enunciation); énoncé (enounced)

The theory of **énonciation** is particularly associated with the French linguist Benveniste (1966) and indicates the then strong French interest in DISCOURS(E) and CONTEXT (see also Greimas and Genette in NARRATOLOGY, in the 1970s). The term has no exact equivalent in English, although **enunciation** is sometimes used, which normally means 'pronunciation'. Pronunciation is certainly part of its meaning. An alternative rendering is UTTERANCE (q.v.), but this has an 'active' and 'passive' meaning: the act of uttering or speaking, and the product of speaking. The first would correspond to enunciation; the second to Benveniste's **énoncé**, the 'narrated event' or **enounced**.

L'énonciation refers to the realization of language (as COMPETENCE) in language (as PERFORMANCE), i.e. the physical act of producing an utterance within a given context in time and space, part of the SUBJECTIVE mode of *discours* or the SPEECH EVENT. **L'énoncé**, in contrast, is highlighted in HISTOIRE, the 'objective' mode of narration of events in the past, which abstracts the utterance produced from its context.

Important linguistic indicators of enunciation are the DEICTIC pronouns or shifters denoting speaker and listener, *I* and *you*. However, the *I* in an utterance like *Next year I will run away to sea* is also the subject of what is uttered as well as the subject of the enunciation.

In LITERARY DISCOURSE, fictive acts of enunciation are EMBEDDED in the act of enunciation between writer and reader, which may or may not be made prominent. A crude distinction has sometimes been made (see Eagleton 1983) between 'realist' fiction which suppresses its mode or mechanics of production (also scientific or legal texts), and MODERNIST, which make enunciation part of their meaning, exposing their essential artifice. (See also Easthope 1983 on the development of English poetry since the Renaissance.)

entailment

Entailment was taken into SEMANTICS from logic, like PRESUPPOSITION (q.v.), which it resembles, since both are kinds of implication. However, while it has attracted considerable attention in semantics, it has not, unlike presupposition, been taken up significantly in STYLISTICS or TEXT/DISCOURSE ANALYSIS. (But see Stubbs's (1983) work on PLOT summaries for possibilities.)

Entailment means 'logical' or 'truthful' consequence: by saying that p^1 **entails** p^2 we mean that if p^1 is true, p^2 has to be true. So given the PROPOSITION *The cow jumped over the moon*, the proposition *The cow moved* follows logically from, or is entailed by it. The reverse does not, however, apply: *The cow moved* does not necessarily entail that she jumped over the moon.

As it can be noted, any entailments made or deduced are essentially less specific, more general, or GENERIC. (Indeed, entailment has been seen as the sentential equivalent of HYPONYMY (q.v.) at word level.) We are probably largely unconscious of the entailment process in our comprehension of utterances, yet it must be continual.

The explicit use of entailment, as a kind of loose PARAPHRASING technique, can be seen in summary, whether of plot, or (commonly) in newspaper headlines. *Soldier killed in riot* is a usefully brief and truthful essential entailment of a more informative proposition which can be amplified in the article itself. At word level, it can function as a means of COHESION in a (usually formal or literary) text: to avoid repetition, a 'specific' item may be replaced by its entailed generic equivalent in a following sentence: *The Chelsea Flower Show opened yesterday. The event was marred by heavy rain.*

entropy

Originally a concept developed in the study of energy in thermodynamics in the nineteenth century, **entropy** was taken into COMMUNICATION and INFORMATION THEORY by Shannon & Weaver (1949) in opposition to REDUNDANCY (q.v.).

Both refer to degrees of predictability in a message: an **entropic** message has high unpredictability, and therefore high information value; a redundant message is highly predictable, and therefore low in information value. PHATIC utterances such as *Good morning, how are you today? – Very well, thank you* would be obvious examples of redundancy in speech; whereas LITERARY LANGUAGE, especially poetry, is characteristically entropic.

A text with no redundancy, however, is rare, and would be difficult or irritating to comprehend: a certain amount of predictability is necessary for ease of mental processing. It is no wonder, therefore, that Joyce's entropic *Finnegans Wake* remains largely unread.

There may be a shift of entropy and redundancy within a text, or within a sentence. Given a sentence beginning *The _____*, it is difficult to predict the rest; but given the sentence *I went to the opticians to have my eyes _____*, it is possible to supply a plausible completion. The longer the message, the more abundant the information. Even in poetry, the pattern of general entropy may be locally reduced by RHYME patterns, which set up expectations: *moon* rhyming with *June*, for instance.

epanalepsis

From Gk 'a taking up again' a RHETORICAL FIGURE of REPETITION; but critics vary in their descriptions of it.

(1) The simplest is to see it (e.g. Cuddon 1998) as the repetition of words after intervening words, effective for EMPHASIS or emotion, perhaps: e.g. Othello's *Put out the light and then put out the light*. This is also known as **epanadiplosis**, and Puttenham (1589) calls it the 'Echo sound'. (See also PLOCE.)

(2) Nash (1980), however, sees it more specifically as repetition of the beginning of a line or sentence at the end: e.g. *Cassius from bondage will deliver Cassius* (*Julius Caesar*).

(3) Leech (1969), by contrast, sees it as a kind of double repetition involving PARALLELISM (a . . . a) (b . . . b), as in Milton's *With ruin upon ruin, rout upon rout* (*Paradise Lost*).

epanodos

The *OED* gives two meanings for this RHETORICAL FIGURE:

(1) the return to the regular 'thread' of discourse after a digression;

(2) a kind of CHIASMUS (q.v.) in which elements of a sentence are repeated in reverse order (ab:ba). (See also ANTISTROPHE.)

There are frequent examples in Joyce's work, in passages of description, often combined with ALLITERATION. So at the end of *The Dead*: ... *the snow <u>falling</u> <u>faintly</u> through the universe and <u>faintly falling</u> ...* , and in *Portrait of the Artist: Her bosom was as a bird's <u>soft</u> and <u>slight</u>, <u>slight</u> and <u>soft</u> as the breast of some darkplumaged dove.*

(3) Cuddon's (1998) definition seems to be similar to EPANALEPSIS above, i.e. the repetition of words at the beginning and middle, or middle and end of a sentence.

epic preterite

Epic preterite, a translation of Ger. *Episches Praeteritum* or 'historical past TENSE', has been used in European criticism to refer specifically to the past tense of the FREE INDIRECT STYLE (FIS) (see Bronzwaer 1970; Stanzel 1959). This fuses the present and the past time in the consciousness of a narrator's recollections, and in effect, is no longer 'past'. The time is the 'now' of thought, and DEICTICS of present reference can co-occur: e.g. ... *and of course he <u>was</u> coming to her party <u>tonight</u>* (Woolf: *Mrs Dalloway*). The 'present' deictics represent the now of story-time [HISTOIRE] not the 'now' of DISCOURS.

As Banfield (1982) notes, the event narrated and the act of consciousness are at one. Interestingly, the epic preterite can occur in narrative passages where there is no apparent representation or thought of speech, but it still suggests a perspective of awareness or consciousness overriding the events themselves: e.g. *They were moving now, closer to the enemy; This time he saw that the danger was real.*

Hamburger (1957) sees the epic preterite as the defining feature of narration or *histoire*, and even as the distinctive marker of FICTION v. non-fiction. Although FIS is found outside literature (e.g. in newspaper reporting), certainly the combination of past tense and consciousness seems a literary device.

epic: ~ style; ~ simile

(1) The **epic** or GRAND (q.v.) or **heroic style** is a descriptive phrase for any elevated or elaborate STYLE imitative of the mode of the classical poetic epics of Homer and Virgil. So Milton's *Paradise Lost* has lengthy and intricate CLAUSE structures, Latinate DICTION, the 'machinery' of invocations, **epic similes**, and a universal seriousness of TONE.

(2) **Epic** or **homeric similes** themselves are characteristically lengthy and detailed comparisons, often complex in syntax, and formally introduced by *like* or (*just*) *as*: e.g. in the description of Satan in Book II of *Paradise Lost*:

> Incenst with indignation Satan stood
> Unterrifi'd, and *like* a Comet burnd,
> That fires the length of Ophiucus huge
> In th'Artick sky, and from his horrid hair
> Shakes Pestilence and Warr ...

Fielding in *Tom Jones* has many amusing 'mock'-epic similes, in a work which as a whole presents a comic PARODY of this GENRE. Note the EMBEDDED clauses in the following example:

> As a vast herd of cows in a rich farmer's yard if while they are milked they hear their calves at a distance, lamenting the robbery which is then committing, roar and bellow, so roared from the Somersetshire mob an hallaloo . . .

epilogue

(1) In drama, one of the FORMAL and RHETORICAL conventions which presents the play explicitly to the audience: if the **prologue** is the initial presentation, the **epilogue** is the conclusion, often spoken by a character in the play itself who may offer a 'moral', or ask for the audience's applause and indulgence (e.g. the fairy Puck at the end of *A Midsummer Night's Dream*). The actor thus breaks FRAME, steps out of the play's own WORLD; yet at the same time heightens the sense of CLOSURE.

(2) In the tradition of the novel it is a formal CODA (q.v.) or closing device, which provides the *Nachgeschichte* (details of the ultimate fates of the characters), shifting the time-scale or ORIENTATION from that of the immediate narrative to some later period. George Eliot's sentiments in the 'Finale' of *Middlemarch* are echoed by other nineteenth-century novelists, and no doubt readers:

> Every limit is a beginning as well as an ending. Who can quit young lives after being long in company with them, and not desire to know what befell them in their after-years?

epistrophe, also epiphora

A RHETORICAL device of REPETITION, the opposite to ANAPHORA (q.v.), by which the last words in successive lines, clauses or sentences are repeated: as in Othello's ironic *A fine woman! a fair woman! a sweet woman!* (IV.i).

epithet

(1) In ordinary usage, an **epithet** is likely to be taken as a descriptive (ADJECTIVE) phrase or appellation used to characterize someone, and may often be abusive (*You clumsy idiot; Fatso*, etc.). Epithets may become nicknames, as in *King Aethelred the Unready; William the Conqueror; Spotty Muldoon; Nat 'King' Cole; Jimmy 'Schnozzle' Durante.*

(2) Banfield (1982) restricts the term to a kind of NOUN PHRASE with the structure 'X of Y' involving EVALUATIVE nouns, e.g. *that idiot of a doctor, he's a devil of an organizer*; and to evaluative adjectives like *blasted; sweet; poor; bloody.*

(3) In traditional RHETORIC and POETIC DICTION, however, it refers to an 'ornamental' adjective or adjective phrase which co-occurs either with a proper

name in a kind of FORMULA, as in *bold Zeus; pious Aeneas*; or with a noun in a similar habitual COLLOCATION: *rosy-fingered dawn; wine-dark sea*. These examples, taken from classical epic, are also known as **Homeric epithets**.

Semantically, such adjectival epithets are often redundant: poetic phrases like *liquid wine* or *golden sun* illustrate **non-restrictive** MODIFICATION, i.e. the adjectives offer additional information, which is not, however, necessary to distinguish the object referred to from another: contrast *red* v. *white wine*, for instance. **Poetic epithets** are found in poetry of all periods, in oral poetry and ballads (*green sod; white bones*) and mainstream English verse alike (e.g. Keats's *creamy curd; fiery noon; green hill*).

(4) In SYSTEMIC GRAMMAR (see Halliday 1985), the term **epithet** is used very generally and FUNCTIONALLY to refer to a modifying 'slot' in the structure of the noun phrase (nominal group). This is typically filled by (most) adjectives, since it indicates 'some quality' of the noun, whether 'objective' (describing the thing itself) or 'subjective' (the speaker's attitude to it), e.g. *blue car* and *fantastic car*. PARTICIPLES also function as epithets, as in *lost cause* and *fallen idol*.

(See also TRANSFERRED EPITHET.)

epizeuxis

Colourfully called the 'cuckoo spell' by Puttenham (1589) **epizeuxis** is a FIGURE of REPETITION, with no words intervening. An artful naturalism, it is used effectively in Shakespeare's plays to suggest great intensity of feeling or emotion:

Howl, howl, howl, howl, O, you are men of stones

(*King Lear*, V.iii)

Thou'lt come no more,
Never, never, never, never, never!

(ibid.)

equivalence

(1) **Equivalence** is particularly associated with the work of Jakobson (1960) on POETIC LANGUAGE, and what he saw as its predominant characteristic: patterns of REPETITION and PARALLELISM on all levels, of sound, syntax, lexis and meaning.

Basic to all language structure and use, he argued, are the principles of CHOICE or selection (**paradigmatic**) and combination (**syntagmatic**): we choose words from equivalent expressions (*sofa*) rather than *chair* or *settee*, for instance), and combine them with others contiguously in an utterance or sentence. But in poetic language the **principle of equivalence** is extended to the syntagmatic or linear dimension; or, in other words, the paradigmatic equivalent or related elements recur contiguously. As a result, patterns of similarity (and also opposition) in sound, form and meaning are created.

To take an example from the PHONOLOGICAL level. In speech we will select the PHONEME /b/ rather than /p/ and /ɪ/ rather than /æ/ and /n/ rather than /t/ to produce /b+ɪ+n/ *bin* rather than /p+æ+t/ *pat*. But in poetic language in particular the sound /b/ may well recur in a sequence of syllables in a line, i.e. in ALLITERATION.

In the following lines from Auden's *Look Stranger*, phonological equivalences combine with syntactic equivalences (repetition of ADVERBIAL 'where'-CLAUSE; repetition of verbal nouns *pluck* and *knock*):

> Here at the small field's ending pause
> Where the chalk wall falls to the foam, and its tall ledges
> Oppose the pluck
> And knock of the tide . . .

It is one thing to isolate equivalence relations (of which, in any case, there would appear to be almost an infinite number), and another to indicate those which are poetically significant, and further, those which are thematically significant. While Jakobson's critics pointed to equivalences in non-poetic texts (e.g. advertising, legal documents, telephone directories), the sheer density in poetry of all kinds of equivalences cannot be denied, especially involving METRICAL form. However, there is a danger in Jakobsonian analysis (e.g. 1962, 1970) of seeing equivalence as the only structural device of importance.

(2) **Equivalence** is also used in the study of COHESION (q.v.) to refer to a kind of SYNONYMIC relation or VARIATIONAL device used to avoid repetition of lexical items. While it is largely associated with formal writing, it is found, for example, in popular journalism, in sentences of the kind: *Film star Rocky Clint arrived at Heathrow yesterday. The macho six-footer and father of six had the fans swooning in the arrival lounge.*

erlebte rede

(1) Literally meaning 'experienced speech', a German term coined by Lorck (1921) for the French *style indirect libre*, first discussed extensively by Bally (1912) and which in British and American criticism is now termed FREE INDIRECT STYLE/SPEECH (FIS) (q.v.). It has itself been used in English works (e.g. Quirk 1959), but FIS has largely superseded it.

Erlebte rede is a kind of INDIRECT or **reported** SPEECH in which the speech (or thoughts) of a CHARACTER and the words of the NARRATOR are blended, with no verb of reporting indicated, e.g.

> Dorothea coloured with pleasure, and looked up gratefully to the speaker./Here was a man who could understand the higher inward life, and with whom there could be some spiritual communion . . .
>
> (George Eliot: *Middlemarch*)

The second sentence evokes the character's 'experience' rather than the narrator's. Pascal (1977) reveals that German scholars themselves have never really liked the term, but it stuck: presumably out of simple convenience.

(2) Cohn (1966) uses it specifically for FREE INDIRECT THOUGHT rather than speech, or what she also calls NARRATED MONOLOGUE (q.v.).

(See also EPIC PRETERITE.)

estrangement

(1) **Estrangement** as a principle of art (see also ALIENATION and DE-AUTOMAT-IZATION) was much discussed by the **Russian** FORMALISTS and the PRAGUE SCHOOL linguists, and put into practice by artists of the Weimar Republic, notably Brecht in his *Verfremdung* effect in the epic theatre.

Shklovsky (1917) believed that the function of art was *ostranenie* 'making strange', making the familiar unfamiliar, heightening awareness, in painting, sculpture and photography as well as in literature. The degree of estrangement may vary: surrealism and absurdist theatre represent a radical distortion of reality, PARODY less so; fresh METAPHORS force the reader to look again at every-day objects or well-known experience. LITERARY LANGUAGE generally may be seen to be characteristically **estranging**, FOREGROUNDING the features of ordinary language by REPETITION or DEVIATION, and in consequence forcing our renewed attention to the meaning.

(2) **Estrangement** or **alienation devices** have also been exploited as an analytical technique in DISCOURSE ANALYSIS and ETHNOMETHODOLOGY (q.v.) (see, e.g., Garfinkel 1967). Even transcribing conversation into writing or a phonetic transcription is useful for revealing aspects of speech which may normally elude our ears: making the familiar strange.

(3) The specific phrase **words of estrangement** has been used in novel theory as an aspect of FOCALIZATION or PERSPECTIVE, following Uspensky (1973). These are MODAL expressions which signify the narrator's clear distance from the con-sciousness of the character being described (and so contrasts with FREE INDIRECT STYLE (q.v.)): VERBS and ADVERBS of speculation, interpretation or tentativeness (*seem, apparently, as if*, etc.).

Such estrangement devices may suggest realism: that the OMNISCIENT NAR-RATOR, however omniscient, cannot enter the minds of the characters. But since entering minds is so evidently 'normal' in fiction, it is the estranging, in any case usually sporadic, which is 'marked'. Austen and George Eliot make playful, even irritatingly arch use of the device, switching outside and inside the minds of their heroines, as in this example from *Northanger Abbey*:

> Whether Catherine thought of Tilney so much, while she drank her warm wine and water, and prepared herself for bed, as to dream of him when there, cannot be ascertained . . .

As Fowler (1977) notes, techniques of estrangement can more generally be exploited to suggest other kinds of distance: e.g. for moral distance (as with unpleasant or villainous characters); or for enigmatic distance, to heighten the sense of mystery.

ethical: ~ stylistics

Ethical stylistics is Wales's term (1995) for what she sees as a future direction for STYLISTICS, in line with developments elsewhere and the logical implication of its own position. Recent developments in such disciplines as CRITICAL LINGUISTICS and CRITICAL DISCOURSE ANALYSIS (CDA), FEMINIST CRITICISM, cultural studies and DECONSTRUCTION have revealed that not only is there no such thing as a 'neutral' or 'objective' STYLE, but no such thing as a neutral speaker or writer. Areas of bias and SUBJECTIVITY frequently exposed and analysed include journalism, politics, police interrogations, warfare and pornography, which are also areas where ethical issues can be raised. The question arises, therefore, as to whether stylistics can or should avoid moral or value judgments; and whether also it might not intervene pragmatically in the non-academic world, along the lines of forensic linguistics. Certainly, one aim of CDA is to raise 'critical language awareness' (Fairclough 1992b), especially in schools; and supposedly it is committed to making social changes through forms of direct intervention involving language, but its success is open to dispute. More successful in English-speaking societies, certainly, has been the gradual elimination by the end of the twentieth century of sexual and other forms of linguistic discrimination following the interventions of feminists and the 'political correctness' movement.

It is a notable fact, nonetheless, that stylistics has fought shy even of value judgments, of EVALUATION; possibly as a back-lash from the Leavisite tradition in LITERARY CRITICISM on the one hand, and the PRESCRIPTIVISM tradition in grammar on the other. Yet outside academe, issues to do with the reformation of style in order to cut out obfuscation and ambiguity in legalese and bureaucratese, have met with practical success in Britain by the Plain English Campaign.

(See also VERBAL HYGIENE. See further Toolan 1997.)

ethnography of communication/speaking

Not to be confused with ETHNOMETHODOLOGY below, **ethnography** is a kind of large-scale sociolinguistic study which investigates patterns of speaking in relation to ethnic and social groups and cultural differences (see the work of Dell Hymes 1962f in particular).

Ethnography has been important in the study of COMMUNICATIVE COMPETENCE (q.v.) and CODE-SWITCHING (q.v.), with the probing of the 'rules' of social interaction and of variables of REGISTER or SPEECH EVENT (topic, setting, participants, etc.). More generally, interesting cultural differences have been revealed in 'norms' of conversational behaviour (e.g. the role of silence).

(See further Coulthard 1977, ch. 3.)

ethnomethodology

A branch of sociology, concerned with the study of social interaction, in which linguistic interaction clearly plays an important part. In particular it has led to closer scrutiny of conversational behaviour and structures, of relevance to DISCOURSE ANALYSIS and PRAGMATICS. (See the work of Sacks of Schegloff in the 1970s, e.g. Sacks, Schegloff and Jefferson 1974, on ADJACENCY PAIRS and TURN-TAKING, for instance.)

etymological: ~ meaning; ~ fallacy

(1) In everyday usage we are largely unaware of or unconcerned about the **etymological** or original **meaning** of words, and even in linguistics, the study of word origins (**etymology**) has a minor place today, although it has played an important part in DIACHRONIC studies.

However, for words derived from classical languages, which make up a large proportion of scientific vocabulary, for instance, a knowledge of origins can help us to know their meanings: e.g. *micro-scopic* (Gk 'small-seeing'); *stereo-phonic* (Gk 'solid-sounding'); *quadri-lateral* (Lat. 'four-sided').

In LITERARY LANGUAGE many writers have deliberately invoked the original classical meanings of words for particular effects, aware that their readers would share the same knowledge. In Milton's *Paradise Lost*, such etymological licence is part of his EPIC STYLE. So when he compares Satan to the comet with burning tail like *horrid hair*, he means it is 'bristling, rough' (cf. Lat. *horridus*).

(2) Although changes in meaning are inevitable, it has been a long-held belief or desire by many people that words should maintain a stable meaning, and that the **etymological meaning** is the CORRECT or 'true' one. (Indeed, etymology itself is derived from the Greek *etumos* meaning 'true', and it was the Greek Stoics in the fifth century BC who first stated this view.) This **etymological fallacy** is not supported by linguists, who point out that for many words the etymology is not known. And although (mostly older) people might complain about the 'misuse' of *genocide* or *viable*, there are thousands of words in everyday speech patently being used in senses far removed from their original ones (*black* originally meant 'pale', for instance).

The 'etymological' or 'original' meaning is in any case a fiction, since the earliest recorded or reconstructed meaning of a word or its root is the result of prehistoric developments which we cannot recover. (See also USAGE.)

euphemism

From the Gk 'well-speak', the substitution of an inoffensive or pleasant expression for a more unpleasant one, or for a term which more directly evokes a distasteful or TABOO subject.

Offensive topics vary from period to period and from society to society. We are not so coy about pregnancy and sex as our forebears, although we may resort to substitutions (or SLANG equivalents), e.g. in front of children (*She's in the family way; they're 'living together'*). Bella Wilfer's revelation of her pregnancy to her husband in Dickens's *Our Mutual Friend* strikes the modern reader as distinctly cloying:

> Do you remember, John, on the day we were married, Pa's speaking of the ships that might be sailing towards us from the unknown seas?
> – I think – among them – there is a ship upon the ocean – bringing – to you and me – a little baby, John.

But defecation and death, for example, continue to be topics for **euphemisms** (*If anything should happen to me; passed away/on; powder room*, etc.).

In DECONSTRUCTIONIST terms, the process of euphemistic substitution is endless 'deferral' (see DIFFÉRANCE). For the euphemism, precisely because it is itself associated with a distasteful subject, can itself also be displaced by another. So *coffin* replaces *box*, and *casket* replaces *coffin*; ME *shit-house* is replaced by *lavatory* is replaced by *toilet* is replaced by *loo*, etc.

In ordinary conversation euphemism can be seen as a natural result of what Leech (1983) has termed the POLITENESS **principle**: we will 'avoid unpleasantness' so as to spare other people's feelings, or to maintain our own FACE (q.v.). Many unpleasant or unskilled occupations are semantically 'up-graded' by JARGONISTIC euphemisms: *rotating delivery officer* (postman); *street cleansing operative* (road-cleaner).

In certain REGISTERS, however, euphemism is more consciously exploited in the mitigation of unpleasant subjects by what Leech (1981) aptly terms ASSOCIATIVE ENGINEERING to promote a more positive or brighter image. In the domain of advertising, fat old women do not exist, only fuller, mature figures; and in house-selling ads, a 'character' house 'in need of some redecoration' is probably falling apart. More seriously, euphemism, can promote a false 'rose-coloured' WORLD-VIEW. Anthony Burgess (*TLS*, 12 April 1985) nicely referred to **euglots** for the regular euphemistic vocabulary of DOMAINS such as politics, where *deterrent* means 'bomb', and *peacekeeper* 'missile', and where ACRONYMS can be used euphemistically if we don't know what they stand for (e.g. *GSD* applied to radiation): an aspect of Orwellian 'nukespeak' (Chilton 1985).

euphony

(1) From Gk 'well-sound', used in traditional LITERARY CRITICISM to mean 'pleasing sound(s)'. (Its opposite is **cacophony**, 'ill-sound'.)

However, it is hard to imagine a term less critically useful and more highly subjective and impressionistic. **Euphony** is certainly less useful than ONOMATOPOEIA (q.v.), for at least that relates sound effects to meaning. What is euphonious depends on the critic's ear and AESTHETIC tastes, and notions of an AFFECTIVE response (producing pleasurable sensations, e.g. of regularity).

(2) However, the avoidance of rather awkward conjunctions of sounds seems to be a factor in certain sound changes where pronunciations of words have been simplified, and **euphony** could describe such processes. So *Leicester* and *Worcester* are pronounced /lestə/ and /wustə/ to avoid repetition of the FRICATIVE /s/. And in NEOLOGISMS, too, euphony may play a part: a brand name for a new kind of soap powder must be easy to pronounce, otherwise no-one will ask for it by name: *Persil* is more acceptable than *Pseril*.

evaluative meaning; evaluation

(1) For Palmer (1981) **evaluative meaning** is akin to EMOTIVE MEANING (q.v.): there are words which affect our emotions because they have CONNOTATIONS of approval or disapproval (e.g. *bitch* v. *lady*; and exclamations and oaths typically). Generally, he argues, in everyday language much of what we say is not a statement of fact, and CONCEPTUAL MEANINGS not necessarily paramount. We are continually assessing situations, people, others' speech (see also FEEDBACK).

In certain types of discourse **evaluation** plays an important part, and is 'built into' the GRAMMAR and LEXIS: in reviews, project or experiment assessments, certain kinds of journalistic article, etc.

(2) So in CONTEXTUAL GRAMMAR (see Winter 1982) **evaluation** is one of the major CLAUSE RELATIONS (q.v.), realized in constructions such as *There is no justification for . . . ; It is not true that; This sounds strange, but it's true*; and phrases or disjuncts like *in my opinion, speaking frankly*, etc.

(3) And in DISCOURSE ANALYSIS, **evaluation** is the name of a functional MOVE in a unit of exchange, e.g. between teacher and pupil in the classroom (see Coulthard 1977). An initial question (*What is the capital of Greece?*) can produce the answer, *Athens*, and the teacher's feedback, *Good* or *Well done*, etc. (Outside the classroom, this kind of evaluation can sound patronizing.)

(4) In the analysis of (oral) NARRATIVES, Labov & Waletsky (1967) proposed **evaluation** as a component part, following ORIENTATION and **complication**, and preceding **resolution** and CODA. Evaluation indicates the point or interest of the story on the part of the speaker. However, in Labov (1972) he revised the schema, and rightly proposed that evaluation could occur more freely in a narrative sequence. It can obviously occur at the beginning: *I've just had this wonderful experience/heard this fantastic joke*, etc.

In the novel, 'evaluation' is hard to delimit solely in terms of a structural component or division. Explicit evaluation, often ethical, is the mark of the PERSPECTIVE of an OMNISCIENT NARRATOR, and may be found anywhere, e.g. as a comment on a character's actions or thoughts, or a device for arousing the reader's ESTRANGEMENT or sympathy. And actual endings, or EPILOGUES (q.v.) are traditionally places where moral conclusions can be drawn (as in 'fables').

(5) In the larger discourse situation involving the reader's response to a literary text, **evaluation** has an important, if contentious and problematic role. In traditional LITERARY CRITICISM the criteria by which judgments of 'goodness' and 'badness' have been made have varied. Truth to life, or degree of realism is

one such criterion; interesting plot or unusual theme, another. Generally, however, evaluation appears to be a kind of disciplined subjectivity.

More influential on academic criticism (and university syllabuses) have been the ideas of Leavis in the 1930s, who postulated a literary CANON of texts, the 'great tradition', based on cultural, social, ethical and formal criteria. 'Major' and 'minor' authors were distinguished, as well as 'major' and 'minor' texts. Not all critics have agreed with Leavis; and many writers have been subsequently re-appraised or 'elevated' (women writers like Elizabeth Gaskell, for instance).

More radically, this whole evaluative process has been rejected by some critics for its subjectivity and IDEOLOGICAL bias (see Eagleton 1983); and rejected too is the evaluation implied in LITERARINESS. All kinds of discourse are deemed equally worthy of study, and no evaluative comparisons are made between them.

In so far as criticism implies INTERPRETATION, interpretation involves evaluation, if only of those features intrinsically deemed worthy of consideration, or significant for the elucidation of the text's adjudged meaning, or for their contribution to its 'unity'.

(6) In STYLISTICS, the role of **evaluation** has been something of an embarrassment. In the early days of stylistics in the 1960s, any kind of 'literary criticism' was frequently voiced as being undesirable (e.g. Crystal & Davy 1969); but stylistics typically combines the linguistic approach of systematic description of textual features, and the critical approach of literary appreciation, so that it is of necessity concerned with interpretation: with the literary effect of linguistic features, and their contribution to the overall meaning of the text.

Where evaluations are made, these are intrinsic to the text, i.e. assessments of the effectiveness or APPROPRIATENESS of linguistic features to their perceived function. Frequently, however, unless it is explicitly stated otherwise, assessments are assumed to be positive. As Leech (1985) says, stylistic analysis does not result in a value judgment, but rather assumes it: a kind of 'prejudice' in favour of the work being examined. (See also Short 1961, ch. 1.)

For ordinary language users, however, evaluation of styles may be brought to the attention by failures in communication: through AMBIGUITY, prolixity, JARGON, REPETITION, etc. Certainly, in society at large, certain modes of discourse are valued more than others (excessive CO-ORDINATION is regarded as 'unsophisticated', for example); and perhaps stylistic studies generally should pay more attention to the RHETORIC of composition, and the pragmatic assessment of 'models' of style, along the lines of Nash (1980). (See also ETHICAL STYLISTICS.)

existential sentence

Despite the name, this has nothing whatever to do with the philosophy of existentialism! On the contrary, **existential sentence** in GRAMMAR describes a construction which states that something 'exists', and which is formally identifiable by the pattern *there* (= non-locative ADVERB as 'dummy' SUBJECT and THEME) + *be* ('exist') + logical subject + X (= rest of CLAUSE), as in *(Waiter, waiter) there is a fly in my soup; There's no business like show business;* etc. Such sentences can be seen to be related in form to more straightforward patterns, such as: *A fly* (subject) *is in my soup; No business is like show business*; but as these very paraphrases suggest, the existential equivalent is by far the commoner alternative, since it allows the desired special FOCUS to fall on a post-VERBAL, rather than pre-verbal element, i.e. the normal position for focussing, or for NEW INFORMATION. The subject slot is normally reserved for less significant, or for GIVEN INFORMATION (i.e. as theme).

Existential sentences are particularly useful if the grammatical subjects are 'heavy' or complex, and accord with the **principle of** END-WEIGHT (q.v.): *There wasn't one word of sympathy or understanding for the departing Foreign Minister* (an example not paraphrasable, in fact, in terms of subject + *be*).

In FORMAL, especially LITERARY, English other verbs than *be* can be found, e.g.: *Once upon a time there lived a poor woodcutter; There may come a time when you will regret your actions; There rose in the distance a huge cloud of yellow dust.*

exophoric reference

One of a pair of terms popularized by Halliday & Hasan (1976), referring to CONTEXTUAL or SITUATIONAL REFERENCE (**exophoric**); as distinct from TEXTUAL reference (ENDOPHORIC, q.v.).

Exophoric reference may be 'specific', i.e. referring to the immediate situational context in which the discourse is taking place; or 'generalized' or **homophoric**, referring to the larger cultural context or shared knowledge. Contrast the functions of the DEFINITE ARTICLE *the* in phrases like *Mind the step; and the world today*. The **first** and **second** PERSON PRONOUNS (*I, we* and *you*) are typically exophoric, singling out the participants in the discourse; whereas the **third** person pronouns (*she, it, he, they*) are typically endophoric, referring to NOUN PHRASES in the CO-TEXT. However, in sentences like *They're always digging up the roads round here, they* functions exophorically.

Exophoric reference is particularly important in dramatic texts for helping to establish the situational dimensions of the WORLD of the play, its **universe of discourse**.

exordium

In classical RHETORIC a **division** of an oration which marks the opening or intro-duction. An alternative name is **proemium**. One function is to put the listener in the right frame of mind by the 'capturing of good will' (**captatio benevolentiae**), so as to be receptive to what follows: as in Mark Antony's *Friends, Romans and countrymen, lend me your ears* (Shakespeare: *Julius Caesar*). Jests or fables were attention-catching devices, means of insinuation (**insinuatio**). Such devices are still used by politicians and lecturers.

Many openings of novels can be regarded similarly as formal introductions. So Fielding devotes the first chapter of *Joseph Andrews* to putting his own novel in context, with a consideration of 'biography' and of Richardson's *Pamela*.

expression

(1) As a count noun, **expression** is used in linguistics and STYLISTICS to refer very generally to words or phrases which 'express' a meaning, especially in a particular context. So we can say that the expression *finny tribe* was used to refer to 'fish' in eighteenth-century POETIC DICTION.

(2) As a non-count noun, **expression** is also used in linguistics following de Saussure (1974/1916) to describe a level or plane of language, opposed to CONTENT (q.v.). Very crudely, a distinction is made between 'what' is said, and 'how' it is said (expression).

What expression consists of is not always made clear, and it is frequently used synonymously with FORM (q.v.). But they can be seen to be distinct. Expression, involving PHONOLOGY and SYNTAX, 'expresses' or realizes content or meaning through the mediation of form: the actual patterns of sound and syntax, and also LEXIS. Halliday (1978) has argued that in the early stages of linguistic development, children have only the two-level contrast of expression and content, and that form, the more abstract level relating expression to content, comes later. Their CODING system is thus comparable to traffic lights, where the coloured signals are the expression, and their meanings the content. Expressions (*sic*) like *Teddy* and *choo-choo* may be invariable, and may not be conjoined with others in UTTERANCES.

Hjelmslev (1943) refined the Saussurean distinction to include **substance** as well as form, and argued in any case that form cuts across content. So the **substance of expression** is its material nature, the sounds or their GRAPHEMIC subsitutes in writing.

Chatman (1978) applied the whole model to the novel, where **expression** corresponds generally to DISCOURS, and content to HISTOIRE (q.v.). The substance of expression is the actual physical manifestation of the narrative, whether verbal or cinematic, for example; the **form of expression** is the narrative in its sequence. The **substance of content** is the whole universe on which the novelist draws for inspiration; the **form of content** is the PLOT.

expressive: ~ meaning; ~ function; ~ stylistics, etc.

(1) **Expressive meaning** is sometimes used in SEMANTICS as an alternative to AFFECTIVE or ATTITUDINAL or EMOTIVE MEANING in referring to the emotional ASSOCIATIONS of words evoked in the user; and also to meanings which indicate the attitudes or feelings of the user.

Many of the exclamations and metaphoric IDIOMS of colloquial speech have expressive meaning: *down in the dumps; in the doldrums; sick to the teeth;* etc.

Expressive devices are affective or CONATIVE in so far as they can also trigger a response in the listener.

(2) LITERARY LANGUAGE is often said to be **expressive**, in that it generally evokes associations over and above CONCEPTUAL MEANINGS, and also in its

manipulation of the FORM of language through RHYTHM, sound patterns, REPE-TITION, etc., to 'express' or emphasize feelings or attitudes. It is also evocative or affective in its design on the responses of the reader. Related is Leech's (1983) **expressivity principle**, an aspect of textual RHETORIC.

Often, however, **expressive** and **expressiveness** are simply used to mean 'vivid(ness)' or 'effective(ness)'.

(3) Various FUNCTIONAL classifications of language distinguish an **expressive function**.

Lyons (1977) distinguishes the **expressive** from the **descriptive** (i.e. factual or informative) and the **social** (interactive). Utterances that are expressive in this sense identify the speaker's feelings or personality. He acknowledges that the distinctions are far from clear-cut, and that in any case an utterance may have more than one function. So *I'd love a cup of coffee* is informative as well as expressive, and may be interactive in the sense of implying that the hearer should actually fetch or make one.

Influential was the similar distinction of Bühler (1934), between the functions of **representation**; VOCATIVE (*Appel*); and **expression** (*Ausdrück*), according to whether reference is made to the outside world; the hearer; or the speaker. Essentially characterizing the speaker, the expressive function is thus marked by IDIOLECTAL features of rhythm and IDIOM, etc.

More controversial, however, is the connection he made between the express-ive function and POETIC LANGUAGE. Even in lyric poetry we cannot assume that it is the feelings of the poet that are being expressed. (See also (4) below.) However, given the common assumption of an *I*-PERSONA, the lyric poetry of Wordsworth or Shelley, for instance, characteristically FOREGROUNDS the feelings of the 'speaker'.

From Bühler developed Jakobson's (1960) model of the SPEECH EVENT (q.v.), identifying the main components involved in COMMUNICATION, and the different functions of language correlated with them. His EMOTIVE FUNCTION (q.v.) sim-ilarly reveals an orientation towards the speaker and his or her feelings, and can be equated with the expressive function.

(4) Plett (1977) uses the term **expressive stylistics** as a general category of stylistic approaches which are speaker or writer-centred, and which imply an old-fashioned view of STYLE itself as revealing the personality or 'soul' of the writer. It is particularly associated with the work of Croce (1922), Vossler (1932) and Spitzer (1948).

On a more objective basis, however, expressive stylistics may be seen to survive in notions of style as IDIOLECT: in the idea that Dickens has a style that is different from Trollope's or Thackeray's. Certainly this view of style is central to STYLOMETRY, involved in historical questions of authorship.

(5) In SPEECH ACT THEORY the **expressive** (noun) is one of Searle's (1975f) categories of ILLOCUTIONARY ACTS (q.v.). It is a type of UTTERANCE in which speakers make known their feelings or attitudes to the state of affairs at issue. Apologies, congratulations, thanks and condolences are common expressives.

extradiegesis; extradiegetic

In Genette's (1972) work on NARRATIVE, **extradiegesis** arises in the discussion of narrative or DIEGETIC levels, or the EMBEDDING of one narrative in another. (See also FRAMING.)

Third PERSON NARRATORS are commonly **extradiegetic**, telling the STORY which constitutes the main narrative level (e.g. in the novels of Jane Austen). An **intradiegetic** narrator is on the same level of reality as the characters in the story told: e.g. Gulliver, Ishmael, Jane Eyre (usually **first** person narrators). Stories embedded within stories constitute a level 'below', i.e. METADIEGETIC or **hypodiegetic**.

(See further Rimmon-Kenan 1983.)

extrafictional voice

A rather subtle distinction introduced into the discussion of the DISCOURSE of the novel by Lanser (1981) as a refinement on the notions of AUTHOR (q.v.) and IMPLIED AUTHOR (q.v.).

Attention in LITERARY CRITICISM, where it has not focussed on the responses and role of the READER, has focussed on the implied author figure (see Booth 1961): the 'Fielding' or 'Austen' who may address the reader directly or indirectly through the work, and whose opinions may or may not coincide with those of the real Fielding or Austen.

However, Lanser argues that even the implied author is inevitably constructed by the reader partly from what is known about the real author, whose presence cannot utterly be banished even from the text. (It is the real author, for instance, who normally subdivides the novel into chapters and gives them titles.) Readers, in fact, respect the AUTHORITY of a novel as a criticism of society or human nature as being based not only on the author-PERSONA within the text, but also on the posited or assumed real author: the **extrafictional voice**. This VOICE is therefore the textual counterpart of the historical author: e.g. the voice of Dickens criticizing the society of Victorian England in his novels like *Oliver Twist* and *Hard Times*.

eye-dialect

The use of non-STANDARD spelling in LITERATURE (e.g. DIALOGUE in drama and novels) to suggest non-standard pronunciations, which in fact, are not non-standard at all; or rather, no different from standard pronunciations: e.g. *woz* or *wuz* (was), *wimmin* (women). These are sometimes interspersed with forms that do attempt to record DIALECTAL pronunciations or forms, as in Dickens's Mrs Gamp: *Oh Sairey, Sairey, little do we know wot lays afore us!* (*Martin Chuzzlewit*).

Visually, the effect is to give an illusion of speech that is different from standard English. However, the disturbing implication is that such DEVIANT spellings may suggest spelling errors, and so a view of dialectal speech that aligns it with social inferiority and illiteracy. In the novel tradition it is usually the 'lower' class characters whose speech is so transcribed (and certainly not the main characters).

eye-rhyme

A licence in RHYME which has developed particularly in the modern period, by which associations are made through spelling and not sound: e.g. *great/meat; find/wind* (noun). (See also HOMOGRAPH.)

In poetry of earlier periods, what seem to be such imperfect rhymes are simply reflections of true pronunciations now obsolete: e.g. Shakespeare's *wind* (noun)/*unkind*.

F

fabula

One of a pair of terms (see also SJUŽET) introduced into the theory of NARRAT-IVE by the **Russian** FORMALISTS in the 1920s (notably Shklovsky 1925).

For any narrative there are two levels: the SURFACE level with the actual sequence of events as narrated (*sjužet*); and the DEEP level, the abstracted chronological or logical ordering possible of the events (i.e. **fabula**). Readers of novels and spectators of plays and films will gradually work out the underlying logic of the action from the succession of events before them, from the flashbacks or anticipations, and from inferences, or actual GAPS, in the narrative. In simple narratives *fabula* and *sjužet* will normally coincide; in a novel like Faulkner's *The Sound and the Fury* the relationship is more complex.

There is no precise equivalent for this term in English (cf. Lat. *fabula* 'discourse') since the literal 'fable' already has an accepted meaning as a story with a moral (cf. Aesop's Fables). It corresponds to the French STRUCTURALIST term HISTOIRE (q.v.), and STORY has sometimes been used to translate *fabula* and *histoire* alike (see Chatman 1978), despite the ambivalence of this term itself in English.

An interest in the level of *fabula* is reflected in the Formalist study of what Propp (1928) calls the MORPHOLOGY of folk-tales, the underlying (universal) structural configurations of participant ROLES and actions, e.g. 'hero' and 'villain', and the 'quest' MOTIF.

(See also PLOT; RÉCIT.)

face

Face in sociology is much associated with the work of Goffman (1955f), which was subsequently developed by Brown & Levinson (1978, 1987) in connection with the social norms of conversational behaviour into an influential theory known as POLITENESS THEORY (q.v.).

Face is the 'positive social value' we claim for ourselves, based on approved social attributes. It is related to the CO-OPERATIVE PRINCIPLE: we tacitly agree to maintain the faces or images of others, and others will maintain ours. So in many cultures it is not considered polite to be disagreeable, aggressive or tactless, even among friends; and if we have to confront people we will resort to indirect methods and expression, so as not to 'lose face', or to threaten that of our interlocutor's by **face threatening acts** (FTAs).

In addition to **positive face**, politeness theory distinguishes **negative face**, which refers to basic rights to freedom of action, of ourselves and our interlocutors. Again, mitigating strategies such as HEDGES (*I hate to impose but . . .*) avoid imposition and lessen the threat to another's face.

The more a person is in the public limelight, the more important will be the public image, and the presentation of self through language. Politicians now employ spin-doctors to 'sell' their images as well as party policies; and will often release carefully worded statements, involving, e.g. EUPHEMISM or PERIPHRASIS, to avoid controversy or public loss of face (e.g. *We had a frank exchange of views*).

(See also ROLE.)

feedback

Taken into DISCOURSE ANALYSIS (and other disciplines such as the theory of education) from COMMUNICATION studies, **feedback** refers to the process whereby a receiver's reactions to a MESSAGE are picked up by the sender and monitored, so that adjustments can be made if necessary.

In the context of public speaking, a lecturer, for example, will normally respond to NON-VERBAL signals or **back-channelling** (facial expressions of incomprehension, boredom or somnolence). In ordinary conversation the signals can be verbal as well as non-verbal, since the listener as potential interlocutor has an active rather than passive role: items such as *Yes, Mmm, really?, I see*, etc., acknowledge the listener's understanding, and also serve to endorse or query the speaker's words, without actually interrupting the other's flow. In telephone conversations such verbal signals are important, in the absence of face-to-face contact. Extended silence on the part of the listener is likely to provoke utterances like *Are you still there?* Extended silence even in face-to-face contact is likely to appear MARKED in some way.

In the theatre or in the television studio, silence on the part of the audience is a highly negative signal to the performers, and feedback in the way of laughter, applause and even booing, is welcomed. (In the dramatic DIALOGUE on stage, however, the feedback signals of 'real' speech are not always present.)

For literature, direct feedback from the reader is impossible; but dramatic rises or falls in sales of books are one kind of indirect feedback, and critical reviews another. The writer may anticipate potential feedback, however, from an IMPLIED READER, and so 'build' it into the discourse of the text. For a nineteenth-century serial novelist like Dickens, it was actually possible for an author to respond week by week to the critical reception of the serial parts of a novel published in magazine form.

felicity conditions

In SPEECH ACT THEORY **felicity conditions** refer to particular kinds of APPROPRI-
ATENESS valid for the successful functioning of speech acts, e.g. promising,
ordering, threatening, requesting, etc. Utterances which do not satisfy various
conditions are regarded as infelicitous, and, in a sense, as invalid speech acts.

One kind of felicity or **appropriateness condition (preparatory)** depends on
the utterer having the cultural 'authority' to perform a given type of speech
act: not everyone can christen a baby, or open Parliament, for example. And
a marriage ceremony that is not conducted by a minister or registrar would
normally be regarded as 'null and void' (sea-captains are an exception).

So-called **sincerity conditions** assume that the speaker is telling the truth: a
fact which is of immense importance in a law court (see also Grice's **maxim of**
QUALITY (q.v.)). **Essential conditions** mean that the speaker is normally committed to certain beliefs or INTENTIONS in performing a speech act. There is no
point in asking someone to fetch you a cup of tea if you do not want it; or
promising someone a present if you have no intention of keeping your promise.

feminine rhyme

This has come into English PROSODY from French, where it more properly
belongs. It is based on the extra syllable needed in the METRE when, for example,
the adjective is feminine: e.g. *petit; petite*. In English, **feminine rhymes** are multi-
syllabic, involving unstressed endings, e.g.

> / ×
> Little Jack Horner
> / ×
> Sat in a corner

They are contrasted with so-called MASCULINE rhymes which are monosyllabic
and therefore STRESSED or 'strong': as in *June, moon*.

Rhymes containing final unstressed syllables are not so common in the
English verse tradition generally as monosyllabic rhymes. Attridge (1982) suggests that this is because they lack a sense of CLOSURE. They are exploited for
humorous purposes in Byron's *Don Juan*, where words rhyme with phrases,
and so unstressed words are highlighted: *pudding/mud in; persuaded/they did;
intellectual/hen-pecked you all*, etc.

feminist: ~ criticism; ~ linguistics; ~ stylistics, etc.

(1) **Feminist (literary) criticism** is a discipline that rapidly developed within
the last two decades of the twentieth century, particularly in the United States,
Britain and France, as an offshoot of the larger feminist movement concerned
with the political, social and economic equality of the sexes. It has many forms,

and no single theoretical approach, although DECONSTRUCTION THEORY and READER-RESPONSE CRITICISM have been influential. One strand has probed the understanding of literature (predominantly written by men) through the experience of reading as a woman, and queried the supposed 'objectivity' or 'neutrality' and 'universality' of the written discourse. Another has queried the EVALUATIVE procedures which have established a CANON of literary works where 'minor' writers are predominantly women writers. Another has discussed the (frequently misogynistic) images of women in the literary works themselves. The work of Cixous (1975) and other French critics exposed the strong PHALLO-CENTRIC (q.v.) bias of the influential psychoanalytical theory of Freud. And what Showalter (1979) called **gynocriticism** is the study of women writers by women, and here the critical writings of Virginia Woolf have been a major influence. Generally, feminist criticism in more recent years has tended to emphasize, in all sorts of ways, the differences between the sexes and the whole idea of 'gender' as a linguistic or textual construct. However, in the early period of the feminist movement as a whole the emphasis was on 'sameness', in attempts to argue and fight for women's equality with men. (See further Mary Eagleton 1996; Moi 1985.)

(2) Not surprisingly, feminism has inevitably influenced views about lan-guage, the very medium of literary reality, and the real-world codification of social values. In **feminist linguistics** the early work of Spender (1980) and of others influenced by LINGUISTIC DETERMINISM, has drawn attention to sexual stereotyping in language, and the way women are MARKED in GRAMMAR and also in the MEDIA as if inferior, subordinate or simply non-existent.

Such work has been influential in linguistic 'engineering' to eliminate sexual bias. Even in Britain, SUFFIXES like -man, -woman and -ess are now avoided in job advertising as a result of public policy to eliminate sexual discrimination: e.g. *draughters* not *draughtsmen*, *flight attendants* not *air hostesses* are needed. The use of the pronoun *he* as a GENERIC to include male and female (as in *the speaker/reader/character . . . he*) is now mostly avoided in critical writings, for example, in favour of *he or she; (s)he;* or *she*. In colloquial speech and informal writing anyway, *they*-forms are commonly used (e.g. *If a customer wants their account queried . . .*).

Parallel to the critical view that men and women may differ in their ways of thinking and perceiving reality, is the interest in sociolinguistics in investigating differences between male and female speech. In Western societies general differ-ences have certainly been assumed: e.g. that women 'gossip' and 'rabbit on' (cf. Dickens's garrulous Flora Finching and Mrs Nickleby); but objective evidence has been hard to collect. And it may well be that loquacity is itself measured against a male 'norm'. Certainly from studies in DISCOURSE ANALYSIS there is evidence to suggest that men are far more likely to interrupt other speakers, and 'hold the floor', than women although general issues of 'power' are raised here. (See further Cameron 1992; Coates 1986; Wales (ed.) 1994.)

(3) From developments in both (1) and (2) has come the more recent sub-discipline **feminist stylistics** or **feminist text analysis**. The first term has been popularized by Mills (e.g. 1995), and generally feminist stylistics aims to provide

a gender perspective on the critical analysis of literary and media texts, using 'tools' from stylistics and CDA. It looks at issues of sexism and IDEOLOGY, of agency and FOCALIZATION, etc., in textual practices, and addresses also relations between IMPLIED READERS and their 'real' socially and historically situated counterparts. (See also Threadgold 1997 on a **feminist poetics**.)

fiction; fictionality, etc.

(1) **Fiction** is most likely to be thought of as a GENRE consisting of imaginary and imaginative prose NARRATIVES, chiefly novels, but also short stories: the essence of LITERATURE, in other words.

This is fine, as long as we recognize that fictional literature is not all fiction (e.g. some novels may refer to 'real' events or people not **fictitious**); not all literature is fiction (there is poetry and drama as well as the novel, and lyric as well as narrative poetry); nor is all literature **fictional** (we may study Donne's sermons, or the Authorized Version of the Bible as literature). Conversely, not all fiction is literature: fictional (i.e. imaginative) discourse is found in jokes (*There was an Englishman, an Irishman, and a Scotsman* . . .); mathematical problems (*Two plumbers take three hours to fill a tank* . . .) and TV and radio advertising particularly.

The fictional status of certain kinds of DISCOURSE or SPEECH ACT may be hard to determine: e.g. avowedly autobiographical novels, or the so-called **factional** novels of D. M. Thomas. The criterion may simply be PRAGMATIC: whether we EVALUATE it by the standards of truth and falsehood. We assume an auto-biography to be true, but not necessarily an autobiographical novel. So news-reporting is assumed to be **non-fictional**, whether or not it actually always is.

(2) To the extent that most literature of all kinds (novel, poetry, drama) creates an imaginative WORLD, **fictionality** can be seen to be an important characteristic, and has sometimes been seen as a significant aspect of LITERARINESS. But just as some critics see 'degrees' of literariness, so it is arguable that some **fictional worlds** are closer to the real world than others: historical novels versus Terry Pratchett's 'Discworld' novels, for example. Moreover, what is debated in philo-sophy is the relations between these worlds, the 'real' world, and POSSIBLE WORLDS (q.v.). (See also SIMULACRUM. See further Ronen 1994; Ryan 1991; Walton 1978.)

field: semantic ~; lexical ~; ~ of discourse

(1) In SEMANTICS the ideas of **semantic** or **conceptual fields** derives chiefly from the work of German and Swiss scholars in the 1920s and 1930s (e.g. Trier 1934), although it is close to earlier principles of thesaurus-making like Roget's.

The vocabulary of a language is seen not as a vast number of simple LEXICAL ITEMS, but as comprising groups of items which 'realize' or give structure to areas or DOMAINS of REFERENCE in the real world. So the semantic field of colour, for instance, is reflected in English by the **lexical field** or LEXICAL SET of items of colour terms, whether basic (*red; yellow; blue*) or descriptive (*pillar-box/flame red*, etc.). Lexical fields, because of continual changes in the vocabulary, are not normally as stable as the semantic; and different communities lexicalize semantic fields in different ways. (See further Lyons 1977.)

Certain semantic fields of cultural importance attract a high density of overlapping, partially or wholly SYNONYMOUS items: e.g. the field of modern technology; or of Anglo-Saxon heroic warfare. Many words, because of their multiplicity of meanings, may be associated with more than one semantic field. It is (SITUATIONAL) CONTEXT that tells us that the notice *Heavy plant crossing* has more to do with the field of machinery than nursery gardening (or science fiction). In POETIC LANGUAGE particularly, semantic and lexical fields may overlap because of the prevalence of METAPHORIC associations. So the seasons and nature contribute to the semantic density of Shakespeare's sonnet on old age (Sonnet 73):

> That time of year thou mayst in me behold
> When yellow leaves, or none, or few, do hang
> Upon those boughs which shake against the cold,
> Bare ruined choirs, where late the sweet birds sang.

(2) The term **field (of discourse)** is particularly associated with the study of REGISTER (q.v.) developed by Halliday *et al.* (1964) and is one of the distinguishing criteria by which certain TEXTUAL features can be correlated with certain contexts of situation. (See also TENOR; MODE.) Not always clearly determined, it refers largely to subject matter or type of activity: e.g. the field of newscasting, advertising, children's comics.

Field clearly influences choice of LEXIS: certain words and phrases are particularly associated with certain activities (see also JARGON).

(3) In the work of the social theorist Bourdieu (1993), **field** is close to DOMAIN (q.v.) as a socially and functionally significant 'structured space', e.g. economic, political, educational.

figurative: ~ meaning; ~ language; figuration

(1) In SEMANTICS **figurative meaning** describes a very common type of extension of meaning for a word (resulting in POLYSEMY or multiple meaning), i.e. by METAPHORIC transfer of senses.

So there is the LITERAL or basic or CONCEPTUAL MEANING of words like *mouth* and *head* and *foot* (which corresponds normally to the basic definitions in dictionaries), and also the figurative or metaphorical meaning, as in phrases like *mouth of the river; head of the school*, and *foot of the bed*.

In some instances, the figurative meaning of a word may become so common that the original, literal meaning may be superseded: so-called **dead metaphors**. So we rarely, unlike the Anglo-Saxons, talk of *keen* (i.e. 'sharp') weapons; although we may be *keen* (i.e. 'enthusiastic') to learn such things. Many words borrowed from Latin have really been used in English only in their figurative

151

senses: e.g. words with the root *-prehend* ('take; seize'), as in *comprehend, appre-hend*. It may well be the case that we use many hundreds of words of classical origin in 'figurative' senses that we assume now to be literal.

De Man and other DECONSTRUCTIONISTS would go so far as to deny any clear-cut distinction between literal and figurative meaning; and further speculate on the figural 'roots' of all language (see also Foucault (1966) on CATACHRESIS). This is a far cry from those seventeenth- and eighteenth-century scholars like Thomas Sprat who believed that figurative meanings 'deviated' from the 'true' meanings of words, and who viewed, through rationalist eyes, all figurative language with suspicion.

COGNITIVE LINGUISTS such as Lakoff *et al.* (1980f) and Gibbs (1994) would go further than deconstructionists and argue not only for the fundamental import-ance of figurative 'language', ubiquitous and not 'DEVIANT', but also of what they term **figuration**, for human thought. The mind is not seen as inherently literal, and figurative processes are basic to many of our conceptualizations of experi-ence. They further argue, as do RELEVANCE THEORISTS, that therefore figurative language isn't necessarily more difficult to produce and understand than literal language.

(2) As (1) suggests, however, **figurative** can be closely identified with metaphor-ical, and **figurative language** is frequently used to mean simply metaphorical language; or else metaphor is seen as a very important or basic aspect of figurat-ive language. So Leech (1969) considers metaphor, and also SYNECDOCHE and METONYMY under this heading.

(3) More generally still, **figurative language** sometimes embraces in LITERARY CRITICISM all kinds of devices or features which are semantically or grammati-cally MARKED or unusual in some way, notably all the rhetorical FIGURES OF SPEECH below as well as metaphor, metonymy and synecdoche.

In this sense figurative language can be seen to be characteristic of LITERARY, especially POETIC, LANGUAGE, although it is also associated with advertising. Here SIMILES, PUNS and other word-play are particularly striking for persuasive or eye-catching effects (*cool as a mountain stream; H2eau; Go to work on an egg*, etc.). But as cognitive linguists in (1) above stress, even in ordinary conversation figurative language is not infrequent, e.g. in the form of racy SLANG metaphors (e.g. *pickled; canned; stewed* for 'drunk'), HYPERBOLE or exaggeration (*I was scared to death*), simile (*daft as a brush*), etc. (See also IMAGERY; POETICALITY.)

figure: ~ of speech; ~ of thought

(1) A **figure of speech** is popularly associated with such EXPRESSIVE devices of language as METAPHOR and SIMILE, by which IMAGES are evoked through comparison of one 'object' with another: e.g. *Women are angels, wooing; Time is like a fashionable host* (Shakespeare: *Troilus and Cressida*).

(2) In RHETORIC, whence the origin of the term, **figures of speech** are actually much more numerous than those given in (1), and far more diverse in their nature, so that it is difficult to define their essential feature. And even here, and

in LITERARY CRITICISM generally, there is variation in the use of the term, as to what is or is not 'included' in it. (See (3) and (4) below.)

Plett (1977) defines the **figure** as 'the smallest DEVIANT language unit', which implies controversially that figures generally depart from the linguistic 'norms' of everyday language in some way, whether semantically, or syntactically. This is possibly the case if we see deviations as not only rule-breaking, but also over-regular (as in REPETITION); but see FIGURATIVE LANGUAGE above. Originating in classical oratory as devices to structure and elaborate an argument, and to move the emotions of an audience, figures of speech soon came to be associated with the art of literary composition.

Broadly, figures are traditionally divided into SCHEMES (q.v.) and TROPES (q.v.), of which schemes are by far the most frequent.

Schemes are FOREGROUNDED by their patterns of regularity of FORM, SYNTACTIC or PHONETIC. So ANAPHORA and EPISTROPHE show syntactic repetition (of clause- or line-initial words and clause- or line-final words). Tropes (from Gk 'turn') twist words away from their usual meanings or COLLOCATIONS to produce semantic or lexical 'deviation', as in metaphor (*You are my sunshine*); METONYMY (Antony's *I am dying, Egypt, dying*, in Shakespeare's *Antony and Cleopatra*); and SYNECDOCHE (*a new hand for the job*). Leech (1969) succinctly defines tropes as 'foregrounded irregularities of CONTENT'; whereas schemes are 'foregrounded regularities of EXPRESSION'.

(3) Traditionally, however, **figures of speech** have also been restricted to schemes: a usage (rather confusingly) opposite to the common modern one in (1), where it is the trope rather than the scheme which is identified with figure of speech.

(4) Sometimes **figures of speech** are also distinguished in traditional rhetoric from so-called **figures of thought**, which are otherwise rather loosely associated with the other figures of speech, although rather different in their form and function. They have a PRAGMATIC role at SENTENCE or TEXT level in the presentation of the argument or theme to the listener: commonly structures with particular SPEECH ACT functions, e.g. RHETORICAL QUESTION; APOSTROPHE; AMPLIFICATIO(N). (See further Dixon 1971.)

Literary interest in, and use of, figures of speech reached its zenith in the Renaissance: Peacham's (1577) handbook lists nearly 200 different types. (Four hundred are listed in Sonnino 1968.) Poets handled them with verve and ostentation, having learned their names as part of their grammar school education and their study of ELOCUTIO. A decline in the study of classics, and a growing suspicion of the rhetorical, have led to a decline in their use in literary composition and public speaking, although a 'hard core' of figures still persists, and some are known reasonably well by name. Devices of repetition are common in public speaking (see Atkinson 1984); and FIGURATIVE LANGUAGE is generally characteristic of advertising, for example (see Dyer 1982). Indeed, new figures unknown in traditional rhetoric have to be accounted for here: e.g. GRAPHEMIC deviations in brand names (*Kleen-eze; Hi-Glo*).

Undoubtedly, a knowledge of rhetorical figures is of considerable importance for our understanding of stylistic effect in literary language in earlier periods.

Their Greek forms are admittedly difficult to pronounce or remember; and many confusingly overlap with others in meaning, or appear to have more than one meaning (see, e.g. EPANODOS).

In the second half of the twentieth century, however, renewed interest in figures of speech came from French STRUCTURALISM (e.g. the work of Barthes, Genette, Todorov) influenced by the earlier **Russian** FORMALISTS; from DECONSTRUCTION THEORY; from STYLISTICS in work on text analysis; SPEECH ACT THEORY; COGNITIVE LINGUISTICS and PRAGMATICS. As a result, there have been several attempts at new classifications of figures. (See Nash 1989; Plett 1977, 1985.)

finite: ~ verb; ~ clause

(1) In the grammatical categorization of the English VERB PHRASE, the **finite verb** is the form which is marked for TENSE, and matched for singular number with a **third** PERSON SUBJECT in the PRESENT or **past tense** (e.g. *She touch-ed the elephant*). Such verb forms are thus 'finite' in that they refer to an event which is related to a moment of time: they are thus useful DEICTIC elements, providing temporal orientation.

So-called NON-FINITE VERB (q.v.) forms in English are not marked in this way, and comprise INFINITIVES (*touch; hate*; etc.) and PARTICIPLES (*touch-ing; touch-ed; eat-en*).

Complex verbal groups expressing ASPECT and/or VOICE as well as tense (and/or MODALITY) combine one (initial) finite form with non-finite forms, e.g.:

> She is feeding the elephants
> She has fed the elephants
> She shouldn't have been feeding the elephants

(2) A **finite** CLAUSE usually has a subject (except for IMPERATIVES, where the subject is implied); and these may be MAIN or SUBORDINATE CLAUSES; e.g. both clauses in the sentence *She likes elephants/ although she dislikes hippos*. Non-finite clauses, containing non-finite verb forms, can only be subordinate: as in *Feeding the elephants,/ she was deafened by their noise*.

focalization; focalizer

Following the work of Genette (1972), **focalization** is used in the study of literary NARRATIVE and DISCOURS(E) for what is also known, in similar metaphorical terms, as PERSPECTIVE (q.v.) or POINT OF VIEW (q.v.).

As Rimmon-Kenan (1983) says, focalization refers to the 'angle of vision' through which the story is focussed, but in a sense which includes not only the angle of physical perception (e.g. close or distant, panoramic or limited), but also cognitive orientation (complete or restricted knowledge of the world described) and emotive orientation ('subjective' or 'objective'). These last two senses are emphasized by Fludernik (1996).

NARRATORS are commonly the **focalizers** (or what Stanzel 1984 calls **reflectors**, following Booth 1961 and Henry James): the OMNISCIENT NARRATOR typically adopting an external, panchronic and objective stance: the ZERO DEGREE. **First** PERSON narrators, however, commonly provide **internal focalization**, information regulated by their view of events, and often a subjective viewpoint (e.g. Pip in Dickens's *Great Expectations*). A special kind of internal focalization is found in INTERIOR MONOLOGUE (q.v.).

The narrator, as one who speaks, is not always the main focalizer, or the one who sees. In Henry James's *The Ambassadors*, for example, it is crucial that we distinguish Strether's view of events from the narrator's, however hard this may be to do, and however teasingly and dynamically ambiguous the interplay. In FREE INDIRECT SPEECH (q.v.) the VOICE of a CHARACTER is typically mediated through the voice of the narrator; yet the focalization remains that of the character.

(See further Chatman 1990.)

focus; focus(s)ing, etc.

(1) In TEXT LINGUISTICS and linguistics attention is paid to the INFORMATION structure of UTTERANCES and TEXTS, to the recognition that patterns of prominence and importance of information are ever changing at SENTENCE level and beyond: what can be termed **focus(s)ing** (or linguistic FOREGROUNDING). (See also FUNCTIONAL SENTENCE PERSPECTIVE (FSP).)

However, there is a certain NORM of USAGE, and certain recognized DEVIATIONS. The centre of interest or EMPHASIS in an utterance is the **focus**, which in speech coincides with the INTONATION NUCLEUS, the last ACCENTED or STRESSED element of a LEXICAL ITEM. In English important or NEW INFORMATION is normally reserved until the ends of utterances, so the term END-FOCUS (q.v.) is often used, e.g.: *I can resist everything except temptation* (Wilde: *Lady Windermere's Fan*).

Focus is contrasted with the THEME (q.v.), the point of initiation of an utterance (the pronoun *I* in the quotation above): normally of relatively low informational value; or possibly comprising GIVEN or PRESUPPOSED information in certain contexts. So while a sentence like *A lorry is waiting to overtake me* is not unacceptable, the EXISTENTIAL equivalent [*There's*] *a lorry waiting to overtake me* allows the focus to fall on a post-verbal element which is of some importance. Such syntactic devices are called **focus markers** (see Taglicht 1985).

As this example also illustrates, the focus may be shifted from end-position depending on the utterance (**marked focus**); or an utterance may have more than one focus (*lorry, overtake* in the last example). Theme and focus may sometimes coincide in initial position (**marked theme**), with, for example, FRONTING (q.v.) of the OBJECT: *Yet one tree you must not touch* (Milton: *Paradise Lost*).

(2) Certain ADVERBS commonly function as **focus markers**: what Quirk *et al.* (1985) term **focussing subjuncts**: words like *only; also; particularly*. In *She also likes Schubert* attention is drawn to the final element (*Schubert*).

(3) In DISCOURSE ANALYSIS of the Birmingham school **focus** is a kind of MOVE which acts as a FRAME or transition from one topic or ACT to another. It is a METAstatement, describing what the conversation is going to be about, or, retrospectively, what it has been about: e.g. *Today I thought we'd discuss the sexual imagery in 'Troilus and Cressida'; That's all we've got time for this week on Marxist criticism.*

Such explicitness, associated with the prepared or planned discourse of lecture-room and classroom, for example, would be odd in ordinary conversation, which is characteristically unplanned; but may occur in telephone conversation (e.g. *I'm just ringing about my washing-machine . . .*).

(4) In sociolinguistics **focus(s)ing** has sometimes been used, following le Page (1968), to refer to a high degree of linguistic conformity characteristic of closely-knit societies or groups: e.g. the DIALECT of the working-class networks of Belfast (see Milroy 1980). It is contrasted with **diffusion** associated with loosely organized groups (e.g. the Romany spoken by travellers).

foot

Used in traditional METRICS or verse **scansion**, and introduced by Gascoigne (1575) to refer to a unit or division of a line of verse containing a STRESSED syllable or **ictus**. (See also RHYTHM.) The characteristic repetition of the **feet** (e.g. three, four, five feet) constitutes the metrical pattern of the verse line.

Some critics (e.g. Cummings & Simmons 1983; Sinclair 1972) have said that the foot starts at the onset of one stressed syllable, and continues until the onset of the next: e.g. I / xx I (/ x x).

This works well for the traditional DACTYLLIC and TROCHAIC patterns, but not the IAMBIC or ANAPAESTIC ((x) x /). It is therefore better to take the (vaguer) descriptions of the *OED* or of Leech (1969), which refer only to its consisting of a number of syllables, one of which must be stressed, e.g.:

  x / x / x   / x / x /
IBut beIcontentIed: whenIthat fellIarrest . . .

(Shakespeare: Sonnet 74)

However, since it is not always easy to decide how the lines should be 'scanned' or analysed, modern metrists prefer to use the concepts of MEASURES (q.v.) or BEATS (q.v.). (But see Halliday 1985.) GENERATIVE METRICS also works without the concept of foot.

foregrounding

A popular term in STYLISTICS (especially in the analysis of poetry) introduced by Garvin (1964) to translate the PRAGUE SCHOOL term of the 1930s, *aktualisace*, literally ACTUALIZATION (q.v.).

(1) As Mukařovský (1932) and Hávranek (1932) believed, like the **Russian** FORMALISTS before them, it was the FUNCTION of POETIC LANGUAGE to surprise the reader with a fresh and dynamic awareness of its linguistic MEDIUM, to DE-AUTOMATIZE what was normally taken for granted, to exploit language AESTHETICALLY. **Foregrounding** is thus the 'throwing into relief' of the linguistic SIGN against the BACKGROUND of the NORMS of ordinary language. (An analogy with visual arts was intended by the Prague School.) So the regularized patterns of METRE, for example, are foregrounded against the natural RHYTHMS of speech.

(2) But within the literary text itself linguistic features can themselves be **foregrounded**, or 'highlighted', 'made prominent', for specific effects, against the (subordinated) background of the rest of the text, the new 'norm' in competition with the non-literary norm. It is on this 'internal' foregrounding that critical attention is largely focussed.

Foregrounding is achieved by a variety of means, which have been largely grouped under two main types: DEVIATION and REPETITION; or **paradigmatic** and **syntagmatic foregrounding** respectively (Leech 1965). Deviations are violations of linguistic norms: grammatical or semantic, for example. Unusual METAPHORS or SIMILES (the traditional TROPES) produce unexpected conjunctions of meaning, forcing fresh realizations in the reader:

> ... the air on his face
> Unkind as the touch of sweating metal
>
> (C. D. Lewis: *Departure in the Dark*)

Foregrounding, following the emphasis of the Prague School, has not uncommonly been defined in terms of deviation: cf. Leech and Short's 'artistically MOTIVATED deviation' (1981). In one sense repetition is a kind of deviation, as the entry for that term reveals: it violates the normal rules of usage by overfrequency. Repetitive patterns (of sound or syntax, for example) are superimposed on the background of the expectations of normal usage, and so strike the reader's attention as unusual. ALLITERATION, PARALLELISM, and many FIGURES OF SPEECH or SCHEMES involving repetition of LEXICAL ITEMS are thus commonly exploited in foregrounding in poetic language:

> I've heard them lilting at loom and belting,
> Lasses lilting before dawn of day ...
>
> (C. D. Lewis: *I've Heard them Lilting*)

Such devices are not unknown, of course, in non-literary language (e.g. advertising, jokes, oratory), but it is the very consistency and COHERENCE of use which seems to be characteristic of poetic language particularly. But what is or is not foregrounded may well be difficult to establish in some contexts, and an element of subjectivity of response seems inevitable. Indeed, van Peer (1986) and Short (1996) emphasize the perceptual prominence of foregrounded features, their existence signalled by the reader's conscious attention.

form

(1) **Form** in linguistics is sometimes defined as a 'level' of language, its structure, consisting of the PHONOLOGICAL, GRAMMATICAL and LEXICAL patterns which express CONTENT or meaning. The level of form thus mediates between the levels of EXPRESSION and content. (See also (7) below.)

(2) Commonly, however, a simple distinction is made between **form** and meaning, especially in regard to linguistic units: the SENTENCE, CLAUSE, **phrase** and **word**. GRAMMAR traditionally deals with the structural characteristics of these units and their FUNCTION (q.v.) to give a **formal** description; SEMANTICS deals with meaning.

(3) In LITERARY CRITICISM, **form** is a very common term in the non-linguistic general sense of 'structure'. It often overlaps with GENRE in phrases like *the novel/lyric form*; and with METRICAL structure in phrases like *the sonnet/ballad/ iambic pentameter form*.

(4) It also commonly refers to the structure or shape of a single text, be it novel or poem; and so figures prominently in those critical movements (e.g. NEW CRITI-CISM) concerned with organic unity or AESTHETICS. (See also GESTALT theory.)

(5) An interest in unity, combined with a stronger interest in formal features in the linguistic sense of (2), characterizes the movement known as **Russian** FORMALISM (q.v.). Here the emphasis is on the study of the features' aesthetic function; and the literary work itself defined as 'pure **form**' (Shklovsky 1925). A concern with form in the linguistic sense is also prominent in STRUCTURALISM.

(6) In formalism and structuralism, and also MARXIST CRITICISM and CRITICAL LINGUISTICS, there is a tendency to argue that literary works are about language; that the MEDIUM is the MESSAGE; that **form** is content (see (1) above); that there is no content before form.

Even in linguistics the dichotomy between form and content has been questioned. Formalized (crudely) as the SURFACE and DEEP STRUCTURE of GENERATIVE GRAMMAR, in recent work these levels reveal considerable overlap.

Their relationship has also been a much debated topic in literary criticism and STYLISTICS. That form and content are inseparable is sometimes known as the MONIST (q.v.) view. To change a form, it is argued, will produce a different 'meaning'. In POETIC LANGUAGE certainly, with the aesthetic focussing on form, this is quite plausible.

However, common notions of SYNONYMY and PARAPHRASE depend on the so-called DUALIST (q.v.) view that the 'same content' can be expressed in different forms. In NARRATOLOGY it can be argued that the same 'story' can be represented in verbal or visual form (i.e. film), and the dichotomy resembles the French HISTOIRE V. DISCOURS. STYLE itself is commonly seen as a CHOICE of form ('manner') to express content ('matter').

(7) The use of **form** to ENACT or mirror content is a common literary device, an extension of the literary principle of MIMESIS. PHONETIC and SYNTACTIC devices are especially exploited to enact the content or subject matter of auditory and KINETIC experience especially (see also ONOMATOPOEIA), and are a feature too of concrete poetry.

formalism; Russian ~; formalist stylistics

(1) **Russian Formalism** was one of the most important linguistic and literary movements of the early twentieth century, but comparatively unknown in the West until Todorov's translation of some of the important texts into French in the 1960s. The term had pejorative connotations to the contemporaries of the Formalists who so labelled them.

There were two main groups: the Moscow Linguistic Circle, founded 1915, and the St Petersburg group, *Opayaz*, founded 1916. Their members included Viktor Shklovsky (see, e.g., DE-AUTOMATIZATION; ESTRANGEMENT; FABULA; PLOT); Vladimir Propp (see, e.g., FUNCTION; MORPHOLOGY of folk-tales); and Roman Jakobson (see, e.g., DOMINANT; EQUIVALENCE; METAPHOR; POETIC FUNCTION; SPEECH EVENT). Jakobson provided a significant link with the PRAGUE SCHOOL (q.v.) which he later helped to establish, and western STRUCTURAL LINGUISTICS and POETICS, after his emigration to the United States. The Formalists flourished until 1930. They were considerably occupied by literary, especially poetic, FORM (q.v.), inspired both by the ideas of Saussure on the structure of language, and by the AESTHETIC ideas of the SYMBOLIST movement.

Though a wider scope of issues was covered in their work (e.g. literary evolution), it is for their ideas about the internal formal differences between poetic and non-poetic language, and about the structure of NARRATIVE, that they are best known. Like the Prague School they were extremely interested in the related art forms of film and painting (see also FOREGROUNDING). With their scientific approach to the linguistic devices of literature, they present an early precursor of modern (formalist) STYLISTICS (see also (4) below). (On the history of Formalism, see Erlich 1965; see also Bennett 1979.)

(2) **Formalism/formalism** is sometimes found as a generic term to cover not only Russian Formalism (itself confusingly sometimes written with lower case *f*), but other critical movements independently concerned with the formal autonomy of literature e.g. NEW CRITICISM.

(3) In linguistics **formalism** is sometimes found opposed to FUNCTIONALISM (q.v.), reflecting two broad approaches to linguistic analysis (see Leech 1983). The GENERATIVE GRAMMAR of Chomsky 1965 illustrates formalism: language studied as an autonomous system, with the emphasis on grammatical forms and the PROPOSITIONAL MEANING of sentences at the expense of their PRAGMATIC FUNCTION and communicative CONTEXT.

(4) By analogy with linguistics, a distinction has been made, following Taylor & Toolan (1984), between **formalist** and FUNCTIONALIST STYLISTICS (q.v.). The approach of Jakobson (Jakobson & Lévi-Strauss 1962; Jakobson & Jones 1970) to the analysis of poetic texts, clearly influenced by his own Russian background, illustrates his reliance on purely formal linguistic criteria in identifying stylistic patterns (see also EQUIVALENCE). This reliance was shared by GENERATIVE STYLISTIC analyses common in the 1960s (e.g. Fowler 1972; Ohmann 1964).

A formalist, and also generative, approach has recently been revived, however, under the heading of **literary linguistics**, by Fabb (1997), interested in the adaptation of linguistic form to literary forms, e.g. metrical, and in underlying 'universals' of literary form.

formality, degrees of

In sociolinguistics and STYLISTICS **formality** refers to the way in which the STYLE or TONE of language will vary in APPROPRIATENESS according to the social CONTEXT: the SITUATION and the relationship between ADDRESSER and ADDRESSEE(s).

There is not a simple choice between **formal** and **informal**, but linguists generally recognize a scale or continuum ranging from very formal to very informal. Joos (1962) specifically identified five 'degrees' or KEYS or styles, which he labelled **frozen, formal, consultative, casual** and **intimate**, each correlated with certain linguistic features. It is fairly easy to distinguish the frozen style of (written) legal documents, with their latinate DICTION and impersonal SYNTAX, from the intimate style of (spoken) interchanges between close friends, with their SLANG and ELLIPTICAL syntax. But it is not so easy to categorize neatly the intervening degrees, or relate them to DISCOURSE types or formal features. So advertising language can be formal and informal; and the PASSIVE sentence, often associated with formality, is not uncommon in everyday speech.

But certainly (in-)formality is an important factor in everyday USAGE, perhaps more important than choice of MEDIUM. Writing in many situations has become less and less formal, approaching the informality of 'casual' or colloquial speech. We tend generally to associate LITERARY LANGUAGE with formality, but allowances must be made for GENRE and MIMETIC principles. A modern dramatist, for example, will frequently seek to reproduce the informality of colloquial speech.

All in all, factors such as public v. private occasion; size and status of audience; degree of acquaintance, etc., are important social constraints on formality: sometimes giving rise to CODE- or DIALECT-SWITCHING (q.v.). **Terms of** ADDRESS are ready indicators of degrees of formality: from *Madam* to *Prof. K. M. Wales; Kathleen; Katie; Chuckles*, etc.

(See also DECORUM; TENOR.)

formula; formulaic: ~ language; ~ system

(1) **Formulaic language** is used by some linguists to describe all those **formulas** or repeated phrases of fixed COLLOCATION and grammatical structure in everyday usage which form part of the ritual of social behaviour, or PHATIC COMMUNION. They include greetings and farewells (*Hello; How are you?; Cheerio*); and expressions of condolence and congratulation now formalized by the greetings card industry (*Many happy returns; In deepest sympathy*). In the written MEDIUM formulas are most noticeable in letter writing, varying in degrees of FORMALITY (*yours faithfully* v. *much love*).

(2) In the study of oral poetry, classical and modern European, and of Old English poetry (particularly) in the English verse tradition, a **formula** is a collocation of words which recurs identically in FORM and CONTENT and in METRICAL PATTERN in a line of verse, within a poem and even beyond: i.e. it belongs to a common poetic stock known to many poets or 'singers'. Interest in formulas developed out of the work on the composition of Homeric verse by Parry in the 1920s and 1930s (e.g. 1930) and by his student Lord (e.g. 1960), and was first applied to (Old) English verse by Magoun (1953). (See further ORAL-FORMULAIC THEORY.)

Anglo-Saxon poets, even the educated clerics who presumably composed pen in hand, found formulas useful for the demands of their written ALLITERATIVE VERSE: e.g. *heard under helm* ('hardy under (his) helmet'); *dreame bidrorene* ('of joy deprived').

Originality and personal idiosyncracy of expression were clearly not aesthetic requirements in early English verse; although some variation in collocations is certainly found. Again, however, these **formulaic systems** or **variants** tend to become conventionalized between poems. So given the GRAMMETRICAL 'mould' ADJECTIVE (/×) plus NOUN (/×) (e.g. *Drihten* 'Lord'), one can find variations expressing a similar idea: *halig* ('holy') *Drihten*; *mihtig* ('mighty') *Drihten*, etc.

Formulaic language is also found in the alliterative verse tradition of the fourteenth century, and survives in the TAGS (q.v.) of other Middle English verse and ballads.

frame: ~ of reference; framing

With basic senses of 'structure' and 'enclosure' **frame** has become an exceedingly popular term in various aspects of linguistics and LITERARY CRITICISM.

(1) In discussions of the LITERARINESS of literature, and the place of an AESTHETIC function or response, the extent to which literature demands a frame, or can be seen to be **framed**, is much debated.

It might be argued that any piece of language deemed to be framed, i.e. consciously set apart in some way from 'ordinary' language (e.g. in verse lines), constitutes a literary artefact; conversely, it can also be argued that once we regard a piece of language as 'literary' (e.g. the opening words of a novel, however mundane), we thereby frame it: semiotize it as a special SIGN.

It is easier perhaps to use the term frame in visual art (where it originates); although the DECONSTRUCTIONIST Derrida (1978a) raised here interesting questions about its aesthetic status, and the difficulty of distinguishing the marginal or extrinsic from the intrinsic or central.

The framing of art is also made apparent in the theatre: the literary status of a play confirmed by the so-called **picture-frame** stage of traditional design; or by dimmed lights and lowering and raising of the curtain. The term **breaking frame** is commonly used to describe those devices whereby the character withdraws from the WORLD of the play to address the real-world audience directly: e.g. in an ASIDE or EPILOGUE. Paradoxically, such devices also serve to heighten the COUNTERFACTUAL status of the play's world (see Elam 1980).

(2) But, as Elam also notes, the theatrical frame is also heavily dependent upon a set of conventions about theatrical and dramatic activity known to the audience, which governs their expectations, and is part of their COMPETENCE. Such **frames of reference**, often culture-specific, which help to determine GENRE are characteristic of our experience of the novel, and poetry also. And what is termed INTERTEXTUALITY (q.v.) involves frames of reference or models of COHERENCE based on our knowledge of other texts within a genre, as well as our knowledge of the world. (See also CODE; DOMAIN.)

(3) The habit of **framing** in this sense is not only characteristic of our appreciation of literature, but of our dealings in society generally.

First used in artificial intelligence and in sociology (e.g. Goffman 1974) COGNITIVE LINGUISTICS in particular has drawn attention to the extent to which our ordinary behaviour is framed: i.e. organized into conventional conceptual structures which map out the many typical situations of our daily lives: e.g. shopping in a supermarket; supper in a bed-sit; a board-room meeting, etc. In each case we have a rough idea or 'blue-print' of what to expect in terms of place, actions and participants, etc., drawing on our memory and encyclopedic world knowledge. And as Eco (1979) says each of these frames is already an inchoative text or condensed story: not far removed from a TV sit-com, perhaps. (See also SCHEMA.)

(4) Such views on frames have now also contributed to research into NARRATIVE comprehension. Readers interpret characters ongoingly, for example, by relying on known frames of reference in order to 'fill out' their actions, situations, etc., whether this knowledge is CONTEXTUAL (i.e. drawn from the 'real' world in their own period, or at the time the text is set), or CO-TEXTUAL (i.e. drawn from the text itself). (See further Emmott 1997; Werth 1999.)

(5) In DISCOURSE ANALYSIS a **frame** is more precisely a transition marker between one topic or section of a discourse and another. Frames are realized by a small set of linguistic items such as *well, right, OK, now* and *good*. They are commonly found in, for example, doctor–patient or teacher–pupil exchanges, in telephone conversations, and in ordinary conversation where explanation or clarification is involved (e.g. *well it's like this*); but are mostly absent from any but the most informal kind of writing.

They frequently co-occur with FOCUS (q.v.) devices which explicitly state what the new topic is to be about: *OK, Now today I thought we'd move on to the Crimean War . . .*

(6) In LITERARY CRITICISM a **frame-story** or **frame-narrative** is a story linking a further series of stories told by individual characters: the most notable example in English being Chaucer's pilgrimage frame to his *Canterbury Tales*. (See also DIEGETIC; EXTRADIEGETIC.)

free direct: ~ speech; ~ style; ~ discourse

(1) By analogy with DIRECT SPEECH (q.v.), **free direct speech** (FDS) has been commonly used since the late 1950s to describe a method of representing speech in the written medium.

The term **free** is variously interpreted, however, but traditionally, by analogy with FREE INDIRECT SPEECH/STYLE (FIS) (q.v.), describes speech which is given directly or idiosyncratically without the accompanying reporting clause or TAG, characteristic of direct speech, e.g.:

She said, 'I want to see the elephants.' (DS)
'I want to see the elephants.' (FDS)

also called **abruptive dialogue** by Genette (1980). The quotation marks may also be lacking; in which case it may be hard to distinguish speech from narrative in a story or novel (and also from FIS). In this example from Dickens's *Bleak House* the ambiguity suggests empathy between NARRATOR and courtroom activity: *Now. Is there any other witness? No other witness.*

However, Leech & Short (1981), Simpson (1993) and Short *et al.* (1996f), for example, rather confusingly also categorize as FDS sentences without speech marks but with a reporting clause present, e.g.: *She said I want to see the elephants.*

FDS commonly occurs within the context of DS, to save repetition of reporting clauses, e.g.: *She said, 'I want to see the elephants. What is a zoo without them?'* The switch or **slipping** from narrative report and INDIRECT SPEECH (q.v.) to FDS was noted by Longinus (*On the Sublime*) as an effective RHETORICAL device (**polyptoton**) to suggest an outburst of emotion.

Hard to classify as either DS or FDS are sentences where indication of LOCUTIONARY ACT and speaker occurs after the quoted words, in a following sentence, e.g.: *'I want to see the elephants.' She tugged her father's hand as she said this.*

As the entry for DS reveals, even when it occurs within the same sentence the grammatical status of the reporting clause is disputed. When it occurs medially or finally it is hard to see it as determining or governing the reported clause, so that it can be seen to be 'free' in the sense of being 'independent' or 'non-embedded'. Hence it might be possible, following Leech & Short, to categorize as FDS *'I want to see the elephants', she said.*

I take here the conservative and less confusing view that the presence of any kind of *verbum dicendi* means DS, not FDS. Functionally, however, as Short *et al.* recognize, there seems to be little difference between the two, although FDS tends to minimize the narrator's role and FOREGROUND the character and his or her speech. The omission of a tag makes it economical to use in (popular) newspaper headlines, and also eye-catching and dramatic (e.g. *Britons easy to sack*). FDS + speaker's name is also the common mode of representing dramatic discourse in the written medium.

(2) The terms **free direct discourse** (McHale 1978) and **free direct style** tend to have a wider reference, including the representation of thought as well as speech (see also FREE DIRECT THOUGHT). Where emphasis in discussion falls on MODE rather than what is represented, then a more inclusive term is useful. *Discourse*, however, has connotations very much of the spoken word, whereas *style* is more neutral.

free direct thought

Free direct thought describes the representation of thought(s) in the written MEDIUM, established by analogy with FREE DIRECT SPEECH, and introduced by Leech and Short (1981).

Here the apparently verbalized thoughts of characters are reported directly (e.g. with **first** PERSON PRONOUN, PRESENT TENSE, etc.), but without the reporting clause. Cf.:

> She suddenly thought: 'Am I too late?' (DIRECT THOUGHT (DT))
> 'Am I too late?' (FDT)

The quotation marks are commonly omitted in FDT; otherwise only the context will determine whether a character is talking or thinking.

As with DT, FDT is characteristic of literary NARRATIVE rather than of any non-literary register, since access to 'thought processes' is implausible in real life. As with FDS it may be found in the larger context of DT. It is particularly common in INTERIOR MONOLOGUE (q.v.) as a twentieth-century novelistic device, where the lack of reporting clause leads to a smoother text, and reinforces the absence of an apparently controlling NARRATOR. The words are supposed to represent only those thoughts that pass through the CHARACTER's mind, so POINT OF VIEW is limited. In contrast with FREE INDIRECT THOUGHT (q.v.), FDT appears much more dramatic.

free indirect: ~ speech; ~ style; ~ discourse

(1) Terms owing their origin to the French term *le style indirect libre*, first discussed extensively by the stylistician Bally (1912). This refers to a kind of INDIRECT SPEECH (IS) or **reported** speech in which the speech of a CHARACTER and the words of the NARRATOR are blended, but with no reporting clause indicated (hence 'free'). It is also known as REPRESENTED SPEECH. (See also ERLEBTE REDE.)

Like indirect speech, the ILLOCUTIONARY FORCE and the PROPOSITIONAL MEANING of the supposed UTTERANCE of the speaker are represented in **free indirect speech** (FIS), but not necessarily the actual words (as in DIRECT SPEECH (DS)). In the process of 'reporting', the direct words appear to be transmuted: normally PRESENT TENSE back-shifted to past; **first** PERSON and **second** PERSON PRONOUNS becoming **third** PERSON; e.g.:

> She said, 'We are bound to see the elephants.' (DS)
> She said that they were bound to see the elephants. (IS)
> They were bound to see the elephants. (FIS)

However, FIS is often more vivid than IS, since other transpositions characteristic of IS do not usually occur: notably the shift from proximity reference to distance in ADVERBIALS of time and place, e.g.:

> She said, 'We are bound to see the elephants here today.' (DS)
> She said that they were bound to see the elephants there that day. (IS)
> They were bound to see the elephants here today. (FIS)

The blend of character's FOCALIZATION and narrator's VOICE is here confirmed as a combined discourse, or what Pascal (1977) terms the DUAL VOICE (q.v.) and Banfield (1982) the **unspeakable**, since there is no 'real' speaker. Such markers, if they occur, along with other emotive and idiosyncratic speech features of idiom, etc., help to distinguish FIS from simple narrative report. (This is not always easy, however, as the novels of George Eliot illustrate.) The DEICTICS refer not to the 'now' of the narrative DISCOURS, but to the 'now' of story-time (HISTOIRE). In effect the past tense fuses the event narrated and the moment of utterance (see EPIC PRETERITE).

Also striking is the preservation of the INVERSION of SUBJECT and VERB order characteristic of direct questions in standard English, but not indirect:

'Am I too late?', she asked. (DS)
She asked whether she was too late. (IS)
Was she too late? (FIS)

Yet, despite some immediacy, FIS clearly lacks the impact of FREE DIRECT SPEECH, and suggests a narrator's voice in some control. It commonly arises in the novel, or in parliamentary reports, for example, in a context of NARRATIVE REPORT or IS. It can be effectively exploited, like the other modes of speech representation, in the FOREGROUNDING and BACKGROUNDING of characters and viewpoints, manipulating the reader's degrees of sympathy. So in Dickens's *Hard Times* FIS can suggest the (social) distance between employer and worker: *Mr. Bounderby was at his lunch. So Stephen had expected. Would the servant say that one of the Hands begged leave to speak to him?*

Examples of FIS have been traced back to eighteenth-century novels, and it can be found also earlier in non-literary texts, and in Chaucer and even in Ælfric's prose (tenth century). But its systematic use is found in the novels of Jane Austen onwards.

(2) **Free indirect style** usefully covers the representation of thought(s) as well as speech, suggesting the mode is similar. This is otherwise termed FREE INDIRECT THOUGHT (q.v.). **Free indirect speech** itself is also (confusingly) sometimes so used; but **free indirect discourse** is more common (Fludernik 1993; McHale 1978).

In some cases it is actually difficult to tell whether technically speech or thought is involved: both reflect, of course, a character's consciousness. So in the opening lines of Woolf's novel, *Mrs. Dalloway*, IS is followed by either FIS or FIT: *Mrs. Dalloway said she would buy the flowers herself. For Lucy had her work cut out for her . . .*

(See also COLOURED NARRATIVE; HYBRIDIZATION.)

free indirect thought

Coined by analogy with FREE INDIRECT SPEECH (q.v.) by Leech & Short (1981) to make a FUNCTIONAL, rather than FORMAL, distinction between the representation of speech and of thought. (See also NARRATED MONOLOGUE; REPRESENTED THOUGHT.)

As with FIS, there is no reporting clause, and a prevailing INDIRECT SPEECH mode of representation (the PRESENT TENSE of the DIRECT SPEECH mode shifted to past; **third** PERSON PRONOUNS replacing **first and second** person), but with a direct or 'present' DEICTIC orientation rather than an indirect or distant one, e.g.:

> She suddenly thought, 'I've seen this man before.' (DT)
> She suddenly thought that she had seen that man before. (IT)
> She had seen this man before. (FIT)

The blend of character's FOCALIZATION and narrative VOICE, so characteristic of the free indirect style generally, is especially effective in this (essentially literary) rendering of thoughts, feelings and sensations, for it allows the NARRATOR to 'get inside' the CHARACTER without breaking the flow of the narrative by continual insertions of TAGS like *she thought*, etc. FIT also keeps some of the subjectivity of DIRECT THOUGHT without its staginess, and its commitment to (unrealistic) faithful representation. It is particularly exploited therefore in STREAM OF CONSCIOUSNESS FICTION (q.v.), and for major rather than minor characters. It is also found in first person narratives of recollection, e.g. Dickens's *David Copperfield* (where the pronoun *I* remains unchanged).

(See also PSYCHO-NARRATION.)

free verse

From Fr. *vers libre*, verse only 'free' in the sense that it does not conform to the usual regular METRES associated with poetry. Still, this was enough to make Robert Frost say that it was like playing tennis without a net. It is certainly not un-RHYTHMICAL, nor, in the absence of RHYME, necessarily prosaic. SYNTAX and INTONATION are very important in determining the verse lines, which are FRAMED or marked visually in any case by the GRAPHOLOGICAL conventions of spacing and (often) typography. With no fixed patterns or NORM to follow, readers can create their own individual speeds and EMPHASES, etc. Easthope (1983) calls it **intonational metre**.

A typical example of **free verse** is Lawrence's *Snake*:

> A snake came to my water-trough
> On a hot, hot day, and I in pyjamas for the heat,
> To drink there.
> In the deep, strange-scented shade of the great carob-tree
> I came down the steps with my pitcher . . .

Although it is found in poetry of earlier periods, free verse is particularly associated with modern poetry, arising out of MODERNISM and imagism and the experiments of such poets as Pound, Eliot and Carlos Williams. (See further Eliot's essay, 1932.)

fricative

In PHONETICS, a type of consonant where the air passage in the mouth is narrowed without complete closure so that audible friction is produced.

In English many consonants are **fricatives**. For VOICELESS /f/ and VOICED /v/ the friction is produced between the bottom lip and upper teeth (**labiodental fricatives**); for /θ/ and /ð/ (as in *thin* and *this*, respectively) between the tongue and upper teeth (**dental**). For /s/ and /z/ the air escapes narrowly behind the teeth (ALVEOLAR); and for /ʃ/ and /ʒ/ (as in *ship* and *pleasure*, respectively) friction occurs between the tongue and roof of the mouth (**palato-alveolar**); for /h/ the friction occurs in the larynx (**glottal**).

The prolonged 'noisy' nature of fricatives is often exploited for ONOMATOPOEIC effects, to suggest whistling, sizzling, buzzing, etc. Their written representation is formalized in children's comics and elsewhere to represent snores (*z-z-z-z-z*) and silencers (*shhh!!!*), for example.

fronting

(1) **Fronting** refers to the SYNTACTIC shifting of elements, usually for highlighting or EMPHASIS, from their normal post-VERBAL position to the beginning of the SENTENCE or CLAUSE: DIRECT OBJECTS, for instance, as in *Yet one tree you must not touch* (Milton: *Paradise Lost*) and with INVERSION of SUBJECT and verb, e.g. *In came a fiddler, and tuned like fifty stomach-aches* (Dickens: *A Christmas Carol*). In RHETORIC known as **hysteron proteron**.

Fronting is also found in everyday speech (e.g. *tight these shoes are; the wine you'll find in the cupboard*). Some examples in speech, however, may be the result of lack of clear planning of the utterance.

In terms of the PROSODIC and INFORMATIONAL STRUCTURE of such sentences, fronting affects the normal or usual pattern of prominence and importance of information, which normally builds up to a FOCUS, at the end of the sentence. (See also FUNCTIONAL SENTENCE PERSPECTIVE.) Here the centre of interest coincides with the NUCLEUS, the last ACCENTED element of the final LEXICAL ITEM. The beginning of a sentence, however, is normally of relatively low informational value, or possibly comprises GIVEN or PRESUPPOSED information (see THEME). The fronting of elements therefore gives them extra importance or emphasis (and often sentences have a double focus). The coincidence of focus and theme has been called **marked theme** or **thematic fronting** (Quirk *et al.* 1985); or **thematization** (Young 1980).

(2) A special kind of **fronting** occurs in DIRECT SPEECH or DIRECT THOUGHT, where the speech reported commonly precedes the reporting clause: *'Come on! Come on!' puffed Gordon to the coaches.* (Rev. Awdry: *Thomas the Tank Engine*.)

function

(1) It is now a commonplace in the study of language to recognize that as a system of COMMUNICATION language has many **functions**; and that it is part of our COMPETENCE as speakers not only to know how to produce utterances, but also how to use them in the different SITUATIONS of our social life. Developments in linguistics in the last quarter of the twentieth century in fact turned towards the study of function rather than FORM: expecially in PRAGMATICS and SPEECH ACT THEORY, and in DISCOURSE ANALYSIS. (See also FUNCTIONAL GRAMMAR.)

Language can be seen to have a multitude of functions or communicative ROLES: for naming, quarrelling, persuading; for expressing feelings, giving orders, providing information; for newscasting, weather reporting, creating novels, poems and plays, etc.

There have been many attempts to categorize the functions of language, the number of categories varying according to perspective or discipline. Many have centred specifically on the ACT of communication itself.

(i) Influential was Bühler's (1934) broad threefold classification based on what are seen as the essential elements of ADDRESSER, ADDRESSEE and SIGN: to express the speaker's feelings, etc. (*Ausdruck*: EXPRESSIVE FUNCTION); to appeal to, or influence the addressee (*Appell*: appellative or CONATIVE FUNCTION); and to represent the real world (*Darstellung*: descriptive or REFERENTIAL FUNCTION).

The **functions** are not regarded as mutually exclusive: an utterance may well have more than one function. But to this essentially practical classification, the PRAGUE SCHOOL linguists added a fourth category: an AESTHETIC FUNCTION ((q.v.); and see (5) below).

(ii) To this scheme Jakobson (1960) added three other **functions** in his equally influential model of the SPEECH EVENT (q.v.). The PHATIC FUNCTION (q.v.) establishes and maintains CONTACT between participants; the METALINGUAL FUNCTION (q.v.) focusses on the language itself; and the POETIC FUNCTION (q.v.) corresponds to the Prague School aesthetic function.

(iii) A modified form of Bühler seems to underline the tripartite system of so-called MACRO or META-**functions** which forms the theoretical base of Halliday's SYSTEMIC FUNCTIONAL GRAMMAR (e.g. 1973, 1985). The conative and expressive functions merge in Halliday's INTERPERSONAL FUNCTION (q.v.): language used to express the relations between, and attitudes of, speaker and listener. The referential function would correspond to Halliday's IDEATIONAL FUNCTION (q.v.) (the expression of experience). In addition Halliday has a TEXTUAL FUNCTION (q.v.): language making reference to itself, in text building.

(iv) Halliday's work has also reflected his strong interest in the development of language in children, and changes in **functions** are an aspect of this. Here more functions are given, seven in all: **instrumental** ('I want'); **informative** ('I've got something to tell you'); **imaginative** ('Let's pretend'); **regulative** ('Do as I tell you'); **interactional** ('Me and you'); **personal** ('Here I come'); and **heuristic** ('Tell me why').

(v) An interest in linguistic development, and in the comparison of human language with animal communication systems, combines with Bühler in the work of Popper (1972). He distinguishes two 'lower' **functions** characteristic of primitive systems: **expressive** and **signalling** (the latter communicating information about feelings to others); and two 'higher' (i.e. only human functions: **descriptive** and **argumentative** (the latter presenting and evaluating arguments, etc.). Each successive function presupposes the others.

Popper's model is broader than some in that he is concerned overall with the function of language generally in society, and not only with single utterances or exchanges.

(vi) A similar broad interest in the social **functions** of utterances informs speech act theory as developed by Austin and Searle in the 1960s. Here the problem is attempting to classify speech acts and their communicative functions (e.g. promising, complaining, swearing, etc.), the number of which appears to be enormous. Stubbs (1983) notes how some appear late in life (e.g. expressing condolences); and some functions of language are not easily described systematically (e.g. to release tension).

(2) Some of these speech acts or MICRO-**functions** have been traditionally related to formal features in GRAMMAR, notably SENTENCE types. So an INTERROGATIVE is used for a question; and IMPERATIVE for a directive or command; a DECLARATIVE for a statement. However, it is also recognized that there is no strict correlation between form and function: a declarative sentence can be used for a directive (e.g. *I'd rather you sit down*) and a question (e.g. *You've finished your homework already?*).

(3) Grammatical theory has always paid great attention to syntactic **function** at the level of the sentence unit and below. For example, NOUN PHRASES can be defined functionally as well as formally in terms of their role as SUBJECT, OBJECT and ADVERBIAL in the clause; ARTICLES have different functional roles in determining the noun phrase, etc.

(4) In STYLISTICS, the study of the **function** of linguistic elements in TEXTS is central, not only of their grammatical function, but more importantly of their function in relation to the 'meaning' of the text, their contribution to the overall theme and structure: what is termed 'stylistic significance'.

Consideration, too, has to be given to communicative functions in the sense of (1).

Non-literary stylistics in particular and REGISTER studies have related situational types of language to predominant functions; e.g. advertising with persuasion; TV commentary with information. Such typologies according to dominant functions are also an aspect of TEXT LINGUISTICS. So de Beaugrande & Dressler (1981) distinguish between **descriptive**, **narrative** and **argumentative** texts.

But what are the functions of literary texts themselves? Is it sufficient to isolate a narrative function, or an aesthetic or poetic? Is literature simply a function of language? As a communicative act between addresser (writer) and addressee (reader) a literary text has potentially a number of wider functions than self-indulgence (expressive) or SELF-REFLEXIVITY, the writer's consciousness of language. Poems may be declarations of love, eulogies or political propaganda; novelists may wish to make us think deeply about problematic yet crucial aspects of experience. (Within the WORLD of the literary text, of course, real-world functions are characteristically imitated: characters argue, command, write letters, etc.) Traditional RHETORIC, out of the pragmatics of oratory, recognized the persuasive power of language, and the ability of the GRAND STYLE of the epic to 'move' the emotions. It also distinguished two other functions/types of literature: to entertain (popular); to instruct (educational or moral).

(5) In the pioneering work of Propp (1928) on the analysis of common patterns of PLOT using a corpus of Russian folk-tales, **function** was one of the main components. It refers to an act of a CHARACTER which is significant for the plot or action; and Propp's thesis is that functions can remain constant from tale to tale, and that the number is limited (he found thirty-one). So a hero may receive a special or magic gift (be it horse or eagle) which subsequently enables him to be transported away.

Other NARRATOLOGISTS have queried Propp's model and proposed refinements: e.g. Brémond (1966, 1973). (See also NARRATIVE GRAMMAR. See further Culler 1975; Rimmon-Kenan 1983.)

(6) In the narrative structural analysis of Barthes (1966) a **function** (*fonction*) is the smallest narrative unit, which combines with others into sequences to make ACTIONS. Functions have degrees of significance: **cardinal** or KERNEL (*noyaux*) functions, the 'nodes' or 'hinges' of the story, are opposed to CATALYSTS (*catalyses*): the former advance the action, the latter delay or amplify it. (See also INDEX. See further Chatman 1969.)

functional: ~ change; ~ shift

See CONVERSION.

functionalism; functional: ~ grammar; ~ stylistics

(1) In linguistics a broad distinction is sometimes made between the two approaches of FORMALISM and **functionalism**. The former, as illustrated in Chomsky's GENERATIVE GRAMMAR in the 1960s, studies language as an autonomous system, emphasizing grammatical FORMS and the PROPOSITIONAL MEANING of SENTENCES; the latter, as illustrated in PRAGUE SCHOOL linguistics and in the **functional grammar** or SYSTEMIC GRAMMAR developed by Halliday since the 1970s, lays stress on the PRAGMATIC function of language in its communicative CONTEXT. Particular attention is also paid to the grammatical FUNCTION or ROLES of linguistic units, as defined in (3) in the entry for **function**, which are seen to implicate MACRO-functions. Fundamental to Halliday's model is the belief that uses of language shape the system. (See also Dik's, 1978, Functional grammar.)

(2) A distinction can also be made, following Taylor & Toolan (1984), between FORMALIST STYLISTICS and **functional stylistics**. Again, GENERATIVE STYLISTIC models and the analyses of Jakobson, e.g. Jakobson & Lévi-Strauss 1962, Jakobson & Jones 1970 with their heavy reliance on the study of formal features, can be opposed to more recent approaches where particular note is taken of the stylistic

function or effects or thematic significance of linguistic features in literary texts, and where various grammatical models are adopted.

CRITICAL LINGUISTICS looks at the function of elements, non-LITERARY as well as literary, from the particular perspective of IDEOLOGY. Its concern is to correlate language with social and political assumptions.

(See also DISCOURSE ANALYSIS; PRAGMATICS; SPEECH ACT THEORY.)

functional sentence perspective (FSP)

Developed particularly by Firbas in the late 1950s and early 1960s, in the post-Second World War PRAGUE SCHOOL of linguists, but owing its origins to the work of the first generation of that school (e.g. Mathesius: see further Vachek 1964).

It is an analysis of SENTENCES and TEXTS based on relative INFORMATIONAL values. According to the principle of COMMUNICATIVE DYNAMISM (CD) (q.v.), different elements will contribute with different effect to the development of the communication. So GIVEN INFORMATION determined by the CO-TEXT or by the CONTEXT (the so-called THEMATIC elements or THEME), will have the 'lowest' degree of CD; NEW INFORMATION or elements with significant semantic content (RHEMATIC/RHEME) will have the 'highest' degree. The overall functional pattern therefore in a sentence provides the **FSP**. In any text basic distributions of CD will vary according to co-text and semantic structure of sentences, but in English the normal pattern is to move from 'low' to 'high', and WORD ORDER is important here, as well as INTONATION (see also END-FOCUS).

Although ideas of theme and rheme have been used by other linguists (e.g. Halliday 1985), the advantage of FSP is that it provides a scale or cline of values rather than an opposition. Linking theme and rheme there are **transitional elements** (usually VERBS); and rhematic elements themselves may have degrees of semantic weight. So in this sentence which opens *Live and Let Die* by Ian Fleming: *There* (thematic) *are* (transitional) *moments of great luxury in the life of a secret agent* (rhematic), the complex NOUN PHRASE which marks the rheme is itself graded dynamically, culminating in the most important phrase *secret agent*.

(See further Firbas 1992. For a critique, see Taglicht 1985.)

function word

Sometimes used in GRAMMAR and SEMANTICS to describe words which have little LEXICAL MEANING, but rather grammatical meaning, and which contribute to the structure of the clause or phrase. They are also known as **form words, empty words** or **kenemes**; and are opposed to CONTENT WORDS or **full words** or **pleremes**, like NOUNS, ADJECTIVES and VERBS, which have lexical meaning.

Typical **function words**, therefore, are CONJUNCTIONS, ARTICLES, and miscellaneous items hard to classify, but with considerable structural significance:

e.g. *not; let's; yes*. Some so-called function words have some semantic content, notably AUXILIARY verbs like *can, shall*, and *may*.

Function words are CLOSED CLASS items, closed to change or renewal in the LEXICON. They are normally unstressed in speech. The natural REDUNDANCY of language means that in normal CONTEXTS relations between words can often be assumed, and so some function words in types of text where economy matters can be omitted: e.g. newspaper headlines (e.g. (*A*) *scout patrol* (*is*) *lost on* (*a*) *mountain*).

G

---

gap

(1) In linguistics **gap** refers to a missing unit or value in the system, be it PHONETIC, LEXICAL, SEMANTIC; an absence possible according to the rules of the language.

So, for example, in English we have *brother* and *sister* but no LEXICAL ITEM apart from the archaic or specialized *sibling*, to denote both, as a HYPERONYM (q.v.) (cf. Ger. *Geschwister*). Phonetically, /bl/ is an acceptable initial consonant cluster in English (e.g. *black*), and /ɪŋ/, *ing* an acceptable vowel + final consonant, but there is no word *bling*. Of course it is open for someone (product manufacturer, scientist, science-fiction writer, etc.) to introduce such words at any time.

(2) In LITERARY THEORY, and in RECEPTION THEORY (q.v.), **gaps** or **blanks** have arisen in a discussion of the INFORMATIONAL content of a text, and the reading process. (See, e.g., Iser 1978 on *Leerstellen*.)

It is a basic fact that no story or drama can ever tell everything; it would be far too tedious anyway. Much information can be taken for granted or PRESUPPOSED as a common or cultural knowledge, what is not said therefore being left to the reader to supply, from FRAMES OF REFERENCE, to make the text COHERENT. The same is also true of non-literary texts, e.g. newspaper articles: we must 'read between the lines'. (Legal language is designed to reduce gaps, and therefore 'loopholes' in the law: hence the tedious repetition, which would elsewhere be redundant.) Complex stories, however, or OPEN TEXTS (q.v.) often make the reader work harder, to fill in gaps of some significance for the plot or characterization (e.g. Conrad's *Lord Jim*); and many gaps arise from the narrative perspective of a restricted POINT OF VIEW (e.g. in Faulkner's *The Sound and The Fury*). Novelists often usefully exploit the physical breaks or 'gaps' between chapters, and dramatists exploit act or scene divisions, to pass over blocks of time. The MEDIUM tends to create its own specific gaps: it is difficult to enter the thoughts of characters in film.

(See also INDETERMINACY.)

generative: ~ grammar; ~ semantics; ~ poetics; ~ phonology; ~ metrics; ~ stylistics

(1) The term **generative** was first introduced into linguistics from mathematics by Chomsky (1957) to describe a specific group of GRAMMARS which explicitly aim by a set of finite rules to describe and produce (**generate**) all and only the GRAMMATICAL sentences of a language. Chomsky was fascinated by human linguistic CREATIVITY, which he defined as our ability or COMPETENCE to produce and understand an infinite number of utterances from the finite set of linguistic resources.

The most significant of these rather complex grammars, and the one Chomsky himself later developed (1965) was TRANSFORMATIONAL GRAMMAR (TG) (q.v.), hence the terms **generative grammar**, **transformational generative grammar** and **TG** have often been used synonymously. TRANSFORMATIONS (q.v.) were supposedly special powerful and economic rules designed to change forms in the DEEP STRUCTURE of sentences into their actual SURFACE STRUCTURE forms, by deletion, movement, etc.

(2) **Generative semantics** grew directly out of TG in the late 1960s and early 1970s, as a result of considerable discussion about the nature of deep structure, and the role of semantic interpretation. For semanticists like Lakoff (1971) and McCawley (1968) a semantic component was the base of deep structure; whereas 'standard' TG proposed a syntactic (and lexical) deep structure, from which the 'meaning' of a sentence could be derived. In other words, a different 'model' was proposed, but equally formalized and rule-determined.

(3) Only gradually did the limitations of the TG approach to language come to be strongly felt: mainly that it was idealized and SENTENCE-based. Attempts to apply a **generative** framework to language in use, e.g. to TEXT analysis in TEXT LINGUISTICS in the 1970s, exposed the fallacy of assuming that a text was simply a string of separate grammatical sentences in sequence; simultaneously as variant transformational models were proposed, which essentially derived complex NARRATIVES from simple ones or from sets of narrative components. (See the work of Petöfi 1971, 1975; and van Dijk 1972; also Prince 1973; and see Pavel 1985, for survey.) (See also GRAMMAR; NARRATIVE GRAMMAR; NARRATIVE SEMIOTICS.)

(4) Although now no longer in favour **generative grammar** proved appealing to STYLISTICS in the 1960s (see Ohmann 1964, also 1966), with early Chomskyan clausal transformations providing the framework for a comparison of IDIOLECTAL prose STYLES (e.g. Hemingway and Faulkner). Generally, TG was felt to be an appropriate model for analysis, since the notions of deep and surface structure seemed to correspond with the popular DUALIST (q.v.) approach to style, namely that there are 'different ways' of saying the same thing. So ACTIVE and PASSIVE sentences like

> The sparrow killed Cock Robin
> Cock Robin was killed by the sparrow

and clauses and NOMINALIZATIONS like

Caesar fortified the camp
Caesar's fortification of the camp

would have the same deep structure as the source of their surface meaning. Differences in WORD ORDER between sentences were regarded as the result of superficial (and optional), 'stylistic' (*sic*) transformations.

However, the basic premise of TG, namely that all and only grammatical sentences would be generated, caused problems to stylisticians, who in the process of their discussions of GRAMMATICALITY (q.v.) merely confirmed the difficulty inherent in the TG aim itself (see Hendricks 1969; Thorne 1965, 1969). Clearly LITERARY LANGUAGE is as much a part of English as any other variety, but there may be grammatical structures acceptable to it that would be regarded as DEVIANT in 'ordinary' everyday usage, through the use of, e.g. METAPHOR and PERSONIFICATION, especially in poetry. To try to devise rules that are general enough to include literary usages would be a forbidding task, and it is not surprising, therefore, that TG theory concentrated on a rather narrow linguistic 'competence'. The alternative is to provide a grammatical description of literary text(s) quite separately: to assume that a text (e.g. poem) has its own (regular) 'grammar' or 'dialect'.

(5) In LITERARY THEORY, a combination of STRUCTURALISM, generative theory and READER-RESPONSE CRITICISM gave rise to a kind of **generative POETICS** in the work of Bierwisch (1970) and Culler (1975). Culler suggested a **literary** COMPETENCE by analogy with Chomsky's linguistic competence. Such a poetics was to make explicit the IDEAL's knowledge of the set of conventions needed for the interpretation of literary texts, whether linguistic, cultural or INTERTEXTUAL.

(6) More substantial has been the impact of generative grammar on METRICS, especially in the USA, beginning with the work of Halle & Keyser (1966), on Chaucerian IAMBIC PENTAMETER, aligning itself with Halle's work (with Chomsky) on **generative phonology** (Chomsky & Halle 1968). In 'standard' TG theory the PHONOLOGICAL component of the grammar interpreted the outcome of the syntactic component in terms of actual surface realizations, the phonetic DISTINCTIVE FEATURES of which are themselves rule-governed.

In **generative metrics** the 'deep' structure or abstract metrical pattern is related to the surface RHYTHMS by a set of actualization realization rules, which account for permissible positions of stressed and unstressed syllables within the line.

In principle, a generative approach to metre seems attractive, with its speculation that metre may be 'innate', and its aim of providing a definitive set of rules which will generate all and only the metrically 'correct' iambic lines for the oeuvre of any one poet. A concern with metrical styles is reflected in the work of Kiparsky (1977), for instance, on Wyatt, Shakespeare, Milton and Pope. However, in practice, it has proved easier to define 'unacceptable' lines than it has to predict acceptable ones; and the whole approach is rather too idealized, despite its corpus basis. (See Attridge 1982, ch. 2; but see further Fabb 1997.)

generic: ~ meaning; ~ proposition; ~ reference, etc.

Generic is used in SEMANTICS and GRAMMAR for classes of objects, etc. (cf. Lat. *genus*) as opposed to specific entities. So *flower, animal, vegetable* have a natural **generic meaning**; whereas *daisy, rose, elephant, cat, onion* and *carrot* all have a more specific meaning, as types or HYPONYMS of the generic words.

However, it is also possible to speak of daisies or elephants as a class, if we wish to make generalizations about their typical characteristics as a species. Conjoined with the ARTICLES (q.v.), the nouns then have **generic reference** in propositions like

An elephant is herbivorous
The elephant(s) is/are herbivorous
Elephants are herbivorous.

Although the CONNOTATIONS of the articles may well be different (e.g. seeing an elephant as the representative of its class, versus thinking of the class as a whole), and philosophers argue about the possibility of there being different kinds of **generic statements**, nonetheless we can assume the same basic meaning is shared. (See further Quirk *et al.* 1985, 5.52f.)

PRONOUNS, too, can have generic INDEFINITE REFERENCE, as in *You/one never can tell; They're putting up the mortgage rate again*: referring to people in general or indeterminate groups (building societies; banks).

In English **generic propositions** are most frequently expressed in the PRESENT TENSE; and can be grouped with other kinds of generalizing expressions like proverbs (*Many hands make light work*); gnomic or sententious statements (*Hope springs eternal in the human breast* (Pope's *Essay on Man*)); scientific or universal truths (*The moon goes round the earth*); which have the same timelessness (see Lyons 1977). Propositions that are valid for all time are also characteristic of laws and rules (although these can be changed by decree), instructions and recipes. (See also APHORISM.)

Generic propositions are also found in novels, especially those characterized by an 'intrusive' author–narrator figure (e.g. Fielding, George Eliot), e.g.: *Every physician almost hath his favourite disease* (Fielding: *Tom Jones*). One function is to link the world of the novel and its values to those of the society at large and familiar to the reader. (See also REFERENTIAL CODE. See further Fowler 1981.)

genre; genre analysis, etc.

From Fr. (and ultimately Lat.) meaning 'kind' or 'class' **genre** is widely used in LITERARY CRITICISM, and has become very popular in DISCOURSE ANALYSIS and TEXT LINGUISTICS. It has also become commonplace in MEDIA studies to classify films or TV programmes according to such genres as horror film, 'soap opera', documentary, etc.

(1) Since classical times it has been customary to think of literature as consisting of different kinds of works, and one function of a POETICS from Aristotle

onwards has been to try and classify them, from theoretical, stru
historical perspectives. In the twentieth century there are, for instance,
of Frye (1957) and of Todorov (1971) and Fowler (1982).

The broadest and commonest division is that between poetry, prose
drama; and then further (sub-)genres can be distinguished within each: e.g.
lyric, epic, ode, ballad, sonnet within poetry; tragedy and comedy within drama.
Even these are broad types: the number of possible sub-genres is difficult to
estimate; many do not have names. But the significant point is that, whatever the
level of abstraction, no literary work exists in isolation: it is related to other texts,
belongs to an INTERTEXTUAL 'system', and so cannot properly be understood
except in relation to its place in that system.

However arbitrary may appear to be the boundary between one genre
and another, what distinguishes them, and what determines how genres are
traditionally defined, is usually the set or cluster of structural and STYLISTIC
properties that have come to be associated with them, which have come to be
DOMINANT in the FORMALIST sense; also certain functions, TONES, subject matter,
WORLD-VIEWS and audiences. So Elizabethan sonnets prototypically were not
only written to a strict metrical form, but assumed certain postures (the scorned
lover, for example) and tones (of eulogy, lament, etc.) and were read by a courtly
educated circle. Well into the eighteenth century different literary kinds were
governed by the inherited classical principle of DECORUM (q.v.), of an appro
priate matching STYLE (e.g. the GRAND STYLE for epic).

Not that the 'rules' for a genre were always slavishly followed: practice may
differ from precept, and literary innovation has always balanced conformity.
Viewed historically, and in any one period, genres present a more dynamic,
flexible aspect, one genre developing out of another (the novel out of prose
romances, for example). The novel as 'super-genre' (Bakhtin 1981) is the most
difficult genre to characterize, and one precisely in which formal experimenting
is equally characteristic. And there are so-called mixed genres, which blend one
variety with another: e.g. mock-epic, tragi-comedy.

If a genre is a model of writing, it also becomes a model of expectation for the
reader. It is part of our literary COMPETENCE (Culler 1975) that we FRAME a text
within a genre from our general knowledge of reading, and so tolerate the death
of the hero in a tragedy, but not in a comedy. Of course our expectations may
be thwarted by a new twist to the normal or typical pattern (e.g. accepting a
detective story where the murderer is revealed at the beginning).

(2) For Bakhtin (see Morson (ed.) 1986) literature is itself a culturally complex
genre (secondary) which is learnt alongside primary speech genres from our
earliest experiences with language. As kinds of cultural practice non-literary
discourses have their own relatively stable generic categories and structures,
with their characteristic formal properties, social functions, and contextual
APPROPRIATENESS: what Hasan (1978) in the Australian SYSTEMIC 'genre school'
describes as genre/generic structure potential (GSP). Conversation as a discourse
genre (see Hymes 1974) or even as a meta-genre (Fludernik 1996) can be
subdivided further into the (sub-)genres of intimate, telephone, public debate,
interview, etc. A distinction is sometimes also made between simple and

service, as an example of the latter, comprises con-
prayer, hymn, etc.

tinguishing these uses of *genre* from those of REGISTER
linguists have abandoned the latter term altogether.
an SYSTEMIC 'school' which pioneered register studies,
ontradiction. If a distinction can be made, it is best to
rthy & Carter (1994), who see genre at a 'higher level'
ake a **core generic function** like reporting, there are the
ither reports, progress reports, etc.; and within the genre
of weather.   re are specific registers such as TV weather forecasts and
newspaper reports, marked by quite specific medium-determined linguistic
features and structures, etc. So any group of texts which show a similarity of
register can be said to belong to the same genre. Another model is to see genre
at a 'deeper' level, with register the 'surface' manifestation of genre. In CDA
genres or **discourse types** are sociocultural practices related to institutions and
issues of social difference and power. (See further Bex 1996.)

(3) The social dimension of genre is particularly stressed in the field of **genre
analysis**, particularly associated with the work of Swales (e.g. 1990) and Bhatia
(1993), in relation to the teaching of English for Academic Purposes and the need
for the acquisition of generic as well as other linguistic skills. (See also CONTRASTIVE
RHETORIC.) Genres are classes of discourses recognized by expert members of the
DISCOURSE COMMUNITY with the same primary social function and communicative goals and intended audience.

gestalt

From the Ger. meaning 'form' or 'shape', this word has figured in European
theories of:

(1) AESTHETICS of the early twentieth century: in the discussion of FORM and
CONTENT (*Gehalt*) in art.

(2) more influentially, psychology: in the so-called **gestalt psychology** originating in the early twentieth century in Germany, which stresses the tendency
of the human brain to make wholes out of parts, and wholes which are more
than simply the sum of the parts.

(3) **Gestalt** as a complex of properties has been taken up in SEMANTICS and
TEXT LINGUISTICS, as part of a larger interest in cognitive processes: of CONCEP-
TUALIZATION (see, e.g., Lakoff & Johnson 1980); and of textual comprehension.
So in the RECEPTION THEORY of Iser 1971, *Gestalten* (plural) are the complexes of
signs or FRAMES (q.v.) significant for interpretation which are formed (and often
re-formed) by readers as they read.

It can also be argued that readers aim for an overall, global gestalt of a text;
and so (2) and (3) relate to (1) and ideas of unity and CLOSURE much discussed
in LITERARY THEORY (e.g. Smith 1968).

(4) **Gestalt** has also come to be loosely or metaphorically used for any
underlying structure perceived as a whole: e.g. in METRICS, groups of stresses
or rhythmic patterns.

given information

One of a pair of terms (see also NEW INFORMATION (q.v.)) commonly used in DISCOURSE ANALYSIS and TEXT LINGUISTICS with reference to the INFORMATIONAL content of UTTERANCES.

As its name suggests, **given** refers to information stated or already known to the participants: either supplied in the CO-TEXT; or PRESUPPOSED from the situational CONTEXT, or from the (wider) context of assumed common knowledge. It is contrasted with **new information**, which is not known, or not assumed to be known, to the addressee; or which is regarded as particularly 'newsworthy'.

Each utterance or sentence in an extended discourse will present different patterns of **givenness** and **newness**. Typically, opening sentences will contain new information; sentences in sequence will contain a distribution of both given and new. DEFINITE ARTICLES commonly indicate given information; and so do SUBORDINATE CLAUSES: *Besides being a well-known literary critic, he also writes books on the history of aviation.* ELLIPSIS is an economical way of disposing of known information in contexts where it is readily understood: e.g. answers to questions:

. . . How does your garden grow?
[My garden grows] with silver bells and cockle shells . . .

Given and new are often associated with THEME (q.v.) and RHEME (q.v.) (see the post-war PRAGUE SCHOOL work on FUNCTIONAL SENTENCE PERSPECTIVE); but linguists like Halliday (1985) have taken pains to distinguish them. The association is understandable, since theme and rheme are also aspects of TEXT structure involving information, but its value and importance rather than degree of newness. However, the theme as 'point of departure' in an utterance often coincides with given information; just as the rheme, the part of the sentence (usually post-VERBAL) that is communicatively most important or significant, will coincide with new information.

gradatio

See CLIMAX.

grammar

(1) **Grammar** commonly denotes a level or component of language subsumed under the general level of FORM (q.v.), and distinct from meaning and sound, specifically the words, phrases and clauses of which sentences are composed. Grammar itself can be subdivided into SYNTAX (the structure of clauses and sentences) and MORPHOLOGY (word structure).

In English it is syntax which is the most significant aspect of grammatical structure, and syntax and grammar are therefore sometimes used interchangeably in this sense.

(2) **Grammar** also describes the systematic classification or description of the linguistic structure itself, its forms and grammatical FUNCTIONS.

Traditionally, some grammars have tended to be PRESCRIPTIVE rather than descriptive in their 'rules': advising people what they ought to say, and what is considered CORRECT according to some ideal standard not necessarily based on the observation of actual USAGE.

(3) Much modern grammatical study engages broadly with all levels, pronunciation and meaning included; and may be concerned with grammatical universals (features common to all languages), and a general theory of language, as in GENERATIVE GRAMMAR (q.v.). In this sense, therefore, the term **grammar** is used very broadly indeed.

(4) In generative theory and also RELEVANCE THEORY the term refers not only to the model of analysis, but also to the system of rules generated which supposedly formalizes a native speaker's COMPETENCE, or internalized knowledge: so we can speak of an individual's **grammar** in any speech community.

(5) **Grammar** as an IDIOLECTAL set of rules is also manifested in studies of 'Shakespeare's grammar' or 'the grammar of Spenser'; or of individual texts such as poems by Cummings, Donne or Dylan Thomas. In such studies, the notion that the grammar of poetry (particularly modern) involves a systematic DEVIATION from a NORM has sometimes been implied.

(6) The 'upper limit' of grammatical analysis has been traditionally the SENTENCE, but the interest in inter-sentence relations and TEXT structure developed since the 1970s has led to notions of TEXT GRAMMAR (q.v.) where linguistic theory (e.g. generative grammar) is applied to structural descriptions of whole texts (e.g. Petöfi 1971, 1975; van Dijk 1972f).

(7) Well established, however, are studies of NARRATIVE text which use **grammar** in a looser, metaphorical sense. For example, the grammatical SUBJECT is seen to be analogous to the ACTANT (q.v.) in a PLOT or the 'actor'; the OBJECT analogous to the 'receiver' of an action. A pioneering work in abstract structures is Propp's (1928) on the MORPHOLOGY (*sic*) of the folk-tale; and other grammars, using degrees of linguistic METALANGUAGE, include those of Todorov (1969) on *The Decameron*; Greimas (1966f); Kristeva (1970); Prince (1973); and Souriau (1950), on dramatic plots. (See also NARRATIVE GRAMMAR.)

grammaticality, also grammaticalness

An UTTERANCE or SENTENCE is strictly **grammatical** if it conforms to the rules of a language's GRAMMAR (q.v.) and **ungrammatical** if it does not; but the terms are not always so strictly used.

In popular use an utterance like *I ain't done nothing*, however ACCEPTABLE to a DIALECT speaker, would be regarded as ungrammatical by those upholding STANDARD ENGLISH as the NORM. For others, sentences ending in a preposition, or constructions like *It is me* would be regarded as ungrammatical, however widespread in usage, because they do not conform to an idealized English grammar based on centuries of precept rather than practice.

But even with the usage of English as a whole as a basis for formalization of definitions there are problems, as Chomsky's GENERATIVE GRAMMAR revealed in the 1960s. This stimulated discussion of the whole subject of **grammaticality** or **grammaticalness**, since a generative grammar explicitly aimed to describe and produce all and only the grammatical sentences of a language. Even allowing for the fact that no model for English has ever been fully worked out, the rules devised were for an English narrow in scope and variety, to the extent that structures of LITERARY, especially POETIC, LANGUAGE, and METAPHORIC language, would technically not be generated and therefore dubbed ungrammatical or DEVIANT (q.v.).

It is not always easy to tell whether 'deviation' is semantic or grammatical. Chomsky's own famous example of *Colourless green ideas sleep furiously* certainly seems nonsensical (although contexts have been suggested for it); and in terms of the 1965 generative model it is ungrammatical; although the basic syntactic categories of adjective + adjective + noun + verb + adverb are grammatical. Such sentences have therefore been seen as **semi-grammatical**, and grammaticalness itself as a scale or cline.

However, it has been argued that the whole notion of grammaticalness is too ideal. Aside from obvious cases of marked ungrammaticalness as in jumbled anagrammatic WORD ORDERS (*Ears elephants have big*), in speech, and in literary language, violations of grammatical rules may pass unnoticed, or be considered perfectly acceptable, if utterances in their contexts make good sense (*Do like I do; Him who disobeys me disobeys* (Milton: *Paradise Lost*)). Moreover, what may cause problems of interpretation for hearer or reader (especially) are structures technically grammatical but difficult to process because of their complexity: PERIODIC SENTENCES in the prose of Milton or James; or the verse lines of Donne or Hopkins.

grammatology

(1) The term **grammatology** first appears meaning 'science of writing' (Gelb 1952) coined from Gk *gramma* ('thing written, letter'). Such a study considers, for instance, the history and development of writing-systems, principles and techniques, and the functions of writing in different societies. (See also GRAPHOLOGY.)

(2) **Grammatology** acquired a DECONSTRUCTIONIST gloss through the work of Derrida (1967a), as part of his philosophical critique of language generally. He had much to say about what he saw as the traditional PHONOCENTRIC over-valuing of the spoken word at the expense of the written. The term 'writing' itself is commonly used in LITERARY THEORY not only in its normal, GRAPHIC sense, but also in a Derridean, metaphysical sense to refer to a generalized 'inscription', **archi-writing**, basic to speech as well, and to language itself. For Derrida, language is basically 'inscribed' in a network of DIFFERENCES: the signification of signs comes as much from what they are not, as from what they are. (See also Norris 1982.)

The study of **applied grammatology** stretched Derrida's ideas into contemporary (popular) culture and art (see Ulmer 1985).

grammetrics

Grammetrics came into STYLISTICS in the 1960s, from a blend of *grammar* and *metrics*, to describe the relations in poetry between SYNTAX and METRICAL units.

So **grammetrical** studies of Old English verse have examined the grammatical and rhythmical patterns of the A- and B-VERSES in terms of their FORMULAIC structure. And appreciation of ENJAMBMENT as a poetic device involves consideration of the degree of tension between metrical pausing and syntactical pausing, at line-endings.

(See further Sinclair 1966.)

grand style

The **grand** or **high** STYLE is one of a set of three terms (the others are MIDDLE, and PLAIN or **low**) formalized in classical RHETORIC, and influential in literary composition up to the Renaissance and after.

According to the principle of DECORUM (q.v.), style should be fitted to subject matter, genre, characterization or situation, etc. Thus a grand or elevated style was considered suitable for the epic genre, itself concerned with heroic deeds and grand passions; and is marked by a complex, PERIODIC clause structure, elaborate EPIC SIMILES, rhetorical devices of AMPLIFICATION and EMPHASIS, etc. designed to move the emotions of the reader or listener. Such a style is characteristic of Milton's *Paradise Lost*, and much of Chaucer's *Knight's Tale*.

grapheme; graphemies; graphology, etc.

From Gk *graphos* 'written', present-day linguistics has spawned a whole set of terms to do with the study of written language, most by analogy with the study of speech in PHONETICS and PHONOLOGY.

(1) So, by analogy with PHONEME (q.v.), a **grapheme** is the smallest distinctive unit in the writing system of a language: popularly known as 'letter' or SYMBOL. In English ORTHOGRAPHY or spelling there is no one-to-one relationship between grapheme and phoneme: so <c> represents /k/, /s/ in *cut, ceiling*; and /ʃ/ is symbolized by <sh>, <ch>, <ssi> and <ti>, etc., in *ship, charade, mission* and *caution*.

Each grapheme is potentially realized as a set of **allographs** or variants, due to variations in typefaces or handwriting. Stylistically, such variations will be associated with **degrees of** FORMALITY: printed graphemes associated with the formal language of published materials, hand-written with personal correspondence, etc.

(2) The study of such units in a language is called **graphemics**, or **graphology**. (In popular usage **graphology** also refers confusingly to the study of handwriting as a means of character analysis.)

Graphemics also embraces other features associated with the written or **graphic** MEDIUM: punctuation; paragraphing; spacing, etc. Different REGISTERS make particular use of such **graphological** features as: size of print and capitalization in newspaper and advertising lay-outs; different typefaces and sizes in dictionaries such as this one; special line lengths in poetry, etc. Halliday's (1985) term for the particular units of lines and stanzas associated with written poetry is **graphometric units**. In prose, the term **graphic unit** refers to pieces of text separated by punctuation, e.g. commas and full-stops (Leech & Short 1981). Different texts will have different **graphological** STYLES according to the density and degree of 'weight' of punctuation.

(3) **Graphology** can also refer to the writing system of a language, as manifested in handwriting and typography; and to the other related features noted in (2), e.g. capitalization and punctuation.

(4) In theory, just as phonology is a branch of the wider and more theoretical discipline of phonetics, concerned with universals of sound-making, so **graphetics** is the term needed to describe the study of graphic universals, general features of the written medium influential on all (or many) systems (e.g. shape; size; spacing; material; etc.).

(5) But **graphetics** is also used for the study of typographical and visual devices in art, **graphicology** being a less confusing alternative term. These devices are also studied in **visual grammar**.

In literature, novelists have occasionally experimented with aspects of the written medium for expressive effects since Sterne's *Tristram Shandy*, with its blank pages, false chapter headings and varied typography. Layout is exploited ICONICALLY in certain kinds of poetry, from the metaphysical poet George Herbert's *Wings*, through to 'Fury said to a Mouse' in Carroll's *Alice in Wonderland*, and many modern so-called concrete poems. Iconic resemblance is also the basis of many of the characters in the Egyptian (**hieroglyphic**) writing-system. And the close relationship between writing and art is reflected in the painstaking attention taken to their complex system of characters by Chinese and Japanese artists, who practise **calligraphy** (Gk 'beautiful writing') as an art form.

H

___

habitus

A term borrowed from Aristotle by the French sociologist Pierre Bourdieu to refer to a set of dispositions, acquired by cultural and social inculcation which make people act and react in certain ways in different FIELDS. There are linguistic consequences of this: different professions have their own JARGONS, ways of speaking, and presenting arguments which may be unconsciously assimilated, but which are a necessary condition of acceptance and validation. (See further Bourdieu 1991.)

half-rhyme

An imperfect RHYME which rests on likeness of sounds rather than strict identity. It usually takes the form of the repetition of final consonants with variation in preceding vowels: a kind of CONSONANCE (q.v.) (e.g. *bend, sand*). Common in Celtic poetry, it became very popular at the end of the nineteenth century, and is found in the work of Hopkins, Dickinson, Yeats, Owen, Auden and Hughes, for example. So in Yeats's *Easter 1916*:

> I have met them at close of day
> Coming with vivid faces
> From counter or desk among grey
> Eighteenth-century houses . . .

(See also PARARHYME.)

head

(1) In GRAMMAR the **head** or **headword** frequently describes the word in a NOMINAL GROUP which is both lexically and grammatically most important: usually the NOUN, with any adjectives as MODIFIERS (e.g. *Blue Moon*). Heads can be found in other syntactic groups: e.g. the main VERB in a verbal group.

(2) In the study of INTONATION, especially amongst British phoneticians, all the ACCENTED syllables before the NUCLEUS in a TONE UNIT. American linguists tend to use **pendent** for **head**.

(3) More recently, in Carter & McCarthy's study of informal spoken English (1997) **head** refers to the FRONTING of a noun or noun phrase at the beginning of an utterance in anticipation of a structure which then forms the main SUBJECT. Heads are thus used for FOCUSSING and orienteering, for identifying key information or establishing a shared FRAME of reference for what the speaker thinks is important: e.g. *This friend of mine, Tim, his cousin, he actually met Elton John.* Cf. written English *The cousin of Tim, a friend of mine, has actually met Elton John.* (See also PROLEPSIS.) The amplification or extension or reinforcement of something at the end of an utterance they call the **tail**. (See TAG.)

hedging; hedge

(1) In DISCOURSE ANALYSIS and SPEECH ACT THEORY **hedging** is the qualification and toning-down of utterances or statements, so common in speech and writing, by CLAUSES, ADVERBIALS, etc., in order to reduce the riskiness of what one says.

Mitigation of what may otherwise seem too forceful may be one reason; politeness or respect to strangers and superiors another (*That may be true, but . . .; Would you mind awfully if . . .*).

In this connection **hedged** PERFORMATIVE has been used, following Fraser (1975), for a kind of clause structure which METALINGUISTICALLY refers to the ILLOCUTIONARY FORCE of the utterance: e.g. *We regret to inform you that; May I suggest that.*

In NARRATIVES hedging is likely to be the sign of an obtrusive NARRATOR or IMPLIED AUTHOR; or of the subjective POINT OF VIEW of a character. So in Woolf's *To the Lighthouse* Mrs Ramsey ponders: *Like all stupid people, he had a kind of modesty, too, a consideration for what you were feeling, which, once in a way at least, she found attractive.*

(2) In SEMANTICS **hedges** are modifiers in a narrower sense: Lakoff (1975) uses the term for modifiers which qualify **prototypes**: e.g. phrases ranging from *par excellence* to *technically; loosely speaking; in certain respects.* So a cabbage is a vegetable par excellence, but a tomato is only one loosely speaking. For various purposes (e.g. law; insurance) HYPONYMOUS categories may be redefined, and hedges are therefore useful (see Lakoff & Johnson 1980).

hendiadys

From Gk 'one thing by two', and what Puttenham (1589) dubbed the 'figure of twinness', **hendiadys** is a relatively uncommon FIGURE OF RHETORIC where two NOUNS connected by *and* are used instead of the more usual ADJECTIVE + noun construction, to give added EMPHASIS, e.g.:

> The heaviness and the guilt (i.e. heavy guilt) within my bosom
> Takes off my manhood
>
> (Shakespeare: *Cymbeline*, V.ii)

hermeneutics; hermeneutic: ~ circle; ~ code, etc.

(1) From Gk 'interpretation', **hermeneutics** or **hermeneutic theory** is precisely the art or science of understanding and INTERPRETATION.

Traditionally **hermeneutics** has been concerned with 'correct' textual interpretation, of the scriptures and patristic writings in the early Christian Church; later it covered legal and also literary texts, e.g. poetic ALLEGORY. Nowadays, however, hermeneutics has a broader, more philosophical base, and also relates to psychology and scientific methodology. It particularly developed amongst German-speaking scholars after the Second World War, notably Gadamer (much influenced by earlier philosophers like Heidegger). (See Gadamer 1972, 1976.) It was also developed in the USA (in particular) through the work of Hirsch (1967) on INTENTION (q.v.).

Interesting is the notion of the **hermeneutic circle**, borrowed from early Biblical hermeneutics, which represents the dynamic process of interpretation in terms of a continual interplay of interpreter and text, of whole context and individual parts. (For another 'circle' of interpretation, see PHILOLOGICAL CIRCLE.)

Gadamer's insistence on the historical nature of understanding has important implications for disciplines such as LITERARY CRITICISM, NEW HISTORICISM and historical PRAGMATICS, and the knotty question of a text's 'meaning' for a modern reader. He convincingly argues for a compromise position, in that any act of understanding is a fusion (*Verschmelzung*) of one's own **horizon** with the historical one, with no clear boundary between. The text, as it were, seems to beckon towards us, be 'relevant' to our age; at the same time we must of necessity reach back to the earlier period: the historical horizon is both present and absent, and our understanding involves a 'dialogue' between past and present, between the original and accrued meaning. (For a resumé of hermeneutics, see further Holub 1984; also Palmer 1969.)

(2) This dialectical position is also at the heart of Barthes's early writings, culminating in his work of 1964; yet later, under the influence of DECONSTRUCTION THEORY, he turned anti-historical.

But Barthes (1970) himself used the term **hermeneutic** in a very particular way that has been influential in NARRATOLOGY. He distinguishes certain CODES (q.v.) which readers draw upon in making sense of a text. The **hermeneutic code** foregrounds interpretation negatively, in that it involves all those units whose function is to delay INFORMATION to the reader, to pose questions and ENIGMAS, to delay answers and solutions. Certainly suspense and 'riddle' are common PLOT lines in novels, not only in detective fiction, e.g. Conrad's *Lord Jim* and *Heart of Darkness*; and there are various devices of equivocation, suspension, obliqueness and obscurity which can be exploited. SYNTAX and LEXIS can be clearly involved, as Barthes's own analysis of Balzac's *Sarrazine* reveals.

heteroglossia

A translation of the Russian linguist Mikhail Bakhtin's coinage *raznorecie* in the 1930s, **heteroglossia** (Gk 'different tongue') refers to the internal differentiation or stratification of language. There is the interaction of different VARIETIES: social and regional DIALECTS; the JARGON of different occupational and social groups; the conjunction of archaic and innovatory tendencies, etc. Bakhtin emphasizes that there are no 'neutral' words or TONES in a language, and that language itself is not single-voiced.

For Bakhtin, part of the particular fascination of the novel as a GENRE compared with poetry is the ready incorporation of heteroglossia as a principle of its structure. The ALIEN voices of different social groups are all present, as well as different sub-genres, and the VOICES of the NARRATOR and the different CHARACTERS. The discourse of the novel is essentially heterogeneous and interactive, and manifestations of this POLYPHONY include the DOUBLE VOICE of FREE INDIRECT SPEECH, COLOURED NARRATIVE and CHARACTER ZONE.

(See also CARNIVAL(ESQUE); DIALOGIC; HYBRIDIZATION; POLYPHONY. See further Bakhtin 1981.)

high style

See GRAND STYLE.

histoire

One of a pair of terms (see also DISCOURS) introduced into French linguistics and NARRATOLOGY by Benveniste (1966), and frequently used untranslated in British and American criticism. This is advisable, for a literal translation as 'STORY' (and 'DISCOURSE') (e.g. Chatman 1978) adds to the vagueness and polysemy of these words.

(1) Benveniste himself was interested in UTTERANCE, and distinguishes two modes: the 'objective' mode of *histoire* concerned with the NARRATION of events in the past (L'ÉNONCÉ); and the SUBJECTIVE mode of *discours*, highlighting the present mode of ÉNONCIATION (q.v.). Linguistic characteristics of *histoire* are the **third** PERSON PRONOUNS and the **past** TENSE; of *discours* the **first** and **second** PERSON pronouns, DEICTICS, and the PERFECT.

Benveniste sees *histoire* as abstracting the *énoncé* from the CONTEXT OF UTTERANCE, from speaker and listener, and hence is the 'pure' narrative mode; but as others have pointed out (e.g. Genette (1980)), even a third person narrative is hardly neutral or anonymous, and has a characteristic narrative VOICE, and a *discours*-frame of IMPLIED AUTHOR and IMPLIED READER.

(2) So *histoire* and *discours* are now taken as 'levels' rather than modes of utterance: every utterance is both an event and an enunciative act. In narrative terms they correspond to CONTENT (*histoire*) and FORM (*discours*), or DEEP and SURFACE STRUCTURE: what is being told v. how it is told; and so align themselves with the **Russian** FORMALIST distinction between FABULA (q.v.) and SJUŽET (q.v.): the abstracted chronological or logical ordering of events v. the actual sequence

of events as narrated. (But see also RÉCIT.) Hence the study of *histoire* in narratology has involved research into universals of PLOT across folk-tales, and also into NARRATIVE GRAMMARS. (See also ACTANT; FUNCTION.)

historic present

The special use of the PRESENT TENSE (q.v.) in oral or written, anecdotal or literary NARRATIVE, where the **past** TENSE might be expected, the shift creating a more dramatic or immediate effect. The listener/reader is 'drawn into' the account. So the **historic present** is common in jokes: *A man walks into a bar with an elephant on a lead and asks for a pink gin* . . . ; personal stories: *I wake up and hear this horrible howling outside* . . . ; and passages descriptive of activity in novels and poems:

> . . . Loud sounds the Axe, redoubling Strokes on Strokes;
> On all sides round the Forest hurles her Oaks
> Headlong . . .
>
> (Pope: *The Iliad*)

In some modern short stories and novels it is not uncommon to find the present tense used as the narrative mode throughout (e.g. Brookner's *Family and Friends*).

Related to the historic present is probably the use of the present tense in newspaper headlines to record events in the recent past (*England fails to win vital match*).

historical pragmatics

See PRAGMATICS.

homonymy; homography; homophony

Terms used in SEMANTICS to refer to words which have the same FORM, but different, i.e. unrelated meanings.

Homonymy refers to words which are identical in both spelling and sound (e.g. *bear* (NOUN, VERB); *mole*). **Partial homonymy** or **heteronymy** due to variation in MEDIUM is shown in words which have the same spelling but different pronunciations (e.g. *lead; bow*), i.e. **homographs**; and in words which have the same pronunciation but different spellings (e.g. *pale; pail*), i.e. **homophones**. The conservative nature of English spelling has given rise to a considerable amount of **homophony**.

Problems of AMBIGUITY or **homonymic clash** do not frequently arise, because CONTEXT will help us to decide on the most appropriate meaning; but potential ambiguity can certainly be exploited in PUNS and jokes:

Q: Why is a tree surgeon like an actor?
A: Because he's always taking boughs (bows).

Homophony is naturally exploited in RHYME; **homography** in EYE-RHYME (q.v.).

There is much discussion about the relation between homonymy and POLY-SEMY (q.v.), double or multiple meaning also arising from identical forms, but of the same not different words. It may not be easy to distinguish between them, unless we actually know the ETYMOLOGY of the words. So *weeds* in the senses of 'garments' (archaic) and 'plants' may well be thought to be derived from the same word referring to plants by some kind of metaphoric association, whereas they are homonyms. Conversely *metal* and *mettle*, although distinguished by spelling since Johnson's *Dictionary* (1755) and widely divergent in meaning, are technically derived from the same root. Some linguists, therefore, also include under homonymy words derived from the same origin, but whose senses now widely diverge: e.g. *sole; game; pupil; gay* (see Allan 1986).

hybridization

(1) In LEXICOLOGY a **hybrid** is sometimes used for words made up of elements from different languages, e.g. OE (i.e. native) root + Fr. or Lat. SUFFIX (e.g. *wash-able*); or (common in scientific vocabulary) two foreign roots (e.g. Gk *tele* + Lat. *vision*).

(2) **Hybridization** was developed particularly by Bakhtin in the 1930s in his work on the variety of STYLES or HETEROGLOSSIA (q.v.) in the novel. It refers to the mixing within a single utterance or sentence of two different VOICES or con-sciousnesses: e.g. that of the NARRATOR and a CHARACTER or a social group, but with no formal speech boundaries.

Bakhtin has many examples from Dickens, where hybridization is used for IRONY and satire. In *Little Dorrit*, for example, hybrid constructions effectively highlight the social hypocrisy by means of a COLLECTIVE DISCOURSE (q.v.) mer-ging with the narrator's voice: *But Mr Tite Barnacle was a buttoned-up man, and consequently a weighty one* ... The adverb *consequently* signifies a shift to the cultural values of 'society' in the novel.

Hybridization may also define FREE INDIRECT SPEECH (q.v.), which Pascal (1977) terms DOUBLE VOICE. There is a similar blend of a character's and narrator's PERSPECTIVES, often with an ironic distancing. (See also COLOURED NARRATIVE.)

hyperbaton

From Gk 'over-step', a FIGURE OR SPEECH in which 'normal' WORD ORDER is trans-posed by INVERSION or FRONTING, etc. Also known in RHETORIC as **anastrophe**.

Although often used for EMPHASIS, such DEVIATIONS are common in traditional POETIC LANGUAGE: e.g. NOUN + ADJECTIVE order, as in

Meadows trim with daisies pied,
Shallow brooks and rivers wide

(Milton: *L'Allegro*)

189

hyperbole

From Gk 'exceed', a common FIGURE or TROPE in speech as well as literature, popularly known as **exaggeration** or **over-statement**. (For **understatement**, see LITOTES.)

In drama, **hyperbole** is often used for EMPHASIS as a sign of great emotion or passion; as when Hamlet tells Laertes of his love for Ophelia:

> . . . Forty thousand brothers
> Could not, with all their quantity of love,
> Make up my sum

> (V.i)

In PRAGMATIC terms hyperbole superficially violates Grice's **maxims of** QUALITY and QUANTITY, since it distorts the truth by saying too much. But hyperbole is not the same as telling lies: there is normally no intent to deceive one's listeners, who will no doubt INFER the true state of affairs anyway. We juggle with the facts and the apparent meanings, as we do in the case of METAPHOR, a related trope. Common phrases, often involving metaphor, like *It made my hair stand on end/my blood boil*, at least imply an intensity of feeling, and add vividness and interest to conversation (see further Leech 1983, for his **interest principle**). As for Hamlet above, the strength of his emotions is such that he himself believes he is telling the truth.

However, there is a danger of deception in the hyperbole of sensational reporting. Headlines often reveal discrepancies of numbers in the reporting of accidents, e.g.: *Thousands feared dead after nuclear leak.*

Hyperbole is often popularly assumed to distinguish female from male speech. But there is no firm evidence that women exaggerate more than men do. It's an absolutely preposterous claim.

(See also METALOGISM. See further Gibbs 1994, ch. 8.)

hyper-fiction; ~ text, etc.

Hyperfiction as a term was used by Robert Couver in a book review in the *New York Times* (1992), to describe what is also termed **interactive fiction** (IF) readable only on a computer and made possible by **hypertext**. Fittingly POSTMODERN and INTERTEXTUAL, hypertext provides the means of arranging information in a non-linear way, and accommodates not only printed texts, but digitized sound, graphics, animation, etc., so that hyperfictions themselves have no single beginning or end and little sense of 'unity' or CLOSURE, different on each 'reading'. Spatial, labyrinthian, and journey metaphors commonly describe the readerly experience: readers 'enter' and 'leave' and the WORLD they 'go to' is an imaginative **cyber-space** (a term coined by William Gibson in his novel *Neuromancer* 1984). Problem-solving, role-playing adventure games of the 1970s anticipated more developed narrative frameworks.

However, despite interest in hypertext and -fiction in LITERARY THEORY, a **hyperstylistics** has yet to emerge.

(See further Bolter 1991; Gibson 1996, Appx; Graddol 1994; Landow 1992.)

hyponymy

Hyponymy is a coinage (Gk 'under-naming') that has entered modern SEMANTICS through Lyons (1963). It refers to a relationship between the senses of LEXICAL ITEMS of 'inclusion', involving specific (**subordinate** or **hyponymic**) items and more general (**superordinate** or **hyperonymic**). So, for example, *cabbage, pea* and *sprout* are (**co-)hyponyms** of *vegetable*.

Although **hyperonyms** frequently are GENERIC (q.v.) words, in different contexts or classificatory systems the same word may be both a hyponym or a hyperonym: *tree* is superordinate to *oak* and *ash*, but itself subordinate (along with *shrub* and *flower*, etc.) to *plant*.

Co-hyponyms can be seen as kinds of SYNONYMS, since their CONCEPTUAL MEANINGS partly overlap in respect of their superordinate. If synonymy is symmetrical (a = b), hyponymy is asymmetrical (a → b): an oak is a tree, but a tree is not necessarily an oak. But hyponymy, like synonymy, often functions in discourse as a means of lexical COHESION by establishing referential EQUI-VALENCE to avoid repetition: *Did you see the policeman flag down that old car? I bet the vehicle wasn't taxed or insured properly.*

hypotaxis

From Gk 'under-order', common in traditional GRAMMAR and RHETORIC and revived by Halliday (e.g. 1985) to refer to what is also commonly known as SUBORDINATION (q.v.) in CLAUSES. **Hypotaxis** refers to a kind of dependent element which is explicitly linked to the MAIN CLAUSE by a CONJUNCTION, e.g.: *The time will come/when he will regret it.*

Heavy use of hypotaxis is more likely in writing than speech, and in kinds of writing that need qualification, clarification, argument or concession, etc.

(See also PARATAXIS.)

191

iambic pentameter

Iambic was taken from classical PROSODY into English during the Renaissance to refer to a FOOT or METRICAL unit of RHYTHM consisting of an unstressed syllable followed by a STRESSED ($\times$/). In the English verse tradition, the commonest kind of line pattern containing iambic feet or **iambs** is the five-BEAT or **pentameter**, introduced by Chaucer (with RHYME). After Surrey's use of it in his translation of the *Aeneid*, the iambic metre became widespread in the **blank verse** of Elizabethan poetry and drama, and flourished later in the **heroic couplets** of the eighteenth century. It is only since the twentieth century, indeed, that the iambic pentameter has been seriously challenged by other verse forms, notably FREE VERSE (see Easthope 1983).

What is remarkable throughout its history is the degree of stability of the iambic pentameter. The metrical NORM is a line of ten syllables, beginning with an unstressed syllable and ending with a stressed ($\times$/ $\times$/ $\times$/ $\times$/ $\times$/). Apart from iambic pentameter, syllable-counting is not native to English metre, preferred instead is the counting of ACCENTS or stresses in the ACCENTUAL (q.v.) tradition inherited from Old English, as in popular four-beat verse. So we can note the 'regular' pattern of

> $\times$ / $\times$ / $\times$ / $\times$ / $\times$ /
> But wherefore do not you a mightier way . . .
>
> (Shakespeare: Sonnet 16)

whereas the second line of the sonnet has the same number of syllables, but there is a departure from strict iambic rhythm in the placement of stresses. These follow the 'natural' rhythm of English, where major word classes (NOUNS; ADJECTIVES; **main** VERBS) are stressed:

> /   / $\times$ $\times$ $\times$ /$\times$ / $\times$ /
> Make war upon this bloody tyrant, Time?

Even allowing for variation in stress placement (beginning the line, for example, with a stressed syllable rather than unstressed is very common), and allowing also for IDIOLECTAL variations between poets, there are still fairly strict rules about what patterns may or may not be permitted in a line, which have been implicit throughout the history of iambic pentameter (e.g. /// does not normally open a line, nor ××/×).

Nonetheless, there is enough variety in an iambic line for it to avoid monotony, since prominent syllables are determined by the verse CONTEXT. We can read it fairly naturally according to the rhythms of speech, only aware of the norm, or the GESTALT, in our minds. COUNTERPOINTING or tension can result from the interplay of the regular and varied pattern; or between what some see as the SURFACE and DEEP patterns. An actor reciting the famous line from *Henry V*

```
 /     / × × × /   /   /   /   /
Once more unto the breach, dear friends, once more
```

(III.i)

is clearly going to stress seven words not five in the interests of naturalism; the extra stresses in effect signalling Henry's urgent exertions to rally his troops.

The iambic pentameter particularly attracted the attention of GENERATIVE METRISTS in the 1960s, beginning with the work of Halle & Keyser (1966) on Chaucer.

(See further Attridge 1982, ch. 2, for a critique.)

icon; iconicity

(1) In SEMIOTICS, and in the work of Peirce particularly (1931–1958), an **icon** is one of three major types of SIGN (q.v.): one which resembles in its form the object to which it refers (cf. Gk 'image'). (See also INDEX; SYMBOL.)

An obvious kind of resemblance, and most common, is the visual one, and examples of **iconic signs** would be photographs, certain map symbols and road signs, all with varying degrees of **iconicity** depending on the 'accuracy' of representation. In principle, such signs should be readily and universally understood across cultural and linguistic boundaries (hence the value of road signs); but in practice some kinds of resemblance have indeed to be 'learned'.

Iconic signs are said to be highly MOTIVATED; whereas symbols, with the relations between sign and object determined by convention, are unmotivated, i.e. **arbitrary**. Since human language is characteristically symbolic, iconicity does not play a large part; yet resemblance between sound and sign lies behind ONOMATOPOEIC words like *cuckoo*, *moo* and *sizzle*, etc. Both visual and aural iconicity are obviously dependent on MEDIUM.

At the level of sound, what is sometimes termed **secondary iconicity** (Lyons 1977) covers a not insignificant number of lexical items like *grind*, *grate*; *flip*, *flop*, *flutter*; *bump*, *thump*, etc., where, regardless of ETYMOLOGY, the forms are certainly felt by native speakers to be appropriate to their SIGNIFIEDS, whether noises, movements or other sensations. (See also PHONAESTHESIA; SOUND SYMBOLISM.)

(2) Literature, in fact, can be regarded as iconic in the broad sense that its FORM may strive to IMITATE in various ways the reality it presents: the so-called

ENACTMENT or **iconicity principle** or **maxim**. So variations in CLAUSE structure, and RHYTHM, can suggest to the reader auditory or KINETIC phenomena; and the WORD ORDER of elements in a sentence can reflect order of real-world events or actions. This is true also of non-literary texts, as instruction manuals or guide books illustrate. Generally, also, grammatical SUBORDINATION and FOCUS can be seen to work iconically; subordinating or highlighting information of different degrees of importance. So, in this example from Austen's *Sense and Sensibility*, the manipulation of sequencing suggests the enactment of events from the PERSPECTIVE of the characters involved:

> Not a syllable passed aloud. They all waited in silence for the appearance of their visitor. His footsteps were heard along the gravel path; in a moment he was in the passage; and in another, he was before them.

The principle of iconicity is often considered to be of limited value because of the relatively narrow range of experiences that can be enacted, and also seen as being vulnerable to impressionism and subjectivity in the **isomorphic** correspondences that are often further identified generally between FORM and CONTENT. Nonetheless, it is arguable that iconicity has a pervasive influence on CHOICE of expression in a way that neither critics nor linguists have succeeded in explicating.

ideal: ~ speaker; ~ reader; ~ subject

(1) **Ideal speaker** is a term particularly associated with Chomsky and GENERATIVE GRAMMAR in the 1960s, and the notion of COMPETENCE (q.v.), which formed the basis of his theory. Competence refers to the internalized knowledge speakers of a language supposedly have about its system, which enables them to construct and understand an inifinite number of CORRECT sentences. To the extent that competence is distinguished from PERFORMANCE (what we do when we actually speak or write), then it is a rather idealized notion; and the native speaker whose intuitions about language Chomsky regarded as important, and whose knowledge of language is perfect, is an ideal speaker.

(2) The competence–ideal-speaker model proved attractive to LITERARY THEORY, popularized particularly by Culler (1975), who proposed a POETICS which would make explicit the knowledge of the conventions needed for the interpretation of literary texts by the **ideal reader** (see also Fillmore 1981). But the notion of an ideal reader of literature has a long history, and also came into prominence in French STRUCTURALISM (e.g. the work of Barthes) and RECEPTION THEORY or READER-RESPONSE CRITICISM (q.v.). References to an ideal reader have been found in French and German criticism of the nineteenth and early twentieth centuries (e.g. Valéry Larbaud): i.e. the reader who would properly and completely understand the meaning and significances of a text, without the inadequacies or subjectivity of response of real readers. Leavis (1952) referred to the **perfect reader**. To some extent, seen from the point of view of the author writing for a readership in mind, this ideal reader coincides with what is now popularly termed the IMPLIED READER (q.v.).

But as used in reader-orientated criticism, the ideal reader is not an image of a reader so much as a more theoretical construct, who materializes in the process of reading, of re-creation. There is the related AVERAGE READER (q.v.) or **super-reader** of Riffaterre (1959, 1966), a composite figure based on the sum of reactions by informants to linguistic features of texts in terms of their stylistic (or non-stylistic) value. In the AFFECTIVE STYLISTICS of Fish (e.g. 1970, 1973), concerned with the mental operations involved in the process of reading, there is the **informed reader**: actually real, but capable of an extremely sensitive and astute response to literature. (See also INTERPRETATIVE COMMUNITIES.)

One problem with the ideal reader concept, as with that of ideal speaker, is that it is so ideal: divorced from all contextual considerations of society and time. Real (or lay) reading might be open to subjectivity, but responses to literature are richly fascinating precisely because they are governed by social and historical perspectives. In a way, ironically, the ideal reader concept does reflect this: it is an ideal modern reader – no-one has suggested that the ideal reader in Shakespeare's time was very different.

(3) Closer to the sense of 'implied' is Fairclough's (1989) notion within CDA (q.v.) of an **ideal subject**, whether viewer, listener, or reader, projected by media directors and advertising agencies, etc., to represent the many real 'consumers' who will read or watch their messages.

idealized cognitive model (ICM)

In COGNITIVE METAPHOR THEORY (see Lakoff 1987), the idea that each conceptual metaphor arouses in our minds a highly complex and IDEOLOGICAL set of structured assumptions or GESTALT about what any particular piece of reality is for us. So, for example, each society will have their own folk beliefs and particular ICMs of marriage (which are influential on popular romance fiction, of course: namely that prototypically it is based on love and enduring). ICMs can change conceptually over time: in Middle English texts we can see sin and temptation conceptualized in terms of a military invasion by devils.

(See also FRAME.)

ideational: ~ meaning; ~ function

(1) In SEMANTICS **ideational meaning** is sometimes found as an alternative to terms like CONCEPTUAL, PROPOSITIONAL or REFERENTIAL, to refer to the basic meaning of words expressing the external world around us.

(2) This representation of experience is one of the important FUNCTIONS of language; and in Halliday's grammatical theory, which he developed into a FUNCTIONAL or SYSTEMIC GRAMMAR (see 1985), the **ideational** or referential **function** is one of three major functions (see also INTERPERSONAL; TEXTUAL). Included here is not only the representation of physical experiences, but also internal experiences, thoughts and feelings, etc.

Halliday also distinguishes, aside from this **experiential** (subfunction), a **logical** subfunction: the expression of fundamental logical relations, which are ENCODED or manifested linguistically by the syntactic devices of CO-ORDINATION, HYPOTAXIS, INDIRECT SPEECH, etc., and which are important in the communication of complex experiences such as scientific experiments or philosophical arguments.

The possibility (even probability) that different speech communities represent experience in different ways through language has fascinated many linguists and anthropologists. Some would argue that language itself influences perception of the world (see DETERMINISM).

Even within a speech community, no two speakers will have the same experiences, the same WORLD-VIEWS. (See also IDEOLOGY; MIND STYLE.) In literature such experiences are brought to the foreground of attention, and analysis of ideational meaning is therefore prominent in LITERARY CRITICISM. An interest in the vehicle and mode of representation (e.g. POINT OF VIEW, degree of FOCUSSING) is very popular in STYLISTICS and NARRATOLOGY.

ideology

A buzz-word widely used in many disciplines, with differing but overlapping shades of meaning. Three main areas can be isolated:

(1) **Ideology** is very commonly associated with MARXIST CRITICISM, where it can be defined as the ideas or mode of thinking characteristic of a class or political–economic system; particularly ideas which are claimed to be 'natural' or universally valid, although basically legitimating a class or materialistic interest. In this sense we can speak of, for example, a 'capitalist', 'communist' or a 'bourgeois' ideology. The ideas themselves may be not only political in origin, but moral, religious, philosophical and aesthetic. The significant fact, however, is that ideology in this sense is definitely associated with the power relations in society, although ordinary people might not be aware of the extent to which what they say and believe is influenced by these. But in any society, important **ideological state apparatuses** (Althusser 1971) are the educational system and the MEDIA. Ideological discourse is thus authoritative: whether this be explicit political propaganda, TV documentary or IAMBIC PENTAMETER (Easthope 1983).

Marxist criticism is anti-FORMALIST: concerned to unearth the ideological assumptions of literary texts, and also to analyse literature, its writing, RECEPTION, and AESTHETIC VALUES, in the larger social context. (On Marxist criticism in Britain, see Eagleton 1976b; Thompson 1984.)

(2) Outside the Marxist framework, with its associations of dogma or doctrine, **ideology** is often simply used as in SEMIOTICS to mean any system of values based on ideas and prejudices and cultural and social assumptions which amounts to a pervasive, unconscious, WORLD-VIEW.

Each individual will have his or her own ideology, or set of ideologies whose linguistic realization constitutes a CODE (q.v.); each literary and non-literary text will express a particular ideology, or competing ideologies, some of which may indeed be political in the sense of (1) above. To the Russian linguists Bakhtin and Voloshinov in the 1930s every word and every discourse is ideological, and every speaker an **idiologue**: markedly realized in the CHARACTERIZATION of novels and drama. Critical work on literary POINT OF VIEW (q.v.), following Uspensky's work in the 1970s, for example, is concerned to stress its ideological function, its role in revealing, and also shaping, attitudes. (See also MIND STYLE.)

(3) It is ideology in this broader sense, but with the political–authoritative overtones also of (1), that has become since the 1980s the concerns of the kind of textual and stylistic analysis known as CRITICAL LINGUISTICS and CRITICAL DISCOURSE ANALYSIS (q.v.). Their aim is to examine the relationship between language and meanings, which influence thought and reflect ideological assumptions, in discourses such as newspaper headlines, regulations and advertising as well as the media. Like Marxist criticism they argue in effect that no discourse is 'neutral', 'transparent' or 'innocent'. (See further Lee 1992; Simpson 1993.)

idiolect

(1) Popular in sociolinguistics since the 1940s, and first used in the USA, to refer to the speech habits of an individual in a speech community, as distinct from those of a group of people (i.e. DIALECT).

The usage of an individual may well be constrained by his or her place of origin, but **idiolect** covers those features which vary from REGISTER to register, MEDIUM to medium, in daily language use; as well as the more permanent features that arise from personal idiosyncracies, such as lisping, monotone delivery, favourite exclamations, etc. Idiolect thus becomes the equivalent of a finger-print: each of us is unique in our language habits. Such 'voice-prints' are of great value to dramatists or novelists as a ready means of characterization, along with physical attributes: see Alfred Jingle's 'telegraphic' style in Dickens's *Pickwick Papers*; Jay Gatsby's 'old sport' as a term of address in Fitzgerald's *The Great Gatsby*. (For Dickens's idiolects in detail, see Golding 1985.)

(2) **Idiolect** has also figured in discussions of STYLE (q.v.), and defined as a system of individual stylistic features. Personal identity is seen not only in speech, then, but in writing habits: each author will have his or her own stylistic idiolect or authorial style.

We may well recognize that an unnamed poem is Milton's rather than Hopkins's, that certain grammatical or lexical features are characteristic of different authors. Such recognition lies behind PARODY (q.v.). But differences are not always so obvious, so that it is notoriously difficult, for example, to attribute authorship to parts of Jacobean plays, composed in collaboration. STYLOMETRY (q.v.), however, does consider authorship attributions on a statistical basis (sentence and word lengths; clausal CONNECTIVES, etc.), on the supposition that stylistic individuality is often unconscious, and relatively stable, moreover, throughout a writer's career.

An older view of style saw it as idiolectal in a less linguistic, more psychological or philosophical sense. Comments like Sir Thomas Browne's 'stylus virum arguit' in the seventeenth century, and Buffon's 'Le style, c'est l'homme même' in the eighteenth century argue for style as the revelation of personality, or of the psyche: a view taken up by early twentieth-century European stylisticians such as Spitzer (1948).

idiom; idiomaticity

(1) **Idiom** is sometimes used as a loose equivalent to language or VARIETY or even IDIOLECT (as in *the French idiom; the idiom of prose; the Miltonic idiom*), and so meaning any set of linguistic features peculiar to a speech community, group or individual.

(2) But in linguistics **idioms** most usually denote phrases or strings of words which are idiosyncratic (**idiomatic**) in that they are language-specific, not easily translated into another language and in that their meaning is not easily determined from the meanings of their constitutive parts.

In English such phrases are characteristically fixed in COLLOCATION, 'opaque' in meaning and of restricted grammatical mobility. So *bury* and *hatchet* collocate in *Let's bury the hatchet*, or *They buried the hatchet* meaning 'let's make peace', etc.; but we don't normally find **The hatchet was buried*.

However, it is probably best to think of idioms as revealing degrees of **idiomaticity** in respect of opaqueness and grammatical fixity. As the example above suggests, idioms are commonly METAPHORICAL (cf. *She let the cat out of the bag/spilled the beans/split hairs*, etc.). Partial idioms have one word with a literal meaning, the other FIGURATIVE (e.g. *red hair; white coffee*). To pull one's leg ('tease') is a common idiom and is found in grammatical variants such as *You're pulling my leg; She doesn't like having her leg pulled; Pull the other leg*, etc.

Not all idioms are lexical: some are grammatical peculiarities, e.g. *I'm not friends with you; I can't help it; How do you do*. **Idiomatization** seems an almost inevitable consequence of social interchange and the need to be polite. FORMULAS like *How do you do*, and *please* have become institutionalized or fossilized; and also structures such as *Can you/could you . . . ?* used as requests. (See Leech 1983.)

Many lexical idioms are clearly associated with the vividness of colloquial speech (*He's kicked the bucket/snuffed it* = 'died'), and many phrasal verb idioms are particularly associated with **informal** rather than FORMAL situations (*make up, do away with, turn on, get off with*, etc.). (For such idioms see especially Cowie *et al.* 1993.) As with SLANG, certain FIELDS of reference may be more 'productive' of idioms than others (e.g. death; sex). However, it is hard to imagine any kind of discourse without some idioms occurring. There are stylistic CONNOTATIONS in idioms like the EUPHEMISTIC *to pass away* ('die'); and social connotations for *the little woman*, or *(h)er indoors*. Like slang, proverbial phrases, CLICHÉS and SIMILES, they represent the POETIC DICTION of non-poetic, everyday language.

Origins of idioms are varied, usually anonymous. But *Nice one Cyril* comes from a football chant, while *salad days, primrose path, caviar to the general*, from Shakespeare.

illocutionary: ~ act; ~ force; ~ verb

All terms primarily associated with PRAGMATICS and particularly with SPEECH ACT THEORY, as developed by Austin (1962) and Searle (1969f). This is concerned with linguistic ACTS made while speaking which have some social or INTERPERSONAL purpose and effect.

Speech act and **illocutionary act** have often been used interchangeably, but technically, a speech act consists of a LOCUTIONARY ACT (q.v.), the physical act of uttering; the illocutionary act, performed through speaking (e.g. making a promise, giving orders, forecasting a match result, etc.); and the PERLOCUTIONARY ACT or **effect** (q.v.), the effect achieved by the utterance on the ADDRESSEE, e.g. frightening or persuading.

Greatest attention has focussed on illocutionary acts, on the communicative purpose of speakers' utterances rather than on the effects, since the former are on the face of it easier to describe: we may intend to insult someone, but the insult may not be perceived as such, and so lose its effect. But even for illocutionary acts, the listener's recognition of the speaker's INTENTION is important (Austin would say essential): continuing chatter after a teacher's request for silence does not ordinarily suggest misinterpretation (or lack of uptake), but disobedience.

Numerous attempts have been made to categorize illocutionary act, the numbers, labels and basis for distinction varying considerably. So Austin has five major groups (**verdictives; exercitives; commissives; behabitives; expositives**), which clearly cannot hope to cover all the acts in English (even Austin admitted there may well be up to 10,000 different ones). Yet such labelling is useful: the term **directive**, for instance (see Searle 1975) has come to be used now instead of 'command' in grammar (Quirk *et al.* 1985), deriving from a commonly distinguished category of illocutionary act designed to get the addressee to do something: as in requests, orders, pleading and daring. Moreover, classifications can help in the study of TEXT typology and description. Expositives (arguing, postulating, conceding) will be markedly characteristic of such REGISTERS as technical papers and newspaper leaders; **acknowledgments** (Bach & Harnish 1979) such as apologies, condolences and greetings, will be characteristic of ordinary PHATIC COMMUNION.

The kinds of illocutionary act prominently discussed and categorized tend to be those markedly distinguished by the use of so-called PERFORMATIVE or **illocutionary verbs**: e.g. *I promise to pay the bearer on demand the sum of ten pounds*; or *I vote we adjourn till tomorrow* (cf. also *apologize; affirm; offer; request*, etc.). However, outside FORMAL or written situations where clarity or emphasis is important, such explicit marking is rare; yet **illocutions** are the very stuff of discourse: all utterances can be said to have an **illocutionary force** or communicative function. So *I will see you tomorrow* with the MODAL verb has the illocutionary force usually of a promise; and *Cigarettes can seriously damage your health* the force of a warning. In each case, it is argued, the speech act can be as successful as those marked explicitly by performatives (*I warn you that*, etc.), since the same FELICITY CONDITIONS (q.v.) or criteria of APPROPRIATENESS apply, pertaining to the nature of the situation, speaker's beliefs, etc. And in terms of GENERATIVE

GRAMMAR, it has been argued that implicit illocutions are marked by a performative clause in the DEEP STRUCTURE (see Lakoff 1971).

However, many statements may be AMBIGUOUS and have potentially more than one illocutionary force: a reader may well interpret the statement above as simply a factual assertion, and not as an admonishment about the perils of smoking. (For non-native speakers, a major problem always is learning how to express illocutionary forces in the appropriate syntactic or prosodic forms.) CONTEXT can often help us to identify forces more precisely; but speech act theorists have nonetheless underestimated the complexity of actual discourse (and the INDETERMINACY of even speakers' intentions), concentrating instead on single sentences. In DISCOURSE ANALYSIS, in fact (e.g. Coulthard 1977; Edmondson 1981), illocutionary acts have themselves been seen as units in larger ACTS (q.v.), which may well comprise several utterances or exchanges, and even a whole DISCOURSE (see below; see also SPEECH ACT).

Speech act theorists, however, recognized one important kind of illocutionary act arising out of the vagaries and inexplicitness of natural conversation, namely the INDIRECT SPEECH ACT (q.v.): an utterance which ostensibly performs one act but actually has the force of another. A major type is the request framed in the form of a question about the ADDRESSEE's willingness or ability to do something (*Would you mind opening the window?*). But as the entry also reveals, the term **indirect** could well apply (and often is applied) to many illocutionary acts of the kind discussed above, not explicitly marked by a performative verb.

The study of illocutionary acts has been taken up in the analysis of LITERARY DISCOURSE, especially that of dramatic DIALOGUE. (See Elam 1980.) In drama, where all speech is functional and a kind of action, the illocutionary force of each utterance is especially heightened (Ohmann 1973). Illocutionary acts may well offer clues to complexity of character: 'stock' figures, it is suggested, lack the range of illocutionary modes of such quick-witted characters as Volpone or Richard III; so Polonius in *Hamlet* tends mostly towards directives.

Different illocutionary modes can also help distinguish the different VOICES in the novel: NARRATOR v. CHARACTER(s). A wider range of illocutions is open to the characters in their fictional WORLD, mimetic of the real; the modes of the narrator more appropriate to relations with the READER or IMPLIED READER: identifying, generalizing, evaluation, etc.

Early speech act theorists following Austin, were disinclined to take the illocutions of literary discourse seriously because of their status as FICTION: promises could not be 'valid' on stage because they were not literally 'true'; nor Donne's request *Come live with me and be my love* (*The Bait*). Yet such speech acts are valid in the fictional world (see MIMESIS). Ohmann (1971) sees literature generally as a **quasi-speech act**, without illocutionary force, raising the age-old question about its autonomy, and its place and function in society. Arguably, the 'art for art's sake' slogan is balanced in different periods and in different GENRES by intentions to instruct, to preach, to persuade.

Conversely, it has been argued (see Culler 1983; Lanser 1981; Pratt 1977) that speech act theory has taken too narrow a view of 'normal' (*sic*) discourse, and underestimated the FICTIONALITY of even non-literary behaviour. Literary discourse could belong in a larger class therefore of 'hypothetical' illocutions (mathematical problems, computer projections, illustrative sentences in grammars and dictionaries, parables, jokes, white lies, etc.).

image; imagery

Image and **imagery** are used in LITERARY CRITICISM with varying, often overlapping, senses.

(1) Originally **image** had a visual meaning, still common in SEMIOTICS, of a physical IMITATION of an object, as in sculpture, painting, masque.

(2) In literary criticism, the common sense of a mental picture of an object, etc., is combined with the sense of a 'picture' evoked in works. Depending on the critic, this literary picture or description may or may not involve FIGURATIVE LANGUAGE or **imagery**: such as SIMILE and METAPHOR, by which **images** are evoked by comparing one REFERENT with another (*My love is like a red, red rose,* Burns). Studies. of imagery in this sense have traditionally been common: so Spurgeon (1935) catalogued the different **semantic** FIELDS from which Shakespeare's major images are drawn; and Tuve (1947) described imagery characteristic of Elizabethan and metaphysical poetry. (See also VEHICLE.)

Literary images, whether in prose or poetry, are not simply decorative, but serve, for example, to DE-FAMILIARIZE: to reveal aspects of experience in a new light; or to reinforce theme, setting or characterization. In the first paragraphs of Dickens's *Bleak House* the literal description of the London fog quickly becomes SYMBOLIC of the befogging practices of Chancery; in Sitwell's *Winter the Huntsman,* the PERSONIFICATION of the title is realized in the LEXIS of hunting which unifies the poem, e.g.:

Through his iron glades
Rides Winter the Huntsman.
All colour fades
As his horn is heard sighing.

Far through the forest
His wild hooves crash and thunder
Till many a mighty branch
Is torn asunder. . . .

As this extract also reveals, descriptions may evoke not only visual images, but also sound (*heard sighing; crash and thunder*), and other sensory experiences.

(3) In popular usage and in MEDIA studies **image** has acquired CONNOTATIONS of falseness, e.g. a **brand image** of a consumer product or the perceived identity of a politician promoted by advertising agencies or publicity campaigns may involve a certain amount of engineering in the presentation of the 'real' thing. What Leech (1974) calls **image-building** depends on the suppression of undesirable ASSOCIATIONS and the promotion of desirable ones in both visual and verbal terms: a shampoo or cake of soap promises romance or luxury, a breakfast cereal health and 'sunshine'. (See further Pope 1998.)

imitation

In LITERARY CRITICISM **imitation** is traditionally used in two senses:

(1) As a translation of the Greek MIMESIS (q.v.) following the writings of Plato and Aristotle, it is seen as the characteristic function of literature: the **imitation**, or the illusion of a realistic representation of the world and human action. This is strikingly revealed in the nineteenth-century so-called 'realist' novels, for instance, of Dickens or Balzac; or in much of English drama since the sixteenth century.

An extension of the principle of imitation applies to FORM as well as CONTENT: LITERARY DISCOURSE often strives to ENACT the reality it presents in its SYNTAX or LEXIS (see ICONICITY; see also ONOMATOPOEIA).

(2) Advocated by Cicero, Longinus and Horace, in RHETORIC and in the later Renaissance and neoclassical literary traditions, **imitation** (**imitatio**) was a kind of translation exercise much favoured by 'advanced' students and poets. As Johnson explains in his *Dictionary* (1755), it is a method of translating poetry 'looser than PARAPHRASE, in which modern examples and illustrations are used for ancient, or domestick for foreign'. The skill is to find apt equivalences, and also to capture the STYLE and form of the original as far as possible. Celebrated examples of imitation are Pope's *Imitations of Horace's Epistles and Satires* as well as Johnson's own imitation of the *Tenth Satire of Juvenal* in his *Vanity of Human Wishes*.

With the later stress on originality as an AESTHETIC principle, *imitatio* as a poetic GENRE grew into disfavour. Yet to the extent that poets have continually found inspiration and models in their poetic predecessors, in a looser sense imitation may be seen to be creatively influential. (See also INTERTEXTUALITY.)

imperative

Common in GRAMMAR to refer either (1) to one of the major SENTENCE types: the others being DECLARATIVE (q.v.) and INTERROGATIVE (q.v.); or (2) to a form of the VERB, which in English is marked by no special grammatical SUFFIX, no TENSE distinction, and normally by the absence of an overt SUBJECT in concord when it occurs in a sentence. So *Go away!* is an **imperative sentence** containing the imperative verb form *go*; *Stop!* is an **imperative verb** also functioning as a complete imperative sentence.

In some grammars, the **imperative** is also described as (3) a MOOD (see also MODALITY), and so alternates with the terms **indicative** (the normal sentence mode for 'facts') and SUBJUNCTIVE (expressing the uncertain or hypothetical), to express will or desire.

Despite the overt absence of a subject, the latter is assumed implicitly to be the **second** PERSON PRONOUN *you*, since the imperative is used in direct address: see also reflexive verb forms (*Do it yourself*) and TAG QUESTIONS (*Come here, will you*). The presence of the ADDRESSEE is often indicated, however, by a VOCATIVE element (a name or TERM OF ADDRESS): *Batter my heart, three personed God* (Donne: *Holy Sonnet*, XIV).

Imperatives are typically used with the ILLOCUTIONARY FORCE of 'commands' or directives, if we interpret these in a broad sense to include orders (*Stop*); orations (*Hear us, O heavenly Father*); pleas (*Have mercy upon us*); requests (*Kindly refrain from smoking*); instructions (*Check that the wiring is correct*); greetings (*Have a nice day*), etc. In most cases the speaker expects some action to be taken as a result.

STYLISTICALLY, however, the bare imperative verb form occurs rarely, and sounds perfunctory even rude outside formalized or authoritative settings or the intimate family circle (*Go and brush your hair!*). The force of a command may be softened for reasons of POLITENESS by modifiers such as *please* or *kindly*; or the imperative itself replaced by a declarative or interrogative. Compare:

Please put the cat out
I wonder if you'd mind putting the cat out, please
Could you put the cat out, please?

TRANSFORMATIONAL GRAMMAR variously saw all the major sentence types as being related in DEEP STRUCTURE; or argued for an underlying PERFORMATIVE VERB construction for the imperative: *I order you to put the cat out.*

As a form of direct address, the imperative is most commonly found in face-to-face interchanges or correspondence. Where it occurs in literature, we assume that it is directed either towards a character within the WORLD of the text, at the level of HISTOIRE (q.v.), as in Donne's: *For God's sake hold your tongue, and let me love* (*The Canonization*); or towards the IMPLIED READER, at the level of DISCOURS, as in Pope's

A little learning is a dang'rous thing;
Drink deep, or taste not the Pierian spring

(*An Essay on Criticism*)

impersonality

Any DISCOURSE that is described as **impersonal** is marked by a distinct lack of the personal and informal mode: i.e. makes no reference to the immediate CONTEXT OF SITUATION between ADDRESSER and ADDRESSEE by the use of the PERSONAL PRONOUNS *I* and *you*, for example, nor to the feelings and opinions of the participants. If a pronoun is needed as a SUBJECT, and if generalizations are to be made, then there is the INDEFINITE or GENERIC pronoun *one*: as in *One should always be careful when talking to strangers.* (However, even *one* has acquired personal overtones in some (social) dialects, especially those of the upper classes and Royal Family: *one was glad when one's daughter got engaged.*)

A common alternative is the PASSIVE with AGENT-deletion, which is characteristic of such impersonal REGISTERS as scientific textbooks, 'officialese', legal documents, public notices, etc.: *Smoking is not permitted in rear seats.*

Impersonal language tends to be avoided in technical advertising, however, and increasingly official documents are being rephrased into a simpler and less distancing style. Yet even in ordinary speech it is difficult to avoid some impersonal constructions, especially those involving the use of the pronoun *it* (e.g. the first clause of this sentence; and constructions such as *it's raining*). Certain novels and short stories also reflect a scrupulous avoidance of the personal in their narration or DISCOURS to produce a narrative that is close to 'showing' (MIMETIC) rather than 'telling' (DIEGETIC): see the work of Henry James or Hemingway, for instance.

implicature

See **conversational implicature**.

implied: ~ author; ~ reader

(1) The **implied author** in LITERARY CRITICISM was popularized by Booth (1961) who had seen, along with others (e.g. Tillotson 1959), the role of the real author diminished in critical interpretation as part of the NEW CRITICAL and ANTI-INTENTIONALIST APPROACH: the argument being that an author's INTENTIONS, even when possible to ascertain, are critically irrelevant.

The implied author is thus a TEXTUAL construct, created by the real author to be the (ideal?) image of him- or herself, and also created anew by the reader; and who may or may not intrusively address the reader directly (see (2)); and whose opinions and POINT OF VIEW as NARRATOR may or may not coincide with those of the author, be it Austen or Dickens. (See further Chatman 1990, chs 5, 6.)

Technically then, since the 1960s, when critics refer to 'Dickens's view of Victorian society', they mean the IDEOLOGY of 'Dickens' and not of the historical Dickens (d. 1870), unless explicitly making use of such biographical material as his letters and essays. However, even allowing for artistic licence and the metamorphosis of the autobiographical into fiction, it is difficult to dissociate finally the real from the implied author, especially when external evidence invites comparisons (as in the case of Lawrence or Joyce, for instance). (See also EXTRAFICTIONAL VOICE.)

(2) By analogy, the term **implied reader** has been created: what Booth himself termed the **postulated** or **mock reader**. Very obvious examples occur in those novels where a reader is explicitly addressed, and assumes almost the status of a character in the fictional world, as in Sterne's *Tristram Shandy*. (See also NARRATEE.)

But the implied reader, especially in RECEPTION THEORY (see Iser 1974, 1978) is rather a complex concept, hovering between the real reader of the text at any one moment of time, and the image of an IDEAL READER (q.v.), who would properly and completely understand the meaning and significances of a text. The implied reader is basically what the textual RHETORIC itself implicates or involves; not, then, only characteristic of literature, but of all kinds of texts, an illustration of Bakhtin's DIALOGICAL (q.v.) principle. (See also Eco's **model reader**, 1979.)

From the viewpoint of the author, clearly he or she may well write for a particular readership, which may then be inscribed in the text in the form of

PRESUPPOSITIONS or assumed shared knowledge; or explicit direct addresses (e.g. *gentle reader*).

From the viewpoint of the real reader, we are constantly comparing our own capabilities with those the implied author assumes we have. Also, our response is often very complex, especially to works from earlier periods. Here a discrepancy between the real and implied is more obvious. So, in reading Hardy's *Tess of the d'Urbervilles*, we are aware of the (sympathetic) reactions expected to Tess's plight from the way the text constructs them; we match them with what we infer to be those of many of the novel's contemporary readers to 'fallen women'; but we also match them inevitably with our own from a present-day perspective.

in medias res

(1) This Latin phrase meaning 'in(to) the middle of things' was originally applied to epic poetry by Aristotle, to describe how poems such as *The Iliad* and *The Aeneid* do not begin at the beginning of an action, which is more usual in storytelling (*ab ovo* 'from the egg'), but in the middle. In such poems, however, there are still formal introductory FORMULAS which mark an 'opening': *Sing, O Goddess, the wrath of Peleus's son* (Homer: *The Iliad*); *I sing of arms and the man who came from Troy* (Virgil: *The Aeneid*).

(2) In modern STYLISTICS and criticism of the novel (e.g. Leech & Short 1981; Watson 1979) the term is more usually used to describe an opening technique for plunging the reader into the apparent middle of a situation, as if 'interrupting' it, with no preliminaries of introduction.

The technique gained in popularity in the twentieth century, along with the decline in fashion for the obtrusive, OMNISCIENT NARRATOR, and along with a METAFICTIONAL awareness of the arbitrariness of beginning anywhere; but it is by no means unusual in nineteenth-century fiction: e.g. Charlotte Bronte's *Jane Eyre: There was no possibility of taking a walk that day.* In the interests of realism, it has always been exploited in epistolary novels, or those taking the form of a personal journal: e.g. Richardson's *Pamela* in the eighteenth century:

Dear Father and Mother,
I have great trouble and some comfort to acquaint you with.

In medias res is obviously the commonest way of opening a play, and marks many 'dramatic' poems, e.g. those of Donne.

Linguistically, the technique is marked by DEFINITE ARTICLES, PRONOUNS and other DEICTIC words giving the illusion of a world already created to which familiar reference can already be made: what Leech (1969) calls an INFERRED SITUATION: e.g. John Wain's *Rafferty: He* (who?) *kept trying to take her* (whose?) *arm, as they walked home* (where?) *from the cinema on that* (which?) *sweltering Saturday night.* (See also ANAPHORA; CATAPHORA.) Such ENIGMATIC openings clearly violate the **maxim of** QUANTITY (q.v.), since the reader must read on, hoping for clarification of identities, etc.

inanimate

A basic conceptual distinction is that between entities possessing life or animacy (human beings, animals) and which are ANIMATE (q.v.), and those which do not: objects natural and man-made, etc., which are **inanimate**.

Lexically, this distinction is reflected in COLLOCATIONS (*brand-new fridges*, but not (unless for humour) *brand-new husbands*); and the selection of SUBJECTS and VERBS: *creak, clatter* bring to mind inanimate subjects; *laugh* and *chatter* animate. However, violation of these rules occurs frequently in FIGURATIVE LANGUAGE. So in PERSONIFICATION inanimate objects are made animate: tables *groan* with food; whistles blow *forlornly*. Speech is full of such figures which have become (dead) METAPHORS: the *leg* of the table, *hand* of the clock, *foot* of the bed, etc.

In LITERARY, especially POETIC LANGUAGE, the anthropomorphic tendency is strong, particularly with features of the natural world. Hardy's trees in *The Woodlanders* have *jackets of lichen and stockings of moss*; but then plants and trees do have a kind of 'life', and according to Wordsworth and others, even a Divine Spirit. In the device of **pathetic fallacy** (a term coined by Ruskin in 1856), human feelings are ascribed to objects often in keeping with the speaker/character's own: as in Verlaine's *Il pleure dans mon cœur comme il pleut sur la ville* ('It cries in my heart as it rains on the town').

indefinite: ~ article; ~ reference; ~ pronoun

(1) The **indefinite article**, *a* (*an* before words beginning with a vowel), grammatically classed as a DETERMINER (q.v.) in English, is a CLOSED CLASS item in the NOUN PHRASE which pertains to the REFERENCE of the noun, specifically 'count' nouns like *chair(s)* and *table(s)* not non-count nouns like *furniture*. It is used when the noun has not been mentioned before (in the CO-TEXT) or is not already known (in the situational CONTEXT): hence 'indefinite'. It thus contrasts with the DEFINITE ARTICLE which functions to indicate GIVEN INFORMATION rather than NEW INFORMATION. Thus the indefinite article commonly occurs at the beginning of simple stories or (narrative) poems, to introduce referents:

I had a little nut-tree,
Nothing would it bear
But a silver nutmeg
And a golden pear . . .

Semantically, the indefinite article, which is etymologically related to the (stressed) numeral *one* in Old English, has shades of indefiniteness. *I'm looking for a hotel* could mean any hotel; *I'm looking for a cat*, a particular one (which is lost); *I'm buying a pound of sausages* means one pound (rather than two).

(2) **Indefinite** is also used as a label for a subclass of PRONOUNS, which lack the definiteness of PERSONAL PRONOUNS like *I, you, she*, etc. They include the 'universal' forms *everybody* (*everyone, everything*) and the negatives *nobody* (*no-one, nothing*), as well as *somebody*, etc., and the GENERIC *one* meaning 'people in

general', as in <u>One</u> *should never underestimate an elephant's intelligence.* (See also IMPERSONAL.) The personal pronouns can at times be used indefinitely: *you* is a popular alternative to *one;* and *they* and *it* are indefinite in utterances such as *They say it will rain tomorrow.*

indeterminacy

(1) In linguistics **indeterminacy** arose because of the problems posed by many grammatical theories which were over-categorical (e.g. GENERATIVE GRAMMAR). It is not always easy, for example, to say what is grammatical and what is not, and easier to suggest that there are **degrees of** GRAMMATICALITY. But indeterminacy of classification has dogged even traditional grammars: certain words are difficult to classify grammatically: are *mine, yours, hers,* etc. PRONOUNS or DETERMINERS, or both? What 'part of speech' is *please?* In SEMANTICS too, the predilection for BINARISM, as in COMPONENTIAL ANALYSIS, leaves no room for indeterminacy or pluralism of semantic category: is mud liquid or solid?

(2) Those linguists who analyse language in use rather than as a system, in DISCOURSE ANALYSIS and PRAGMATICS, for instance, are aware of a different kind of **indeterminacy** arising from the nature of the SPEECH EVENT between speaker and hearer. The MESSAGE communicated may not be clearly expressed, or clearly received, so that AMBIGUITY arises. Sometimes indeterminacy is planned or strategic: the ILLOCUTIONARY FORCE is negotiable (Leech 1983). So, in Shakespeare's *Othello* Iago's false insinuations to Othello about Cassio are interpreted by Othello as true facts and accusations of his wife's adultery.

(3) It may well be argued that strategic **indeterminacy** is a special characteristic of LITERARY, especially POETIC LANGUAGE.

In READER-RESPONSE or RECEPTION THEORY, developed in the 1970s, indeterminacy was commonly discussed. One view is of the text as a determinate structure but with inevitable information GAPS or 'spots of indeterminacy' (*Unbestimmtheitsstellen*) that the readers must fill in from their own cultural knowledge, 'reading between the lines' as it were. (See the work of Iser, drawing on Ingarden 1931 (1973); also PHENOMENOLOGY.) Another view sees the text itself as indeterminate, not given shape or substance until readers interpret it – a more substantial 'concretization' (see Fish 1970). (See also CLOSED V. OPEN TEXT; READERLY V. WRITERLY.)

index; indices

(1) In SEMIOTICS, particularly following the work of Peirce, an **index** is one of three major types of SIGN (q.v.) (see also ICON and SYMBOL). It is related to its REFERENT by relations of contiguity or proximity or causality. (See also METONYMY.)

Obvious natural examples are thunder and lightning (indicating a storm), smoke (indicting a fire) and spots (indicating a disease like measles). Human attributes are often interpreted **indexically**: a staggering walk indicating drunkenness or exhaustion; a stutter nervousness. Watching a play performed on stage we are especially alert to such **indexical signs** from gestures, posture and voice quality and TONE, for CHARACTERIZATION, emotions and PLOT. So too in the novel: as well as physical attributes, Dickens exploits turns of phrase and speech idiosyncracies (Mr Micawber's *in short*, Mark Tapley's *jolly*, Mr Sleary's lisp) as **indices** of IDIOLECT; and regional DIALECT for characters such as Sam Weller and Peggotty as indices of regional and social group (see Abercrombie 1967).

Linguistically, DEICTIC words, such as the DEMONSTRATIVES *this* and *that*, are sometimes referred to, following Peirce, as **indexical expressions** or **subindices**: pointing (like the index finger) to something in the CONTEXT.

(2) **Indices** (singular **indice** or **index**) had a special sense in the structural analysis of NARRATIVE of Barthes (1966). Narrative units are divided into those significant for the action of a story (FUNCTION (q.v.)) and those which provide details of characterization or background relevant to the themes (**indices**). Some narratives depend heavily on functions (e.g. folk-tales); others, such as psychological novels, on indices. A subgroup of indices (**informants**) provides information of a locational or deictic nature; but even here a description may be evocative of an atmosphere significant for the theme of the narrative as a whole. Many openings of novels are on one level informants, but also indices: the first sentences of Orwell's *1984* prepares us for the bleakness and austerity of the Big Brother IDEOLOGY:

> It was a bright cold day in April, and the clocks were striking thirteen. Winston Smith, his chin nuzzled into his breast in an effort to escape the vile wind, slipped quickly through the glass doors of Victory Mansions, though not quickly enough to prevent a swirl of gritty dust from entering along with him . . .

indicative

See MOOD; SUBJUNCTIVE.

indirect object

Commonly used in GRAMMAR to describe the NOUN PHRASE which follows the grammatical SUBJECT and VERB in a CLAUSE or SENTENCE, and which refers to the usually ANIMATE 'beneficiary' or 'recipient' of the process described. In languages such as Latin and Old English, this would be expressed by the **dative** CASE.

Where the **indirect object** (IO) does occur, it must always accompany the DIRECT OBJECT (DO) (q.v.), which refers to an entity directly 'affected' by the action in the clause, e.g.:

> I fed the elephant (DO)
> I fed the elephant (IO) a bun (DO)
> I gave the elephant (IO) a bun (DO)

but not

*I gave the elephant (IO).

The indirect object can usually be paraphrased by a PREPOSITIONAL PHRASE with *to* or *for*: as in *I gave a bun to the elephant*, following the DO in this case, not preceding it. Here grammars differ in their treatment of such phrases. For example, Sinclair (1972) classes them strictly as ADVERBIALS; Quirk *et al.* (1985) class them as **prepositional objects**; but SYSTEMIC GRAMMARS (e.g. Young 1980) as indirect objects also. Functionally, there is certainly no difference between *I gave the elephant a bun* and *I gave a bun to the elephant*. The difference is STYLISTIC not grammatical: the FOCUS falling on a different element in each sentence.

indirect: ~ speech; ~ thought; ~ discourse

(1) **Indirect speech** (IS) or **reported speech** is the term given, by analogy with DIRECT SPEECH (DS) (q.v.), to a prime method of representing speech in the written MEDIUM. In classical RHETORIC and traditional GRAMMARS it is also known as *oratio obliqua*.

The words of a speaker are presented in a NOMINAL *that*-clause after a SPEECH ACT verb/clause (e.g. *say, tell; ask, enquire*, etc.) or TAG. In the process of reporting, the 'direct' words appear to be transmuted, e.g.:

'I shall come here again tomorrow,' she said

becomes

She said [that] she would go there again the next day.

The PRESENT TENSE in the *that*-clause is normally 'backshifted' to the past; the **first** PERSON PRONOUN, *I*, becomes the **third** person, *she*; VERBS and ADVERBIALS expressing 'proximity' shift to those of 'distance'.

There has been a tendency for IS to be described as TRANSFORMATIONALLY equivalent to DS, but the relationship between the two modes has been a matter of much discussion (see especially Banfield 1982). Syntactic 'rules' of equivalence for statements as above are certainly more straightforward than for other sentence types:

'Is it raining?', she asked → She asked whether it was raining
'Go home!', she ordered him → She ordered him to go home.

Moreover, in the process of reporting, there is a tendency for the bare PROPOSITIONAL content only to remain, and for the colloquial characteristics of actual speech, the IDIOMS and PROSODIC features, to be lost: filtered or interpreted, as it were, through the mind of the reporter or narrator. So an utterance like: *'Gosh!', she exclaimed, 'How dreadful!'* is difficult to report indirectly, resulting only in a loose PARAPHRASE or variant: *She exclaimed how dreadful (it was)/ that it was dreadful.*

Since the function of indirect speech is to 'report', then fidelity of reporting to content, rather than to exact wording, is often more important. Indeed, in the context of minute-taking, for example, sentences like *The committee agreed that they would appoint a new Chairperson before the vacation* most probably present a summary of many actual utterances (and by more than one speaker); and an indirect command such as *She ordered him to go home* could well be ENTAILED by *'Get the bloody hell out of here!' she shouted at him.* (See also NARRATIVE REPORT OF SPEECH ACTS.)

So indirect speech is a useful economical device for novelists who wish to keep a firm control on the NARRATIVE, and a steady pace. And by a kind of ICONIC resemblance, the opposition between DS and IS can be exploited in terms of FOREGROUNDING and BACKGROUNDING, in terms of prominence in PLOT, or moral 'directness' or warmth of feeling, versus muted status, coldness or evasiveness, etc. So in Dickens's *Bleak House*, for example, the conversations between the Dedlocks are always reported rather than quoted, suggesting the distance of feeling between them: *Sir Leicester is apprehensive that my lady, not being very well, will take cold at that open window. My lady is obliged to him, but would rather sit there, for the air* . . . (FREE INDIRECT SPEECH).

However, this is not to deny that IS cannot at times be EXPRESSIVE, or be 'coloured', to use Page's (1973) term, by features associated with DS. This device is much exploited for comic effect by Dickens: e.g. Kit Nubble's mother in *The Old Curiosity Shop*:

> To this, Kit's mother replied, that certainly it was quite true, and quite right, and quite proper, and Heaven forbid that she should shrink, or have cause to shrink, from any inquiry into her character or that of her son . . .

So too McHale (1978) distinguishes between **indirect content paraphrase**, and **indirect discourse**, 'MIMETIC to some degree'. Rather confusingly, however, Leech & Short (1981) define IS very strictly, and instead classify utterances with DS features as free indirect speech (FIS).

In older literature, and in journalism today, it is quite common to find **slipping** from one mode to the other, from IS to DS within a discourse: *Then Sir Bors lened upon his bed's side and told Sir Launcelot how the queen was passing wroth with him, 'because ye wore the red sleeve at the great jousts'* . . . (Malory: *Morte d'Arthur*); also from IS to FIS: *The journalist asked whether the Minister had really tried hard enough. Had she considered going to Liverpool herself?*

Leech & Short also give FIS status to sentences where there is INVERSION of the reporting and reported clauses, the reporting clause functioning as a kind of parenthetical 'comment'-clause: *There was a possibility of success, the doctor suggested; Would the government give such an assurance, she wondered.* (See also Halliday 1985.) In the last example, the WORD ORDER of the direct question is retained. These are sometimes called **pseudo-report structures**.

(2) By analogy with indirect speech, the term **indirect thought** (IT) has been coined to refer to the representation of thought processes. Some writers use the term IS to cover both speech and thought; **indirect discourse** is also popular as an inclusive term (McHale 1978).

Unlike IS, indirect thought is chiefly characteristic of LITERARY DISCOURSE: the OMNISCIENT NARRATOR having privileged access to the thoughts of the characters.

The syntactic features are identical to those of IS, but a verb of cogitation or reflection replaces a verb of speaking in the reporting clause: *She pondered whether she was dreaming*. (See also DIRECT THOUGHT; **indirect** INTERIOR MONOLOGUE.)

indirect speech act

A term taken from SPEECH ACT THEORY (see Gordon & Lakoff 1971; Searle 1975) in recognition of the fact that in speaking we often say one thing and mean or implicate something else. So one ILLOCUTIONARY ACT (q.v.) is performed indirectly by what appears to be another.

A common type of **indirect speech act** or **indirect illocution** is a request framed in the form of a question about the ADDRESSER's willingness or ability to do something: e.g. *Can you put the kettle on?* Such utterances are felt to be more polite, less brusque than a request in the IMPERATIVE (*Put the kettle on please!*), and in ordinary conversation the LITERAL force of such questions has become increasingly incidental, a matter of convention. A lot depends on the CONTEXT: if the addresser has recently broken her arm, the question may well be an inquiry about her ability.

The notion of indirect speech act is also commonly evoked in the discussion of illocutionary act and ILLOCUTIONARY FORCE generally. Indeed, in the numerous utterances where there is no explicit speech act verb (such as *inquire; beseech; order; complain*, etc.) and where there is instead the DECLARATIVE or statement, it is possible to give indirect status to the different illocutionary forces or meanings generated (see Allan 1986). So an utterance like *Waiter, there's a fly in my soup* may well have the primary force of a statement or description, but is usually interpreted as having the force of a question (*What's this fly doing in my soup?*) and/or a request (*Please replace this soup by another bowl, without a fly in it*).

In general, it can be argued, following Leech (1983) that it is better to think of degrees of directness and indirectness in speech acts, and to allow for considerable variability of interpretation.

(See also INFERENCE; CONVERSATIONAL IMPLICATURE.)

inference

(1) The process of deduction, of working something out, of making explicit what is unspoken or unwritten, is recognized in TEXT LINGUISTICS, PRAGMATICS, RELEVANCE THEORY and DISCOURSE ANALYSIS as an important element in the understanding of others' speech, and in the making of textual COHERENCE.

For example, by drawing on background knowledge or on the CONTEXT OF SITUATION, we can **infer** as addressees the appropriate ILLOCUTIONARY FORCE of UTTERANCEs that superficially seem indirect, or appear to flout the CO-OPERATIVE PRINCIPLE (q.v.) of conversation. *Are you doing anything this evening?* is not usually inferred in the context of a phone-call as a simple question asking for information, but as an invitation. (Cf. *Are you doing anything this evening? No? In that case, would you like to/please come out with me?*) For the speaker's part, an invitation may be IMPLICATED.

In the construction and interpretation of NARRATIVES, **inference** is absolutely necessary. Without the taking for granted of facts, details and cultural knowledge, a story would be exceedingly tedious to read: much information is PRESUPPOSED on the basis of our understanding of what happens in the 'real' world. (See also GAP; INDETERMINACY; SCRIPT.) So we assume that the hero or heroine goes to sleep, eats breakfast and lunch every day, even though those events may not be described; what then is FOREGROUNDED are events more significant for the PLOT or CHARACTERIZATION. This too involves another kind of inferencing: continually assessing (and reassessing) events in terms of their potential significance for the theme of the story.

Texts, non-literary as well as literary, vary in the degree of inferencing that has to be made: instruction leaflets for DIY kitchen units are normally highly explicit; whereas letters between close friends will assume a considerable amount of shared knowledge. In FICTION, the use of INTERIOR MONOLOGUE (q.v.) as a device for the representation of characters' thought processes, leads to a high degree of inference on the part of the reader, in order to see logical connections between superficially random impressions:

> My missus has just got an. Reedy freckled soprano. Cheese-paring nose. Nice enough in its way: for a little ballad. No guts in it. You and me, don't you know? In the same boat. Soft-soaping. Give you the needle that would . . .
>
> (Leopold Bloom, in Joyce's *Ulysses*)

(2) The term **inferred situation** is used by Leech (1969) to describe the poetic device of creating the WORLD of the poem, its own SITUATION. Hardy's poems often invoke a scene from the first lines: e.g. *The Self-Unseeing*:

> Here is the ancient floor,
> Footworn and hollowed and thin,
> Here was the former door
> Where the dead feet walked in . . .

infinitive

Well-established in GRAMMAR for that part of the VERB which is its basic form as cited in dictionaries (e.g. *speak, write*), and which is NON-FINITE (q.v.), i.e. unmarked for TENSE or MOOD, etc.

It is also that form of the verb which follows AUXILIARY VERBS, as in *I can come, you must go*. Where it occurs with other kinds of verb, and where it is used as a CLAUSE or phrase, it is normally preceded by *to*: as in *I want to come; To be or not to be, that is the question.* So strongly associated is *to* with the **infinitive** that many people, following a PRESCRIPTIVE grammatical tradition, or notions of CORRECTNESS, dislike 'splitting' the phrase with an ADVERBIAL, at least in writing. Yet **split infinitives** occur commonly in speech without being noticed. A notorious example is immortalized in the popular TV series *Star Trek: To boldly go where no man has gone before*. Split infinitives seem rhythmically more natural than the alternative, and FOCUS attention on the verb: cf. *to boldly go where* . . . (× /× /×) v. *to go boldly where* . . . (× / /× ×). (See further Crystal 1984.)

Infinitives as clauses are commonly found in instructions or book-titles as **directives**: *To Paint a Water Lily; How to succeed in business without really trying*. For brevity, they are also common in newspaper headlines, to express future time: *Foreign Minister to visit Peru*, the probable equivalent of *is to*.

information: ~ theory; ~ processing; ~ structure; informativity, etc.

(1) **Information** in a technical sense is derived from COMMUNICATION THEORY, particularly the work of Shannon & Weaver (1949) on systems of SIGNALS. So-called **information theory** is concerned with the efficiency of a system in the transmission of a MESSAGE, and **informational value** or weight is measured in terms of degrees of predictability. The greater the unpredictability, the higher the informational value of a signal. (See also REDUNDANCY.)

Applied to human language, its different components and discourse types, we can see how information works in this sense. In spelling, for example, given the letter *q* the high statistical probability that it will be followed by *u* in English means that that the latter has low informational value. FORMULAIC LANGUAGE, fixed in syntactic patterns and COLLOCATIONS, is also highly predictable, so that the REGISTERS in which it occurs will be low in information value. LITERARY LANGUAGE, by contrast, tends to be high in such value, with its unusual METAPHORS and striking turns of phrase.

However, taken to a logical extreme, the technical sense of information clashes with the general sense of information, which describes semantic content value. Joyce's *Finnegans Wake* is the ultimate example of a text that is unpredictable on phonological, grammatical and lexical levels, and hence highly 'informative'. But, in the ordinary sense, to most readers it is too complex to be understandable, and therefore uninformative.

(2) In TEXT LINGUISTICS informational value has been focussed on content rather than system, and notions of **informativity** (de Beaugrande & Dressler 1981) or **information dynamics** (Enkvist 1985) or **information processing** (Quirk *et al.* 1985), etc., are concerned with the degree of unexpectedness and familiarity of a message to the hearer, and the way such information is presented. Each UTTERANCE or SENTENCE in an extended DISCOURSE reveals different patterns of GIVENNESS (q.v.): information stated but already known to the participants, whether supplied in the CO-TEXT or PRESUPPOSED from the situational CONTEXT; and NEW INFORMATION (q.v.): information which is either not assumed to be known to the hearer, or which is not regarded as particularly 'newsworthy'.

While many sentences will contain all new information, many others reveal degrees of given and new, with the highest degree of informativity occurring towards the end, the FOCUS of interest, PROSODICALLY often coinciding with the NUCLEUS of INTONATION when spoken:

> My conscience hath a thousand several tongues,
> And every tongue brings in a several tale,
> And every tale condemns me for a villain

> (Shakespeare: *Richard III*, V.iii)

In SYSTEMIC GRAMMAR especially, discussions of **information (units)** have been interrelated with discussion of units of intonation or TONE GROUPS (q.v.) and consequently the spoken MEDIUM (see Halliday 1985; see further Allan 1986, vol. 2, ch. 7). But even in writing, the organization of the sentence by SYNTACTIC means will highlight the **information structure**: by the use of the PASSIVE, for instance.

Halliday has also been keen to distinguish the information system as described above very strictly from what he calls THEMATIZATION (q.v.), a concept borrowed from the PRAGUE SCHOOL linguists, but which, in fact, is also concerned with information. Studies of FUNCTIONAL ṢENTENCE PERSPECTIVE (FSP) (q.v.) involving the concept of COMMUNICATIVE DYNAMISM (CD) describe the dynamic 'development' of an utterance in terms of degrees of givenness and newness of information, and also the semantic value or weight of sentence elements. However, despite the close association of THEME/given, and RHEME/new, it is true that relative importance of information can be distinguished from newness. Thematization applies to all utterances regardless of context; whereas information processing must operate in the context of the preceding DISCOURSE or SITUATION. An opening sentence of a poem, novel or fairy-tale must obviously be 'new' information; yet it can be thematized internally in terms of the semantic value of its elements: *Once upon a time there* (thematic)/*were* (transitional)/*three little pigs* (rhematic).

(3) The general notion of **information** as new knowledge, and as knowledge being exchanged between participants in a SPEECH EVENT, is also important to consider. One of the FUNCTIONS of language is to communicate factual information (and many REGISTERS are primarily informative in this sense), but language (including 'body language') also conveys EXPRESSIVE or SUBJECTIVE information about feelings and emotions, and information INDEXICAL of a speaker's social status, age and origin, etc.

In LITERARY DISCOURSE, the information-exchange is only 'one-way': there is no FEEDBACK or response from the reader. Nonetheless the process is complex (see Genette 1972). In the novel we can distinguish between the information imparted by a character, and that by a NARRATOR or IMPLIED AUTHOR, the distribution of which may well not be 'straightforward'. Withholding vital pieces of information leads to ENIGMA and suspense. The more information provided in a novel, the more MIMETIC it seems; and the more information given about a character, the more our feelings will be roused, whether of sympathy or dislike. Significant events will be described in great detail; although certain areas of life have remained unexpressed until the modern period. As in many films today, sexual consummation must frequently be INFERRED, i.e. be read into the GAPS or cuts between scenes. Once a novel is read, we may ask ourselves why we read it again; and what kind of 'information' is then sought or received.

inkhorn term

Coined in the 1540s and current throughout the sixteenth century to describe the device of over-using Latinate words in writing, as if flowing from the ink-pot, in order to 'elevate' the STYLE. Thomas Wilson gives this example in his *Art of Rhetoric* (1553):

> Pondering, expending, and revoluting with my selfe, your ingent affability, and ingenious capacity for mundane affairs: I cannot but celebrate, and extol your magnifical dexterity above all other.

Not surprisingly, such a style was frequently PARODIED: e.g. in Jonson's *Poetaster* (1601). But some words have remained, and are well-established in the language: e.g. *irrevocable; compatible; depopulation.*

(See also AUREATE STYLE.)

integrational linguistics

An anti-FORMALIST, anti-CODE, pro-CONTEXT theory of communication (in the widest sense), associated particularly with Roy Harris (e.g. 1995) and still being developed. It arose out of his critique (1981) of what he terms the 'myths' of contemporary linguistic theory. (See also Toolan 1996.)

As its name suggests, it seeks to stress the harmonious integration of language with other human activities in their social context (an idea also stressed by Bakhtin and Bourdieu); and also emphasizes the role of the individual in the continuous creation of language as part of their total behaviour. It is argued that human beings inhabit what can be seen semiotically speaking as a 'communicative space' in which language is not neatly 'segregated' as a pre-existing code. Interesting for further research is the significance given to the 'folklinguistic' views of the ordinary language user: especially on the many linguistic BINARISMS that integrationalists would seek to undermine: e.g. LANGUE V. PAROLE; COMPETENCE V. PERFORMANCE; FIGURATIVE V. LITERAL; LITERARY V. non-literary; STANDARD V. non-standard, etc. For Harris and others, 'yer real chappie' replaces the notion of the IDEAL SPEAKER.

intention; intentionality; intentional(ist) fallacy

(1) Underlying most modern LITERARY CRITICISM is the supposition that the 'meaning' of a work is primarily to be derived from the TEXT and/or the READER, and not the (external) **intentions** of its AUTHOR: what is termed the ANTI-INTENTIONALIST APPROACH, versus **intentionalism**.

Intentionalism was chiefly described and decried as a **fallacy** by the American NEW CRITICS in the 1940s (see Wimsatt (ed.) 1954) as part of a general reaction against impressionistic and subjective criticism. For them the text as artefact belongs not to the author but to the public; in any case, the intention or design of an author is not necessarily accessible to use as a means of INTERPRETATION (if he or she is dead, for example); or the finished text may differ from an author's original intention. As a result, literary criticism offers a potential multiplicity of textual interpretations, since intention and meaning do not coincide.

Nonetheless, the danger is that we approach texts in a critical vacuum (which is not what the New Critics advocate). Some writers actually proclaim their intentions as part of the text: so Milton announces his intention in the first lines of *Paradise Lost* to sing 'of Man's first disobedience'. In such cases the intention can be judged as part of the meaning of the text, built into it, part of a larger, more abstract and comprehensive 'intention', as it were, which the text itself creates (see Culler 1983; Iser 1978; or what Charman (1990) calls **intent**). In other cases, a writer may write a preface, like Wordsworth to his *Lyrical Ballads*. It is difficult not to take account of the poet's intention here, if ultimately precept is matched against practice; presumably the same applies to comments in letters, autobiographies, essays, etc.

For some kinds of writing it is difficult to ignore the question of intention: PARODY, for instance, and IMITATION, depend for their success on the reader's awareness of the author's critical or appreciative intent to mimic or distort; again, perhaps, inscribed in the GENRES themselves (see Hutcheon 1985).

The whole question of intention was revived in the 1960s in the HERMENEUTICS of the American critic Hirsch (e.g. 1967), who argued for a literary meaning based on what is assumed to be the author's meaning, resistant to the historical fluctuations in interpretation.

(2) If the author's intentions are not seen to be of prime critical importance, nonetheless we still assume that the text was consciously intended and is not the product of automatic or automatized writing. We also assume that it was written for a particular purpose, whether as a piece of self-indulgence, a means of making money, or as political propaganda, etc.

That texts have specific 'goals' is more easily demonstrated in non-literary discourse, and de Beaugrande & Dressler (1981) use the term **intentionality** as one of their standards or criteria of TEXTUALITY. Having a plan or a goal, whether to describe an experiment, or to complain about shoddy workmanship, leads the speaker or writer to structure an argument COHERENTLY.

(3) **Intentionality** plays a prominent role in SPEECH ACT THEORY (q.v.), especially in the work of Austin (1962) and Searle (e.g. 1983); and also in RELEVANCE THEORY. Here, unlike literary criticism, interest is centred on the **communicative intention** of the speaker in performing an ILLOCUTIONARY ACT successfully, and the hearer's recognition of this intention. It is argued it is easier to describe acts from the point of view of the speaker rather than the hearer, since the listener may misinterpret 'intentions'.

However, the same problems arise as in (1): can we always be sure that we know the intentions of speakers? These are clearest in the case of explicit PERFORMATIVES (*I hereby pronounce you man and wife*), and clearer perhaps in one-to-one conversation or simple exchanges (e.g. request–response); but not so clear, as DISCOURSE ANALYSTS have stated, in extended DIALOGUE or in discourse that is written, and so also LITERARY DISCOURSE. In understanding speech acts in written texts it is the reader's interpretation which is the determining factor, albeit based on the assumption of a recognition of the writer's 'intention'. This, in the end, can only be a textual construct. (For Derrida's criticism of speech act theory and intentionality, see further Culler 1983.)

interior: ~ monologue; indirect ~ monologue; ~ dialogue

(1) **Interior monologue** was first used in French to describe a technique in the novel for representing the direct thought processes of characters. There is uncertainty surrounding the coiner of the term, but it was certainly made prominent by Valéry Larbaud who applied it to Joyce's *Ulysses* on its publication (1922). Joyce himself acknowledged that he had derived the technique (without its name) from a SYMBOLIST novel by Dujardin (1887) *Les Lauriers sont Coupés*, which describes the events in a day through the eyes and thoughts of a young man in love.

Interior monologue is an extended form of FREE DIRECT THOUGHT (q.v.), making up a considerable part of the structure of a novel. It is marked by the **first** PERSON PRONOUN, **present** ORIENTATION in TENSE and DEICTICS, and the absence of a reporting CLAUSE and GRAPHOLOGICAL marks of quotation, and so any signs of a NARRATOR. The FOCALIZATION or POINT OF VIEW is entirely internal and subjective. Moreover, the STYLE represents an attempt to suggest inchoate thought processes, or the rapid succession of thoughts or topic shifts, and also non-verbal IMAGES, by the use of dislocative or rambling SYNTAX, NOMINAL GROUPS as SENTENCES, METAPHOR, etc. So, Leopold Bloom, watching the diners in the pub, contemplates:

> Chump chop from the grill. Bolting to get it over. Sad booser's eyes. Bitten off more than he can chew. Am I like that? See ourselves as others see us. Hungry man is an angry man. Working tooth and jaw. Don't! O! A bone! . . .
>
> (Joyce: *Ulysses*)

A term often used synonymously is STREAM OF CONSCIOUSNESS (TECHNIQUE) (q.v.); but the latter term is better applied, and less confusingly, to the general representation of thought processes in the novel by a whole variety of means; or to the fictional GENRE developed in the early years of the twentieth century and associated with writers like Joyce and Woolf, where internal focalization is so FOREGROUNDED, and the OMNISCIENT NARRATOR unobtrusive.

(2) One less striking method of representing thoughts, for instance, is what has been termed **indirect interior monologue**, by analogy with INDIRECT SPEECH and THOUGHT (q.v.) (see Humphrey 1954). Here the reader is aware of the author's presence by the use of **third** person pronouns, but the syntax and focalization are that of the character. Again in *Ulysses*, Joyce's portrayal of Gerty Macdowell is a good example:

> Yes, it was her he was looking at and there was meaning in his look. His eyes burned into her as though they would search her through and through, read her very soul. Wonderful eyes they were, superbly expressive, but could you trust them? People were so queer . . .

(3) **Interior dialogue** is used by Hawthorn (1985) to describe an older novel technique which seems formal and rather stilted today (but see Hemingway's *The Old Man and The Sea*): namely, to depict thought processes as a debate between distinct VOICES (whether of the character, or summoned in the imagination). Hawthorn's illustrations from Charlotte Bronte's *Jane Eyre* suggest that it was a device that served to highlight mental anxiety or anguish:

> A kind fairy, in my absence, had surely dropped the required suggestion on my pillow; for as I lay down it came quietly and naturally to my mind: 'Those who want situations advertise; you must advertise in the -shire Herald.'
> 'How? I know nothing about advertising.'
> Replies rose smooth and prompt now: 'You must include the advertisement and the money to pay for it under a cover directed to the Editor of the Herald . . .

Interior dialogue could well describe MONOLOGUE as well: the concept of 'single-voice', indeed, is challenged by the Bakhtinian DIALOGICAL (q.v.) **principle**. So Bloom in *Ulysses* continually engages in questions and answers with himself (as in (1)). Also, it is not always easy to ascribe utterances to Bloom or to the narrator, in the absence of formal identification.

interpersonal: ~ function; ~ rhetoric

(1) In Halliday's grammatical theory (e.g. 1971) the **interpersonal** FUNCTION or **component** is one of three major or META-functions or components of language (see also IDEATIONAL; TEXTUAL). This is concerned with the relations between ADDRESSER and ADDRESSEE in the DISCOURSE situation or the SPEECH EVENT, and corresponds therefore to the EXPRESSIVE (addresser-oriented) and CONATIVE (addressee-oriented) functions of language described by Bühler (1934) and Jakobson (1960) for instance.

Obvious linguistic markers of the interpersonal mode include the **first** and **second** PERSON PRONOUNS *I* and *you*; **terms of** ADDRESS; DEICTIC elements; and SPEECH ACTS such as questions and directives.

(2) The term **interpersonal rhetoric** is used by Leech (1983) as part of his theory of PRAGMATICS, and as an extension of Grice's (1975) CO-OPERATIVE PRINCIPLE (q.v.) of conversation. Leech argues that other tacit rules are part of our **communicative** COMPETENCE, notably those of POLITENESS; which includes being tactful and sympathetic to others, and being modest about ourselves. INDIRECT SPEECH ACTS, which mitigate the offensive or impolite, such as *If I were you, I'd be careful where I put that cigarette end* are also interpersonal rhetorical strategies.

interpretation; interpretive community

(1) **Interpretation** is very common in LITERARY CRITICISM and STYLISTICS, disciplines which are heavily orientated towards the study of individual works or the oeuvre of particular writers. The theory and philosophy of interpretation is studied in HERMENEUTICS (q.v.) and in DECONSTRUCTION THEORY.

In a basic sense it means 'understanding': understanding the language of a text, and understanding its meaning and theme(s). In STYLISTICS it is the interpretation of the language derived from the analysis of the formal and semantic patterns which leads to the assessment of the significance of findings for the interpretation of the text's overall meaning. And interpretation at this level is guided by our COMPETENCE as readers of literature; by our knowledge of literary conventions such as GENRE, and by our cultural knowledge.

All this might suggest, however, that there is simply a meaning to be unlocked and expounded if we have the key (like the 'interpretation' of dreams); but the process is more complex and dynamic than that. On the one hand, a text may give rise to more than one interpretation, because of the complexity or plurivalence of its language or themes (e.g. *Hamlet*); on the other, the reader or listener can be said to produce the meaning just as much as the author or the text does. Or rather, there is a continual interaction between the text and the reader, which (ideally) acts as a constraint on the degree of freedom or (im)plausibility of any interpretation. Inevitably, the process of interpretation will be coloured by subjectivity, and even by changes in fashion and taste from one period to another. All these CONNOTATIONS, of exposition, creativity and subjectivity, are also there when we talk of an actor's 'interpretation' of a role on stage.

(2) In the work in AFFECTIVE STYLISTICS of Stanley Fish (e.g. 1980), the individual response to a text is played down in favour of the notion of **interpretive communities** to which a reader belongs, and which determine his or her reading. Fish's own equivalent of the IDEAL READER (q.v.), his **informed reader** (informed in the sense of being sensitive and astute), is so precisely by virtue of 'membership' to a community of like-minded readers.

If Fish's community idea seems vague and also elitist, this does reflect a significant point about reading and discussing literature today, namely that it largely takes place in academic establishments such as schools and (especially) institutes of higher education; and that literary criticism as a subject is practised largely by academics who talk to other academics. But, of course, there is not necessarily 'like-mindedness' of interpretation even within this apparently totalitarian 'community': there are many different theoretical frameworks informing the interpretation of literature, from NEW HISTORICISM to MARXISM and POSTMODERNISM. Moreover, teachers are always anxious to encourage a personal, individual response to literature in students; but Fish would query the extent to which this is not already predetermined: by previous pedagogic experiences, by acquired **literary** COMPETENCE, by general cultural knowledge, etc.

(See also EVALUATION.)

interrogative: ~ pronoun

Interrogative is very commonly used in GRAMMAR to distinguish one of the major SENTENCE structure types; the others being the DECLARATIVE (q.v.) and IMPERATIVE (q.v.). It is the type standardly used for questions. (See also MOOD.)

There are two main types of **interrogatives** in English:

(i) the so-called **'yes–no' questions**, which as their name suggests, often expect an answer 'yes' or 'no', and which have INVERSION of the SUBJECT and AUXILIARY VERB (to form interrogatives with **lexical** VERBS, the auxiliary *do* is used), e.g.: *Shall I compare thee to a summer's day?; Listen, do you want to know a secret?*

(ii) the so-called *wh*-**question** formed with **interrogative pronouns** and other forms (e.g. *who; which; where; when; how*, etc.). Here again, unless the *wh*-form is the subject so that the WORD ORDER is that of the declarative sentence, there is inversion of the subject and auxiliary after the initial interrogative word: *Who killed Cock Robin?; Where have all the flowers gone?*

It is usual to distinguish sentence types in this way from their meanings, or SPEECH ACT functions. A declarative sentence can have the ILLOCUTIONARY FORCE of a question simply by changing the INTONATION pattern from a (normal) falling to a rising (represented in writing by a question mark): *You are getting bored?* Although interrogatives are very commonly uttered with a rising intonation, the falling pattern is also frequently found, especially with *wh*-forms. Interrogatives themselves are popularly used instead of imperatives for polite requests (*Could you answer the phone, please?*) (see further Allan 1986); and a special type called RHETORICAL QUESTIONS (q.v.) (**interrogatio**) are semantically statements, even though syntactically interrogative:

Where's the man could ease a heart
Like a satin gown?

(Dorothy Parker: The Satin Dress)

Interrogative sentences, demanding as they do an ADDRESSEE, are more commonly found in face-to-face interaction than other types of discourse (except examination papers and joke-books). A fictional interchange is assumed by the reader for Shakespeare's *Shall I compare thee to a summer's day?* above; it is not common for a NARRATOR to ask questions of the IMPLIED READERS even if they are sometimes directly addressed.

NB: as the example of joke-books and examination papers reveal, we do not always ask questions in ignorance of the answer elicited (cf. also teacher–pupil interchanges).

intertextuality; intersubjectivity

(1) Now common in LITERARY THEORY and TEXT LINGUISTICS, **intertextuality** was introduced first into French criticism in the late 1960s by Kristeva (see 1969) in her discussion and elaboration of the ideas of Bakhtin, especially his general DIALOGICAL (q.v.) **principle**. The equivalent term **transtextuality** has sometimes been found (see Genette 1979).

Basically, it can be defined as UTTERANCES/TEXTS in relation to other utterances/ texts. So even within a single text there can be, as it were, a continual 'dialogue' between the text given and other texts/utterances that exist outside it, literary and non-literary: either within that same period of composition, or in previous centuries. Kristeva argues, in fact, that no text is 'free' of other texts or truly original.

GENRE is thus an intertextual concept: a poem written in the genre of a sonnet conforms to conventions that belong to a particular tradition inherited by the poet and which are also perhaps being exploited by the poet's contemporaries. When Shakespeare writes: *My mistress' eyes are nothing like the sun* (Sonnet 130), the *I*-PERSONA is reacting against the conventional sonnet CONCEITS in a kind of interactive dialogue, conceits which his contemporaries also must have known about. For the reader, therefore, intertextuality functions as an important FRAME OF REFERENCE which helps in the INTERPRETATION of a text (see Eco 1979).

In this example, the text is a transformation of another, a common way that intertextuality works. Borrowing is a more obvious process, whether in the form of a phrase in POETIC DICTION (e.g. *finny tribe*); a QUOTATION or allusion (as in Wilde's *A little sincerity is a dangerous thing . . .* , or titles like Huxley's *Brave New World*); larger-scale insertions (as in Eliot's *The Wasteland*); or structural models (myths and legends for science fiction); or all these modes (as in Joyce's *Finnegans Wake* and other MODERNIST fiction). IMITATION (q.v.) and PARODY (q.v.) depend on both borrowing and transformation of previous forms: what Genette termed **paratextuality**. Intertextuality is also a feature of non-literary discourse (e.g. advertising); and of non-verbal forms: film and music, for instance. (See also TEXTUALITY. See further Leitch 1983, ch. 6; Widdowson 1992, ch. 9.)

(2) Intertextuality shades into **intersubjectivity**, which is sometimes used as an alternative: but essentially intersubjectivity concerns the relations a text has with wider or vaguer spheres of knowledge, which the reader must also draw upon for interpretation (see Fowler 1977). In oral cultures, for instance, the Old English epic or the medieval ballad PRESUPPOSES in its composition a shared knowledge between poet and audience comprising stock RHETORICAL devices, DICTION and FORMULAE, as well as a shared set of values and social beliefs.

intonation

(1) In PHONETICS **intonation** describes the distinctive PROSODIC patterns or contours of rise and fall in pitch or TONE in speech UTTERANCES. We rarely speak on one level continuously; that would be monotonous.

Interest generally centres on the final direction of pitch movement in utterances, as being the most significant in function. Four basic contrasts (or KINETIC TONES) are characteristic of English: **Low Fall** (LF); **High Fall** (HF); **Low Rise** (LR); **High Rise** (HR). Intonation is variedly, but systematically, used in English to convey ATTITUDINAL MEANING, ILLOCUTIONARY FORCE, grammatical structure and INFORMATION **value**. The 'higher' the rise or fall of the voice, the greater the degree of involvement or emotion: a final HF marks incredulity or astonishment, and so is used in exclamations (*What a lovely surprise!*); a HR indicates considerable uncertainty, and so is characteristic of INTERROGATIVES (*Are you sure you've got the date right?*). Generally, the voice falls at the end of an utterance if it is a statement; it may fall also at clause boundaries, but LR is also common, especially in reading verse, or reading aloud. There are also variations in intonation patterns between regional ACCENTS (Tyneside and Welsh English v. RP, for instance); between REGISTERS (pulpit oratory v. horse-racing commentary); and STYLES of speaking (formal v. impromptu informal conversation). Less well researched are potential differences in intonation patterns between the sexes.

Phoneticians have evolved several different methods of analysing intonation and transcribing it on the printed page: there are differences between British and American terminologies, and between British and British. The minimum unit for analysis is called the TONE GROUP or TONE UNIT (q.v.) which is marked by several ACCENTED syllables at different pitch levels (or KEYS) and one prominent peak called the NUCLEUS, which carries the significant pitch contrast (HF, LF, etc.). The nucleus also coincides on the level of information with the utterance element with the highest degree of informativity, the FOCUS (q.v.), e.g.:

> What passing-bells for those who die as *cattle*?
> Only the monstrous anger of the *guns* . . .
>
> (Wilfred Owen: *Anthem for Doomed Youth*)

Traditionally, the study of intonation has concentrated very much on sentences or clauses because they commonly coincide with individual tone (and sense) groups. However, work in DISCOURSE ANALYSIS has drawn attention to the role of intonation as a COHESIVE device, and as a means of signalling the distribution of GIVEN and NEW INFORMATION between utterances as well as within them. So Brazil (1975) distinguished two basic tones: the **referring** or **invoking** (FR) when the information is known or expected; and the **informing** or **proclaiming** (F) when the information is new or FOREGROUNDED. (See also KEY.)

Although intonation is hardly indicated in writing (the exclamation and question marks give some clues), it can be reconstructed in silent or public reading of poetry, for instance, and also dramatic performance, using sense and SYNTAX as guides. In fictional DIALOGUE novelists will use speech TAGS like *her voice rising in anger; in a low tone of resentment*, etc.

(2) In the work of the Russian linguists and critics who followed Bakhtin in the 1920s and 1930s (e.g. Voloshinov 1973, first published 1929) **intonation** is used metaphorically in the discussion of the heterogenous, DIALOGICAL nature of novel discourse. In FREE INDIRECT SPEECH in particular there is a DOUBLE VOICE within the syntax: that of the narrator's and that of the character's evaluations: a special 'intonation'.

intransitive

In the categorization of VERBS and CLAUSES in GRAMMAR, **intransitive** describes structures which have a SUBJECT and verb but no DIRECT OBJECT. Verbs like *come*, *go* and *die* do not need objects; contrast verbs like *make* and *catch* (*I'll make the tea then catch the train*), which are called TRANSITIVE VERBS (q.v.).

Some verbs can function both **intransitively** and transitively: cf. *Are you reading?* and *I am reading a new book.* Halliday (1985) has noted how in many of such verbs there is a causative semantic relationship, which he calls the **ergative**, e.g.: *The boat sailed* v. *The boy sailed the boat* (ergative).

Common in colloquial speech is a verb–object construction which can be seen as the equivalent of an **intransitive verb**. In phrases like *have a bath/smoke; take a shower/nap*, etc., the verb has little lexical meaning which derives instead from the direct objects as deverbal nouns.

(See also TRANSITIVITY.)

inventio

Inventio or **invention** is one of the five classical **divisions** of RHETORIC concerned with the 'finding out' (cf. Lat. *invenire*) or selection of material and arguments for a composition. This might be 'invented' by the writer in the modern sense of the word, but originality of idea was by no means necessary. The arrangement of the argument was far more important, and writers like Aristotle and Cicero gave guidance on structuring: by definition, division into genus and species, causes and effects, etc.

inversion

(1) In modern GRAMMAR the reversal in normal WORD ORDER of the major SENTENCE elements, particularly SUBJECT and VERB.

Inversion was also sanctioned in RHETORIC, known under the FIGURE of HYPERBATON (q.v.). Inversion of subject and verb is extremely common in poetry, often after FRONTING of the OBJECT for EMPHASIS, e.g. from Wordsworth:

Ten thousand saw I at a glance

(I Wandered Lonely as a Cloud)

Strange fits of passion have I known

(Lucy)

Many kinds of inversion are also common in non-poetic and non-literary language: after (semi-)negative ADVERBIALS in FORMAL discourse (*Scarcely had I left the room . . .*); after *here* in phrases like (*Here comes the milkman*). Also formal is the SUBORDINATE CLAUSE of concession or condition where inversion replaces an initial CONJUNCTION: *Had I known you were ill, I'd have come and seen you* (cf. *If I'd known . . .*).

Where there are 'heavy' adverbials inversion is often usefully combined with FRONTING to leave the FOCUS on the (important) subject, e.g.: *On stage here tonight is comedian Jack Dee.*

Inversion in the reporting clause of TAG for DIRECT SPEECH commonly occurs; with the clause as a whole 'inverted' from initial position, cf.:

Thomas said 'I'll show the other engines'. (Rev. Awdry: *Thomas the Tank Engine*)
'I'll show the other engines,' *Thomas said.*
'I'll show the other engines', *said Thomas.*

(See also JOURNALESE.)

An obligatory grammatical inversion is that of subject and AUXILIARY VERB in INTERROGATIVES, e.g. *Shall we dance?*; *Do you come here often?*; and also TAG QUESTIONS, e.g. *It's quiet here, isn't it?*

(2) **Inversion** was also used in sixteenth-century rhetoric to describe the device of turning an argument against one's opponent.

(3) In classical METRICS, it describes the substitution of one kind of FOOT for another. So, in a predominantly IAMBIC pattern (×/) there may be found an **inverted** TROCHAIC pattern (/×). So in Shakespeare's Sonnet 29, which describes the narrator's condition:

```
 /  ×  ×  /   ×  / ×  ×    /   /
When in disgrace with fortune and men's eyes
×/   ×  /    ×/   × /   ×    /
I all alone beweep my outcast state
```

The substitution of a trochaic foot initially in the line can match a dramatic shift of mood:

```
 /  ××  /  ×   /
Haply I think on thee . . .
```

irony: ~ dramatic

(1) A FIGURE OF SPEECH or TROPE derived from Gk *eironeia* via Latin, and meaning 'dissimulation'. **Antiphrasis** used to be an alternative RHETORICAL name.

Irony is found when the words actually used appear to contradict the sense actually required in the CONTEXT and presumably intended by the speaker: utterances like *Aren't you clever!* or *What lovely weather!* (when it's raining) found in speech are not to be taken LITERALLY. Directed against another person, irony is often sarcastic, serving as an oblique polite form of criticism. But if the INTENDED irony is not perceived then its force is lost. Extended examples of irony can be found in novels, e.g. Fielding's *Jonathan Wild*. Here words of approbation and HYPERBOLE apparently extol vices as virtues, and irony has a satirical, distancing function. In PARODY (q.v.) irony is a major rhetorical strategy, and it is often characteristic also of FREE INDIRECT SPEECH.

It can be argued that the use of tropes like irony and hyperbole (and also LITOTES) which involve doubleness of meaning violate the CONVERSATIONAL MAXIM of QUALITY (q.v.): in the interest of effectiveness of communication we normally tell the truth.

(2) **Irony** is not only verbal, as phrases like *the irony of the situation* or *tragic irony* suggest. Here the discrepancy or incongruity is between what appears, or is believed, to be the case and the real state of affairs. Irony in this sense is often

used in PLOTS in themes in LITERATURE, e.g. in Hardy's and James's novels; and plays like Shakespeare's *Macbeth*, where Duncan trusts the thane who plans to kill him; and *King Lear*, where Lear rejects the daughter who actually loves him the best.

It is quite common for the reader to perceive the irony of situations before the characters do: this is known as **dramatic irony**. But the double PERSPECTIVE (of reader and of character) applies equally to FICTION as to the stage. Booth (1974) distinguishes another kind of literary irony, namely where it is at the expense of the NARRATOR rather than the character. In novels like Ford's *The Good Soldier*, for instance, the reader 'reads between the lines' and sees the events being described from quite a different angle from the POINT OF VIEW of the gullible and hence **unreliable** (in Booth's terms) narrator.

(See further Gibbs 1994; Muecke 1982.)

isochrony, also isochronism

Used in PHONETICS and METRICS since the 1950s to describe the characteristic nature of RHYTHM in English, at least as it sounds to the ear. From Gk 'equal-timed', isochrony refers to the tendency for STRESSED syllables or BEATS to occur at fairly equal intervals, both in speech and verse. So each of the proper names with varying numbers of syllables in the following utterance will take up the same amount of time:

      × / × × / × /
    The (Kensington) (Kenton) (Kent) road was deserted

isocolon

From Gk 'equal-member', a FIGURE OF SPEECH in which phrases or CLAUSES in a SENTENCE are of equal length and PARALLEL in SYNTAX and hence RHYTHM. A MARKED device, **isocolon** is especially frequent in the prose style of writers influenced by Latin RHETORIC. Johnson uses it for elaboration of argument and for EMPHASIS: e.g. his letter to Lord Chesterfield (1754):

> The notice which you have been pleased to take of my labours, had it been early, had it been kind; but it has been delayed till I am indifferent, and cannot enjoy it; till I am solitary, and cannot impart it; till I am known, and do not want it.

J

jargon

It is hard to imagine that this word, which is often used pejoratively in ordinary speech, derives from an OF word meaning 'the warbling of birds', and is so used in Chaucer's *Merchant's Tale* to describe the old man, January: *And ful of jargon as a flekked pye* (= 'magpie'). But it is an easy semantic shift from bird noises to unintelligible human language, and then to a REGISTER or VARIETY of language which non-users fail to understand because of the kind of specialized vocabulary used, which has been its common significance since the seventeenth century.

Different professions and disciplines have of necessity evolved their own terminologies for specialized needs, from science to STYLISTICS, marketing to the Internet; and jargon can be used quite neutrally to describe these. What is often objected to, however, is the (sometimes wilful) manipulation of jargon for obfuscation, pomposity or mere verbosity; and groups like the Campaign for Plain English in Britain have attracted much sympathy for their attacks on the language of legal contracts, Civil Service leaflets and politics, etc. Consider also PARODIES, like this revised version of the *23rd Psalm*:

> The Lord and I are in a shepherd / sheep situation, and I am in a position of negative need. He prostrates me in a green belt grazing area . . .

(See also ARGOT; CANT; HABITUS; METALANGUAGE; SLANG. See further Nash 1993.)

jouissance

(1) One of a pair of terms (with *plaisir*) popularized in LITERARY THEORY by Roland Barthes (1975), and remaining untranslated in English. (*Jouissance*, meaning 'pleasure' or 'merriment' was once used by poets like Spenser, and then fell out of use in English, according to the *OED*.) **Jouissance**, for Barthes, is a heightened and radical kind of reading pleasure, an enrapture, almost sexual. *Plaisir* is a quieter pleasure, maintaining cultural equilibrium. So we can think of the different kinds of enjoyment potentially effected by rhetorical TROPES like METAPHOR on the one hand, and many SCHEMES on the other: literary metaphor

working disruptively by DE-FAMILIARIZATION; schemes pleasing by the comforting familiarity of repetition.

(2) The sexual connotations of the word *jouissance* had been highlighted by the psychoanalyst Jacques Lacan in his 1972–3 seminars, and it has also been used in FEMINIST CRITICISM for the 'orgasmic' pleasure afforded by women's writing (*écriture feminine*) with its qualities of excess and defiance against patriarchal forms of representation.

journalese

Although **journalese** can be used simply as a useful descriptive term for the linguistic features of the REGISTER of journalism, the use of the SUFFIX -*ese* (cf. **Johnsonese** = '(polysyllabic) style of Johnson'; **officialese** = 'JARGON of official forms, etc.') undoubtedly reinforces its more usual pejorative sense in common usage.

Originating in the nineteenth century, when journalism had a distinctive style even then but of a rather more FORMAL kind, the term today is normally reserved for the description of the STYLISTIC features associated with the popular 'tabloid' newspapers, features which were derived after the Second World War chiefly from the influential American journal *Time*. Noteworthy is the use of 'heavy' PREMODIFICATION and APPOSITION in NOUN PHRASES as SUBJECTS, as the attributes of the speaker are compactly listed (by age, sex, occupation, etc.); often linked with INVERSION of subject and VERB, e.g.: *Declared the shapely blonde divorcee, mother of three . . .*

Journalese is also noticeably FORMULAIC: drawing upon a stock of short LEXICAL ITEMS for all contingencies (e.g. *drama, dash, bid, shock,* etc.); and of CLICHÉS and fixed COLLOCATIONS (e.g. *the smile that says it all; battling granny; love-nest,* etc.).

(See further Reah 1998.)

K

---

kenning

In Old English criticism since the late nineteenth century, **kenning** is a term borrowed from ON RHETORIC (cf. *kenna við* 'to name after') to describe a poetic PERIPHRASIS or a descriptive METAPHORICAL COMPOUND, in the DICTION of OE poetry. So *hilde-nædre* ('battleadder') is a spear; *heafod-gemma* ('head-gem') an eye; and *hwæl-rad* ('whale-road') the sea. Once coined, such kennings became part of the common stock of OE POETIC DICTION, to be drawn upon at will by secular or religious poets, being vivid, and useful METRICALLY in the ALLITER-ATIVE VERSE form.

Kennings represent about 20 per cent of the compounds in *Beowulf*, yet OE kennings were not so elaborately CONCEITED as those found in ON poetry: e.g. poetry itself described as 'the sea of Odin's breast'.

A simpler kind of kenning (ON *kent heiti*) in OE poetry identifies the REFERENT with something it actually is: e.g. boat as 'wavefloater', or deer as 'heath-stepper'. These are not unlike the periphrases of eighteenth-century poetry: e.g. *scaly tribe* ('fish'), *feathered choirs* ('birds').

(See further Brodeur 1959.)

---

kernel: ~ sentence

(1) In very early TRANSFORMATIONAL GRAMMAR (TG) Chomsky (1957), in-fluenced by the work of Harris (1951), used **kernel sentence** to describe a basic un MARKED SENTENCE type from which all other sentences (e.g. negative, INTER-ROGATIVE, PASSIVE) were said to be derived according to TRANSFORMATIONAL **rules**. It largely corresponds to the DECLARATIVE sentence, simple in its structure (e.g. *The cow jumped over the moon*). Certainly the ordinary speaker is likely to feel that sentences such as *Did the cow jump over the moon?* and *The cow didn't jump over the moon* are related in some way, if only in PROPOSITIONAL content.

The concept had some vogue in the 1960s in STYLISTICS, before Chomsky's TG model changed. Ohmann (1964), for example, distinguishes prose STYLES of different authors, such as Faulkner and Hemingway, on the basis of (simple) kernels and COMPLEX SENTENCE types. (See also MATRIX.)

(2) By analogy, the term has also been used in NARRATIVE theory (e.g. Chatman 1978) to describe the kind of analysis practised by Propp (1928) on Russian folk-tales and Todorov (1969) on *The Decameron*: where PLOTS are reduced to a basic number of **kernel types** or FUNCTIONS (q.v.). Different CHARACTERS realize similar ROLES or perform similar actions from tale to tale.

(3) Confusingly, however, Chatman (1978) also uses the term to translate Fr. *noyau* in Barthes's (1966) system of structural units or functions. **Kernels** here are specifically units which advance the action, the 'nodes' or 'hinges' of the story, v. CATALYSTS (Fr. *catalyses*) which delay or amplify it. So in Hardy's *Tess of the d'Urbervilles*, Tess's decision towards the end of the novel to follow Angel Clare is crucial to the plot, causing Alec d'Urberville's murder. An alternative name is **cardinal function** (Heath's translation of Barthes 1966); and an equivalent would be van Dijk's (1977) **macro-proposition**.

Barthes's own subsequent word developed along more general lines, with his concept of textual CODES (1970). Kernels can be seen to operate in the HERMENEUTIC CODE (q.v.), which involves plot structure, and raising of questions and ENIGMAS.

key: ~ term; keying

(1) In LITERARY CRITICISM **key** occurs in collocations or phrases close to its sense in ordinary speech of 'chief' or 'prevailing'. Williams (1976) entitles his glossary of words that are significant in modern culture and society '**Keywords**', a phrase also used to describe predominant words used in specific poetic periods, e.g. the Augustan (see Tillotson 1961). Along with **key** METAPHOR and **key** SYMBOL, the phrase also describes words in a TEXT significant for the THEME. And any discipline, be it sociology or DECONSTRUCTION, has its **key terms** which reflect its IDEOLOGY or set of beliefs. (And see Carter's title 1995.)

(2) More technically, in Old English METRICS **key** ALLITERATION refers to the first STRESSED word in the B-VERSE of the poetic line which determines the alliterative pattern of the whole line also known as **head-stave** (Ger. *Hauptstabe*).

(3) Some senses of **key** evoke musical associations. In ETHNOGRAPHY, for instance, **key** refers to the TONE or manner in which a SPEECH EVENT is performed (see Hymes 1974): e.g. solemn, light-hearted, teasing. A funeral service is normally solemn; an interview serious, but not necessarily solemn. The key may be signalled not only in CHOICE of language, but also in gestures and facial expressions (smiling, frowning, winking, etc.).

(4) Popular in the 1960s was the use of **key** to refer to a STYLE of DISCOURSE according to **degree of** FORMALITY, following Joos (1962). He distinguished five keys, ranging from the **frozen** or **oratorical** at the most formal end of the scale, to **intimate** at the most informal end. The central, un MARKED key, used in everyday polite interchange with acquaintances, etc., is the **consultative**. The others are **formal** or **deliberate**; and **casual**.

(5) In DISCOURSE ANALYSIS the term **key** was popularized as a result of the work of Brazil (1975) in particular, who took it from the early twentieth-century phonetician and linguist Henry Sweet in the sense of INTONATION pitch.

Concerned with the function of intonation between UTTERANCES in discourse, Brazil suggests that there are three significant pitch-level contrasts between TONE GROUPS, working relative to each other. The use of a **high key** typically signals 'contrastive' or reactive material or relations; it is also often used for elicitations. **Low key** is typically used to signal that the speaker has no more to say; and **mid key** that there may be more to come.

Key also correlates with INFORMATIVITY (q.v.): elements of high informativity, which normally appear at the end of utterances, often have a high key; whereas elements of low informativity, found at the beginning, have a low key.

In general we may also note that in public speaking a 'descending' scale from high to low is often heard; whereas in sports commentary (e.g. of horse racing) a consistently high key reinforces the emotional excitement of the announcer from start to finish.

(6) Somewhat confusingly, the term **key** has also been used in the description of intonation by Halliday (e.g. 1985), but in a different sense. For him key relates selection of (KINETIC) tones to the system of MOOD (q.v.). So a DECLARATIVE SENTENCE uttered with a rising or falling or fall–rise tone may vary in the ATTITUDES conveyed: reservation, contradiction, assertion, etc.

(7) The term **keying** is particularly associated with the work of the sociologist Goffman (1974) on FRAME analysis. So much of our ordinary behaviour is organized into conventional frameworks, and it is part of our social and communicative COMPETENCE that we know how to deal with the different activities of meetings, interviews, ordering meals in restaurants, etc. There are also secondary frameworks or keyings which involve a shift of MODE from the 'real' to the 'fabricated': activities like ceremonials and contests, games and play-acting. LITERATURE itself can be seen as a secondary framework, formally marked by special conventions such as chapter headings and EPILOGUES, etc.

kinesics; kineme; kinetic tone; kinaesthetice, etc.

(1) From Gk *kineo* meaning 'move', **kinesics** in SEMIOTICS describes the COMMUNICATION system of gestures and motion, i.e. 'body language'. The word is also used to describe the study of this.

Kinesics was first systematically analysed in the 1950s by the anthropologist Birdwhistell, who showed how much of our body behaviour was conventionalized and socialized. There are thousands of potential facial expressions, for instance, but each society selects only a limited number for significant use: what were called **kinemes**, by analogy with PHONEME.

It is only fairly recently, with the advent of video recording, that DISCOURSE ANALYSTS have begun to take serious interest in those aspects of face-to-face interaction which are not verbalized, or even vocalized, but which are an integral part of communication. Facial expressions and body movements not only act as important reinforcements to speech, indicating ATTITUDINAL or EMOTIVE MEAN-INGS in smiles or frowns, fist-clenching or feet-tapping, for example, but provide significant 'clues' to participants about speaking and TURNTAKING rights, and also FEEDBACK about how INFORMATION is being received. Eye contact, length of gaze, eyebrow movements, body position are all important signals, for instance. In writing, as in the novel, this sort of information can be provided as clues to attitudes, etc., but is not consistently provided.

(2) Each culture also develops special systems of gesture and movement for specific, often ritualistic purposes. **Kinetic art** is sometimes used to describe those art forms like ballet, mime and drama where body movement and gesture are significant, even prime, carriers of meaning. But as Elam (1980) notes for drama the **kinesic** CODE of the theatre is really part of a kinesic continuum, since 'real-life' body language is also exploited on stage. Gesture is particularly FOREGROUNDED in the Brechtian epic theatre; and in melodrama and farce.

Fish (1970) has argued that literature is also kinetic art because while we read it is 'moving': we turn the pages, and read along the lines.

(3) It is not only art that moves, but speech as well. Without the movement of our mouth, throat and chest, etc., sounds would not be articulated; and various aspects of speech (STRESS and RHYTHM, for example) are accompanied by muscular tension or actual movement of the body (cf. the swaying of football supporters to their rhythmic chants). The particular study of the precise bodily movements which produce speech is called **kinaesthetics**.

Some critics have tried to argue for the kinaesthetic appeal or response in LITERATURE. So Epstein (1978) claims that by a kind of MIMESIS the sound struc-ture of poetic lines, the movements of the tongue, mime movements referred to in the text. His own examples fail to convince.

(4) PHONETICIANS sometimes use the term **kinetic** TONE in INTONATION to refer to the direction of pitch movement associated with the most prominent syllable or NUCLEUS in a tone unit: common tones being 'falling' and 'rising'.

(See also PARALANGUAGE.)

koiné

From Gk koiné (*dialektos*) meaning 'common (language)', and originally applied to the common LITERARY LANGUAGE of the Greeks to the Byzantine period. The term **koiné** is sometimes found as the equivalent to STANDARD LANGUAGE/ DIALECT: a VARIETY used as a common language or LINGUA FRANCA between speakers from different areas and backgrounds, with marked regionalisms being levelled out as a result. Such dialects developed in North America and Australia, for example, as a result of colonization.

The term can also be applied to a written dialect which serves as a common MEDIUM of LITERATURE: e.g. West Saxon for Old English literature; Caxton's dialect for his printed texts in the fifteenth century.

L

langue

One of a commonly cited pair of terms in linguistics (see also PAROLE) introduced by Saussure (1916) and usually left untranslated because it has no direct equivalent in English.

(*La*) **langue** refers to one of the senses of 'language', namely, the system of communication produced by a speech community, and is thus distinguished from language as the general faculty possessed by human beings (*le langage*), and language as the specific verbal behaviour of individuals in speaking and writing (*la parole*).

For Saussure, and for generations of linguists after him, the analysis and codification of the system of language underlying actual USAGE was the main objective in linguistics and GRAMMAR, and his dichotomy between *langue* and *parole* was reinforced by Chomsky's (1965) distinction between COMPETENCE (q.v.) and PERFORMANCE (q.v.), which is not, however, identical.

But it is not easy to identify where the language 'system' originates and how; nor is it always easy to distinguish it from *parole*. We all seem to have access to *langue*, but it is presumably first acquired from our contact with actual usage (*parole*) in accordance with our in-built faculty for language (*langage*). Linguists like Jakobson and Bakhtin would prefer not to see an opposition or dualism here, but a dialectical relationship. There is the danger, too, of seeing language idealistically, as having a 'pure' form (*langue*) which is 'contaminated' when transformed into *parole*. (See further Harris 1995.)

Trends in certain disciplines (e.g. sociolinguistics) reflect a concern with aspects of language which would earlier have been categorized as *parole* (e.g. concrete SPEECH ACTS and DISCOURSE), but which rather reflect another aspect of the system of language not hitherto explored. Stylisticians, too, like the FORMALISTS before them, have argued that LITERARY works need not necessarily be seen as *parole*, but as a kind of language system, a *langue* in their own right (see Widdowson 1983).

lect

Derived from the pattern of established words like DIALECT and IDIOLECT, **lect** is used in sociolinguistics as a generic term equivalent to a language VARIETY for any set of features with a definite functional or situational identity. So there are **genderlects** which distinguish male and female speech. (See also SOCIOLECT.) Adamson (1998) has the useful term **chronolect** for a variety distinctive in time, dividing people in terms of language change. So we can talk of the chronolect of the late sixteenth century, relevant for the understanding of Shakespeare.

Lect is well established in work on CREOLE LANGUAGES, e.g. Bickerton's notion in the 1970s of a **continuum** of **lects** ranging from broad creole as the **basilect** and the local standard as the **acrolect**.

leitmotif

Leitmotif (Ger. *leitmotiv*) was taken into LITERARY CRITICISM from music, where it was first used in Germany in the nineteenth century to describe the characteristic feature of the music of Weber and especially Wagner's musical dramas. Meaning 'leading MOTIF', it refers to the use of repeated orchestral phrases to suggest a particular character, situation, emotion, etc., often interwoven with each other.

Wagner may well have been influenced by literary composition, but the term seems to have been first applied in literary criticism in 1896, to the work of Zola, by Havelock Ellis. Certainly the device was particularly appropriated in MODERNIST literature, and is much discussed in connection with Joyce's later novels, *Ulysses* and *Finnegan's Wake*.

In the 'dream-world' of Joyce's last novel repeated phrases, and even PHONEMES and MORPHEMES, are of considerable structural importance for the interpretation of THEME, and for the signalling of the presences of the principal 'characters' (e.g. /p/, /t/ and /s/ for the daughter Issy).

In a looser sense it is often used, like motif, to mean recurring or favourite themes throughout an author's oeuvre: e.g. the relationship between Destiny and Fate in Hardy's novels. In both senses leitmotif can be applied to other NARRATIVE forms, such as film.

lexicology; lexis; lexical: ~ item; ~ set; ~ meaning; lexicon; lexicalization; lexeme, etc.

(1) The Gk *lexis*, meaning 'word', has spawned a number of derivatives in modern vocabulary studies (or **lexicology**). The work **lexis** is used as a general more technical term for vocabulary or DICTION.

In descriptions of language lexis is sometimes linked with GRAMMAR as a component of language comprising the level of FORM; Halliday (e.g. 1985), combines both in the term LEXICOGRAMMAR. Lexis is the most important means we possess for expressing or encoding our ideas and experience. (See also **lexicalization** below.)

The term is also used in STYLISTIC analyses of both LITERARY and non-literary TEXTS. Different FIELDS (q.v.) of lexis are associated, for example, with different REGISTERS: the JARGON of legal terminology in contracts; words to do with food and methods of preparation in cookery recipes, etc. Habitual COLLOCATIONS are a recognizable feature of different registers, e.g. *desirable residence* (estate agents); *mercy dash* (popular press). Words having similar collocational ranges, and recurring in similar CONTEXTS, are said to belong to the same **lexical set**. The days of the week present an obvious and simple example. In Hopkins's poetry characteristic lexical sets are words to do with religion and nature, reflecting his major THEMES. (See further Cummings & Simmons 1983, ch. 4.)

(2) **Lexical items** are drawn from the stock of words belonging to the language as a whole: the **lexicon**. In Greek this word meant 'dictionary', which is still one of its meanings in English today, especially with reference to 'exotic' languages like Hebrew, Arabic and Greek itself. A lexicon or dictionary is a handy means of cataloguing vocabulary for reference under its **lexical entries**.

We can also speak of the lexicon of an individual, i.e. the personal word-stock of a speaker of a language. Since it is impossible to know every word in a language (and no-one knows just how many thousands of words there are in the English language today), the lexicon of an individual is of necessity smaller than the lexicon of the language. Also, people understand more words than they actually use (i.e. their passive vocabulary is bigger than their active vocabulary). We can estimate Shakespeare's and Milton's vocabularies only very roughly from the words in their works (15,000 v. 7–8,000).

Moreover, we learn new words all the time, and forget others; just as new words, by a variety of lexical processes (e.g. COMPOUNDING, DERIVATION, borrowing) are added to the word-stock, and other words fall obsolete and are replaced (e.g. much of the Old English vocabulary after the Norman Conquest). The lexicon is thus OPEN-ended, whereas GRAMMAR and PHONOLOGY present CLOSED systems. The process of finding words for new concepts is commonly known as **lexicalization**. (See also OVER-LEXICALIZATION; UNDER-LEXICALIZATION.)

(NB: some lexicologists like Bauer 1983, however, have used this term in rather the contrary sense of 'fossilization' or 'petrification': e.g. for words like *warm-th*, which are formed by a derivational pattern unproductive in Modern English.)

The two senses of **lexicon** as a 'register' of words and as part of an individual's COMPETENCE as user of a language came together in Chomsky's (1965) use of the term to describe a feature of his GENERATIVE GRAMMAR. The lexicon here is a sub-component of the 'base' or DEEP STRUCTURE of his model, and provides information about items in terms of semantic FEATURES, and syntactic categories.

(3) Lexicologists and other linguists commonly use the term **lexical item** or **lexeme** instead of simply 'word'. This is because, from a lexical point of view, words can have different FORMS, but are felt to be the 'same word', and would be so cited in a lexicon. *Laugh, laughed* and *laughing* are all forms of the lexeme *laugh*. There is also the possibility of a lexical item comprising more than one

word: e.g. phrasal verbs (*make up*) and IDIOMS (*pins and needles*). Loosely related is the notion of **lexical bundle** (Biber *et al.* 1999, ch. 13) to refer to combinations of words (from 3 to 6) which recur in any given REGISTER, e.g. *I don't know* in conversation; *on the other hand* in academic prose.

(4) A distinction is sometimes made between lexemes which have **lexical meaning** and those which have **grammatical meaning**: so-called CONTENT or **full** words on the one hand, and **form** or FUNCTIONAL or **empty words** on the other. Words with lexical meaning (typically NOUNS, VERBS and ADJECTIVES), by far the biggest category, make reference to objects and experiences in the world; functional words (CONJUNCTIONS, PREPOSITIONS, etc.), a CLOSED CLASS, indicate grammatical relationships.

(See further Lyons 1977, vol. 2, ch. 13.)

liminality

From Lat. meaning 'threshold', the term **limina(ity)** first came to prominence in anthropology to describe marginal or transitional phases in rites of passage in so-called 'primitive' cultures (see Turner 1967). It has struck a chord in POSTCOLONIAL THEORY, with its interest in the marginal; and in studies of CODE-SWITCHING, where speakers move between different spheres of reference.

Out of a state of 'in-betweenness' can come literary creativity. So, for example, for the Northern working-class boy Tony Harrison, going to grammar school was his 'rite of passage', forcing a linguistic divide between his Leeds dialect and the language of education. But the in-betweenness of provincial and metropolitan intellectual underpins his poetry (see, e.g., *Them and [uz]*).

lingua franca

From It. 'Frankish tongue', it is believed **lingua franca** originally described a trade language developed in the Mediterranean regions in the medieval period between people who did not understand each other's language. Now the phrase is commonly used for any language which serves as an 'auxiliary' language of communication between communities, not only for purposes of trade (like Titano in the north-west Amazon), but also for political purposes. The English language is the foremost language in the world for international communication.

(See also KOINÉ; PIDGIN.)

literal: ~ translation; ~ meaning

(1) Originally derived from Lat. *litera* 'letter', a **literal translation** is one which follows the original text 'to the letter', i.e. in a word-for-word translation.

(2) **Literal** came to be applied to the reading or INTERPRETATION of any TEXT (particularly religious texts at first), where the words are taken in their usual senses, and not on an ALLEGORICAL level, for instance.

(3) Most commonly today **literal** is opposed to FIGURATIVE or METAPHORICAL and refers to any word which is used with its basic CONCEPTUAL (often ETYMO-LOGICAL) MEANING.

In everyday interchange, our usual expectation is that **literal meanings** are the NORM: we only look for a non-literal interpretation of an utterance if we can't otherwise make sense of it. Yet IDIOMATIC usages often cause problems for foreign speakers, who may 'back the wrong horse' in working out a phrase's meaning.

In LITERARY LANGUAGE, however, our expectations are reversed: we look for figurative or SYMBOLIC meanings, or THEMATIC resonances in apparently literal usage. The distinction then, between literal and figurative becomes not so much an objective linguistic fact as a PRAGMATIC one. Words are commonly found with metaphorical meanings in the ostensibly 'matter-of-fact' REGISTER of scientific discourse (e.g. *black hole* in astronomical terminology): here the figurative meaning serves as its basic meaning, to LEXICALIZE a concept that needs to be named.

In the work of DECONSTRUCTIONISTS like Derrida and De Man the question of the relationship between literal and metaphorical meaning has been continually raised. So too in COGNITIVE LINGUISTICS/POETICS, where it is argued that human language and mind are not inherently literal; and in RELEVANCE THEORY, where distinction between literalness and figurativeness can be seen as a matter of degree (see also Goatly 1997).

literary competence

See COMPETENCE.

literary criticism

Literary criticism, the dominant discipline in literary studies in British universities today, emerged at the end of the nineteenth century and became fully established in the 1920s and the 1930s with the rise of English studies and the decline of classical studies (see Eagleton 1983).

The Cambridge scholars Leavis and Richards, and also T. S. Eliot, are particularly associated with formulating the aims and methods of literary criticism, chiefly the concentration on the critical INTERPRETATION of a CANON of texts from Chaucer onwards deemed 'worthy' of attention: in the 1930s for their moral and spiritual value, and for their value in ENACTING the complexity of experience. (See also EVALUATION.) Literary critics have also discussed the authorship of texts, and the historical and cultural backgrounds.

Although some literary critics, following Richards (1925) and Empson (1930), have focussed attention on the language of literary texts (see, e.g., Lodge 1966;

Nowottny 1962 in the 1960s), many critics have traditionally been suspicious of STYLISTICS because they feel that, like linguistics, it is too 'objective' and runs the risk of destroying the sensitivity of response that readers need. There is a tendency, too, for critics to concentrate on CONTENT rather than FORM, and to see language as a 'transparent' MEDIUM. (See also LITERARY LANGUAGE; LITERARY THEORY; NEW HISTORICISM; PRACTICAL CRITICISM.)

literary: ~ language; ~ discourse; literature; literariness

One of the commonest questions continually asked in LITERARY CRITICISM, LITERARY THEORY and in STYLISTICS, is 'What is literature?'. A related question, equally popular, is 'Literary language, does it exist?'.

What is meant by **literature** has, since the nineteenth century, very much involved imaginative or FICTIONAL writing, in the GENRES of prose, poetry and drama. (See also MIMESIS.) However, earlier senses of the word included other forms of learned compositions, and other cultured disciplines such as philosophy and history. (There is an inclusive sense currently in colloquial use today, namely when we talk of reading all 'the literature' on cat-breeding, skiing holidays or air pollution.) Derived from Lat. *litera* 'letter', literature has always been associated predominantly with the written MEDIUM, although literature is in many societies orally composed and delivered, and such a body of compositions existed in English society in the early days of the Anglo-Saxon settlements. (See ORATURE.)

One problem arising from the definition of literature as imaginative writing is that some works which are not imaginative have come to be classed as **literary**; e.g. the *Authorized Version* of the *Bible*, and Gibbon's *Decline and Fall of the Roman Empire*. This suggests either that literature characteristically has certain features of FORM which distinguishes it from other writing, or that it has a special effect on readers different from the response to other DISCOURSE, or both. The question of the **literariness** (Jakobson) of literature has preoccupied many schools of thought. Literature is often discussed in terms of AESTHETIC VALUE or effect, for instance: texts, expecially poetic, which are admired for their formal 'beauty' arising from their structural COHERENCE or patterning, or EXPRESSIVE and CONNOTATIVE qualities of meaning and their IMAGERY. Certainly literature, especially poetry, has commonly FOREGROUNDED language and meaning consciously and creatively in a way that overrides a simple informative function, as the FORMALISTS and PRAGUE SCHOOL linguists stressed. Yet there are many literary works, expecially prose, which employ no remarkably unusual or DEVIANT language. Their language is literary not in a special sense, but only in the sense that it belongs to a work regarded generically as literature, as opposed to a newspaper or recipe. But part of literature's aesthetic value also comes from its AFFECTIVE appeal to the emotions of the reader. In various ways, then, literature is seen as an art form, to be compared with music, painting, sculpture, etc.

Yet it has to be admitted that aesthetic appeal is not wholly intrinsic, but is based somewhat subjectively on what is regarded as beautiful by a culture or society in any given period. We should also note that some works of literature seem to be distinguished from others, equally 'fictional', in subjectively EVALUAT-IVE terms: we can talk of 'serious' and 'popular' literature. The novels of Hardy or James, for instance, are more highly regarded in traditional literary criticism than the novels of Dick Francis or Barbara Cartland. Indeed, for many people, literature is only used as term in this qualitative sense, and hence CANONS of 'major' and 'minor' authors are established, on the basis of ajudged moral vision or universal appeal, etc. However, evaluation is 'objective' to the extent that it is usually based on the appraisal of features of form, on structuring and the DE-FAMILIARIZING use of language, as well as on the complexity, depth and range of subject matter, CHARACTERIZATION and THEME.

Early stylistics of the 1960s followed those literary critics who stressed the autonomy of literature and concentrated attention on texts whose language was stylistically MARKED in some way. Now, under the influence of such disciplines as various as DISCOURSE ANALYSIS, MARXIST CRITICISM and POST-MODERNISM, critical perspectives have shifted to the study of literature and its language in relation to other discourses such as the MASS MEDIA, in terms of a continuum rather than a polarity. Neither approach cancels out the other: **literary language** can be different and yet not different from 'ordinary' or non-literary language; there is, as it were, a 'prototype' of literary language, and also numerous variants. But it is the impossibility of defining it in any simple way that is its most defining feature.

(See also POETIC LANGUAGE; STANDARD DIALECT. See further Carter 1999; Carter & Nash 1990; Eagleton 1983, ch. 1; Widdowson 1992.)

literary pragmatics

A term that came into prominence in the 1980s (see especially Sell 1985, 1991). It follows developments in the field of linguistic PRAGMATICS (q.v.), in SPEECH ACT THEORY, TEXT LINGUISTICS and also in STYLISTICS itself, concerned with literature as DISCOURSE in its interactional and social context, and with READER reception.

Hence **literary pragmatics** looks at the linguistic features of texts which arise from the real INTERPERSONAL relationships between AUTHOR, TEXT and reader in real historical and sociocultural CONTEXTS. Consideration is made of features such as DEIXIS, MODALITY, mutual knowledge, PRESUPPOSITION, POLITENESS and TELLABILITY, etc.

(See further van Dijk 1976; Traugott & Pratt 1980; van Peer & Renkema 1984.)

literary semantics

Particularly associated with the work of Eaton (1966f), who established a journal on the subject in 1971.

Broadly defined, **literary semantics** is a branch of LITERARY THEORY (q.v.) concerned with the philosophy of LITERATURE, its value and status as knowledge, and drawing eclectically on a number of other disciplines such as psychology, sociology and logic, as well as linguistics.

In a narrower sense, it is concerned, as the term SEMANTICS suggests, with the 'meaning' of literary TEXTS, on all levels of sound, syntax and lexis, as well as in terms of their historical context. It is also concerned with meaning as developed in the mind of the READER while reading (see also SEMICS); and the relations of text WORLDS to the 'real' world.

literary theory

Now in common use, like the related POETICS (q.v.), amongst critics of LITERATURE to describe an approach to literature which is predominantly abstract and speculative.

In principle, **literary theory** is distinguishable from LITERARY CRITICISM (q.v.) in that the object of focus is not the description and EVALUATION of individual literary TEXTS, but the nature of literature and criticism itself. (See also META-**criticism**.) In practice, however, many literary critics today, and many STYLISTICIANS also, frequently discuss works and authors from a theoretical perspective, indeed often more than one.

There is no single literary theory, but several. The twentieth century saw the development of many theories arising from the discussion begun in classical poetics of the nature of literature, its AESTHETIC status and its features of FORM, for instance (see FORMALISM). But literary theory has also become increasingly involved with wider IDEOLOGICAL issues reflecting the complexity of literary activity when seen from broader intellectual perspectives. So **critical theories** have been drawn from disciplines such as European philosophy (DECONSTRUCTION), Freudian psychoanalysis, FEMINISM, MARXISM, and linguistics (STRUCTURALISM).

(See further Baldick 1996; Culler 1983, Preface; Eagleton 1983.)

litotes

From Gk 'small' or 'meagre', a RHETORICAL FIGURE or TROPE common in ordinary speech which depends on understatement for its effect. It is thus the opposite of HYPERBOLE (q.v.) or overstatement.

Litotes often takes the form of a negative phrase or statement used to express the opposite: whether praising, e.g. *She's no fool*, or damning, e.g. *She's no oil painting*. In PRAGMATIC terms it strictly violates Grice's **maxims of** QUALITY and QUANTITY, distorting the truth by saying too little. However, in social terms litotes is often a useful indirect strategy for reasons of modesty or POLITENESS, if we wish to understate the bad, for example, as in testimonials or reviews (*The applicant's academic record is not overimpressive . . .*), or downplay our own achievements (*It was nothing*). (See further Leech 1983.)

In appropriate contexts, where speaker and listener are aware of the discrepancy between LITERAL phrasing and actuality, litotes is often used in IRONY. It is a characteristic device of Old English poetry: the narrator of the *Battle of Brunnanburh*, for instance, tells us that the Vikings *had no cause to exult* at the result of the battle; they had every reason to weep, in fact, since they were defeated.

locutionary act; locution

Locutionary act is primarily associated with SPEECH ACT THEORY (q.v.) as developed particularly by Austin (1962), which is concerned with linguistic ACTS made while speaking. Technically, a speech act is threefold: the **locutionary act** is the physical act of uttering the words; the ILLOCUTIONARY ACT (q.v.) is what is performed through speaking (e.g. making a wish); and the PERLOCUTIONARY ACT (q.v.) is the effect achieved by the utterance on the ADDRESSEE (e.g. persuading).

Every UTTERANCE is a locutionary act if it conforms to the PHONETIC and SYNTACTIC rules of the language and has a PROPOSITIONAL MEANING. Different **locutions** can express similar illocutions: e.g. requests such as *Could you close the door, please* or *Would you mind closing the door*, etc. Conversely, a locution may have more than one ILLOCUTIONARY FORCE: e.g. *I'll give you a ring sometime* may be a promise or a (polite) brush-off.

In later speech act theory (e.g. Searle 1969) the **locutionary act** was replaced by the **utterance act** and **propositional act**, referring to the physical production of utterances, and their meaning.

logocentrism; phonocentrism

Terms derived from the DECONSTRUCTIONIST metaphysics of Derrida (e.g. 1967b), which are often used interchangeably.

Taking *logos* (Gk 'word') in its broadest sense, Derrida challenges what he sees as the closed and authoritative traditions of Western philosophy and linguistics which have exerted such a powerful influence on the way we think, and the way we view language. In this last respect, more specifically, Derrida challenges the Saussurean idea that the spoken word has primacy or authority and is the origin of 'truth' (i.e. **phonocentrism**), and that writing is secondary (i.e. ABSENT).

(See further Culler 1983; Norris 1982.)

loose: ~ sentence; ~ style

(1) In LITERARY CRITICISM a **loose sentence** is traditionally a COMPLEX SENTENCE in which the MAIN CLAUSE comes first, followed by several (usually)

SUBORDINATE clauses: what some linguists have termed a **right**-BRANCHING structure, e.g. the long rambling opening sentence of Dickens's *Barnaby Rudge*.

Supposedly easier for our minds to process, such structures are commoner and generally more informal than **left-branching** structures, i.e. sentences in which complex dependency precedes the main clause, sometimes known as PERIODIC SENTENCES (q.v.). Most writing, literary or non-literary, normally presents a mixture of loose and periodic sentences.

(2) Although loose sentences are found in the writing of all periods, the term **loose style** has been applied by critics like Croll (1929) and Williamson (1951) to the so-called 'baroque' prose of the seventeenth century. Also a feature of this designated STYLE, in direct contrast to loose, was the use of CURT sentences, marked by short clauses and ASYNDETON (i.e. lack of explicit CONNECTIVES).

low style

See PLAIN STYLE.

ludism

See PARONOMASIA.

M

---

main clause; matrix

(1) In SENTENCE analysis a **main clause** or **free clause** is one which can stand alone (*I love pizzas*); or be CO-ORDINATED with another. (*I love pizzas, / but my son prefers hamburgers*). It is opposed to a **dependent** or BOUND or SUBORDINATE clause (e.g. NOUN clause, ADVERBIAL clause). So in the opening sentence of Bunyan's *Pilgrim's Progress*, the first clause is a dependent, the second a main: *As I walked through the wilderness of this world, / I lighted on a certain place* . . .

(2) In GENERATIVE GRAMMAR main clauses have been designated **matrixes** or **matrix sentences**. They are **superordinate** to the subordinate clauses, which are EMBEDDED within the sentence as a whole.

Rather confusingly, the term **matrix** was adopted by Quirk *et al.* (1985: 14.4) to refer to a main/superordinate clause minus its subordinate clause: *I'll wash the dishes (matrix) / (if you'll dry them)*. Structurally, therefore, their main/superordinate clause consists of both a matrix and subordinate clause (here functioning as an ADVERBIAL), and so is identical with a sentence.

(3) In Riffaterre's (1978) theory of poetry the term **matrix** is equivalent to KERNEL (q.v.), in that he argues that any TEXT is generated from a matrix or minimal sentence by rules of expansion and CONVERSION. The titles of poems (e.g. Yeats's *An Irish Airman Foresees his Death*) or newspaper headlines (*From riches to rags*) often give some clue as to what such a matrix might be. (See also THEME.)

malapropism

Coined in the early nineteenth century after a character in Sheridan's play *The Rivals* (1775) called Mrs Malaprop (cf. Fr. *mal à propos* 'not to the purpose'), who characteristically and comically muddled polysyllabic or Latinate words: *Illiterate him, I say, quite from your memory; She's as headstrong as an allegory on the banks of the Nile*.

Malapropisms are therefore a kind of CATACHRESIS, lexical DEVIATIONS due to ignorance of the true word. They are commonly heard in speech or read in notices (*These sausages contain conservatives*), and often produce unintentional PUNS (*We are all cremated equal*).

Sheridan was not the first dramatist or writer to exploit malapropism for comic effect: there was Fielding and Smollett just before him. And Shakespeare too evidently heard 'abuses' of learned words in Cockney speech, since several of his London characters, like Dogberry in *Much Ado*, are prone to them (e.g. *Comparisons are odorous*, III.v): termed **cacozelon** in sixteenth-century rhetoric.

manner, maxim of

One of four CONVERSATIONAL MAXIMS (see also QUALITY AND QUANTITY; RELATION) distinguished by the philosopher Grice (1975) as playing an important if usually implicit role in our COMMUNICATIVE behaviour.

Ideally we expect clarity in speech, which enables information to be quickly understood. The **maxim of manner** means we should avoid obscurity, AMBIGU-ITY and prolixity, and be orderly. As Grice himself points out, the maxims don't always apply, or are easily violated. Speech is often rambling or ambiguous on INFORMAL occasions, when the need for absolute COHERENCE can be relaxed. And out of POLITENESS we may 'beat about the bush' in our efforts not to offend others. More seriously, legal and tax documents seem often deliberately obscure or prolix to obfuscate the unsuspecting, unsure of their rights.

In literature, STREAM OF CONSCIOUSNESS WRITING regularly violates this maxim for the representation of thought processes, which do not in themselves, of course, follow the structures of speech.

marked/unmarked

Markedness and the opposition between **marked** and **unmarked**, is extremely common in all areas of linguistics including STYLISTICS.

(1) It arose in the work of the PRAGUE SCHOOL in the 1930s, first in PHONOLOGY (e.g. Trubetzkoy 1939), and was particularly developed by Roman Jakobson (see Jakobson & Pomorska 1983, ch. 10). **Markedness** is basically an extension of the structural principle of BINARISM (q.v.) which sees in language a dichotomy between two mutually exclusive contrasting constituents or COMPONENTS. So, for example, many consonants in English are in opposition to each other through the contrasting feature of VOICE (q.v.) and **voicelessness** (voice absent): e.g. /b/ versus /p/; /d/ versus /t/. However, the two terms in an opposition may not simply be equally neutral: one may have a positive or unusual value or force (**marked**); the other be negative, normal or neutral (**unmarked**). The symbols + and − are often used as notation for these assymetric values respectively. In MORPHOLOGY, for example, marked forms are those which indicate a meaning by AFFIXES added to the 'base' of a word (itself neutral or unmarked) to indicate number or gender: e.g. *elephant-s* (plural); *lion-ess* (feminine). Many languages, not only English, mark the feminine gender explicitly, the unmarked forms also being used with GENERIC as well as male reference (cf. *man*; *dog*). FEMINIST LINGUISTICS has been concerned lest the markedness of the female sex in language

(and the inclusiveness and unmarkedness of the male sex) is taken evaluatively, with CONNOTATIONS of 'abnormality' or inferiority (cf. *governor–governess*).

(2) In linguistics and stylistics **markedness** has been used to refer to any features or patterns which are prominent, unusual or statistically DEVIANT in some way. So there is **marked** FOCUS, for example, **marked** WORD ORDER, or **marked** INTONATION. In LITERARY LANGUAGE, ALLITERATION, with its repetition of initial sounds, is a marked phonetic device. The opening paragraphs of Dickens's *Bleak House* are marked syntactically by the unusual absence of main verbs. e.g.: *London. Michaelmas Term lately over, and the Lord Chancellor sitting in Lincoln's Inn Hall . . .*

Marxist criticism

The **Marxist** approach to LITERARY CRITICISM is originally indebted to the revolutionary theory of economic structures and political superstructures as formulated by Marx and Engels in the mid-nineteenth century. Yet it owes its major perspective to the subsequent development of Marxism by latter generations of writers and thinkers (e.g. Lukács 1925). In England the work of Williams has been particularly influential (e.g. 1958, 1977), also Eagleton (1976a, 1976b); in America, Jameson (1971); in France, Macherey (1966) and Althusser (e.g. 1971).

Marxist criticism is anti-FORMALIST: the distinction between FORM and CONTENT effectively neutralized in its concerns to unearth the historical and IDEOLOGICAL assumptions of literary texts, which might reflect, for instance, the mode of thinking of dominant social classes and political systems. It generally analyses literature, its production, reception and AESTHETIC values, in the larger social context (sometimes known as the **sociology of literature**).

Particularly interesting is Eagleton's work on 'literary modes of production' (LMPs). In different periods, and for different kinds of writing, there will be specific social and material forms influencing, and influenced by, the production of literary texts. In the medieval period, and down to the eighteenth century, for instance, much literature was supported by patronage of the cultured; and 'pulp' fiction today (romances and thrillers) is produced for MASS consumption through deals and advances between writer and publishing-house. (For a summary of Marxist criticism, see Bennett 1979; for poetry and Marxism, see Easthope 1983.)

Outside Eastern Europe, Marxist thought has made little impact on linguistics. In the Soviet Union itself the first systematic rapprochement was made by Voloshinov (1929) who showed the need to examine language in its broad political and social CONTEXTS, often conflicting. Echoing a specific Marxist framework, the more recent work in CRITICAL DISCOURSE ANALYSIS examines the relations between language, power and ideology.

(See also CULTURAL MATERIALISM.)

masculine rhyme

One of a pair of terms (see also FEMININE RHYME) used in traditional PROSODY since the end of the sixteenth century, and borrowed from French, where they properly belong. A **masculine rhyme** is typically a monosyllabic CONTENT WORD and therefore a stressed or 'strong' rhyme:

> Stands the Church clock at ten to *three*?
> And is there honey still for *tea*?
>
> (Bridges: *The Old Vicarage, Grantchester*)

The term is also applied to polysyllabic words, where the last syllable is stressed: so *desire*, rhyming with *fire*.

mass media

The **mass** MEDIA are not strictly media for the 'masses', i.e. the public at large, although the size of the audience/readership is a distinctive characteristic and so confusion is understandable. Mass media or **mass communication** (often referred to popularly as the MEDIA (q.v.)) essentially provide information for public consumption, through the complex technological and 'mass-produced' media of print, broadcasting, film, etc. The main examples are newspapers, television, radio and cinema. Also included can be popular forms of culture such as 'pulp' fiction and pop music; and advertising.

LITERARY CRITICS have become increasingly interested in **mass culture**, for long ignored in the first half of the twentieth century as a subject worthy of critical attention under the influence of Leavis, although studied in MARXIST CRITICISM. And linguists, too, following the lead of sociology and media studies (see, e.g., McLuhan in the 1960s), have become increasingly concerned with ways in which the institutionalized media in particular, reflecting the IDEOLOGIES of partisan politics or consumerism, influence the language in which these are encoded and also the WORLD-VIEWS of their audiences (see, e.g., CRITICAL DISCOURSE ANALYSIS and CRITICAL LINGUISTICS). What is debatable, in fact, is the assumption of a 'neutral' or 'objective' public voice of discourse.

(See further Bell & Garrett (eds) 1998.)

matrix

See MAIN CLAUSE.

measure

A traditional term used by some twentieth-century metrists (e.g. Leech 1969) to refer to the basic RHYTHMICAL unit or METRICAL group in a line of verse, comparable to the **bar** in musical scansion as a unit of temporal regularity. It contains one STRESSED syllable and a number of unstressed syllables, normally between one and three.

In the scansion or analysis of verse the **measure** begins with the stressed syllable, e.g.:

```
  ×     /     ×     /    ×     /   ×      /
The  |  guests are  |  met, the  |  feast is  |  set . . .
```

(Coleridge: *The Ancient Mariner*)

The measure is similar to the FOOT (q.v.) taken from classical PROSODY, although this may begin, at least according to some definitions, with an unstressed syllable. Coleridge's four-BEAT line above, therefore, would be analysed as ×/ ×/ ×/ ×/, an IAMBIC pattern. However, Leech feels that there are problems sometimes with classical scansion, since the distinction between an iamb and a TROCHEE (/×) can be lost in some lines; whereas the scansion by measures is simpler, and especially suitable for the rhythms of the native poetic tradition.

medias res

See IN MEDIAS RES.

medium; media, etc.

Used in the study of COMMUNICATION systems, including language, to refer to the physical or technical means by which MESSAGES are transmitted.

(1) **Medium** is often used synonymously with CHANNEL, although the two can be distinguished. Language is primarily transmitted via the medium of speech (or **phonic medium**) along the channel or 'route' of sound-waves in the air; and secondarily via the medium of writing (**graphic medium**) along the channel of the written or printed page. Language is much affected by medium: STRESS and INTONATION are conveyed in speech, but not in writing; writing, which can be perused and re-perused across distances of space and time, tends to be more FORMAL and more complex in structure and meaning than speech. Certain REGISTERS are associated particularly with one or other of these **media** (e.g. parade-ground commands v. income-tax forms); others with both (e.g. lectures).

The human body itself acts as a medium of communication, through the use of gestures, facial expressions and movement, etc.: what has been termed a **presentational medium** (see Fiske 1982). (See also KINESICS; NON-VERBAL COMMUNICATION.)

For art forms, or **representational media**, medium is a term loosely used for 'material': so the painter works through the medium of paint, the sculptor stone, the novelist language.

(2) The advent of modern technology has meant the development of complex **media** which use more than one channel: e.g. television and film, in their use of

vision and sound. The study of such MASS MEDIA (q.v.), popularly known simply as **the media**, was stimulated in the 1960s with the work of McLuhan – 'The medium is the MESSAGE' (q.v.) – who was concerned with the effects of technological media on their audiences.

(3) Norman Fairclough (1995) has coined the punning term **mediatized discourse** with particular reference to the domain of British politics, arguing that the media, manipulated by 'spin-doctors', play a central role in mediating between politicians and the public.

mental space(s) theory

A fairly recent branch of COGNITIVE LINGUISTICS particularly associated with Gilles Fauconnier and also Mark Turner (e.g. 1985, 1995f). A **mental space** is a set of local conceptual configurations which we build up in our minds as we talk or listen, prompted by particular language forms (**space builders**). Utterances are often structurally complex, and thus combine more than one mental space. So it is argued that an utterance like *The doctor told me she would come tomorrow* combines three mental 'time' spaces: current (between speaker and listener); past (the time of the doctor's telling) and future (the prediction of the action of coming). Two 'location' spaces are indicated also: the 'reality' space between speaker and listener, and the place where the doctor currently is.

Mental space theory has tended so far mostly to be concerned with single decontextualized sentences, albeit complex. (But see Freeman 1997 on the idiosyncratic reflexives in Emily Dickinson's poetry.)

(See further Werth 1999, chs 1, 3.)

meronymy

In SEMANTICS, a term to describe a 'part-whole' relation of meaning; as distinct from HYPONYMY, which is a 'member-class' relation. The **holonym** is the whole, and the **meronyms** its component parts.

Dictionaries for foreign learners of English often rely on **meronymy** as a substitute for definition: providing pictures of cars or the human body, and labelling their distinctive parts. Elizabethan poets commonly 'catalogued' or 'enumerated' their lovers' bodies in this way; and it was one of the devices of rhetorical structuring of an argument (INVENTIO).

(See also SYNECDOCHE. See further Cruse 1986.)

message

Taken into linguistics from COMMUNICATION THEORY (see Shannon & Weaver 1949) as part of the model of (human) communication. A **message** or piece of

INFORMATION is ENCODED by a speaker/writer as ADDRESSER into a linguistic form or CODE and transmitted via the MEDIUM of speech or writing along a CHANNEL to an ADDRESSEE who DECODES it.

Human language, however, is much more complex than technical signals, so that it is possible for a message to be AMBIGUOUS in its form and so have more than one possible interpretation. Conversely, the message may be 'encoded' in more than one way with no radical difference in meaning, although there may well be differences in CONNOTATION. Moreover, in face-to-face interchanges, as in theatrical, the total impact of a message comes not only from what is spoken, but from facial expression, gesture, TONE of voice, CONTEXT, etc. In LITERATURE, the message as realized in the TEXT comes only from the words on the printed page, and it is only through these that its WORLD is created. For Jakobson, this SELF-REFERENCE, the 'set towards the message for its own sake', is the essence of LITERARINESS. And the study of literature as message has been very much the province of traditional LITERARY CRITICISM.

Many linguists and critics, however, have challenged the basic notion of a communication model that sees message as a CONTENT that pre-exists independently of the language in which it is encoded; and which is passed inviolate or neutral to the waiting addressee. They have also wished to emphasize the creative aspect of decoding or INTERPRETATION, especially for written messages, with meanings produced from the very interaction of text and reader. McLuhan's work in the 1960s focussed attention on the interplay of medium and message, and on the way what is said is conditioned by aural or visual transmission in broadcasting, film, etc.

meta-

A prefix from Gk meaning variously 'beyond', 'after', 'along with', etc., **meta-** has come to be a common formative element in linguistics and LITERARY THEORY since the 1960s, in the sense particularly of 'beyond' or 'above'.

Undoubtedly influenced by the well-established term METALANGUAGE (q.v.) **meta**-words reflect an increased awareness of, and theoretical engagement with, levels of language and discourse. Of the many listed here, only a selection will be singled out for comment. So we find: **metacommunication; metacriticism; metadrama; metafiction; metafunction; metagrammar; metaimplicature; meta-irony; metapoetics; metapoetry; metasemiotic; metastatement; metastructure; metatalk; metatext; metatheatre; metatopia**, etc.

Closely related to **metalanguage** are terms in DISCOURSE ANALYSIS like **metacommunication, metatalk** and **metastatement**, which all describe communication about communication, second-order discourse. In speech or informal writing, wherever we are concerned that our MESSAGE be understood, INTERPERSONAL utterances such as *What I meant was . . . , Do you see that?*, sensitively monitor the situation. *That's all for now, folks!* is a **metatextual** comment at the end of a 'Loony Tunes' cartoon.

Metacriticism defines a strain of LITERARY THEORY which, influenced by POST-STRUCTURALISM, looks at criticism itself as a kind of literary activity, and discusses critically the principles and procedures of the discipline (see, e.g., the work of Derrida and de Man in the 1970s; and Leitch 1983 for a summary). Generally, any text which comments on another text is a **metatext**; the term also used for a text which self-consciously takes as its subject its own artform or GENRE (e.g. **metafiction**).

Such SELF-REFLEXIVITY is common in drama. **Metadramatic** devices draw attention to the very theatricality and artificiality of the world of the play: ASIDES, prologues and EPILOGUES, plays within plays. And as Calderwood (1969) points out, the very IMAGERY of a play can have a metadramatic function: e.g. Shakespeare's recurring images of acting, 'shadows' and stage, etc. **Metatheatre** has sometimes been used synonymously (e.g. Elam 1980); but as used originally by Abel (1963), it refers to the anti-naturalistic tradition which makes life a dream and the world of the play reality: as in Brecht and Beckett.

metadiegesis; metadiegetic

One of a set of **-diegetic** terms (see also DIEGESIS; EXTRADIEGESIS) in Genette's (1972) work on NARRATIVE and narrative levels. **Metadiegesis** is the story within a story, a narrative of the second degree, e.g. the Tales told by the pilgrims EMBEDDED within the framework of Chaucer's *Canterbury Tales*.

Not all critics have liked Genette's choice of term here, since **meta-** seems to mean 'below' rather than the accepted 'beyond' or 'above': so Rimmon-Kenan (1983) prefers **hypodiegesis**. It is possible to have complex narratives of further degrees: in Emily Bronte's *Wuthering Heights*, for instance. Lockwood notes in his journal a story told to him by Nelly Dean which is in fact a story told to Nelly herself by Isabella. Much research still needs to be done on the particular functions and effects of **metadiegetic** stories.

Note here can also be made of Genette's term **metalepsis** which refers to the explicit transgressions of diegetic levels by the intrusions of NARRATORS or CHARACTERS into their diegetic or metadiegetic worlds. The effect is to give a greater illusion of reality to the fictional world. So 'Sterne' is always in *Tristram Shandy* exhorting the reader to help his characters in some way.

metalanguage; metalingual function

The use of **metalanguage** in linguistics is particularly associated with the work of Hjelmslev (1943). It is a SIGN-system developed to talk about another sign-system as CONTENT, or a higher-level language to talk about another language (the **object-language**). Mathematicians and scientists have developed special systems of SYMBOLS to talk about concepts more easily; other subjects, including linguistics, have developed metalanguages or JARGONS, creating words out of existing elements in the language or extending senses of ordinary words, so that explanatory dictionaries like this one are needed.

Even in ordinary speech we use language **metalinguistically**, to FRAME utterances by drawing attention to them for some reason: to check on a particular pronunciation, to query a DIALECT word, to note an AMBIGUITY, etc. Specific metalinguistic features of language include ADVERBIALS like *frankly* or *bluntly*, and the TAGS of DIRECT and INDIRECT DISCOURSE in the representation of speech (e.g. '*Go away*', *she ordered*). It is the **metalingual** FUNCTION of language (see Jakobson 1960) which helps to distinguish human communication from animal.

metaphor

In RHETORIC, a very common FIGURE or TROPE, derived from Gk 'carry over'. When words are used with **metaphoric** senses, one FIELD or DOMAIN of reference is carried over or mapped onto another on the basis of some perceived similarity between the two fields: so when Hamlet says the world

> is an unweeded garden,
> That grows to seed . . . (I.ii)

the features of gardens are applied to the world.

Aristotle in his *Poetics* saw **metaphor** as a trope based on similitude, and many other critics since have noted an apparent implied relationship with SIMILE (q.v.). So in Johnson's *Dictionary* metaphor is defined as 'a simile compressed in a word'. In the example above, Hamlet could have compared the world to an unweeded garden quite explicitly using the CONNECTIVE *like*. But PROPOSITIONS of the form *X is Y* appear more forceful and dramatic than those with the form *X is like Y*. For one moment we may actually believe X is Y, interpret a metaphor in its PRAGMATIC context LITERALLY, not FIGURATIVELY. As Davidson (1978) has argued, 'all similes are (trivially) true; but most metaphors are (patently) false'; they thus appear to flout the Gricean **maxim of** QUALITY.

What is of interest in SEMANTICS and LITERARY CRITICISM is the motivation behind the analogies made, and the particular semantic features which bind X and Y together: or in the terms of Richards (1936), the TENOR (q.v.) (topic) and VEHICLE (q.v.) (analogue). When Romeo, looking at the sky, says, *Night's candles are burnt out* (*Romeo and Juliet*, III.v) we make sense of the riddle – identify the candles as stars – because they are both sources of light. Here, the shape and material of candles are irrelevant, and so these details we mentally suppress. Tenor and vehicle must have some similarity in order for the analogy to seem appropriate, yet enough difference, in dramatic or descriptive metaphors, for the analogy to seem striking and fresh. Indeed, in some cases it may not always be easy to identify precisely, or at first reading, the **ground** or motivation for the analogy, and the INDETERMINACY or AMBIGUITY that results in Empson's (1930) terms makes metaphor a powerful source of multiple meaning. (And in such cases a PARAPHRASE by a simile is not always obvious. See further Leech 1969; Nowottny 1962.)

Metaphor, in its expression of the familiar by the unfamilar, and in its reconceptualization of experience is a good example of the process of DE-FAMILIARIZATION and is particularly significant, therefore, in POETIC LANGUAGE. For the same reasons it is also exploited, visually and linguistically, in the REGISTER of advertising (cornflakes associated with sunshine, etc.).

As *Night's candles* further illustrates, not all metaphors take the syntactic and propositional form of *X is Y*; and as this equation itself illustrates, a full appreciation of metaphor depends not only on the senses of individual words but also on the interpretation of the lexical items and syntax in the CONTEXT. Not all metaphors are NOUNS, moreover; with metaphorical VERBS the figure of PERSONIFICATION is particularly associated. So Romeo's utterance continues:

Night's candles are burnt out, and jocund day
Stands tiptoe on the misty mountain tops

In terms of GENERATIVE GRAMMAR, echoing seventeenth-century thinking, the metaphor in the second line would be a DEVIATION, since the SELECTION RESTRICTIONS of SUBJECT and verb are here violated: *stands tiptoe on* would normally co-occur with nouns marked with ANIMATE/human reference (as also *jocund* normally). The substitution of the familiar verb phrase (*appears over?*) by the apparently anomalous affects not only the verb here but contiguously the subject: it is *day* which is personified, and acquires by 'contagion' the CONNOTA-TIONS also perhaps of youthful impishness.

Metaphors can work in even more extended ways, across whole passages or stanzas, to provide a FRAME OF REFERENCE, or means of thematic COHERENCE. In Arnold's *Dover Beach* the metaphor of the 'sea' of Faith informs the IMAGERY of most of the sonnet, and appears to give rise to related metaphors (the world as a beach). (See also Nowottny 1962 for **extended metaphor**, Werth 1999 for **sustained metaphor**.)

Metaphor is not peculiar to literary or semi-literary language like advertising. We use or hear hundreds of metaphors in everyday speech, in SLANG, in public speaking, in news reporting, etc. As COGNITIVE LINGUISTS like Lakoff *et al.* (1980f) and POST-STRUCTURALISTS like de Man (1979) have also stressed, they are part of the fabric of language, even of thought. But they are so commonly used that, unlike the striking metaphors of poetry, we have in many cases ceased to be aware that figurative meaning is involved (*the pound recovers; the war against inflation; black hole*). Metaphors also help to fill lexical GAPS in the language: e.g. (computer) *mouse*.

So-called **dead metaphors** are words whose literal meaning is no longer current, and whose sense has therefore been transferred to the figurative: e.g. words of Latin origin like *comprehend, dilapidated, precocious*.

(See also COGNITIVE METAPHOR THEORY; METONYMY; SYMBOL. See further Black 1954; Brooke-Rose 1958; Gibbs 1994; Goatly 1997; Hawkes 1972; Levin 1977; Ricoeur 1975; Steen 1994.)

metonymy

From Gk 'name change', a RHETORICAL FIGURE or TROPE by which the name of a REFERENT is replaced by the name of an attribute, or of an entity related in some semantic way (e.g. cause and effect; instrument; source). So in the advertising slogan *Singapore girls – you're a great way to fly*, the apparent eye-catching anomaly is explained by the substitution of *girls* for *airline* (for whom the girls work). In SEMIOTIC terms, **metonymy** is an INDEXICAL SIGN: there is a directly or logically contiguous relationship between the substituted word and its referent.

Metonymy is very common in everyday language: phrases like *the press* ('newspapers'), *the stage* ('theatre'), *the Crown* ('monarchy') and *The White House* ('US Presidency'), are used almost without our realizing that an object associated with an occupation has come to stand for the office itself. Many common nouns derived from proper names show metonymy in their semantic shift from proper name to object associated with the name (e.g. *cardigan, burgundy, jacuzzi*).

Metonymy is easily confused with SYNECDOCHE (q.v.), and understandably the latter is often regarded as a special type of metonymy. In synecdoche the name of the referent is replaced strictly by the name of an actual part of it: e.g. *strings* ('stringed instruments'); *set of wheels* ('car'); *keel* ('ship'), etc.

In both metonymy and synecdoche the meanings associated are in the same conceptual domain or on the same semantic plane; there is no transfer of FIELD of reference as with metaphor, and no flouting, moreover, of the **maxim of** QUAL-ITY: 'truth' is maintained. And yet like metaphor, it works by substitution: of an expected word by the unexpected. Since the work of Jakobson (1956) on language disorders, and on the structural dichotomy between metaphor and metonymy and their formal similarities and differences, the two figures have often been discussed as a BINARY pair, and come to stand as SYMBOLS of further dichotomies in culture and literature. It is argued, for example, that film and drama work most naturally through metonymy (synecdoche): a tree can stand for a stage forest; a row of houses for a town; scene links scene by contiguity. POETIC LANGUAGE, in contrast, exploits associations by similarity, by metaphor, at least in general. Here, too, a distinction has been made in LITERARY CRITICISM between different modes of writing: if 'realistic' prose is seen as primarily metonymic, some kinds of modern poetry work through metonymy rather than metaphor. The IMAGERY in Larkin's poetry, for example, is characteristically realized by detailed enumerations: the countryside in *Here* made up of *skies and scarecrows, haystacks, hares and pheasants* . . .

In DECONSTRUCTION THEORY, as well as COGNITIVE LINGUISTICS, on the other hand, the opposition between metonymy and metaphor is erased. Many common metaphors have a metonymic basis: when prices go *up*, things cost more money; just as the more things in a pile (cause) the higher it gets (effect).

(See further Gibbs 1994, ch. 7; Latré 1985; Lodge 1977 on MODERNISM; Connor 1985 on metaphor and metonymy in Dickens's *Dombey and Son*.)

metre; metrics; metrical pattern, etc.

Metre is the name given to the regular patterning in verse of STRESSED and unstressed syllables, the FOREGROUNDING of the more variable RHYTHM of everyday speech.

Traditionally in the study of metre (**metrics** or PROSODY), interest has centred on recurring units of rhythm within the line, measured in FEET (from classical prosody), or MEASURES (q.v.). So the IAMBIC PENTAMETER metre has a recurring pattern of five groups of x (unstressed) / (stressed) or five BEATS. Generally, English metre is and always has been ACCENTUAL or stress-timed; the actual number of syllables per line of less importance (unlike the syllabic metre of French poetry).

Metre also encompasses the use of RHYME and non-rhyme as structural devices (as in the five-beat heroic couplet and BLANK VERSE); and the patterns of lines in **stanza** forms as units. For instance, alternating four- and three-beat lines in groups of four are common in nursery rhymes and ballads (the so-called BALLAD METRE).

Metrists are interested not only in the NORMS of verse structure, but also in the DEVIATIONS that arise by displaced stresses or INVERSIONS, unusual rhymes, etc. A **metrical pattern** is sometimes thought of as a GESTALT or an abstract pattern or underlying structure, which can be varied for particular effects. Chatman's (1964) terms are **verse design** opposed to the **verse instance**. Viewed from the reader's experience, patterns of metrical repetition establish expectations of recurrence, what is termed the **metrical set**: metre, as Fowler (1971) says, is located as much in the eye and mind of the reader as in the lines and language of a poem.

There is also variation in **metrical styles** between poets, in their handling of the same rhythmical patterns (e.g. Wyatt and Shakespeare's treatment of the sonnet form).

(See also GENERATIVE METRICS. See further Attridge 1995.)

middle style

One of a set of three STYLISTIC distinctions (the others being GRAND or **high**; PLAIN or **low**) formalized in classical RHETORIC and which were influential on literary composition through to the eighteenth century.

The principle of DECORUM (q.v.) was the determining influence: STYLE should be fitted to subject matter, GENRE, CHARACTERIZATION, SITUATION, etc. The **middle style** represented the 'mean' between the ornate and elevated style as used for epic, and the very plain style used for comic narrative. It was the style generally adopted for the discourse of education and edification, for argument and analysis: making use of some rhetorical FIGURES in the interests of persuasion and emphasis, but the TONE generally fairly neutral. The English homiletic or sermon tradition, from writers like Ælfric in the Anglo-Saxon period, through to Wyclif and beyond to Sir Thomas More, can be seen as an illustration of the middle style.

mimesis

(1) From Gk IMITATION (q.v.) **mimesis** has been a much discussed concept in LITERARY CRITICISM since first discussed by Plato and Aristotle in their reflections on the nature of LITERATURE and of NARRATIVE. (See further Auerbach 1957.)

Plato's use of the term in Book III of *The Republic* has to do specifically with modes of speech representation. He makes a distinction between 'pure' narrative (*haple* DIEGESIS) and mimesis: the first the discourse of the poet as NARRATOR, the second the directly imitated or ENACTED speech of the characters themselves. This distinction corresponds to Henry James's between 'telling' and 'showing'. Dramatic dialogue is most clearly mimetic, whereas the novel is primarily diegetic.

Aristotle in his *Poetics* takes a broader view of mimesis, which came to dominate literary criticism until the twentieth century: namely, that art and literature were essentially mimetic in their aim to give the illusion of a representation of the real world. Either diegesis is not art, because it is not imitation, or else it is a special kind of mimesis. Modern critics have tended to agree that there are degrees of directness in the representation, at least, of speech (see Chatman 1978; McHale 1978); but would also argue, in opposition to Aristotle, that mimesis is a kind of diegesis, that there are degrees of telling: a narrator always being 'implied', who may explicitly provide the TAGGING (*she said*, etc.) But this is to take mimesis in Plato's narrower sense; Aristotle's is broader.

That literature can give a reflection of life is only an illusion, since words must replace the actions and scenes more successfully mimed by drama and painting; but it is an illusion, a 'lie' (Plato) which we have prized and evaluated. (See also VERISIMILITUDE.) 'Realism' is the quality of many English and European nineteenth-century novels, such as Balzac's *Le Pere Goriot* or Tolstoy's *War and Peace*; which appear to give us life as it is, in its social and dramatic detail. Here again, any sense of completeness is an illusion: there must be GAPS. Novelists rely on their readers' powers of INFERENCE for a considerable amount of information and WORLD-building.

Mimesis so far can be seen as mimesis of CONTENT. It is obvious that the linguistic techniques exploited by writers in their efforts to represent the 'truth' of life may be varied and DEVIANT. ALIENATING and FOREGROUNDING devices such as IMAGERY and COMPOUNDING can highlight perceptions about the nature of things (as in Hopkins's poetry). At the same time, language can draw attention to itself, and to literature as an art form, as in metafictional novels, or the poems of e.e. cummings.

(2) Language can also draw attention to what it describes through **mimesis** of FORM: by an isomorphic process of ENACTMENT (q.v.) or ICONICITY (q.v.). Sounds and movement are best enacted in this way by ALLITERATION or ASSONANCE and flexible SYNTAX. (On different kinds of mimetic syntax, see further Davie 1955; Epstein 1975.)

Mimetic or MOTIVATED forms are a feature of the ordinary LEXIS of the language, in ONOMATOPOEIA (*sizzle; bang; cuckoo*, etc.). (See also CRATYLISM; SOUND SYMBOLISM.)

mind style

A popular term coined by Roger Fowler (1977) to describe the linguistic presentation in the novel tradition of an 'individual mental self', whether of a CHARACTER, NARRATOR or IMPLIED AUTHOR.

The presentation of the thought-IDIOLECTS of characters is highlighted in INTERIOR MONOLOGUE and in STREAM OF CONSCIOUSNESS WRITING: the work of Joyce and Woolf, for instance. James in *The Ambassadors* focusses the events described almost entirely through the complex feelings and observations of the main character Lambert Strether, using more traditional methods of NARRATIVE REPORT. In **first-person** fiction character and narrator's **mind styles** are merged: as in Salinger's *Catcher in the Rye*, for example, or Nabokov's *Lolita*.

In its broadest sense, **mind style** can be used to describe the individual authorial conceptualization of events, however MARKED or apparently 'neutral'. No language of fiction, whether that of Dickens, Lawrence or Hemingway, is a transparent window onto reality; and mind style reflects the fact that all our conceptualizations of existence are different, and to some extent controlled by the language we use. (See also IDEOLOGY.)

mise en abyme

On the pattern of **mise en scene** (Fr. 'put/sent into the scene', i.e. stage scenery; surroundings) is the phrase **mise en abyme**, literally 'thrust into the abyss'.

(1) In novel theory (see Hutcheon 1985; Rimmon-Kenan 1983) it has been used for textual structures which mirror themselves: e.g. stories within stories reduplicating the narrator's narrative. In Gide's *The Counterfeiters* the author invents the character of a novelist (Edouard) who invents the character of a novelist writing a novel very similar to *The Counterfeiters* itself.

(2) If we hold a mirror to our own reflection, endless reflections of ourselves will appear *ad infinitum*. In American DECONSTRUCTION THEORY of the 1970s the phrase was used with the emphasis on 'abyss' as a vivid way of illustrating the deconstructionist preoccupation with the endless play and instability of signification and with INDETERMINACY (see also DIFFÉRANCE). (See further Lentricchia 1980, I ch. 5 for a critique.)

modality; modal verb

(1) **Modality** as used in logic, SEMANTICS and GRAMMAR is concerned with speakers' ATTITUDES and STANCE towards the PROPOSITIONS they express. It is

essentially a subjective and qualifying process: judging the truth of propositions in terms of degrees of possibility, probability or certainty; and expressing also meanings of obligation, necessity, volition, prediction, knowledge and belief, etc.

Attempts to classify different kinds of modality have been made, and some terms have passed from logic into semantic studies. Necessity and possibility are basic concerns in logic, and **alethic modality**, dealing with the 'truth' of propositions. Also prominent is a distinction between **epistemic modality** (from the Gk meaning 'knowledge'); and **deontic modality** (from the Gk meaning 'what is binding') concerned with 'obligation' and 'permission'. In Halliday's SYSTEMIC GRAMMAR this particular aspect is termed **modulation** rather than modality. Sentences like *You may be right* and *She must have arrived by now* express degrees of (un)certainty and knowledge; *You may go now* and *You must leave at once* express permission and obligation.

(2) As these sentences illustrate, **modality** is very commonly expressed by the so-called **modal verbs**, a major category of AUXILIARY VERBS in English. Other means of expressing modality include ADVERBS (*possibly; perhaps*), CLAUSES (*I'm certain that . . .*) and MOOD (q.v.). The modal verbs commonly used to indicate different kinds of modality are *can, might, must, should* and *may*. In the broadest sense the modal meanings expressed by these verbs include also volition and prediction (*will; shall*), ability and potentiality (*can; be able to*), etc. (See further Coates 1983; Halliday 1985, ch. 4, 10; Palmer 1979.)

(3) **Modality** came to be discussed in STYLISTICS, TEXT LINGUISTICS and LITERARY SEMANTICS as a result of increased interest in DISCOURSE and INTERPERSONAL relations between IMPLIED AUTHOR or NARRATOR and READER, and the broad issue of POINT OF VIEW in fiction. (See also NARRATIVE SEMANTICS.)

It can be argued that fiction operates in the non-alethic modal system, since no fictional utterance is true or factual, except in the fictional WORLD created. What is at issue is what might or could happen if . . . Moreover, utterances in fiction are always told from the point of view of someone, whether the implied author as narrator, or a character, or both: a subjectivity is inevitable. The more qualified or evaluated the statements, the more a sense of the narrator's personality is conveyed, and the greater awareness revealed of an implied ADDRESSEE. MARKED qualification is characteristic of **first-person** narratives: as in this example from the opening of Madox Ford's *The Good Soldier*.

> . . . We had known the Ashburnhams for nine seasons of the town of Nauheim with an extreme intimacy – or, rather with an acquaintanceship as loose and easy and yet as close as a good glove's with your hand. My wife and I knew Captain and Mrs Ashburnham as well as it was possible to know anybody, and yet, in another sense, we knew nothing at all about them . . .

Marked modality is also characteristic of the representation of characters' thought processes in FREE DIRECT and INDIRECT THOUGHT, or INTERIOR MONOLOGUE (q.v.).

Moreover, PLOTS themselves, whether in drama, epic or the novel, are frequently structured on conflicting modalities: on dreams and reality, obligations and desires, beliefs and dogmas. So in *Paradise Lost* Adam falls because of his violation of the divine deontic modality of prohibition: *Yet one tree you must not touch . . .*

(See further Elam 1980; Fowler 1977, 1996; and Simpson 1993, on modality in drama.)

(4) In their work on situational VARIETIES of (non-literary) language Crystal & Davy (1969) used **modality** in quite a different sense to refer to a dimension of linguistic characterization which has to do with format or GENRE, itself linked to the purpose of the variety. So, for example, we can send a written message to someone in the form of a postcard, letter or fax; or publish details of an Anglo-Saxon treasure-hoard in a newspaper article, periodical paper, monograph or coffee-table book. In each case differences of modality will influence the CHOICE of linguistic features.

In the work on REGISTER by Halliday *et al.* (1964) this dimension is probably covered under MODE below, but this is rather vaguely defined.

mode (of discourse)

(1) Particularly associated with the study of REGISTER (q.v.) as developed by Halliday *et al.* (1964): one of the distinguishing SITUATIONAL factors that help to determine the linguistic and TEXTUAL features characteristic of different varieties (see also FIELD and TENOR).

Mode is not easily defined since it covers the MEDIUM of communication (e.g. speech or writing), and the degree of preparedness and FEEDBACK; what Halliday terms the **symbolic mode** or CHANNEL. The **rhetorical mode** is the format or GENRE (e.g. DIALOGUE v. MONOLOGUE; letter v. report).

In 1964 Halliday also appeared to include the purpose or FUNCTION of the communication under mode (e.g. expository, didactic) (see Halliday *et al.* 1964); although later (e.g. 1978) this is also discussed under **field**. It is perhaps better to regard purpose as a separate factor: what Gregory (1967) includes under **functional tenor**.

(2) In NARRATOLOGY, in the work of Stanzel (1984) **mode** is one of three main axes of his TYPOLOGICAL CIRCLE (q.v.), a model for different kinds of NARRATION. A distinction in the axis of mode is made between NARRATORS who tell the story and **reflectors** or FOCALIZERS who do not, yet who present what is thought or felt directly to the reader.

modernism

A general term for a wide spectrum of literary and artistic movements which emerged in Europe and the United States towards the end of the nineteenth century, at a time of political and spiritual unrest, and which challenged traditions of composition and AESTHETIC theory in radical ways until the 1930s. As Lodge (1981) says, instead of following the principle of art as IMITATION ('art imitates life'), **modernism** espoused Wilde's dictum of 'life imitates art'. Language was not a transparent MEDIUM of reality, but an activity in itself, self-consciously FOREGROUNDED by the use of SYMBOLISM, unconventional SYNTAX, AMBIGUITY, word-play, illogicality and ENIGMA. In a way modernism anticipated the linguistic and literary movements of STRUCTURALISM and FORMALISM, whose own research could be illustrated by modernist writings: the poems of Pound, Yeats and Eliot, for example, or the novels of Woolf and Joyce.

(See further Faulkner 1977; Hawthorn 1998.)

modifier

(1) Used in modern GRAMMAR to describe the **dependent** elements in a NOUN PHRASE or NOMINAL GROUP, occurring before or after the NOUN as HEAD. DETERMINERS (e.g. *the, a*) characteristically function as **modifiers** (*the elephant*), and so do ADJECTIVES (*the old grey African elephant*). A distinction is normally made between such PREMODIFICATION, and POSTMODIFICATION: the latter being modifiers that follow the noun (also known as **qualifiers** in Hallidayan or SYSTEMIC GRAMMAR). RELATIVE CLAUSES, NON-FINITE CLAUSES and PREPOSITIONAL PHRASES are used in postmodification, which tends to be more grammatically complex than premodification.

(2) **Modifier** is also used more generally in grammar to describe structurally dependent elements in other groups of phrases: e.g. *very* in the adjectival phrase *very nice*. These are also known as **submodifiers**. In traditional grammar ADVERBS are often defined as either **sentence** or **verb modifiers** (as in *She angrily stormed out of the room*).

monism

Also known as **text** or **aesthetic monism** a theory of meaning espoused by certain literary critics (e.g. the NEW CRITICS) and stylisticians (e.g. in RADICAL STYLISTICS and CRITICAL LINGUISTICS), which argues for the inseparability of FORM (q.v.) and CONTENT (q.v.).

The opposite view, DUALISM (q.v.) argues that form and content can be distinguished, and thus it is possible for the 'same' content or meaning to be expressed in different ways, by PARAPHRASE or SYNONYMY.

To the **monists**, however, every change of form is a change of meaning, and even dualists acknowledge that, at a surface or superficial level, there will be changes in CONNOTATIONAL values of words. Although it often appears that we have a CHOICE of structures and expressions, different nuances of meaning will be conveyed: (*Stop talking; Please be quiet; I can't hear myself think*, etc.). In POETIC LANGUAGE in particular, where the AESTHETIC focus is as much on form as on content, the extent to which paraphrase is really possible except at a deeper level of PROPOSITIONAL equivalence, is debatable. For the monist, all stylistic choices are linguistic choices, and vice versa; STYLE is not simply a 'manner' of expression, but something more meaningful.

(See further Leech & Short 1981, for a summary.)

monologue; monologic; dramatic monologue

(1) A **monologue** is a self-address, a DISCOURSE of one speaker with no expectation of a response from an ADDRESSEE.

Monologues take many forms: from the 'talking aloud' to oneself in private, to the prepared public lecture. Many DIALOGUES can contain stretches of speech by a single speaker which are actually monologues: descriptions, narratives, jokes and confessions, for example. Monologues are more common in the written MEDIUM: very few kinds of written discourse, other than letters, have a direct expectation of a response; even though articles, reviews, instruction leaflets, etc., are written with a readership in mind.

There are several kinds of literary monologues. The so-called **dramatic monologue**, of which poems like Browning's *My Last Duchess* and *Fra Lippo Lippi* are notable examples, presents a kind of pseudo-dialogue: the speaker–character addresses an 'audience' whose presence is implied (by the use of INTERPERSONAL elements), but whose response is not stated:

I am poor brother Lippo, by your leave!
You need not clap your torches to my face.
Zooks, what's to blame? you think you see a monk! . . .

In the theatre, there is a tradition of comic monologues, such as Stanley Holloway's tale of Albert Ramsbottom and the lions, which are delivered to a listening audience. In drama, the SOLILOQUY is the verbalization aloud of a character's thoughts; and in the novel, INTERIOR MONOLOGUE 'represents' directly a character's thoughts. (See also NARRATED MONOLOGUE.)

(2) The term **monologic** 'single-voiced' is particularly associated with the writings of the Russian linguist Mikhail Bakhtin (first published 1920s onwards), in opposition to DIALOGIC 'double-voiced'. Bakhtin argues persuasively for a distinction that depends not so much on the number of participants but on the nature of the discourse itself. Thus monologue can be dialogic, containing an inherent or implicit 'conversation', addressed to Self as Other. Conversely, dramatic dialogue can be seen as monologic in the sense that, unlike natural dialogue, it is single-voiced, unified, controlled by the dominant voice of the author. So too, for Bakhtin (controversially), is poetic discourse. The language of the novel, however, is characteristically dialogic, open to all the socially diverse languages of everyday life around it, and giving freer play to the voices of characters and narrator within it. (See also POLYPHONY.)

mood

(1) In traditional GRAMMAR a category largely signalled by differences in VERB forms which gives rise to different SENTENCE types, and basic semantic contrasts of MODALITY (q.v.). (See also Lyons 1977.)

The basic or UNMARKED **mood** in English is the **indicative** or 'fact mood', which is signalled, in the **third** PERSON PRESENT TENSE form at least, by the -*s* inflection (*She very obviously like-s elephants*). It is contrasted with the SUBJUNCTIVE (q.v.), the mood of non-fact, expressing the uncertain, hypothetical, or desirable, etc., which is signalled in the third person present by no ending at all: *I suggest that she visit a psychiatrist*. In modern English the subjunctive has been replaced in many usages by MODAL VERBS, prime exponents of modality: *I suggest that she should visit a psychiatrist*; and also the plain indicative: *I suggest she visits a psychiatrist*. In some grammars the IMPERATIVE (q.v.) is also described as a mood, expressing 'will' or 'desire'.

In other grammars (e.g. Hallidayan or SYSTEMIC GRAMMAR) the basic contrast involves distinctions in ILLOCUTIONARY FORCE, and is closely related to the INTERPERSONAL component of grammar. Thus the indicative mood is normally used for DECLARATIVE sentence types which have the force of statements; whereas the imperative mood is used for imperative sentences which have the force of commands or requests. Included here also is the INTERROGATIVE sentence type as a mood: used to ask questions.

(2) The term has also been applied metaphorically to aspects of the study of NARRATIVE in work which adopts a NARRATIVE GRAMMAR as model. Todorov (1966) proposed **mood**, TENSE and ASPECT as dimensions of study, although he later changed mood to the term REGISTER (1967f). A fairly broad category, it is generally concerned with the type of DISCOURSE used by a NARRATOR, modes of speech representation, and degrees of explicitness of narrator and 'reader' presence.

Genette (1972, ch. 4), also has a category of mood, which follows Todorov's concern with modes of speech along a DIEGETIC–MIMETIC continuum, but which also more closely identifies with studies of POINT OF VIEW (Todorov's aspect), termed **modality** by other critics. As he argues, the unmarked mood in narrative, as in ordinary discourse, is that of the indicative, to report facts. Yet there are also degrees of affirmation possible; degrees in QUANTITY of information provided (and hence degrees of 'distance' between narrator and reader); and differences in point of view or FOCALIZATION.

morphology; morpheme

(1) In GRAMMAR and LEXICOLOGY **morphology** (from Gk *morphe* 'form') concerns the internal patterning of words, their 'roots' or 'stems' and AFFIXES.

The **morpheme** (coined in 1896 by analogy with PHONEME) is the smallest distinctive unit of grammatical analysis: it may be a word or **free form**, or an affix or BOUND **form**. So *sausage-s* is composed of a free form *sausage* as stem, plus a bound form, the grammatical SUFFIX or inflection *-s* marking the plural. Grammatical inflections, like the marker of plurality or CASE or TENSE, etc., are all suffixes in English. Most suffixes, and all PREFIXES, are **lexical morphemes** in English, characteristically used to build new LEXICAL ITEMS: as in *pre-shrunk; dry-clean-able; anti-static*. Lexical morphemes have more LEXICAL MEANING than grammatical morphemes like *-ing* or *-ed*. (See also AFFIXATION; DERIVATION.)

Some (mostly grammatical) morphemes have different PHONETIC realizations according to their phonetic contexts: called **allomorphs** or **morphemic** (or

morphophonemic) variants. /t/, /d/ and /ɪd/ are all variants of the past tense morpheme {ED}, in words like *missed, slammed* and *hoarded*. Other alternants are found in words like *loaf – loaves; illegal, irresponsible* (from the Latin negative prefix *in-*) and *commerce – commercial* (/s/ – /ʃ/).

(2) **Morphology** in its more general, biological sense of 'the study of the forms of things' is also known in NARRATOLOGY from the pioneering work of the RUSSIAN FORMALIST, Vladimir Propp. In 1928 he published a book on the forms of Russian fairy-tales, noticing how differences of PLOT action between each story were really variants of the 'same' plot(s); whose basic elements he called FUNCTIONS (q.v.). (See also MOTIF below.)

motif

(1) In studies of NARRATIVE GRAMMAR undertaken by the **Russian** FORMALISTS (e.g. Tomashevsky), and their forerunner Veselovsky at the beginning of the twentieth century (see Lemon & Reis 1965), **motif** is used for the simplest narrative thematic units in folk-tales and stories: e.g. a stepmother hates the beautiful stepdaughter; the sun's light is stolen, etc. Motifs can be combined in any story, and recur from one story to another in different manifestations. (See also the work of Doložel (1976, 1979) in NARRATIVE SEMANTICS.)

(2) **Motif** is more commonly used in LITERARY studies as a synonym for LEITMOTIF: a recurrent THEME or idea in a text or group of texts. So contempt for worldy pleasures is a motif in medieval religious lyrics; the passing of time in Shakespeare's sonnets.

motivation

(1) In SEMIOTICS, following the work of de Saussure (1974/1916), Peirce (pub. 1931–58) and others, a term used in the description of the relations between SIGNS or SIGNIFIERS and their SIGNIFIEDS and REFERENTS.

In human language most of the relationships between sign and referent are arbitrary or **unmotivated**: there is no direct relation between a word and the 'object' it refers to. However, classes of signs known as ICONS (q.v.), since they visually resemble what they represent (as in paintings or photographs or holograms), are highly **motivated**. There are obviously degrees of **motivation**, even within the class of iconic signs: road-signs are less motivated than cartoons, which are less motivated than photographs; and some kinds of painting (abstract, surrealist) are SYMBOLIC rather than iconic. The class of signs known as INDEXICAL (q.v.) signs are partly motivated to the extent that there is a connection between signified and signifier, of causality.

Even technically arbitrary signs can come to appear 'motivated' to the society who uses them, by a kind of 'folk' or 'creative' ETYMOLOGY (see Bolinger 1965; see also Derrida's critique of Saussure, 1967a). Some words, in fact, are motivated to the extent that they are probably of ONOMATOPOEIC origin: their form being MIMETIC of the sound they represent (as in *moo, crash*). To these can be added words whose PHONEME **clusters**, in initial or final positions, have acquired PHONAESTHETIC associations, regardless of possible ONOMATOPOEIC origin, and which can therefore be grouped together and seen as motivated or 'remotivated' (Derrida) by association: e.g. *gl-eam, gl-ow, gl-itter; fl-ip, fl-utter, fl-it; b-ump, th-ump, cl-ump.*

Motivation in this sense can be seen as a kind of 'naturalization', and as Barthes (1967a) has noted, applies to other sign systems such as clothes. There is no reason why a linen coat should be any more suitable for a cool summer evening than a polyester one, or a cardigan; but fashion magazines make the first choice seem perfectly natural and rational (see also Culler 1975, ch. 2). Some lexicologists also distinguish **secondary motivation** in language. So the relationship between the basic CONCEPTUAL MEANING of a word and its derived associated meanings can be seen to be motivated; or the elements of a COMPOUND word or BLEND, since we can justify their origins (*apple tree* ('a tree with apples on'); *smog* ('smoke and fog together')).

(2) **Motivation** in the sense of a relationship deliberately suggested or actively perceived between sign and referent is particularly striking in LITERARY LANGUAGE. As the entry for CRATYLISM reveals, for example, poets such as the SYMBOLISTS have sought to remedy what they considered to be a 'defect' of ordinary language, namely its arbitrariness; and seek instead a highly motivated language, with a close correspondence between words, sounds and meanings. Other poets, too, by COLLOCATION of similar sounding words, suggest relations between them: e.g. Hopkins's *Whatever is fickle, freckled* (*Pied Beauty*); or *And all is seared with trade; bleared, smeared with toil* (*God's Grandeur*).

In a general way, we expect POETIC LANGUAGE, and literary language overall, to be motivated in the sense of it being consciously designed to serve particular themes and designs; and motivation as an artistic principle was very much the concern of the **Russian** FORMALISTS. So for Shklovsky (1917) the forms of art are to be explained by their conformity to the laws of art, not to those of everyday reality. These laws then provide a FRAME OF REFERENCE by which the literary WORLD is made COHERENT.

For the novel in particular, however, we do expect some kind of artistic motivation of PLOT and action that is realistic in terms of the world we know, at least in novels which profess to be realistic (not necessarily fantasy, or science-fiction, for instance). (See also VERISIMILITUDE.) Narrators have to work harder at convincing readers to 'suspend their disbelief' the more apparently implausible an action or event might seem at first glance. So in *Middlemarch* the narrator must tell us a great deal about Dorothea's hopes and illusions in order to justify her attraction to the aged pedant Casaubon.

(3) In PRAGMATICS a distinction can be made following Leech (1983) between rules of grammar as fundamentally conventional, and principles of pragmatics as **motivated**, in terms of conversational goals. So a promise is a promise in recognition of the speaker's **motive**.

In MARXIST CRITICISM and indeed CRITICAL DISCOURSE ANALYSIS, pragmatic motivation has an IDEOLOGICAL spin: discourse goals not seen as 'interest-free' but determined by issues of social power.

N

narrated monologue

Used by Cohn (1966, 1978) to describe one of the modes used in fiction for the representation of consciousness.

It is equivalent linguistically to the more commonly used term FREE INDIRECT THOUGHT (q.v.), since it is marked by the absence of a reporting clause and by a prevailing INDIRECT mode (the use of past TENSES and **third** PERSON PRONOUNS, for example), along with a 'present' DEICTIC orientation as in DIRECT THOUGHT. As a result, the voice of the NARRATOR blends with the POINT OF VIEW of the CHARACTER, without breaking the flow of the narrative.

One advantage of having a term like **narrated monologue**, which might otherwise appear superfluous, is that it can be used to describe not simply the individual or occasional transposition into a character's consciousness within an utterance, but whole stretches of text or 'monologues', such as are found in the STREAM OF CONSCIOUSNESS novels of Woolf, for example.

(See also PSYCHO-NARRATION.)

narratee

As a translation of his own *narrataire* and on the pattern also of ADDRESSEE in English, **narratee** was introduced in NARRATOLOGY in the work of Prince (1971, 1973). Popularized by Chatman (1978), it refers to a participant in the COMMUNICATIVE situation, the recipient of a NARRATIVE communicated by the NARRATOR (q.v.).

Narratees vary in status from work to work, and in degrees of explicitness. Very obviously they may be fictional characters addressed by other characters within a story (Miranda listening to her father's history at the beginning of *The Tempest*, for instance): what Lanser (1981) calls **private narratees**. Or they may be 'listeners' whose presence is invoked explicitly at the outset, and for whom the DISCOURSE of the story as a whole is apparently FRAMED. In epistolary novels, like Richardson's *Pamela*, there is Pamela's 'Father and Mother'; for confessional novels, however, like Nabokov's *Lolita* or Salinger's *The Catcher in the Rye*, the narratee, although explicitly addressed, is not named: *If you really want to hear about it, the first thing you'll probably want to know is where I was born ...* (*The Catcher in the Rye*).

In such cases, it is often difficult to distinguish the narratee from the IMPLIED READER, who ostensibly is situated EXTRADIEGETICALLY 'outside' the fictional world, but who is often similarly explicitly addressed, and is the recipient of the narrative (as in Fielding's novels, for instance). Hence from a functional point of view, implied reader and narratee are merged. We, as real readers, are also narratees; and are continually matching our own responses against those of the presumed reader and/or fictional listener.

narration; narratio

(1) **Narration** often overlaps with NARRATIVE; but as Genette (1972) has emphasized, in the study of FICTION and stories it is useful and important to make a basic distinction between the ACT and process of telling a story (narration), and what is actually told (narrative). An alternative term is **narrating**, as in the English translation of Genette (1980).

Narration is an aspect of the whole process of COMMUNICATION or DISCOURS(E) between AUTHOR and READER, and between NARRATOR and NARRATEE. In critical studies and NARRATOLOGY it has involved the discussion of VOICES and POINTS OF VIEW, of the different kinds and levels of narration (**first** PERSON; **third** person, OMNISCIENT, etc.), and perspectives of vision: the MODALITY of fiction. (See further Chatman 1978; and Stanzel 1984, on narrative transmission.) In some novels the reader is made very aware of the act of narrating (as in Sterne's *Tristram Shandy*); in others, as in INTERIOR MONOLOGUE, the narration is covert, impersonal. Apparently 'transparent', covert narration would deny its own status as an act of telling; yet it is just as marked as overt narration. Covert narration would also appear to characterize drama and film, but no narrator. Bordwell (1985) would allow narration in film, but no narrator.

(2) In traditional RHETORIC, **narratio** 'narration' is that part of a speech or discourse in which the facts are presented, or a story as *exemplum* ('example'), before the conclusion or 'moral'. It is still present in the law courts of today in the summaries of defence and prosecution, and the testimonies of witnesses, etc. In LITERARY DISCOURSE, *narratio* is characteristic of fables. In religious poems, such as the Anglo-Saxon *The Seafarer* and *The Dream of the Rood* (= 'cross') there is a very clear division between the *narratio* and the moral or exhortation.

narrative: ~ proposition; narrativity

(1) A **narrative** is basically a STORY, of happenings or events, either real or imaginary, which the NARRATOR considers interesting or important. 'Real' narratives are those of newspaper reports, confessions and historical records; FICTIONAL narratives are those of comic strips, epic poems, ballads and narrative fiction, such as novels and short stories. Narratives are most commonly narrated

in words, in speech (as in oral literature and jokes) or (chiefly) in writing; but they can be enacted dramatically on stage, or visualized in the images of film and gestures of mime.

Narratives are structured in the sense that they characteristically consist of the NARRATION of a succession of (related) events or experiences, rather than just one. **Narrative propositions** are usually related temporally or causally, explicitly or by PRESUPPOSITION; and are usually marked by the PAST TENSE. The so-called HISTORIC PRESENT (q.v.) is sometimes used, however, especially in oral anecdotes, to create a more vivid and dramatic effect.

The actual sequence of events as narrated is often termed SJUŽET or DISCOURS, following FORMALIST and STRUCTURALIST distinctions between how a story is told and what is being told, the CONTENT or abstracted chronological ordering of events. Genette's (1972) term for the actual verbal representation of narrative discourse is RÉCIT.

Narratives also often have a recognizable and enduring shape, and a distinctive pattern of opening and closing sequences, which are gradually learned or assimilated by tellers and readers alike as part of a general narrative COMPETENCE. Typical structural and thematic units are those of ORIENTATION (the setting of the scene at the beginning of novels, for example, or the fairy-tale FORMULA of *Once upon a time*); 'initiating action'; 'complication' of action; CLIMAX; DÉNOUEMENT or resolution and CODA or closing act (e.g. *And they all lived happily ever after*). (See further Labov & Waletsky 1967 on oral narratives.)

(2) The POSTMODERN theorist Jean-Francois Lyotard (1984), like others before him, has stressed the fundamental importance of narrative in culture, human thought and knowledge. But Lyotard is uneasy. Scientists, for example, need the META-**narrative**, the **grand narrative** (*grand récit*), an overarching intellectual scheme, which claims to help us understand some aspect of modern life in order to 'legitimate' their own knowledge (e.g. Darwinian evolutionism). Claiming that this is out-dated, a mere 'language game', he argues instead in favour of the 'small-scale' narratives (*petits récits*), not totalizing or totalitarian. Narrative, in essence, rather than 'reality' is the source of all value and truth.

(3) Some works on narrative use the term **narrativity** (coined by Greimas 1970) to refer to the text's apparent ability to bring a WORLD to life, to populate it with characters and stories and to convey the feeling of its actuality. Terry Pratchett's 'Discworld' novels succeed by this principle. Ryan (1991) sees PLOT as fundamental to narrativity; Chatman (1978, 1990) the dynamic tensions between *discours* and HISTOIRE; Prince (1987) the feature of TELLABILITY; Fludernik (1996) experientiality: i.e. the quasi-mimetic evocation of real-life with an 'experiencer'.

(See further Emmott 1997; Frye 1957; Rimmon-Kenan 1983.)

narrative grammar

Narrative grammar has been a favoured approach in NARRATOLOGY and POETICS, especially in France, which analyses NARRATIVE structures and PLOTS using a framework analogous to the grammatical CANONICAL structure of a SENTENCE: **macro-structures** in terms of **micro-structures** or **narremes**. So the grammatical SUBJECT corresponds to the ACTANT (q.v.) in a plot or the 'agent' or 'actor' (terms also traditionally used by grammarians); the VERB corresponds to the event or action; the OBJECT to the 'receiver' of an action: as in *The Fairy Godmother helped Cinderella*; or *Captain Ahab killed Moby Dick*.

A pioneering work was the study by the FORMALIST Propp (1928) of the Russian fairy-tale, which reduced his corpus to a basic set of abstract structures or KERNELS using the components of ROLE (of characters) and FUNCTIONS (acts significant for the plot).

The notion that a finite number of elements will produce a wide variety of stories is not unlike the GENERATIVE principle of TRANSFORMATIONAL GRAMMAR; and other narratologists building on Propp's work, e.g. Souriau (1950) on drama; Brémond (1966, 1973); Greimas (1966, 1970); Todorov (1969) on *The Decameron*; and Kristeva (1970), took the grammatical analogy further, and developed a (metaphorical) linguistic METALANGUAGE in their rule-based analyses of stories as PREDICATES, some of it generative. (See also NARRATIVE SEMIOTICS. See further Prince 1973; van Dijk 1976.)

Todorov's narrative grammar is one of the most consistently grammatical; yet like the others it reveals the strengths and weaknesses of this kind of approach. Although we can appreciate that a corpus of apparently disparate tales is more consistently structured than at first glance, such an approach inevitably plays down idiosyncracies and individual variations at the expense of the common elements. It is also open to question whether narrative grammars can really work successfully on kinds of narrative which are more 'sophisticated' than folk- or fairy-tales, or detective fiction.

narrative report of speech (thought) act (NRS(T)A), etc.

(1) Introduced by Leech & Short (1981) to refer to a mode of speech and thought representation in FICTION and non-fiction where a character's speaking or thinking is related by the NARRATOR in a summary. It is therefore also known as DIEGETIC **summary** (McHale 1978); as well as **submerged speech** (Page 1973).

As Leech & Short say, **NRSA** and **NRTA** are more 'indirect' than even INDIRECT SPEECH/THOUGHT. There is simply a report that a SPEECH ACT or thought act has taken place, with no details of what specifically was said or thought, or the exact phrasing. Cf. *She put to her son a series of questions* (NRSA); *She put to herself a series of questions* (NRTA). It is therefore a very useful device in any REGISTER where conversations need to be reported in a condensed form: accounts of parliamentary proceedings; minutes of meetings, etc. Novelists use the technique to indicate that an interchange or utterance has occurred, of not significant enough importance to need precise details: e.g. the opening sentence of James's *The Ambassadors*:

> Strether's first question, when he reached the hotel, was about his friend; yet on his learning that Waymarsh was apparently not to arrive till evening he was not wholly disconcerted.

Here it is of no importance who Strether is likely to have spoken to (probably, of course, the hotel receptionist), so that his interlocutor need not appear; and the question itself is an obvious one to ask in the circumstances.

The use of **narrative report** where DIRECT SPEECH might be expected can be exploited for humour, as in Dickens's *Little Dorrit*: the crowd *recommending an adjournment to Bedlam*.

(2) Rather confusingly, Short *et al.* in their more recent corpus-based studies (e.g. Semino *et al.* 1997) have adopted the terms **Narrator's Report of Speech/ Thought (NRS/T)** for the TAGS or reporting clauses of speech/thought; and so now talk of Narrator's **Representation** of Speech and Thought Acts.

(3) They have also introduced two new related categories of minimal speech and thought report. **Narrator's Report** (*sic*) **of Voice (NRV)** indicates verbal activity, but no explicit indication of particular speech acts (e.g. *She talked on*). **Narration of Internal States (NI)** reports a character's emotional or cognitive experiences: e.g. *Mrs Dale was worried about Jim.*

(4) In more recent work still (e.g. Short *et al.*, forthcoming) they consider analogous categories for the representation of writing activity: e.g. **Narrator's Report of Writing (NRW)** (*She wrote furiously*), and **Narrator's Representation of Writing Act (NRWA)** (*She wrote her letter of resignation last night*).

narrative semantics; ~ semiotics

Terms involving the application of theories of meaning to the study of NARRATIVE.

In **narrative semantics** discussion of topics also debated in philosophy is prominent: e.g. FICTIONALITY; real and POSSIBLE WORLDS; and MODALITY. The work of Doložel (1976, 1979) has been particularly important, one of whose prime concerns is a semantic theory of MOTIFS (q.v.), or representations of states and events.

Narrative semiotics is centrally associated with the writings of Greimas (1966f) who developed a complex GENERATIVE model of NARRATIVE involving a SURFACE structure of a NARRATIVE GRAMMAR and a DEEP level of semantic features or SEMES. Greimas's work in origin was much influenced by the earlier STRUCTURALIST theories of Lévi-Strauss, in particular his work on the structure of myths (1958).

(See further Hamon 1974.)

narratology

A term that came into favour from the 1960s onwards from French under the influence of STRUCTURALISM referring to the theoretical study and analysis of NARRATIVE and its levels and structures; also known as **narrative theory**. It embraces the manifestation of narrative in language and MEDIA, e.g. film; and also covers a wide range of approaches. It is commonly applied to those studies which concentrate on PLOT structures, as in NARRATIVE GRAMMAR (q.v.).

(For a survey of work in **narratology**, see Pavel in van Dijk 1985. See further also Fludernik 1996; Gibson 1996, ch. 3.)

narrator

A person or agent who narrates, who tells a story, whether factual or FICTIONAL.

Following Plato's distinction between a **narrator** who speaks in his or her own VOICE and one who assumes the voice of a CHARACTER (see also DIEGESIS and MIMESIS), modern critics normally include the IMPLIED AUTHOR as narrator in so-called **third** PERSON NARRATION. In some approaches, however, narrator excludes this (as in FORMALIST studies), so that the narrator is a character (e.g. the pilgrims in Chaucer's *Canterbury Tales*; the speakers in Browning's dramatic MONOLOGUES). However, the average reader of a novel will normally equate narrator and 'author'.

Narrators vary in the extent to which they also participate in the action which they describe. So-called **first** person narrators characteristically are the heroes or heroines of their stories (e.g. Jane Eyre and David Copperfield): what Genette (1972) terms **autodiegetic narrators**. In contrast, the OMNISCIENT NARRATOR, the implied author, is typically **heterodiegetic**, detached from the events, and may not even establish a DISCOURSE 'relationship' with the IMPLIED READER: James and Joyce, for instance, in comparison with Fielding, George Eliot or Dickens. Yet even in Dickens's novels the kinds of narrators vary: as in *Bleak House*, for instance, with the dual narrators of Esther Summerson and the omniscient narrator. There is variation also in the amount of detail provided by narrators. In 'realist' novels settings and descriptions of characters are given in great detail and evaluated; thoughts of characters are interpreted, and generalizations made on the society and values portrayed. (See also Stanzel 1971.)

A distinction is sometimes made also between **reliable** and **unreliable** **narrators**, following Booth (1961). Readers normally assume that narrators are reliable, especially if they are the implied author: namely, that what is being told is the (fictional) 'truth'. However, in narratives particularly where the FOCALIZA-TION is limited to the narrator's (as in first person novels), we may sometimes become aware of partiality of judgment: as in Defoe's *Moll Flanders*, for instance. Dramatic IRONY in the novel is often the result of the double PERSPECTIVE of reader and narrator.

N.B. The narrator poses problems in the application of narrative theory to film, since it is difficult to see any 'agency' corresponding to this, aside from the (infrequent) voice-over or character breaking FRAME. Chatman (1990) argues somewhat unconvincingly for 'its' retention; but see rather Bordwell (1985). (See also NARRATION.)

neologism

Borrowed from a French term based on Gk elements, a **neologism** in LEXICOLOGY means 'a newly invented word'.

Each year brings its spate of neologisms which may eventually find their way into dictionaries, if they become widely accepted through a speech community (e.g. *mobile phone; Teletubbies; e-commerce* of the 1990s). Words coined in literature, however, are less likely to be 'borrowed' by others, since their MOTIVATION for creation comes from the CONTEXT of the text, and not from some more larger-scale pragmatic need; yet they may be re-used by later generations of writers (as in POETIC DICTION). Many literary words, therefore, remain NONCE WORDS (q.v.), like Hopkins's *twindle* in *Inversnaid*. However, even literary words may fill a lexical GAP: we have kept Milton's *pandemonium* and Shakespeare's *bare-faced*.

As the examples illustrate, neologisms reveal a wide range of MORPHOLO-GICAL processes: e.g. COMPOUNDING, AFFIXATION, BLENDS and ACRONYMS (e.g. *laser; Aids*, etc.).

New Criticism

(1) From the 1930s to the end of the 1950s the most influential movement in American LITERARY CRITICISM in particular, but which owed much to the ideas of British critics like I. A. Richards and William Empson. Despite the popularity of later movements, such as STRUCTURALISM, the influence of **New Criticism** is still felt in some university departments of literary studies, an influence which was exerted also on modern STYLISTICS at its inception in the 1960s.

New Criticism itself was a reaction against a kind of approach to literature prevalent in the nineteenth century which saw texts as literary history only, and which did not sufficiently appreciate LITERATURE as art or analyse literary texts autonomously and objectively as unified artefacts in their own intrinsic terms. New Critics placed a much-needed emphasis on the language of literature. In many respects, and in their particular interest in poetry, their ideas come close to the **Russian** FORMALISTS. As Eagleton (1983) points out, however, the study of poetry to the New Critics was almost a 'religion', a haven or retreat from what they saw as the threatening IDEOLOGY of science and industry.

The major critics associated with New Criticism in the US were Monroe Beardsley, R. P. Blackmur, Cleanth Brooks, John Crowe Ransom (who named the movement), Robert Penn Warren, René Wellek and W. K. Wimsatt (a member of the PRAGUE SCHOOL before the Second World War). It is with their work that ideas of ANTI-INTENTIONALISM are associated: the 'meaning' of a text being primarily to be derived from internal evidence, and not the 'intentions' of its author. Noteworthy also is their MONIST approach to FORM and CONTENT, taken over by many other literary critics: the text (especially the poetic text) is to be read as a whole, its 'content' inseparable from the whole. (See also AFFECTIVE FALLACY; EMOTIVE MEANING. See further Baldick 1996.)

(2) The term **New Criticism** in French (*la Nouvelle Critique*) takes quite a contrary view of criticism and its objectives. It was a slogan applied to the 'liberal' and exploratory philosophical ideas of Roland Barthes in particular, whose work from 1953 onwards, MARXIST and STRUCTURALIST in character, was a reaction against traditional French criticism or *explication de texte*.

New historicism

A relatively recent development in LITERARY CRITICISM since the 1980s which is fashionably anti-NEW CRITICAL, anti-Leavisite (and so anti-CANONICAL) and anti-FORMALIST; and much influenced by the work of Foucault and also MARXIST CRITICISM in its emphasis on the historical and socio-political contexts of textual production and consumption. As with POSTMODERNISM too it problematizes the relations between 'facts' and 'TEXTS' (talking of the 'textuality' of history and the 'historicity' of texts); and problematizes also the relations between LITERATURE and other kinds of non-literary discourse, especially that of history itself. Much influential work has been written particularly on the Renaissance and Romantic periods, beginning with Greenblatt (1980).

(See further Ryan 1996.)

new information

One of a pair of terms (see also GIVEN INFORMATION) used in DISCOURSE and TEXT ANALYSIS with reference to the INFORMATION content of UTTERANCES or SENTENCES.

As its name suggests, **new** refers to **information** which is pragmatically not known, or not assumed to be known, to the ADDRESSEE; or which is regarded as particularly 'newsworthy'. Given information refers to that stated but already known to the participants, either supplied in the CO-TEXT, or PRESUPPOSED from the situational CONTEXT or common knowledge.

Each utterance in an extended discourse will present different patterns of givenness and newness. We expect opening sentences to contain all new information. INDEFINITE REFERENCE is normally associated with new information; DEFINITE with given.

New information most commonly occurs towards or at the end of an utterance (see END-FOCUS), and PROSODICALLY often coincides with or is signalled by the INTONATION NUCLEUS, e.g.:

But the merriest month in all the year
Is the merry month of <u>May</u>

(*Robin Hood and the Three Squires*)

Given and new are often associated with the PRAGUE SCHOOL notions of THEME (q.v.) and RHEME (q.v.), which are also aspects of text structure involving information: but its value and importance, rather than degree of newness. However, despite assertions that information structure and thematic structure are to be distinguished (see Halliday 1985, for instance), the popular association is understandable. The rheme, for example, the part of the sentence (usually post-VERBAL) that is communicatively most important or significant, will often coincide with new information.

Newspeak

(1) Coined by Orwell (1949) and explained in his Appendix to *1984* as refer-ring to a set of vocabularies invented by the totalitarian authorities of *Ingsoc* which were specifically designed to be self-reductive and to repress ('heretical') thought processes.

The principle behind **Newspeak** was therefore DETERMINISTIC, and also polit-ical, in that Orwell realized the ways in which language could be manipulated for propagandist aims. One influence on Newspeak was not itself political: C. K. Ogden's *Basic English* (1930), designed as a 'universal' means of communica-tion, a LINGUA FRANCA, and which attracted a great deal of attention during the 1930s. Here English was 'reduced' to a select vocabulary of 850 words.

Orwell's Newspeak made considerable use of CONVERSION (*think* as noun and verb, for example); AFFIXATION (*un-* as negative PREFIX in *ungood, undark*); COMPOUNDING (*sexcrime*). Semantically, many of the Newspeak words were EUPHEMISMS, intended to impose desirable mental attitudes: *joycamp* ('forced labour camp'), *Minipax* ('Ministry of War').

(2) Not surprisingly, therefore, the word **Newspeak** itself has passed into common usage: sometimes loosely used to refer to NEOLOGISMS, it particularly refers to new words that are associated with propagandist JARGON, especially those with sinister undertones. It has also inspired related words like **nukespeak** (e.g. *demographic targeting* for 'weapons aimed at people/towns').

noise

Taken into linguistics from COMMUNICATION THEORY (see Shannon & Weaver 1949) **noise** refers to the distortions produced in the CHANNEL to the SIGNAL being transmitted.

Such interference may lead to a complete breakdown of communication, but often it does not, because of the phenomenon of REDUNDANCY (q.v.), the surplus of INFORMATION normally produced in communication, which counteracts dis-turbances. We can often still understand telephone conversations, for instance, even if the wires and equipment hum or crackle. However, a combination of faulty equipment and poor acoustics (itself a kind of **noise** in an extended sense) is often a serious threat to railway station announcements or public oratory, for example. Noise, therefore, is not only auditory interference. Misprints, common in newspapers, are a kind of noise in the GRAPHEMIC MEDIUM; the 'snow' on the television screen is another.

Some linguists have used the term to refer to anything which makes a MESSAGE difficult to DECODE accurately: e.g. sitting in an uncomfortable seat while listen-ing to a lecture (see Fiske 1982). Here the noise originates not in the channel but in the ADDRESSEE. An example of noise originating in the message itself would be linguistic AMBIGUITY or marked DEVIATION (as in Joyce's *Finnegans Wake*, for example).

nominal group; noun phrase (NP); nominalization

(1) **Nominal group** and **noun phrase** (**NP**) are synonymous terms found in different GRAMMARS: SYSTEMIC GRAMMAR favouring the former, for instance, and traditional and GENERATIVE GRAMMAR the latter.

They refer to a structure which has a **noun (nominal)** or PRONOUN as HEAD, with or without MODIFIERS: e.g. [*God's*] *Grandeur*; [*pied*] *beauty*; [*the*] *windhover*; *habit* [*of perfection*]. Heavy nominal groups involving modification by other nouns rather than ADJECTIVES are characteristic of REGISTERS such as newspaper headlines or placards, e.g. [*Parking meters credit card*] *plan*; [*Moors killer confession*] *hopes*. In general, according to Biber *et al.* (1999, ch. 8), complex NPs are most frequently found in academic prose.

(2) In LEXICOLOGY **nominalization** refers to an aspect of the word-formation process of AFFIXATION or DERIVATION whereby nouns are derived from VERBS by nominalizing SUFFIXES: hence **deverbal nouns**: e.g. *nationaliz-ation; derail-ment; convers-ion* (from *convert*). Nominalizations are characteristically ABSTRACT.

(3) Deverbal nouns have themselves been seen as part of a syntactic and stylistic process also known as **nominalization**, in which nominal structures are TRANSFORMATIONS, in Generative Grammar terms, of underlying SENTENCES as DEEP STRUCTURES (see Lees 1960). Not only deverbal nouns, but also **verbal nouns** (marked by the suffix-*ing*: as *singing, dancing*, etc.) are used in such nominalizations, cf.:

> The conversion of the Anglo-Saxons to Christianity took place in the sixth century.
> The Anglo-Saxons were converted to Christianity. This took place in the sixth century.

> Smoking is not allowed on the University Campus any more.
> You are not allowed to smoke on the University Campus any more.

Such compact nominalizations, combined with the PASSIVE, are common in IMPERSONAL and FORMAL REGISTERS such as official notices and scientific articles. In LITERARY LANGUAGE the effect of a consistent use of a nominalizing STYLE is to render static the potentially dynamic or active; and to reify feelings. (See Fowler 1977, who notes the characteristic use in Henry James's novels; see further Ohmann 1964.)

nonce word

A term from ME *for than anes* 'for the once', used for a word newly coined (NEOLOGISM) which is used only once and is never accepted through wider circulation. An alternative term is the Gk *hapax legomenon* ('once said').

In the sixteenth century, many Latinate **nonce words** arose through the influence of INKHORNISM; others appear in individual works, like Joyce's special 'dream' language in *Finnegans Wake*. Other nonce forms remain nonce simply because they do not 'catch on'. The Duke of Edinburgh's formation *dontopedology* ('to put one's foot in one's mouth') is worthy perhaps of wider circulation.

non-finite: ~ verb; ~ clause

In the categorization of the VERB PHRASE in GRAMMAR, a **non-finite** form is not FINITE, i.e. it is not marked for TENSE or matched with a **third** PERSON SUBJECT in the PRESENT TENSE for singular number (e.g. *He snore-s heavily*); and it is not marked for MOOD (q.v.). Non-finite forms comprise INFINITIVES (e.g. *snore, snigger*, etc.) and PARTICIPLES: the *-ing* forms and *-ed* forms (*opening; opened*).

Non-finite verb forms can be quite complex, since they can combine with each other to express distinctions of ASPECT and VOICE: e.g. *She was the last person to have been seen there*. They are commonly used in POSTMODIFICATION of the NOUN, and also function as NOMINAL clauses, e.g. *To be, or not to be, that is the question*; and as ADVERBIAL clauses, e.g. *Crossing the road one day* (= 'while'), *I bumped into an elephant*. **Non-finite clauses**, unlike finite clauses, are always SUBORDINATE.

Because of their lack of finiteness, their lack of DEICTIC orientation in time, non-finite clauses can be exploited in LITERARY LANGUAGE to suggest thoughts or impressions that are continuing or universal, not precisely fixed at one moment: e.g. in the opening descriptions of London in Dickens's *Bleak House*:

> Smoke lowering down from chimney-pots, making a soft black drizzle . . . Horses . . . splashed to their very blinkers . . . Foot pasengers, jostling one another's umbrellas.

non-verbal communication (NVC)

Popularized by the work of Argyle (1972) to distinguish language (verbal) from other SEMIOTIC systems of COMMUNICATION among human beings (non-verbal).

Non-verbal communication can be subdivided into **vocal** and **non-vocal**: i.e. those means of communication which depend on the voice for utterance (see PROSODY; PARALANGUAGE); and those which depend on other parts of the body (facial expressions, gestures, KINETIC movements, etc.). 'Non-verbal' is very frequently used in the sense of 'non-vocal'.

Obviously NVC is of prime importance in the DISCOURSE situation of face-to-face communication. Studies in DISCOURSE ANALYSIS helped by the technology of video now stress the importance of body signals in interaction, for EMPHASIS, for giving clues as to TURN-TAKING, or indicating FEEDBACK to the speaker. Facial expressions and gestures are also important clues to ATTITUDINAL MEANINGS, e.g. of friendliness or hostility.

norm

A widely discussed concept in linguistics and STYLISTICS but not without its problems. Strictly, **norm** is a statistical concept, referring to what is statistically average. DEVIATION (q.v.) refers to the divergence in frequency from the norm. But, whatever its area of application, norm quickly becomes a 'loaded' concept, acquiring the CONNOTATIONS of 'standard' or 'normality', or 'typicality' opposed to 'non-standard' or 'abnormality' or 'untypicality'. Outside language we are aware, for example, that each society has its own norms of social behaviour, or its own images of such norms, and violations of those norms are considered anti-social, abnormal and potentially reprehensible. The MASS MEDIA and advertising are powerful means of presenting and reinforcing norms of social behaviour.

Yet a consideration of even social behaviour shows an important fact about the concept of norm, namely that it is not absolute, but relative. What is abnormal social behaviour to one group of people may be normal to another, and vice versa. The behaviour and dress of certain groups of young people habitually shock the older generations, and is meant to; yet is perfectly acceptable and conventional to the young themselves.

Language as a part of social behaviour is similarly affected. It is common and often practical (for the makers of GRAMMARS) to presuppose that there is a normal set of rules for the English language on each of the linguistic levels: phonological, grammatical, lexical and semantic; and that violation of these rules constitutes deviation and MARKEDNESS. To a great extent this is true. We speak of 'normal' spelling, 'normal' WORD ORDER, etc. However, it must be noted that it is easier to establish phonological norms, the norms of word building, than the norms of grammar or meaning (especially). A form like */tkɪs/ is not an English phonological pattern, and *elephant the grey not a GRAMMATICAL ordering. But there are linguistic norms more relative than these: Wait while (= 'until') tea is 'ungrammatical' to some speakers, but not to others whose dialect it belongs to. Green thought is an odd COLLOCATION, yet in the context of Marvell's poem The Garden is perfectly acceptable and understandable.

In many approaches to LITERARY LANGUAGE there has been the supposition of a norm and deviation. The norm is presumably the language of non-literature, a sort of undifferentiated language, from which literary language deviates. Such a notion lies behind the PRAGUE SCHOOL concept of FOREGROUNDING; and behind ideas common in the early 1960s of poetic grammars whose 'rules' would be different from those of ordinary language (see further Widdowson 1983).

But what, in effect, this also suggests is that literary texts themselves set up their own norms, whose rules can then be described: **secondary norms** or **second-order norms**, as distinguished from **primary** or **first-order norms** (of ordinary language). At the level of METRE and RHYTHM such norms are readily apparent; and the concept of GENRE works by 'rules' and normal expectations. Although there are poets whose language appears markedly deviant (e.e. cummings, Hopkins or Dylan Thomas), these are outnumbered by the poets whose language in differing degrees approximates to that of everyday language (see also POETIC LANGUAGE).

Even 'non-literary language' contains the poetic deviations (sic) of word-play and METAPHOR, for instance, and generally is not as homogeneous as appears to be assumed. The concepts of 'speech community' and COMMON CORE, for example, are very much idealized. Comprising numerous VARIETIES according to social groups and REGISTERS, with differing **degrees of** FORMALITY, and differences according to MEDIA, etc., non-literary language really comprises a set of norms. (On the particular norms of conversation, see CO-OPERATIVE PRINCIPLE.)

It was common in the formative years of stylistics in the 1960s and in COM-PUTATIONAL STYLISTICS to define STYLE itself in terms of a deviation from a norm (see, e.g. Bloch 1953; Levin 1962). And ideas of IDIOLECT, of certain writers using certain constructions very or less frequently, presuppose some norm against which individual variation can be measured. We can see for various reasons how such an approach must be carefully considered. Style in this sense appears 'abnormal'; and what is assumed to be 'normal' would therefore have no 'style'. (See also ZERO DEGREE.) Presumably the norm from which style departs is the norm of ordinary language; but this is itself composed of many, different, norms. Stylisticians, in making comparisons between writers, and between texts, have therefore to work on the basis of CONTEXTUAL norms: measuring Johnson's essay style, for instance, against that of other essayists of the period, or the larger context of eighteenth-century prose style, if necessary. (See further Leech & Short 1981.)

noun; noun phrase

See NOMINAL GROUP.

nucleus; nuclear syllable

In the study of INTONATION and INFORMATION structure, especially amongst British linguists, **nucleus** or **nuclear syllable** is commonly used to refer to the most prominent ACCENTED syllable in a TONE UNIT, and which carries the significant pitch contrast or KINETIC TONE (**High Fall; Low Rise**, etc.). It is also known as the **tonic accent** or **tonic syllable** (and in RHETORIC, the CADENCE).

The nucleus also coincides, on the level of information, with the utterance element with the highest degree of informativity, i.e. the FOCUS (q.v.), e.g. *Why don't elephants like penguins?* This is normally the last accented syllable or LEXICAL ITEM in an utterance (see END-FOCUS); but for EMPHASIS or contrast the nucleus and focus can occur elsewhere, e.g. *A national scandal I call it*. The occurrence of several nuclei (with falling tones) within an utterance would be especially associated with insistent or dogmatic speech: *How many times do I have to tell you* . . .

O

object

In GRAMMAR, a NOUN PHRASE that normally follows the VERB PHRASE (which must be TRANSITIVE) and is directly dependent on it.

There are two kinds of **objects**, the DIRECT (DO) (q.v.) and the INDIRECT (IO) (q.v.). The direct object is semantically directly 'affected' by the action denoted in the CLAUSE or SENTENCE; the indirect object (optional) refers to the (commonly human) 'beneficiary' or 'recipient' of the process described. For example: *She gave him* (IO) *a big hug* (DO). As this example shows, IO normally precedes DO.

In languages like Latin and Old English these functions are expressed by the **accusative** and **dative** CASES respectively. In Modern English, the accusative case survives only in the PRONOUNS, the so-called **objective** case like *me, us, him, her, them, whom*.

In PASSIVE constructions, both DO and IO can become SUBJECTS, e.g.:

Cinderella was given a beautiful coach by her fairy godmother.
A beautiful coach was given to Cinderella by her fairy godmother.
(cf. Her fairy godmother gave Cinderella a beautiful coach.)

occupatio

A FIGURE of RHETORIC in which the narrator says (s)he will not have time or space to describe something, but then actually does so.

A famous example occurs in Chaucer's *The Knight's Tale*. The narrator declines to describe in full the preparations for Arcite's funeral, but what he is going to omit takes seventeen lines to recount.

Occupatio is not a dead figure. It survives in the digressive style of joke-telling, e.g. of British comedian Ronnie Corbett, who regularly told his TV audience in the 1980s that he was not going to tell them the joke about X, and then proceeded to tell it anyway.

(See also PARALIPSIS.)

omniscient narrator

Widely used in LITERARY CRITICISM to describe the characteristic NARRATOR of **third** PERSON NARRATION, here normally identical with the IMPLIED AUTHOR, who is privileged to 'know everything' about the story being told, and to enter into the thoughts of all the CHARACTERS. Summary, and shifts in temporal reference (from past to present and future), are common in **omniscient narration**; so too are FREE INDIRECT DISCOURSE and DIRECT THOUGHT.

Omniscience of narration is the opposite pole to limited FOCALIZATION, where events are told from the PERSPECTIVE of one character (common in **first** person narration). Moreover, there are degrees of omniscience from novel to novel (see Stanzel 1971). Even within the same novel there can be selective omniscience: the narrator may be 'unable' to reveal information, or to have access to a character's thoughts. (See also PARALIPSIS.) Often done to appear 'realistic', this can nevertheless be irritatingly arch, since omniscience may be so prevalent in the rest of the novel.

onomatopoeia

From Gk 'name-making', the LEXICAL process of creating words which actually sound like their REFERENT, e.g. *bang; crash; cuckoo; sizzle; zoom.*

There has been much speculation since Plato whether the first human language was MIMETIC and MOTIVATED in this way. Linguists nowadays since Saussure pay very little attention to **onomatopoeic** forms, since they comprise but a small part of the LEXICON, whose name–reference relationship is characteristically conventional and arbitrary. To some extent, however, onomatopoeic words are as conventional as other words, in that their PHONEMIC shape conforms to the language-system of their coiners, despite the apparent universality of their reference. If ducks say *quack, quack* in English, they say *coin, coin* in French. Many noises are not easily verbalized, so that it requires considerable interpretative power to recognize the references of *iiiaaaauch* as a yawn in children's comics; *phut* or *vrach* as bomb shells in the First World War poems; or *krandle* as the sound of a tram in Joyce's *Ulysses*.

In LITERARY LANGUAGE onomatopoeia is often much exploited as an EXPRESSIVE ICONIC device, along with other sound associations that can be grouped under the general heading of PHONAESTHESIA (q.v.) or SOUND SYMBOLISM (q.v.).

open class

Used in LEXICOLOGY to distinguish those parts of speech or word classes whose membership is open to innovation and renewal by borrowing or NEOLOGISM.

Open-class words comprise the bulk of the LEXICON of the language, and they are grammatically mainly NOUNS, VERBS and ADJECTIVES: the so-called CONTENT WORDS or lexically **full words**, which have LEXICAL meaning, referring to objects and experiences in the world.

They are contrasted with CLOSED-CLASS words, the FUNCTION WORDS like ARTICLES, PREPOSITIONS and CONJUNCTIONS, whose membership is closed to innovation and which are used in the basic syntactic structure of sentences.

open text; openness

(1) **Open text** is one of a pair of terms popularized by Eco (e.g. 1979) to refer to kinds of INTERPRETATIVE interaction between TEXT and READER (see also CLOSED TEXT).

An open text, unlike a closed text such as a work of popular fiction, is not aimed at a specific reader in a specific social context. It is also open in that its theme, structure and language are more complex, less explicit, more 'open-ended': what other critics in RECEPTION THEORY have called INDETERMINATE. (See also Barthes's READERLY and WRITERLY texts.)

Somewhat confusingly, however, Eco argues that open texts are 'closed' in the sense that their readers must mentally engage with the text, organize it in a particular way and not in any sort of way. The open text constructs the model of its own reader as part of its structural strategy. This is certainly true of that most open of novels, Joyce's *Finnegans Wake*. The infinite complexity of this novel is such that some critics have argued that the IMPLIED READER (and IDEAL READER) can be only another Joyce.

(2) **Openness** is also a term used in discussion of narrative CLOSURE. Conventionally, we expect literary texts to work towards a sense of completion. In many novels, for instance, as in drama, closure comes from the 'tying up' of all the strands of the PLOT and the resolution of all the ENIGMAS. Yet some texts, especially modern, work against closure, which has become identified generally with plots or themes of political conservatism, and lack of formal or linguistic experimenting. Hence openness in this sense aligns itself with (1).

oral-formulaic theory

From the late 1920s and early 1930s onwards the work of Milman Parry and then his student Albert Lord (1960) on Homeric verse attracted considerable attention. They decided, on the basis of a comparison with modern oral Serbo-Croatian poetry, that the Greek poems had been composed orally in the same conditions and manner: namely, that they were built up by FORMULAS (q.v.), 'a group of words which is regularly employed under the same metrical conditions to express a given essential idea' (Parry 1930). Examples would be phrases or EPITHETS like *godlike Odysseus* and *rosy-fingered dawn*. Such formulas, it was argued, would be indispensable to an essentially improvisatory technique for the rapid re-creating of a stock of stories in epic verse.

While controversy continued about Homeric verse, the oral-formulaic theory was applied in 1953 by F. P. Magoun Jr to Old English verse. OE verse was undoubtedly oral in its Germanic pagan origins; and its repetitive DICTION and habitual COLLOCATIONS had long been recognized. But Magoun's insistence that if OE poems used formulas as the smallest units of composition, therefore they must have been orally composed, pushed oral composition further into the OE period than had traditionally been considered. It is more probable that the cleric-poets, converted to Christianity and to literacy, used techniques favourable to them from the flourishing oral secular poetry, and which were useful for oral delivery to a listening audience.

(See also ORATURE below.)

orature

A term popular in POSTCOLONIAL THEORY, coined by analogy with LITERATURE, to refer to either (1) oral literary genres in oral cultures stored in memory; or (2) the infusion of oral techniques or performance into Black writing: for example, the work of Jamaica Kincaid.

For Ong (1982) oral literature exhibits **primary orality**; literate societies which have reintroduced forms of orality because of new technologies (e.g. radio, TV, film, video) exhibit **secondary orality**.

(See also SKAZ.)

orientation

(1) Following the work of Labov & Waletsky (1967; also Labov 1972) on the structuring of oral NARRATIVES, **orientation** is frequently used to describe one of the key 'stages' of narrative. Commonly placed at the beginning of stories, it refers to the description of the necessary background of time, place and/or participants in order to fix the story in its setting.

The amount of such information varies from story to story. *Once upon a time* provides the simplest orientation FORMULA. In George Eliot's *The Mill on the Floss* the description of Dorlcote Mill and the surrounding countryside extends to one chapter; in Hardy's *Tess of the D'Urbervilles* time, place and one of the characters are presented in the very first sentence:

> On an evening in the latter part of May a middle-aged man was walking homeward from Shaston to the village of Marlott, in the adjoining Vale of Blakemore or Blackmoor.

For stories or novels beginning IN MEDIAS RES such initial orientations are lacking; the information must be gradually provided elsewhere.

Orientations are also characteristic of other discourse types such as newspaper articles and lectures, e.g. the initial ADVERBIALS in *In Parliament today the Home Secretary revealed new plans to fight street crime.*

(2) In Brazil's work (1985) on the study of INTONATION, **direct orientation** refers to the immediate or CANONICAL discourse between speakers; **oblique** to that kind of discourse which has a pre-determined script to be performed or read aloud. In Jakobsonian terms, the 'set' towards the hearer is replaced by the set towards the discourse itself as a specimen of the language.

orthography

From Gk 'correct spelling' a term in linguistics which refers to the (STANDARD) spelling system of a language.

The English spelling system is decidedly traditional in that it represents pronunciations current in the sixteenth century; but its usefulness lies in the fact that it is standardized, and therefore consistent from one regional DIALECT to another within the British Isles, and most of the major VARIETIES of English throughout the world (apart from the US).

DEVIATIONS from standard spelling are found in dialect literature that attempts to represent dialect speech phonetically (e.g. the Dorset poems of William Barnes); and to reproduce colloquial speech (see also EYE-DIALECT).

over-lexicalization

Popularized by Fowler (e.g. 1996) to refer in LEXICOLOGY and STYLISTICS to the existence of a stock of SYNONYMS for a particular concept (see also UNDER-LEXICALIZATION).

Over-lexicalization in a language occurs when a particular concept or a set of concepts are of vital concern to a culture. Old English poetry, for instance, reveals many synonyms for concepts such as 'lord', 'battle' and 'courage'. The JARGONS of certain trades or professions with their profusion of terms are also examples. (See ANTI-LANGUAGE.)

In a text sets of related terms can be FOREGROUNDED to emphasize what is being described. So Fowler himself notes the extensive vocabulary of 'abundance' which is prominent in Keats's *Ode to Autumn*.

oxymoron

From Gk 'sharp-dull', a FIGURE of RHETORIC which juxtaposes apparently contradictory expressions for witty or striking effects (e.g. *Heathrow: The world's local airport*). It presents a kind of condensed PARADOX (q.v.).

Oxymoron is commonly associated in poetic convention with the fluctuations or contradictions of the feelings of love: so Pandarus in Chaucer's *Troilus and Criseyde* exclaims *I have a jolly wo, a lusty sorwe* (sorrow). The lament of the 'love-sick' Romeo in *Romeo and Juliet* (I.i) is a parody of the contemporary sonnets:

Why, then O <u>brawling love</u>, O <u>loving hate</u>,
O <u>any thing</u>! of <u>nothing</u> first create.
O <u>heavy lightness</u>! serious vanity!
Mis-shapen chaos of <u>well-seeming</u> forms!
<u>Feather</u> of <u>lead</u>, <u>bright smoke</u>, <u>cold fire</u>, sick health!

Lanham (1991) rather cynically invites his readers to find oxymoronic meanings in contemporary phrases like *academic administration; airline cuisine; business ethics* and *military intelligence.*

(See further Shen 1987.)

P

---

paradox

From Gk 'against-opinion', a **paradox** is a statement which is apparently self-contradictory, a kind of expanded OXYMORON (q.v.): e.g. Orwell's *War is peace, Freedom is slavery* and *Ignorance is strength (1984)*; or Rousseau's *Man is born free and everywhere is in chains (Du Contrat Social)*.

The reader must probe beyond the LITERAL MEANING to find a deeper, usually more philosophical meaning which will reconcile the apparent absurdity. Because of the initial puzzlement however, paradox is a TROPE that can be effectively exploited: in advertising slogans to attract attention; and in the larger puzzle context of riddles, e.g. *I devour words, yet am not any the wiser* (a bookworm). It has also been a prominent device in love poetry, both secular and religious, through the ages, to express the conflicting emotions that love inspires. So Donne writes of his relations with God:

> For I
> Except you enthrall me, never shall be free,
> Nor ever chaste, except you ravish me
>
> *(Holy Sonnets, 14)*

paralanguage; paralinguistic feature

Definitions of **paralanguage** vary considerably, according to what is included or excluded. But generally it is recognized that communication in the spoken MEDIUM involves not only the UTTERANCES that realize language (VERBAL), but also other systems of SIGN also, that are NON-VERBAL (q.v.).

In this respect paralanguage is often regarded as a non-verbal, but vocal system, along with PROSODIC FEATURES (q.v.) such as pitch and loudness. And characteristic **paralinguistic features** would be noises that do not function as PHONEMES (i.e. in building words), but nonetheless do communicate a 'meaning' or ATTITUDE in speech: e.g. giggles, snorts, exclamations of disgust, disapproval, boredom, etc. But other definitions or discussions would include prosodic features also (see Elam 1980); and still others non-vocal signs like facial expressions and gestures, hence virtually synonymous with NON-VERBAL COMMUNICATION (q.v.) (see Lyons 1977).

Paralanguage significantly interacts with language in spoken discourse in ways that DISCOURSE ANALYSTS have been keen to study. It is not easily represented in the GRAPHIC MEDIUM of novelistic DIALOGUE. Speakers rely on paralinguistic FEEDBACK from their ADDRESSEES; the audience watching and listening to a play can catch a whole range of emotional and attitudinal CONNOTATIONS from the vocalizations of the actors. They in turn can judge from the laughs, boos, hisses or coughs something of the audience's reactions to their own performances.

(See further Trager 1958.)

paralepsis; paralipsis

Both these terms, easily confused, are found in the work of Genette (1972) on NARRATIVE DISCOURSE:

(1) **Paralepsis**, Genette's own coinage, involves the giving of more information than is strictly the NORM for any novel, given the degree of constraint on such information according to the FOCALIZATION or PERSPECTIVE from which the story is being told. Discrepancies are particularly obvious in narratives with internal focalization, or with **first** PERSON NARRATORS. So in James's *What Maisie Knew* we are told details about a scene that Maisie, the main focalizer in the novel, would not have witnessed. In Fitzgerald's *The Great Gatsby*, Nick Carraway, the narrator, clearly has access to the thoughts and feelings of other characters: a situation which is only thinly justified by his explanations that they have been reported to him.

(2) **Paralipsis**, already an accepted term in RHETORIC, meaning 'false omission' as in (3), is the converse of paralepsis; namely, the giving of less information than the norm of focalization would seem to require. A simple example would be the narrator's omission of some action or event pertaining to the main characters focalized. In detective stories, for example, sometimes vital clues are concealed from the reader, to be revealed only at some later stage. And the whole force of Balzac's novella *Sarrasine* depends on the fact that the sex of the beautiful singer is not immediately obvious.

(3) In traditional rhetoric **paralipsis** is a device in which something is emphasized by suggesting that it is too obvious to discuss. In formal speech situations **paraliptic phrases** are quite common: e.g. *not to mention; leaving aside; to say nothing of.* (See also OCCUPATIO.)

parallelism

A device common in RHETORIC which depends on the **principle of** EQUIVALENCE (q.v.) in Jakobson's (1960f) terms, or on the REPETITION of the same structural pattern: commonly between phrases or clauses. So in the proverb *Out of sight, out* *of mind* there is the repetition of the PREPOSITIONAL PHRASE; in *He came, he saw, he conquered* the repetition of the clause. As a RHETORICAL FIGURE **parallelism** is also known as **parison**.

There is usually some obvious connection in meaning between the repeated units which reinforces the equivalence, but they need not be SYNONYMOUS. Parallelism with contrast or ANTONYMY is known as ANTITHESIS, as in: *When one is in love one begins by deceiving oneself. And one ends by deceiving others. That is what the world calls a romance* (Wilde).

Parallelism has been defined by Leech (1969) as 'FOREGROUNDED regularity'. Sometimes the parallelism is made more prominent by ALLITERATION and other patterns of sound: common in some sixteenth-century prose styles, for example. Parallelism has often been influenced by Latin models, and is a feature of public oratory, for EMPHASIS. The influence of Hebrew poetry, where parallelism is a striking feature, is felt in the liturgy, and the language of the *Psalms*:

> They have mouths, but they speak not:
> eyes have they, but they see not.
> They have ears, but they hear not;
> noses have they, but they smell not (Psalm 115)

Jakobson notes its striking use in POETIC LANGUAGE; and Leech considers METRE nothing more than parallelism of RHYTHM. For Jakobson, indeed, it is the PROSODIC structure of verse that dictates the parallel structures; whereas in prose it is meaning.

(See further Short 1996, ch. 1.)

paraphrase

(1) In translation studies **paraphrase** is a kind of translation which is neither slavish (**metaphrase**) nor too free: what Steiner (1975) calls a 'faithful but autonomous restatement'. The OE poems *Genesis* and *Exodus*, for example, are METRICAL paraphrases of the books of the Bible, admittedly rather free and amplificatory in places.

(2) What is often involved in such a translation is the rendering of the PROPOSITIONAL MEANING of a SENTENCE in one language in different words in another language, and linguists interested in SEMANTICS therefore use the term **paraphrase** to describe such alternatives of expression within one and the same language. It is thus a kind of SYNONYMY (q.v.) but at clause rather than word level.

What is PRESUPPOSED in (1) and (2) alike is that sentences apparently dissimilar in their expression can actually have the 'same' meaning. This was an important presupposition in Chomsky's development of TRANSFORMATIONAL GRAMMAR, with the notions of DEEP and SURFACE STRUCTURES; and also lies behind the DUALIST theory of meaning common in STYLISTICS, namely that the same CONTENT can be expressed in different FORMS (see Ohmann 1964). And paraphrase as an explanatory technique is used commonly in lectures and informative articles in order to communicate complex ideas more simply.

But the notion of paraphrase has not gone unchallenged by critics and translators, expecially in connection with LITERARY LANGUAGE. What has to be qualified are notions of 'sameness' of meaning or content. It is better to think in terms of 'similarity', or in terms of DENOTATION V. CONNOTATION or THEMATIC MEANING. At one level it may well be the case that, for example, *Shut up* and *Can't you be quieter,* or ACTIVE and PASSIVE sentences refer to the same propositions; but the very existence of 'alternatives' hints that CHOICE of construction depends on other factors: degree of situational FORMALITY, for instance.

pararhyme

One of a confusing group of terms differently and overlappingly used in LITERARY CRITICISM to refer to kinds of imperfect RHYMES.

(1) With some critics **pararhyme** appears to be synonymous with HALF-RHYME and CONSONANCE in that it refers to the REPETITION of final consonants with variation in the preceding vowels: e.g. *pest; last.*

(2) Leech (1969) uses the term for what others call APOPHONY: the repetition of both initial and final consonants with variation in the medial vowels: e.g. *pest; past.*

parataxis

In traditional GRAMMAR and RHETORIC **parataxis** describes the linking of clauses by juxtaposition rather than through explicit SUBORDINATION (HYPOTAXIS) or CO-ORDINATION. Some discussions, however, include co-ordination under parataxis (e.g. Fowler 1996; Turner 1973).

The connection between clauses has thus to be inferred. Simple logical or temporal linkage is characteristic, as in

Humpty Dumpty sat on a wall,
[and then] Humpty Dumpty had a great fall

also causal:

Boys and girls come out to play,
[because] The moon doth shine as bright as day

and manner: *Save trees – [how?] Eat a beaver.*

Parataxis is common in popular and unsophisticated literary forms, like nursery rhymes, ballads and prose chronicles (e.g. Malory's *Morte d'Arthur*), as well as ordinary speech. It is particularly associated with oral literature, and survives in OE poetry.

(See also ASYNDETON.)

parody; pastiche

(1) If the Greek roots of **parody** are taken to mean 'counter-song', then it can be seen as a kind of IMITATION which borrows the STYLE and techniques of a text or writer's IDIOLECT and fits new subject matter to it, often for a humorous or satirical purpose. So the lexical REPETITIONS and striking RHYTHMS of Longfellow's *The Song of Hiawatha* are parodied in a modern anonymous version, with a more commonplace CONTENT:

> He killed the noble Mudjokivis.
> Of the skin he made him mittens,
> Made them with the fur side inside,
> Made them with the skin side outside.
> He to get the warm side inside,
> Put the inside skin side outside.

What makes parody so amusing often is not simply recognizing what features are being parodied and why, but also appreciating the parodist's own creative talents: fusing creativity or wit with critique (Waugh 1984). It is not confined to LITERARY DISCOURSE: graffiti artists will parody advertising campaigns, for example: *Jesus saves – with the Woolwich.*

On the one hand parody FOREGROUNDS or ALIENATES, exposes and makes prominent, certain stylistic features of the original text or idiolect; on the other hand, in its own freedom of subject matter, it promotes its own identity and exposes its difference. Even the 'imitation' is not exact: a style is 'generated' which only partly resembles that of the source. As Bakhtin (1981) has said, parody is a DOUBLE-VOICED discourse, engaging in a DIALOGIC relationship with its parallel text. Parody need not be satirical: Hutcheon (1985) argues that another sense of the prefix *para-* could be 'with' or 'beside', so that parody could be seen as sometimes working almost in collusion with its source. Self-confessed parodists like Nash (1985) certainly admit that their work is a kind of tribute.

In its appropriation or QUOTATION of an anterior text, parody is an important means of INTERTEXTUALITY: what Genette (1979) calls **paratextuality**. Some critics see parody as a basic principle of literary development, especially in the (self-)conscious trends of 'anti-novel' and METAFICTION. But readers of novels like Fielding's *Joseph Andrews* and Austen's *Northanger Abbey*, for instance, have also to be aware of the contribution of parodic INTENT to the formation of these novels, with their exposure of conventions considered ridiculous.

(2) **Pastiche** is another paratextual form, often difficult to distinguish from parody, since its borrowings are often also for humorous or satirical purposes. But, as its name suggests, (from It., meaning 'paste'), pastiche is characteristically a 'pasting together', a patchwork or medley of borrowed styles. So Joyce's 'Oxen of the Sun' Episode in *Ulysses* is overall a pastiche of English prose styles from Anglo-Saxon times to the present day; comprising in several places specific parodies of well-known authors (Malory; Bunyan; Dickens, etc.); and in others, pastiche of 'period' styles (OE, ME, Elizabethan Chronicle style, etc.).

(See also REGISTER(-SWITCHING); STYLIZATION.)

parole

One of a commonly cited pair of terms in linguistics (see also LANGUE), introduced by Saussure in the early twentieth century, and usually left untranslated because they have no direct equivalents in English. They are often compared with Chomsky's (1965) distinction between COMPETENCE (q.v.) and PERFORMANCE (q.v.), although they are not identical.

Langue and **parole** both mean 'language', but whereas *langue* refers to it as the general system or CODE of COMMUNICATION within a speech community, *parole* is more specifically the verbal behaviour or UTTERANCES of individuals in speech and writing, the individual instantiations of the *langue*.

As Saussure himself acknowledges, obviously there is a close relationship between the two: utterances are formulated according to the 'rules' of the system; the system itself changes DIACHRONICALLY under the strong influence of the actual USAGE of *parole*. More recent developments in disciplines like socio-linguistics have blurred the distinction: so SPEECH ACTS, hitherto categorized as *parole*, can in fact be regarded as yet another aspect of the linguistic system.

Parole has traditionally been seen as the province of LITERARY LANGUAGE and of STYLE, with the stress on the individual realization or CHOICE of the code. Yet the FORMALISTS argued that literary language was itself a kind of *langue*; and that any work of art as *parole* must be seen in relation to that *langue*, as well as to the language as a whole (see also Widdowson 1983). Stylisticians, in their analysis of *parole*, must inevitably describe any choices or significant features in relation to the *langue*.

paronomasia

From the Gk root *onomasia* 'naming', **paronomasia** is a general RHETORICAL term for word-play, expecially PUNS, involving words that sound similar: e.g. as in jokes or graffiti: *Nuclear food here – fission chips*. So also Hamlet's complex word-play in his cynical ASIDE to Claudius, who addresses him as *cousin* and *son*: *A little more than* kin *and less than* kind! (I.ii).

The importance of language play in everyday language is stressed by Carter (1999), who sees it as an important means of social 'bonding'. COGNITIVE LINGUISTS like Gibbs (1994) would see paronomasia an important **ludic principle**, as part of the 'poeticality' of human thought, fulfilling a basic need of the human species as a whole. (On its significance in language development, see Crystal 1998; on word-play in advertising, see Cook 1992, Tanaka 1994. See also DECONSTRUCTION.)

participle

In GRAMMAR describes a NON-FINITE part of the VERB PHRASE.

A **participle** has two forms: an *-ing* form and an *-ed/en* form (as in *running; jumped; fallen*). These are conventionally known as **present** and **past participles** respectively, but the terminology is inexact and confusing. Strictly, non-finite forms do not show TENSE distinctions, and are not fixed in time. Rather, their distinction is one of ASPECT: the *-ing* form used for actions that are not completed but continuing/continual; the *-ed* form used for actions that are completed. They thus combine with FINITE and AUXILIARY verb forms to make up the PROGRESSIVE ASPECT (e.g. *She is writing a book*) and the PERFECT (*She has written a book*), as well as the PASSIVE VOICE (*The book was written*). They are also often used ADJECTIVALLY as MODIFIERS in the NOUN PHRASE: e.g. *a sneezing elephant*; *a squashed banana*. Such modification is characteristic of traditional POETIC DICTION: *purling brooks; twined flowers*. Some participles have acquired permanent adjective status: e.g. *an interesting/smashing elephant; a bored/disgruntled elephant*. Participle CLAUSES also act as modifiers; so that participles altogether are very common in descriptive writing, e.g.:

> To hear each other's <u>whispered</u> speech;
> <u>Eating</u> the Lotos day by day,
> To watch the <u>crisping</u> ripples on the beach,
> And tender <u>curving</u> lines of creamy spray . . .

> (Tennyson: *Song of the Lotos-Eaters*)

passive

Passive is widely used in GRAMMAR to refer to a subtype of the category VOICE concerned with the relations of SUBJECT and OBJECT and the 'action' expressed by the VERB. It is opposed to the ACTIVE (q.v.).

The active voice is more usual, hence **un**MARKED. Here the grammatical subject of the clause or SENTENCE is the AGENT of the action which is expressed by a TRANSITIVE VERB; and the object has the role of the 'affected' participant, e.g.:

(a) Labour Eurosceptics accuse BBC of bias.

In the **passive voice**, the affected object is the grammatical subject and the agent is expressed in a PREPOSITIONAL PHRASE; the verb form consists of the AUXILIARY verb *be* plus the *-ed* PARTICIPLE, i.e.:

(b) BBC accused of bias by Labour Eurosceptics.

There is obviously a close complementary relationship between active and passive sentences: they appear to have the same PROPOSITIONAL MEANING, to be PARAPHRASES of each other. In some models of GENERATIVE GRAMMAR both types have been seen to be derived from the same DEEP STRUCTURE. Yet equally obviously, the very existence of an apparent grammatical CHOICE means that the passive must have particular CONNOTATIONS of its own.

Its significance lies in its INFORMATIONAL and THEMATIC values. In the unmarked active sentence, the CANONICAL distribution of information is to begin with GIVEN INFORMATION and end with NEW, which is highlighted by END-FOCUS. The subject is normally the point of departure, i.e. the THEME. So in (a) above, *Labour Eurosceptics* is the theme, and the focus naturally falls on the object of his or her criticism. In (b), however, the BBC is thematized, and the focus falls on the AGENT.

It is also possible, however, for the agentive phrase to be omitted, i.e.:

(c) In the Commons today the BBC was accused of bias.

Such passive constructions are extremely useful when the agent, in fact, is not known to the speaker or can only be vaguely defined; the active sentence would force an agent to be expressed e.g.:

(d) In the Commons today someone (many people?) accused the BBC of bias.

In REGISTERS such as scientific writing, for example, where the personal tone is often undesirable and where the agents of actions (the scientists themselves) are not as important as the experiments, etc., the elimination of the 'logical' subject is very useful, as in *When X is added to Y the substance Z is formed*. (See further Biber *et al.* 1999, chs 6 & 11.)

Stylisticians, especially CRITICAL LINGUISTS (q.v.), are interested in the extent to which the CHOICE of active or passive, with the differences of focus and EMPHASIS, affects the PERSPECTIVE of the action so as to influence the reader's or listener's view of events. In other words, the choice can have distinct IDEOLOGICAL implications.

perfect, also perfective

The **perfect** or **perfective** is the traditional term in GRAMMAR for a subtype of the category of ASPECT applied to VERBS: also known as **phase** in the work of Palmer (1979).

Aspect refers to particular ways of viewing the temporal constraints of an activity or event. The PROGRESSIVE (q.v.) indicates whether an action is in progress (*be + ing*): e.g. *She is feeding the elephant*; and the perfect(ive) indicates whether an action is completed (*have + -ed/-en*): e.g. *She has fed the elephant*.

It is difficult to dissociate aspect from TENSE, the verbal category that normally denotes temporal distinctions. *She fed the elephant* marks a past action, but also equally a completed action; *She has fed the elephant* marks a completed action, and hence one that is now past. Some grammars do treat the perfect as a tense. Often the perfect and the **past tense** appear to be used synonymously, both within STANDARD ENGLISH, and between DIALECTS (British and American, for instance):

(a) She handed in her essay this morning.
(b) She has handed in her essay this morning.

Certain ADVERBIALS of time seem more usual with the perfect than with the past tense: cf.

Has she handed it in (yet) (since) (so far)?
Did she hand it in (yesterday) (last week) (on Monday)?

Grammarians usually explain this by suggesting that the perfect has certain connotations: of recent past time, for instance; or of an action completed but with some current 'relevance' still. This does not easily account for examples (a) and (b), however. In such cases the perfect seems to be more EXPRESSIVE in some way, more vivid or immediate.

(See further Biber *et al*. 1999, ch. 6.)

performance

Usually discussed in opposition to COMPETENCE (q.v.), both terms made famous in the GENERATIVE GRAMMAR of Chomsky (1965). They have often been compared with Saussure's dichotomy between PAROLE and LANGUE, but the context of discussion is really quite different.

Chomsky's main stress was on competence, the internalized linguistic knowledge speakers of a language supposedly have, which enables them to construct and interpret an infinite number of grammatically CORRECT SENTENCES. **Performance** was seen as secondary to competence: what we do when we actually speak, i.e. the process of speaking and writing. UTTERANCES may or may not conform to system sentences, because of hesitations, slips of the tongue, etc., all seen as aspects of performance.

Performance was therefore something of a 'rag-bag', yet the development of disciplines like DISCOURSE ANALYSIS, PRAGMATICS, sociolinguistics and SPEECH ACT THEORY led to more serious attention being paid to performance, and so to aspects of linguistic behaviour largely ignored by Chomsky. The dichotomy is now much blurred: the notion of competence extended to a general **communicative** COMPETENCE which incorporates 'rules' based on actual linguistic behaviour in social contexts. Even the 'messiness' or NOISE of slips and hesitations can be seen to have important discourse or INDEXICAL functions. Linguists like Halliday (1978) preferred to drop the distinction between competence and performance altogether, and work with as low a degree of idealization as possible.

performative: ~ verb

Terms introduced by the philosopher J. L. Austin (1961f) as part of a classification of SENTENCES, and which came to be of considerable importance in what is known as SPEECH ACT THEORY.

At first, **performatives** were opposed to CONSTATIVES (q.v.), which are essentially DECLARATIVE SENTENCES, statements which describe a state of affairs and which are 'true' or 'false' (e.g. *Prince Charles is the heir to the throne*). Performatives, however, not only 'say' something, but 'do' something verbally: e.g. *I promise to pay you back tomorrow; I swear I'll be good; I name this ship Good heavens, this is Mumm Cordon Rouge champagne* (advert). What is at issue is not truth and falsehood but degree of successfulness (see FELICITY CONDITIONS).

Austin himself then came to the conclusion that constatives themselves 'do' something, that they are part of some action performed by the speaker. They can be made into performatives by prefixing something like *I tell you/state that* (*Prince Charles is the heir to the throne*). Other linguists after Austin, indeed, favoured an underlying performative clause as part of the DEEP STRUCTURE of all sentences (see Ross 1970; for problems, however, see Allan 1986, II ch. 8).

Austin also refined and expanded his notion of performatives. All the examples quoted so far are marked by a specific **performative verb**, the **first** PERSON PRONOUN and the PRESENT TENSE. Such sentences clearly effect what they utter rhetorically but they are very MARKED. In actual DISCOURSE they would sound formal or authoritative, if obviously unequivocal (e.g. *I forbid you to smoke*); and indeed are more characteristic of ritualistic or institutionalized REGISTERS (cf. also *I hereby pronounce you man and wife*). Nonetheless, Austin's insight into the ACTS we make while speaking was a significant one, and he came to make a threefold distinction between LOCUTIONARY ACT (the physical act of speaking); ILLOCUTIONARY ACT (act performed in saying something); and also PERLOCUTIONARY ACT (act performed as a result of saying something, e.g. persuading).

So performatives take their place under the heading of illocutionary act. Here Austin and others (e.g. Searle 1969†) have argued that all sentences have an ILLOCUTIONARY FORCE which is often indirectly or implicitly expressed, i.e. without an explicit performative verb. So *I'll pay you back tomorrow* can be intended as a promise; *Don't smoke in here* as a prohibition: what Austin calls **primary performatives** (v. **explicit performatives**), and what are also called INDIRECT SPEECH ACTS (q.v.). Interestingly, our ability to understand illocutionary force is shown in INDIRECT SPEECH (q.v.). In reporting sentences like *I'll see you tomorrow*, the reporter must introduce an appropriate performative in the reporting clause, and *promise* is most likely here (see further Leech 1983). With or without performative verbs, illocutionary acts are frequently classified on the basis of explicit performatives as METALANGUAGE, which linguists like Edmondson (1981) and Leech feel is misleading.

For a DECONSTRUCTIONIST critique of performatives and constatives, see Derrida (1977a,b); see further de Man (1979).

periodic sentence; also period

(1) In traditional LITERARY CRITICISM terms since the eighteenth century which describe a COMPLEX SENTENCE in which the MAIN CLAUSE is delayed until the end. A **periodic sentence** can be contrasted with a LOOSE SENTENCE, in which the main clause comes first.

A periodic sentence is supposedly harder for our minds to process, dominated as it is by **left**-BRANCHING (q.v.) structures rather than **right-branching**. As Leech & Short (1981) say we must hold all the elements in memory until we reach the end when we can fit the SUBORDINATE elements to the main point. Periods are especially useful, therefore, for EMPHASIS, or for a CLIMAX. They are generally characteristic of writing rather than speech, and of FORMAL prose styles and kinds of prose in which other syntactic structures are exploited for RHETORICAL effects: e.g. ANTITHESIS and PARALLELISM, e.g.:

> Since then the imaginary night of vengeance must be at last remitted, because it is impossible to live in perpetual hostility, and equally impossible that of two enemies, either should first think himself obliged by justice to submission, it is surely eligible to forgive early.
>
> (Johnson: *The Rambler* no. 125, 1751)

(2) From Gk 'circuit', for Renaissance rhetoricians as for Aristotle **period** referred to a 'circuit' of speech, so any kind of well-rounded sentence, often leading to a climax as in (1). Hence there was a close link between a period and a sense of CLOSURE: giving **period** the still-used sense of full stop. (See further Adamson 1999.)

periphrasis

From Gk 'about-speech' (cf. **circumlocutio(n)** as the Latin equivalent), a statement or phrase which uses more words than are strictly necessary. (See also REDUNDANCY.)

In everyday speech **periphrasis** is associated with politeness and the wish to avoid giving offence. It is often characteristic of EUPHEMISM and JARGON, where unpleasant associations can be avoided: e.g. *young offenders rehabilitation centre* for 'Borstal'; *gone to join the choir invisible* or *turned up his toes* for 'died', etc. It is also associated with FORMAL or elevated styles of speech and writing.

Over the centuries periphrasis has become particularly identified with the descriptive phrases of traditional POETIC DICTION (q.v.): from the Old English KENNINGS (e.g. 'swan-road' = 'sea') to the phrases of eighteenth-century poetry (*finny tribe* = 'fish'; *fleecy care* = 'sheep'). The desire for elaboration and for elevation of the mundane according to the principle of DECORUM, is an important motive. Hackneyed as such **periphrastic** phrases appear when we meet them from poem to poem, on first reading at least they have a distinctive ESTRANGING effect.

perlocutionary: ~ act; ~ effect; ~ force

Terms primarily associated with SPEECH ACT THEORY as developed by Austin (1961), concerned with linguistic ACTS made while speaking which have some social or INTERPERSONAL purpose and effect.

A speech act consists of the LOCUTIONARY ACT (q.v.), i.e. the very act of uttering; the ILLOCUTIONARY ACT (q.v.), which is what is performed through speaking (e.g. making a promise, giving orders, etc.); and the **perlocutionary act**: the effect achieved by the UTTERANCE on the ADDRESSEE through the illocutionary act: e.g. frightening; amusing; persuading; intimidating.

The greatest attention in speech act theory and other disciplines, like PRAG-MATICS, has focussed on the communicative purpose or ILLOCUTIONARY FORCE of utterances rather than on the **perlocutionary effects**, since the former are on the face of it easier to describe. We may intend to insult someone, but the insult may not be perceived as such, and so the effect is lost. In other words, we can't control perlocutionary effects. Illocutionary acts are also more closely tied to specific utterances, and linguistic behaviour generally. Illocutionary acts with PERFORMATIVE VERBS are most clearly understood as such; but even without them many can be recognized: cf.

I promise to see you tomorrow.
I will see you tomorrow.

and the PARAPHRASE in INDIRECT DISCOURSE:

She promised to see him tomorrow.

However, such formulae as *By saying X speaker convinces/persuades hearer that P* . . . (Leech 1983), which seem like paraphrases, are not easily converted into direct utterances. What is the speaker likely to have actually said? Perhaps it was a whole complex of illocutions or interchange that convinced the hearer. It is noteworthy that examples commonly given of perlocutionary acts are all in the **third** PERSON, not the first person, as with illocutionary acts: e.g. *She flattered him by talking of his great achievements*. Such sentences are more akin to NARRATIVE REPORT (q.v.) than indirect discourse. Moreover, perlocutionary effects can be directly attributable to non-linguistic behaviour. A considerable amount of NON-VERBAL COMMUNICATION, such as looks and gestures, for instance, has characteristically a **perlocutionary force**: threatening; amusing; boring; annoying; consoling; embarrassing; irritating. All these actions have been listed as potential (verbal) perlocutionary acts.

It is perhaps partly because of this that linguists such as Leech have argued that the study of perlocutionary acts is not properly part of pragmatics; yet it is difficult to know where else they should be studied (psycholinguistics?). In any case, it is not always easy to distinguish between illocutionary and perlocutionary force. Certain kinds of illocutionary acts, despite the problems noted above, are specifically intended by the speaker to get the addressee to do something (e.g. ordering; requesting); complimenting usually ENTAILS pleasing, etc. Certain ritualistic performatives have inextricable perlocutionary implications: to name a ship is to name it, and to baptize a baby is to baptize it.

One discipline that has traditionally concerned itself with perlocutionary effects has been RHETORIC: particularly with the effects of persuasion and of moving the emotions. But again, as Lanser (1981) states, the rhetorical impact comes from the totality of a performance: the illocutionary force and the PRO-POSITIONAL content of all the sentences in the text, together with the speech act CONTEXT and a whole host of variables which depend on the participants' knowledge and values, etc.

persona; personal pronoun; person

(1) **Persona**, meaning 'mask', is the Latin term for (dramatic) character following the masking conventions of classical Greek drama (see also DRAMATIS PERSONA). It has been borrowed into LITERARY CRITICISM to refer to the ROLE constructed by the NARRATOR or IMPLIED AUTHOR of a text: the persona of a rejected lover in Elizabethan sonnet sequences, for instance; or the meditative solitary walker in Wordsworth's poetry. For Yeats the concept of the persona or 'mask' is of considerable importance in his theory of poetic art.

(2) The term was adopted in Latin GRAMMARS for the classification of the so-called **personal pronouns**, and of VERBS. As Lyons (1977) says, the language event was thus viewed as a drama, in which the principal DEICTIC role was played by the speaker or ADDRESSER (**first person**: *I, we*), and the other important role by the ADDRESSEE (**second person**: *you*); all other roles (i.e. people who may or may not be present) by the **third person**: *he, she, it, they.*

(3) These terms have been taken over into NARRATIVE theory. A **first person** NARRATION is one in which a character tells his or her own story: what Genette (1972) terms auto DIEGETIC; the **third person** narration is one in which an IMPLIED AUTHOR as NARRATOR tells a story about a CHARACTER (**heterodiegetic**), by far the commonest type of narration. In the former, the narrator is inside the story; in the latter, outside. (See further Stanzel 1984.)

personification

A FIGURE OF SPEECH or TROPE in which an INANIMATE object, ANIMATE non-human, or ABSTRACT quality is given human attributes.

Personification is particularly associated with LITERARY, especially POETIC, LANGUAGE, e.g. lines like Gray's

> Here rests the head upon the lap of Earth
> A youth to fortune and to fame unknown.
> Fair Science frowned not on his humble birth,
> And Melancholy marked him for her own

(Elegy Written in a Country Churchyard)

In TRANSFORMATIONAL GRAMMAR (TG) sentences involving personification would be strictly DEVIANT: the normal SELECTIONAL RULES for NOUNS and VERBS are violated. Yet when personification occurs in ordinary speech we are often hardly aware of it: in METAPHORS, IDIOMS and proverbs (e.g. *Time flies; Necessity is the Mother of Invention; the hand on a clock; the leg of a table*, etc.); and a REGISTERS such as journalism. Here especially, ships, planes and countries are regularly personified as female: at least, they co-occur with the PRONOUN *she.* (See Wales 1996, ch. 6.) Personification adds vividness to political RHETORIC: inflation *eating up* profits for instance.

(See also PROSOPOPOEIA.)

perspective

Used by some critics of the novel (e.g. Fowler 1977; Genette 1972; Stanzel 1984; Uspensky 1973) to refer to what is also known more commonly as FOCALIZATION (q.v.) or POINT OF VIEW (q.v.).

Perspective is a mode of controlling INFORMATION according to whether or not it is viewed through the consciousness of the NARRATOR or (usually main) CHARACTERS. So Fowler, following Uspensky, distinguishes between **internal** and **external perspective**. In the former, the WORLD of the novel is filtered through the thoughts and impressions of the characters; very obviously in modes like INTERIOR MONOLOGUE and SOLILOQUY, but also through FREE INDIRECT DISCOURSE and NARRATIVE REPORT. With the external perspective it is the narrator's point of view which prevails, and the characters' inner thoughts are not revealed to us.

It must be noted that most novels seem to offer some kind of inner perspective. The external perspective seems MARKED, and is often exploited for specific effects of ESTRANGEMENT or playfulness within the more general 'open' context. Not to be allowed to know what characters are thinking can heighten a sense of their mystery or inscrutability: we can contrast Hardy's presentation of Tess with that of Alec d'Urberville, for instance.

phallocentrism, also phallologocentrism

Terms used within the disciplines of FEMINIST CRITICISM and DECONSTRUCTION particularly since the 1970s to describe any work which portrays a PERSPECTIVE or IDEOLOGY heavily biassed towards the male's, to the subordination and even exclusion of the female's. The writings of Hélène Cixous (e.g. 1975) can be particularly noted for their exposure of **phallocentrism**, in the psychoanalytical theory of Freud, for example. It also pervades many literary works. In Lawrence's novels, for instance, the voices and actions of the women characters are frequently dominated or overshadowed by those of the men.

phatic: ~ communion; ~ function

Phatic communion (Gk *phasis* 'utterance') owes its origin and popularization to the work of the anthropologist Malinowski (1923). He was struck by the fact that not only the English talked about the weather, but that sociable talk with very little meaningful content is found in many languages, his own studies centring on those of the Pacific islands. Other terms are sometimes found: e.g. **ritual equilibrium** (Stubbs 1983).

It is therefore simply a 'verbal signalling', a highly REDUNDANT means of establishing social bonds between people, who may be strangers to each other. As Leech (1983) says, there ought to be a **phatic maxim** in conversation: 'Avoid silence' or 'Keep talking'. Greetings and other such FORMULAS (e.g. *How are you?*)

are typically used with a **phatic** FUNCTION, a term associated with Jakobson's (1960) model of the SPEECH EVENT, and its concomitant functions of language. The phatic function establishes and maintains CONTACT, keeps the CHANNELS of communication open.

Precisely because it lacks informative value, phatic language is not frequently found in LITERATURE, even drama. In the plays of Pinter, however, especially his short sketches, phatic utterances are FOREGROUNDED for humorous or 'realistic' effects.

phenomenology; phenomenological criticism

(1) Although we tend to use *phenomenon* in ordinary speech for anything which is remarkable or rare, in its technical or philosophical sense the word refers to something in the outside world which is perceived by the mind or the senses. **Phenomenology** in twentieth-century philosophy is particularly associated with the work of the German thinker Husserl, who denied the independent existence of objects in the external world; they are rather mediated through our consciousness. (See further Eagleton 1983; for a critique, see Derrida 1967a.)

(2) **Phenomenological criticism**, which is particularly associated with the so-called Geneva school of the 1940s and 1950s, is also concerned with the relations between object (the TEXT) and consciousness: the author's, as manifested in the text itself, in its THEMES and IMAGERY. The WORLD of the text takes its form and IDEOLOGY from the consciousness of the author.

In its concentration on the immanence of the text, and its disregard for historical context, such criticism resembles NEW CRITICISM, and indeed phenomenology influenced critics like Wellek; yet it differs from New Criticism in its concentration on CONTENT at the expense of FORM. Husserl himself inclined to an INTENTIONALIST approach to meaning, which again, the New Critics opposed.

The notion of consciousness was taken up by the Polish theorist Ingarden in the 1930s, but with particular reference to the READER. (See Ingarden 1973.) In this respect Ingarden's work was very influential on later RECEPTION THEORY (q.v.), as developed by Iser (1971f) in particular. Literary texts only fully exist in his view with the active participation of the reader: they require 'concretization'. (See also INDETERMINACY. See further Lentricchia 1980, ch. 3.)

philology; philological: ~ stylistics; ~ circle

(1) Nowadays **philology** is reserved in language studies at tertiary and research level for the comparative or historical study of languages, mainly on the evidence of written texts, established on a learned and scientific basis in the nineteenth century. But the term (from Gk 'love of learning') has also traditionally been applied to the study and criticism of literature.

(2) Terms like **literary philology** and **philological stylistics** therefore have a decidedly old-fashioned ring to them, but they are associated particularly with

the work of the European scholar Spitzer (e.g. 1948), widely regarded as an important forerunner of the 'modern' STYLISTICS of the 1960s. For Spitzer, impressionistic judgments of the style and language of a text should be avoided, or at least checked against the objective linguistic evidence that comes from a detailed examination of linguistic features, and from a comparison with other texts if necessary.

(3) Spitzer's concept of the **philological circle** in one sense reflects the kind of process that stylisticians commonly perform in their analysis and INTERPRETA-TION of a text: constantly moving between hypothesis, linguistic analysis and critical explanation. (For another 'circle' of interpretation, see HERMENEUTIC.) Yet Spitzer's ultimate aim is to find the 'inward life-centre', the creative principle of the text. (See also EXPRESSIVE STYLISTICS. See further Freeman 1970.)

(4) Adamson (1998) makes the case for a **New Philology** which will combine stylistics with NEW HISTORICISM in the form of a newly historicized re-engagement with the language that the readers of earlier periods were reading, and with which their acts of interpretation were conducted. As with any DIACHRONIC perspective however, and as with a subject like HISTORICAL PRAGMATICS, it is hard to avoid present values and interpretations, and a 'dialogue' is inevitable between original and accrued meanings.

phonaesthesia; phonaestheme

Phonaesthesia is the study of the EXPRESSIVENESS of sounds, particularly those sounds which are felt to be appropriate to the meaning of their LEXEMES: also known as **phonaestasia, protosemanticism, secondary** ONOMATOPOEIA and SOUND SYMBOLISM.

The term **phonaestheme** (Firth 1957) is therefore given to the sounds, or clusters themselves, which, although not separable units of meaning, function rather like MORPHEMES in that they form **phonaesthetic** networks with recurring 'meanings'. Alternative terms are **psychomorphs** or **submorphemic differentials** (Bolinger 1965). As Allan (1986) notes, in words like *flail, flap, flare, flush, flick, fling, flop* and *flounce* the initial *fl-* suggests sudden movement; in *bash, crash, smash* and *thrash, -ash* suggests violent impact.

An interest in phonaesthesia goes back to Plato's *Cratylus*, in which the whole question of the relations between name and 'object' is discussed. (See also CRATYLISM.) While linguists are generally agreed that language is mostly arbitrary, non-ICONIC, nonetheless whatever the origin of individual words, it is clear that many words within different languages can be grouped together in this way, and are felt to be associated by ordinary speakers. It can be noted that most English phonaesthemes are in monosyllabic words, and seem 'Germanic' in origin. A poet like Hopkins, interested in both ETYMOLOGY and expressiveness makes great play with phonaesthetic effects:

And all is seared with trade; bleared, smeared with toil;
And wears man's smudge and shares man's smell

(*God's Grandeur*)

The study of expressive PHONETIC effects in literature is sometimes called **phonostylistics**.

(See further Nash 1986; Wales 1990.)

phonetics; phoneme; phonology

Phonetics is the well established term for the technical study of the vocal aspect of language: speech sounds and how they are produced (**articulatory phonetics**), transmitted (**acoustic phonetics**) and perceived (**auditory phonetics**); also PROSODIC features of speech, such as INTONATION and STRESS.

Out of the numerous sounds that our speech organs can produce a limited number are used significantly in each language to form words: these distinctive functional sounds are known as **phonemes**. Replace /b/ by /p/ in the word *big*, for example, and a word with a completely different meaning results. (See also DIFFERENCE.) Not everyone may pronounce /b/ in exactly the same way, and there are variations according to its position in a word: e.g. /bɪg/ v. /rʌb/ *rub*; but these so-called **allophonic variations** make no difference to the meanings of words. That aspect of phonetics concerned specifically with the study of the inventory of phonemes within a language, their patterns and distribution, is known as **phonology** (or **phonemics**). (See further Gimson 1989.)

Phonology also describes the system of sounds itself, whether of a language or DIALECT, etc. So we can speak of the phonology of English, or of the Durham dialect, or of Alfred's ninth-century prose. We also speak of phonology as a level (**phonological**) of language, which is the EXPRESSION or realization of language in its spoken FORM.

In POETIC LANGUAGE we are often aware of the conscious FOREGROUNDING of phonology through the COHESIVE patterns of REPETITION of sound, by ALLITERATION, ASSONANCE, PHONAESTHESIA and RHYME, etc. Also characteristic of poetry is the kind of phonological DEVIATION due to ELISIONS: of initial, medial or final sounds (*'gainst; ne'er; oft*, etc.). (See also APHESIS; APOCOPE. See further Cummings & Simmons 1983, ch. 1; Leech 1969, ch. 6.)

phonocentrism

See LOGOCENTRISM.

pidgin

A hybrid CONTACT language which is specially created for the purposes of communication, e.g. in trading, between groups of people who do not know each others' language. **Pidgins** partly combine the features of one language (e.g. the LEXIS of English) with those of another (e.g. the GRAMMAR of African or Chinese

VERNACULARS), but also develop their own distinctive SYNTAX, often very simple in its SURFACE form. So from West African Pidgin English (WAPE) quoted in Traugott & Pratt (1980, ch. 9):

> Som boi i bin bi fo som fan kontri fo insai afrika
> Some boy he (past)-be in some fine country inside Africa

The origin of the word 'pidgin' is uncertain and controversial: it may or may not derive from a corruption of the word 'business', as is popularly supposed (see further Todd 1974).

Over a period of time some pidgins have become well established in their communities, being especially useful as a LINGUA FRANCA. WAPE is used in popular oral literature and sermons; Neo-Melanesian or Tok Pisin has rapidly acquired the status of an official language in Papua New Guinea. In some cases, as in Haiti and Jamaica, a pidgin becomes the mother tongue (i.e. transmitted as a first language from parents to children), and becomes what is technically known in sociolinguistics as a CREOLE (q.v.).

plain style, also low style

The **plain** or **low** STYLE is one of a set of three terms (the others are GRAND or **high**, and MIDDLE) formalized in classical RHETORIC and influential on literary composition through to the Renaissance and beyond.

According to the principle of DECORUM (q.v.), style should be fitted to subject matter, GENRE, characterization or situation. The plain style was therefore considered appropriate for the lower classes and for comedy, satire, exposition and NARRATIVE. Switching from one style to another within one and the same work was also possible, to reflect shifts in tone, etc. (See further Gilbert 1979.) The plain style approached colloquial speech in its linguistic features and unpretentiousness, yet was generally more 'artful' in its construction than speech, if less rhetorical than the middle and grand styles.

The style of Chaucer's comic *fabliau* tales (e.g. *The Miller's* and *The Reeve's*) are often cited as examples of the plain style, yet one suspects that Chaucer's style here, in line with his general treatment of his material, is far more sophisticated than that of the originals on which his tales are based.

plaisir

See JOUISSANCE.

ploce

Pronounced /ˈpləʊsiː/ this FIGURE of RHETORIC appears to be recorded with two uses:

(1) Some sixteenth-century handbooks define it as the use of a proper name to refer to a person and his or her qualities: as in *Hamlet* (V.ii):

> Was't Hamlet wronged Laertes? Never Hamlet.
> If Hamlet from himself be ta'en away,
> And when he's not himself does wrong Laertes,
> Then Hamlet does it not, Hamlet denies it . . .

(2) More commonly **ploce** is defined as a figure of REPETITION: words repeated intermittently within a line or sentence (see also EPANALEPSIS). We can note the PUN on his own name in Donne's *A Hymn to God the Father*, in a context of other noteworthy repetition in his self-scrutiny:

> Wilt thou forgive that sin, where I begun,
> Which was my sin, though it were done before?
> Wilt thou forgive that sin through which I run,
> And do run still, though still I do deplore?
> When thou hast done, thou hast not done,
> For I have more . . .

plosive, also stop

In PHONETICS **plosive** describes a type of consonant articulation.

There is a complete closure at some point in the mouth behind which air pressure builds up and is then released 'explosively'. It is easiest to hear this for the BILABIAL plosives /b/ (VOICED) or /p/ (VOICELESS), as in *Peter Piper picked a peck of pickled pepper*; other plosives are the ALVEOLAR /t/ and /d/, and the VELAR /k/ and /g/.

plot

A very commonly used term in LITERARY CRITICISM and NARRATOLOGY, but one which is extremely ambiguous.

(1) On the face of it **plot** seems easy enough to define, since in ordinary usage it means what the *COD* defines it as: 'plan of main events or topics in play, poem, novel, etc.'. So we can usually tell someone the plot of *Hamlet* or *Oliver Twist*, which means summarizing the action essentially. As Stubbs (1983) says, the word implies FICTION since we don't normally talk of the 'plot' of a newspaper article or scientific article; rather we use *summary* in these instances.

To the average person it is the element of 'action' which might most spring to mind, and the word is often used synonymously with STORY (q.v.; but see also below, *passim*). Brooks (1984) notes how many people read books for their plots: they talk of 'good' and 'bad' plots, 'simple' or 'complicated'; 'exciting' or 'dull'; some books, indeed, may have 'no plot' to them. Certain fictional GENRES are popularly associated with plot in this sense: folk-tales, melodrama and thrillers, for instance; versus STREAM OF CONSCIOUSNESS WRITING. Indeed, the word plot, as Kennedy (1983) says, commonly has the CONNOTATIONS of 'intrigue' that we associate with plot in another of its senses (as in *Gunpowder Plot*).

One implication behind this is that plot involves more than simply the stringing together of actions, but that reader and author alike are aware of relations between the events, particularly cause and effect. This was how Forster defined plot in 1927: a 'story' was a NARRATIVE of events arranged chronologically, whereas a plot was also a narrative, but with the emphasis on causality (e.g. *The clock struck one, the mouse ran down*). On a larger scale, it is easy to see how a pattern of causality within the frame of a novel can take on ethical implications. (See also Barthes's ACTIONAL and HERMENEUTIC CODES.)

It is the sense of pattern, of 'plan', that has traditionally been focussed on in literary criticism, since Aristotle's extensive discussion in his *Poetics* of plot (Gk *mythos*) as one of the six elements of tragedy. He was interested in the different orders or arrangements of incidents, and it is to him that we owe some commonly used terms and concepts which identify different plot elements: e.g. PERIPETEIA ('reversal') and **anagnorisis** ('recognition'). An interest in plot structure and plot typology on the basis of CONTENT has been maintained ever since (see Chatman 1978 for a useful survey).

Quite a different approach to plot typology was introduced with the **Russian FORMALISTS** in the early years of this century and continued with the (French) STRUCTURALISTS like Todorov, Brémond and Greimas (see also MORPHOLOGY; NARRATIVE GRAMMAR). What attracted Propp (1928), for instance, in his analysis of the plots of Russian folk-tales, was the basic similarity in structures of many of them in terms of character ROLE and significant actions (FUNCTIONS).

(2) It is precisely because of the Formalist and Structuralist interest in narratives that the definition of plot becomes more complicated; or rather, it is because of attempts to render key terms from Russian and French into English that the term **plot** (and *story*) becomes confusingly ambiguous.

The Formalists made a distinction in a narrative between FABULA (q.v.) and SJUŽET (q.v.): the abstracted chronological or logical ordering of events v. the actual sequence of events as narrated: DEEP V. SURFACE STRUCTURE, so to speak. These were aligned with the French terms HISTOIRE (q.v.) and DISCOURS (q.v.) of Benveniste (1966); but because the latter is itself ambiguous, the term RÉCIT is sometimes used to render *sjužet*. As the entries reveal, the rendering of all these terms into English is problematic.

It is in this connection, however, that the term plot is often used: as an equivalent or rendering of *sjužet* (e.g. Chatman 1978; van Dijk 1972; Elam 1980), and meaning something like 'story-as-discoursed' (see Brooks 1984; Chatman 1978).

But there are some discrepancies between the concept of *sjužet* and the traditional home-grown uses of plot in (1). For Elam (1980), for example, *sjužet* will include 'omissions, changes in sequence, flashbacks, incidental comments', etc. But is this what we ordinarily mean by plot? Asked to recount the plot of *Hamlet* or *Oliver Twist*, we are hardly likely to include incidental comments, only details considered highly significant. Indeed, it is perfectly possible to summarize a plot in one sentence or a (set of) PROPOSITIONS (e.g. *In 'Pride and Prejudice' Elizabeth Bennett and Mr Darcy begin by disliking each other but end up getting married*); and propositions indeed are the bases of narrative grammars. Moreover, given that we also can recount the plot of a film or play as well as a novel, there is a sense in which plot can be seen less as a surface/*discours* phenomenon than a 'deeper' one (since *fabula* is the basic stuff of film as well as verbal narrative). It is interesting in this connection that Fowler's (1977) discussion of plot comes in a section on the deep structure of novels. If plot is to be seen abstractedly as a 'level' of narrative, then it seems best placed between *sjužet* and *fabula*, rather than identified with either.

pluralism

(1) **Pluralism** can be applied to any discipline in which a variety of approaches or theories is applied, e.g. linguistics and LITERARY CRITICISM.

But it has become increasingly common for an individual teacher or critic to specialize in one predominant theory: RELEVANCE THEORY within PRAGMATICS, for example; NEW HISTORICISM within LITERARY THEORY. The motivation behind this may well be that it is better to know one theory thoroughly than many theories superficially; or that this is less damaging to one's health. As Eagleton (1983) puts it: 'trying to combine structuralism, phenomenology and psycho-analysis is more likely to lead to a nervous breakdown than to a brilliant literary career'.

Yet many scholars do adopt a pluralist, eclectic approach, perhaps believing that no one theory can provide all the answers, and that there is a lot to be gained from combining the best of several approaches. Certainly, developments within linguistics since the 1960s led to a reaction against a narrow theoretical perspective centred on 'system' and COMPETENCE, and opened up avenues of investigation which place language firmly in a rich sociocultural context. And as the entry for STYLISTICS reveals, this discipline, from its rise in the 1960s, has typically absorbed many ideas from neighbouring subject areas such as linguistics, DISCOURSE ANALYSIS and POETICS, in response to the nature of its subject matter, the multi-levelled discourses of literary and non-literary language. Hence stylisticians like Fowler and Leech & Short have inevitably in their textbooks covered a wide range of concepts drawn from as wide a range of theories.

(2) Leech & Short (1981) themselves discuss **pluralism** not so much in terms of diverse viewpoints but as part of a discussion about the relations between FORM and CONTENT, and the MONIST (q.v.) v. DUALIST (q.v.) approaches. The pluralist approach, which they favour, is a kind of compromise, since there is not just 'meaning' but various kinds of meaning, distinguished according to different FUNCTIONS, as in Halliday's grammatical theory (see Halliday 1985).

poetic diction

A very commonly used phrase in LITERARY CRITICISM to describe a kind of LEXIS used in poetry but which rarely occurs outside it.

One motivation for the existence of **poetic diction** is the recurring belief that POETIC LANGUAGE is or should be 'different' from other discourses. Poets today prefer to search out the colloquialisms and plain words of speech, but up until the early years of the twentieth century ARCHAISMS and FORMAL Latinate lexis were common in poetry, along with poetic RHETORICAL devices such as APOSTROPHE and PERSONIFICATION: words like *maiden* for *girl*; *billows* for *sea*; *bough* for *branch*; *vernal* for *Spring*, etc. By the rhetorical principle of DECORUM such a diction was felt to be appropriate to a GENRE which elevated and intensified aspects of experience, DE-FAMILIARIZED them.

However, the process of de-familiarization can itself become familiarized, or AUTOMATIZED. Poetic NEOLOGISMS and COLLOCATIONS are readily seized upon by the next generation of poets, the forces of convention pulling against those of innovation. Poetic diction therefore particularly describes those LEXICAL ITEMS which become part of a stock vocabulary of poetry, recurring from one poet's work to another. So critics like Groom (1955) have traced the transmission of a poetic diction from Spenser in the sixteenth century to Bridges in the twentieth. ADJECTIVE (as EPITHET) and NOUN combinations are the most frequent, the adjectives often displaying AFFIXATION, by -*y* or -*ing* or -*ed*: e.g. *purling brooks*; *honied flowers*.

In the eighteenth century such a diction became markedly frequent in poetry, so that the phrase itself is often particularly associated with that period. The adjective and noun combinations are chiefly PERIPHRASES: ordinary words, considered too 'low' for poetry, are replaced by circumlocutory phrases of descriptive epithet and generic noun: e.g. *finny tribe* ('fish'); *feather'd tribe* ('birds').

It is interesting to compare the poetic diction of this period, so pervasive and standardized, with that of the OE period, which was similarly conventional and periphrastic (see FORMULA; KENNING).

poetic: ~ language; ~ function

In LITERARY CRITICISM since classical times the focus of attention has most frequently centred on the language of poetry. In the analysis of LITERARINESS, of ways in which LITERARY LANGUAGE may be said to be different from, or similar to, non-literary language, it is **poetic language** which is seen as the most significant discourse.

Poetic language is popularly regarded as the most CREATIVE of discourses, original in its ideas and inventive in its FORMS. (See also POETIC LICENCE.) Our tolerance of DEVIATION is very high in poetry: we have almost come to expect striking METAPHORS, unusual COLLOCATIONS, irregular WORD ORDER, etc., as we sense the poet striving after fit expression. Not that creative language is confined solely to poetry; but in poetic discourse unusual words and structures, and phrases rich in CONNOTATIONS, seem most heavily concentrated. (But see also POETIC DICTION.)

It is to the **Russian** FORMALISTS and PRAGUE SCHOOL linguists in the early decades of this century that we owe much of the theory of poetic language that has proved influential on POETICS and STYLISTICS, given added impetus through the work of Roman Jakobson. One main thesis is that the characteristic POETIC FUNCTION consists in FOREGROUNDING and ESTRANGING language and meaning consciously and creatively against the BACKGROUND of non-literary language, by devices of deviation and also REPETITION or PARALLELISM. For Jakobson, patterns of repetition, on all levels of sound, syntax, lexis and meaning, are the most important feature of poetic language, in many languages if not all (see EQUIVALENCE). An obvious example is poetic METRE, which can be seen as foregrounded against the natural RHYTHM of speech, regularized into repetitive patterns. It is metre which distinguishes poetry most obviously from prose.

The East European critical focus on the formal features of poetry arises quite naturally out of a belief that this, in fact, is what poetry is 'about': that poetic language is SELF-REFERENTIAL and perceptible in a way that non-literary language is not. The meaning of a poem comes as much from the form as from the CONTENT, which in any case is created within the poem. This WORLD autonomy, and lack of 'proper' SPEECH ACT relevance has been commented on by others; yet it must not be overstressed. Many poets from the Anglo-Saxon clerics to Blake and Wilfrid Owen have seen their work as fulfilling an important social or ethical function. What Lotman (1971) aptly calls the 'semantic saturation' of a poem comes as much from the INFORMATION (in the technical sense) of the different linguistic levels as also from its INTERTEXTUAL and INTERSUBJECTIVE relations with other texts and (social and cultural) knowledge at large. And critics as diverse as Johnson, Wordsworth and Eliot have argued for the suitability of poetry for themes universal and permanent; and the MEDIUM also best suited for intense emotion.

The EMOTIVE FUNCTION or meaning of poetic language, celebrated in Wordsworth's Preface to the *Lyrical Ballads,* was stressed by I. A. Richards in the 1920s and 1930s, and taken up by the NEW CRITICS. Through its IMAGERY or SYMBOLISM and rhythm, etc., the function of poetic language was to arouse the feelings of its readers or listeners in a way that scientific language, mainly REFERENTIAL, did not. This is a very sweeping generalization: registers of propaganda like political oratory and advertising exploit RHETORIC for emotive ends; conversely, poetic language has referential meaning like any other discourse.

poetic licence

The conflicting tendencies of convention and innovation noted under POETIC LANGUAGE and POETIC DICTION come together in the traditional concept of **poetic licence**.

In one sense the term suggests 'freedom', and generally poetic language has been marked at different periods and by different poets by a high degree of CREATIVE DEVIATION from the linguistic NORMS of grammar, lexis and meaning. But the term as it is usually applied refers to particular kinds of deviations: those which have become conventionalized, re-used by generations of poets often as simple technical devices to fit METRICAL requirements, and often also sanctioned in RHETORIC. PHONOLOGICAL licences, for example, commonly involve the ELISION of syllables: initially (APHESIS: *'gainst*); medially (SYNCOPE: *e'er*) and finally (APOCOPE: *oft*). A common SYNTACTIC licence is that of unusual WORD ORDER (HYPERBATON): e.g. OBJECT before VERB, as in Cowper's

> God moves in a mysterious way
> His <u>wonders</u> to perform . . .
> Ye fearful saints, <u>fresh courage</u> take . . . (*Olney Hymns*)

(See further Leech 1969, chs 1, 2, 3.)

poetics

(1) The term suggests that it should be concerned with the art or theory of poetry, and indeed it has commonly been so since classical times (e.g. Horace's *Ars Poetica*). Yet etymologically **poetics**, like poetry, means simply 'making', so that it can be concerned with the art of any GENRE. Aristotle's *Poetics*, for instance, the most celebrated example, discusses the art of drama and epic, but not specifically poetry.

Poetics as the 'science' of literature particularly developed as a discipline in the twentieth century. In Eastern Europe, the work of the **Russian** FORMALISTS and the PRAGUE SCHOOL linguists (including Jakobson) which flourished after the First World War was particularly significant for the understanding of LITERARINESS and POETIC LANGUAGE. It also illustrates one distinct tendency of modern poetics, that it is very much influenced by linguistic theory or theories.

The Formalists (e.g. Shklovsky (1925) and Propp (1928)) were also pioneers in the systematic analysis of NARRATIVE structure, and influential therefore on what came to be called the **poetics of the novel** or the **poetics of fiction** (see also NARRATIVE GRAMMAR; NARRATOLOGY). West European critics like Barthes and Todorov in the 1950s and 1960s and later assimilated their ideas with STRUCTURALISM to produce a discipline primarily concerned with identifying the essential properties or conventions of form of all texts rather than individual ones (as in LITERARY CRITICISM). Naturally theoretical, there is not INTERPRETATION or EVALUATION of texts, although a considerable interest, under the influence of GENERATIVE GRAMMAR and READER RESPONSE criticism, in the activity of interpretation itself, and notions of LITERARY COMPETENCE.

The Bakhtinian critics Morson & Emerson (1990) nicely propose **prosaics** as against poetics: to refer to a theory of literature that privileges prose in general and the novel in particular; and as a form of thinking that presumes the importance of the everyday and the ordinary.

In drama, despite, or because of, the precedence of Aristotle, a modern poetics has still to emerge.

(2) Also to be noted is the narrower use of the term in collocations like 'a **poetics** of point of view/expressiveness'; 'Dostoevsky's poetics'. Here it means simply 'a theory (of form)'.

(See also COGNITIVE POETICS; GENERATIVE POETICS; PSYCHO-POETICS; STRUCTURALIST POETICS. See further Bierwisch 1970; Culler 1975; Jakobson 1960; Todorov 1971, 1981. For a critique of Jakobsonian poetics, see Fowler 1981, ch. 9.)

point of view

One of the most commonly discussed concepts in twentieth-century criticism of the novel. Discussion is complicated, however, by the fact that **point of view** can be defined in more than one way; and also by the fact that novels themselves reveal a variety of techniques not easily classifiable.

(1) Like the related term, PERSPECTIVE (q.v.), **point of view** in the basic AESTHETIC sense refers to 'angle of vision', as in art and film theory: so the angle of vision or perception by which the events of a novel are narrated and the information presented. When the FOCALIZER or **reflector** is the AUTHOR as NARRATOR, then the artistic sense of perspective is particularly noticeable, in descriptions of setting as ORIENTATION: for example, a scene described in close-up, or as from a distance. So Hardy describes the Vale of Blackmoor as from a height and with an artist's eye:

> Here, in the valley, the world seems to be constructed upon a smaller and more delicate scale; the fields are mere paddocks, so reduced that from this height their hedgerows appear a network of dark green threads overspreading the paler green of the grass. The atmosphere is languorous, and is so tinged with azure that what artists call the middle distance partakes also of that hue, while the horizon beyond is of the deepest ultramarine.
>
> (*Tess of the D'Urbervilles*)

(2) Even in ordinary speech we use **point of view** in the figurative sense of the way of looking at a matter, rather than a scene, through someone's 'eyes', or thoughts. So in novels with an OMNISCIENT NARRATOR or IMPLIED AUTHOR, he or she will provide the prevailing point of view (as in Fielding's or Jane Austen's novels); what Chatman (1990) calls **slant**. In **first** PERSON NARRATION the prevailing perspective is usually that of the main character-as-narrator (*David Copperfield; Catcher in the Rye*): Chatman's **filter**. Yet in many such memoir-novels there may well be a double perspective revealed: of the main character as maturer or wiser than the younger self whose adventures are related.

With the twentieth-century development of kinds of fiction that moved away from the omniscient narrator directly into the consciousness of the characters themselves, as in STREAM OF CONSCIOUSNESS WRITING and INTERIOR MONOLOGUE, point of view has become increasingly internalized, and the main events quite strikingly presented through the impressions of the characters themselves.

As critics like Genette (1972) and Chatman (1978) have stressed, it has therefore become increasingly important to distinguish point of view from VOICE, i.e. who is speaking the narrative. The centre of consciousness in Joyce's *Portrait of the Artist*, for example, is Stephen Dedalus; yet the teller is the traditional implied author. With modes of thought presentation, however, (FREE) (IN)DIRECT, etc., telling and perceiving are very closely intertwined: here the mode of narration simultaneously allows us to see things from the character's point of view.

(3) **Point of view** in the figurative sense entails not only the presence of a conceptualizing character or focalizer, but also a particular way of conceptualizing: a WORLD-VIEW or IDEOLOGY, whether the focalizer is a character or an implied author. With strong centres of consciousness the model of reality presented in fiction will inevitably be subjectively coloured or evaluated, even politically or ethically (e.g. *Gulliver's Travels; Lolita; Confessions of Felix Krull*); but it is impossible for any discourse not to reveal some sort of ideological STANCE. (See also MIND STYLE.) Moreover, since it is perfectly possible for a novel to contain more than one focalizer, the perspective shifting from one character to another, or from narrator to character, a number of different ideological perspectives may be revealed: as in Dickens's *Hard Times* or Joyce's *Ulysses*: what Bakhtin and others would call DIALOGISM (q.v.) or POLYPHONY (q.v.).

(4) An aspect that has been particularly developed relates **point of view** to the larger DISCOURSE situation of narrator–text–reader. (See, e.g., Fowler 1977 on MODALITY; Lanser 1981.) So on the ideological level the implied author may communicate explicitly or implicitly to the readers a sense of his or her ATTITUDE to the story narrated ('Dickens', for instance, on the social abuses of his time); and this affects TONE: the use of satire or IRONY, for example. Or the narrator may reveal a particular attitude to the readers: of deference, friendliness, etc. In this sense point of view clearly applies to any kind of discourse, non-literary as well as fictional.

There have been many attempts to classify point of view in fiction. Two attempts much discussed are those by Friedman (1955) and Stanzel (1971); see also Uspensky (1973). For surveys of the subject, see further Fludernik 1993; Fowler 1996, ch. 9; Simpson 1993.

politeness theory

A very popular theory in PRAGMATICS currently, in FEMINIST LINGUISTICS and in stylistic analyses of dramatic and fictional dialogue, **politeness theory** has largely been developed by the cultural anthropologists Brown and Levinson out of SPEECH ACT THEORY and the sociologist Goffman's work on FACE (q.v.) since the late 1970s (see particularly 1978, 1987). Also influential has been the work of Leech (1983) on **politeness maxims**, as a social refinement of Grice's CO-OPERATIVE PRINCIPLE.

Somewhat paradoxically, however, Brown & Levinson's theory presents a rather self-interested view of politeness; it's not just a question of public manners or the avoidance of giving offence. As Short summarizes it (1996), if we don't pay attention to the 'face' or public image needs of others, we are unlikely to be very expert in getting things done. So we avoid tactics which threaten face.

One set of politeness strategies works by the appeal to **positive** face, the speaker's positive self-image oriented towards the addressee's: marked by the use of compliments, words or noises of sympathy or approval, the assertion of common ground and the avoidance of disagreement. **Negative** politeness strategies are oriented towards the addressee's negative face needs, i.e. their preference for freedom of action. So a speaker will apologize, claim their profound indebtedness, avoid being direct, use HEDGES, etc.

Feminist linguists, like CRITICAL DISCOURSE ANALYSTS generally, are interested in the particular social contexts in which such politeness strategies operate, and issues of discourse and institutionalized power. (See Holmes 1995 for a critique of theories of gender difference.) Monarchs need fear little threat, so can afford to be less polite (the Queen in *Alice in Wonderland*, for example, shouting *Off with his head!*).

Politeness theory is ambiguous about any claims to universality, but there are clearly cross-cultural differences, as there are historical, and these must not be underestimated in pragmatic studies. (In Igbo, for example, requests are not seen as impositions.) Moreover, there may be more complex nuances than the binary opposition between 'positive' and 'negative' implies. So, in the wrong context, positive 'solidarity'-promoting devices will appear patronizing.

(See further Herman 1995 on drama.)

polyphony

In music **polyphony**, from Gk 'many voices', refers to the putting together of different melodies in harmony; and the term has been borrowed into LITERARY CRITICISM, especially in the discussion of the structure of the novel. Related terms are **polyvocality** and **polyvalence**.

Polyphony is particularly associated with the work of the Russian Mikhail Bakhtin and his writings on Dostoevsky translated into English in 1973 (first published 1929). Bakhtin argues that novels like Dostoevsky's challenge the traditional novel with its authoritarian authorial VOICE (i.e. MONOLOGIC) by permitting the POINTS OF VIEW and the IDEOLOGIES and voices of the characters to have free play.

Polyphony is sometimes used as a synonym for DIALOGIC (q.v.), another of Bakhtin's key terms (see Bakhtin 1981); but the latter is best used to cover a more complex notion involving the sense not only of a DIALECTIC but also of language engaging with anticipated responses. Polyphony would therefore refer simply to the potential plurality of IDIOLECTAL or SOCIOLECTAL voices and consciousness so characteristic of the novel as a GENRE. (See Fowler 1983.)

(See also HETEROGLOSSIA.)

polyptoton

A FIGURE of RHETORIC in which a word is repeated in different case forms (as in Latin or Greek); or, as in English, in which words are repeated derived from the same root (by CONVERSION; AFFIXATION, etc.). For example, Shakespeare's Sonnet 28:

But day doth daily draw my sorrows longer,
And night doth nightly make grief's strength seem stronger

It was also known as **adnominatio, traductio** and **paragmenon.**

Polyptoton occurs very commonly in present-day advertising as a means of EMPHASIS. In the course of the script of an advert for face cream, for example, words relating to *moisture* (e.g. *moisturizer; moisturizing*) are likely to appear several times.

polysemy

In SEMANTICS **polysemy** describes a very common phenomenon, that many words have more than one meaning. Hence the need for dictionaries and glossaries.

New meanings develop for words over a period of time, but often without the more established meanings being lost. A language can normally tolerate such a semantic 'overload', because CONTEXT aids the selection of the appropriate meaning of a word; but occasionally AMBIGUITY can result (e.g. *Do you mean drinking glasses, or reading glasses?*). This ambiguity can also be exploited in PUNS: e.g.

Q: What holds the moon up?
A: Moon beams.

polysyndeton

In RHETORIC **polysyndeton** describes the MARKED use of several CONJUNCTIONS in succession (especially the same one) particularly for CO-ORDINATE CLAUSES or phrases. It is thus opposed to ASYNDETON (q.v.), without conjunctions.

Often associated with an unsophisticated speech or prose style, it occurs frequently in medieval Chronicle writing, such as Malory's *Morte d'Arthur*:

And anon there came in a dove at a window, and in her mouth there seemed a little censer of gold, and therewithal there was such a savour as all the spicery of the world had been there.

(Book XI, 2)

(See further Short 1986.)

possible worlds (theory)

Possible worlds have traditionally been much studied in philosophy, logic, SEMANTICS and some theories of GRAMMAR, especially in relation to issues of truth/falsehood, MODALITY and COUNTERFACTUALS; but especially since the 1980s they have also come into prominence in LITERARY THEORY and TEXTLINGUISTICS, and into many discussions of FICTIONALITY.

A possible world is essentially any state of affairs which can be conceived. 'World' is thus a metaphor, but therein lies the trouble. What is endlessly debated is the relation of the 'real' WORLD to possible worlds and to fictional worlds; and the differences, if any, between possible worlds and fictional worlds. The philosopher David Lewis (1986) has argued that all possible worlds exist, and that our world or actual world is but one among many worlds, and that fictional worlds are a special subtype of possible worlds. For Pavel (1986) it is the fictional world which 'inaugurates' possible worlds; and our world has definite onto-logical priority. Others argue, however, that our world is a possible world, but that others are located in 'logical space'. Ryan (1991) proposes that a fictional world is an alternative possible world which functions as the actual world of the universe projected by the text. Fictional worlds are underspecified of necessity in relation to the real world, but are not necessarily false. On the other hand, possible worlds aren't as 'rich' as text worlds, argues Werth (1999).

(See also TEXTWORLD THEORY. See further Ronen 1994.)

post(-)colonialism; post(-)colonial: literature; ~ theory

Covering one of the most popular courses of study currently in English depart-ments of higher education, the label **post(-)colonial theory** hides a potential IDEOLOGICAL minefield, while at the same time economically embracing a wide variety of approaches and foci of study.

The term **post-colonial** literally suggests 'after colonial rule', i.e. after official de-colonization, and it has been used to describe the literature produced in the British Commonwealth, traditionally featured in Commonwealth studies; also known as 'New Literatures in English'. The academic interest in such literature has done much to problematize the notion of a literary CANON.

The term was politicized and theorized particularly after the publication of Ashcroft *et al.*'s influential *The Empire Writes Back* (1989), who stressed the par-ticular tensions of literature emerging from under the influence of imperialism, and the differences of cultural assumptions. This in turn had been influenced by Said's *Orientalism* (1978), which popularized the idea of the colonized as an invented 'Other' projected by the colonizing power, a DISCOURSE in Foucault's sense. (See Baldick 1996.) For Ashcroft *et al.*, however, and other critics not only writing from Singapore, India, Bangladesh and the Caribbean could be embraced, but the historically more established writings of the USA, Canada and Ireland, for example; and post-colonialism could also embrace pre-independence writ-ing, under conditions of imperialist subordination. Writers of so-called 'New Literature in Britain', after post-war immigrations, can also be classed under this heading: e.g. Salman Rushdie, Timothy Mo, Jean Rhys.

Post-colonial, therefore, a temporal term, has become more of a theoretical term, **postcolonial**, and so a site of many positions and perspectives, some related to POSTMODERNISM. Novels like Coetzee's *Foe*, for example, have aroused dis-cussion of narrative representations and re-writings of colonization; the novels of Salman Rushdie, discussion of the relations between fantasy and realism. FEMINIST CRITICISM has melded discussions of women and subordination with issues of minority cultures and race. (Socio-) stylistic studies have looked at phenomena such as CODE-SWITCHING, the use of PIDGINS and CREOLES, INTER-TEXTUALITY and the rhetoric of ORATURE and SKAZ.

(See further Boehmer 1995; McLeod 2000; also Pennycook 1998 on 'colonialism' in English language teaching.)

post-modernism; postmodern theory

(1) **Post-modernism** was coined in the 1960s to describe a current literary movement which is a progression from MODERNISM (q.v.), the latter flourishing in Europe and America in the early years of this century until the 1930s. Like modernism, post-modernism challenges literary traditions and conventions, but more radically. In the novels of American writers like Barth, Nabokov and Pynchon, and of British writers like D. M. Thomas and Fowles, there is considerable undercutting of realism and of unity and neat resolutions. Writing is highly self-conscious, aware of itself and of the reader reading it. (See also HYPERFICTION. See further McHale 1989.)

(2) Somewhat confusingly, **post-modernism** or **postmodern theory** is also currently very popularly used as a synonym for POST-STRUCTURALISM below, to describe a reactionary intellectual movement, similarly French-inspired, influential on LITERARY THEORY from the late 1960s and early 1970s. Since this movement values many principles illustrated by postmodern writing, and since both can be seen to represent an IDEOLOGICAL shift in late twentieth-century Western culture, the extension of meaning is to be understood: e.g. the idea that 'reality' is constructed by language, and that no 'objective' truth exists. (See further Gibson 1996. For a critique see Eagleton 1996.)

The shift in sense appears to have been accelerated by the publication of Jean-François Lyotard's study of the **postmodern condition** (1984) of the late twentieth century. Ostensibly a commissioned report for the Quebec government to guide university policy on knowledge, Lyotard argued that in post-industrial societies the status and nature of knowledge had changed with the collapse of what he called the **grand** NARRATIVES (q.v.) which had traditionally determined the methods and grounds for acquiring knowledge. He denied the possibility of objective truth altogether; instead reality was absorbed into image, production into consumption. (See also SIMULACRUM.)

postmodification

In modern GRAMMAR **postmodification** describes all those elements in a NOUN PHRASE or NOMINAL GROUP which are subordinate to the noun as **head** word, and occur after it. Structures which typically function as **postmodifiers** include PREPOSITIONAL PHRASES (e.g. *A Man for All Seasons*); RELATIVE CLAUSES (*The Man who would be King*); and NON-FINITE CLAUSES (*A Woman Killed with Kindness*).

For modification of the noun head by elements occurring before it, see PREMODIFICATION. Heavy **pre-** and **postmodification** is most likely to be found in written REGISTERS of the technical or LITERARY type. Complex NOMINALS with heavy postmodification are characteristic of legal language, for example, or of any register where explanatory detail is felt necessary, e.g.:

> You will be offered the choice/ of an alternative holiday of at least comparable standard/ or a full refund/ of any monies you have already paid less only our reasonable expenses if cancellation is due to a *force majeure*/ . . .

(See further Biber *et al.* 1999, ch. 8.)

post-structuralism

The name given to a reactionary intellectual movement originating in France and very influential on LITERARY THEORY from the late 1960s/early 1970s especially in France and the United States. It is also now popularly known as POST-MODERNISM (q.v.).

As the term suggests, **post-structuralism** amongst other things sets out to challenge and subvert some of the basic principles of STRUCTURALISM (q.v.), not the least of which is that there are such things as 'structures' which are stable and have determinate meanings. For post-structuralists the relations between SIGNIFIER and SIGNIFIED are unstable, meaning is INDETERMINATE and therefore difficult to grasp. TEXTUAL unity is also an illusion: the aim of post-structuralist criticism is to tease out the contradictions of logic and meaning inherent in the works themselves, to 'deconstruct' them.

Post-structuralism is sometimes therefore identified with DECONSTRUCTION THEORY (q.v.) and the writings of Jacques Derrida, but the latter is only part of this larger 'style of thought' (Eagleton 1983), albeit the most well-known. Post-structuralism in France embraces also the later writings of scholars like Jacques Lacan in psychoanalysis and Julia Kristeva in FEMINIST CRITICISM, as well as the later writings of the critic/SEMIOTICIAN Roland Barthes.

Along with its philosophical speculations, post-structuralism has created its own esoteric jargon and its own linguistic word-play: it is creative as much as it is critical, but often turgid as much as it is stimulating.

(See further Culler 1983; Harari 1980; Lentricchia 1980, ch. 5.)

practical: ~ criticism; ~ stylistics

(1) Also known as **critical appreciation** or **commentary and analysis**, **practical criticism** is a way of looking at LITERARY texts first advocated in English

Studies at Cambridge in the 1930s, and still a feature of the syllabus and examinations of many schools and institutions of higher education today.

It is particularly associated with the names of I. A. Richards (1929) and F. R. Leavis in the 1930s, who reacted against what they considered to be inadequate and imprecise approaches to the teaching and understanding of literature, and emphasized the need for close attention to be paid to the literary text itself, its structure and THEMES. What makes practical criticism different from say the traditional *explication de texte* of the French is that it pays little attention to the social or historical contexts. It has been common examination practice for texts to be analysed or criticized without their titles or authors being given; or simply extracts of a text to be studied. What matters is the effect of the work on the reader, and his or her own intuitive responses.

However, it is one thing for Cambridge scholars in their INTERPRETIVE COMMUNITY to 'read' a text, and quite another for the layperson. What if we don't all respond to texts in the same way? There is no accepted methodology for practical criticism, so that analysing a text can pose considerable problems for students unless some guidance and critical concepts are provided by teachers. In any case, it is hard to analyse a text without drawing on some **literary** COMPETENCE drawn from a knowledge of other literary texts apparently similar (or dissimilar), and some knowledge of its cultural or historical milieu.

(2) However, the idea of looking closely at texts is basic to STYLISTICS, which generally attempts to integrate LITERARY CRITICISM and linguistics. It is, in fact, more 'practical' than practical criticism, since it bases INTERPRETATION on an analysis of significant linguistic features, and tries to avoid impressionism or subjectivity.

The term **practical stylistics** can be used to describe the work of stylisticians like Widdowson (e.g. 1992) who are primarily interested in the stylistic analyses of texts as teaching aids for literature and language study by native and foreign speakers of English. (See also **pedagogical** STYLISTICS.)

pragmatics

(1) **Pragmatic** is well established in everyday use to mean 'practical' even 'dogmatic'; from Gk *pragma* 'deed'. Very much a down-to-earth philosophy is **pragmatism**, the doctrine 'that evaluates any assertion solely by its practical consequences' (*COD*). The term and discipline pragmatics (also known as **pragmalinguistics**) is a relatively recent development, so that it is hard to define in a simple way.

But since the 1970s pragmatic studies of various kinds have become increasingly more numerous, with the growth of sociolinguistics, DISCOURSE ANALYSIS and FUNCTIONAL GRAMMARS; and with the reaction in many linguistic circles against what was seen as a narrow approach to problems of language in the influential work of Chomksy and his followers.

The term pragmatics was first used by scholars interested in questions of meaning. The linguist philosophers Morris and Peirce, for instance, writing in the late 1930s, and early 1940s, were interested in the relations of SIGNS to 'interpreters' and to 'users'. Pragmatics at its simplest, therefore, but also broadest, can be defined as the study of language use.

The exact relationship between SEMANTICS and pragmatics has been much discussed ever since, but basically pragmatics is concerned with the meaning of UTTERANCES rather than of SENTENCES or PROPOSITIONS; and meaning that comes from the CONTEXTUAL and INTERPERSONAL SITUATION involving speaker and listener. An utterance like *Can you drive a car?* will have a different 'meaning' if the context and participants vary: spoken by a girl to a young man in a pub, for instance, or by a driver to his passenger when taken suddenly ill. SPEECH ACT THEORY, CONVERSATIONAL IMPLICATURES and PRESUPPOSITION have been very influential on pragmatics in this respect, as the work of Leech (1983) and Levinson (1983) illustrates. Pragmatists ask not *What does X mean?* but *What do you mean by X?*. They are interested in the FUNCTIONS, INTENTIONS, goals and effects of utterances, and ultimately in the kind of linguistic COMPETENCE required to use language in specific social situations. Hence the inevitable overlap of pragmatics with related fields of linguistic inquiry and the interest taken by STYLISTICS. (For the application of pragmatic theory to the relations in the written MEDIUM between author, reader and text, see LITERARY PRAGMATICS.)

Of relevance to literary study is the recently emerged **historical pragmatics** (see Jucker 1995), which looks closely at the communicative context of texts in different historical periods, e.g. their particular audiences and purposes; or else traces the development of pragmatic features and functions across periods. This would be particularly interesting, for example, in relation to POLITENESS THEORY (q.v.). So it is possibly the case that plain speaking was more positively evaluated in the Early Modern period than today; and that 'sincerity' was more valued in private than in public. Such shifts in values are also an issue in **cross-cultural pragmatics**: see, e.g., Blum-Kulka & Kasper (1989).

(2) Some linguists now recognize an additional linguistic level or grammatical component in addition to PHONOLOGY, SYNTAX and semantics, namely the **pragmatic**, which links constructions with uses of language in context.

(See also POLITENESS THEORY; RELEVANCE THEORY. See further Thomas 1995.)

Prague School

The **Prague School**, properly the **Prague Linguistic Circle**, like **Russian** FORMALISM (q.v.), was one of the most important linguistic and literary movements of the early twentieth century, and its work still continues to this day (see, e.g., FUNCTIONAL SENTENCE PERSPECTIVE; THEME and RHEME). Only gradually did the ideas of Mathesius, Mukařovský, Trubetskoy and others become known in the west: partly through Roman Jakobson, who (like Trubetskoy) had moved from Moscow and Formalism to Prague, and helped found the Circle in 1926, later emigrating to the United States at the outbreak of the Second World War; and also through the translations of their work into English in the early 1960s (see Garvin 1964; Vachek 1964).

Greatly influenced by the STRUCTURALISM of Saussure, the Prague linguists made significant contributions to PHONETICS, PHONOLOGY and SEMANTICS through their ideas on COMPONENTS or 'distinctive features'. (See also MARKEDNESS.) Yet they developed Saussure's ideas of LANGUE and PAROLE along essentially FUNCTIONALIST lines: i.e. what shape the language system are the functions it must perform. So Jakobson's model of the SPEECH EVENT is based on their ideas. Functionalism is also the basis of their study of LITERARY LANGUAGE and its AESTHETIC qualities, with prime importance given to the POETIC FUNCTION. Building on the ideas of the Formalists, the Prague School developed the influential notions in STYLISTICS of FOREGROUNDING and (DE-)AUTOMATIZATION: the characteristic function of poetic language as highlighting and ESTRANGING language and meaning consciously and creatively by means of DEVIATION or patterns of PARALLELISM against the BACKGROUND of non-literary language.

praxis

(1) For Aristotle in his *Poetics* **praxis** meaning 'practice' was the action of the play. In recent drama criticism the term is extended to theories of practice and performance.

(2) The term has also been used more generally for the practice of the craft of writing, as opposed to theory; and also for the process of writing, particularly as generated through negotiation in groups or in mixed media or genres.

(3) In MARXIST CRITICISM it stands for a broad view of literary creation that includes both culture and the author's social milieu; also an active engagement in social and political movements, as distinct from abstract philosophizing (Hawthorn 1998).

All three senses are combined in Birch's (1991) approach to the language of drama, within a general **social** SEMIOTICS frame.

predicate; predicator

(1) In GRAMMAR **predicate** refers to a major constituent of the SENTENCE other than the SUBJECT. A sentence is sometimes said to be 'complete' if it consists of a subject and predicate, which is realized by a VERB (PHRASE) in English, with or without a following OBJECT and other elements, such as ADVERBIALS. For example, sentences like

She /swallowed.
She /swallowed hard.
She /swallowed a fly.

all have subjects and predicates. The verb as main exponent of the predicate is sometimes known as the **predicator**.

(2) Semantically, the subject–predicate distinction corresponds to THEME–RHEME, or 'topic' and 'comment', in that the predicate is what is said about the

subject. Together they make up a PROPOSITION (q.v.). More finely, on the basis of the verbs, the predicate can be seen to indicate an action, a process, or state of affairs. SEMANTICS and logic have their own kind of predicates, or **predications**, which do not wholly correspond to the grammatical. They are linking elements with **arguments** which provide additional information about something in a proposition. Not only verbs can be predicates in this case, but also ADJECTIVES: *grey*, for example, in combination with the argument *elephant*.

(3) Both **predicate** and argument can be found in the CASE GRAMMAR as developed by Fillmore (1968). The sentence as DEEP STRUCTURE predication consists of a set of arguments (NOUN PHRASES in different ROLES or cases) and a choice of predicate (state, event, process, etc.). A kind of predication analysis is also found in GENERATIVE SEMANTICS (see Traugott & Pratt 1980 for summary); and, as Fowler (1977) has argued, such a deep structure framework can in some respects be applied to NARRATIVES (see also NARRATIVE GRAMMAR). A PLOT may be thought of as a sequence of predicates (actions) and roles (characters).

(4) In Leech's (1983) discussion of SPEECH ACT THEORY, the semantic concept of (ILLOCUTIONARY) **predicate** is preferred to the syntactic one of ILLOCUTIONARY VERB. So **assertive predicates**, for example, introduce reported statements (e.g. *She announced that she wanted to get married*) and **rogative predicates** introduce reported questions (e.g. *She asked whether there were any offers*).

prefix; prefixation

In LEXICOLOGY a **prefix** is a type of AFFIX (see also SUFFIX) or formative which can be added to the base or root of a word to make new words: here, at the front of a word. Examples of **prefixation** include (for NOUNS) *anti-abortion* and *pre-war*; (for VERBS) *de-bunk* and *dis-possess*; (for ADJECTIVES) *hyper-modern* and *non-stick*.

Prefixes reveal varying degrees of productivity in Modern English, and have come from other language (chiefly French, Latin and Greek) as well as native stock. Prefixes like *be-* and *en-* to derive verbs from nouns are not used much today, but were once common in the POETIC DICTION of Elizabethan poets like Spenser and Shakespeare. Certainly *bedew*, *becloud*, *engarland* and *engirdle* have formal or poetic CONNOTATIONS.

(See further Bauer 1983.)

premodification

In modern GRAMMAR, **premodification** is used to describe all the elements in a NOUN PHRASE/NOMINAL GROUP which are subordinate to the noun, and occur directly before it.

The two main types of elements which function in this position are DETERMINERS and ADJECTIVES (in that order), e.g. *The White Peacock*. Nouns are also commonly modified by other nouns, and whole strings are found in newspaper headlines and placards (e.g. *Heathrow bullion robbery trial verdict*). Determiners can themselves be preceded by words like *all* and *both* (**predeterminers**), as in *all the right notes*; and followed by numerals (e.g. *those three blind mice*). What can make premodification heavy is the combination of several adjectives in this attributive position, e.g.: *A London Transport big six-wheeler, scarlet-painted, diesel-engined, 97 horse-power omnibus* (song by Flanders & Swan).

Rare in colloquial speech, heavy premodification is characteristic of descriptive REGISTERS such as advertising, catalogues, scientific articles and LITERARY prose.

(See further Biber *et al.* 1999, ch. 8.)

preposition: ~ phrase

A **preposition** is a FUNCTION word used to relate a NOUN PHRASE which it precedes with another part of the SENTENCE, the whole forming a **prepositional phrase**. It expresses meanings of space, time, position, etc., as in *between the houses; at mid-day; on the beach*. Prepositional phrases are therefore very useful to indicate ORIENTATION, i.e. settings in place and time, as part of NARRATIVES:

> Fog up the river, . . . fog down the river, . . . Fog on the Essex marshes, fog on the Kentish heights . . . Fog in the eyes and throats of ancient Greenwich pensioners . . .
> (Dickens: *Bleak House*)

Some kinds of prepositional phrases in English would be expressed by CASES in other languages, e.g. **dative** (*to; for*); **ablative** (*from*); **instrumental** (*with*); cf. also the GENITIVE CASE in English (mostly ANIMATE) nouns (cf. *the house of her uncle; her uncle's house*). Prepositional phrases commonly function as ADJUNCTS or ADVERBIALS in clause structure (e.g. *I'll see you/ in my dreams*); and many prepositions are formally identical with adverbs: e.g. *up, down, on, off, in, over*: cf.

> The train went off on time (adverb)
> The train went off the rails (preposition)

Prepositional phrases also commonly function as POSTMODIFIERS in a noun phrase (e.g. *The Hound of the Baskervilles*).

(See further Quirk *et al.* 1985, ch. 9.)

prescriptive grammar; prescriptivism

(1) Traditional GRAMMARS have very often been **prescriptive** in their approach: i.e. describing the language not as it is used (**descriptive**), but as it is thought the language ought to be used; even condemning certain USAGES (**proscriptive**).

Grammatical **prescriptivism** is the belief in CORRECTNESS, that certain usages are 'right' and 'wrong' according to what amounts to be a highly subjective or ideal standard. It originated in the late seventeenth and eighteenth century, when ideas of 'fixing' and 'improving' the language were particularly rife, and when English dictionaries and grammars became popular (e.g. Lowth's *English Grammar*, 1762). Latin was an influential model, and so were appeals to 'logic'. (See also CATACHRESIS.)

In one sense prescriptivism has made little impact on general usage (although 'double negatives' (e.g. he should*n't never* have done that) are no longer a feature of STANDARD ENGLISH); yet in another sense its influence has remained. There are a small number of usages which are still the subject of controversy today, and which tend to be avoided in FORMAL REGISTERS and formal writing: 'dangling' PARTICIPLES, for instance, and PREPOSITIONS at the end of sentences. Moreover, authoritative handbooks on English usage continue to be written or reprinted (e.g. H. W. Fowler 1998). Clearly the general public feels the need for guidance in usage, and, needing to know what is 'right' or 'wrong', does not question the grounds on which rules are made.

The need for guidance is acknowledged increasingly by modern grammarians, who are acutely aware of the needs of students and foreign learners of English, for instance. The older prescriptivism has been replaced by a milder form based on APPROPRIATENESS and ACCEPTABILITY: recommendations based on the observation that certain constructions are more likely to be found, and hence are more appropriate, in some CONTEXTS or registers than others: e.g. *let's* as a **first** PERSON singular IMPERATIVE in very colloquial English (e.g. *Let's have a look*); and *hereupon* and *thereafter* as CONNECTIVES in very formal English.

More generally, linguists have taken more notice of 'abusage', the ways language can be manipulated, through EUPHEMISM, JARGON, AMBIGUITY and sexism, for deceitful or demeaning ends. (See also CRITICAL LINGUISTICS; ETHICAL STYLISTICS; FEMINIST CRITICISM. See further Bolinger 1980.)

(2) The public need for guidance in usage applies to more general matters to do with TEXTUAL structure and organization of material, CHOICE of level of formality and appropriate DICTION: matters of STYLE. Traditionally, RHETORIC has provided such guidance, with treatises on all kinds of composition and appropriate FIGURES and levels of style. (See also DECORUM.) In the United States, where composition skills are a feature of high school and college courses, there are modern equivalents to the traditional treatises (e.g. Brooks & Warren 1972). But in Britain there are no such publications on the same scale. (But see Nash 1980.)

(3) The Leavis tradition of LITERARY CRITICISM is prescriptive in its CANONIZATION of certain works and authors in the 'great tradition' at the expense of others; but all critics can be said to be prescriptive in the sense that they wish to persuade readers to read texts in the way they read them. The normative influence of critics and INTERPRETIVE COMMUNITIES is stressed in the work of Fish (1980); and the 'authority' of critics is well attested by student responses.

(See also VERBAL HYGIENE.)

present tense

TENSE in the VERB is the most significant grammatical means of indicating time, so that the **present tense** is used to refer to present time: marked MOR-PHOLOGICALLY in Modern English only in the **third** PERSON singular of LEXICAL verbs (-s).

Yet the relationship between tense and time is complex. On the one hand the temporal continuum itself is not easily divided up into past, present and future, nor is present time easily defined (the present moment? the present year? century?); so *I feel hungry* or *I live in London* or *English is the most widely known language in the world* have different shades of present reference. On the other hand there are not enough tenses in English verbs to indicate the main time divisions: there are only two tenses, the present and the **past**, but no future. Consequently, the present tense is one of the means used to express future time (e.g. *The plane leaves for St Lucia tomorrow*). Moreover, there is the added complication that for certain kinds of (dynamic) verbs, it is the PROGRESSIVE ASPECT (q.v.) that most commonly indicates actions happening at the present moment, rather than the present tense: e.g. *I'm mending the car (just at the moment/right now,* etc.). In older English the simple present was the norm, and this survives in the grammar of poetry into the twentieth century:

> The showers beat
> On broken blinds and chimney pots,
> And at the corner of the street
> A lonely cab-horse steams and stamps
>
> (T. S. Eliot: *Preludes, 1*)

However, the present tense is certainly commonly used in sports commentaries for actions described simultaneously with the moment of speaking: the so-called 'instantaneous present', as in *Botham bowls to Border, who plays a beauty of a stroke.* The present tense is also used with similar reference in rituals and ceremonies with PERFORMATIVE VERBS: e.g. *I name this ship Marie Celeste.*

There are other MARKED temporal uses of the present tense in different RE-GISTERS. In newspaper headlines the present is used for the (longer) PERFECT ASPECT for events that have just happened and with present relevance: e.g. *Soviets save Aussie boffins.* In narratives, the HISTORIC PRESENT (q.v.) is used for the more usual past tense for vividness and immediacy, e.g. *Suddenly the door opens, and a large shape looms out of the darkness.*

This makes the present tense a very general category. It also has certain uses that are not strictly temporal in reference, so that some linguists prefer to label it the **non-past tense**. It is very commonly used in GENERIC statements for universal truths (e.g. *A rolling stone gathers no moss*), and where these occur in novels with third person NARRATION, they are a characteristic sign of the OMNISCIENT NAR-RATOR: *With a single drop of ink for a mirror the Egyptian sorcerer undertakes to reveal to any chance comer far-reaching visions of the past* (opening sentence of George Eliot's *Adam Bede*).

In LITERARY CRITICISM and newspaper articles, etc., the present tense is also used for statements about writers and works which have relevance beyond the biographical: e.g. *In his poetry Hopkins expresses his love of God and of nature.*

presupposition

Used in SEMANTICS and PRAGMATICS and taken from logic to refer to the necessary preconditions or assumptions made in speaking or writing an UTTERANCE, distinct from what may actually be asserted. So *I'm surprised she's leaving* assumes the fact that someone is leaving, but actually asserts the speaker's surprise. The **presupposition** would be the same even if the speaker had not been surprised.

Presupposition is an important element in the distribution of GIVEN and NEW INFORMATION in DISCOURSE. Communication would be impossible if everything had to be defined or explained every time we spoke; but the degree of necessary explicitness will vary from SITUATION to situation, and depend on the knowledge that speakers and hearers will assume of each other.

In some REGISTERS the assumption of presumed knowledge can be manipulated, either for economy, or for the insinuation of information or a value system or a WORLD-VIEW, etc. So adverts of the kind *Why does slow reading let you down?* or *Why is your memory so poor?* use the *wh*-question (a common structure for revealing presuppositions) as an artful and economic means of revealing the basis of their sales campaign: namely that slow reading or a poor memory is a social disadvantage. What is also assumed, of course, presumptuously, is that the readers of the adverts are themselves slow readers or have poor memories.

Presupposition is also commonly exploited in FICTIONAL discourse as a means of establishing the 'reality' of the fictional world. In the zany world of riddles, for example, we have to accept that elephants can paint their toenails or climb trees, etc., in order to appreciate the joke:

Q: How do elephants get down from trees?
A: They sit on a leaf and wait till autumn.

Presupposition is also exploited in the IN MEDIAS RES technique of opening poems and novels, etc., the illusion of a world already in existence, e.g. *Hale knew, before he had been in Brighton three hours, that they meant to murder him* (first sentence of Greene's *Brighton Rock*). Here the existence of a man called Hale who is visiting Brighton is taken for granted.

(For other kinds of implied meaning, see also CONVERSATIONAL IMPLICATURE; ENTAILMENT; INFERENCE. See further Gazdar 1979; Kempson 1975; Wilson 1975.)

productivity

See CREATIVITY.

progressive

One of two types of ASPECT in English (see also PERFECT(IVE)), which is a grammatical category of VERBS referring to particular perspectives on the temporal constraints of activities or events. The **progressive** is concerned with duration of activities (so is also known as the **durative**). It is expressed by a part of the verb *be* plus the *-ing* form or PARTICIPLE, and can be used with the PRESENT or **past** TENSE: e.g. *She is/was reading Proust*. Since it involves actions, **stative verbs** don't normally occur in the progressive aspect (**I am believing in Father Christmas*).

The use of the progressive normally implies that the action is not yet finished: e.g. *I am eating a pie*. It has therefore become very common in Modern English to use the progressive instead of the simple present tense of the LEXICAL verb to refer to an action happening at the moment of speaking or writing: *The kettle's boiling* v. *The kettle boils*, for example. In appropriate contexts or with certain ADVERBIALS it can also indicate habitual or iterative actions:

> At the moment, she is having weekly sessions (habitual)
> She's always getting into trouble (iterative)

When used in conjunction with the simple tenses, the progressive provides a kind of temporal BACKGROUNDING to events, a point of ORIENTATION or FRAME OF REFERENCE, so in narratives or anecdotes: *I was walking home from the station one night when suddenly a car screeched to a halt alongside*.

prolepsis

From Gk meaning ANTICIPATION (q.v.), a term used in RHETORIC and traditional GRAMMAR in various senses.

(1) The narration of an event at a point earlier than its strict chronological place: a sense revived by Genette (1972) in his discussion of the DISCOURS(E) of narrative. For him **prolepsis** is a subtype of ANACHRONY (*sic*), and opposed to ANALEPSIS or flashback, the narration of an event at a later point. It occurs commonly in older or oral literature, where suspense does not seem to have mattered so much in storytelling as in later literature. In the novel, prolepsis is a MARKED sign of the OMNISCIENT NARRATOR, e.g.:

> In observing this small winter scene, we are on safe ground. The tall young man would to the end of his days wear double-breasted suits, would, being something of an engineer, always be gratified by large dazzling vehicles, would, though a German and at this point in history a German of some influence, always be the sort of man with whom a Polish chauffeur could safely crack a large, comradely joke.
>
> (Keneally: *Schindler's Ark*)

Prolepsis occurs more frequently, however, in **first** PERSON NARRATION as the 'natural' result of a character looking back on his or her life from a later standpoint.

Generally, it might be argued, following Brooks (1984), that in our reading there is a double movement of prolepsis and analepsis: the constant anticipation of the moment when, looking back, everything falls into place.

(2) **Prolepsis** in rhetoric is also used to describe the kind of ANACHRONISM in literary works where places or people are alluded to, but which would not yet in reality exist.

(3) Also it is the device of referring briefly to something in anticipation of elaboration at a later point: remarks like *As we shall see* . . . , also noted by Genette. It is common to open orations or even narratives in this way as a form of prologue: cf. the epic openings of *The Iliad* and *The Odyssey*, and Milton's *Paradise Lost*:

> Of Man's first disobedience, and the fruit
> Of that forbidden tree, whose mortal taste
> Brought death into the world, and all our woe, . . .
> Sing Heavenly Muse . . .

Such 'foreshadowing' often has connotations of foreboding.

(4) The element of foreboding may also be present in **prolepsis** as the FIGURE OF SPEECH in which ADJECTIVES are used in anticipation to describe something which has not yet happened: a kind of TRANSFERRED EPITHET, e.g.

> . . . when Jove
> Will o'er some high-vic'd city hang his poison
> In the sick air' (*Timon of Athens*, IV.3)

and *mortal* in the quotation from Milton above.

(5) Orators were accustomed to anticipate the objections or counter-arguments of their opponents, and so forestalled them by **proleptic** METAstatements, such as *I know it will be said that* . . . Such anticipatory strategies occur also in ordinary discourse (see Edmondson 1981).

(6) In traditional grammar **prolepsis** is the term used to describe any structure which anticipates another later in the sentence or in a following clause: usually NOUNS or NOUN PHRASES anticipating PRONOUNS. As a result, the sentence structure is rather LOOSE or informal, but the noun phrase receives special EMPHASIS as a MARKED THEME, e.g. *That old tramp, I saw him again yesterday.*

In modern grammar this is sometimes known as **anticipated identification** (Quirk *et al.* 1985, ch. 17.78), HEAD or **left dislocation**. It is opposed to **postponed identification** or **right dislocation**, where pronouns precede a NOMINAL, which appears finally, as a kind of amplification, often in a TAG phrase, e.g. *She's completely mad, your sister (is).*

pronoun

In GRAMMAR a FUNCTION word of a CLOSED SET generally used to substitute for a NOUN or NOMINAL GROUP, and standing alone as a HEAD **word**.

The main class of pronouns is the PERSONAL pronouns. Some make reference to a nominal in the CO-TEXT and have an important COHESIVE function with ANAPHORIC or CATAPHORIC REFERENCE, i.e. the **third person** pronouns: *she; it; he; they. She* and *he* have largely ANIMATE reference. Others identify participants in the SITUATIONAL CONTEXT, the ADDRESSER and ADDRESSEE, i.e. the **first** and **second person** pronouns: *I, we, you.* (See also ENDOPHORIC and EXOPHORIC reference.)

These pronouns have three CASE forms, the **subjective, objective** and **genitive** (e.g. *I, me, mine; she, her, hers*). There are some case USAGES which are frowned upon in PRESCRIPTIVE GRAMMARS, but which occur commonly in informal speech and writing: e.g. *It is me; I'm taller than him*. The RELATIVE PRONOUN *who* also distinguishes case forms: *whom* and *whose; whom*, particularly associated with FORMAL contexts.

Other important pronoun types are the **reflexives** (e.g. *myself; yourself*) and INDEFINITES (*someone; anybody*, etc.).

(See further Wales 1996.)

proposition: propositional meaning

Proposition was borrowed from philosophy into SEMANTICS; and the **propositional meaning** of an UTTERANCE or SENTENCE is its basic or core or CONCEPTUAL MEANING.

A proposition is an abstract unit of meaning, composed of a **name** or an **argument** (what is to be talked about, generally corresponding to the grammatical SUBJECT) and a PREDICATE (an action or a state attributed to the 'name', which may or may not correspond to the grammatical predicate). Hence a proposition resembles the SPEECH ACT of a statement or assertion, and usually corresponds grammatically to a DECLARATIVE SENTENCE composed of subject and predicate. However, the levels of grammar and meaning should be carefully distinguished: ACTIVE and PASSIVE sentences, for example, with different subjects and predicates, can be seen to express the same propositions: cf.

> Children sweeten labours (Bacon).
> Labours are sweetened by children.

(See also DUALISM.) Conversely, one sentence may express two or more propositions, if it is AMBIGUOUS: e.g. *General flies back to front*. According to Halliday (1985) propositions may be affirmed or denied: e.g. *He loves me, he loves me not*. Moreover, they may not be directly asserted, but also PRESUPPOSED (q.v.) or ENTAILED (q.v.). So *In time the savage bull sustains the yoke* (Kyd; *The Spanish Tragedy*) presupposes the proposition that bulls are savage.

Our ability to understand and abstract propositions is revealed in our LITERARY COMPETENCE to abstract PLOTS from NARRATIVES, and to provide plot summaries (see Fowler 1977, 1996; Stubbs 1983, ch. 10). Indeed, what is often seen as the CONTENT of a literary work can be defined as a network of propositions. NARRATIVE GRAMMARS characteristically work on the basis of the plots of stories being reduced to simple propositions (e.g. *Hero rescues maiden from evil creature*).

prosody; prosodic feature

(1) From Lat. 'accent' (ultimately from Gk) **prosody** has since the fifteenth century traditionally been defined as the study or rules of versification, now more commonly known as METRICS.

The focus of attention has always been the recurring units of RHYTHM within the line, scanned or analysed in FEET if the model has been classical prosody, or in MEASURES. Classical terminology, based on a verse in which syllables were counted, and their degrees of length, has not proved satisfactory for a native verse which depends on ACCENTED or STRESSED syllables; yet still survives in terms like IAMBIC PENTAMETER (q.v.).

In the twentieth century there have been various metrical theories proposed, some using linguistic ideas as a basis. So GENERATIVE METRICS (q.v.) proved influential in the 1960s, following GENERATIVE GRAMMAR (e.g. Halle & Keyser 1966); and also STRUCTURALIST approaches (e.g. Chatman 1964). (See further Attridge 1995.)

(2) It was out of the study of versification that much of the earliest work on aspects of PHONETICS was initiated, patterns of versification being based on the sound and rhythm of speech. One of the senses of **prosody** in the sixteenth century was 'correct pronunciation', and prosody formed part of GRAMMAR until well into the eighteenth century. In Lindley Murray's *Grammar* (1795) prosody included not only versification, but also accent, EMPHASIS and TONE in speech, all features which linguists today regard as **prosodic features**.

(3) For modern linguists and phoneticians **prosody** is a level or contour of sound features over and above the level of the VERBAL component of language; and prosodic features (or **supra-segmentals**) characteristically function over longer stretches of speech than PHONEMES: e.g. stress or emphasis (over LEXICAL ITEMS in English) and INTONATION or pitch variation (over UTTERANCES). Usually discussed also are pausing, rhythm, tempo (variations in speed of utterance) and degree of loudness; although in some sources there is some confusing overlap with features of PARALANGUAGE (q.v.).

Although intonation and stress are characteristic of all English spoken utterances, certain prosodic features will be more MARKED in some REGISTERS than others. Different kinds of sports commentaries, for instance, vary in their rates of delivery and degrees of loudness. An interest in the textual and social functions of prosodic features in different types of spoken discourse has increased due to the influence of such disciplines as DISCOURSE ANALYSIS and ETHNOMETHODOLOGY.

In the representation of speech in the written MEDIUM, prosodic features are hardly or inadequately indicated, since the alphabet represents phonemes only. Italics can indicate emphasis, and so too capitals. Punctuation is only a rough guide to degree of pausing (comma, colon and full stop) and possibly a rising intonation (question mark) or high fall (exclamation mark). (See further Allan 1986, II, ch. 6; Crystal 1975.)

prosopopoeia

(1) From Gk 'person/face making', best known as a FIGURE of RHETORIC whereby an INANIMATE object is represented as being able to speak. It is a common device in riddles (e.g. *My first is in butter but not in bread . . . What am I?*), and poems like Tennyson's *The Brook* (*I come from haunts of coot and hern*).

Prosopopoeia is thus an extension or variation of PERSONIFICATION (q.v.), in which an inanimate object is given human attributes. Almost half the people who withdraw money from cashpoint machines speak to them; and half the British drivers talk to their car (and men more than women).

(2) Traditionally, however, other uses of the figure apply to human beings: e.g. a dead or absent person may be represented as present and speaking (e.g. the ghost of Hamlet's father); a fictitious speaker may be created (as in dramatic MONOLOGUES; also known as **ethopoeia**); or fictitious speeches assigned to 'real' characters (e.g. Tolstoy's Napoleon in *War and Peace*).

pseudo-cleft

In modern GRAMMAR, a kind of structure whereby for EMPHASIS or FOCUS a simple SENTENCE is split or 'cleft' into two parts connected by a form of the verb *be* with a RELATIVE CLAUSE as SUBJECT(S) (commonly) or COMPLEMENT(C). (The **pseudo-cleft** is related to the CLEFT SENTENCE (q.v.) which is more clearly divided into two clauses.) Alternatives terms are **equated-relative** (Taglicht 1985); **thematic equative** (Halliday 1985); and *wh*-**cleft** (Biber *et al.* 1999). So *We want cheaper petrol* (subject–VERB–OBJECT) will produce

What we want (S) is cheaper petrol (C)
Cheaper petrol (S) is what we want (C)

With the relative clause as subject and as THEME, the focus still falls on *cheaper petrol* as in the simple sentence, but there is more a sense of anticipation, of building up to a climax. Pseudo-clefts are commonly used where the focus coincides with NEW INFORMATION, and the relative nominal with GIVEN INFORMATION.

Q. What do you want?
A: [What we want is] cheaper petrol

As Halliday notes, with pseudo-clefts there is also the connotation of exclusiveness (. . . *and nothing else*).

With ANIMATE REFERENCE the relative NOMINAL is usually expressed by phrases such as *the one/person who*, as in *The person who stole my bicycle must be an idiot* (cf. *An idiot must have stolen my bicycle*). Here the pseudo-cleft more naturally allows the focus to occur in post-verbal position.

psycho-narration

Used by Cohn (1978) to describe one of the modes she identifies as found in FICTION for the representation of consciousness.

In **psycho-narration** a **third** PERSON NARRATOR reports a CHARACTER'S thoughts and feelings. This is not exactly McHale's (1978) DIEGETIC **summary**, nor Leech & Short's (1981) NARRATIVE REPORT (NR), since there is some 'colouring' of the report by the character's own PERSPECTIVE or (verbalized) thoughts. It thus inclines towards FREE INDIRECT THOUGHT (FIT) (or what Cohn calls NARRATED MONOLOGUE), with which it naturally co-occurs in extended passages, as in this extract from Hardy's *Tess of the D'Urbervilles*:

> She thought of her husband in some vague warm clime on the other side of the globe, while she was here in the cold [psychonarration]. Was there another such wretched being as she in the world? Tess asked herself; and thinking of her wasted life, said, 'All is vanity'. She repeated the words mechanically, till she reflected that this was a most inadequate thought for modern days [NR]. Solomon had thought as far that more than two thousand years ago; when herself, though not in the van of thinkers, had got much further [NR; or FIT] . . .

psycho-: ~ poetics; ~ stylistics, etc.

Just as disciplines like psychology and psychoanalysis have influenced linguistics and led to fields such as **psycholinguistics**, basically concerned with investigating the mental processes involved in human communication, so influence has also been felt in the areas of LITERARY THEORY and CRITICISM, in AFFECTIVE STYLISTICS, etc.

(1) The term **psycho-poetics**, for example, refers to literary theory, common in France and the United States, much influenced by the psychoanalytical theories of the unconscious of Freud and Lacan; also known as **psychoanalytical criticism** or **Freudian poetics**. (See the work of Kristeva and Bloom in the 1970s; and Brooks on PLOT, 1984.) For a political interpretation of the unconscious, the work of the MARXIST CRITIC Jameson (1981) is particularly significant. (See further Durant & Fabb 1990; Eagleton 1983, ch. 5.)

(2) **Psycho-stylistics** applies psycholinguistic research to the study of LITERARY effects. So van Peer (1986) studies FOREGROUNDING from this perspective. In other studies, for example, the salience of particular devices such as RHYME, METAPHOR and IMAGERY is related to memorability from listening to TEXTS.

Early work in STYLISTICS this century was interested in psychology in a less technical sense: the so-called EXPRESSIVE STYLISTICS (q.v.) associated with Croce (1922), Vossler (1932) and Spitzer (1948). STYLE was thought to reveal the personality or psyche of the writer: *stylus arguit hominem* (Thomas Browne). This seems not unrelated to work in (1), of American critics like Holland (1975), part of which concerns relations between poetic style and total personality.

pun

According to the *OED* the word **pun** (of uncertain origin) did not appear in English until 1662 with Dryden; yet this word-play is found in English literature since earliest times, and different kinds of word-play involving different kinds of puns were termed collectively PARONOMASIA in RHETORIC.

A pun is an AMBIGUITY: specifically, a FOREGROUNDED LEXICAL ambiguity (Leech 1969). It involves the use of a POLYSEMOUS word to suggest two or more meanings (commonly LITERAL V. FIGURATIVE); or the use of HOMONYMS, i.e. different words which look or sound the same but which have different meanings. The whole point of a pun, however, is the user's intent to produce a humorous or witty effect from the juxtaposition of meanings. Thus puns commonly occur in jokes, e.g.:

Q: How do you get down from elephants?
A: You don't, you get it from ducks.

They are pervasive in newspaper headlines as eye-catching/attention-getting devices, e.g. *GNER back pedalling over cycle ban; No toast for breakfast television*.

A stretching of the conventions is found in the near-puns termed **jingles** by Leech (1969). Here the pronunciation must be distorted for the pun to be appreciated: common in adverts (e.g. *Porky and Best*: sausages) and in 'Knock-knock' jokes like:

Q: Who's there?
A: Martini.
Q: Martini who?
A: Martini hand is frozen.

And in puns based on BLENDS (e.g. *An amayonnaising offer from Heinz*) (see also Joyce's *Finnegans Wake, passim*).

A special kind of pun known as **antanaclasis** involves the repetition of the same word or form or sounds but in different senses in the near CO-TEXT: e.g. *A tanker at anchor; You won't wind up the evening being wound up by the bill*; or *Gaunt am I for the grave, gaunt as a grave* (*Richard II*, II.i).

Once common in Elizabethan drama and poetry, and not only for laughs, punning was regarded as a 'degenerate' kind of wit in the eighteenth century. In LITERARY THEORY it has achieved high respectability as a serious means of revealing nuances of concepts, and the 'endless play' of meaning, as in the DECONSTRUCTION THEORY of Derrida and his followers (see, e.g., DIFFÉRANCE).

Q

---

quaesitio

In RHETORIC **quaesitio** is a FIGURE in which several questions are uttered one after the other. Characteristically they are suggestive of heightened emotion, as in Shylock's defence of his race and religion:

> Hath not a Jew eyes? hath not a Jew hands, organs, dimensions, senses, affections, passions? fed with the same food . . . as a Christian is? If you prick us, do we not bleed? If you tickle us, do we not laugh? if you poison us, do we not die? and if you wrong us, shall we not revenge? . . .
>
> (Shakespeare: *The Merchant of Venice*, III.i)

Since these particular questions do not expect an answer, and are really equivalent to statements (*A Jew does have eyes*, etc.), they can be identified individually as RHETORICAL QUESTIONS (q.v.).

quality and quantity, maxims of

Two of four maxims (see also MANNER and RELATION) distinguished by the philosopher Grice (1975) as playing an important underlying role in our communicative behaviour: part of a general CO-OPERATIVE PRINCIPLE.

(1) The **maxim of quality** concerns truthfulness: normally we are not expected to tell lies, or to say things for which we have no evidence. This seems comparable to some of Searle's (1969) sincerity conditions in SPEECH ACT THEORY (see FELICITY CONDITIONS).

The maxim makes conversation sound as if it were always taking place in a law court, where, of course, such a maxim is strictly observed. But truthfulness is still a goal or NORM in speech, since telling lies impedes COMMUNICATION (amongst other things).

However, for various PRAGMATIC reasons, it may not always be desirable to tell the straight truth: 'white lies' are often necessary for reasons of POLITENESS, to save our ADDRESSEE's feelings, for example. Politicians might claim that to tell the whole truth would not be in the nation's interest; advertisers might not exactly lie, but not exactly tell the whole truth (e.g. about the state of a house for sale).

In METAPHOR (e.g. *She's an elephant*) the maxim is patently flouted, yet we accept the falsity as conventional. And there is always an element of truth nonetheless. Other FIGURES that contravene the maxim are HYPERBOLE (distorting the truth by exaggeration) and IRONY (saying the opposite).

(2) The **maxim of quantity** concerns the degree of INFORMATION normally demanded: participants should be as informative as is required, not more nor less than. We certainly think it very rude if no reply at all is given to a question; and very tedious if minute details are provided which seem REDUNDANT in the CONTEXT. Yet not all conversation is informative: PHATIC COMMUNION, for instance, is factually quite uninformative, telling others what they know already (e.g. *Very cold today, isn't it?*), yet socially acceptable as a means of making CONTACT.

Flouting the maxim of quantity is a common means of CONVERSATIONAL IMPLICATURE, of meaning more than we actually say. If we ask someone a question, and the answer appears insufficient, we will INFER either that our interlocutor doesn't really know enough, or that he or she is unwilling for some reason to give the right amount of information. Children will infer both from answers like *We'll see* to questions like *Can we go to the seaside on Sunday?*.

The two maxims are interrelated to some extent. Not to give enough information can in some ways be seen as withholding the truth: the house agent omitting to mention that a house described as *in need of some redecoration* actually has dry rot understandably violates the maxim of quantity in order to avoid violating the maxim of quality. The figure of LITOTES flouts the maxim of quantity by saying too little (e.g. *It's not bad*), which can also be seen as distorting the truth. Hyperbole, mentioned above, distorts the truth by saying too much. (See further Leech 1983.)

quotation

We tend to think of **quotation** as academic: the citation of words from other authors or sources of reference to highlight or confirm some viewpoint. Scholars and students make extensive use of quotations, which conventionally are attributed.

A TEXT with quotations is clearly POLYPHONIC in the sense of Bakhtin (1973), or 'multi-voiced': the VOICE of the writer interwoven with the voices of his or her sources. It is also DIALOGIC in Bakhtin's sense, in that much of the dynamism and tension of criticism comes from the engagement of the writer with the quotations since (s)he may or may not agree with them. It is also INTERTEXTUAL, since a text with quotations depends on the writer's (and reader's) knowledge of previous discourses.

Unattributed quotation, however, in modern scholarship, if not classical or medieval, is regarded as an offence and dubbed **plagiarism**. It is especially disapproved of if the quotations are borrowed without the quotation marks or inverted commas of DIRECT SPEECH. As the controversy over D. M. Thomas's novel *The White Hotel* revealed, the extensive borrowing of material, or appeals to voices of authority whether in agreement or disagreement, must be fully acknowledged, at least in print. But as Bakhtin also argues, ordinary speech is full of the (unconsciously) appropriated ALIEN words of other people. Such borrowed words may even be quotations: foreign phrases (*C'est la vie*), phrases from the Bible (*An eye for an eye*) or Shakespeare (*hoist with his own petard*).

Special kinds of intertextual quotation are IMITATION (q.v.) and PARODY (q.v.) which appropriate and also transform a previous discourse on an extensive scale. But as Hutcheon (1985) argues, even a LITERAL quotation is a kind of parody, because of the shift in context that it must undergo.

R

rank: ~-shift

Terms especially associated with Halliday (1961) and what has now come to be known as SYSTEMIC GRAMMAR. **Rank** is a hierarchical unit or level of SENTENCE structure composed of items at the rank below. So there are five significant ranks in English grammatical description: sentence; CLAUSE; **group** (or phrase); **word**; MORPHEME. A sentence is made up of clauses; a word made up of morphemes, etc.

It is sometimes possible for items at a certain rank to be downgraded or **rankshifted** to a FUNCTION at a lower level. So a sentence like *Do it yourself* functions at word level within a (NOMINAL) group in a phrase like *A do-it-yourself shop*. RELATIVE CLAUSES characteristically function at word level, EMBEDDED within a nominal group, equivalent to ADJECTIVAL MODIFIERS: cf.

The elephants, <u>which were big and noisy</u>, marched into the ring.
The <u>big noisy</u> elephants marched into the ring.

The idea of a rank scale was borrowed by the Birmingham school of DISCOURSE ANALYSIS in the 1970s and applied to units of classroom discourse. So there were established the (progressively smaller) units of **lesson**; **transaction**; **exchange**; **move** and ACT. (See further Burton 1980; Sinclair & Coulthard 1975.)

reader: ~ response criticism; readerly

(1) **Reader response criticism** or **theory** describes various kinds of critical approaches popular from the 1970s which focus on the activity of the reader in the INTERPRETATION of a work. So, for example, there was the AFFECTIVE STYLISTICS of Fish (1970f) in the United States and of Riffaterre (1959f) in France; the STRUCTURALIST POETICS of Culler (1975) with his **literary** COMPETENCE; and the SEMICS of Eaton (1966f). (See also, importantly, RECEPTION THEORY.) Reader response criticism, like POST-STRUCTURALISM, tried to move away from the TEXT as critical focus, and even more so from (the INTENTIONS of) the AUTHOR.

One result has been a proliferation of terms to describe the **reader**, a complex role, with varying degrees of 'realness' according to critic. Common has been the notion of an IDEAL READER (q.v.), who properly and completely understands the meaning and significance of a text, without the inadequacies or subjectivity of response of 'real' readers: very much a theoretical and functional construct. A related term and concept is the AVERAGE or **super-reader** (Riffaterre 1959f), based on the sum of reactions by informants to linguistic features in texts and stylistic values. Fish's (1970f) **informed reader** is partly real, but also partly ideal: a reader capable of a highly sensitive and intelligent response to literature. Under the influence of Iser's work in reception theory in the 1970s emerged the concept of the IMPLIED READER, the image of a reader created by the textual rhetoric itself, inscribed in the language or PRESUPPOSITIONS, whom the author may explicitly or implicitly address, and who thus combines real and ideal qualities as an addressee. (See also Eco's 1981 **model reader**.)

One problem with all these reader figures, apart from their vagueness, is that they seem much more static than seems credible; and rather imply that a response to a text is a straightforward process, that will be the same on re-reading; or for another reader of a different gender or culture; or for another generation. Clearly it is not so easy to analyse the 'receiving'/interpreting end of a communicative act. And in many approaches the actual impetus for interpretation comes still from the text which 'releases' information as readers 'respond' to the patterns or devices in the text. While it seems right, however, to stress that readers ENCODE or create meanings as much as DECODE them, it is misleading to play down the whole DIALOGIC process of author–text–reader, and the possible correlations between textual features and 'effects' on readers. A lot of work is currently being done, on what happens during the process of reading: how coherent hypotheses based on textual and PRAGMATIC knowledge, are made about PLOT and THEMES, which may be confirmed, or overturned and so redeveloped, etc.; and how these correlate with the distribution of INFORMATION in the text itself, which may be delayed or suspended, or left implicit, etc. (See, e.g., Emmott 1997.)

(2) One detailed attempt to expose the activity of reading and interpreting a text was Barthes's (1970) analysis of Balzac's short story *Sarrasine*. Barthes was in general keen to distinguish two kinds of text and so two kinds of reader: the *lisible* ('**readerly**') text of the classical novel with a rather passive reader as consumer; and the *scriptible* ('WRITERLY') text of the twentieth century, especially the POST-MODERNIST, which because of its structural and linguistic DEVIATIONS requires a more active participation of its readers.

Although the distinction, not unlike Eco's CLOSED TEXT (q.v.) and OPEN TEXT (q.v.), is broadly plausible, nevertheless, as Barthes's own analysis of Balzac rather ironically reveals, even with classical novels the reader is far less passive than might be supposed. While the implied cultural values that make up the REFERENTIAL CODE of nineteenth-century novels are not to be questioned, there is still a lot of interpretative work for the reader to do at the levels of plot and theme. And as is obvious in (1), other critics argue for the reader as producer rather than simply consumer of meaning, irrespective of period of textual composition.

received pronunciation (RP)

Introduced by the phonetician and dialectologist Alexander Ellis over a hundred years ago, and the established term for the unofficial social STANDARD pronunciation or ACCENT understood throughout the British Isles if not widely used. **Received pronunciation (RP)** is, however, recognized or 'received' as a model for foreign learners of British English, being thought of as 'typically' English.

For Ellis, as for others before him since the first emergence of a spoken standard at the end of the sixteenth century, such an accent was 'received' in the social sense of being 'accepted'. For it was spoken by those professions or social groups of high status: the upper classes (cf. the phrase **The Queen's English**), lawyers, Oxbridge dons, etc., especially those in London (i.e. the capital) and the Home Counties. (See also SOCIOLECT.) By the end of the nineteenth century RP was associated also with public schools, anywhere in the country. Even today RP enjoys considerable social prestige to the extent that some regional accents are judged 'inferior' in many ways even by their speakers. People are prone to evaluate varieties of speech stereotypically, and RP speakers are commonly rated as being particularly intelligent and articulate: an image much heeded by MEDIA advertisers.

The advent of radio broadcasting brought a new kind of prestige to RP, also therefore sometimes known as **BBC English**. The first announcers were recruited from public schools and the universities, so in one sense RP was used quite naturally. However, it was also regarded as an accent which was intelligible to the British population in a way that some regional accents would not be. Yet today many radio and TV announcers have regional accents, although on BBC Radio 3 and 4 and the World Service (especially) the accents are still predominantly RP, or 'educated Southern British English' (Gimson 1989).

By comparing newsreels of the pre-war years with those of the 1990s, it is clear that RP, as an accent, is as prone to phonetic changes as any other variety of speech. Only the oldest generation of RP speakers tend to say /ɔːf/ for *off* or /krɔːs/ for *cross*, for example. Gimson distinguishes **conservative RP** from **general**; and general also from **advanced**, spoken by such social groups as the younger members of the Royal Family. Advanced and conservative RP are most likely to be judged 'affected' by non-RP speakers on the grounds of pronunciations like /fɛmɪlɪ/ (*family*) or /graɪnd/ (*ground*). General or **mainstream** (Wells 1982) or **unmarked RP** seems to be acquiring features associated with the London regional dialect of Cockney (e.g. the glottal plosive), to the extent that it has been dubbed **Estuary English**.

Despite RP's image, and the fact that many educated British people tend to modify their regional pronunciations in the direction of RP, they nevertheless remain content with their modified speech. By analogy with CREOLE studies, Honey (1985) speaks of a LECT continuum, ranging from the **basilect** (the broad regional accent) to the **acrolect** (RP), with many people reaching a **paralect** (i.e. an approximate acrolect) stage. In addition, there is the **hyperlect**, the kind of RP associated with such speakers as the Royal Family, traditionally the socially privileged. (See further Wales (1994) on **royalese**.)

reception theory, also reception aesthetics

This is the German strain of READER RESPONSE CRITICISM developed systematic-ally as a complex and rather technical discipline from the late 1960s and early 1970s, particularly at the University of Konstanz. It is primarily associated with the work of Jauss (see 1974) and Iser (1971f), the latter's writings especially mak-ing a considerable impact on reader response criticism and LITERARY THEORY generally in Britain and the United States. (See also IMPLIED READER.)

Reception theory draws on other disciplines such as linguistics, LITERARY CRITICISM, psychology, philosophy, sociology, AESTHETICS and the PHENOMENO-LOGY of Ingarden in the 1930s in order to discuss theoretical models of the TEXT–READER relationship, the (dynamic) reading process, and textual production and reception (in the work of Jauss in particular). For Iser as for Ingarden, literary texts only fully exist with the active participation of the reader: they require concretization. Inevitably, in any text there will be 'spots of INDETERMINACY' (*Unbestimmtheitsstellen*) or information GAPS (Iser's *Leerstellen*) that readers must fill in from their own cultural knowledge in order to make the text fully COHER-ENT and consistent. According to Jauss such cultural knowledge, along with INTERTEXTUAL knowledge, makes up the **horizon of expectations** by which any text will be measured. Most importantly, he has stressed that horizons will change in different historical periods, producing as a result different definitions of literature. (For a slightly different kind of 'horizon', see HERMENEUTICS and Gadamer (1972).)

Reception theory, especially the work of Iser, has not been without its critics. The reader response critic Stanley Fish (1981) believes the theory is actually more traditional and FORMALIST than it might at first appear. The text is seen very much as a determinate, fixed structure, whose meaning must be DECODED by the attentive reader. (For a general critique of reception theory, see also Holub 1984).

As Elam (1980) rightly noted, the impact of reception theory on the criticism of dramatic discourse has been underwhelming, despite the fact that it is to Aristotle that we owe the first critical interest in the effect of drama on the audience. The notions of IDEAL and IMPLIED spectators, for example, certainly seem reasonable.

récit

Introduced by Genette (1972) in his discussion of NARRATIVE structure, and often left untranslated because of the lack of an unambiguous equivalent in English.

Genette was dissatisfied with the BINARY DEEP v. SURFACE oppositions of HISTOIRE v. DISCOURS, or narrative v. NARRATION: the abstracted chronological ordering of events as narrated, or what is being told, v. how it is told and the ACT of narration. It is the surface oppositions that cause most difficulty, since what they embrace is wide and they are not at all synonymous. *Discours* in particular includes not only the ordering of events but also the wider relations between AUTHOR and READER, POINT OF VIEW, etc. Genette therefore distinguishes between the basic story stuff (*histoire*; what the FORMALISTS term FABULA (q.v.)); the act of narration or narrating; and **récit**, the actual verbal representation in the TEXT (the Formalists' SJUŽET (q.v.)).

Récit is translated as 'text' by Rimmon-Kenan (1983), but this adds to the semantic load of this term in English. So too does the English translation (1980) of Genette's term as 'narrative'.

redundancy

(1) A term taken into linguistics from COMMUNICATION and INFORMATION THEORY, in opposition to ENTROPY (q.v.), both concerned with the degrees of predictability of a MESSAGE.

A **redundant message** is one which is highly predictable, and therefore low in information value. Human language in a technical sense is highly redundant, conveying an excess of meaning, because 'messages' or bits of information are conveyed on several levels simultaneously. So given the sequence *She closed the —or*, we can confidently predict even out of CONTEXT that the missing symbols are *d* and *o*, from our knowledge of GRAMMAR (a NOUN following the DEFINITE ARTICLE), of LEXIS (likely COLLOCATES with *closed*) and of the spelling patterns of English. In circumstances where NOISE may interfere with communication, e.g. faults on a telephone line, **redundancy** can enable the listener still to understand what has been said. And it is because of redundancy that ELLIPSIS features prominently in spoken DISCOURSE, and ASSIMILATIONS and ELISIONS can be tolerated.

Generally, LITERARY LANGUAGE is less predictable or redundant than most other types of discourse, because of its DEVIATIONS and unusual collocations and IMAGERY. Yet on the level of PHONOLOGY patterns of RHYTHM and RHYME are characteristically redundant because of their regularity or predictability (*June and moon*, for instance). (See further Fiske 1982, ch. 1.)

(2) In non-technical usage **redundancy** has acquired definite pejorative connotations of superfluity. The RHETORICAL term for an excess of meaning is **pleonasm**, as in *I can see with my own eyes*; related to **tautology**, where the same PROPOSITION is repeated in different words.

Such REPETITION may be due to lack of careful planning, but may also be used deliberately for EMPHASIS or to suggest strong feelings. Redundancy of meaning and expression is also characteristic of oral poetry, of Old English ALLITERATIVE VERSE and the later ballads, for instance:

It was <u>mirk</u>, <u>mirk night</u>, there was <u>nae starlight</u>.
They waded thro' <u>red blude</u> to the <u>knee</u> . . .

(Thomas Rhymer)

Its use here may well owe something to the technicalities of communication as in (1). Repetition is useful to a listening audience unable to 'go over' a text to catch the drift; and useful also in situations where background noise can impede reception (as in crowded halls and streets).

reference; referent; referential: ~ meaning; ~ function; ~ code

(1) In philosophy and SEMANTICS these terms are all concerned with the relations between words and extra-linguistic reality: what words stand for or **refer** to in the outside WORLD or UNIVERSE OF DISCOURSE. So the **referent** of the word *elephant* is the animal, elephant. **Referential meaning** is sometimes used instead of CONCEPTUAL or **cognitive** or DENOTATIONAL MEANING to describe that aspect of the meaning of a word which relates it precisely to its extra-linguistic **reference**. So **reference** itself is often opposed to **sense**: respectively, meaning in the world of experience v. linguistic meaning (relations of SYNONYMY, ANTONYMY, etc., which are internal to language). Note that for Ogden & Richards (1923) reference is used more specifically for the mental image of the referent produced by the word, and corresponds to Saussure's SIGNIFIED (q.v.).

The **referential** FUNCTION of language is basic to COMMUNICATION, and its significance has been recognized in many categorizations of the functions of language, e.g. Bühler (1934) and Jakobson (1960); see also Halliday's IDEATIONAL FUNCTION (e.g. 1973). It has sometimes been argued that the referential function or referential meaning is FOREGROUNDED or more prominent in certain types of discourse than others: e.g. technical or factual reporting v. POETIC LANGUAGE.

(2) The orientation towards the outside world, a world of physical, social and cultural experiences, is also reflected in Barthes's (1970) use of the term **referential code** as part of his categorization of the CODES or FRAMES OF REFERENCE readers draw upon to make sense of LITERARY texts. The referential code also includes social IDEOLOGY and cultural stereotypes as well as facts. Novels are characteristically MIMETIC, rendering an illusion of the real world. (See also VERISIMILITUDE.) But whatever the degree of 'realism' in a novel, it is economical for authors to PRESUPPOSE a certain amount of general knowledge in their readers and to assume shared values. These are often made explicit in the GENERIC statements of the OMNISCIENT NARRATOR, as in Dickens's *Bleak House*:

> This is the Court of Chancery; which has its decaying houses and its blighted lands in every shire; which has its worn-out lunatic in every madhouse, and its dead in every churchyard . . .

Even SYMBOLISM may depend on the referential code: the use of seasons to suggest birth and death, or the use of journeys for the 'road' of life, depends on assumed general cultural meanings. (For a discussion of the referential code, see especially Fowler 1981, ch. 6.)

(3) In GRAMMAR and TEXT LINGUISTICS **reference** is used in a much broader sense to mean any kind of designation, TEXTUAL as well as SITUATIONAL. Even in semantics it is recognized that not all elements of a language refer to specific objects in the outside world, chiefly the grammatical or FUNCTION WORDS, such as PREPOSITIONS, CONJUNCTIONS, DETERMINERS and PRONOUNS. Pronouns, however, like other classes of DEICTIC words, can 'point' to something in the environment, whose semantic reference will yet change from situation to situation. (See also EXOPHORIC REFERENCE.) In a text, the terms reference and refer are convenient to describe the function of words like pronouns and determiners to designate

a NOUN PHRASE they identify with in the immediate CO-TEXT (i.e. ENDOPHORIC REFERENCE), e.g.:

Mary had a little lamb,
His fleece was white as snow;
And everywhere that Mary went
The lamb was sure to go.

This CO-REFERENCE by 'backward-looking' (ANAPHORIC, q.v.), and also 'forward-looking' (CATAPHORIC, q.v.) reference, is an important means of COHESION within a text, of linking sentence with sentence, and at the same time avoiding REPETITION.

In grammar, other kinds of reference are distinguished: so pronouns like *you, I, she, he* have PERSONAL reference; the ARTICLES have DEFINITE (*the*) or INDEFINITE (*a*) reference, and GENERIC or specific.

register; ~ -switching, etc.

(1) Used in musical studies since the early nineteenth century to refer to the ranges of TONES that can be produced by the voice (e.g. 'upper'; 'middle'; 'lower'), **register** has been taken into PHONETICS to describe potential pitch ranges in speech. Although male voices are usually lower in pitch than female, the normal unMARKED register for both sexes is low. High registers are marked in some way: to indicate intense emotion, for example. Musical terms like **falsetto** and **soprano** are sometimes used to describe such different registers.

The term is also used to describe kinds of voice quality: e.g. 'breathy voice' or 'creaky voice'.

(2) More widely known is the use of **register** in STYLISTICS and sociolinguistics to refer to a VARIETY of language defined according to the SITUATION.

First introduced in the 1950s, the term retains some of the connotations of the musical sense, presumably its analogy, in that it suggests a scale of differences, of **degrees of** FORMALITY, APPROPRIATE to different social uses of language. It is part of the COMMUNICATIVE COMPETENCE of every speaker that he or she will constantly switch USAGES, select certain features of sound, grammar, lexis, etc., in the different situations of everyday life: a domestic chat, a business letter, a telephone conversation, etc. All these uses of language serve different social ROLES.

The codification of the significant linguistic features which determine overall the STYLE of the register was much to the fore in the 1960s, in the work of Enkvist, Spenser & Gregory (1964), for instance, and particularly Halliday (1964f) and later SYSTEMIC linguists. Three main variables were distinguished which are felt to be significant for the CHOICE of situational features: FIELD or subject matter; MEDIUM or MODE (e.g. speech or writing; format, etc.); and TENOR, the relations between participants (e.g. social roles) which influences degree of formality, etc. To these can be added the FUNCTION of the variety: e.g. expository, didactic. TV sports commentary, for instance, is obviously distinguished as a variety, with its special vocabulary reflecting the subject, the audio-visual medium, the functions of describing and evaluating and the fairly informal relations between commentator and mass audience. Different registers will overlap with each other in respect of function or medium or even field (e.g. a prayer v. a sermon), so that many linguistic features will be common to several registers. Yet a considerable proportion of the features will be drawn from COMMON CORE language. (See, however, RESTRICTED LANGUAGE.)

Our awareness of the distinctive varieties of language is confirmed when we are confronted by **register-switching** and **register-mixing** or -**borrowing**. For example, converting a lecture into a printed text means switching style to a different degree of formality, and manipulating the GRAPHIC conventions: also known as **recontextualization**. As for register-mixing, many adverts, for instance, take the form of letters. Register-mixing is a kind of PARODY: the formal features of one kind of discourse are borrowed for new subject matter. There is often the same humorous or satirical effect: so a trade union's version of *Psalm 23* begins:

> The Union is my Shepherd I shall not work,
> It leadeth me to lie down on the job . . .

Another kind of register-borrowing is commonly found in the novel, which absorbs the conventions of non-LITERARY varieties for MIMETIC effects: e.g. 'reproducing' newspaper articles, telegrams or personal letters. This is also termed **re-registration**. (See also INTERTEXTUALITY.)

Since the 1960s and outside Hallidayan influence, other terms for register have come into fashion: e.g. **diatypic language variety**; **sublanguage**; **discourse genre**; **text type** and even GENRE itself (q.v.). However, it is the prominent term in Biber *et al.* (1999). Some linguists have found it difficult to maintain a distinction between 'genre' (or 'subgenre') and 'register'. It is probably easiest to see registers as particular situational configurations of linguistic resources, quite specifically contextually determined; genres are larger or 'higher-level' structures, groups of texts which are recognized as performing broadly similar functions in society. So advertising comprises specific types which vary in choices of linguistic features, for example, according to medium (TV, radio, magazine, etc.), field (beauty products, mobile phones), tenor (target audience, etc.). Register is thus a usefully flexible concept: we can appreciate genres for their shared elements; but no two registers will ever be identical. (See further Bex 1996.)

(3) For Todorov's (1967) use of the term **register** in relation to his NARRATIVE GRAMMAR see MOOD, the term he first used in 1966.

relation, also relevance, maxim of

(1) The **maxim of relation** is one of four maxims (see also MANNER, QUALITY and QUANTITY) distinguished by the philosopher Grice (1975) as playing an important underlying role in our COMMUNICATIVE behaviour: part of a general CO-OPERATIVE PRINCIPLE (q.v.).

We normally expect each other's utterances to be **relevant** to the situation and topic at hand. As other linguists have argued (e.g. Sperber & Wilson 1982), it is a central principle, for we easily detect irrelevance and try very hard to make apparently irrelevant remarks relevant, by **inference**. (And see RELEVANCE THEORY below.) Answers to requests are very commonly phrased indirectly in this way, as polite refusals:

A: Can you babysit for me on Tuesday evening?
B: West Ham United is playing at home.

A will assume that B cannot babysit, precisely because he or she is going to the match. If we cannot find relevance, we will either assume that our interlocutor has misunderstood, or is deliberately being obscure for some reason, wishing to 'change the subject' perhaps. The violation of this maxim, more than the others, can lead to frustration, even a breakdown in communication.

In extended MONOLOGIC utterances, however, irrelevance in conversation is quite common, since one train of thought will inspire another, and the lack of premeditation and advance planning means the topic can easily be lost sight of. Prolixity is often a consequence, so the maxim of manner is also violated. Dickens frequently exploits both maxims for comic effect and to suggest a particular scatterbrained mental 'set': as with Flora Finching in *Little Dorrit*:

'Dear, dear', said Flora, 'only to think of the changes at home Arthur – cannot overcome it, seems so natural, Mr Clenham far more proper – since you became familiar with the Chinese customs and language which I am persuaded you speak like a Native if not better for you were always quick and clever though immensely difficult no doubt, I am sure the tea chests alone would kill ME if I tried, such changes Arthur . . .'

Yet phrases we commonly use like *I'm/ you're wandering off the point* or *digressing* testify to the idea of relevance as a NORM or ideal. In written discourse the maxim of relation is even more highly regarded and irrelevance not so much tolerated as in speech, for there is time to review material for COHERENCE.

(2) In LITERARY LANGUAGE the maxim of relation assumes the greatest significance, and relevance itself takes on added meaning: a 'super-relevance'. Readers presume that every word of a text is relevant to an overriding design and theme; and so find it exceedingly difficult to decide whether anything is in fact 'irrelevant'. Moreover, the maxim of super-relevance means that dramatic DIALOGUE is more 'informative' in the fullest sense of the word than ordinary conversation.

relative: ~ clause; ~ pronoun

A **relative clause** is a SUBORDINATE CLAUSE which most commonly functions as a POSTMODIFIER in a NOUN PHRASE. It is thus 'related' to an antecedent, the noun phrase. It is introduced by a set of **relative pronouns**: *wh*-forms (*who; whom; whose; which*), or *that*; or (in inFORMAL discourse usually) in some constructions nothing at all (the so-called ZERO-**relative**), e.g.:

The yellow fog *that* rubs its back upon the windowpanes
(Eliot: *Love Song of J. Alfred Prufrock*)

Footfalls echo in the memory
Down the passage <u>which</u> we did not take
Towards the door [Ø] we never opened . . .

(Eliot: Four Quartets)

Who is used for ANIMATE, chiefly human, antecedents; *which* for INANIMATE. The CASE of the *wh*-forms depends on the function of the relative within its own clause: so, in the following quotation, *whom* is in the **objective case** because it is the OBJECT of *overthrow*:

For, those *whom* thou thinkst, thou dost overthrow
Die not, poor death

(Donne: Holy Sonnets X)

However, in informal speech *whom* is rarely heard, and *that* or the zero-relative is commonly used here instead of *who*: *That woman (who/that /Ø/) I met is an old school friend.* (See further Quirk *et al.* 1985, ch. 6.)

Relative clauses function like ADJECTIVES to add information to the preceding noun phrase. If the information is specific or particularizing, then it is called a **restrictive** or **defining** relative clause; if the information could easily be omitted, it is called a **non-restrictive** or **non-defining** or **parenthetical** relative (a less common type). The non-restrictive is often separated from the MAIN CLAUSE by commas in writing, or a separate INTONATION contour in speech, and occurs with *wh*-forms usually: cf.

The vase <u>which</u> is in the cupboard needs a good clean (i.e. a particular vase; not the vase which is on the dresser).
The vase, <u>which</u> is in the cupboard, needs a good clean (only one vase, which happens to be in the cupboard if you want to know).

Sometimes relative clauses function as the head noun phrase of a clause themselves, as in PSEUDO-CLEFTS, e.g.: *What we want/is a nice cup of tea.*

relevance theory

(1) A pragmatic and cognitive theory of communication particularly associated with the work of Sperber & Wilson (1994 [1986]f) and their associates, and based on the concept of **relevance** from Grice's MAXIM OF RELATION (q.v.). Like Grice, they are interested in the types of INFERENCES and assumptions that interlocutors draw on in communication. This is said to be 'successful' when the hearer infers the speaker's (intended) meaning from an utterance. The smaller the processing effort involved in interpretation ('cost'), the greater the relevance ('benefit'). For relevance theorists, the act of interpreting is most definitely premised on the addressee's assumption that an utterance will be 'optimally relevant'.

In general, they argue that a CODE model of communication is inadequate, in that the actual linguistic forms, etc., can only provide clues as to speakers' meanings, rather than full representations of them.

One important difference between relevance theory and Grice is that indirectness strategies are not seen as 'floutings' of his CONVERSATIONAL PRINCIPLES, but that the interpretation of indirectness follows a search for interpretation consistent with the principle of relevance. It is assumed on the hearer's part that indirectness will lead to what are termed extra 'contextual effects', which compensate for the extra processing effort involved.

(2) Some relevance theorists have focussed their attention on literary communication, as part of a LITERARY PRAGMATICS, and precisely the issues of processing effort and 'richer' contextual effects, particularly in relation to tropes like METAPHOR and METONYMY. (See Pilkington 1996.) For relevance theorists the Gricean 'violation'-view of such tropes is rejected; and metaphoric and LITERAL utterances do not involve for them distinct levels of interpretation; however, the more effort involved in processing a metaphor, the more 'poetic' it will be.

Relevance theoretical approaches to literary language have been dubbed **relevance stylistics** by Green (1997), who provides a critique of this approach, and the extent of its usefulness to literary questions and readings.

See further Bex (1996), Goatly 1997 (ch. 5) and Toolan (1996, 1999) for a general critique of what is seen as the rigidity of relevance theory, and its underplaying of the significance of social context, for example.

repetition

(1) **Repetition** in ordinary conversation can be seen both as a problem, i.e. of REDUNDANCY ('You're repeating yourself'), and also as a powerful resource of INTERPERSONAL involvement and rapport: the latter much emphasized by Tannen (1989), who sees it as the primary rhetorical device of spoken language. It may also be used for EMPHASIS, or out of intensity of feeling.

(2) It is difficult not to appreciate the significance of repetition, on all linguistic levels, in LITERARY LANGUAGE. However, since LEXICAL repetition is very obviously drawn to the attention, it is often therefore avoided in favour of VARIATION by SYNONYMY, or SUBSTITUTION by PRONOUNS, important means of COHESION. Such repetition is felt to suggest the lack of premeditation characteristic of ordinary speech, and is often associated with 'unsophisticated' styles, e.g. of children's narratives or medieval chronicles, e.g. Malory's *Morte d'Arthur*:

> This beast went to the well and drank, and the noise was in the beast's belly like unto the questing of thirty couple hounds, but all the while the beast drank there was no noise in the beast's belly . . .

This kind of repetition may go back to oral techniques of composition and delivery: certainly it is common in Old English poetry, and the repetition of whole lines or sentences is a feature of ballads. What is termed **incremental repetition** or **adding style** refers to the characteristic ballad technique of repetition interwoven with lines which advance the narrative:

> And what will ye leave to your ain mither dear, Edward, Edward?
> And what will ye leave to your ain mither dear,

Me dear son, now tell me, O?
The curse of hell frae me sall ye bear, Mither, Mither:
The curse of hell frae me sall ye bear:
Sic counsels ye gave to me, O

(Edward)

Other kinds of repetition are exploited in narratives, e.g. of phrases or themes for LEITMOTIFS (q.v.).

Another kind of lexical repetition, in conjunction with grammatical repetition or PARALLELISM, is a feature of many different kinds of SCHEMES of RHETORIC: e.g. ANAPHORA (repetition of words at the beginning of successive clauses); EPISTROPHE (repetition at the end of clauses) and SYMPLOCE (repetition at beginning and end). (See also EPIZEUXIS and PLOCE). Elaborate though these devices may be, they are significant means for heightening emotion and 'pointing' an argument whether in literature or political speeches. Such figures are particularly frequent in sixteenth- and seventeenth-century poetry, when the vogue for the arts of rhetoric was at its height, e.g.:

Tell zeal it wants devotion;
Tell love it is but lust:
Tell time it is but motion;
Tell flesh it is but dust

(Ralegh: *The Lie*)

Obvious patterns of repetition on the PHONOLOGICAL level in poetry are those of regular RHYTHMS, to produce different METRES; also repetition of vowels and consonants in ALLITERATION, ASSONANCE and RHYME.

(See also EQUIVALENCE.)

reported speech

See INDIRECT SPEECH.

representation: ~ of speech; ~ of thought; represented: ~ speech; ~ thought

(1) The problems of rendering speech, a temporal MEDIUM with its own distinctive features, in the written linear medium, have exercised both writers and critics alike; the latter particularly concerned with trying to categorize methods of presentation, or better, **representation**. The representation of thought processes, which has become prominent in the novel since the early twentieth century, is even more difficult, since a great deal of our thoughts are not verbalized at all, and where they are, are not obviously structured by normal patterns of SYNTAX.

For different classifications of speech and thought (re)presentation, see particularly Banfield (1982), Cohn (1978), Fludernik (1993), Genette (1972), Leech & Short (1981), McHale (1978), Page (1973) and Short *et al.* (1996f). See also DIRECT SPEECH and DIRECT THOUGHT; FREE DIRECT SPEECH and FREE DIRECT THOUGHT; INDIRECT SPEECH/THOUGHT; INTERIOR MONOLOGUE; NARRATED MONOLOGUE; NARRATIVE REPORT; PSYCHO-NARRATION, etc.

(2) **Represented speech** and **thought (RST)** are terms Banfield uses to describe what is more commonly termed FREE INDIRECT SPEECH/STYLE. In this sense represented speech was first used by Jespersen (1922).

(3) **Represented speech** is also used by Bakhtin (e.g. 1981) to cover most of the different modes of (1). It is sometimes useful to have a general term, since (free) direct and indirect modes characteristically co-occur in novels; and there is often **slipping** from one type to another. So too in the representation of consciousness (e.g. in the novels of Virginia Woolf).

restricted: ~ code; ~ language

(1) **Restricted code** is one of a pair of controversial terms (see also ELABORATED CODE) coined by the sociologist Basil Bernstein in the 1960s as part of a theory of educational development and social class. They replaced his earlier terms **public** and **formal language**.

The terms refer to types of meaning or cultural values generated by the social system and realized in VARIETIES of language (see Halliday 1978). They have, however, even in Bernstein's own work, frequently been used as variants of variety or DIALECT. The assumption is that social class determines the variety of English available to a child. Restricted code users (working class), as the term 'restricted' rather pejoratively suggests, were orientated supposedly towards particularistic or context-tied meanings, so that the language is concrete and personal, often REDUNDANT or predictable, reinforced by considerable use of NON-VERBAL COMMUNICATION. By contrast, elaborated code users (middle and upper classes) were oriented towards context-free, more universal meanings, so using a more impersonal and abstract language. Bernstein claimed generally that the educational system is dominated by the elaborated code; and that working-class children are prevented from doing well at school because of their lack of access to this code: in other words, are linguistically 'deprived'.

What has never been actually 'proved', however, is that the codes are SOCIOLECTS, that there is a linguistic difference between classes on the linguistic basis he describes. Speakers from any class will switch between such codes as linguistically defined according to different situations: so restricted code in the sense of simple context-tied constructions and a reliance on shared knowledge is a feature of PHATIC COMMUNION in anyone's speech. Many aspects of the language of the school curriculum may well be complex (certainly not all), but it is part of any child's education to master them, or at least acquire a passive COMPETENCE in being able to understand them. (For the application of restricted and elaborated code to Lawrence's *Sons and Lovers*, see Fowler 1977.)

(2) **Restricted language** has been commonly used in studies of REGISTER from Halliday *et al.* 1964 onwards to describe varieties of language which have a very restricted purpose and therefore a limited range of linguistic choices: e.g. parade-ground drills; knitting patterns.

rheme

(1) One of a pair of terms (see also THEME) particularly developed by the post-war PRAGUE SCHOOL of linguists as part of their general interest in the INFORMATIONAL value of UTTERANCES. (See also COMMUNICATIVE DYNAMISM (CD); FUNCTIONAL SENTENCE PERSPECTIVE (FSP).)

The **rheme** or **rhematic element** carries most semantic importance in the utterance, most commonly coinciding with NEW INFORMATION, and in English at least, occurring in FOCUS position towards the end of the utterance. The theme carries least significance in CONTENT, and commonly occurs initially. Linking theme and rheme are **transitional elements**, usually VERBS, e.g. *Here we* (thematic) *go round* (transitional) *the mulberry bush* (rhematic). There is thus a scale of 'dynamism', the rheme pushing forward the MESSAGE. Rhematic elements can themselves be graded dynamically: as in (*There was*) *an Old Man/with a beard.*

(2) Outside the Prague School the terms **theme** and **rheme** are commonly found, but in a much more schematized way, as initial and non-initial elements, corresponding to SUBJECT and PREDICATE grammatically, and sometimes para-phrased as **topic** and **comment**. (See the work of Halliday 1985 on THEMATIZATION.) What is said about a topic is, in fact, the meaning of *rhema* in the original Greek.

Yet one consequence of this dissociation from FSP is that irrespective of informational values the theme will always be at the beginning and the rheme (now incorporating 'transitional' elements) will always simply be 'the remainder': it loses its significance. So SENTENCES with MARKED WORD ORDER, for instance where significant information is FRONTED, will not be distinguished from those with normal, e.g.:

Monday's child (theme)/ is fair of face (rheme).
Fair of face (theme)/ is Monday's child (rheme).

rhetoric

(1) From Gk *techne rhetorike* 'art of speech', originally a discipline concerned with the skills of public speaking as a means of persuasion. The influence of **rhetoric** extends even to the twentieth century in many other kinds of dis-course, although the formal study of classical rhetoric has declined, as the study of classical languages has declined.

Certain STYLISTIC techniques were developed by the forensic orators of the fifth century BC, which were later formalized in treatises or handbooks: particu-larly the so-called FIGURES OF SPEECH (q.v.): SCHEMES and TROPES which helped to structure and elaborate an argument, and to move the emotions.

In the Renaissance, particularly under the influence of the reformist Peter Ramus, such figures became increasingly identified with the whole art of rhetoric, which was defined simply as the art of speaking well (*bene dicendi*); but the study of these figures under the heading of ELOCUTIO or STYLE, was technically one of the five major aspects or **divisions** of rhetoric. The others were INVENTIO (the finding of topics): DISPOSITIO (the arrangement of ideas); **memory** (prepared, not spontaneous speaking); and **pronunciation** or **delivery** (enunciation, including accompanying gestures).

Rhetoric was one of the major courses of study in the European education curriculum, one of the Seven Liberal Arts, closely allied to the other 'communication' skills of GRAMMAR and DIALECTIC. It became a valuable training for would-be writers, who applied what we would call methods of PRACTICAL CRITICISM to earlier writers, as well as composing their own works.

One recurring concern among the theorists, still reflected today in some of the connotations of the term rhetoric itself, is the extent of the rhetor's or orator's honesty. As early as Socrates, rhetoric had been condemned as the 'mother of lies' in its possible manipulation to conceal rather than reveal truth; and its association with artificiality of thought and expression, and with 'bad style', has persisted ever since. (On the definition and development of classical rhetoric, see especially Dixon 1971; on the use of rhetoric in advertising, see Dyer 1982; and in public speaking, see Atkinson 1984.)

(2) With the development of subjects such as SEMIOTICS, STYLISTICS and PRAGMATICS, an interest in traditional rhetoric has been revived; and, indeed, new areas of rhetoric have been suggested for development. Earlier interest in the 'philosophy' of rhetoric had been aroused by the (1936) work of Richards, which bridged the past with then current work in LITERARY and practical CRITICISM. In the United States in particular, handbooks which give guidance on composition skills continue the rhetorical tradition, in what is sometimes called **modern rhetoric** (see, e.g., Brooks & Warren 1972).

In one sense modern stylistics can be seen as a development of the main branch of rhetorical study, namely *elocutio*, with its interest in the relations between FORM (*verba*) and CONTENT (*res*), and a concentration on the analysis of characteristic features of (especially literary) expression. In particular, the early work of Leech (e.g. 1969) was an attempt to fuse modern linguistic insights with traditional work on rhetorical figures: what he calls **descriptive rhetoric**. Other scholars, e.g. the Belgian Groupe μ, have focussed specific attention on rhetorical figures, and proposed new classifications on a rigorous linguistic basis (see further Plett 1985 on this **rhetorical stylistics**). In contrast, American DECONSTRUCTIONISTS like de Man in the 1970s speculated philosophically on **rhetoricity**, the semantics of FIGURATIVE and LITERAL MEANING. (See de Man 1979.)

More recently, Leech (1983) and also other linguists like Leith and Myerson (1989), have approached rhetoric from a broader pragmatic perspective, and so have brought into the foreground again traditional rhetoric's own broader sense of a means of public persuasion, producing a social discourse with AFFECTIVE MEANING, or a PERLOCUTIONARY EFFECT on the ADDRESSEE(s).

(3) Not surprisingly, therefore, the term **rhetoric** has now come to be used in modern linguistic and literary theory in new senses which reflect current rather than traditional perspectives; or in senses that are only loosely connected with the more traditional ones. So for Leech (1983) for example, rhetoric is a set of conversational 'principles' and 'maxims', INTERPERSONAL and TEXTUAL; for Jordan (1984) on the 'rhetoric' of everyday English texts, it refers to principles of INFORMATION STRUCTURE and 'signalling' strategies (**rhetorical structure theory**). Common and less linguistic is the sense of '(a set) of formal techniques', as in Booth's (1961) title, *Rhetoric of Fiction* (i.e. techniques of 'telling' and 'showing'); or Sucksmith's (1970) sub-title 'the Rhetoric of Sympathy and Irony in [Dickens's] Novels'.

rhetorical question

RHETORIC distinguished four types of questions in FIGURES **of thought** (see, e.g., QUAESITIO), but the one most commonly known as a **rhetorical question** was called **interrogatio** (or **erotema** in GK). This is a question which does not expect an answer, since it really asserts something which is known to the ADDRESSER, and cannot be denied. It is thus the equivalent of a statement, often negative: as in the last line of Shelley's *Ode to the West Wind: If Winter comes, can Spring be far behind?* (which implies Spring can't be far behind).

Ohmann (1971) argues that because it only appears to be a question, it is 'insincere': a quasi-SPEECH ACT. Yet de Man (1979) amongst others has argued that, despite intentions, it could be taken literally: for example the last line of Yeats's *Among Schoolchildren*:

> O body swayed to music, O brightening glance,
> How can we know the dancer from the dance?

In classical oratory, as in public speaking still, rhetorical questions were useful as persuasive devices to appeal to the listeners' reason; or as EMOTIVE devices to suggest the speaker's outburst of natural feeling (see Longinus *On the Sublime*, ch. 18). In fiction, they are the obvious sign of the OMNISCIENT NARRATOR, making a direct appeal to the reader.

rhyme: ~ scheme

(1) **Rhyme** is a kind of PHONETIC echo found in verse: more precisely, a PHONEMIC matching.

In English **end rhyme** is the most frequent type: two units (commonly monosyllabic words) matched by identical sequences of sounds stretching from the vowel (usually STRESSED) to the end of the word, with the initial sound varied: e.g. *June/moon; rose/toes*. Such rhymes occur most commonly at the ends of METRICAL lines; within the lines they are called **internal rhymes**. And as *rose/toes* illustrate, it is sound, not spelling, that is primary. Identical spellings but with different pronunciations produce EYE-RHYME (q.v.), e.g. *bough/cough*. Some apparently imperfect rhymes may be due to sound changes that have taken place since the verse was written: e.g. Pope in the eighteenth century rhymes *obey* and *tea*. Others may be deliberate distortions, often for comic effect (in RHETORIC called **antisthecon**), as in:

> There was a good canon of Durham,
> Who fished with a hook and a worrum.

More common in limericks, actually, are perfect rhymes but with altered spellings, e.g.:

> An innocent maiden of Gloucester
> Fell in love with a coucester named Foucester.

As this example also reveals, sometimes the repeated syllables may involve unstressed or 'weak' rather than stressed or 'strong' endings of words: also termed FEMININE RHYME (q.v.) v. MASCULINE RHYME (q.v.). There are other variations on the **full** rhyme pattern, that have become popular especially since the nineteenth century: e.g. HALF-RHYME, with repetition of final consonants only, with variation in the vowels, e.g. *bend/sand*; APOPHONY or **slant rhyme**, with repetition of both initial and final consonants, e.g. *bend/band*. (See also CONSONANCE; PARARHYME.) ALLITERATION is sometimes termed 'initial rhyme', since it is the initial sound which is repeated, e.g. *four fat frogs*. The repetition of initial consonant and vowel is termed REVERSE RHYME (e.g. *cash/carry*).

Until the present rhyme has been a predominant feature of English metrical structure since the Norman Conquest, when it was introduced in this way under French influence. Anglo-Saxon verse had used alliteration as a COHESIVE feature of form. With the simultaneous introduction of various stanza patterns, several dominant **rhyme schemes** were established. Rhyming in adjacent lines (aa, bb, etc.) is a feature of the **heroic couplet**; the pattern abab is known as **alternate rhyme**. Common rhyme schemes for four-BEAT verse in four lines are abab or abcb (as in BALLAD METRE and nursery rhymes). There are other, more elaborate schemes: in so-called **rime couée** the pattern is aab, bbc, as in Gray's *Ode on the Death of a Favourite Cat*; with **rhyme royal**, introduced by Chaucer, the pattern is seven lines of ababbcc; **ottava rima** is eight lines of abababcc; and the **Spenserian stanza** is nine lines of ababbcbcc, as in *The Faerie Queene*. Distinctive patterns are also associated with the GENRE of the 14-line sonnet, both Italian and Elizabethan.

Nowadays, rhyme is not favoured outside popular verse of songs and jingles in contemporary poetry; FREE VERSE is the fashion. This may be because rhyme so obviously draws attention to the MARKEDNESS of poetry as distinct from prose. Traditionally, however, in five-beat or IAMBIC verse, absence of rhyme has always been a noteworthy feature: so-called BLANK VERSE. Attridge (1982) suggests that it does not need the CLOSURE of rhyme in the way that four-beat verse does, which is more perceptibly salient.

(2) **Rime**, with the archaic spelling of *rhyme* (as in Coleridge's *Rime of the Ancient Mariner*), is a term used by some phoneticians to describe the vowel (with or without following consonants) which follows the **onset** of any syllable (the

consonants(s)). Since this term is now favoured by the National Literacy Strategy for primary stage pupils, it is to be hoped that they can distinguish it from **rhyme**.

rhythm

(1) Both RHYME and **rhythm** derive from the same Gk word *rhuthmos* 'flow'. In PHONETICS and PROSODY rhythm is generally described as the perceptual pattern of ACCENTED or STRESSED and unaccented or unstressed syllables in a language. Even in speech rhythm is fairly regular, the stressed syllables recurring at roughly equal intervals (see also ISOCHRONY); in verse the regularity is heightened to produce METRICAL patterns, cf.

```
 ×  / ×    /  ×    /  × /  ×    /  × / ×
In Scotland, Wales and Northern England, snow will fall on high ground;
 × /    × /    × /  ×    / ×    /
Around his tomb let Art and Genius weep
 ×  /  × /    × /      / ×    /
But hear his death, ye blockheads! hear and sleep
```
(Johnson: Vanity of Human Wishes)

Pronounced regularity of rhythm is also found in many literary prose works, and was much cultivated along with the syntactic regularity of PARALLELISM and ANTITHESIS by eighteenth-century essayists like Johnson. A rhythmical prose very close to verse was also cultivated in the Anglo-Saxon period by homilists such as Ælfric and Wulfstan. Rhythm is sometimes FOREGROUNDED for EXPRESSIVE or ICONIC effects by novelists: so Dickens suggests the regularity of movement and sound of a speeding train in *Dombey and Son*:

> Through the hollow, on the height, by the heath, by the orchard, by the park, by the garden, over the canal, across the river, where the sheep are feeding, where the mill is going, where the barge is floating, where the dead are lying, where the factory is smoking, where the stream is running . . .

(2) In LITERARY CRITICISM the term rhythm has sometimes been used rather loosely and vaguely following the (1927) work of Forster on the novel, to refer to patterns of REPETITION which apply to the text as a whole, and so give it its characteristic TEXTURE and structure, comparable to the overall 'rhythm' of a piece of music.

role: social ~; discourse ~; semantic ~; narrative ~, etc.

(1) That 'all the world's a stage' is well known in sociology and sociolinguistics where the dramatic concept of **role-playing** has been adapted to the study of our social behaviour.

Role is a relational concept: each of us has a number of different parts to play in our daily encounters with different people in different social situations: the same person may be variously a lecturer, mother, socialite, customer, etc. For each of these **social roles** we have certain NORMS or expectations of behaviour; we are accustomed to 'act' in particular ways, and to make choices of appropriate language. (See also REGISTER; TENOR.) Unfortunately social stereotyping can occur, which may be further fixed in the images of advertising: the image of the housewife, for instance, in the role of administering angel. Not all roles are compatible with each other: **role conflict** can result. So the role of housewife notoriously conflicts with the role of breadwinner. Some roles have more social status than others: a housewife is lower in status than many other occupations. Some social roles are acquired through definite achievement or competition; others arise naturally through circumstances (e.g. daughter, sister, fiancée, wife, mother, aunt, divorcee, mistress).

Some roles are more obviously similar to dramatic roles because of their ritualistic nature: special clothes and/or distinctive features of language accompany the role of bride or groom, freemason or guest at a royal garden party. TERMS OF ADDRESS characteristically reflect differences of social role: *Professor Wales* in public or FORMAL situations v. *Mum* at home, for instance. In some languages differences of social role are built into the grammatical system of PRONOUNS. English PERSONAL pronouns indicate only DEICTIC roles, i.e. they identify participants in the speech SITUATION: ADDRESSER (*I*), ADDRESSEE (*you*) and any others (*she, he, they*). (See also FACE; PERSONA.)

(2) Attracting interest in DISCOURSE ANALYSIS are the various and complex **discourse roles**. For instance, a speaker may not be the author of an utterance, but a spokesperson or mouthpiece; the receiver of a message may not be the addressee but a bystander.

(3) In linguistics what has sometimes been termed **role structure analysis** applies to those grammatical theories or models such as CASE GRAMMAR (q.v.) (see Fillmore 1968) and TRANSITIVITY in Halliday's SYSTEMIC GRAMMAR, where NOUN PHRASES (NP) can be expressed in terms of their semantic relationships. So grammatical SUBJECTS with human REFERENCE commonly have an AGENTIVE role as instigator or doer of an action (e.g. *Jack and Jill went up the hill*); DIRECT OBJECTS with human reference are commonly **patients**, the recipient of an action (e.g. *I took him by the left leg,/And threw him down the stairs*). Other **semantic roles** for NPs may be **beneficiary, instrument**, etc.

As the work of Halliday (1971) himself has shown on Golding's *The Inheritors*, the concept of semantic roles has proved of value in STYLISTICS for the analysis of the semantic structure of texts in terms of IDEOLOGY and WORLD-VIEW. The CHOICE of semantic roles can powerfully alter the PERSPECTIVE of a text, to suggest, for example, an overall 'agency' or an overall 'passivity' on the part of the main characters. (See further Burton 1982; Fowler 1977, 1996.)

(4) In earlier NARRATIVE studies, **role** structure had already been explored in the analysis of PLOTS by the FORMALIST Propp (1928) in his study of Russian folktales. His corpus, he argued, could be reduced to a basic set of configurations, based upon CHARACTERS recurring in a set of roles and actions (FUNCTIONS): e.g. 'hero', 'villain', 'dispatcher' and 'helper'. A character may have more than one role (a hero may turn into the villain); conversely, a role may be filled by more than one character (there may be several helpers for the hero).

Propp's work was later taken up by French STRUCTURALISTS in the 1960s such as Greimas (1966) and Todorov (1969), who developed NARRATIVE GRAMMARS (q.v.) on the basis of characters and events viewed functionally and schematically as ACTANTS or participants in a series of actions or PROPOSITIONS.

Russian formalism

See FORMALISM.

S

---

schema; schema theory

(1) **Schema** from Gk 'form, shape', basically referring to skeletal organizations of conceptual knowledge, was originally so used by the philosopher Kant at the end of the eighteenth century. It is particularly associated with psychology and the work of Bartlett (1932), to explain how information from stories is frequently re-arranged in the memories of readers from other cultures to fit in with their own expectations and conceptual knowledge or mental pictures. Connected bits of general cultural information based on verbal and non-verbal experience, etc., are stored as packages or schemas or **schemata**, which, although often stereotypical, are continually being 'updated'. Schemata are crucially important for us to make INFERENCES about what is going on in a text or discourse, to fill in GAPS and to make it COHERENT. (See also TEXT WORLD.) They are also influential on our general COMMUNICATIVE COMPETENCE: so that we know how to buy a ticket for the train, and what to say or do (or not) in the presence of the Queen. Developed by AI research and cognitive psychology in the 1970s, **schema theory** is now influential in COGNITIVE LINGUISTICS and cognitive approaches to literature and text comprehension.

Related and confusingly overlapping terms to describe subtypes of mental representations include **script** (information stored as a 'narrative': e.g. what 'normally' happens in an interview or a restaurant: Schank & Abelson 1977), **scenario**, **plan** and FRAME (q.v.). (See further Emmott 1997; Fairclough 1989.)

(2) Cook (1994) suggests that literature in particular tends to be **schema-refreshing**, rather than **schema-reinforcing**, i.e. our conventional ways of perceiving the world are challenged or disrupted. Adverts tend to confirm stereotypical assumptions, on the other hand. Although he does make the point that schema-refreshment is reader-dependent, his idea seems to be very close to the traditional FORMALIST idea of DE-FAMILIARIZATION (q.v.) as an inherent property of texts. In any case, if schemas are mental representations, then different readers will respond differently to texts: the same text may well be schema-reinforcing to one reader, schema-refreshing to another, depending on their own experiences (e.g. a 'bonkbuster' novel). Despite an assumption of cultural homogeneity, there will be some variation in these generic mental representations from person to person. (On schema theory and poetry, see Semino 1997.)

(3) In COGNITIVE METAPHOR THEORY **image-schemata** are basic simplified mental representations of common physical experiences which are projected in conventional metaphors to classify more complex physical or mental phenomena: e.g. containers, links, movement up and down, balance. (See especially the work of Lakoff *et al.* (1987f). For an application to the imagery of *King Lear*, see Freeman 1993.)

scheme

In RHETORIC it was customary to divide FIGURES OF SPEECH into **schemes** and TROPES (q.v.); although the term *scheme* itself from Gk SCHEMA 'form', since it was first used in English in the sixteenth century has often been used simply as a synonym for figure of speech generally.

Schemes comprise those figures which arrange words into schematized patterns of FOREGROUNDED regularity of FORM, syntactic, lexical or phonetic (see Leech 1969). Common are those which depend on PARALLELISM or REPETITION between clauses, e.g. ANAPHORA, EPISTROPHE; or some sort of contrast or INVERSION (ANTITHESIS; CHIASMUS). Schemes of sound include ASSONANCE and ALLITERATION.

script

See SCHEMA.

selection(al): ~ feature; ~ restriction; ~ rule

Terms which came into popular use through GENERATIVE GRAMMAR as it was revised from 1965, after Chomsky and others (e.g. Katz & Fodor 1963) reconsidered the relations between SYNTAX and meaning.

Working on the principle that LEXICAL ITEMS would be drawn from the LEXICON in DEEP STRUCTURE into their appropriate 'slots' in SURFACE STRUCTURE, Chomsky also recognized that there were certain constraints or restrictions on the co-occurrence of items in the grammatical CONTEXT, seemingly part semantic, part syntactic. So while *Elephants* (SUBJECT) *eat* (VERB) *peanuts* (OBJECT) is grammatical, **Peanuts eat elephants* is not, despite its NOUN PHRASE (NP) + VERB PHRASE + NP structure. One can say that the verb *eat* must 'select' a NP as subject which is marked or **subcategorized** with the semantic **feature** or COMPONENT [+ ANIMATE]. The verb itself would be marked with this **selection restriction**: i.e. [+ [+ 'animate']].

Selection(al) rules proved of interest in early STYLISTICS (see, e.g., Hendricks 1969; Thorne 1969), at least for their violations. For they raised the same sort of problems about GRAMMATICALITY and DEVIATION as other aspects of generative grammar: namely, that there are violations of these quite commonly in language, but which are regarded as ACCEPTABLE. METAPHOR and PERSONIFICATION would be good examples of regular violation of selection rules. The native speaker may well accept that there is some ANOMALY in utterances like *Rust eats iron* or *Time eats away our lives*; but a grammar that cannot generate such surface structures does little justice to the complete workings of language.

Selectional features are therefore best dealt with outside such a syntactic model, in terms of a sentence-semantics theory (see Leech 1974); or of COLLOCATIONS (q.v.). On the basis of normally compatible features, for example, we will find the likely ADJECTIVE combinations *tall trees* or *tall people*, but not **tall cushions* or **tall ants*. Certainly interesting grammatical information comes to light in the study of such patterns, of use for foreign learners of English: e.g. the kind of objects which co-occur with the verbs *narrate, chide* and *mar*; or subjects with *recede, screech* and *nonplus*.

(See also SEME. See further Allan 1986, I, ch. 5.)

self-reference, also self-reflexivity

A recurring idea in discussions of LITERARY LANGUAGE in different critical approaches is that it is characteristically 'narcissistic': i.e. **self-referential**. So Jakobson and other FORMALISTS and PRAGUE SCHOOL argued that the essence of LITERARINESS is the 'set towards the MESSAGE' for its own sake, the POETIC FUNCTION of language. There is an awareness of language and MEDIUM that is not so significant in other types of discourse.

In (POST-)MODERNIST writings, self-reference appears heightened in the anti-realist mode. The meaning of a text comes primarily through the patterns and play of words and structures within the text, rather than through reference to an external WORLD and its truth-values: Joyce's *Finnegans Wake*, for example. Such works further illustrate the related notion that FORM and CONTENT are inseparable.

semantics

See SEMIOLOGY.

seme; semic code; semics

(1) From Gk *sema* 'sign' (cf. SEMANTICS, SEMIOTICS), and by analogy with PHONEME and MORPHEME, **seme** has been used in European STRUCTURALISM and semantics (e.g. Coseriu 1967; Greimas 1966) to describe a minimal distinctive feature of meaning or COMPONENT.

Semes define the essential DENOTATIONS of different LEXICAL ITEMS within a lexical FIELD in terms of BINARY OPPOSITIONS: e.g. items of clothing can be

MARKED as being 'with [+] or 'without [−] sleeves' (e.g. *jacket* v. *waistcoat*); [+ or − 'hood'] (e.g. *jacket* v. *anorak*), etc. The problem is that there appears to be an unlimited number of discriminations that could be made along these lines.

(2) **Seme** has sometimes been more loosely applied (e.g. Fowler 1977) to more general semantic components common to several semantic fields, and which may even be universals: what in GENERATIVE SEMANTICS are termed **markers** (v. **distinguishers**, which are semes proper), and what French linguists strictly call **classemes**. These are oppositions such as ANIMATE V. INANIMATE; 'male' v. 'female', etc. which determine the SELECTIONAL FEATURES (q.v.) of lexical items. (See further Lyons 1977, I.)

(3) Fowler (*op. cit.*) also followed Barthes's (1970) use of the term **seme** and the related notion of **semic** CODE, for the application of semic analysis to the study of NARRATIVE, especially CHARACTER. Here semes are compared to the set of attributes (physical, psychological, etc.) by which each character is distinguished. The more components a character has, the seemingly more complex or 'rounded' they are; stereotype characters will have few semes. The 'humour' characters of Elizabethan drama (e.g. the braggart, the fool) can be seen to be **monosemic**; and this is also reflected in the dramatic and novel tradition of naming characters by attributes, e.g. Downright and Wellbred (Jonson); Squire Alworthy (Fielding).

Greimas (1966) himself was interested in the application of semic analysis to narratives, but on a more extensive scale than character. The complexity of his semantic theory is partly due to his development of structuralist approaches such as the work of Lévi-Strauss (1985) on myths, and partly to his ambitious yet desirable aim to relate semes (in DEEP STRUCTURE) to the larger units and meanings of SURFACE STRUCTURE. (See also NARRATIVE SEMIOTICS.)

(4) Rather confusingly, Eaton (1972) used **semics** to refer to quite a different area of study, namely his own version of READER-RESPONSE CRITICISM, which comes close to RECEPTION THEORY. **Theoretical semics** focusses on the mental activity of the reader in the INTERPRETATION of texts; **empirical semics**, like Riffaterre's AFFECTIVE approach, uses readers' actual responses in texts to define distinctive STYLES. (See also LITERARY SEMANTICS.)

semiology, also semiotics; semantics

(1) **Semiology** and **semiotics** are terms which are virtually synonymous; the former, following Saussure, favoured especially in France; the latter, following Peirce, favoured especially in America. From the Gk root *sema* 'sign' they refer to a discipline which did not yet exist in the early years of the twentieth century, but which Saussure and Peirce coincidentally felt should exist: the theory or science and analysis of SIGNS and sign systems and their meanings, specifically those involved with COMMUNICATION between human beings in different societies and cultures. (The study of animal communication systems is called **zoosemiotics**.)

Semiotics/semiology is exceedingly comprehensive, since it must cover verbal language in its different MEDIA of speech and writing, and also NON-VERBAL

COMMUNICATION systems, such as gesture and body movement (KINESICS), and other CODES of proximity/distance (**proxemics**), dress and MASS MEDIA, etc. Semiotics thus overlaps with other disciplines, such as COMMUNICATION THEORY, linguistics, sociolinguistics and **semantics**.

As Barthes (1953b, 1967b), has stressed, almost anything in society can be a significant sign: 'meaningful' to the speech community, even IDEOLOGICALLY coded. So we may assign a stranger to a certain social group or class, even political party, on the basis of clothes, hair style, ACCENT and make of car owned, etc. In this respect also semiotics takes as much interest in the MESSAGES of photography, myth, advertising and television as the written discourse of literature, and concerned equally with how 'meaning' is produced as with what it may be.

By extension *semiotics* is also used as a collective noun to refer to any system of signs itself: e.g. the semiotics of fashion-writing, or of drama.

The theoretical basis of semiology owes much to the STRUCTURALIST preoccupation, following Saussure, with the process of signification (**semiosis**), the relationship between SIGNIFIER (q.v.) (EXPRESSION/FORM) and SIGNIFIED (q.v.) (concept), the two components of the sign. From American semiotics has come also much theoretical discussion of different kinds of signs according to degree of MOTIVATION (q.v.), i.e. degree of relations between signifier and REFERENT: so ICON (q.v.), INDEX (q.v.) and SYMBOL (q.v.) are distinguished. (See further Eagleton 1983, ch. 3; Eco 1976; Hawkes 1977, ch. 4; Innis 1986.)

(2) What is called **literary semiotics** studies the verbal signs of literary texts as systems in their own right, and is close to (STRUCTURALIST) POETICS. (See also NARRATIVE SEMIOTICS.) Some early work in this area was done by the FORMALISTS and the PRAGUE SCHOOL, and is continued in **Russian structuralist semiotics** or the **New Soviet Semiotics** (see Shukman 1980): the work of Lotman (1971, 1972) on poetry, for instance. For Lotman, poetry is particularly 'rich' semantically, interweaving several different CODES (phonetic; syntactic, etc.) each with their own dynamic patterns. Drama offers a potentially wider field of analysis, since not only verbal but also visual and kinesic sign systems are exploited in the theatre. Surprisingly, however, as Elam (1980) notes, relatively little attention has been paid outside the Formalist tradition to the semiotics of the theatre. His own work yet provides a comprehensive survey of the potential, if embracing also much material traditionally regarded as the province of STYLISTICS or DISCOURSE ANALYSIS (e.g. SPEECH ACT THEORY).

(3) A cross-disciplinary **social semiotics** that combines the European semiotic traditions of Jakobson and the Prague School with SYSTEMIC-FUNCTIONAL approaches to language was initiated by Halliday (1978), and now has its own journal. Broadly, the forms of language 'encode' a socially constructed representation of the world; language's functional organization as a system is a symbol of the structure of human interaction in society. (See further Threadgold 1997.) One recent offshoot has been Kress & van Leeuwen's work on the **visual semiotics** of Western society, a GRAMMAR of visual design (1996).

(4) **Semantics**, the term from the same Gk root as *semiotics*, is specifically the study of linguistic meaning, of words and sentences, and has been much influenced by philosophy and logic. **Lexical semantics** has traditionally studied

the different sense relations of words, e.g. SYNONYMY, ANTONYMY, HYPONYMY and MERONYMY; and also sense COMPONENTS or features and semantic FIELDS.

A recent offshoot deals with **prototypes** and 'fuzzy' concepts: the idea that concepts can be classified with reference to a 'central' type, but that category membership is graded, and boundaries between concepts are 'fuzzy'. (So our concept of a tomato is fuzzy, between a fruit and a vegetable.)

Sentence semantics focusses on meanings that hold between parts of the sentence in terms of ROLES (e.g. 'agent', 'patient'); and on issues of PARAPHRASE, ENTAILMENT, PRESUPPOSITION, and PROPOSITIONAL MEANING, as well as of POSSIBLE WORLDS.

Its relations with PRAGMATICS has been much debated, but it essentially remains the study of the meaning potential of linguistic units, rather than the meaning of these in actual contexts of use.

(See also GENERATIVE SEMANTICS; LITERARY SEMANTICS; NARRATIVE SEMANTICS. See further Lyons 1977.)

sentence

Not easily defined, despite being a common term in GRAMMAR. The **sentence** is usually taken as one of the most significant units of grammatical analysis, and the largest: the others being CLAUSE, **phrase, word** and MORPHEME. Attention focusses largely on its structural characteristics, although these are not always easily distinguishable from those of the clause. Moreover, it is more readily described in its written realization than the spoken, since in speech sentence boundaries are not easily delimited, and features of form are apt to vary considerably from the NORM. For speech, it is preferable to speak of UTTERANCE (q.v.), despite some problems of usage even here.

Sentences, like many clauses, normally consist of a SUBJECT and PREDICATE; but unlike clauses can stand on their own as independent units. Traditionally, therefore, they are said to contain 'a complete thought'; or a distinct PROPOSITION. They may also contain more than one clause: either one or more SUBORDINATE CLAUSES (hence a COMPLEX SENTENCE); or a CO-ORDINATE CLAUSE (hence COMPOUND SENTENCE); or both (**mixed sentence**): e.g.

> Answer a fool according to his folly, /lest he be wise in his own conceit (complex)
> Pride goeth before destruction, /and an haughty spirit before a fall (compound)
> Whoso diggeth a pit /shall fall therein: /and he /that rolleth a stone, /it will return upon him (mixed)
>
> (*Book of Proverbs*)

A sentence with just a MAIN CLAUSE is called a **simple sentence**: as in *She is obsessed with elephants*.

Sentences are also classified on the basis of structural features correlated with FUNCTION or ILLOCUTIONARY FORCE. So the basic sentence type is the DECLARATIVE used for statements, with a WORD ORDER of subject-VERB(-OBJECT). The other major types are the INTERROGATIVE used for questions (marked by the INVERSION of subject and AUXILIARY VERB); and the IMPERATIVE (with no overt subject actually) used for directives.

(See also LOOSE SENTENCE; PERIODIC SENTENCE.)

signal; sign; signifier; signified; signification

(1) **Signal** in ordinary USAGE is not easy to distinguish from **sign** (see (2) below). In COMMUNICATION THEORY (q.v.) it denotes the electrical impulses or radio waves which are used to transmit MESSAGES from transmitter to receiver, i.e. the physical form of the message. For the transmission of spoken or written messages, the signals would be the PHONEMES and GRAPHEMES. The signal is made INFORMATIVE by the CODE or set of rules assigned to it: so that we know, for example, that a red traffic light signals 'Stop', a green light 'Go'. As a result, signals are INDEXICAL in the sense that there is a cause and effect relationship between signal and meaning; just as a cat's mewing signals, or indicates, that it is hungry or lonely.

(2) **Signs** are the focus of study in SEMIOLOGY/SEMIOTICS (q.v.), which ana- lyses their systems and meanings in different cultures. From Lat. *signum* 'mark, token', sign is sometimes used interchangeably with SYMBOL (q.v.) to denote 'something' which stands for, or REFERS to, something else, in a meaningful way. So we talk of signs of rain, or animal tracks as signs; or words as signs of ideas (Samuel Johnson); or mathematical or astrological signs. As Barthes (1967b) stressed, almost anything in society can be a significant sign, often IDEOLOGICALLY coded: so a Rolls-Royce is a sign of wealth and prestige, rainbow-coloured hair a sign of adolescent rebellion against the values of the Establishment.

Signs have no significance, however, unless users recognize them as signs. The meaning of signs has to be learned by the community, and their values can change. To this extent they are symbolic in the sense that the pioneering American semiotician C. S. Peirce (1931–1958) distinguishes, namely that there is an arbitrary relationship between sign and REFERENT. Other types of signs show varying degrees of MOTIVATION (q.v.): the ICON (q.v.) visually resembling what it represents (e.g. holograms; photographs); and the index causally connected (e.g. smoke to fire). Icons and indices are sometimes termed **natural signs** (v. symbols as **artificial signs**). But even icons need some form of interpretation in the way that symbols do, and may be culture-specific (e.g. male and female signs on public notices).

(3) All signs have in common a FORM and a referent or **significatum**; more specifically, as the STRUCTURALIST linguist de Saussure argued (1916), they conjoin a form and a concept, *signifiant* or **signifier**, and *signifié* or **signified**. So the word *elephant* is a sign: consisting of a signifier, the sequence of phonemes or graphemes that give *elephant*, and a signified, the image of the animal in our mind, the 'real' animal in the outside world (which may or may not be physically

357

present). Peirce's term for signified is **interpretant**. The relationship between signifier and signified is arbitrary to the extent that signifieds can change through time: so words like *lust* and *science* evoke a narrower concept than they used to.

For Saussure and other structuralists after him, the REFERENTIAL MEANING of the sign is not as important as the CONCEPTUAL MEANING, and that too is dependent upon its DIFFERENCE from the conceptual meaning of other signs. The meaning or **signification** of the word *chair* in English, for example, contrasts with that of *chaise* in French, although the latter can be translated as 'chair'. *Chair* as a HYPERONYM can include *armchair* in English; but *chaise* and *fauteuil* ('armchair') are not interchangeable in French.

(NB: Saussure uses the term signification more precisely for the relations between sign and referential meaning.)

POST-STRUCTURALISTS like Derrida and Lacan have probed the process of signification further, however, undermining as a result the apparently stable (if arbitrary) relationship between signifier and signified. But some of the post-structuralist ideas were already anticipated by the early semioticians. Asked to explain the signification of the signifier–signified *elephant*–'elephant', we will, as Peirce acknowledged, inevitably use other signifiers (e.g. *large animal with trunk and tusks*), which can only be explained by other signifiers – so the process is endless: what Derrida calls **deferral**, an aspect of DIFFÉRANCE.

(See further Eagleton 1983, ch. 4; Easthope 1983, pt 1; Eco 1976, ch. 7; Fiske 1982, ch. 3; Leitch 1983, pt 1.)

simile

From Lat. *similis* 'like', **simile** is a FIGURE OF SPEECH whereby two concepts are imaginatively and descriptively compared: e.g. *My love is like a red, red rose; as white as a sheet*, etc.

Like and *as* (. . . *as*) are the commonest connectives; Leech & Short (1981) term **quasi-similes** literary descriptions involving the use of phrases like *as if; resembling; suggesting*, etc. Dickens uses both kinds in his evocative description of the November weather of London:

> As much mud in the streets, as if the waters had but newly retired from the face of the earth, and it would not be wonderful to meet a Megalosaurus, . . . wandering like an elephantine lizard up Holborn Hill.
>
> *(Bleak House)*

Since Aristotle's *Rhetoric*, simile has often been compared with METAPHOR (q.v.), where two FIELDS of REFERENCE are similarly juxtaposed, but without an explicit marker of similitude: *X is Y*, rather than *X is like Y*. Here the FIGURATIVE MEANING must be deduced, but in consequence metaphor is much more dynamic than simile. As Davidson (1978) argues, similes are (trivially) true; but most metaphors are (patently) false. However, in literary IMAGERY and passages of description, like the one quoted above, similes and metaphors frequently co-occur (e.g. *like an elephantine lizard*).

(See also EPIC SIMILE.)

simple sentence

See COMPLEX SENTENCE.

simulacrum

In a POSTMODERN vision the French philosopher and critic Jean Baudrillard (1995) has argued that modern communications and MEDIA have become so pervasive and technically sophisticated that we can no longer claim to have a view of the 'real'; only images of images. These images without 'originals' or REFERENT are **simulacra**. Anyone who has been to a Disney-world, or watched a TV docu-soap, will appreciate the blurring/fusing of the real and fake or FICTIONAL. Baudrillard's own exemplum is the 1992 Gulf War. To adopt Fairclough's phrase (1995) it was MEDIATIZED: (re)presented by selected documentary film footage, computer-enhance images and graphics, etc., so that for many people in the West it existed in a kind of virtual reality.

Even in the pre-photocopier age, the philosopher Walter Benjamin (1935) had argued that, because of modern technology and the cheap reproduction of images, the 'aura' surrounding a unique work of art was dispensed with.

(See further Pope 1995.)

situation

Situation is commonly evoked in linguistics, especially sociolinguistics and PRAGMATICS, and is frequently synonymous with CONTEXT and its collocates: OF SITUATION (q.v.) and OF UTTERANCE (q.v.) in particular.

It refers to the non-linguistic setting or environment surrounding language use, and which can clearly influence linguistic behaviour. There is the immediate DISCOURSE situation in which a TEXT or UTTERANCE is produced, involving an interchange between speaker or writer (*I*) and listener or audience (*you*). (See also speech EVENT.) Discourse itself is set in a larger, social situational context: e.g. a conversation between friends taking place in a pub, or at an art exhibition, where reference can be made in passing to features of the environment (e.g. *It's very crowded in here tonight; What do you think of this painting?*). There are broader contexts even than this: the pub may be in Islington or the Isle of Man; and the participants may refer to a common general background of shared knowledge and cultural assumptions.

Our awareness of these different kinds of situations means that we often need not be quite so explicit in our utterances, since we can assume familiarity or awareness of things. A notice that reads *Keep off* in a public park can assume *the grass* as the OBJECT. However, for written texts such as novels, where the discourse situation is more diffuse and IMPERSONAL, this sort of linguistic economy cannot be exploited. (See further de Beaugrande & Dressler 1981, ch. 8, on **situationality**.)

In our everyday life we are confronted by a range of social situations, and it is part of our COMMUNICATIVE COMPETENCE that we can adjust our language and **degree of** FORMALITY according to the nature of the situation. Some situations seem to depend generally and fairly consistently on a regular set of features, so that distinctive VARIETIES of language result: what are called REGISTERS or **discourse/situation types**: e.g. sports' commentary; newspaper headlines; obituaries.

LITERARY LANGUAGE can be said to create its own context, so that the situation inside the poem or novel is more important than the extra-textual: what Leech (1969) calls the INFERRED (v. the **given**) **situation**. In drama, actors may turn directly from the created discourse situation to address the audience directly in the real-world situation, in ASIDES, for example.

(See also EXOPHORIC REFERENCE; WORLD.)

sjužet

One of a pair of terms (see also FABULA) introduced into NARRATIVE THEORY by the **Russian** FORMALISTS in the 1920s (notably Shklovsky (1925)).

For any narrative there are two levels: the SURFACE level with the actual sequence of events as narrated, with all the flashbacks, ANTICIPATIONS, and GAPS, i.e. **sjužet** or **syuzhet**, and a DEEP level, the abstracted chronological or logical possible ordering of the events, i.e. *fabula*. In simple narratives like fairy-tales the two levels usually coincide; in more complex narratives readers must deduce *fabula* from *sjužet* (as with narratives that begin IN MEDIAS RES, for instance).

The problem is how to find satisfactory equivalents in English, since 'subject' and 'fable' have well established meanings. PLOT (q.v.) is sometimes used as the equivalent to *sjužet*, but that is ambiguous. The terms are usually, therefore, left untranslated. Problems are compounded, however, by the fact that the terms were assimilated in French criticism to the distinction between DISCOURS (q.v.) (*sjužet*) and HISTOIRE (*fabula*), which also yield the ambiguous English terms DIS-COURSE (q.v.) and STORY (q.v.). However, even in French, *discours* is ambiguous, including more elements to do with the act of ENUNCIATION than *sjužet* involves; so that Genette (1972) proposes RÉCIT (q.v.) as the equivalent to *sjužet*, the verbal representation of events in the text.

skaz

A term introduced by the Russian FORMALIST Boris Eichenbaum and also used by the Russian critic Mikhail Bakhtin (1981), which is not usually translated: to refer to a pseudo-oral type of narrative discourse, the stylized imitation of the speech of an individual NARRATOR. A famous example is the so-called 'Cyclops' episode in Joyce's *Ulysses*, narrated as if the monologue of a Dublin bar-fly.

slang

(1) Popularly used as an equivalent to JARGON, as collocations like **schoolboy slang; drug addicts slang; RAF slang**, etc., imply. The term refers to the individual vocabulary used by different social groups. However, jargon is best reserved for technical or professional vocabulary arising from rather specialized needs. **Slang** is closer to ARGOT or ANTI-LANGUAGE, in that STANDARD LEXICAL ITEMS are replaced by **re-lexicalizations** which are characteristically very informal, and designed, like a 'secret language' to be unintelligible to the uninitiated. So Winchester schoolboys may *sport a thoke* ('oversleep'); and tramps *scrump* ('steal').

(2) In a more general sense **slang** has a wide circulation: at least it is associated with larger social groups such as adolescents, or dialect speakers (e.g. Cockney **rhyming slang**). Again, it is characteristically associated with very informal REGISTERS, and speech predominantly; and again it presents an alternative LEXIS, of an extremely colloquial, non-standard kind, sometimes co-occurring with swearing. If *the pictures* is the informal equivalent of *the cinema*, *the flicks* is stylistically even more informal than *the pictures*.

In both (1) and (2), but especially (2), slang words can come and go very quickly: either passing out of the language completely, or being 'promoted' to standard usage. No one says *hard cheese* or *spiffing* any more, which sound very Wodehousian. Some words considered slang in the eighteenth century are now not: e.g. *piano; bully; doggerel*. Some words, however, remain this side of respectability for a long time: *booze* (verb) since the fourteenth century, for example.

Slang reveals a remarkable EXPRESSIVENESS and CREATIVITY in its forms: marking considerable use of NEOLOGISM; CLIPPING; SOUND SYMBOLISM; METAPHOR, etc. Its prime motivation is obviously a desire for novelty of expression; and as Turner (1973) notes, it lacks the finer cognitive distinctions that usually motivates technical jargon. As has often been noted, certain **semantic** FIELDS seem to attract a wealth of slang terms and IDIOMS: e.g. money (*brass; dough; mint; lolly*, etc.); head (*noodle; noddle; chump block; loaf*, etc.); drunk (*slewed; sloshed; plastered; half-cut*, etc.); nonsense (*ballyhoo; piffle; cobblers; guff*, etc.). Many are obviously humorous, and such humour is often exploited in a kind of EUPHEMISM, which softens TABOO subjects, e.g. death (*pushing up the daisies; kick the bucket; a stiff*).

sociolect, also social dialect

Sociolect is a term created by analogy with words like DIALECT and IDIOLECT which is used in sociolinguistics to refer to a VARIETY of language distinctive of a particular social group or class.

Linguists have always had problems in defining speakers' USAGE in English strictly on the basis of social class, since there appears to be no strict correlation between class as defined sociologically, and linguistic features; in any case, the distinction of classes is harder to make than geographical distinctions for more variables are involved: education; occupation; etc. (See the problems associated with notions of ELABORATED and RESTRICTED CODE, for example.) Certain LEXICAL variations have often been popularly pointed out, however, that distinguish (broadly) the 'upper' from the 'lower' classes. (See Ross 1956, for **U** and **non-U** usages like *napkin/serviette*, still a talking point nearly 50 years on.)

The study of sociolects has been intensified and made more complex by research into urban dialects (e.g. the work of Labov in the 1960s in the USA, and Trudgill, Milroy and Cheshire in the UK.). DIALECTOLOGY has tended to concentrate on regional, rural, varieties, where the speakers/informants present a more socially unified community.

Traditionally, RECEIVED PRONUNCIATION (q.v.) was a kind of sociolect, associated with those educated at Oxbridge and public schools, as well as the upper classes.

The term *sociolect* can also be applied to the varieties of language used by different age groups; both sexes; or various occupations, etc. (See also JARGON.) In some languages there are very marked differences between the speech of old and young men (e.g. for the Masai in East Africa); or between male and female speech (e.g. in Thai and Carib and some American Indian languages) sometimes termed **genderlects**.

soliloquy

From Lat. 'alone-speak', **soliloquy** is a well established dramatic practice (found in the medieval 'Morality' plays) whereby a character, normally alone on stage, utters his thoughts and feelings aloud, often directly to the audience like an extended ASIDE. Realistic in the sense that it reflects the practice of 'thinking aloud', this self-address is yet a useful theatrical device since it has many functions. As Hussey (1992, ch. 9) notes, in early Elizabethan drama it was often expository, or informative about a character's intentions. With the development of 'malcontent' introspective characters like Hamlet, soliloquies began to reveal inner DIALOGIC dilemmas and disturbed mental states. Moreover, soliloquy is an effective device for attracting the sympathy of the audience: particularly so if the 'hero' is a villain, like Richard III, or Macbeth. With the decline of poetic drama, however, the extensive use and extended utterances of soliloquy also declined.

Yet as a device for the REPRESENTATION OF THOUGHT, it was taken over into the novel tradition as one of a range of conventions: identical in form with

DIRECT SPEECH, but having the self-address of DIRECT THOUGHT. Its theatrical origins perhaps explain why it is often melodramatic: as in Ralph Nickleby's last words before his suicide, reminiscent of the despair of Faustus's final soliloquy in Marlowe's play:

> 'I know its meaning now,' he muttered, 'and the restless nights, the dreams, and why I have quailed of late. All pointed to this. Oh! if men by selling their own souls could ride rampant for a term, for how short a term would I barter mine to-night!'
> (Dickens: *Nicholas Nickleby*)

sound symbolism

Certain sounds or sound clusters are felt to ENACT or to be in some way appropriate to the meanings expressed: also known as PHONAESTHESIA (q.v.), **protosemanticism** and **secondary** ONOMATOPOEIA.

Although **sound symbolism** is the term generally used, it is something of a misnomer, since the connection between sound or PHONEME and meaning is felt to be more MOTIVATED, less arbitrary, than with SYMBOLISM proper. Nonetheless, the ICONISM varies. Words like *bump, crump, thump* might indicate, onomatopoeically, a dull sound on impact; but *gl-* as in *glitter, glimmer, glint, glisten, gleam, glow,* does not actually mime the light it so evidently suggests.

The extent to which such correspondences are universal has preoccupied many scholars. Certainly the significant opposition between the high front vowels /iː/ and /ɪ/ and back vowels like /ʊ/ and /uː/ in respect of smallness or light v. largeness or darkness is attested in many languages. Sound symbolism has been linked with speculations about the origin of language, incapable of being proved (see also CRATYLISM). The fact remains, however, that in any speech community speakers will associate words together, regardless of original ETYMOLOGY: what Bolinger (1965) calls a 'creative etymology'.

(See further Jakobson & Waugh 1979.)

speech act theory

Speech act theory is particularly associated with the work of the philosopher J. L. Austin (published 1962) and his student J. R. Searle (1969f) who developed it after the former's death. It is concerned with the linguistic ACTS made while speaking, which have some social or INTERPERSONAL purpose and PRAGMATIC effect.

After making an initial distinction between CONSTATIVES (q.v.) and PERFORMATIVES (q.v.), Austin then refined his categories to produce: (i) the act of uttering (LOCUTIONARY ACT, q.v.); (ii) the act performed in saying something, e.g. promising, swearing, warning (ILLOCUTIONARY ACT, q.v., now including performatives); and (iii) the PERLOCUTIONARY ACT (the act performed as a result of saying something, e.g. persuading). Moreover, **speech acts** are not considered to be successfully performed unless certain FELICITY CONDITIONS are fulfilled: e.g. recognizing the speaker's INTENTIONS (as with warnings); or the speaker having the appropriate authority (e.g. to baptize; name a ship, etc.).

The greatest attention in speech act theory has focussed on illocutionary acts, on the communicative purpose of utterances, and the term **speech act** is very frequently used interchangeably with *illocutionary act*. A distinction is also made between **direct** and INDIRECT SPEECH ACTS (q.v.): the former being those illocutionary acts explicitly marked by a performative verb as in *I promise I'll behave*; and the latter those where, for example, one illocutionary act is performed indirectly by another: very commonly requests framed as questions (e.g. *Can you turn the sound down?*).

Austin's work was significant in the 1960s for turning attention from SENTENCES as syntactic units to sentences as UTTERANCES in speech SITUATIONS with specific intentions and goals. Speech acts can be seen as the basic units of DISCOURSE; yet Austin and Searle themselves never pursue the full implications of this. In fact, for them the utterance remains the simple 'ideal' sentence of traditional grammatical citation. In actual discourse it may not always be easy to identify a speech act simply on the basis of one sentence: an accusation, for instance, can be seen as a MACRO-speech act comprised of a series of questions (and responses). Or an utterance, even in CONTEXT, may have more than one possible ILLOCUTIONARY FORCE (recognized by Searle). In any case, different kinds of discourse, different SPEECH EVENTS (q.v.) will comprise a variety of speech acts: in a domestic argument, for example, partners may (verbally) attack, threaten, insult, belittle, wheedle, evade, etc. Generally, the number of potential speech acts in English is impossible to estimate.

The term speech act suggests that Austin and Searle are primarily concerned with speech, however 'idealized' that appears to be. But certainly speech act theory can be applied to the sentences of written discourse. Controversial, however, has been the place of LITERARY LANGUAGE in speech act theory generally, as Derrida (1977a, b) exposed in his DECONSTRUCTIONIST debate with Searle. Considerable emphasis is placed, following Austin, on the FICTIONALITY of literary illocutions: so promises in the dialogue of a play or novel can't be valid because they are not literally 'true': they are, in Austin's own words, 'etiolated' utterances (i.e. sicklied), 'parasitic'. Such metaphors place literary language in the category of DEVIATION, and confirm only 'factual' or REFERENTIAL MEANING as being of value. At the same time Austin confirms the equally common view that literature is MIMETIC of the 'real' world, if only by illusion or pretence. Ohmann (1971) therefore defined literature generally as a **quasi-speech act**, without illocutionary force; Searle (1976) speaks of **quasi-assertions**.

While we might accept that an author does not intend statements such as *Call me Ishmael* (first sentence of Melville's *Moby Dick*, told in the **first** PERSON) to be taken literally as a personal invitation, we certainly judge such speech acts in the literary world in real terms. In drama, where speech is action, such a judgment is indispensable. The fact remains that in the general context of the situation of discourse between author and reader, valid speech acts do take place. On a global level, authors inform, preach, declare their love, etc. in a variety of literary genres; and the traditional FIGURES OF SPEECH have been exploited in RHETORIC for distinct perlocutionary effects. Stories can be seen basically as acts of NARRATION. And within a text, NARRATORS engage with their IMPLIED READERS in speech acts of informing, describing, evaluating, etc. In discussing literary language, therefore, in terms of speech acts, it is important to distinguish different levels and kinds of utterances.

Moreover, viewed from another angle, literary language is not so estranged from other kinds of discourse where fictionality also plays a part: e.g. jokes, scientific projections or problems, TV advertising, etc. So Pratt (1977) warns against a too narrow approach to speech acts generally, on the basis of 'norms' or 'ideals'.

(See further Allan 1986, vol. 2; Fish 1973; Lanser 1981, Appendix.)

speech event

(1) As developed by Jakobson (1960), **speech event** describes an influential model of the CANONICAL SITUATION of DISCOURSE, or CONTEXT OF UTTERANCE, and what he considers to be six key constituends of COMMUNICATION and related FUNCTIONS.

These constituents are not all easily defined or distinguished, but in any situational context (1) an ADDRESSER (2) sends a MESSAGE (3) to an ADDRESSEE (4), which requires a CODE (5) (the language or system of meaning). CONTACT (6) is maintained between them by voice and gestures, for instance, or by psychological or social factors. Language orientated to any one of these constituents has a different function: to addresser the EMOTIVE; to addressee the CONATIVE; to context (which includes also the non-linguistic world generally) the REFERENTIAL; to contact the PHATIC; to code the METALINGUAL; and to message (the SURFACE structure, in effect) the POETIC.

LITERARY DISCOURSE is itself a double, even multiple speech event, requiring more than one set of participants (AUTHOR to READER; NARRATOR to NARRATEE; CHARACTER to character). (See further Burton 1980.)

(2) From the work on ETHNOGRAPHY by Hymes in particular (e.g. 1974), **speech event** is known in sociolinguistics and DISCOURSE ANALYSIS as a well defined unit or structure of social and verbal behaviour that can comprise a series of SPEECH ACTS and even REGISTERS or discourse types. A church service, for instance, has a clearly ordered structure of procedure, and comprises registers of sermon, prayer and reading, etc. Speech events well studied in discourse analysis include school lessons and doctor–patient sessions.

stance

Generally taken to be the use of language in speech and writing to convey personal feelings, attitudes or judgments concerning the PROPOSITIONS being expressed:

also known as MODALITY (q.v.), and a significant aspect of linguistic SUBJECTIVITY. The work of Biber & Finegan (1989) adopts a computational approach, looking at lexical and syntactic markers of stance across REGISTERS (e.g. adverbs and adjectives, verbs and modals: e.g. *happily; might; true; I fear*). They identify six separate STYLES of stance, including 'emphatic expression of AFFECT' (particularly associated with romance fiction, personal letters and telephone conversations); 'faceless stance' (associated with academic prose); and 'expository expression of doubt' (press reportage). As expected, perhaps, conversation has the highest frequency of stance adverbials; the second highest academic prose.

In DIRECT SPEECH, TAG clauses with speech act and adverb are a common device to indicate stance: e.g. *she said angrily/disappointedly*.

(See further Biber *et al*. 1999, ch. 12.)

standard: ~ dialect; ~ English

In any speech community, a **standard** DIALECT or VARIETY of language is one which is regarded as having a special social status and prestige, serving as a 'model' for various functions, and transcending as a result the usual dialect boundaries.

Historically speaking, **standard English** therefore is the model for educated written usage throughout the British Isles and even beyond, and it is that variety which is the basis of modern GRAMMARS of English. There is a fairly uniform orthography or spelling system and a remarkably consistent SYNTAX and LEXIS. A standard spoken grammar has been less easy to establish. On the issue of a 'standard' pronunciation, however, see RECEIVED PRONUNCIATION (RP).

There is a strong connection between the standard and literature in many languages. Modern High German is associated with the Lutheran translation of the Bible; standard Italian with the work of Dante, and standard Russian with the work of Pushkin. Chaucer has in the past been associated with the rise of Standard English, but the real development came after his death. That he wrote in the London dialect was, however, significant. It was the dialect of the government scribes, a **chancery standard**, that proved most influential (see McIntosh 1963; Samuels 1963); and its usefulness as a model was made evident with the development of printing, and large-scale dissemination of texts to a wide reading-public. From the Norman Conquest, writers had used their own dialect for their work, but dialectal differences were such that it might not easily be understood outside their own region. London English in any case avoided some of the extremes of northern and southern forms, as Caxton recognized. A standard acts as both a unifying and levelling force.

The rise of a standard dialect often means that regional forms become socially stigmatized, and marked regional features have slowly disappeared over the centuries. The term **non-standard** applied to regional dialects implies (negatively) that the standard is a NORM. (See also VERNACULAR.) IDEOLOGICALLY, as Halliday (1978) and others have stated, the standard variety can become associated with empowerment, and values of order and conservatism; while dialects, 'ghetto languages' and ANTI-LANGUAGES represent protest or opposition.

As English has spread throughout the world as a first and second language, so there have developed new standard Englishes. Nonetheless, although accents may vary English newspapers printed in the United States, Canada, Australia and Cairo present a remarkably uniform set of linguistic features.

(See also KOINÉ. See further Bex & Watts 1999; Crowley 1989; Milroy & Milroy 1999 on the 'ideology of standardization'.)

stop

See PLOSIVE.

story

(1) In ordinary usage refers to a NARRATIVE, whether fact or FICTION, which is regarded noteworthy of being told (cf. *That's a good/funny/exciting story*, etc.). (See also TELLABILITY.) **Stories**, whether fairy or oral folk, have a distinct structure, and a set of participants (CHARACTERS) and series of events or actions.

(2) In NARRATOLOGY, however, **story** came to be used by some theorists (e.g. Chatman 1978) as a translation of the French term HISTOIRE (q.v.), itself equivalent to the **Russian** FORMALIST term FABULA (q.v.). A distinction is here made between the SURFACE STRUCTURE or FORM of a narrative, the SJUŽET (q.v.) or DISCOURS (q.v.), i.e. the sequence of events as actually narrated, with any flashbacks or anticipations; and the DEEP STRUCTURE or CONTENT, the *histoire/ fabula*, i.e. the basic abstracted chronological ordering of events (which may not coincide with the *sjužet*). Consequently, story takes on a narrower meaning, and we are left with no general term that covers both *fabula* and *sjužet* as in (1).

It is, however, very hard to keep out the connotations of (1). Problems are compounded by the fact that sometimes *sjužet/discours* is translated as PLOT (q.v.), itself an ambiguous word in English, since some of its uses in English actually coincide with story. If one talks about reading a novel *for its story*, for example, the sense is similar to plot (i.e. main events).

stream of consciousness: ~ fiction/writing; ~ technique

Stream of consciousness is widely used in the theory of the novel; but was first used in psychology by William James, brother of Henry James, in his *Principles of Psychology* (1890) to describe the free association or flow of thoughts and impressions in a person's mind at any given moment.

James's interest in the depths of the subconscious coincided with a growing interest generally in this subject at the end of the nineteenth and beginning of the twentieth century, culminating in the work of Jung and Freud. Novelists, too, were bringing the subconscious to the foreground of their fiction, and so developing new techniques for rendering the flow of thoughts that in actuality are only partly verbalized; and if verbalized, only partly formulated. So the term came to be applied to the kind of MODERNIST novels like those of Dorothy Richardson first of all, also Woolf, Proust, Joyce and Faulkner in the 1920s, in which the main FOCALIZATION is through the internal PERSPECTIVE and thoughts of a central character.

Rather confusingly, however, at the same time as stream of consciousness was circulating as a phrase, so too was INTERIOR MONOLOGUE (q.v.), a term applied by Valery Larbaud to Joyce's *Ulysses* (1922). Joyce himself claimed he was influenced by the technique in a SYMBOLIST novel by Dujardin, *Les Lauriers sont Coupés* (1887), which describes the events in a day through the eyes and thoughts of a young man. What Dujardin later in 1930 came to say about his novel, which was hailed as a precursor to stream of consciousness fiction, shows how interested he himself was in trying to capture thoughts closest to the unconscious, without any logical organization. So interior monologue and stream of consciousness have frequently been used synonymously to refer to the technique of inner representation.

Some scholars, however, mindful of the word *flow*, have tried to make a distinction between the terms on the basis that stream of consciousness works specifically by free associations, random ordering; interior monologue by ordinary syntax, if often ELLIPTICAL (see Chatman 1978). Certainly, in Joyce's *Ulysses* Molly Bloom's unpunctuated ramblings suggest the free 'flow' of random thoughts as they pass in quick succession, e.g.:

> . . . what do they ask us to marry them for if were [*sic*] so bad as all that comes to yes because they cant get on without us white Arsenic she put in his tea off flypaper wasnt it I wonder why they call it that if I asked him hed say its from the Greek leave us as wise as we were before . . .

Bloom's thoughts, in contrast, are represented in short phrases:

> Shrunken skull. And old. Quest for the philosopher's stone. The alchemists. Drugs age you after mental excitement. Lethargy then. Why? Reaction . . .

But since Chatman's own illustration of stream of consciousness comes from one of Bloom's cogitations, the distinction seems pointless. In any case, the reader has to work just as hard to see the RELEVANCE of each juxtaposed proposition as with Molly, so prevalent is free association for both characters.

It is probably clearest, therefore, to adopt the distinction made by scholars such as Humphrey (1954): stream of consciousness applied to the general representation of thought processes by a variety of means (including (FREE) DIRECT and INDIRECT THOUGHT, LEITMOTIFS, and IMAGERY, for example); or to the GENRE to which novels like *Ulysses* or Woolf's *Mrs Dalloway* belong, quite different in their overall textures, yet preoccupied alike with the psychology of their characters. Interior monologue would then refer to one kind of technique, namely a sustained free direct thought, with no overt sign of a narrator.

(See also MIND STYLE. See further Edel 1955; Friedman 1955.)

stress

Stress is used in PHONETICS and METRICS to refer generally to the prominence given to, and perceived in, certain syllables in words.

Traditionally this prominence is identified as the force or intensity of air coming from the lungs, perceived as loudness by the hearer: e.g. the first syllable of *el-e-phant*; or the last syllable of *gi-raffe*. Many phoneticians nowadays, however, prefer to talk of ACCENTED syllables rather than stressed syllables (e.g. Gimson 1989), because other features of prominence are involved: length, quality and especially pitch change. The close relation between pitch change or INTONATION and stress is shown at utterance level with the NUCLEUS (q.v.): the syllable which carries the KINETIC TONE is normally the last stressed syllable in the utterance:

'Do you 'come here 'often?

As Cruttenden (1997) says, stressed syllables are 'potentially accentable'.

All LEXICAL ITEMS of the OPEN CLASSES (i.e. NOUNS, ADJECTIVES, VERBS) have an inherent stress pattern; those of the CLOSED CLASSES (i.e. GRAMMATICAL words such as PREPOSITIONS, PRONOUNS and CONJUNCTIONS, etc.) are typically unstressed. A low degree of stress leads commonly to ELISION (q.v.), or loss of sounds in syllables. The succession of stressed and unstressed syllables or words therefore in the stream of speech produces a natural, even fairly regular, RHYTHM which is exploited in verse to produce METRE. (See also ISOCHRONY, i.e. **stress-timing**.)

Phoneticians distinguish several degrees of stress; to the ordinary speaker three degrees are perceived as salient: **main, primary** or **strong; secondary;** and **weak** or **unstressed**. Polysyllabic words like *in-form-a-tion* reveal a pattern of secondary–weak–strong–weak. Many COMPOUNDS can be distinguished from NOUN PHRASES by a stress pattern of strong–weak/secondary rather than two strong stresses: e.g. *greenhouse* v. *green house*. In verse metre, however, secondary stress is usually discounted in scansion or analysis, and only a BINARY contrast is made: (+/– stress).

Stress patterns of words are not fixed for all time: the pronunciation of many words like *controversy* and *formidable* varies from speaker to speaker; and there are DIALECTAL differences. Stress variation marks very strongly, for instance, the difference between English and American pronunciations of words like *laboratory*. Since Chaucer's time many words borrowed from French have shifted their stress from the natural French position of final syllable to the commoner Germanic position of first syllable, e.g.:

```
        ×   / ×   ×   ×   / ×   ×   × /
. . . (So priken hem nature in hir corages):
        ×  /  ×  /  ×     ×   ×  × /
Than longen folk to goon on pilgrimages
```

('Prologue': *Canterbury Tales*)

An extra kind of intensity can be used for EMPHASIS, for contrastive purposes or for special FOCUSSING on parts of an utterance other than the (normal) nucleus: as in *It's white wine I asked for, not red.*

structuralism; structuralist: ~ linguistics; ~ poetics

(1) **Structuralism** describes an intellectual discipline which gradually developed momentum during the twentieth century, influenced by FORMALISM and the PRAGUE SCHOOL. It is particularly associated with a group of French scholars writing after the Second World War, reaching a peak in the 1960s: e.g. Claude Lévi-Strauss (in anthropology); Roland Barthes (LITERATURE and SEMIOTICS); and Michel Foucault (history).

As the term implies, structuralism is concerned with structure(s): of language and other systems of knowledge and cultural behaviour (e.g. kinship systems and myths, as studied by Lévi-Strauss). It was greatly indebted for a model to the ideas of Saussure (1916). The term **structural linguistics** has sometimes been given to Saussurean linguistics, which can be seen as part of the general movement of structuralism (but see also (3) below).

Structuralists followed Saussure in emphasizing the arbitrariness of the relation between SIGNIFIER or FORM and the SIGNIFIED or concept, and in stressing the importance of DIFFERENCE between SIGNS, i.e. their relations with one another, as a determinant of meaning.

(2) Applied to literature, structuralist ideas gave rise to an analytical approach that was more theoretical and broader than some other approaches, and is best viewed as a (**structuralist**) POETICS. Interest centred not so much on the EVALUATION of individual texts as in LITERARY CRITICISM, but on their structural patterns (e.g. the work of Jakobson on selected poems); or interpretative CODES (see Barthes 1970 on Balzac's *Sarrasine*); or the formal properties and conventions of texts within a GENRE (e.g. folk-tales or fabliaux, as in the work of Todorov).

In 1975 the term structuralist poetics became particularly associated with the work of Culler, who shifted attention to the more dynamic activity of the READER, with his notion of **literary** COMPETENCE (q.v.), loosely based on the GENERATIVE paradigm of Chomsky.

Literary structuralism was often criticized for being too formalist, and for studying texts as CLOSED systems, outside of their social and historical context. The French structuralists themselves came to question basic structuralist premises, and so gave rise to POST-STRUCTURALISM (q.v.).

(3) Outside Europe, the term structuralism was applied in the US more narrowly to the grammatical approach popular in the 1950s and 1960s, following the pre-war work of linguists like Sapir and Bloomfield, which parses sentences and describes grammatical features ignoring 'meaning'. This is also known as **descriptive linguistics**.

(See further Eagleton 1983, ch. 3; Hawkes 1977. For a structuralist approach to METRE, see Chatman 1964; and to SEMANTICS, see Lyons 1963.)

style

Although **style** is used very frequently in LITERARY CRITICISM and especially STYLISTICS (q.v.), it is very difficult to define. There are several broad areas in which it is used.

(1) At its simplest, **style** refers to the perceived distinctive manner of EXPRESSION in writing or speaking, just as there is a perceived manner of doing things, like playing squash or painting. We might talk of someone writing in an 'ornate style', or speaking in a 'comic style'. For some people, style has EVALUATIVE connotations: style can be 'good' or 'bad'.

(2) One obvious implication of (1) is that there are different **styles** in different SITUATIONS (e.g. comic v. turgid); also that the same activity can produce stylistic variation (no two people will have the same style in playing squash, or writing an essay). So style can be seen as variation in language use, whether LITERARY or non-literary. The term REGISTER (q.v.) is also used for those systematic variations in linguistic features common to particular non-literary situations, e.g. advertising, legal language, sports commentary.

Style variation occurs not only from situation to situation but according to MEDIUM and **degree of** FORMALITY: what is also sometimes termed **style-shifting**. (See also DECORUM; KEY.) It may vary, in literary language within or between texts, GENRES and periods so we may talk of the style of Augustan poetry. Style is thus seen against a background of larger or smaller DOMAINS (q.v.) or CONTEXTS.

(3) The notion of variation and also variables is the perspective on **style** taken in sociolinguistics. For style is a variable, as distinctive as class, region or gender, in the analysis of phonological or morphological variation, for example, in different speech situations, roles or social networks. Style in this sense roughly corresponds to degrees of formality, and each choice (see (5) below) is thus socially marked or unmarked in any given social situation.

(4) In each case, **style** is seen as distinctive: in essence, the set or sum of linguistic features that seem to be characteristic: whether of register, genre or period, etc. Style is very commonly defined in this way, especially at the level of TEXT: the style of Keats's *Ode to a Nightingale*, for example, or of Jane Austen's *Emma*, even the **house-style** of a journal or newspaper.

Stylistic features are basically features of language, so style in one sense is synonymous with language: we can speak equally of the 'language' of *Ode to a Nightingale*. What is implied, however, is that the language is in some way distinctive, significant for the design or THEME, for example. When applied to the domain of an author's entire oeuvre, style is the set of features peculiar to, or characteristic of an author: his or her 'language habits' or IDIOLECT (q.v.). So we speak of Miltonic style, or Johnsonese, often a feature of PARODY. In parody, individual linguistic features often acquire a particular salience: what Adamson (1998, ch. 7) calls **style markers** (e.g. Samuel Johnson's abstract Latinate vocabulary).

(5) Clearly each author draws upon the general stock of the language in any given period; what makes styles distinctive is the CHOICE of items, and their distribution and patterning. A definition of **style** in terms of choice is very popular, the selection of features partly determined by the demands of genre, form, theme, etc. (See, e.g., Simpson 1993; Traugott & Pratt 1980.)

What is often debated, however, is the extent to which stylistic choice involves variation in meaning. If a writer chooses *steed* instead of *horse*, or *loot* instead of *money*, what subtleties of CONNOTATION or even IDEOLOGY are involved in the selection from a stock of apparent SYNONYMS? (See also DUALISM and MONISM.) For many people, stylistic meaning or variational value is what distinguishes PROPOSITIONS that on a DEEP level express the 'same' meaning, such as:

Pater passed away last summer.
My Dad kicked the bucket last summer.

This is not to say, however, that there is always more than one way to say anything. Nor is it satisfactory to regard style decoratively, to define it as some kind of expressive emphasis 'added' to an utterance (see Epstein 1978; Riffaterre 1959). All utterances have a style, even if they might seem relatively 'plain' or unMARKED: a plain style is itself a style. (See ZERO DEGREE.)

(6) Another differential approach to **style** is to compare one set of features with another in terms of a DEVIATION from a NORM, a common approach in the 1960s (see Enkvist 1973). It would be wrong to imply that style itself is deviant in the sense of 'abnormal', even though there are marked poetic idiolects like those of Hopkins, Dylan Thomas and e.e. cummings. Rather, we match any text or piece of language against the linguistic norms of its genre, or its period, and the COMMON CORE of the language as a whole. Different texts will reveal different patterns of DOMINANT or FOREGROUNDED features.

(7) For Cameron (1995) style is a 'commodity' in the modern marketplace: a text can be 'packaged' in a particular style for a particular kind of customer or consumer: e.g. glossy magazines; university mission statements. This idea echoes the social theorist Pierre Bourdieu's idea that what circulates on the linguistic market is not 'language' as such, but rather discourses that are stylistically marked both in production and reception (Bourdieu 1991).

(See also GRAND, MIDDLE, PLAIN STYLE. See further Carter & Nash 1990; Leech & Short 1981, chs 1, 2; Short 1996.)

stylistics

The study of STYLE (q.v.); yet just as style can be viewed in several ways, so there are several different stylistic approaches. This variety in **stylistics** is due to the main influences of different branches of linguistics and LITERARY CRITICISM.

Stylistics in the twentieth century replaced and expanded on the earlier study of ELOCUTIO in RHETORIC. Following the publication of a two-volume treatise on French stylistics (*stylistique*) by Bally (1909), a pupil of the STRUCTURALIST, Saussure, interest in stylistics gradually spread across Europe via the work of Spitzer (1928, 1948) and others. It was in the 1960s that it really began to flourish in Britain and the United States, given impetus from post-war developments in descriptive linguistics, GRAMMAR in particular.

In many respects, however, stylistics is close to literary criticism and PRACTICAL CRITICISM. By far the most common kind of material studied is LITERARY; and attention is largely TEXT-centred. The goal of most stylistic studies is not simply to describe the FORMAL features of texts for their own sake, but in order to show their FUNCTIONAL significance for the INTERPRETATION of the text; or in order to relate literary effects or themes to linguistic 'triggers' where these are felt to be relevant. Intuitions and interpretative skills are just as important in stylistics and literary criticism; however, stylisticians want to avoid vague and impressionistic judgments about the way formal features are manipulated (not that good literary criticism is necessarily vague or impressionistic). Traditional literary critics were suspicious of an 'objective' approach to literary texts, as the notorious Fowler-Bateson controversy reveals (see Fowler 1971). Unfortunately, this issue has recently been revived by Mackay (1996f; see Short *et al.* for responses, 1998, 1999). Stylistics is only 'objective" (and the scare quotes are significant) in the sense of being methodical, systematic, empirical, analytical, coherent, accessible, retrievable and consensual.

As a result, stylistics continually reassumes its models and terminology in the light of new developments in linguistics. In the late 1960s GENERATIVE GRAMMAR was influential; in the 1970s and 1980s DISCOURSE ANALYSIS and PRAGMATICS; in the 1990s CRITICAL DISCOURSE ANALYSIS and COGNITIVE LINGUISTICS. Stylistics also draws eclectically on trends in LITERARY THEORY, or parallels developments in this field. So the 1970s saw a shift away from the text itself to the READER (see, e.g., AFFECTIVE STYLISTICS; RECEPTION THEORY), and is now broadly concerned with how we understand a text and are affected by it.

Stylistics is sometimes called confusingly **literary stylistics** or **linguistic stylistics**: *literary* because it tends to focus on literary texts; *linguistic* because its models or tools are drawn from linguistics. However, linguistic stylistics has also referred to a kind of stylistics whose focus of interest is not primarily literary texts, but the refinement of a linguistic model which has potential for further linguistic or stylistic analysis: Burton's (1980) discourse model for dramatic texts, for instance. Fowler's term for stylistics was **linguistic criticism** (1980).

Stylistics or **general stylistics** can be used as a cover term to cover the analyses of non-literary VARIETIES of language, or REGISTERS: e.g. Bex 1996. Because of this broad scope, stylistics comes close to work done in sociolinguistics. Indeed, **sociostylistics** studies, for instance, the language of writers considered as social groups (e.g. the Elizabethan university wits; pamphleteers); or 'fashions' in language.

Because of its eclecticism, stylistics has come to be used as a significant teaching tool in language and literature studies for both native and foreign speakers of English: what can be termed **pedagogical stylistics** (e.g. work of Henry Widdowson 1992).

In sum, we may concur with the French linguist Jean-Jacques Lecercle that no one has ever known exactly what the term *stylistics* comprises yet that the subject is forever being reborn.

(See also COGNITIVE STYLISTICS; COMPUTATIONAL STYLISTICS; CRITICAL LINGUISTICS/CRITICAL DISCOURSE ANALYSIS; DISCOURSE STYLISTICS; ETHICAL STYLISTICS; EVALUATION; EXPRESSIVE STYLISTICS; FORMALIST and FUNCTIONAL STYLISTICS; LINGUISTIC CRITICISM; PRACTICAL STYLISTICS; STYLOMETRY; TEXT LINGUISTICS. See further Enkvist 1985; Short 1996, ch. 1; Simpson 1993.)

stylization

Coined by the Russian critic Bakhtin in the 1930s to describe the technique of IMITATION, of the conscious and consistent representation by an author of another style (see Bakhtin 1981). The result is a DUAL VOICED discourse, the style imitated and the 'silent' presence of the author. One clear example is PARODY (q.v.). Novelists like Dickens frequently used stylization for comic or ironic effect: the first chapter of *Pickwick Papers*, for instance, imitating the IMPERSONAL style of minute-taking:

> May 12, 1827. Joseph Smiggers, esq., P.V.P.M.P.C., presiding. The following resolutions unanimously agreed to: –
> That this association has heard read, with feelings of unmingled satisfaction, and unqualified approval, the paper communicated by Samuel Pickwick, Esq., G.C.M.P.C., entitled 'Speculations on the Source of the Hampstead Ponds, with some Observations on the Theory of Tittlebats'.

stylometry, also stylometrics

This subdiscipline of STYLISTICS has nothing to do with *metre* or *-meter* as verse form but *meter* in the sense of measuring (cf. *geo-metry*).

Stylometry uses statistical analyses to investigate stylistic patterns in order to determine authorship of TEXTS: it is concerned, therefore, very much with STYLE as IDIOLECT (q.v.). It has been particularly associated with the work of Andrew Morton (e.g. 1978). Many fourteenth-century poems have been examined for Chaucerian authorship for example; and plays like *Pericles* and *Henry VIII* re-examined as part of the Shakespearean CANON.

Linguistic features commonly examined in stylometry include word length; sentence length; CONNECTIVES; COLLOCATIONS. These are not necessarily FOREGROUNDED features, but those which are assumed to be relatively unconsciously used by an author, and therefore fairly stable throughout his or her career. The procedures are essentially comparative: comparing sets of variables in the disputed text with those in an authenticated text. Otherwise, it is very difficult to establish a NORM for comparison.

(See also COMPUTATIONAL STYLISTICS.)

subject; subjectivity

(1) In GRAMMAR the **subject** is a major SENTENCE element, a NOUN (PHRASE), which typically precedes the VERB in the PREDICATE in DECLARATIVES, and which determines by concord or agreement the form of the verb in the PRESENT TENSE **third person singular**, e.g. *She like-s elephants; They hate elephants*. The PERSONAL PRONOUNS have a special **subjective** CASE, as *she* and *they* above.

The division of sentences into two major constituents, subject and predicate, derives from Greek philosophy. It corresponds to the PRAGUE SCHOOL distinction between THEME and RHEME or **topic** and **comment**. The subject is therefore the concern of the MESSAGE, often the **psychological subject**, and on it rests the truth of the argument (see Halliday 1985, 2.5). In a sentence where there is both GIVEN and NEW INFORMATION, it is most likely to be given rather than new. Theme and subject do not always coincide: in *Money we want* the DIRECT OBJECT *money* is FRONTED to theme position for EMPHASIS before *we*, the GRAMMATICAL SUBJECT.

In sentences like *It is raining* or *It's late* the sentence is hardly about *it*, yet *it* is the grammatical subject, a 'prop' word or **dummy subject**, needed because English favours FINITE CLAUSES with subjects as well as predicates. But not all sentence types have subjects: IMPERATIVES have only an implied subject (*you*). In colloquial speech and personal writing, such as diaries, subjects are often ELIDED where they can be understood from the CONTEXT, e.g.: *Monday morning: felt terrible. Got up late and dashed to work . . .*

In some models of TRANSFORMATIONAL GRAMMAR a **logical** or DEEP STRUCTURE **subject** was distinguished for PASSIVE sentences as the equivalent to ACTIVE. In

The school captain was presented with a book token by Jeffrey Archer.

Jeffrey Archer is the logical, not the grammatical, subject: cf.

Jeffrey Archer presented the school captain with a book token.

If the grammatical subject has human reference, then very commonly it expresses the AGENT(IVE) of the action (as *Jeffrey Archer* in the active sentence above). Other ROLES include **instrument** (e.g. *The sword cut the knot*); and **affected participant** (e.g. *He was presented with a token*). (See also INVERSION. See further Biber *et al.* 1999, ch. 3.)

(2) In philosophy, the distinction between **subject(ive)** and **object(ive)**, between the self and the not-self, is widely recognized. When LITERARY CRITICS talk of a subjective work, they mean that it is highly personal (whether or not, of course, it is autobiographically sincere or true). Stylistic markers of textual subjectivity would include AFFECT and STANCE features, EMOTIVE language and shifts in FOCALIZATION.

It is very difficult for any discourse to be completely objective, and the **subjectivity** of speech is a general fact. An obvious marker of subjectivity is the personal pronoun *I*. The French linguist Benveniste (1966), followed by Lacan in psychoanalysis, made a distinction between two kinds of subjects in discourse: the **subject of the** ENUNCIATION or act of speaking, and the **subject of the** ENOUNCED or the narrated event. So *I* in an utterance like *I promise to come on Sunday* is both subject of the enunciation and of the enounced. The 'I-that speaks' is thus a contextual construct: just one 'position' among others.

Focus on the act of speaking, on the SPEECH EVENT itself, to produce a consciously constructed subjectivity, is sometimes seen as specially characteristic of MODERNIST and POST-MODERNIST writing. Postmodern theorists go further and see subjectivity as connoting its other meaning of subservience: we take up only those roles or **subject positions** that are already ordained for us by language and culture (Baldick 1996).

(See further Green & LeBihan 1996, ch. 4; Pope 1995.)

subjunctive

Traditionally belonging to a category in GRAMMAR called MOOD (q.v.), the **subjunctive** is largely signalled by differences in VERB forms from the **indicative**, and gives rise to different SENTENCE types, or contrasts of MODALITY.

The basic mood in English is the indicative or 'fact-mood', marked in the **third** PERSON PRESENT TENSE form at least by the -*s* inflection: e.g. *She leaves tomorrow.* In contrast, the subjunctive is the mood of non-fact, expressing the hypothetical, or doubtful, also the desirable, or obligatory, etc. (see Lyons 1977), e.g. *I insist that she leave tomorrow.* There is no formal inflection in Modern English for the subjunctive of LEXICAL verbs (cf. Old English, where the ending was -*e* in the singular, -*en* in the plural). For the verb *be*, in the **past tense** of the subjunctive the form *were* (from OE again) occurs in the singular: e.g. *I wish it were true.*

As these examples reveal, the subjunctive is most commonly found in SUBORDINATE CLAUSES. There are FORMULAIC utterances where the subjunctive survives in the MAIN CLAUSE: e.g. *God save the Queen; Glory be to God; Come what may.*

Grammarians in the first half of the twentieth century predicted that the subjunctive would disappear completely, since the indicative, or MODAL verbs like *should* and *may* are in any case stylistic alternatives, especially in inFORMAL usage (e.g. *I wish it was true; I insist that she should leave/leaves tomorrow*). However, possibly because of American English influence, the subjunctive can frequently be heard, and especially read, in what Quirk *et al.* (1985), call **mandative** uses, in NOMINAL clauses which express a future plan or intention. It is especially common in reports of meetings or minutetaking: e.g. *The Board recommended that the proposal be voted upon at its next session.* Note the use of the present subjunctive, even though the verb in the main clause is in the past tense.

subordinate clause; subordination

Common in GRAMMAR to describe a hierarchic structure of CLAUSES within the (COMPLEX) SENTENCE. A **subordinate clause**, unlike a CO-ORDINATE CLAUSE, is a constituent of the sentence as a whole: e.g. an ADVERBIAL clause functions as an adverbial, as in *No longer mourn for me / when I am dead* (Shakespeare: Sonnet 71: adverbial of time).

Other main kinds of subordinate or BOUND CLAUSES introduced by **subordinators** or CONJUNCTIONS are NOMINAL clauses and RELATIVE CLAUSES. There are also subordinate clauses which are NON-FINITE, and which have no formal subordinators, e.g. *I've been to London/to see the Queen.* Subordinate clauses cannot stand alone as independent units, unlike MAIN CLAUSES.

Stylistically, it is sometimes possible to replace a complex sentence by a corresponding COMPOUND (i.e. main + co-ordinate clause), e.g.:

If you move/ I'll shoot
Move/ and I'll shoot

As it was dark,/ we decided to pitch our tent
It was dark,/ and so we decided to pitch our tent

The co-ordinate constructions appear more INFORMAL than the subordinate. Generally, complex sentences with strings of subordinate clauses are much more characteristic of written and formal registers than speech: e.g. technical and legal discourse. A complex sentence in which the subordinate clauses precede the main clause, which is therefore delayed until the end, is termed a PERIODIC SENTENCE (q.v.). In linguistics this is also known as a type of left-BRANCHING structure; opposed to a **right-branching** structure where the main clause comes first.

Subordination is an important means of distributing INFORMATION within a sentence according to its value: the most important information is normally expressed in the main clause, that of lesser significance in the subordinate clause(s): a pattern of FOREGROUNDING and BACKGROUNDING.

(See also EMBEDDING; HYPOTAXIS. See further Quirk *et al.* 1985, chs 14, 15; Winter 1982.)

substitution

Used in GRAMMAR to refer to a means of COHESION in TEXTS.

It is not easy to distinguish from CO-REFERENCE (q.v.), since both are means of avoiding REPETITION, tend to work ANAPHORICALLY, and involve the use of **pro-forms** (e.g. PRONOUNS). But basically, co-reference is a relation on the semantic level, depending on semantic identity between NOUN PHRASES; **substitution** is a relation on the structural level, depending on structural identity (see Halliday & Hasan 1976). It involves the replacement of one expression by another, which 'stands for' it: a common example is the pro-form *one*, e.g.: *I bought a red jumper, and then I saw a nicer blue one.* Here *one* replaces the noun *jumper* which is understood. Notice that it is not, semantically, the same jumper: contrast, with co-reference: *I bought a red jumper, but I didn't like it really.*

Substitution is found also with VERBS (e.g. *do*) and CLAUSES (*so*): often involving ELLIPSIS, e.g. *I bought a red jumper and my sister did too* (i.e. *bought (a red jumper)*); *Did your sister like it? – I don't think so* (i.e. *that she liked it*).

(See further Halliday 1985, 9.3; Quirk *et al.* 1985, ch. 12.8f.)

suffix; suffixation

In LEXICOLOGY a **suffix** describes a type of AFFIX or formative which can be added to the base or root of a word to make new words: here at the end of a word. (See also PREFIX.)

Suffixes very commonly change one word class or part of speech into another: e.g. NOUNS into VERBS (*terror-ize; hospital-ize*); verbs into nouns (*hospitaliz-ation; pay-ment*); ADJECTIVES into nouns (*kind-ness; banal-ity*). But further nouns can be derived from nouns, usually of an ABSTRACT nature: e.g. *friend-ship; rac-ism*.

English has taken its most productive suffixes from French and Latin (e.g. *-able; -ize*). Some noun suffixes have traditionally indicated female ROLES (*waitr-ess, steward-ess; usher-ette* (borrowed from French)); but they are avoided these days on the grounds of their sexual discrimination.

Suffixes in English can also indicate grammatical categories. These are rarer in NE than in earlier stages of the language, but the plural inflection (*-s*), and the verb forms (*-s, -ing, -ed*) are examples of grammatical suffixes, characteristic of 'inflectional' languages like Latin and Modern German.

(See further Bauer 1983; Quirk *et al.* 1985, Appendix I.)

surface structure

One of a pair of terms (see also DEEP STRUCTURE) made famous by Chomsky's (e.g. 1965) GENERATIVE GRAMMAR.

In his 'standard theory', SENTENCES were held to have a deep underlying structure which generates the surface form by means of TRANSFORMATIONAL rules of addition or deletion, etc. The **surface structure** was therefore the linear arrangement of the words (the surface SYNTAX), and the PHONOLOGICAL or GRAPHOLOGICAL representation. It is that which is important for the distribution of INFORMATION values and FOCUS.

Chomsky maintained that there is sometimes a discrepancy between deep and surface structures: a sentence may have two different deep structures, and so give rise to AMBIGUITY in its surface structure, e.g. *Biting flies can be a problem.* Conversely, sentences with different surface forms can yet be regarded as PARA-PHRASES of each other, sharing the same deep structure: e.g. ACTIVE and PASSIVE sentences in some versions of the model: cf.

> Hurricane hits Riviera coast.
> Riviera coast hit by hurricane.

The distinction between surface and deep structure here may help to account for differences in degree of syntactic complexity between writers. Many of Shakespeare's sentences, for example, have a superficially simple construction, which yet on closer examination yields a potentiality of different readings. In contrast, a prose writer like Hemingway has a 'directness' of style that can be explained by a close match between deep and surface structure (see Traugott & Pratt 1980).

As Fowler (1977) pointed out, the notion of surface and deep structure is not unrelated to traditional ideas in LITERARY CRITICISM of FORM and CONTENT; and Chomsky's views of paraphrase align him with the DUALIST stance on STYLE: namely, that it is possible to say 'the same thing' in different words. (See also Ohmann 1964.) The distinction also resembles the dichotomy in NAR-RATOLOGY between SJUŽET/DISCOURS and FABULA/HISTOIRE; and the metaphors of 'deep' and 'surface' structure indeed inform much work in NARRATIVE GRAM-MAR (q.v.).

syllepsis

(1) From Gk 'taking together', a FIGURE OF SPEECH in which one word is used in two senses within the same utterance; and where the effect is of putting together two CO-ORDINATE constructions with ELLIPSIS. It is frequently used with comic or satiric effect, e.g. *She went home in a flood of tears and a sedan chair* (Dickens); *Search your lockers and your consciences.* (See also ZEUGMA.)

(2) **Syllepsis** can also be used as a term to describe the more colloquial construction of a co-ordinate structure with ellipsis of the verb: what linguists term ZERO-ANAPHORA, e.g. *She has deceiv'd her father, and may thee* (*Othello*, I.iii).

(3) Joseph (1947) uses the term to describe a kind of PUN in Shakespeare in which a word conjures up two meanings, largely because of the presence of a related word in the CONTEXT: e.g.

Thou seest the heavens as troubled with man's act,
Threaten his bloody stage (*Macbeth*, II.iv)

(4) **Syllepsis** is used idiosyncratically by Genette (1972) in his study of ANACHRONY (q.v.) in NARRATIVE, i.e. types of discrepancy between logical FABULA/HISTOIRE order and actual SJUŽET/RÉCIT order. Syllepsis is really a-chronous, since there is no chronological relationship between *fabula* and *sjužet*, and the grouping of sequences is random. Sterne's *Tristram Shandy* would illustrate this.

symbol: symbolic code; symbolism

(1) From Gk 'token', a **symbol** is a SIGN, whether visual or verbal, which stands for something else within a speech community. So the cross is a symbol of Christianity, and within British culture black garments a symbol of mourning. So too human language can be seen as a characteristically symbolic system: words standing for REFERENTS in the outside world (and in the world of the imagination); the letters of our alphabet standing for sounds. Disciplines such as mathematics and chemistry have evolved their own sets of symbols to represent logical and numerical arguments, and earth's minerals and elements: πr^2, H_2O, etc.

(2) However natural many of our traditional cultural symbols appear to be (e.g. owls symbolizing wisdom), in SEMIOTICS, following C. S. Peirce, is stressed the arbitrariness of the relationship between symbol and referent. Peirce classifies a **symbol** as a subtype of sign, the most conventional, the least MOTIVATED. The two other main types are INDEX (q.v.) and ICON (q.v.). Nonetheless, the distinctions between these types of signs are not always clear-cut. The use of a pair of scales as a symbol of justice, for instance, seems not unmotivated in the sense that, metaphorically speaking, we 'weigh the pros and cons'. The term symbol is often loosely used for index: for Peirce, a Rolls-Royce would 'point' directly to wealth (index) rather than symbolize it; but it would certainly be a symbol of social status. (See further Barthes 1953b; 1967b, etc.; Innis 1986.)

(3) Different DOMAINS within each culture evolve their own special sets of symbols or **symbolism**. LITERATURE, for instance, draws on general symbols (spring as a symbol of life and birth, winter of death, etc.), and also 'literary' symbols, a popular field of study in LITERARY CRITICISM. These may be part of the literary heritage (e.g. roses symbolizing beauty and love); or IDIOLECTAL, i.e. created by an individual writer (the symbolism of Blake or Yeats, for instance). It is part of our literary COMPETENCE that we tease out the symbolism and what it stands for from our interpretation of the IMAGERY, for example, and from the CONTEXT. Poetic symbols are characteristically METAPHORIC in structure. In novels, symbolism may be more diffuse in its realization: characters, objects or buildings can acquire a symbolic force, a more abstract or generalized significance, and so help towards an understanding of the THEME of the work as a whole. For Barthes (1970) the **symbolic** CODE is one of the FRAMES OF REFERENCE we draw upon for our understanding of a text, which enables us to work out thematic oppositions, such as good v. evil, life v. death.

A text which has a systematic level of meaning other than the narrative is often an ALLEGORY (q.v.). Symbolism is frequently associated with it. In the medieval dream-vision poem *Piers Plowman*, there are allegorical characters such as Lady Mead and Hunger, PERSONIFICATIONS of vices and virtues; and symbolic characters like Piers the ploughman himself, whose significance shifts in different parts of the poem: Peter the Apostle, Jesus Christ, mankind.

(4) **Symbolism** (usually with a capital S) is also used to describe a nineteenth-century literary movement originating in France, particularly associated with the poetry of Baudelaire, Rimbaud, Mallarmé and Verlaine. For them, objects and also the sounds of language are given significant, often esoteric, symbolic meanings, in a poetry that is essentially EMOTIVE, suggestive and anti-naturalistic. Symbolism exerted a strong influence on British and American literature by the end of the century: on Arthur Symons, Yeats, Eliot, Joyce, Pound and Wallace Stevens, for example. (See further Chadwick 1971.)

symploce

Pronounced /sɪmpləʊsiː/, from Gk 'interweaving', a FIGURE OF SPEECH in RHETORIC. It involves the REPETITION of one set of words at the beginning of a series of sentences or verse lines, and of another set at the end: a combination of ANAPHORA and EPISTROPHE, e.g.:

> *Son:* How will my mother for a father's death
> Take on with me and ne'er be satisfied!
> *Father:* How will my wife for slaughter of my son
> Shed seas of tears and ne'er be satisfied!
> *King Henry:* How will the country for these woeful chances
> Misthink the king and not be satisfied!
>
> (*Henry VI*, II.v)

synaesthesia

From Gk 'together-perception', a phenomenon whereby a stimulus applied to one of the 'five senses' produces a response from the other(s).

Synaesthesia is often used in LITERARY CRITICISM, however, to refer simply to the interconnections between the different senses that can be exploited for literary effect, and reflected in synaesthetic METAPHORS, and choice and COLLOCATIONS of LEXICAL ITEMS. So touch is applied to sound, sound to smells, etc. But even in everyday usage we find collocations like *cold voice; sharp noise*; and in advertising, phrases like *Tender Touch Tights: fifteen delicious shades*. As Chapman (1984) says, music critics will talk of the 'colour' of a piece of music; art critics of the 'tone' or 'harmony' of a text.

Although found in poetry of all periods, synaesthesia was particularly exploited by the SYMBOLIST (q.v.) poets, who were keen both to explore the world of feelings and sensations and to attribute unusual suggestive significances to objects, and even language itself. So Rimbaud attributed colours to letters/vowels: *A black, E white, I red, U green, O blue.*

(See further Shen & Cohen 1998.)

synchrony; synchronic linguistics

Synchrony is one of a pair of terms (see also DIACHRONY) introduced by Saussure (1916) which refers to the two basic perspectives for the study of language: looking at it as it exists at a given state or time (**synchronic**); and/or as it changes through time (**diachronic**).

While Saussure acknowledged that a total study of language must involve both dimensions, it is largely owing to his own influence that modern linguistics has come to be dominated by a synchronic perspective (see STRUCTURALISM). Much work has been done on the systematic description of present-day English; and many grammatical theories (e.g. GENERATIVE GRAMMAR) have primarily involved a synchronic perspective: so too in STYLISTICS.

Yet language is never static, and a synchronic perspective is inevitably 'ideal'. Synchronic grammarians record obvious changes, but generally do not seek to account for the function of elements by an appeal to historical factors.

syncope

From Gk via Lat. 'cutting away', a kind of ELISION in RHETORIC in which sounds are omitted from the middle of words, so that, for example, a two-syllable word becomes a monosyllable. This was often very useful METRICALLY, so that **syncope** is commonly found in poetry: forms like *o'er* and *ne'er* for *over* and *never*.

Medial elision of vowels is commonly heard in speech: /medsən/ for *medicine*; /temprɪ/ for *temporary*, etc. (also known rhetorically as **synaeresis**); and it has become fixed in the pronunciation of some place names: /lestə/ (*Leicester*); /glɒstə/ (*Gloucester*), etc.

synecdoche

From Gk 'take up with something else', and pronounced /sɪ'nekdəkɪ/, a TROPE in RHETORIC, in which 'part' of a REFERENT is named and stands for the 'whole'; or vice versa. So *strings* can mean 'stringed instruments' (part for whole); or *England* can mean a sports team (whole for part) in headlines like *England thankful to avoid serious injury*. **Synecdoche** is commonly found in proverbs (e.g. *Many hands make light work; Two heads are better than one*, etc.).

It is not easily distinguished from METONYMY (q.v.), which also works by the principle of contiguity: i.e. there is a directly or logically contiguous or INDEXICAL relationship between the word 'substituted' and its referent. In metonymy the relationship is one of cause and effect, or instrument and material, etc., e.g. *crown* for 'monarchy' (monarchs wear crowns); *willow* for 'cricket bat' (bats are made of willow), etc. Jakobson (1956) includes synecdoche as a subtype of the larger FIGURE of metonymy.

In SEMIOTIC terms, synecdochic SIGNS are found frequently in the theatre: a tree will represent or SYMBOLIZE a forest; a tent a whole battlefield, on the stage where space is at a premium. (See Elam 1980.) Synecdoche is also a common device in film: a row of houses will suggest a city.

(See also MERONYMY; see further Lakoff & Johnson 1980.)

synonymy; synonym

In SEMANTICS, **synonymy** is the expression of the 'same' meaning by different words within a language: e.g. *duvet* v. *continental quilt*.

It is very hard to list **absolute synonyms**: words which are identical both in DENOTATION or basic CONCEPTUAL MEANING, and in their CONNOTATIONS, and so which can be interchanged in all CONTEXTS. Most natural languages make do with **near-synonyms**, words which are 'similar' in meaning but which vary in their STYLISTIC values. So *laryngitis* and *sore throat* have the same denotational meaning, or conceptual equivalence, but differ in their context of use: the first more technical than the second. *Steed* and *charger* are more archaic or poetic than *horse*, which is not as colloquial as *gee-gee*. Many apparent synonyms have different COLLOCATIONAL ranges: we speak of *tall* or *high buildings*, but only *tall people* and *high mountains*.

Nonetheless, synonymy is favoured as a means of COHESION in many FORMAL REGISTERS (especially written), in order to avoid REPETITION; and thesauri like Roget's are popularly resorted to for lists of expressions of certain basic concepts.

As a RHETORICAL device synonymy is frequently found with PARALLELISM; most obviously in BINOMIALS (e.g. *to have and to hold; rack and ruin; toil and moil*), a marked feature also of legal language (e.g. *made and signed; breaking and entering*). Synonymy was a marked characteristic of Old English POETIC DICTION, e.g. *dreng, cempa, ðegn* meant 'warrior'.

(See also HYPONYMY; PARAPHRASE. See further Leech 1974, ch. 12.)

syntax

From Gk 'together-arrangement', the traditional term in GRAMMAR for the core component of SENTENCE structure: the way words, phrases and CLAUSES are ordered and formally grouped.

Syntax provides the skeleton framework of the SENTENCE, and plays a key role in the distribution and FOCUSSING of INFORMATION, in the use of SUBORDINATION, WORD ORDER variations, etc. As debates within GENERATIVE GRAMMAR in the late 1960s highlighted, the contribution of syntax to the overall 'meaning' of a sentence is now recognized to be greater than has traditionally been supposed, and the boundary between syntax and meaning is far from clear. (See e.g., SELECTION RESTRICTIONS.)

systemic: ~ grammar; ~ linguistics

Particularly associated with the work of Halliday from the late 1960s onwards, a development of his earlier so-called **scale and category grammar**, first proposed in 1961, and itself built on the ideas of J. R. Firth. Here Halliday established the major units of linguistic analysis (MORPHEME, **word**, **group**, CLAUSE, SENTENCE) and theoretical categories (**unit, structure, class, system**) which enable the analyst to deal thoroughly with any TEXT.

What is emphasized in **systemic grammar** is the notion of system, but seen as a network, of options or CHOICES. Each major aspect of grammar can be analysed in terms of a set of options, each option dependent upon the CONTEXT or environment. So the system of grammatical MOOD (q.v.), for instance, involves a basic choice of INDICATIVE or IMPERATIVE; the indicative involves a further choice between DECLARATIVE and INTERROGATIVE, while the imperative involves a choice between 'exclusive' and 'inclusive' (i.e. **second person** and **first person**). The interrogative involves a further choice between 'closed' and 'open', and so on.

The choices are not always BINARY; and the systemic approach allows for flexibility and 'delicacy' of subdivision, as approved in the original scale and category theory. One consequence is the breaking down of the boundary between grammar and meaning. This has proved particularly useful in the analysis of VERB functions (see TRANSITIVITY).

As Halliday himself has stressed, systemic grammar is really **systemic-FUNCTIONAL**: the systemic component forming the theoretical aspect of a more comprehensive grammar which interprets grammatical patterns in terms of their configurations of social and linguistic functions. So despite its apparent FORMALISM, systemic grammar is not formalist in the way that GENERATIVE GRAMMAR was. One major tripartite division is that into IDEATIONAL (q.v.), INTERPERSONAL (q.v.) and TEXTUAL FUNCTIONS (q.v.) of language.

Because it provides a fairly exhaustive and semantically sensitive taxonomic and functional approach, systemic grammar has proved a popular and useful framework for stylistic analysis: see Burton and Kennedy, for example, in Carter (1982), and Halliday (1971) on Golding's *The Inheritors*. (But see Fish 1973 for a critique.) Systemic theory has also been applied to other areas of study, e.g. DISCOURSE ANALYSIS (see Berry 1981, in particular).

(See further Berry 1975, 1977; Butler 1985; Cummings & Simmons 1983; Fawcett & Halliday 1985; Halliday 1985; Kress 1976.)

T

tag: ~ question; tagging

(1) In GRAMMAR a **tag** or **tag question** is a short INTERROGATIVE structure comprising an AUXILIARY VERB and a PRONOUN which is attached to a DECLARATIVE.

In languages like French and German the tag question is invariable and therefore FORMULAIC: e.g. *n'est-ce pas?; nicht wahr?* (both negative). In English there is *innit* in informal speech, but usually the auxiliary verb matches the verb of the declarative clause, having the same MODAL, if there is a modal present, otherwise *do*. There is a SUBJECT, co-referring to the subject of the declarative, and INVERSION occurs. Both negative and positive tags are found, which provide a complex grouping as a result.

The commonest type of tag question in standard English is the **reversed polarity** or **checking tag**: in the negative when attached to positive sentences, in the positive when attached to negatives, e.g.:

> Kate likes travelling, doesn't she? (more formally: does she not?)
> Kate doesn't like travelling, does she?

In one sense these checking tags have the same ILLOCUTIONARY FORCE as direct questions like:

> Does Kate like travelling?
> Doesn't Kate like travelling?

but pragmatically their effect is rather different. Direct questions are more open-ended; the checking tags really invite agreement or non-agreement with the speaker (*Yes, she does; No, she doesn't*), who cannot be really sure, however, of his or her information, hence the interrogative. A greater degree of confidence; or of tentativeness, is given depending on the INTONATION pattern of the tags: a falling TONE (NUCLEUS on the auxiliary) is more confident, less tentative than a rising tone, and so makes the tag more like an exclamation.

The **copy tag (same polarity)** is only found with positive statements. And here the tag is also positive: *Kate likes travelling, does she?* These are not really interrogative: the speaker typically echoes, often ironically or suspiciously, what someone else has said, and so conveys his or her attitude to the state of affairs.

It has sometimes been claimed that women use tag questions more than men (e.g. Lakoff 1975), and that tags indicate a lack of confidence, since they serve to request confirmation. But, as Cameron (1992), argues, there doesn't appear to be substantial evidence for the former claim; and tag questions need not sound hesitant if spoken with a falling tone. One of their obvious functions in DIS-COURSE is to ensure FEEDBACK, and to draw the addressee into the conversation. They may be used strategically to initiate a change of TURNS (q.v.).

Tags can also be added to IMPERATIVE sentences: here the PRONOUN is *you*, reflecting the use of imperative in direct address; and there is more variation in the verb forms, e.g.: *Shut the door, will you/can you/won't you/can't you*. Linguists differ in their judgment as to the degree of brusqueness or politeness of these different tags; more significant seems to be the tone of voice with which any and all of them can be uttered.

(2) By analogy with tag question, **tag** is also used to refer to NOUN PHRASES or ELLIPTICAL clauses (often with an auxiliary) which are common in colloquial speech as appendages to statements for EMPHASIS, e.g.: *That was a fight, that was/was that* (simple repetition, with or without inversion); *It's a good drink, is beer/beer is*. Here, in what Quirk *et al.* (1985) call an **amplificatory tag**, a pronoun precedes the more explicit subject which appears as a kind of addition. (Carter & McCarthy's term (1997) is **tail**.)

(3) In the discussion of the modes of REPRESENTATION OF SPEECH and THOUGHT in the novel, the terms **tag** and **tagging** are sometimes found with reference to the presence of reporting clauses containing a LOCUTIONARY or SPEECH ACT verb and a speaker nominal: e.g. *she said/wondered*, traditionally an *inquit* **formula**. In Chatman's (1978) classification **tagged** modes are to be distinguished from the FREE modes: i.e. FREE DIRECT SPEECH/THOUGHT and FREE INDIRECT SPEECH/THOUGHT.

In the direct modes the grammatical status of the reporting clause is not easy to define, since it has considerable mobility in the sentence as a whole, occurring initially, medially and finally:

(i)   She said, 'Will you ring me tomorrow night?'
(ii) 'Will you ring me tomorrow night?', she said
(iii) 'Will you', she said, 'ring me tomorrow night?'
(iv) 'Will you ring me', she said, 'tomorrow night?'

In (i) the reported clause functions like a DIRECT OBJECT; in (ii) like a comment clause (Quirk *et al.* 1985); but in the others more like a parenthesis. INVERSION of verb and subject is possible in examples (iii) and (iv) with a noun as subject: *'Will you ring me', said Daisy, 'tomorrow night?'* In a popular journalistic style such inverted clauses can be found initially: *Said Elton John, 'Watford will definitely win the Cup!'*.

What is in need of further study, with the medial examples particularly, is the possible PROSODIC effect of the inserted tags and their contribution to the RHYTHM of prose. In (iii), for example, the auxiliary verb phrase appears to be more emphatic, since the tag which follows suggests a pause.

As Fowler (1996), points out, the general use of tagging indicates the explicit presence of the NARRATOR, and so a kind of DIALOGIC structure results, between narrator and CHARACTER. (On Dickens's use of what is termed **suspended quotation**, see Lambert 1981.) Some novelists provide considerable detail in the reporting clause: not only offering a wide range of speech act verbs (which are in any case usually more varied for direct speech than for indirect), such as *gasp, giggle, falter, persist, thunder*; but also adding STANCE ADVERBIALS to indicate more clearly the manner of uttering (e.g. *with a shudder; apologetically; in a low voice*, etc.). These are in one sense the equivalent of theatrical stage directions, trying to capture those features of sound and vision that can't be conveyed in the (written) 'words' alone. But by such means overall the narrator controls our reactions to the characters. (See further Banfield 1982.)

(4) **Tag** is found also in the discussion of Middle English poetry to describe the FORMULAIC phrases that recur from poem to poem, which seem merely to fill out the line for METRICAL reasons, or to supply a RHYME. So there occur in the thirteenth-century lyric *Blow, Northern Wind*, the PREPOSITIONAL PHRASES *in boure* ('in (her) bower') and *under hode* ('under (her) hood'). Many such tags survive from the Old English ALLITERATIVE poetic tradition.

tellability

Originally used by Labov (1972) in his analysis of oral narratives and introduced into NARRATIVE theory and LITERARY PRAGMATICS by Pratt (1977) in her application of SPEECH ACT THEORY to LITERARY DISCOURSE.

Tellability simply means 'worth(iness) of narrating', and is an essential factor in 'good' storytelling, whether fact (as in journalism) or fiction. It involves not only the incidents themselves, whether they are considered surprising or eventful or comic enough by the story-teller to be worth relating, but also the manner of narration (DISCOURS). The hearer's or reader's attention is aroused and interest kept during the narration by rhetorical or formal devices of heightening, etc. There is, for example, nothing intrinsically tellable about an old lady swallowing a fly; but in the folk-song our interest is maintained by the accumulation of more and more absurd swallowings, and the RECURSIVE structuring of the narration: *She swallowed the dog to catch the cat to catch the bird to catch the spider . . . to catch the fly . . .* , etc.

(See also NARRATIVITY; see further Leech 1983, on the **interest principle** in discourse.)

tenor (of discourse)

(1) In LITERARY CRITICISM **tenor** is one of a pair of terms introduced by Richards (1936) in his account of METAPHOR (q.v.).

The tenor is the LITERAL (GIVEN) subject or topic of the metaphor; the VEHICLE (q.v.) is the analogy or IMAGE made (NEW). As Leech (1969) says, we are meant to 'believe' that tenor and vehicle are identical, that X is Y, that roses are girls, or fog is a cat, etc. What is of interest to linguists is the MOTIVATION behind the connection between tenor and vehicle, the semantic features of comparison, or what Richards terms the **ground** of the analogy. Tenor and vehicle must have some similarity in order for the metaphor to seem appropriate; yet enough difference in order for the metaphor to appear striking and fresh, DE-FAMILIARIZING our perception of life.

The terms tenor and vehicle can also be applied to SIMILES, where the comparison between objects in different spheres of reference is made explicit:

> . . . When the evening is spread out against the sky (*tenor*)
> Like a patient etherised upon a table (*vehicle*) . . .
>
> (Eliot: *Love Song of J. Alfred Prufrock*)

N.B. In COGNITIVE METAPHOR THEORY, tenor is the **source** domain and vehicle the **target**.

(2) **Tenor** or **tenor of discourse** is also used in sociolinguistics, particularly in the work of Halliday to describe one of the three main variables felt to be significant for the CHOICE of situational features determining characteristic REGISTERS (q.v.). (See also FIELD; MEDIUM.) Halliday himself had first used STYLE in 1964, but because of its more general uses, then adopted tenor, introduced by Spencer & Gregory in Enkvist *et al.* (1964).

Tenor involves the relationships between participants in the situation, their ROLES and status. This will affect the kind of language chosen, particularly in respect of the **degree of** FORMALITY: contrast an interview for a job, a lovers' tiff, two strangers talking at a bus-stop, a research article on the hibernation patterns of toads, etc. There are significant choices of LEXICAL ITEMS, for instance: intimate and colloquial vocabulary in the lovers' tiff, contrasting with a high degree of technical language in the research article. Although written for a mass impersonal readership, it yet presupposes that readership to share the same intellectual or research concerns. Tenor correlates with Halliday's general component or function of language, the INTERPERSONAL FUNCTION, associated with relations between discourse participants, and reflected in choices of MODALITY and INTONATION, etc.

Gregory later distinguished between **personal tenor** and **functional tenor** or purpose: the latter element not easily accounted for in Halliday's tripartite division. In Ellis & Ure (1969) personal tenor is **formality**, and functional tenor is **role**.

tense

From OF *tens* 'time', a category in GRAMMAR of the VERB PHRASE expression relations of time.

In English, as in other languages, there is some (slight) MORPHOLOGICAL indication of **tense**. The PRESENT TENSE is realized by the base form, which is identical with the INFINITIVE except in the **third** PERSON where *-s* is added (realized by /s/, /z/, /ɪz/, depending on the final consonant: e.g. *sits, prods, dozes*); and the **past tense** is realized either by the addition of -(*e*)*d* (/t/, /d/, /ɪd/, e.g. *walked, dozed, prodded*) on the vast majority of verbs; or by a vowel change, in verbs deriving from Old English 'strong' or 'irregular' verbs: e.g. *swam (swim); bound (bind)*, etc.

The correlation between tense and time is not straightforward, since there are only two tenses in English, but three major temporal distinctions: past, present and future. As Lyons (1977) says, however, many other languages lack a future tense: perhaps because it is not seen as so definite and certain as the past, and involving more of an element of prediction. In English, indeed, future time is commonly expressed by MODAL VERBS (*will; shall*, etc.); and also the present tense and ADVERBIALS (e.g. *I go to Paris next week*). In some traditional grammars, however, the phrase **future tense** can be found.

Present time itself is not easily defined, and so can embrace a wide span of reference. As the entry for PRESENT TENSE illustrates, it has a wide range of uses, not all of them strictly temporal, so is sometimes known as the **non-past tense**. The past tense, sometimes traditionally termed the **preterite**, is typically used to mark actions and events that specifically take place in the past, and so is usual in historical accounts and narratives: e.g. *William the Conqueror invaded England in 1066*. Very common, however, is a modal use of the past tense to indicate polite tentativeness, as in *I thought I would ask you if . . . ; Did you wish to see me?*

As Lyons (1977) also notes, tense is a DEICTIC category in that temporal reference is fixed in relation to the speaker's 'now' (v. 'then') in the DISCOURSE situation. In novels, where the world of the fiction intersects with the world of narration, and also the world of the reader reading, temporal relations can become quite complex. So, for example, *Dombey sat in the corner of the darkened room . . .* (Dickens: *Dombey and Son*) has the past tense of straightforward third person narration indicating the time of HISTOIRE (story); but *Whether I shall turn out to be the hero of my own life, or whether that station will be held by anybody else, these pages must show . . . (David Copperfield)* refers to the (future) time of reading outside the time of the novel. Within any one novel there will be shifts of tense according to the shifts of temporal PERSPECTIVE. A uniform sequence of past tenses is more characteristic of folk- and fairy-tales than the novel. In continental criticism the term EPIC PRETERITE (q.v.) refers specifically to the past tense of FREE INDIRECT STYLE, which fuses the present time of thought with the past tense mode of narration.

Tense is sometimes used, especially in older grammars, to cover other uses and forms of the verb which are now also termed ASPECT (q.v.): as in the PERFECT tense/aspect. Strictly speaking, aspect indicates whether an action is in progress: e.g. *She is composing a symphony* (the PROGRESSIVE aspect); or completed: *She has composed a symphony* (the perfect(ive)); but it is difficult to dissociate these meanings from the purely temporal. The present progressive in particular is used much more commonly than the simple present tense to describe actions done at the present time (*The taxi is waiting* v. *The taxi waits*).

(See further Biber *et al.* 1999, ch. 6.)

text; textual function; textuality; texture

Text is commonly used in many branches of linguistics and in STYLISTICS and LITERARY CRITICISM, but is not easily defined, or distinguished from DISCOURSE (q.v.).

(1) Etymologically, **text** comes from a metaphorical use of the Lat. verb *textere* 'weave', suggesting a sequence of sentences or utterances 'interwoven' structurally and semantically. As a count noun it is commonly used in linguistics and stylistics to refer to a sequential collection of sentences or utterances which form a unity by reason of their linguistic COHESION and semantic COHERENCE: e.g. a scientific article; a recipe; poem; public lecture; sermon, etc. However, it is possible for a text to consist of only one sentence or utterance, e.g. a notice or road-sign (*Exit; Stop*), which is semantically complete in itself, and pragmatically tied to a specific situation.

In Halliday's FUNCTIONAL GRAMMAR the **textual function** is one of the three main (META-)FUNCTIONS or components of language, which has to do with the way language is constructed as a text, making links with itself and the situation.

(2) Cohesion and coherence referred to above are not the only features that make a text a text, although they are the most significant: de Beaugrande & Dressler (1981) have seven criteria of what they call **textuality**, the others being INTENTIONALITY (having a plan or purpose); ACCEPTABILITY (having some use for the receiver); SITUATIONALITY (relevance to the context); INFORMATIVITY (degree of NEW INFORMATION); and INTERTEXTUALITY (relations with other texts). Halliday (1978, 1985) stresses also the importance of a text's generic structure, the form it has as a property of its GENRE and of its THEMATIC structure, the means it has for highlighting or FOCUSSING information. (On textuality/texture, see (5); for a different, literary, approach to text and textuality, see (6).)

(3) Since these criteria are generally most prominent in the written MEDIUM, a **text** is very often defined primarily in terms of written or printed material; and in traditional literary criticism often used synonymously with *book*. However, more recently it has been extended to include the filmic and even corporeal (the body as text).

Some DISCOURSE ANALYSTS (e.g. Coulthard 1977) would also reserve text for written language, and have appled discourse to spoken communication, especially the DIALOGIC (v. the MONOLOGIC). But very commonly now discourse is used in a very comprehensive way for all those aspects of the SITUATION or CONTEXT of communication, not only the MESSAGE (written or spoken), but also the relations between ADDRESSERS and ADDRESSEES. In this sense, discourse would subsume the text, as comparable to the 'message'. (See, e.g., Widdowson 1995.) So a sermon can be regarded as a discourse, involving the speaker's awareness of an audience, but also as containing a text, the sermon written to be orally delivered.

Undoubtedly, however, the term *discourse* is often used rather loosely to mean VARIETY, whether spoken or written; and in COLLOCATIONS like *discourse type*, for instance, it does appear to be synonymous with **text type** as used in TEXT LINGUISTICS (q.v.).

However, some text linguists (e.g. van Dijk 1972) see the relations between text and discourse in terms of DEEP V. SURFACE STRUCTURE, or abstract v. physical: text as an abstract, basic linguistic unit manifested or realized as discourse in verbal utterances.

(4) Rather confusingly, in NARRATOLOGY and stylistics **text** has been viewed by some in quite the opposite way (e.g. Fowler 1977; Rimmon-Kenan 1983). Text is the equivalent of Genette's (1972) term RÉCIT, itself a rendering of the FORMALIST term SJUŽET. *Récit* or text refers here to the surface structure of a NARRATIVE, the actual sequence of events as narrated, as opposed to the (possible) chronological ordering, the deep structure.

(5) From a linguistic point of view, it is the surface structure where features of cohesion, as in (1), are realized, such as CO-REFERENCE, CONJUNCTIVES and lexical EQUIVALENCE, contributing altogether to what is sometimes termed **texture**.

From the same root as text, and meaning literally 'the arrangement of threads in a fabric', and by extension, the 'characteristic feel', texture as a metaphor applied to a text involves not only unifying features, but also IDIOLECTAL features: the CHOICES in STYLE which distinguish one text or oeuvre from another, e.g. different kinds and densities of IMAGERY and devices of RHETORIC. Texture can thus be distinguished from textuality in (2) (although it is often not, as in Halliday & Hasan 1976), in that whereas textuality is a characteristic property of all texts, texture is a property of individual texts.

Texture is sometimes used by some literary critics to describe suggestive language and imagery resulting from ICONIC attempts to render phenomena associated with the five senses by PHONAESTHETIC and SYNAESTHETIC devices.

(6) **Text** and **textuality** in recent LITERARY THEORY, such as POST-STRUCTURALISM, have a much vaguer meaning, and come close to ideas of INTERTEXTUALITY (q.v.). The etymological meanings of weaving are revived in notions that all understanding is textual in the sense that words interlink with each other in their associations in an endless 'deferral'; and in the sense also that the process of INTERPRETATION involves our reading of a text interacting with the design of the text itself, and with our readings of other texts, which themselves call forth other texts, and so on. The traditional autonomy of the text is thus undermined. So too in the AFFECTIVE STYLISTICS of Stanley Fish (1970): the text is not an 'object', but an experience or process, created by the reader. Moreover, for NEW HISTORICISM as for POSTMODERN THEORY, relations between text and even history and truth are problematized.

(7) As a non-count noun, **text** is used by some linguists and discourse analysts to describe any stretch of writing or speech, not necessarily complete, which is the object of observation or analysis: e.g. children talking; an interview; extracts from a legal contract. It thus contrasts with the hypothetical, constructed (often single) sentences normally used by linguists as illustrative material.

textual intervention

Rob Pope's term (1995) for writing and re-writing exercises in order to make students aware of stylistic CHOICE on the one hand, and its implications, and the creative role of the READER on the other hand, in the construction of meaning. Pope argues that the best way to understand how a text works is to 'intervene' by changing it: a 'radical rhetoric'. Issues that are particularly highlighted include PERSPECTIVE and degrees of FORMALITY, DIEGESIS/MIMESIS and differences in GENRE and media representations.

text: ~ linguistics; ~ grammar; textworld theory

(1) Known as *Textwissenschaft* and *Textlinguistik* in West and East Germany, **text linguistics** as a comprehensive discipline is particularly associated with work done in that part of Europe and also the Netherlands, the Soviet Union and Finland. In focussing on the TEXT, itself a comprehensive term, as an object of study, it overlaps in many ways with aspects of DISCOURSE ANALYSIS, STYLISTICS, PRAGMATICS, sociolinguistics and NARRATOLOGY. In German, in fact, as Edmondson (1981) points out, the term *Text-* is even broader in its reference than in English, in the absence of a term equivalent to DISCOURSE.

Text linguistics as a sub-branch of linguistics did not really develop until the early 1970s, until linguistics itself began to be less concerned with the SENTENCE as the prime unit of analysis; or at least until it began to be felt that some special discipline should take note of potential units larger than a sentence, or of intra-sentence relations. One major concern is the definition of TEXTUALITY; and also the classification or typology of texts according to their GENRE characteristics. Under the influence of pragmatics and psychology, more attention has also focussed on the production or processing and reception of texts, and on their social function in society. (See further de Beaugrande & Dressler 1981, ch. 2; Enkvist 1985; Graustein & Neubert 1979.)

(2) Particularly influential as a model in early text-linguistic theory was GENERATIVE or TRANSFORMATIONAL GRAMMAR. At first used in **text grammar**, i.e. attempts to reconstruct texts on the basis of generating syntactic 'rules' of sentences, generative–transformational models have been more successfully used in more projective ways: complex NARRATIVES derived from simple ones, or from sets of narrative components, for instance. (See van Dijk 1972f; Prince 1973).

(3) More recently there has been a striking rise of interest in **text** WORLDS, influenced by developments in COGNITIVE LINGUISTICS, SCHEMA THEORY, and ideas in philosophy and logic on POSSIBLE WORLDS, coming together with van Dijk and others' work on text grammar. From the creative interaction of writer, reader, text and context in the construction negotiation of meaning comes a cognitive 'text world' (van Dijk's term; see also Petöfi 1975) that can be experienced as if it contained people, places and events. And within this text world there are also the mental worlds of the characters themselves. Theorists like Emmott 1997 and Werth 1999 are particularly interested in the actual process of text world-building, and the particular textual elements (e.g. DEIXIS) which activate this process.

theme; thematization, etc.

(1) In LITERARY CRITICISM **theme** is the 'point' of a literary work, its central idea, which we INFER from our INTERPRETATION of the PLOT, IMAGERY and SYMBOLISM, etc. Different approaches to literature have foregrounded issues of theme. For example, STRUCTURALISTS like Levi-Strauss were interested in **thematic oppositions** in myths and stories such as life v. death. Much contemporary criticism relates textual themes to questions of cultural codes and IDEOLOGY.

(2) In linguistics **theme** is one of a pair of terms (see also RHEME) particularly developed by the PRAGUE SCHOOL as part of their general interest in the INFORMATIONAL value of UTTERANCES. (See also COMMUNICATIVE DYNAMISM; FUNCTIONAL SENTENCE PERSPECTIVE (FSP). See further Firbas 1961f.)

In effect, theme in (1) coincides more with rheme in that this carries most semantic importance, most commonly coinciding with the FOCUS and with NEW INFORMATION, i.e. 'what is said about a topic' or **comment**. The theme, in contrast, carries least significance in content, commonly coincides with GIVEN INFORMATION, and is also usually found in initial position, generally coinciding with the grammatical SUBJECT of the utterance, i.e. the **topic** or 'starting point' (hence **thematic subject**). Linking theme and rheme are **transitional elements** (usually the VERB PHRASE), e.g.: *Time* (theme) *doth transfix* (transition) *the flourish set on youth* (rheme) (Shakespeare: Sonnet 60). Although the theme commonly occurs initially, it need not always in a connected discourse; but it will always be the element with the lowest communicative value.

Outside the Prague School, however, the terms theme and rheme were taken over in a more schematized way, as in the SYSTEMIC/FUNCTIONAL GRAMMAR of Halliday (1985), under the general heading of **thematization** or **thematic structure** (and what is elsewhere called **topicalization**). Here the theme is any initial element, whether CONJUNCTION, ADVERBIAL or NOUN PHRASE; and not only the subject but also the COMPLEMENT, if placed initially. Theme as 'point' of departure' might seem plausible in some cases, e.g. for adverbials of place as in *In the window* (theme) *stood a candle* (rheme), where the most important part of the message focusses on *a candle*. In other cases, however, the variation of normal WORD ORDER is such to prompt FRONTING or INVERSION for EMPHASIS or prominence, and so to produce what other linguists (e.g. Quirk *et al.* 1985) call a **marked theme**; or what others call (confusingly) 'thematization' or 'topicalization', e.g. *Down* came the rain. It is hard to justify *down* as the topic and *rain* as the comment here; rather the reverse.

In Quirk *et al.* (1985) theme is opposed not to rheme but to FOCUS, normally END-FOCUS, the 'point of completion', carrying usually the most informational interest or value, and thus the element coinciding with the normal NUCLEUS of the INTONATION in speech. With this opposition between point of initiation and point of completion, theme ceases in some ways to have the 'lowest' communicative value, as for the Prague School, but is actually an element of some prominence.

All in all, the thematization of utterances or **thematic meaning** (Leech 1974), the distribution of elements according to degrees of prominence, is an important part of paragraph and TEXT structuring and processing in the written medium: significant also for the understanding of theme in (1). (See further McCarthy & Carter 1994 on **thematic analysis**.)

(3) In ORAL-FORMULAIC THEORY, the study of oral verse composition, a **theme** is a recurrent element of narration and description, a sort of set-piece. It is larger than a FORMULA which occurs within the verse line, which helps the oral poet to compose his songs the more readily. Examples would be the arming of the hero; or a sea-voyage (such as survive in the Old English poem *Beowulf*). It is also known as a **type-scene**. (See further Fry 1968; Lord 1960.)

Such themes correspond in some respects to the conventional *topoi* (sg. *topos*) in RHETORIC, also translated as 'theme' or 'topic', i.e. recurring subjects for argument that appear again and again in literature. These, too, occur in OE poetry under the influence of the Latin homiletic or sermonizing tradition, e.g. the mutability of life and the vanity of human wishes – the subject of Johnson's poem of that name in the eighteenth century. (See also MOTIF.)

tone: ~ group; ~ unit; tonicity; tonality; tune

(1) In ordinary usage, **tone** or **tone of voice** means a particular quality of sound associated with particular emotions or feelings, e.g. *Don't talk to me in that tone of voice*, etc. More loosely the term is used in LITERARY CRITICISM, sometimes to refer to the general tone adopted by the IMPLIED AUTHOR or the NARRATOR as part of the MODALITY of the work, e.g. IRONIC (as in mock-epic or satire) or intimate (as in some love poetry).

(2) In PHONETICS **tone** refers to the pitch level of a syllable, and is very important for distinguishing word meanings in **tone languages** like Cantonese or Mandarin. In English what is more significant is the pitch contour, stretching over part or the whole of an UTTERANCE, called the **tone group** or **tone unit**; and the distinctive pitch movement or contrast associated with the most prominent ACCENTED **(tonic) syllable**, i.e. the KINETIC or NUCLEAR TONE (also known traditionally as **tune**). The commonest nuclear tones in English are **High Fall** (HF) and **Low Fall, High Rise** (HR) and **Low Rise**; also **Fall–Rise** (FR) and **Rise–Fall** (RF). (See also INTONATION.) The higher the rise or fall of the voice, the greater the degree of involvement: e.g. in astonishment (HF) or surprise (HR):

        \\   /

Goodness gracious! What on earth is that?

The tonic syllable also marks the FOCUS of INFORMATION (*that*, for instance) in the tone unit as unit of information. The work in DISCOURSE ANALYSIS of Brazil (1975) has stressed the importance of the Fall–Rise and Fall Tones for distinguishing GIVEN and NEW INFORMATION respectively.

In Halliday's work on intonation since the 1960s, the term **tonicity** refers to the location of the nucleus, and **tonality** to the division of the utterance(s) into tone groups. The tone groups in informal conversation, for instance, are characteristically shorter than in prepared discourse. (See further Crystal 1975.)

topicalization

See THEME.

transfer

See CONVERSION.

transferred epithet

Also referred to as a kind of PROLEPSIS or **hypallage** in RHETORIC (Gk 'changing over'), a **transferred epithet** is a FIGURE OF SPEECH in which an ADJECTIVE properly modifying one NOUN is shifted to another in the same sentence, e.g. *She passed a sleepless night*; or Desdemona's *Alas! what ignorant sin have I committed?* (Shakespeare: *Othello*, IV.ii).

(See also EPITHET.)

transformational grammar (TG); transformation

Variously known as **transformational grammar (TG)**, **transformational–generative grammar** and GENERATIVE GRAMMAR, this influential grammatical theory and model is particularly associated with the work of Chomsky from the late 1950s and 1960s onwards (see especially 1957, 1965).

Chomsky's generative grammar aimed to describe and produce (**generate**) all and only the GRAMMATICAL SENTENCES of a language. Important for the production was a set of **transformation rules** (T-rules) or **transformations**, which are powerfully economic rules for transforming one syntactic element or constituent or 'string' into another. Chomsky was influenced in his development of the idea of transformations by the use of them by his own teacher, Zellig Harris (1952), in his work on TEXT structure. With the introduction of the notion of DEEP and SURFACE STRUCTURE in the 1965 so-called **standard theory**, T-rules enabled conversion to take place between deep and surface forms. So **simple sentences** became COMPOUND or COMPLEX by T-rules of CONJUNCTION or EMBEDDING. There were rules for negation, deletion, NOMINALIZATION, etc.; and optional T-rules (called **stylistic**) for more surface operations such as THEMATIZATION. It is a moot point whether transformations in themselves do not affect meaning, as Chomsky first presupposed. Later, in the early 1970s, he rather changed his mind, as part of his **extended standard theory** (EST).

The implications of a transformational model for a theory of STYLE and meaning were much discussed, especially when the vogue for TG was at its height. (See also DUALISM; PARAPHRASE.) Critics like Ohmann (1964), using the early TG model, and Hayes (1966) have considered the stylistic implications of the

CHOICES of different kinds of transformations in respect of identifying IDIOLECT: the styles of different writers. By 'unpicking' the surface text in terms of different transformations, it is possible both to expose the deep structure and also to project possible alternative surface manifestations. So Henry James's complex yet semantically economic clause structure reveals a layering of transformations, many of them involving degrees of nominalization. For the simpler styles of prose writers like Hemingway it does not need a transformational model to reveal the obvious; nonetheless the 'rewriting' process is helpful in stimulating discussion of the different effects of syntactic choices. (For a critique, however, see McLain 1976.)

The transformational–generative model was also used and applied in TEXT LINGUISTICS from the 1970s. Chomsky's model was soon proved inadequate as a means for generating a whole text, since the theory is essentially sentence-based; but the work in Western Europe of scholars like Petöfi (1975) and van Dijk (1972f), building on GENERATIVE SEMANTICS, illustrates how the concept of transformations could be used in the derivation of complex NARRATIVES from sets of components or MICRO-**structures**. A generative model of narrative structure was also used by the French linguist, A. J. Greimas (see NARRATIVE SEMIOTICS).

(See further Jacobs & Rosenbaum 1971; Traugott & Pratt 1980.)

transitive verb; transitivity

(1) **Transitive** in traditional GRAMMAR, in the categorization of VERBS and CLAUSES, describes structures which have a SUBJECT and verb, and an OBJECT which is 'affected', as it were, by the action of the verb. From Lat. 'going through', the influence of the verb extends to the object as 'goal'. Structures with no object are called INTRANSITIVE (q.v.), e.g. *He wrote a letter* (transitive)/ *then he vanished* (intransitive). It is possible for a verb to function both **transitively** and **intransitively**: *She turned the pages, then turned over*. Where there is both a DIRECT OBJECT and INDIRECT OBJECT in a clause, the verb is sometimes termed **ditransitive** (e.g. *He wrote her a letter*); and where there is a COMPLEMENT as well as object, the verb is termed a **complex transitive** (e.g. *She called him a devil*). (See Quirk *et al.* 1985, 16.18f on COMPLEMENTATION.)

(2) In the FUNCTIONAL/SYSTEMIC GRAMMAR as developed by Halliday, the transitive verb system is part of a broader, semantic configuration of relations involving **processes** (the verb phrase), **participant** ROLES (the NOUN PHRASE) and **circumstances** (ADVERBIALS). (See Halliday 1985.) The different patterns of **transitivity** are the prime means of expressing our external and internal experiences, which is part of the IDEATIONAL FUNCTION of language.

So the traditional transitive verbs themselves are categorized, by grammatical as well as semantic criteria, into different types of processes: the major ones being **material** (*jump, swim*), **mental** (*notice, fear*) and **relational** (*is, stands for*). The traditional categories of subject and object are analysed in terms of the semantic roles of AGENT, **beneficiary, goal**, etc.; and other clausal elements (i.e.

adverbial) are analysed in terms of their function as indicating **manner, cause, instrument**, etc.

Because transitivity is so central to the ideational function of language, and because Halliday's description is expansive and expandible, many stylisticians, including Halliday himself, have used his model in the analysis of FICTION; and particularly in the analysis of MIND STYLE (q.v.). Whether the WORLD-VIEW of a character or a narrator, there is presented in literature an individual interpretation of physical and mental experiences. So Halliday (1971) analyses at length the limited cognition processes in Golding's *The Inheritors*; Burton (1982) the passive role of Sylvia Plath in *The Bell Jar*; and Kennedy (1982) aspects of the narration of Conrad's *The Secret Agent* and Joyce's 'Two Gallants'. Transitivity in relation to IDEOLOGY has also been the focus in CRITICAL LINGUISTICS (q.v.): see, e.g., Fowler (1991).

(See also VOICE.)

triad, also triplet

While BINARY structures are a well-known device in RHETORIC, ranging from PARALLELISM and ANTITHESIS to linked pairs of words or **doublets**/BINOMIALS, series of three units (*oratio trimembris*) are also common: what can be termed **triads** (Nash 1980), or **triplets**. So, in Bacon's *Essays*, three propositions are common: *Wives are young men's mistresses; companions for middle age; and old men's nurses*; the third clause often forming the CLIMAX: *Nuptial love maketh mankind; friendly love perfecteth it; but wanton love corrupteth and embaseth it.* All three NOUNS form a climax in Pope's *Essay on Man*:

> . . . Sole judge of truth, in endless error hurled;
> The *glory, jest*, and *riddle* of the world!

As Atkinson (1984) reveals, such **three-part lists**, as he terms them, are an extremely common feature of the rhetoric of modern political oratory: phrases like 'blood, sweat and tears'; or, as in this report in the *Guardian*:

> Mrs Thatcher yesterday described as 'scandalous, scurrilous and totally false' allegations that she had dealt in shares during her term of office as Prime Minister . . .

trochee

A term taken from classical PROSODY into English during the Renaissance to refer to a FOOT or METRICAL unit of RHYTHM consisting of a STRESSED syllable followed by an unstressed syllable (/ x). The **trochaic** rhythm has a striking marching quality to it that recurs in the four-BEAT verse of nursery rhymes, for example:

```
/    ×  /  ×    /  ×  /  ×
```
Simple Simon met a pieman
```
/ ×    / ×    /   ×   / ×
```
Mary, Mary, quite contrary

Like the DACTYL (/ × ×), the **trochee** is sometimes called a 'falling rhythm'; to be distinguished from the IAMBIC (× /) and ANAPAESTIC feet (× × /), which are called 'rising'. But as Leech (1969) points out, it is not always easy to distinguish iambs from trochees within a verse line. In many instances of verse written in IAMBIC PENTAMETER trochees are found for variation, especially initially in the line:

```
×    /  ×    /    /    / × × × ×        /
```
For sweetest things turn sourest by their deeds;
```
/ ×    ×  /  ×    /  ×   /     ×   /
```
Lilies that fester smell far worse than weeds . . .

(Shakespeare: Sonnet 94)

trope

In RHETORIC, FIGURES OF SPEECH were divided into SCHEMES (q.v.) and **tropes**, schemes basically involving (regular) patterns of FORM, and tropes lexical or semantic DEVIATION of some kind.

From Gk 'turn', a trope twists words away from their usual meanings or COLLOCATIONS: what Leech (1969) describes as a FOREGROUNDED irregularity of CONTENT, and Todorov (1967) terms ANOMALY (q.v.). Common traditional kinds of tropes are METAPHOR, METONYMY and OXYMORON; also figures like HYPERBOLE, LITOTES and IRONY which play with LITERAL meaning. To be included also could be deviations not traditionally labelled, such as unexpected collocations (e.g. *dressed in marvellous sulks*). N.B. Nash's nice term (1989) for a pattern of related tropes in a text is **tropodrome**.

(See further Gibbs 1994 on the significance of tropes in cognition and language.)

turn-taking

In ETHNOMETHODOLOGY and DISCOURSE ANALYSIS, coined as part of research into conversational behaviour, and how the contributions of speakers interact (see Goffman 1974; Sacks *et al.* 1974).

Linguists are interested in how one participant knows when the current speaker is finishing, so that he or she can take a **turn**. The current speaker may indicate implicitly (by body language or PROSODIC features) or explicitly (by inviting a response) that another person can take over (e.g. *What do you think, Fred; That's right, isn't it?*). Alternatively, the other person may 'read' signals from the flow of speech which suggest an opening is possible. Even when a speaker shows signs of wanting to 'hold the floor', another participant can take advantage of a pause or clause-break to make a comment. Most conversation, to be COHERENT, is not naturally confused or confusing; it proceeds in an orderly way, by a series of interactional MOVES, with each participant having a turn to speak. However, in emotional or power-assymetrical conversation one speaker may interrupt another (**turn-stealing**); or, in a group discussion, two or more may speak simultaneously. Certainly ordinary conversation is less ordered than formalized or institutionalized DISCOURSES such as debates, where only the chairperson has the 'authority' to initiate changes of speaker (**turn-controlling**). There are thus different conventions for different types of spoken discourse: compare also the court-room and student seminar. (See further Edmondson 1981, 4.2, for a discussion of turns.)

More orderly than conversation too is the DIALOGUE traditional in drama. Interruptions are rare, as each character unfolds exactly what must be said. In the interests of 'realism', however, or of information-giving without excessive MONOLOGUE, **turn-taking** devices can be set up.

(See also ADJACENCY PAIR. See further Herman 1995.)

typological circle

In the work of Stanzel (1984) on NARRATION the **typological circle** is his complex model for accounting for all the manifold ways in which a story can be told.

There are three main axes each involving an opposition: of PERSON (whether the NARRATOR is inside or outside the world of the story); PERSPECTIVE (internal or external POINT OF VIEW of the CHARACTER); and MODE (narrators telling the story v. **reflectors** or FOCALIZERS who don't, yet who present what is thought or felt directly to the reader).

All narrative situations, Stanzel argues, whether comprising the whole framework of a story or just a part of it, can be seen as being composed of elements of these three axes, shading into one another where necessary. But he argues for three basic types of narrative situation: **first person narrative; authorial narrative** (non-personalized, outside the world of the characters) and **figural narrative** (involving a reflector). Within the first person narrative situation then can be plotted novels which range from the *I* of extreme internal perspective/reflector, the INTERIOR MONOLOGUE (as in *Ulysses*); through the narrating *I* in the world of the characters, as in *Moby Dick*; to the *I* as editor in *Gulliver's Travels*; and so over the boundary into the *I* outside the world of the characters (hence authorial narrative) in a novel like *Tom Jones*.

U

under-lexicalization

Popularized by Fowler (e.g. 1996) to refer in LEXICAL and STYLISTIC studies to the lack of an adequate set of words to express specific concepts. It can be contrasted with OVER-LEXICALIZATION (q.v.), the surplus of words.

In ordinary speech **under-lexicalization** can arise through ignorance of the particular appropriate word; or through momentary forgetfulness or vagueness; or through the natural REDUNDANCY of the CO-TEXT and CONTEXT – note the common use of words like *so-and-so, thingummy,* etc. Across language or DIALECT boundaries, a concept that is under-lexicalized in one community may be over-lexicalized in another (e.g. Anglo-Irish terms for different kinds of potatoes; or West Indian terms for different 'ages' of bananas).

Under-lexicalization may be exploited in LITERARY LANGUAGE to suggest a limited PERSPECTIVE or MIND STYLE: e.g. the immature consciousness of Stephen Dedalus as he starts school in Joyce's *Portrait of the Artist* is reflected in the REPETITION of the vague word *nice*:

> That was not a <u>nice</u> expression. His mother had told him not to speak with the rough boys in the college. <u>Nice</u> mother! . . . She was a <u>nice</u> mother but she was not so <u>nice</u> when she cried.

universe of discourse

See WORLD.

unspeakable sentence

See FREE INDIRECT STYLE; VOICE.

usage

(1) As a singular noun, **usage** is the general linguistic practice at any one period of time in speech and writing of a speech-community.

As Horace recognized in his *Art of Poetry*, usage must inevitably change, and as a result the linguistic system itself (i.e. LANGUE). Modern GRAMMARS characteristically describe current usage (e.g. Biber *et al.* 1999).

Many people through the ages have resisted the idea of usage as an authority for codification, just as they have resisted the idea of usage changing. In the eighteenth century in particular grammarians were concerned to describe the language as they thought it ought to be used, by some ideal or absolute standard of CORRECTNESS, and wished to 'fix' it from further change or 'deterioration' (see also PRESCRIPTIVISM). Even today there are authoritative handbooks on usage being written or continually reprinted (see, e.g., Fowler 1998. See also CATACHRESIS; ETYMOLOGICAL FALLACY).

(2) Although prescriptivism has made little impact on general usage, there are a number of **usages** which are the continual subject of controversy for a variety of reasons. Which syllable should be STRESSED in *controversy*? Does *anyone* raise *his* or *their* hand? Can we *loan* our glasses? Or split an INFINITIVE? Often what people believe they say (or ought to say) is different from their actual usage. They are also more concerned about what to use in (FORMAL) writing, more than in (informal) speech.

More serious than this kind of **abusage** (Partridge) is that in which language can be manipulated to distort the truth, as in propaganda, or to denigrate, as in racist or sexist language – language used, in Bolinger's (1980) phrasing, as a 'loaded weapon'.

(See also EUPHEMISM; JARGON.)

utterance

(1) **Utterance** is not easily distinguished from SENTENCE (q.v.), but can usefully be seen as the physical realization of a sentence in either its spoken or written form. In other words, it belongs to language in use rather than language as a system.

This aspect of utterance is stressed very much in the writings of the Russian linguists Bakhtin and Voloshinov of the 1930s. The Saussurean notion of PAROLE is extended to make utterance quite specifically social, concrete, and fixed in time.

(2) Very commonly, however, utterance tends to be reserved for spoken DISCOURSE (cf. Fr. ÉNONCIATION / ÉNONCÉ); and to describe a stretch of speech before and after which there is silence. This could range from a one-word response to a series of 'sentences'; or even part of a sentence (e.g. *Well, I'll be . . .*). Utterance could also be co-extensive with a MONOLOGUE; although it is natural to think of DIALOGUE as containing several utterances. Any discussion of INTONATION, or of FOCUSSING or THEMATIZATION properly applies to utterances rather than to sentences.

V

variation

(1) Introduced into studies of Old English POETIC LANGUAGE and STYLE in the late nineteenth century to describe a characteristic feature of the ALLITERATIVE VERSE that distinguishes it from the Germanic verse of the Continent: the repetition of an idea, whether expressed in a word, phrase or clause, in different words or SYNONYMS, often with grammatical PARALLELISM.

Accumulatively, the effect is to give a leisurely pace and sense of REDUNDANCY to Old English poetic expression; but in individual descriptive passages, where it most occurs, the effect is also to broaden and deepen an IMAGE because of the additional CONNOTATIONS that are brought. So the description of the monsters' home in *Beowulf* reads (in translation):

> They possess a secret land, wolf-cliffs, windy nesses, a dangerous fen-path, where the mountain-stream falls down under the darkness of the nesses, a flood, down under the earth.

(See further Brodeur 1959.)

(2) In classical RHETORIC, the repetition of the same thought in different words was known as **expolitio** or **exergasia**; and 'elegant **variation**' was a marked feature of prose essay style as a means of avoiding plainness and as a device for EMPHASIS until the twentieth century, e.g. Johnson:

> When the mind is unchained from necessity, it will range after convenience; when it is left at large in the fields of speculation, it will shift opinions. (Preface to his *Dictionary*)

Simpler kinds of LEXICAL variation are found in many REGISTERS as a means of COHESION and to avoid REPETITION (see also EQUIVALENCE).

variety

Common in sociolinguistics especially to describe any system of language which distinguishes one group of people or one FUNCTION from another: whether regional or occupational (see DIALECT); social (see SOCIOLECT); or situational (see REGISTER). More technical-sounding equivalents are LECT and **diatype**.

Varieties can contain **sub-varieties**: within the **national variety** of British English, the dialect spoken in the north-east of England varies in respect of certain features between Newcastle, Durham city and Darlington; the language of television commentary varies between sports coverage and royal weddings, between football, wrestling and snooker. Language, in fact, is far from being a uniform phenomenon, which makes a systematic description exceedingly difficult.

(See also COMMON CORE; HETEROGLOSSIA.)

vehicle

In LITERARY CRITICISM one of a pair of terms (see also TENOR) introduced by Richards (1936) in his account of METAPHOR (q.v.).

Tenor is the LITERAL (GIVEN) subject or topic of the metaphor (x); the **vehicle** is the analogy or IMAGE made (y). So for a metaphor, x is identified as y in some way, one FIELD of REFERENCE (as for the vehicle) is (FIGURATIVELY) transferred to another. The most vivid or telling metaphors arise when the ground of identification is not immediately obvious, or when the field of reference seems at first glance quite removed from that of the tenor's. So in *Macbeth* (V.v):

> Life's but a walking shadow, a poor player
> That struts and frets his hour upon the stage,
> And then is heard no more: it is a tale
> Told by an idiot, full of sound and fury,
> Signifying nothing.

In COGNITIVE METAPHOR THEORY, vehicle is the **source domain** (and tenor the **target**).

What is of interest to many literary critics is the kinds of vehicles that are evoked in a text or a writer's oeuvre. Recurring analogues, e.g. of blood, poison, flowers or light can help the reader to an appreciation of significant THEMES. Certainly books and articles which classify IMAGERY in terms of vehicle are more common than those which deal with tenor (e.g. Spurgeon 1935 on Shakespeare's imagery; Tuve 1947 on Elizabethan and Metaphysical poetic imagery).

velar

Used in PHONETICS in the description and classification of consonants on the basis of place of articulation in the mouth. It refers to a sound made by the movement of the back of the tongue toward the soft palate or **velum**. In (STANDARD) English, the **velar consonants** are the VOICED and VOICELESS PLOSIVES /g/ and /k/, and the nasal /ŋ/ written *ng*. For the plosives the soft palate is raised, for the nasal it is lowered.

verb: ~ phrase, also verbal group

(1) **Verbs** are a major word class in English which function as the PREDICATOR in a CLAUSE, linking SUBJECT with PREDICATE.

There are two major kinds of verbs: **full** or **lexical** or **main verbs** which belong to the OPEN CLASS of LEXICAL ITEMS, and which typically express actions or states (*hop; giggle; think*, etc.); and the CLOSED CLASS of AUXILIARY VERBS (*be; do; will; may*, etc.).

(2) In a **verb phrase** or **verbal group** there will always be a main verb as HEAD, and in many cases accompanying auxiliaries, which help to express distinctions of VOICE (e.g. *is given*); ASPECT (e.g. *is crying; has cried*); negation (*didn't cry*), etc. The forms of the main verb change correspondingly, a basic distinction being between the FINITE and NON-FINITE forms: cf. *I cry, she crie-s* (PRESENT TENSE), *I cried* (**past tense**) v. the PARTICIPLES (*cry-ing; cried*). A small group of verbs have irregular forms involving vowel changes, left over from Germanic MORPHOLOGICAL habits: e.g. *drink–drank–drunk; drive–drove–driven*.

(3) In TRANSFORMATIONAL GRAMMAR, **verb phrase** (VP) conventionally indicates both verb and rest of predicate.

(See also MOOD. See further Biber *et al.* 1999, ch. 5.)

verbal hygiene

Debbie Cameron's striking term (1995) for the manifestation of many people's impulse, whether lay or professional linguists, to regulate or control language; and their defiant refusal to leave it alone. Traditional grammatical PRESCRIPTIVISM is an obvious example, but for Cameron the Campaign for Plain English against JARGON; producing guide-lines on non-sexist language or other 'politically correct' language movements; societies for 'pure English' or spelling reform; and (sadly) societies for the preservation of regional DIALECTS would also come under this umbrella. So too, presumably, would CRITICAL LINGUISTICS and CRITICAL DISCOURSE ANALYSIS, with its efforts to raise awareness of IDEOLOGICAL manipulation in discourse.

verisimilitude, also vraisemblance

Terms in English and French LITERARY CRITICISM meaning 'likeness to truth', and describing the common convention in LITERARY LANGUAGE, especially that of FICTION, whereby an illusion of reality is given through the proliferation of detail. This will fix a story in a definite social and physical setting. In fantasy and science fiction for example, the fantastic and strange are all the more readily accepted or 'naturalized' by the reader (e.g. *Gulliver's Travels*). **Verisimilitude** is only a convention, an illusion: but the reader thus finds MOTIVATION for characters and events; and moreover takes the GAPS or INDETERMINACIES and fills in the details according to the FRAMES OF REFERENCE suggested.

As Culler (1975, ch. 7) points out, verisimilitude in a broad sense is not easily distinguishable from other kinds of **naturalization**. In George Eliot's novels, for instance, the reader is not only expected to know something about nineteenth-century village life or a provincial town, but also works and ideas about art, architecture, religion and philosophy. (See further Barthes 1970 on the REFERENTIAL CODE.) The reader of nineteenth-century 'realistic' novels must also be familiar with the INTERTEXTUAL conventions of the GENRE, which provide their own NORMS of detail.

vernacular

From Lat. 'native, domestic', commonly used term in DIACHRONIC LINGUISTICS and in sociolinguistics to refer to either: (1) the language native to a country, the mother tongue; or (2) one's native DIALECT as opposed to the STANDARD.

So, for example, according to (1) poems and prose were written in the Old English **vernacular** in competition with Latin, dominant as a language of learning during the Anglo-Saxon period; and Chaucer wrote his poems in the vernacular in the fourteenth century rather than Latin, or the politically important language, French.

For (2) one can speak of the vernacular of South Lincolnshire or of Glasgow. Often the term carries with it connotations of very localized, non-prestigious, speech. So Biber *et al.* (1999, ch. 14) somewhat patronizingly define it as the 'popular untaught variety of a language found in colloquial speech' and felt to be 'inappropriate for serious public communication' and as a model for foreign learners. Nonetheless they acknowledge that vernacular forms have an important role in marking 'social solidarity' among speakers. The term *vernacular* is often used interchangeably with **non-**STANDARD, also evaluated negatively often against the 'norm' of the standard hegemonic dialect.

(3) The term **Black English Vernacular** (BEV) is a standard term to describe the urban VARIETY of English spoken mostly by black Americans in the US, and whose origin is much debated; also known as **African-American Vernacular**.

vocative

In traditional GRAMMAR and the study of inflected languages refers to a special CASE form of the NOUN used in direct address: e.g. *Et tu, Brut-e* 'And you, Brutus'. In English it refers to a noun or noun phrase or proper name used in address, separated in speech from the rest of the CLAUSE by its own INTONATION contour, and in writing by commas, e.g.: *Tim, dinner's on the table; I forgot to tell you darling, but I'm joining the Foreign Legion; Don't lie to me, you bastard; What do you think, Doctor Foster?*.

As these examples reveal, the **vocative** is typically used to attract someone's attention (as in the first example), and as such most typically occurs initially; or, in other positions, it simply punctuates a speech to keep someone's attention; to invite TURN-TAKING; or to express a feeling or attitude. Titles and first names and surnames are commonly used in this way as **terms of** ADDRESS (q.v.), indicating **degrees of** FORMALITY from polite respect (e.g. *Mrs Dalloway*) to familiarity (e.g. *Clarissa; Clarry*).

Vocatives are commonly used in traditional POETIC DICTION in the function of APOSTROPHE to absent people or even inanimate objects (*O wild West Wind*). They are also traditionally used in invocations to the gods or Muses; and are still a feature of the traditional liturgy (*Our Father, which art in heaven; Thou who takest away the sins of the world*).

voice

(1) In PHONETICS **voice** or **voicing** refers to the sound made by the vibration of the vocal cords in the larynx in the articulation of vowels and consonants. The vocal cords vibrate for all vowels in English, which are thus **voiced**; but only certain consonants. For many kinds of consonants there is a PHONEMIC opposition between voice and **voicelessness**: the PLOSIVES /b/ v. /p/; /d/ v. /t/; /g/ v. /k/; the FRICATIVES /v/ v. /f/; /z/ v. /s/; /ʒ/ v. /ʃ/; the AFFRICATES /dʒ/ v. /tʃ/.

(2) In GRAMMAR **voice** is widely used to describe a VERBAL category concerned with the relations of SUBJECT and OBJECT and the action expressed by the TRANSITIVE verb.

Where the subject is the AGENT of the action, this is known as the ACTIVE VOICE (q.v.); where the subject is the recipient of the action, or directly affected by it, this is known as the PASSIVE VOICE (q.v.), e.g.:

Jumbo the elephant greatly loved the zoo-keeper. (active)
The zoo-keeper was greatly loved by Jumbo the elephant. (passive)

There are obvious syntactic differences between the two sentences: the forms of the verb, and the introduction of the preposition *by* in the second. It is generally argued that the PROPOSITIONAL MEANING remains the same, however, that active and passive sentences are PARAPHRASES of one another. Yet where a shift of FOCUS or EMPHASIS is required, the passive, which is on the whole less commonly used than the active, is an important STYLISTIC construction. (See further Biber *et al.* 1999, ch. 6.)

(3) **Voice** is popularly used in LITERARY CRITICISM and STYLISTICS, especially in the discussion of modes of NARRATION and REPRESENTATION OF SPEECH, to describe 'one who speaks' in a narrative, whether the IMPLIED AUTHOR, or CHARACTER, or both (as in FREE INDIRECT SPEECH). (See also DUAL VOICE; EXTRAFICTIONAL VOICE.) But as critics like Genette (1972) and Chatman (1978) point out, it is sometimes confused with POINT OF VIEW or PERSPECTIVE. This is not surprising, in view of the fact that an OMNISCIENT NARRATOR, for instance, tends both to tell and view events.

As Gibson (1996, ch. 4) argues, voice seems to be the central focus in narratology, a major point of reference with a human presence as source or origin. But is it possible to have a narrative without 'voice'? Banfield's notion of **unspeak-**

able sentences in the context of FREE INDIRECT SPEECH has problematized the issue: instead of a 'dual voice' there could be no speaking subject at all. In the novels of George Eliot as of James Joyce there are sentences certainly not easily assignable to either a character or narrator.

(4) In the writings of Bakhtin (e.g. 1981) voice in this context takes on the broader connotations of STYLE and DISCOURSE, especially in the collocation DOUBLE-VOICED (q.v.). For him the discourse of the novel illustrates his central DIALOGIC principle: characteristically heterogeneous and interactive, voices of social groups, IDEOLOGIES, as well as of narrator and characters, are all interwoven. (See also POLYPHONY.)

(5) In FEMINIST CRITICISM voice has been a central preoccupation: with women 'finding a voice' with which to speak and write in the public arena of a patriarchal IDEOLOGY and society; with the idea of women as the 'Other' voice in opposition/subordination to the male; or as a voice on the cultural margins.

W

word order

In GRAMMAR that aspect of SYNTAX concerned with the arrangement of words in CLAUSES and SENTENCES in particular, but also phrases (see, e.g. ADJECTIVE).

In Modern English **word order** (WO) is highly significant grammatically for the FUNCTIONAL load it bears. The functions of SUBJECT and OBJECT in some constructions, for instance, are determined solely by position, e.g.:

> Man (subject) eats shark (object).
> Shark (subject) eats man (object).

Hence the order subject–VERB–object (SVO) is the 'neutral' or **un**MARKED order for English. In inflected languages like Old English, Latin and Modern German such functions are indicated by CASES, so that WO variations away from a SVO order are quite plausible.

However, even in inflected languages variation is commonly made for STYLISTIC reasons, as in Modern English. For FOCUS and EMPHASIS variations can occur, with FRONTING of object, for example, or INVERSION of subject and verb: *That man I detest; Up comes Fred no worse for wear.* Such stylistic variation is especially common in LITERARY, especially POETIC, LANGUAGE: in RHETORIC it is known as HYPERBATON. In some cases it seems due to the demands of metre and rhyme; but the effect generally, as Turner (1973) says, is to add interest and emphasis, and to vary the 'intonation':

> Me this unchartered freedom tires (OSV)
>
> > (Wordsworth: *Ode to Duty*)
>
> No motion has she now, no force (OVSO)
>
> > (Wordsworth: *Lucy Poems*)

But even in literary language, marked DEVIATIONS do not normally occur, and would be as **un**GRAMMATICAL as in everyday language. (The language of Joyce's *Finnegans Wake* is one notable exception.)

In non-literary language, however, there are some elements of the sentence or clause which are relatively mobile compared with subjects and objects, namely

ADVERBIALS. They naturally occur in initial, medial and final position, although final position seems the most usual:

Very quickly she walked away from him.
She walked very quickly away from him.
She walked away from him very quickly.

Also, in non-DECLARATIVES, namely INTERROGATIVES, inversion of subject and verb is common in *yes–no* questions (e.g. *Are you sure?*).

word-play

See PARONOMASIA; PUN.

world, also universe of discourse; world-view

(1) **World** frequently occurs in many disciplines related to the study of language: in logic, SEMANTICS, philosophy, LITERARY and NARRATIVE SEMANTICS, DISCOURSE ANALYSIS, COGNITIVE LINGUISTICS, TEXT LINGUISTICS and LITERARY CRITICISM, for example. It has become the prime focus of TEXTWORLD THEORY and POSSIBLE WORLDS THEORY.

There are many different kinds of worlds which language relates to or makes REFERENCE to. Primarily it codifies the real physical world and the world of our thoughts and sensations about the experiences around us (see IDEATIONAL FUNCTION). Thus most of our everyday speech and writing is anchored in a **discourse world** orientated towards the real world as a FRAME OF REFERENCE; as a result of which a large amount of shared or common knowledge can be PRESUPPOSED.

But within the large world there are smaller worlds of reference: the country, town, street, house, etc., where we live. There are other CONTEXTS, situational rather than geographical, which provide frames of reference: what are called DOMAINS or fields of influence. So the domain or 'world' of advertising will refer to a largely different set of entities than that of bee-keeping. This is also known as **universe of discourse**, in one of its senses (but see also below).

However, philosophers and literary critics are interested in other kinds of worlds, which human language has the unique capacity to make reference to, namely the worlds of possibility or of the imagination (see also COUNTERFACTUAL; MODALITY). Not all of our everyday conversation, indeed, is rooted in firm reality: *if only* is the entry to wishes, hopes, dreams and fantasies. The world or universe of discourse, in other words, is broader and more abstract than the real world or **actual world**.

LITERATURE, like film, provides prime examples of another reality: the INFERRED SITUATIONS of poetry, the created worlds of drama and FICTION: what Elam (1980) defines as a 'spatio-temporal elsewhere'. In theory, the **text worlds** created in fiction are infinite: a character can create his or her own counterfactual **subworld**, and so on. And certainly in HYPERFICTION multiple worlds exist. Yet in

409

many respects, especially in 'realistic' fiction, the world of the TEXT bears a close relationship with the real world in the interests of VERISIMILITUDE. In historical novels, for example, real characters and events may be referred to: e.g. the Napoleonic wars in Tolstoy's *War and Peace*; the French Revolution in Dickens's *Tale of Two Cities*. Even fantasies and science fiction with their utopias and dystopias are normally interpreted as having some relation with the real world, if only by contrast (e.g. the extreme worlds of *Alice in Wonderland* and Terry Pratchett's 'Discworld' novels). INTERPRETATION is an important word in this respect: the world of a literary or filmic text is not so much given, as created by the reader; so there are as many different worlds as there are readers (or spectators, in the case of drama and film). (See further Allan 1986, I. 3.3.3; Ryan 1991; Werth 1999.)

(2) The relations between language and the real world are made more complex by the possibility that language not only reflects the world, but also acts as a 'barrier' to the world, and blinkers our perception of it. As a result, our **world-view**, i.e. our pattern of beliefs and cultural assumptions or IDEOLOGY, is constrained by the very language which apparently exists to express it.

The idea that language 'determines' or constrains world-view (in German *Weltanschauung*) has been a pervasive one in philosophy and European and American linguistics even before the twentieth century. It is popularly known as **linguistic** DETERMINISM (q.v.).

writerly

The common English translation of Fr. *scriptible*, introduced by Barthes (1970) into his discussion of kinds of TEXTS and READERS.

A **writerly** text, especially characteristic of the twentieth century and POST-MODERNIST writing and METAFICTION, is difficult to read (yet for Barthes extremely pleasurable) because of its structural and linguistic DEVIATIONS and INDETERMINACY of meaning. It requires therefore the active participation of its readers. Joyce's *Finnegans Wake* would be an extreme example of such a text (and not so pleasurable). *Scriptible* is opposed to *lisible* (READERLY, q.v.): the text being supposedly easier to read, and requiring a passive reader: characteristic in Barthes's view, of the 'classical' French novel.

(See also JOUISSANCE; and Eco's (1979) distinction between OPEN and CLOSED TEXTS.)

Z

zero: ~-article; ~-morph; ~-affixation/derivation; ~-anaphora, etc.

The linguistic concept of **zero** (∅) strikes a chord with DECONSTRUCTION, for it is simply ABSENCE that is meaningful. Superficially there may be no physical element present, yet according to some system or theory, absence may have a function by analogy.

(1) Thus NOUNS in English are normally accompanied by ARTICLES (e.g. *a; the*), but some nouns, notably mass nouns and INDEFINITE plurals, do not (e.g. *cheese; mice*). So the **zero-article** is a commonly used concept to 'fill' the article paradigm or system. Similarly, with the plurals of nouns: the MORPHEME *-s* regularly denotes plurality, but some nouns have an unchanged form with a plural verb (e.g. *The sheep are safely grazing*): hence a **zero-morph** is posited.

(2) In LEXICOLOGY, the terms **zero**-AFFIXATION or **zero** DERIVATION are used as alternatives to CONVERSION or **transfer** to describe a method of word formation that does not depend on the use of affixes to change one word class into another, but simply changes with no alteration in form (e.g. nouns to verbs: *to sandwich; to taxi*).

(3) A slightly different use of zero is found in the concept of **zero**-ANAPHORA, or **gapping**. Here a 'missing' element, through the speaker's ELLIPSIS, can be supplied or recovered by the listener from to CO-TEXT. Zero-anaphora is thus a very useful device to avoid REPETITION, and is commonly found in CO-ORDINATE CLAUSES, e.g.: *Jack fell down and [Jack] broke his crown.*

(See also **zero**-RELATIVE. For a critique of the concept of **zero**, see further Haas 1957.)

zero degree (of writing)

Zero degree and (**writing**) **degree zero** are translations of phrases popularized by the French critic Barthes (1953a).

(1) Strictly, Barthes uses **writing degree zero** to describe the classical French STYLE or *écriture* initiated by Camus, which he sees as a style of ABSENCE, i.e. a

neutral, 'transparent' or **un**MARKED style. It is questionable, however, whether a work can have no style: the very 'absence' of a marked style can itself be seen to be stylistically significant.

(2) In Barthes and elsewhere, **degree zero** has also been used as a synonym for NORM, and any kind of norm, whether of the STANDARD LANGUAGE; or habitual (LITERARY) conventions; or the normal level of NARRATIVE generality, which helps to determine PERSPECTIVE. This is also known as the **threshold of functional relevance**. (For a discussion of **degree zero** NARRATEE, see further Lanser 1981.)

zeugma

From Gk 'yoke', a FIGURE OF SPEECH in which either (i) two NOUNS (commonly) are governed by a single VERB, but where a difference in meaning is involved; or (ii) where one verb serves more than one CLAUSE. It is very difficult to distinguish from SYLLEPSIS (q.v.), e.g.:

(i) Time and her aunt moved slowly.

(Austen: *Pride and Prejudice*)

(ii) But passion lends them power, time means, to meet . . .

(Shakespeare: *Romeo and Juliet*, II, Prologue)

References and Further Reading

Abel, L. 1963 *Metatheatre: a new view of dramatic form.* Hill & Wang: New York

Abercrombie, D. 1967 *Elements of general phonetics.* Edinburgh University Press

Adamson, S. 1998 The code as context: language-change and (mis)interpretation. In Malmkjaer, K. and Williams, J. (eds) *Context in language: learning and language understanding.* Cambridge University Press

Adamson, S. 2000 Literary language. In Lass, R. (ed.) *The Cambridge history of the English language vol. 3 1476–1776.* Cambridge University Press

Aitken, A. J., Bailey, R. W., Hamilton-Smith, N. 1973 *The computer and literary studies.* Edinburgh University Press

Allan, K. 1986 *Linguistic meaning* (2 vols). Routledge & Kegan Paul

Althusser, L. 1971 *Lenin and philosophy.* New Left Books

Argyle, M. 1972 *The psychology of interpersonal behaviour.* Penguin

Ashcroft, B., Griffiths, G., Tiffin, H. 1989 *The empire writes back: theory and practice in post-colonial literatures.* Routledge

Atkinson, M. 1984 *Our masters' voices.* Methuen

Attridge, D. 1982 *The rhythms of English poetry.* Longman

Attridge, D. 1995 *Poetic rhythm: an introduction.* Cambridge University Press

Auerbach, E. 1957 *Mimesis.* Doubleday: Garden City, New York

Austin, J. L. 1961 *Philosophical papers.* Oxford University Press

Austin, J. L. 1962 *How to do things with words.* Oxford University Press

Bach, K., Harnish, R. M. 1979 *Linguistic communication and speech acts.* MIT Press: Cambridge, Massachusetts

Bakhtin, M. 1968 *Rabelais and his world.* MIT Press: Harvard

Bakhtin, M. 1973 *Problems of Dostoevsky's poetics.* Ann Arbor: Ardis (First published in Russian in 1929)

Bakhtin, M. 1981 *The dialogic imagination: four essays.* University of Texas Press: Austin

Baldick, C. 1996 *Criticism and literary theory from 1890 to the present.* Longman

Bally, C. 1909 *Traité de stylistique française.* Carl Winters: Heidelberg

Bally, C. 1912 Le style indirect libre en français moderne, *Germanisch–Romanisch Monatsschrift* **4**: 549–56; 597–606

Banfield, A. 1982 *Unspeakable sentences: narration and representation in the language of fiction.* Routledge & Kegan Paul

Barry, P. 1984 The enactment fallacy, *Essays in criticism* **30**: 95–104

Barthes, R. 1953a *Le degré zéro de l'écriture.* Seuil: Paris (Translated 1967 *Writing degree zero.* Cape)

Barthes, R. 1953b *Mythologies.* Seuil: Paris (Translated 1972 Cape)

Barthes, R. 1964 Rhétorique de l'image, *Communications* **4**: 40–51 (Translated 1977 Rhetoric of the image, *Image – music – text.* Fontana)

Barthes, R. 1966 Introduction à l'analyse structurale des récits, *Communications* **8**: 1–27 (Translated 1977 *Image – music – text.* Fontana)

Barthes, R. 1967a *Système de la mode.* Seuil: Paris

Barthes, R. 1967b *Elements of semiology.* Cape

Barthes, R. 1970 *S/Z.* Seuil: Paris (Translated 1975 Cape)

Barthes, R. 1975 *Le Plaisir du Texte.* (Translated 1976 *The Pleasure of the Text.* Cape)

Barthes, R. 1977 The death of the author. In Heath, S. (ed.) *Image – music – text.* Fontana

Bartlett, F. C. 1932 *Remembering: a study in experimental and social psychology.* Cambridge University Press

Baudrillard, J. 1995 *The Gulf War did not take place.* Indiana University Press: Bloomington

Bauer, L. 1983 *English word-formation.* Cambridge University Press

de Beaugrande, R., Dressler, W. 1981 *Introduction to text linguistics.* Longman

Bell, A., Garrett, P. (eds) 1998 *Approaches to media discourse.* Blackwell

Benjamin, W. 1935 *The work of art in an age of mechanical reproduction.* (In *Illuminations,* translated 1970, Cape)

Bennett, T. 1979 *Formalism and Marxism.* Methuen

Benveniste, E. 1966 *Problèmes de linguistique générale.* Gallimard: Paris (Translated 1971 *Problems in general linguistics.* University of Miami Press: Coral Gables)

Bernstein, B. 1971 *Class, codes and control 1: theoretical studies towards a sociology of language.* Routledge & Kegan Paul

Bernstein, B. 1973 *Class, codes and control 2: applied studies towards a sociology of language.* Routledge & Kegan Paul

Bernstein, B. 1975 *Class, codes and control 3: towards a theory of educational transmissions.* Routledge & Kegan Paul

Berry, M. 1975, 1977 *Introduction to systemic linguistics* (2 vols). Batsford

Berry, M. 1981 Systemic linguistics and discourse analysis: a multi-layered approach to exchange structure. In Coulthard, M., Montgomery, M. (eds) *Studies in discourse analysis.* Routledge & Kegan Paul

Bex, T. 1996 *Variety in English (texts in society: societies in text).* Routledge

Bex, T., Watts, R. J. (eds) 1999 *Standard English: the widening debate.* Routledge

Bhatia, V. K. 1993 *Analysing genre.* Longman

Biber, D., Finegan, E. 1989 Styles of stance in English: lexical and grammatical marking of evidentiality and affect, *Text* **9**: 93–124

Biber, D., Johansson, S., Leech, G., Conrad, S., Finegan, E. 1999 *The Longman grammar of spoken and written English.* Longman

Bickerton, D. 1973 The nature of a creole continuum, *Language* **49**: 640–69

Bierwisch, M. 1970 Poetics and linguistics. In Freeman, D. C. (ed.) *Linguistics and literary style.* Holt, Rinehart & Winston: New York

Birch, D. 1991 *The language of drama: critical theory and practice.* Macmillan

Birdwhistell, R. L. 1952 *Introduction to kinesics.* University of Louisville Press: US

Black, M. 1954 *Models and metaphors.* Cornell University Press: Ithaca

Bloch, B. 1953 Linguistic structure and linguistic analysis, *Georgetown University Monograph Series on Language and Linguistics, 4*

Bloom, H. 1997 *The anxiety of influence: a theory of poetry* (2nd edn). Oxford University Press

Bloomfield, L. 1933 *Language.* Holt, Rinehart & Winston: New York

Blum-Kulka, S., Kasper, G. (eds) 1989 *Cross-cultural pragmatics.* Ablex: New Jersey

Boehmer, E. 1995 *Colonial and postcolonial literatures.* Oxford University Press

Bolinger, D. 1965 *Forms of English.* Harvard University Press: Cambridge, Mass.

Bolinger, D. 1980 *Language – the loaded weapon.* Longman

Bolter, A. D. 1991 *Writing space: the computer, hypertext and the history of writing.* Lawrence Erlbaum Associates: Hillsdale, NJ

Booth, W. C. 1961 *Rhetoric of fiction.* University of Chicago Press: Chicago

Booth, W. C. 1974 *A rhetoric of irony.* University of Chicago Press: Chicago

Bordwell, D. 1985 *Narration in the fiction film.* University of Wisconsin Press: Madison

Bourdieu, P. 1991 *Language and symbolic power* (ed. J. B. Thompson). Polity Press/Blackwell

Bourdieu, P. 1993 *The field of cultural production.* Columbia University Press: New York

Brazil, D. 1975 Discourse intonation, *English Language Research, Birmingham: Discourse Analysis Monographs, 1*

Brazil, D. 1997 *The communicative value of intonation in English.* Cambridge University Press (Originally published 1985, Bleak House)

Brémond, C. 1966 La logique des possibles narratifs, *Communications* **8**: 60–76

Brémond, C. 1973 *Logique du récit.* Seuil: Paris

Brodeur, A. 1959 *The art of 'Beowulf'.* University of California Press: Berkeley

Bronzwaer, W. J. 1970 *Tense in the novel.* Wolters-Noordhoff: Gröningen

Brooke-Rose, C. 1958 *A grammar of metaphor.* Secker & Warburg

Brooks, C., Warren, R. P. 1972 *Modern rhetoric* (3rd edn). Harcourt, Brace, Jovanovitch: New York

Brooks, P. 1984 *Reading for the plot: design and intention in narrative.* Clarendon Press

Brown, G., Yule, G. 1983 *Discourse analysis.* Cambridge University Press

Brown, P., Levinson, S. 1978 Universals in language usage: politeness phenomena. In Goody, E. N. (ed.) *Questions and politeness: strategies in social interaction.* Cambridge University Press

Brown, P., Levinson, S. 1987 *Politeness: some universals in language usage.* Cambridge University Press

Bühler, K. 1934 *Sprachtheorie.* Fischer: Jena

Burton, D. 1980 *Dialogue and discourse.* Routledge & Kegan Paul

Burton, D. 1982 Through glass darkly: through dark glasses. In Carter, R. (ed.) *Language and literature: an introductory reader in stylistics.* Allen & Unwin

Butler, C. S. 1985 *Systemic linguistics: theory and applications.* Batsford

Calderwood, J. L. 1969 *Shakespearean metadrama.* University of Minnesota Press: Minneapolis

Cameron, D. 1992 *Feminism and linguistic theory* (2nd edn). Macmillan

Cameron, D. 1995 *Verbal hygiene.* Routledge

Carter, R. (ed.) 1982 *Language and literature: an introductory reader in stylistics.* Allen & Unwin

Carter, R. 1995 *Keywords in language and literacy.* Routledge

Carter, R. 1999 Common language: corpus, creativity and cognition, *Language and Literature* **8**: 195–216

Carter, R., McCarthy, M. 1997 *Exploring spoken English.* Cambridge University Press

Carter, R., Nash, W. 1990 *Seeing through language: a guide to styles of English writing.* Blackwell

Carter, R., Simpson, P. (eds) 1989 *Language, discourse and literature: an introductory reader in stylistics.* Unwin Hyman/Routledge

Caughie, J. 1981 *Ideas of authorship.* Routledge & Kegan Paul

Chadwick, C. 1971 *Symbolism.* Methuen

Chafe, W. L. 1973 Language and meaning, *Language* **49**: 261–83

Chambers, R. W. 1932 On the continuity of English prose from Alfred to More and his school. In *Introduction to Early English Text Society, 186* (Nicholas Harpsfeld's *Life of Sir Thomas More*)

Chapman, R. 1984 *The treatment of sounds in language and literature.* Basil Blackwell/André Deutsch

Chatman, S. 1964 *A theory of metre*. Mouton: The Hague

Chatman, S. 1969 New ways of analysing narrative structure, *Language and Style* **2**: 1–36

Chatman, S. 1978 *Story and discourse*. Cornell University Press: Ithaca

Chatman, S. 1990 *Coming to terms: the rhetoric of narrative in fiction and film*. Cornell University Press: Ithaca

Chilton, P. (ed.) 1985 *Language and the nuclear arms debate: nukespeak today*. Frances Pinter

Chomsky, N. 1957 *Syntactic structures*. Mouton: The Hague

Chomsky, N. 1965 *Aspects of the theory of syntax*. MIT Press: Cambridge, Mass.

Chomsky, N., Halle, M. 1968 *The sound pattern of English*. Harper & Row: New York

Cixous, H. 1975 Le rire de la Méduse. *L'Arc* **61**: 3–54 (Translated 1980 The laugh of the Medusa. In Marks, E., de Courtivron, I., *New French Feminisms*. Harvester)

Coates, J. 1983 *The semantics of the modal auxiliaries*. Croom Helm

Coates, J. 1986 *Women, men and language*. Longman

Cohn, D. 1966 Narrated monologue: definition of a fictional style, *Comparative Literature* **18**: 97–112

Cohn, D. 1978 *Transparent minds: narrative modes for presenting consciousness in fiction*. Princeton University Press: Princeton, New Jersey

Connor, S. 1985 *Charles Dickens*. Basil Blackwell

Connor, U. 1996 *Contrastive rhetoric: cross-cultural aspects of second language learning*. Cambridge University Press

Cook, G. 1992 *The discourse of advertising*. Routledge

Cook, G. 1994 *Discourse and literature: the interplay of form and mind*. Oxford University Press

Coseriu, E. 1967 Lexicalische Solidaritäten, *Poetica* **1**: 293–303

Coulthard, M. 1977 *An introduction to discourse analysis*. Longman

Cowie, A. P., Mackin, R., McCraig, I. R. 1993 *The Oxford dictionary of English idioms*. Oxford University Press

Croce, B. 1922 *Aesthetics as science of expression and general linguistics*. Macmillan. (First published 1902 in Italian)

Croll, M. W. 1929 The baroque style in prose. In Malone, K., Rund, M. B. (eds) *Studies in English philology: a miscellany in honour of Frederick Klaeber*. University of Minnesota Press: Minneapolis (Reprinted in Fish, S. E. (ed.) 1971 *Modern essays in criticism: seventeenth-century prose*. Oxford University Press: New York)

Crowley, T. 1989 *The politics of discourse*. Macmillan

Cruse, D. A. 1986 *Lexical semantics*. Cambridge University Press

Cruttenden, A. 1997 *Intonation* (2nd edn). Cambridge University Press

Crystal, D. 1975 *The English tone of voice: essays in intonation, prosody and paralanguage*. Edward Arnold

Crystal, D. 1984 *Who cares about English usage?* Penguin

Crystal, D. 1997a *A dictionary of linguistics and phonetics* (4th edn). Basil Blackwell

Crystal, D. 1997b *The Cambridge encyclopedia of the English language*. Cambridge University Press

Crystal, D. 1998 *The language of play*. Cambridge University Press

Crystal, D., Davy, D. 1969 *Investigating English style*. Longman

Cuddon, J. A. 1998 *A dictionary of literary terms* (4th edn). André Deutsch

Culler, J. 1975 *Structuralist poetics*. Routledge & Kegan Paul

Culler, J. 1983 *On deconstruction: theory and criticism after structuralism*. Routledge & Kegan Paul

Cummings, M., Simmons, R. 1983 *The language of literature: a stylistic introduction to the study of literature*. Pergamon

Davidson, D. 1978 What metaphors mean, *Critical Inquiry* (Autumn): 31–47

Davie, D. 1955 *Articulate energy: an inquiry into the syntax of English poetry*. Routledge & Kegan Paul

Derrida, J. 1967a *De la grammatologie*. Minuit: Paris (Translated 1974 *Of grammatology*. Johns Hopkins University Press: Baltimore)

Derrida, J. 1967b *La voix et le phénomène*. Presses Universitaires de France: Paris (Translated 1973 *Speech and phenomena*. Northwestern University Press: Evanston)

Derrida, J. 1977a Signature événément contexte, Glyph 1: 172–97

Derrida, J. 1977b Limited Inc abc, Glyph 2: 162–254

Derrida, J. 1978a *La vérité en peinture*. Flammarion: Paris

Derrida, J. 1978b *Writing and Difference*. Routledge

van Dijk, T. A. 1972 *Some aspects of text grammars*. Mouton: The Hague

van Dijk, T. A. 1976 *Pragmatics of language and literature*. North Holland: Amsterdam

van Dijk, T. A. 1977 *Text and context: explorations in the semantics and pragmatics of discourse*. Longman

van Dijk, T. A. (ed.) 1985 *Discourse and literature: new approaches to the analysis of literary genres*. John Benjamins: Amsterdam

Dik, S. C. 1978 *Functional grammar*. North Holland Amsterdam

Dixon, P. 1971 *Rhetoric*. Methuen

Dollimore, J., Sinfield, A. 1985 *Political Shakespeare: new essays in cultural materialism*. Manchester University Press

Doložel, L. 1976 Narrative semantics, *Poetics and Theory of Literature* 1: 29–57

Doložel, L. 1979 *Essays in structural poetics and narrative semantics*. Victoria University: Toronto

Downes, W., 1993 Reading the language itself: some methodological problems in D. C. Freeman's ' "According to my bond": *King Lear* and re-cognition', *Language and Literature* 2: 121–8

Durant, A., Fabb, N. 1990 *Literary Studies in Action*. Routledge

Dyer, G. 1982 *Advertising as communication*. Methuen

Eagleton, M. 1996 *Feminist theory: a reader*. Blackwell

Eagleton, T. E. 1976a *Criticism and ideology: a study in Marxist literary theory*. New Left Books

Eagleton, T. E. 1976b *Marxism and literary criticism*. Methuen

Eagleton, T. E. 1983 *Literary theory: an introduction*. Basil Blackwell

Eagleton, T. 1990 *The ideology of the aesthetic*. Blackwell

Eagleton, T. 1996 *The illusions of postmodernism*. Blackwell

Easthope, A. 1983 *Poetry as discourse*. Methuen

Eaton, T. 1966 *The semantics of literature*. Mouton: The Hague

Eaton, T. 1972 *Theoretical semics*. Mouton: The Hague

Eaton, T. 1978 *Essays in literary semantics*. Julius Groos: Heidelberg

Eco, U. 1976 *A theory of semiotics*. Indiana University Press: Bloomington

Eco, U. 1981 *The role of the reader: explorations in the semiotics of texts*. Hutchinson

Edel, L. 1955 *The psychological novel 1900–1950*. Hart-Davis

Edmondson, W. 1981 *Spoken discourse: a model for analysis*. Longman

Elam, K. 1980 *The semiotics of theatre and drama*. Methuen

Eliot, T. S. 1932 *Selected essays 1917–1932*. Faber & Faber

Ellis, A. 1867–74 *On Early English Pronunciation*. Trübner

Ellis, J., Ure, J. 1969 Register. In Meetham, A. R. (ed.) *Encyclopedia of linguistics: information and control*. Pergamon

Emmott, C. 1997 *Narrative comprehension: a discourse perspective*. Oxford University Press

Empson, W. 1930 *Seven types of ambiguity*. Chatto & Windus

Enkvist, N. E. 1973 *Linguistic stylistics*. Mouton: The Hague

Enkvist, N. E. 1985 Text and discourse linguistics, rhetoric and stylistics. In van Dijk, T. A. (ed.) *Discourse and literature*. John Benjamins: Amsterdam

Enkvist, N. E., Spenser, J. W., Gregory, M. J. 1964 *Linguistics and style*. Oxford University Press

Epstein, E. L. 1975 The self-reflexive artefact: the function of mimesis in an approach to a theory of value for literature. In Fowler, R. (ed.) *Style and structure in literature*. Basil Blackwell

Epstein, E. L. 1978 *Language and style*. Methuen

Erlich, V. 1965 *Russian Formalism: history, doctrine*. Mouton: 's-Gravenhage.

Fabb, N. 1997 *Linguistics and literature*. Blackwell

Faulkner, P. 1977 *Modernism*. Methuen

Fairclough, N. 1989 *Language and power*. Longman

Fairclough, N. 1992a *Discourse and social change*. Polity Press

Fairclough, N. 1992b *Critical language awareness*. Longman

Fairclough, N. 1995 *Critical discourse analysis*. Longman

Fairclough, N. 1996 Border crossings: discourse and social change in contemporary societies. In *Change and language* (BAAL 10). Multilingual Matters

Fauconnier, G. 1985 *Aspects of meaning construction in natural language*. MIT Press: Cambridge, Mass.

Fauconnier, G., Turner, M. 1996 Blending as a central process of grammar. In Goldberg, A. (ed.) *Conceptual structure, discourse and language*. CSLI: Stanford

Fawcett, R., Halliday, M. A. K. (eds) 1985 *New developments in systemic linguistics*. Batsford

Ferguson, C. 1959 Diglossia, *Word* **15**: 325–40

Fillmore, C. 1968 The case for case. In Bach, E., Harms, R. T. (eds) *Universals in linguistic theory*. Holt, Rinehart & Winston: New York

Fillmore, C. 1981 Ideal reader and real readers. In Tannen, D. (ed.) *Analyzing discourse: text and talk*. Georgetown University Press: Washington DC

Firbas, J. 1961 On the communicative value of the Modern English finite verb, *Brno Studies in English* **3**: 79–104

Firbas, J. 1964 On defining the theme in functional sentence analysis, *Travaux Linguistiques de Prague* **1**: 267–80

Firbas, J. 1992 *Functional sentence perspective in written and spoken communication*. Cambridge University Press

Firth, J. R. 1957 *Papers in linguistics (1934–1951)*. Oxford University Press

Fish, S. E. 1970 Literature in the reader: affective stylistics, *New Literary History* **2**: 123–62 (Also 1972 Appendix to *Self-consuming artefacts*. University of California Press: Berkeley & Los Angeles)

Fish, S. E. 1973 What is stylistics and why are they saying such terrible things about it? In Chatman, S. (ed.) *Approaches to poetics*. Columbia University Press: New York

Fish, S. E. 1980 *Is there a text in this class? The authority of interpretative communities*. Harvard University Press: Cambridge, Mass.

Fish, S. E. 1981 Why no one's afraid of Wolfgang Iser, *Diacritics* **11**: 2–13

Fishman, J. A. 1971 *Sociolinguistics: a brief introduction*. Newbury House: Rowley

Fiske, J. 1982 *Introduction to communication studies*. Methuen

Fludernik, M. 1993 *The fictions of language and the languages of fiction*. Routledge

Fludernik, M. 1996 *Towards a 'natural' narratology*. Routledge

Forster, E. M. 1927 *Aspects of the novel*. Edward Arnold

Foucault, M. 1966 *Les mots et les choses: une archéologie des sciences humaines*. Bibliothèque des sciences humaines: Paris (Translated 1970 *The order of things: an archaeology of the human sciences*. Tavistock Publications)

Foucault, M. 1972 *The archaeology of knowledge*. Tavistock

Fowler, A. 1982 *Kinds of literature: an introduction to the theory of genres and modes*. Clarendon

Fowler, H. W. 1998 *The new Fowler's Modern English Usage*. Rev. 3rd edn. By Burchfield, R. W. Clarendon

Fowler, R. 1971 *The languages of literature*. Routledge & Kegan Paul

Fowler, R. 1972 Style and the concept of deep structure, *Journal of Literary Semantics* **1**: 5–24

Fowler, R. 1977 *Linguistics and the novel*. Methuen

Fowler, R. 1979 Anti-language in fiction, *Style* **13**: 259–78

Fowler, R. 1981 *Literature as social discourse: the practice of linguistic criticism*. Batsford

Fowler, R. 1983 Polyphony and problematic in *Hard Times*. In Giddings, R. (ed.) *The changing world of Charles Dickens*. Barnes & Noble: New York

Fowler, R. 1986 *Linguistic criticism* (2nd edn 1996). Oxford University Press

Fowler, R. 1991 *Language in the news: discourse and ideology in the press*. Routledge

Fowler, R. 1996 On critical linguistics. In Caldas-Coulthard, C. R., Coulthard, M. (eds) *Texts and practices: readings in critical discourse analysis*. Routledge

Fowler, R., Hodge, R., Kress, G., Trew, T. 1979 *Language and control*. Routledge & Kegan Paul

Fraser, B. 1975 Hedged performatives. In Cole, P., Morgan, J. L. (eds) *Syntax and semantics 3: Speech acts*. Academic Press: New York

Freeman, D. C. (ed.) 1970 *Linguistics and literary style*. Holt, Rinehart & Winston: New York

Freeman, D. C. 1993 'According to my bond': *King Lear* and re-cognition, *Language and Literature* **2**: 1–18

Freeman, M. 1997 Grounded spaces: deictic *-self* anaphors in the poetry of Emily Dickinson, *Language and Literature* **6**: 7–28

Friedman, M. 1955 *Stream of consciousness: a study in literary method*. Yale University Press: New Haven

Fry, D. K. 1968 Old English formulaic themes and type scenes, *Neophilologus* **52**: 48–54

Frye, N. 1957 *Anatomy of criticism*. Princeton University Press: Princeton, New Jersey

Gadamer, H.-G. 1972 *Wahrheit und Methode* (expanded from 1960 edn). Mohr: Tübingen (Translated 1975 *Truth and method*. Continuum: New York)

Gadamer, H.-G. 1976 *Philosophical hermeneutics*. University of California Press: Berkeley

Garfinkel, H. 1967 *Studies in ethnomethodology*. Prentice Hall: Englewood Cliffs, New Jersey

Garvin, P. L. 1964 *A Prague School reader on aesthetics, literary structure and style*. Georgetown University Press: Washington

Gascoigne, G. 1575, reprinted 1868 *Certayne notes of instruction in English verse*. Edward Arber

Gazdar, G. 1979 *Pragmatics, implicature, presupposition and logical form*. Academic Press: New York

Gelb, I. J. 1952 *A study of writing*. Routledge & Kegan Paul

Genette, G. 1972 *Figures III*. Seuil: Paris (Translated 1980 *Narrative discourse*. Basil Blackwell)

Genette, G. 1979 *Introduction à l'architexte*. Seuil: Paris

Genette, G. 1980 Valéry and the poetics of language. In Harari, J. V. (ed.) *Textual strategies*. Methuen

Gibbs, R. W. Jr. 1994 *The poetics of mind: figurative thought, language and understanding*. Cambridge University Press

Gibson, A. 1996 *Towards a postmodern theory of narrative*. Edinburgh University Press

Gilbert, A. J. 1979 *Literary language from Chaucer to Johnson*. Macmillan

Gimson, A. C. 1989 *An introduction to the pronunciation of English* (4th edn, rev. S. Ramsaran). Edward Arnold

Goatly, A. 1997 *The language of metaphors*. Routledge

Goffman, E. 1955 On face-work: an analysis of ritual elements in social interaction, *Psychiatry* **18**: 213–31 (Reprinted in Hutchinson, J., Laver, S. (eds) 1972 *Communication in face to face interaction*. Penguin)

Goffman, E. 1974 *Frame analysis: an essay on the organization of experience*. Harper & Row

Goffman, E. 1981 *Forms of talk*. Basil Blackwell

Golding, R. 1985 *Idiolects in Dickens*. Macmillan

Gordon, D., Lakoff, G. 1971 Conversational postulates, *Papers from the 7th regional meeting of the Chicago Linguistic Circle*: 63–74 (Reprinted in Cole, P. and Morgan, J. L. (eds) 1975 *Syntax and semantics 3: speech acts*. Academic Press: New York)

Gordon, I. A. 1966 *The movement of English prose*. Longman

Graddol, D. 1994 What is a text? In Graddol, D., Boyd-Barrett, O. (eds) *Media texts: authors and readers*. Open University Press/Multilingual Matters

Graustein, G., Neubert, A. (eds) 1979 *Trends in English textlinguistics*. Akademie der Wissenschaften, Zentralinstitut für Sprachwissengeschaft, vol. 55: Berlin DDR

Green, K. 1997 Butterflies, wheels and the search for literary relevance, *Language and Literature* **6**: 133–8

Green, K., LeBihan, J. 1996 *Critical theory and practice: a coursebook*. Routledge

Greenblatt, S. 1980 *Renaissance self-fashioning: from More to Shakespeare*. University of Chicago Press

Gregory, M. J. 1965 Old Bailey speech in *A Tale of Two Cities*, *Review of English Literature* **5**: 42–55

Gregory, M. J. 1967 Aspects of varieties differentiation, *Journal of Linguistics* **3**: 177–98

Greimas, A. J. 1966 *Sémantique structurale*. Larousse: Paris

Greimas, A. J. 1970 *Du sens*. Seuil: Paris

Grice, H. P. 1975 Logic and conversation. In Cole, P., Morgan, J. L. (eds) *Syntax and semantics 3: speech acts*. Academic Press: New York

Groom, B. 1955 *The diction of poetry from Spenser to Bridges*. University of Toronto Press

Haas, W. 1957 Zero in linguistic description. *Studies in linguistic analysis*. Basil Blackwell

Halle, M., Keyser, S. J. 1966 Chaucer and the study of prosody, *College English* **28**: 187–219 (Reprinted in Freeman, D. C. (ed.) 1970 *Linguistics and literary style*. Holt, Rinehart & Winston: New York)

Halliday, M. A. K. 1961 Categories of the theory of grammar, *Word* **17**: 241–92

Halliday, M. A. K. 1971 Linguistic function and literary style: an inquiry into the language of William Golding's *The Inheritors*. In Chatman, S. (ed.) *Literary style: a symposium*. Oxford University Press: New York

Halliday, M. A. K. 1973 *Explorations in the functions of language*. Edward Arnold

Halliday, M. A. K. 1978 *Language as social semiotic*. Edward Arnold

Halliday, M. A. K. 1985 *An introduction to functional grammar*. Edward Arnold

Halliday, M. A. K., Hasan, R. 1976 *Cohesion in English*. Longman

Halliday, M. A. K., McIntosh, A., Strevens, P. 1964 *Linguistic sciences and language teaching*. Longman

Hamburger, K. 1957 *Die Logik der Dichtung* (2nd revised edn 1968). Ernst Klett: Stuttgart (Translated 1973 *The logic of literature*. Indiana University Press: Bloomington)

Hamon, P. 1974 Narrative semiotics in France, *Style* **8**: 34–45

Harari, J. V. 1980 *Textual strategies: perspectives in post-structuralist criticism*. Methuen

Harris, R. 1995 *Signs of writing*. Routledge

Harris, R. 1997 *Signs, language and communication*. Routledge

Harris, Z. 1951 *Methods in structural linguistics*. University of Chicago Press: Chicago

Harris, Z. 1952 Discourse analysis, *Language* **28**: 1–30

Hasan, R. 1978 Text in the systemic-functional mode. In Dressler, W. (ed.) *Current trends in text linguistics*. De Gruyter: Berlin

Havránek, B. 1932 The functional differentiation of the standard language (in Czech). (Translated 1964 in Garvin, P. L. (ed.) *A Prague School reader on æsthetics, literary structure and style*. Georgetown University Press: Washington)

Hawkes, T. 1972 *Metaphor*. Methuen

Hawkes, T. 1977 *Structuralism and semiotics*. Methuen

Hawthorn, J. 1985 *Narrative: from Malory to motion pictures*. Edward Arnold

Hawthorn, J. 1998 *A glossary of contemporary literary theory* (2nd edn). Edward Arnold

Hayes, C. W. 1966 A study in prose styles: Edward Gibbon and Ernest Hemingway, *Texas Studies in Literature and Language* 7: 371–86. (Reprinted in Freeman, D. C. (ed.) 1970 *Linguistics and literary style*. Holt, Rinehart & Winston: New York)

Hendricks, W. O. 1969 Three models for the description of poetry, *Journal of Linguistics* 5: 1–22

Herman, V. 1995 *Dramatic discourse: dialogue as interaction in plays*. Routledge

Hirsch, E. D. 1967 *Validity in interpretation*. Yale University Press: New Haven

Hjelmslev, L. 1943 *Prolegomena to a theory of language* (in Danish) (Translated 1961 University of Wisconsin Press: Madison)

Hockett, C. F. 1958 *A course in modern linguistics*. Macmillan: New York

Hoey, M. 1983 *On the surface of discourse*. Allen & Unwin

Holland, N. 1975 *Five readers reading*. Yale University Press: New Haven

Holmes, J. 1995 *Women, men and politeness*. Longman

Holub, R. C. 1984 *Reception theory: a critical introduction*. Methuen

Honey, J. 1985 Acrolect and hyperlect: the redefinition of English RP, *English Studies* 66: 241–57

Hough, G. 1970 Narration and dialogue in Jane Austen, *Critical Quarterly* 12: 201–29

Hudson, R. 1996 *Sociolinguistics* (2nd edn). Cambridge University Press

Hughes, R. 1996 *English in speech and writing: investigating language and literature*. Routledge

Humphrey, R. 1954 *Stream of consciousness in the modern novel*. University of California Press: Berkeley & Los Angeles

Hussey, S. S. 1992 *The literary language of Shakespeare* (2nd edn). Longman

Hutcheon, L. 1985 *A theory of parody*. Methuen

Hymes, D. 1962 The ethnography of speaking. In Fishman, J. (ed.) *Readings in the sociology of language*. Mouton: The Hague

Hymes, D. 1971 Competence and performance in linguistic theory. In Huxley, R., Ingram, E. (eds) *Language acquisition: models and methods*. Academic Press: New York

Hymes, D. 1974 Ways of speaking. In Bauman, R., Sherzer, J. (eds) *Explorations in the ethnography of speaking*. Cambridge University Press

Ingarden, R. 1973 *The literary work of art* (first published 1931 in Polish). Northwestern University Press: Evanston

Innis, R. E. (ed.) 1986 *Semiotics: an introductory anthology*. Hutchinson

Iser, W. 1971 Indeterminacy and the reader's response to prose fiction (first published in German, 1970). In Hillis Miller, J. (ed.) *Aspects of narrative*. Columbia University Press: New York

Iser, W. 1974 *The implied reader: patterns of communication in prose fiction from Bunyan to Beckett*. Johns Hopkins University Press: Baltimore

Iser, W. 1978 *The act of reading: a theory of aesthetic response*. Johns Hopkins University Press: Baltimore

Jacobs, R. A., Rosenbaum, P. S. 1971 *Transformations, style and meaning*. Blaisdell-Ginn: Waltham, Mass.

Jakobson, R. 1935 The dominant. (Reprinted in Matejka, L., Pomorska, K. (eds) 1971 *Readings in Russian poetics*. MIT Press: Cambridge, Mass.)

Jakobson, R. 1956 Two aspects of language and two types of aphasic disturbances. In Jakobson, R., Halle, M. (eds) *Fundamentals of language*. Mouton: The Hague

Jakobson, R. 1960 Closing statement: linguistics and poetics. In Sebeok, T. A. (ed.) *Style and language*. MIT Press: Cambridge, Mass.

Jakobson, R., Jones, L. G. 1970 *Shakespeare's verbal art in 'Th'Expense of Spirit'*. Mouton: The Hague

Jakobson, R., Lévi-Strauss, C. 1962 'Les Chats' de Baudelaire, *L'Homme* 2: 5–21

Jakobson, R., Pomorska, K. 1983 *Dialogues*. MIT Press: Cambridge, Mass.

Jakobson, R., Waugh, L. R. 1979 *The sound shape of language*. Harvester Press

Jameson, F. 1971 *Marxism and form*. Princeton University Press: Princeton, New Jersey

Jameson, F. 1981 *The political unconscious: narrative as a socially symbolic act*. Methuen

Jauss, H. R. 1974 Literary history as a challenge to literary theory (first delivered as lecture in German, Konstanz, 1967). In Cohen, R. (ed.) *New directions in literary history*. Routledge & Kegan Paul (Reprinted in Jauss, H. R. 1982 *Toward an aesthetic of reception*. University of Minnesota Press: Minneapolis)

Jespersen, O. 1922 *Language*. Allen & Unwin

Jespersen, O. 1949 *A Modern English grammar on historical principles*. Allen & Unwin

Johnson, S. 1755 *A dictionary of the English language* (2 vols). Knapton, Longman, Hitch, Hawes, Miller & Dodsley

Joos, M. 1962 The five clocks, *International Journal of American Linguistics* **28**, no 2, pt 5, Bloomington

Jordan, M. P. 1984 *Rhetoric of everyday English texts*. Allen & Unwin

Joseph, M. 1947 *Shakespeare's use of the arts of language*. Hafner: New York

Jucker, A. H. 1995 *Historical pragmatics*. John Benjamins: Amsterdam

Katz, J., Fodor, J. 1963 The structure of semantic theory, *Language* **39**: 170–210

Kempson, R. M. 1975 *Presupposition and the delimitation of semantics*. Cambridge University Press

Kennedy, A. K. 1983 *Dramatic dialogue: the duologue of personal encounter*. Cambridge University Press

Kennedy, C. 1982 Systemic grammar and its use in literary analysis. In Carter, R. (ed.) *Language and literature: an introductory reader in stylistics*. Allen & Unwin

Kermode, F. 1978 *The sense of an ending*. Oxford University Press: New York

Kiparsky, P. 1977 The rhythmic structure of English verse, *Linguistic Inquiry* **8**: 189–247

Kress, G. R. (ed.) 1976 *System and function in language: selected papers by M. A. K. Halliday*. Oxford University Press

Kress, G., van Leeuwen, T. 1996 *Reading images: the grammar of visual design*. Routledge

Kristeva, J. 1969 *Semiotikè: recherches pour une sémanalyse*. Seuil: Paris

Kristeva, J. 1970 *Le texte du roman: approche sémiologique d'une structure discursive transformationelle*. Mouton: The Hague

Labov, W. 1966 *The social stratification of English in New York city*. Center for Applied Linguistics: Washington, DC

Labov, W. 1970 The logic of non-standard English, *Georgetown University Monogram Series on Language and Linguistics*, 22

Labov, W. 1972 *Language in the inner city*. University of Pennyslvania Press: Philadelphia

Labov, W., Waletsky, J. 1967 Narrative analysis: oral versions of personal experience. In Helm, J. (ed.) *Essays on the verbal and visual arts*. University of Washington Press: Seattle

Lacan, J. 1966 *Écrits*. Seuil: Paris (Translated 1977 *Writings*. Tavistock Publications)

Lakoff, G. 1971 On generative semantics. In Steinberg, D. D., Jakobovits, L. A. (eds) *Semantics*. Cambridge University Press

Lakoff, G. 1987 *Women, fire and dangerous things*. University of Chicago Press: Chicago

Lakoff, G., Johnson, M. 1980 *Metaphors we live by*. University of Chicago Press: Chicago

Lakoff, G., Turner, M. 1989 *More than cool reason: a field guide to poetic metaphor*. University of Chicago Press: Chicago

Lakoff, R. 1975 *Language and woman's place*. Harper & Row: New York

Lambert, M. 1975 *Malory: style as vision in 'Le Morte d'Arthur'*. Yale University Press: New Haven

Lambert, M. 1981 *Dickens and the suspended quotation*. Yale University Press: New Haven

Landow, G. P. 1992 *Hypertext: the convergence of contemporary critical theory and technology* (2nd edn 1997). Johns Hopkins University Press: Baltimore

Langacker, R. 1987 *Foundations of cognitive grammar. Vol. 1. Theoretical prerequisites.* University of Stanford Press: Stanford

Lanham, R. 1991 *A handlist of rhetorical terms* (2nd edn). University of California Press: Berkeley

Lanser, S. S. 1981 *The narrative act: point of view in prose fiction.* Princeton University Press: New Jersey

Latré, G. 1985 *Locking earth to sky: a structuralist approach to Philip Larkin's poetry.* Peter Long: Frankfurt

Leavis, F. R. 1948 *The great tradition.* Chatto & Windus

Leavis, F. R. 1952 *The common pursuit.* Chatto & Windus

Lee, D. 1992 *Competing discourses: perspective and ideology in language.* Longman

Leech, G. N. 1965 'This bread I break': language and interpretation, *Review of English Literature* 6: 66–75 (Reprinted in Freeman, D. C. (ed.) 1970 *Linguistics and literary style.* Holt, Rinehart & Winston: New York)

Leech, G. N. 1969 *A linguistic guide to English poetry.* Longman

Leech, G. N. 1981 *Semantics* (2nd edn). Penguin

Leech, G. N. 1983 *Principles of pragmatics.* Longman

Leech, G. N. 1985 Stylistics. In van Dijk, T. A. (ed.) *Discourse and literature.* John Benjamins: Amsterdam

Leech, G. N., Short, M. H. 1981 *Style in fiction.* Longman

Lees, R. B. 1960 *A grammar of English nominalizations.* Indiana University Center in Anthropology, Folklore and Linguistics, 12: Bloomington, Indiana

Leitch, V. B. 1983 *Deconstructive criticism.* Hutchinson

Leith, D., Myerson, G. 1989 The power of address: explorations in rhetoric. Routledge

Lemon, L., Reis, M. J. (eds) 1965 *Russian formalist criticism.* University of Nebraska Press: Lincoln, Nebraska

Lentricchia, F. 1980 *After the new criticism.* Athlone Press

Levin, S. R. 1962 *Linguistic structures in poetry.* Mouton: The Hague

Levin, S. R. 1965 Internal and external deviation in poetry, *Word* 21: 225–37

Levin, S. R. 1977 *The semantics of metaphor.* Johns Hopkins University Press: Baltimore

Levinson, S. C. 1983 *Pragmatics.* Cambridge University Press

Lévi-Strauss, C. 1958 *Anthropologie structurale.* Plon: Paris (Translated 1972 Penguin)

Lévi-Strauss, C. 1966 *The savage mind* (first published in French, 1962). Weidenfeld & Nicolson

Lewis, D. 1973 *Counterfactuals.* Blackwell

Lewis, D. 1979 Scorekeeping in a language game, *Journal of Philosophical Logic* 8: 339–59

Lewis, D. 1986 *On the plurality of worlds.* Blackwell

Lodge, D. 1966 *Language of fiction.* Routledge & Kegan Paul

Lodge, D. 1977 *The modes of modern writing: metaphor, metonymy and the typology of modern literature.* Edward Arnold

Lodge, D. 1981 Modernism, antimodernism and postmodernism. In *Working with structuralism.* Routledge & Kegan Paul

Lorck, E. 1921 *Die 'erlebte Rede'.* Curl Winters: Heidelberg

Lord, A. B. 1960 *The singer of tales: a study in the process of Yugoslav, Greek and Germanic oral poetry.* Harvard University Press: Cambridge, Mass.

Lotman, Y. 1971 *The structure of the artistic text* (in Russian). Brown University Press: Providence, Rhode Island

Lotman, Y. 1972 *Analysis of the poetic text.* (Translated 1976. Ann Arbor: Ardis)

Lukács, G. 1925 *History and class consciousness: studies in Marxist dialectics* (in German). (Translated 1971. Merlin Press)

Lyons, J. 1963 *Structural semantics.* Basil Blackwell

Lyons, J. 1977 *Semantics* (2 vols). Cambridge University Press

Lyotard, J.-F. 1984 *The postmodern condition: a report on knowledge.* Manchester University Press

Macherey, P. 1966 *Pour une théorie de la production littéraire.* Maspero: Paris (Translated 1978 *A theory of literary production.* Routledge & Kegan Paul)

Mackay, R. 1996 Mything the point: a critique of objective stylistics, *Language and Communication* **16**: 81–93

Mackay, R. 1999 There goes the other foot – a reply to Short *et al.*, *Language and Literature* **8**: 59–66

Magoun, Jr., F. P. 1953 Oral-formulaic character of Anglo-Saxon narrative poetry, *Speculum* **28**: 446–67

Malinowski, B. K. 1923 The problem of meaning in primitive languages. In Ogden, C. K., Richards, I. A., *The meaning of meaning.* Routledge & Kegan Paul

de Man, P. 1979 *Allegories of reading: figural language in Rousseau, Nietzche, Rilke and Proust.* Yale University Press: New Haven

Matejka, L., Pomorska, K. (eds) 1971 *Readings in Russian poetics: formalist and structuralist views.* MIT Press: Cambridge, Mass.

Matejka, L., Titunik, I. R. (eds) 1976 *Semiotics of art.* MIT Press: Cambridge, Mass.

McCarthy, M., Carter, R. (eds) 1994 *Language as discourse: perspectives for language teaching.* Longman

McCawley, J. D. 1968 The role of semantics in a grammar. In Bach, E., Harms, R. (eds) *Universals in linguistic theory.* Holt, Rinehart & Winston: New York

McHale, B. 1978 Free indirect discourse: a survey of recent accounts, *Poetics and Theory of Literature* **3**: 249–87

McHale, B. 1989 *Postmodernist fiction.* Routledge

McIntosh, A. 1963 A new approach to Middle English dialectology, *English Studies* **44**: 1–11

McIntosh, A., Halliday, M. A. K. 1966 *Patterns of language.* Longman

McLain, R. 1976 Literary criticism versus generative grammars, *Style* **10**: 231–53

McLeod, J. 2000 *Beginning postcolonialism.* Manchester University Press

McLuhan, M. 1964 *Understanding media.* Routledge & Kegan Paul

Miles, J. 1967 *Style and proportion: the language of prose and poetry.* Little, Brown & Co: Boston

Milic, L. T. 1967 *A quantitative approach to the style of Jonathan Swift.* Mouton: The Hague

Mills, S. 1995 *Feminist stylistics.* Routledge

Milroy, J., Milroy, L. 1998 *Authority in language: investigating standard English* (3rd edn). Routledge

Milroy, L. 1980 *Language and social networks.* Basil Blackwell

Moi, T. 1985 *Sexual/textual politics: feminist literary theory.* Methuen

Morson, G. S. (ed.) 1986 *Bakhtin: essays and dialogues on his work.* University of Chicago Press: Chicago

Morson, G. S., Emerson, C. 1990 *Mikhail Bakhtin: creation of a prosaics.* Stanford University Press: Stanford

Morton, A. 1978 *Literary detection: how to prove authorship and fraud in literature and documents.* Bowker

Muecke, D. C. 1982 *Irony and the ironic.* Methuen

Mukařovský, J. 1932 Standard language and poetic language (Transl. 1964 in Garvin, P. L. (ed.) *A Prague School reader on æsthetics, literary structure and style.* Georgetown University Press). (Also (abridged) in Freeman, D. C. (ed.) 1970 *Linguistics and literary style.* Holt, Rinehart & Winston: New York)

Nash, W. 1980 *Designs in prose: a study of compositional problems and methods.* Longman

Nash, W. 1985 *The language of humour.* Longman

Nash, W. 1986 Sound and the pattern of poetic meaning. In D'haen, T. (ed.) *Linguistics and the study of literature.* Rodopi: Amsterdam

Nash, W. 1989 *Rhetoric: the wit of persuasion.* Basil Blackwell

Nash, W. 1993 *Jargon: its uses and abuses.* Blackwell

Nida, E. A. 1975 *Componential analysis of meaning: an introduction to semantic structures*. Mouton: The Hague

Norris, C. 1982 *Deconstruction: theory and practice*. Methuen

Nowottny, W. 1962 *The language poets use*. Athlone Press

Ogden, C. K., Richards, I. A. 1923 *The meaning of meaning*. Routledge & Kegan Paul

O'Halloran, K. 1997 Why Whorf has been misconstrued in stylistics and critical linguistics, *Language and Literature* 6: 163–80

Ohmann, R. 1964 Generative grammars and the concept of literary style, *Word* 20: 423–39 (Reprinted in Freeman, D. C. (ed.) 1970 *Linguistics and literary style*. Holt, Rinehart & Winston: New York)

Ohmann, R. 1966 Literature as sentences, *College English* 27: 261–7

Ohmann, R. 1971 Speech acts and the definition of literature, *Philosophy and Rhetoric* 4: 1–19

Ohmann, R. 1973 Literature as act. In Chatman, S. (ed.) *Approaches to poetics*. Columbia University Press: New York

Ong, W. J. 1982 *Orality and literacy*. Methuen

Ong, W. J. 1984 Orality, literacy, and medieval textualization, *New Literary History* 16: 1–12

Orton, H., Barry, M., Halliday, W., Wakelin, M. 1962–71 *Survey of English dialects* (4 vols). E. J. Arnold

Page, N. 1973 *Speech in the English novel*. Longman

le Page, R. 1968 Problems of description in multilingual communities, *Transactions of the Philological Society*: 189–212

Palmer, F. R. 1979 *Modality and the English modals*. Longman

Palmer, F. R. 1981 *Semantics* (2nd edn) Cambridge University Press

Palmer, R. G. 1969 *Hermeneutics*. Northwestern University Press: Evanston

Parry, M. 1930 Studies in the epic technique of oral-verse making I: Homer and Homeric style, *Harvard Studies in Classical Philology* 41

Partridge, E. 1973 *Usage and abusage* (revised edn). Penguin

Pascal, R. 1977 *The dual voice: free indirect speech and its functioning in the nineteenth-century European novel*. Manchester University Press

Pavel, T. G. 1985 Literary narratives. In van Dijk, T. A. (ed.) *Discourse and literature*. John Benjamins: Amsterdam

Pavel, T. G. 1986 *Fictional worlds*. Harvard University Press: Cambridge, Mass.

Peacham, H. 1577 *The Garden of Eloquence*. H. Jackson

van Peer, W. 1986 *Stylistics and psychology: investigations of foregrounding*. Croom Helm

van Peer, W., Renkema, J. (eds) 1984 *Pragmatics and stylistics*. Acco: Leuven

Peirce, C. S. 1931–58 *Collected papers* (8 vols). Harvard University Press: Cambridge, Mass.

Pennycook, A. 1998 *English and the discourses of colonialism*. Routledge

Petöfi, J. S. 1971 *Transformationsgrammatiken und eine ko-textuell Texttheorie*. Athenäum: Frankfurt

Petöfi, J. S. 1975 *Vers une théorie partielle du texte*. Buske: Hamburg

Pilkington, A. 1996 Introduction: relevance theory and literary style, *Language and Literature* 5: 157–62

Plett, H. F. 1977 Concepts of style: a classificatory and a critical approach, *Language and Style* 12: 269–81

Plett, H. F. 1985 Rhetoric. In van Dijk, T. A. (ed.) *Discourse and literature*. John Benjamins: Amsterdam

Pope, R. 1995 *Textual intervention: critical and creative strategies for literary studies*. Routledge

Pope, R. 1998 *The English studies book*. Routledge

Popper, K. 1972 *Objective knowledge: an evolutionary approach*. Routledge & Kegan Paul

Posner, R. 1983 *Rational discourse and poetic communication: methods of linguistic, literary and philosophical analysis*. Mouton: The Hague

Pratt, M. L. 1977 *Toward a speech act theory of literary discourse.* Indiana University Press: Bloomington

Prince, G. 1971 Notes toward a category of fictional narratees, *Genre* **4**: 100–6

Prince, G. 1973 *A grammar of stories.* Mouton: The Hague

Prince, G. 1987 *A dictionary of narratology.* Scolar Press

Propp, V. 1928 *Morphology of the folktale* (Translated 1968 University of Texas Press: Austin)

Puttenham, G. 1589 *Arte of English Poesie* (Reprinted 1936 Cambridge University Press)

Quirk, R. 1959 *Charles Dickens and appropriate language.* University of Durham Press

Quirk, R., Greenbaum, S., Leech, G., Svartvik, J. 1972 *A grammar of Contemporary English.* Longman

Quirk, R., Greenbaum, S., Leech, G., Svartvik, J. 1985 *A comprehensive grammar of the English language.* Longman

Rampton, B. 1995 *Crossing: language and ethnicity among adolescents.* Longman

Reah, D. 1998 *The language of newspapers.* Routledge

Richards, I. A. 1925 *Principles of literary criticism.* Kegan Paul

Richards, I. A. 1929 *Practical criticism.* Kegan Paul

Richards, I. A. 1936 *The philosophy of rhetoric.* Oxford University Press

Ricoeur, P. 1975 *La métaphore vive.* Seuil: Paris

Riffaterre, M. 1959 Criteria for style analysis, *Word* **15**: 154–74

Riffaterre, M. 1966 Describing poetic structures: two approaches to Baudelaire's 'Les Chats', *Yale French Studies* **36/7**: 200–42 (Also in Babb, H. S. (ed.) 1972 *Essays in stylistic analysis.* Harcourt, Brace, Jovanovich: New York)

Riffaterre, M. 1978 *Semiotics of poetry.* Indiana University Press: Bloomington, Indiana

Rimmon-Kenan, S. 1983 *Narrative fiction: contemporary poetics.* Methuen

Ronen, R. 1994 *Possible worlds in literary theory.* Cambridge University Press

Ross, A. 1956 U and non-U. In Mitford, N. (ed.) *Noblesse oblige.* Hamish Hamilton

Ross, J. R. 1970 On declarative sentences. In Jacobs, R. A., Rosenbaum, P. S. (eds) *Readings in English transformational grammar.* Blaisdell-Ginn: Waltham, Mass.

Rusiecki, J. 1985 *Adjectives and comparison in English: a semantic study.* Longman

Ryan, K. (ed.) 1996 *New historicism and cultural materialism: a reader.* Edward Arnold

Ryan, M.-L. 1991 *Possible worlds, artificial intelligence and narrative theory.* Indiana University Press: Bloomington

Sacks, H., Schegloff, E., Jefferson, G. 1974 A simplest systematics for the organization of turn-taking for conversation, *Language* **50**: 696–735

Said, E. 1978 *Orientalism.* Routledge & Kegan Paul

Samuels, M. 1963 Some applications of Middle English dialectology, *English Studies* **44**: 81–94

Sankoff, G. 1972 Language use in multi-lingual societies. In Pride, J., Holmes, J. (eds) *Socio-linguistics: selected readings.* Penguin

Sapir, E. 1921 *Language.* Harcourt, Brace & World: New York

Sarris, A. 1968 *The American cinema: directors and directions, 1929–1968.* Dutton: New York

de Saussure, F. 1974 *Course in general linguistics.* Fontana (Originally published 1916)

Schank, R., Abelson, R. 1977 *Scripts, plans, goals and understanding.* Erlbaum: Hillsdale, NJ

Schiffrin, D. 1987 *Discourse markers.* Cambridge University Press

Schmidt, S. J. 1982 *Foundations for the empirical study of literature.* Buske: Hamburg

Searle, J. R. 1969 *Speech acts: an essay in the philosophy of language.* Cambridge University Press

Searle, J. R. 1975 Indirect speech acts. In Cole, P., Morgan, J. L. (eds) *Syntax and semantics 3: speech acts.* Academic Press: New York·

Searle, J. R. 1976 A classification of illocutionary acts, *Language in Society* **5**: 1–23

Searle, J. R. 1979 *Expression and meaning.* Cambridge University Press

Searle, J. R. 1983 *Intentionality: an essay in the philosophy of mind.* Cambridge University Press

Sell, R. D. 1985 Politeness in Chaucer: Suggestions towards a methodology for pragmatic stylistics, *Studioa Neophilogica* **57**: 175–85

Sell, R. D. (ed.) 1991 *Literary pragmatics*. Routledge

Semino, E. 1997 *Language and world creation in poems and other texts*. Longman

Semino, E., Short, M., Culpeper, J. 1997 Using a corpus to test a model of speech and thought presentation, *Poetics* **25**: 17–43

Shannon, C. E., Weaver, W. 1949 *The mathematical theory of communication*. University of Illinois Press: Illinois

Shen, Y. 1987 On the structure and understanding of poetic oxymoron, *Poetics Today* **8**: 105–22

Shen, Y., Cohen, M. 1998 How come silence is sweet but sweetness is not silent: a cognitive account of directionality in poetic synaesthesia, *Language and Literature* **7**: 123–40

Shklovsky, V. 1917 Art as technique. (Translated in Lemon, L., Reis, M. J. (eds) 1965 *Russian Formalist criticism*. University of Nebraska Press: Lincoln)

Shklovsky, V. 1925 *On the theory of prose* (in Russian). Moscow

Short, M. H. 1986 Literature and language teaching and the nature of language. In D'haen, T. (ed.) *Linguistics and the study of literature*. Rodopi: Amsterdam

Short, M. 1988 Speech presentation, the novel and the press. In van Peer, W. (ed.) *The taming of the text: explorations in language, literature and culture*. Routledge

Short, M. 1996 *Exploring the language of poems, plays and prose*. Addison Wesley Longman Ltd

Short, M., Semino, E., Culpeper, J. 1996 Using a corpus for stylistic research: speech and thought presentation. In Thomas, J., Short, M. (eds) *Using corpora in language research*. Longman

Short, M., Freeman, D. C., van Peer, W., Simpson, P. 1998 Stylistics, criticism and mythrepresentation again: squaring the circle with Ray Mckay's subjective solution for all problems, *Language and Literature* **7**: 39–50

Short, M., van Peer, W. 1999 A reply to Mackay, *Language and Literature* **8**: 269–75

Short, M., Semino, E., Wynne, M. (forthcoming) Revising the notion of faithfulness in discourse report/(re)presentation using a corpus approach, *Language and Literature*

Showalter, E. 1979 Towards a feminist poetics. In Jacobus, M. (ed.) *Women writing and writing about women*. Croom Helm

Shukman, A. 1980 *The new Soviet semiotics*. Methuen

Simpson, P. 1993 *Language, ideology and point of view*. Routledge

Sinclair, J. McH. 1966 Taking a poem to pieces. In Fowler, R. (ed.) *Essays on style and language*. Routledge & Kegan Paul

Sinclair, J. McH. 1972 *A course in spoken English*. Oxford University Press

Sinclair, J. McH., Coulthard, R. M. 1975 *Towards an analysis of discourse*. Oxford University Press

Slembrouck, S. 1992 The parliamentary Hansard 'verbatim' report: the written construction of spoken discourse, *Language and Literature* **1**: 101–20

Smith, B. H. 1968 *Poetic closure*. University of Chicago Press

Sonnino, L. A. 1968 *A handbook to sixteenth-century rhetoric*. Routledge & Kegan Paul

Souriau, E. 1950 *Les deux cent mille situations dramatiques*. Flammarion: Paris

Spender, D. 1980 *Man made language*. Routledge & Kegan Paul

Sperber, D., Wilson, D. 1982 Mutual knowledge and relevance in theories of comprehension. In Smith, N. (ed.) *Mutual knowledge*. Academic Press: New York

Sperber, D., Wilson, D. 1995 [1986] *Relevance: communication and cognition* (2nd edn). Blackwell

Spitzer, L. 1928 *Stilstudien* (2 vols). Max Hueber: Munich

Spitzer, L. 1948 *Linguistics and literary history: essays in stylistics*. Princeton University Press: Princeton, New Jersey

Spurgeon, C. F. 1935 *Shakespeare's imagery and what it tells us*. Cambridge University Press

Stanzel, F. K. 1959 Episches Praeteritum, erlebte Rede, historisches Praesens, *Deutsche Vierteljahrfestschrift für Literaturwissenschaft und Geistgeschichte* **33**: 1–12

Stanzel, F. K. 1971 *Narrative situations in the novel*. Indiana University Press: Bloomington (First published in German, 1955)

Stanzel, F. K. 1984 *A theory of narrative*. Cambridge University Press

Steen, G. 1994 *Understanding metaphor*. Longman

Steiner, G. 1975 *After Babel: aspects of language and translation*. Oxford University Press

Sternberg, M. 1982a Point of view and the indirectness of direct speech, *Language and Style* **15**: 67–117

Sternberg, M. 1982b Proteus in quotation-land: mimesis and the forms of reported discourse, *Poetics Today* **2**: 108–56

Strang, B. M. H. 1970 *A history of English*. Methuen

Stubbs, M. 1983 *Discourse analysis*. Basil Blackwell

Sucksmith, H. P. 1970 *The narrative art of Charles Dickens: the rhetoric of sympathy and irony in his novels*. Clarendon

Swales, J. M. 1990 *Genre analysis: English in academic and research settings*. Cambridge University Press

Taglicht, J. 1985 *Message and emphasis: on focus and scope in English*. Longman

Tanaka, K. 1994 *Advertising language*. Routledge

Tannen, D. 1989 *Talking voices: repetition, dialogue and imagery in conversational discourse*. Cambridge University Press

Taylor, T. J. 1981 *Linguistic theory and structural stylistics*. Pergamon

Taylor, T. J., Toolan, M. 1984 Recent trends in stylistics, *Journal of Literary Semantics* **13**: 57–79

Tesnière, L. 1959 *Éléments de syntaxe structurale*. Klinksieck: Paris

Thomas, J. 1995 *Meaning in interaction: an introduction to pragmatics*. Longman

Thomas, J., Short, M. (eds) 1996 *Using corpora for language research*. Longman

Thompson, J. B. 1984 *Studies in the theory of ideology*. Polity Press

Thorne, J. P. 1965 Stylistics and generative grammars, *Journal of Linguistics* **1**: 49–59 (Reprinted in Freeman, D. C. (ed.) 1970 *Linguistics and literary style*. Holt, Rinehart & Winston)

Thorne, J. P. 1969 Poetry, stylistics and imaginary grammars, *Journal of Linguistics* **5**: 147–50

Threadgold, T. 1997 *Feminist poetics: poesis, performance, histories*. Routledge

Tillotson, G. 1961 *Augustan studies*. Athlone Press

Tillotson, K. 1959 *The tale and the teller*. Rupert Hart-Davis

Todd, L. 1974 *Pidgins and creoles*. Routledge & Kegan Paul

Todorov, T. (ed.) 1965 *Théorie de la littérature*. Seuil: Paris

Todorov, T. 1966 Les catégories du récit litteraire, *Communications* **8**: 125–51

Todorov, T. 1967 *Littérature et signification*. Larousse: Paris

Todorov, T. 1969 *Grammaire du Decameron*. Mouton: The Hague

Todorov, T. 1971 *La poétique de la prose*. Seuil: Paris (Translated 1977 *The poetics of prose*. Cornell University Press: New York)

Todorov, T. 1981 *Introduction to poetics*. Harvester Press (First published in French, 1968)

Toolan, M. 1996 *Total speech*. Duke University Press: Durham, North Carolina

Toolan, M. 1997 What is critical discourse analysis and why are people saying such terrible things about it? *Language and Literature* **6**: 83–103

Toolan, M. 1999 Integrational linguistics, relevance theory and stylistic explanation: a reply to MacMahon, *Language and Literature* **8**: 255–68

Torgovnick, M. 1981 *Closure in the novel*. Princeton University Press: Princeton, New Jersey

Trager, G. L. 1958 Paralanguage: a first approximation. In Hymes, D. (ed.) *Language in culture and society*. Harper & Row, New York

Traugott, E. C., Pratt, M. L. 1980 *Linguistics for students of literature*. Harcourt Brace Jovanovitch: New York

Trier, J. 1934 Das sprachliche Feld. Eine Auseinandersetzung, *Neue Jahrbücher für Wissenschaft und Jugendbildung* **10**: 428–49

Trubetzkoy, N. S. 1939 *Grundzüge der Phonologie*. Cercle linguistique de Prague

Trudgill, P. 1995 *Sociolinguistics: an introduction*. Penguin

Turner, G. W. 1973 *Stylistics*. Penguin

Turner, M., Fauconnier, G. 1995 Conceptual integration and formal expression, *Metaphor and Symbolic Activity* **10**: 183–203

Turner, V. 1967 The liminal period in rites of passage. In *The forest of symbols: aspects of Ndembu ritual*. Cornell University Press: Ithaca

Tuve, R. 1947 *Elizabethan and metaphysical imagery*. University of Chicago Press: Chicago

Ulmer, G. 1985 *Applied grammatology: post(e)-pedagogy from Jacques Derrida to Joseph Beuys*. Johns Hopkins University Press: Baltimore

Uspensky, B. 1973 *A poetics of composition*. University of California Press: Berkeley

Vachek, J. (ed.) 1964 *A Prague School reader in linguistics*. Indiana University Press: Bloomington

Voloshinov, V. 1973 *Marxism and the philosophy of language*. Seminar Press: New York (First published 1929 in Russian)

Vossler, K. 1932 *The spirit of language in civilization*. Routledge & Kegan Paul

Wales, K. 1990 Phonotactics and phonaesthesia: the power of folk-lexicology. In Ramsaran, S. (ed.) *Studies in the pronunciation of English*. Routledge

Wales, K. (ed.) 1994 *Feminist linguistics in literary criticism*. D. S. Brewer/English Association

Wales, K. 1995 The ethics of stylistics: towards an ethical stylistics, *Moderna Sprak* **89**: 9–14

Wales, K. 1996 *Personal pronouns in present-day English*. Cambridge University Press

Walton, K. L. 1978 How remote are fictional worlds from the real world? *Journal of Aesthetics and Art Criticism* **37**: 11–23

Watson, G. 1979 *The story of the novel*. Macmillan

Waugh, P. 1984 *Metafiction: the theory and practice of self-conscious fiction*. Methuen

Wells, J. C. 1982 *Accents of English* (3 vols). Cambridge University Press

Werth, P. W. 1976 Roman Jakobson's verbal analysis of poetry, *Journal of Linguistics* **12**: 21–73

Werth, P. 1999 *Text worlds: representing conceptual space in discourse*. Pearson Education Ltd

Whorf, B. L. 1956 *Language, thought and reality*. MIT Press: Cambridge, Mass.

Widdowson, H. G. 1972 On the deviance of literary discourse, *Style* **6**: 292–308

Widdowson, H. G. 1975 *Stylistics and the teaching of literature*. Longman

Widdowson, H. G. 1979 *Explorations in applied linguistics*. Oxford University Press

Widdowson, H. G. 1983 The deviant language of poetry. In Brumfit, C. J. (ed.) *Teaching literature overseas: language-based approaches*. Pergamon

Widdowson, H. G. 1992 *Practical stylistics*. Oxford University Press

Widdowson, H. G. 1995 Discourse analysis: a critical view, *Language and Literature* **4**: 157–72

Widdowson, H. G. 1996 Reply to Fairclough: discourse and interpretation: conjectures and refutations, *Language and Literature* **5**: 57–69

Williams, C. B. 1970 *Style and vocabulary: numerical studies*. Griffin

Williams, R. 1958 *Culture and society 1780–1950*. Chatto & Windus

Williams, R. 1976 *Keywords: a vocabulary of culture and society*. Fontana

Williams, R. 1977 *Marxism and literature*. Oxford University Press

Williams, R. 1980 *Problems in material culture: selected essays*. Verso

Williamson, G. 1951 *The Senecan amble: a study in prose form from Bacon to Collier*. Faber & Faber

Wilson, D. 1975 *Presupposition and non-truth-conditional semantics*. Academic Press: New York

Wilson, T. 1553 *The arte of rhetorique*. R. Graftonus

Wimsatt, Jr., W. K. (ed.) 1954 *The verbal icon*. University of Kentucky Press: Lexington

Winter, E. 1982 *A contextual grammar of English*. Allen & Unwin

Young, D. J. 1980 *The structure of English clauses*. Hutchinson

Young, D. J. 1984 *Introducing English grammar*. Hutchinson